The International Legal Régime for the Protection of the Stratospheric
Ozone Layer

International Law
in Japanese Perspective

Series Editor

Yuji Iwasawa

VOLUME 13

The titles published in this series are listed at *brill.com/iljp*

The International Legal Régime for the Protection of the Stratospheric Ozone Layer

Second Revised Edition

By

Osamu Yoshida

BRILL
NIJHOFF

LEIDEN | BOSTON

The Library of Congress Cataloging-in-Publication Data is available online at http://catalog.loc.gov

Typeface for the Latin, Greek, and Cyrillic scripts: "Brill". See and download: brill.com/brill-typeface.

ISSN 0929-7111
ISBN 978-90-04-24767-3 (hardback)
ISBN 978-90-04-29087-7 (e-book)

Copyright 2019 by Koninklijke Brill NV, Leiden, The Netherlands.
Koninklijke Brill NV incorporates the imprints Brill, Brill Hes & De Graaf, Brill Nijhoff, Brill Rodopi, Brill Sense, Hotei Publishing, mentis Verlag, Verlag Ferdinand Schöningh and Wilhelm Fink Verlag.
All rights reserved. No part of this publication may be reproduced, translated, stored in a retrieval system, or transmitted in any form or by any means, electronic, mechanical, photocopying, recording or otherwise, without prior written permission from the publisher.
Authorization to photocopy items for internal or personal use is granted by Koninklijke Brill NV provided that the appropriate fees are paid directly to The Copyright Clearance Center, 222 Rosewood Drive, Suite 910, Danvers, MA 01923, USA. Fees are subject to change.

This book is printed on acid-free paper and produced in a sustainable manner.

Contents

Foreword   XI
Editor's Preface   XII
Preface to the Second Revised Edition   XIII
About the Author   XV
Abbreviations   XVI
Cases   XX

Introduction   1

PART 1
International Legal Régimes

1   **International Environmental Régimes**   9
   I   Preliminary Examination of 'International Régimes'   9
   II   International Régimes in International Environmental Relations   16
   III   International Environmental Régimes and International Law   21
     A   *Law-Making in International Cooperation Régimes for Environmental Regulation*   21
     B   *The Institutionalisation of International Environmental Cooperation*   28
     C   *'Soft Enforcement' of Treaties: Implementation of and Compliance with Legal Obligations of International Environmental Régimes*   32
     D   *Non-Governmental Organizations as Actors of International Legal Régimes*   35
   IV   The Emergence of the 'Self-Contained' Régime for Obligations *Erga Omnes*: Ensuring Universal Compliance   39
   V   Conclusions   49

PART 2
The International Treaties for the Protection of the Ozone Layer

2   **The 1985 Vienna Convention for the Protection of the Ozone Layer and Principles of Modern International Environmental Law**   53
   I   Introduction   53

II   The Negotiation of the 1985 Vienna Ozone Convention   54
  A   *National and Regional Regulation of Major Chlorofluorocarbons (CFCs)*   55
  B   *The Vienna Convention Negotiation within the UNEP as a Law-Making Forum*   57
III The 1985 Vienna Convention for the Protection of the Ozone Layer   65
  A   *The Definition of 'Adverse Effects' Caused by Ozone Depletion*   66
  B   *The Legal Status of the Ozone Layer in General International Law*   68
  C   *The Vienna Ozone Convention and the 'Principle' of the Precautionary Approach in Modern International Law of the Environment*   74
  D   *The Provisions of the Vienna Ozone Convention*   85
IV   Assessment of the Vienna Ozone Convention   94

3   **The Montreal Protocol: the Evolution of the International Regulatory Régime for the Protection of the Ozone Layer**   97
  I   Introduction   97
  II   The Montreal Protocol Negotiation: Preparation of the Protocol on the Protection of the Ozone Layer within the UNEP   100
    A   *The First Session of the Working Group*   100
    B   *The Second Session of the Working Group*   105
    C   *Toward a Final Decision in Montreal in September 1987*   107
  III International Legal Regulation of Specified ODSs under the Montreal Protocol   109
    A   *The Final Agreement: Provisions of the Montreal Protocol*   109
    B   *International Control Measures for ODSS*   111
    C   *The Internal Mechanisms for Amendments and Adjustments: Strengthening the System of the International Control Measures*   116
    D   *The European Community as the 'Regional Economic Integration Organisation': the Joint Implementation of the ODS Control Measures*   118
    E   *Special Situation of Developing Countries: The 'Grace Period' for Article 5 Countries*   120
  IV   The Development of the International Cooperative and Regulatory Ozone Régime: the Evolution of International Control Measures and Other ODSs-Related Issues   126

CONTENTS VII

A   *The Need for Revisions of the 1987 version of the Protocol: New Scientific Knowledge on the State of the Ozone Layer*   126

B   *The 1989 Helsinki Ozone Meeting and Its International Soft Law*   128

C   *The 1990 London Ozone Meeting: Strengthening the Control Measures and the Establishment of the Multilateral Fund*   130

D   *The 1992 Copenhagen Ozone Meeting: Strengthening the Control Measures of HCFCs and the Establishment of the Montreal NCP*   131

E   *The 1995 Vienna Ozone Meeting: the Control Measures for HCFCs and Methylbromide, and the Extension of the Grace Period*   134

F   *The 1997 Montreal Ozone Meeting: Control Measures of Methylbromide and Illegal Trade in CFCs and ODSs*   136

G   *The 1999 Beijing Ozone Meeting: a Freeze in HCFCs Production and the Control of a New ODS – Bromochloromethane*   139

H   *The 2007 Montreal Ozone Meeting: Adjustments for Accelerating HCFCs Phaseout*   141

I   *The 2016 Kigali Ozone Meeting: Phasing Down of Hydrofluorocarbons (HFCs)*   143

V   The Domestic Implementation of the International Treaties for the Protection of the Ozone Layer   150

A   *Introduction*   150

B   *Domestic Implementation of the Ozone Treaties in Japan*   152

VI   Conclusions   157

PART 3
The Ozone Régime and the WTO/GATT Régime

4   The Montreal Protocol and the International Trade Law Régime of the WTO/GATT   163

I   Introduction   163

A   *Multilateral Environmental Agreements and WTO/GATT Law*   163

B   *Multilateral Environmental Agreements (MEAs)*   164

II   The International Régime for Trade Restrictions of ODSs   168

A *The Background of Article 4 of the Montreal Protocol: Resolving the Problem of Non-Participation in the* MEA *Régime* 168

B *Article 4 of the Montreal Protocol: Process and Production Method-Related Arguments* 170

III WTO/GATT Trade Law 175

A *The* WTO/GATT *Law* 176

B *The Governing Economic Principles of* GATT *Law* 177

C GATT *Case-Law* 180

IV The Legal Conflicts between MEAS and WTO/GATT Trade Law 182

A *The Legal Conflicts between* MEAS *and* WTO/GATT *Trade Law* 183

B *The Relationship between* MEA *Dispute Settlement Procedures and the* WTO *Dispute Settlement System: the Montreal* NCP *or the* WTO *Dispute Settlement Procedures?* 186

V GATT Article XX and the Global Protection of the Ozone Layer under the Montreal Protocol 190

A *The Exceptions under* GATT *Articles* XI(1) *and XX* 190

B GATT *Article* XI(2) *Exceptions and the Montreal Protocol* 195

C *The Preamble Conditions for* GATT *Article XX Exceptions and Article 4 of the Montreal Protocol: Compliance with the Terms of the Chapeau* 195

D GATT *Article XX(b) and the Protection of the Ozone Layer* 198

E GATT *Article XX(g) and the Protection of the Ozone Layer* 203

VI Conclusions 206

PART 4
The Compliance System of the Montreal Protocol

5 **The Montreal Non-Compliance Procedure and the Functions of the Internal International Organs** 211

I The Montreal Non-Compliance Procedure (NCP) 211

A *The Judicial Settlement of International Environmental Disputes* 211

B *The Avoidance and Quasi-Judicial Settlement of Multilateral Environmental Disputes: the Non-Compliance Procedure* (NCP) 212

CONTENTS

II	The Negotiation of the Montreal NCP	217
III	The Meaning of 'Non-Compliance' in the Montreal Protocol: a Grey Area of the International Ozone Régime	221

    A   *The Meaning of 'Non-Compliance' in the Evolving Ozone Régime*   221

    B   *Depoliticising Multilateral Environmental Disputes? The Relationship between the NCP and the Dispute Settlement Mechanisms in the Vienna Ozone Convention*   224

IV   The Mechanics of the Operation of the Montreal NCP: the Function of the Specialised Internal Treaty Bodies   227

    A   *The Structure of the Montreal NCP*   227

        (1)   The Actors of the NCP   227

        (2)   The Principle of Good Faith (*Bona fides*)   227

    B   *The Functions of the Internal International Agencies in the Montreal Non-Compliance Procedure*   228

V   The Principal Features of the NCP: The Montreal NCP, International Conciliation and Other Dispute Settlement Procedures   244

    A   *The Montreal NCP as a Multilateral Conciliation Mechanism*   245

    B   *The Dispute Settlement Mechanisms Used by Other International Institutions*   249

VI   The Montreal NCP Theory: Soft Enforcement of International Environmental Law   257

VII   The Montreal NCP in Practice   263

    A   *Ensuring Compliance with Reporting Requirements, Control Measures and Trade Restrictions*   263

    B   *Case Study: Non-Compliance by the Russian Federation and the Reactions of the NCP Organs*   272

VIII Conclusions   281

6   The Financial Mechanism of the Montreal Protocol and the International Transfer of Ozone-Friendly Technology: Capacity Building in the Ozone Régime   286

I   The Concept of Capacity Building in International Environmental Law   286

    A   *The Definition of Capacity Building*   286

    B   *Capacity Building and MEAS*   288

II   The Negotiation Process of the Montreal Multilateral Fund and Issues Related to Technology Transfer   290

X CONTENTS

  A *Capacity Building under the Vienna Ozone Convention and the Montreal Protocol* 290

  B *The Negotiation of the Multilateral Fund and Technology Transfer* 292

 III The Structure of the Financial Mechanism of the Montreal Protocol 297

  A *General Legal Aspects* 297

  B *The Role of the International Agencies in the Financial Mechanism* 301

  C *The Global Environment Facility (GEF)* 315

  D *Strategies: Work Programmes, Country Programmes and Institutional Strengthening* 318

 IV Special Considerations for the International Transfer of Ozone-Friendly Technology 323

  A *International Technology Transfer* 323

  B *International Technology Transfer of ODS Reduction* 324

 V The Operation of the Financial Mechanism of the Montreal Protocol 326

  A *The Effectiveness of the Montreal Multilateral Fund* 326

 VI Conclusions 329

PART 5
Conclusions

7 The International Legal Régime for the Protection of the Ozone Layer 335

 Appendix I The 1985 Vienna Convention for the Protection of the Ozone Layer 343

 Appendix II The Montreal Protocol on Substances That Deplete the Ozone Layer 359

 Appendix III Non-Compliance Procedure (1998) 397

 Bibliography 401

 Index 418

Foreword

The development of a treaty régime for the protection of the ozone layer is one of the success stories of modern international environmental diplomacy. The Ozone Convention and the Montreal Protocol have provided one of the more sophisticated models of international regulation and supervision for environmental purposes, and have influenced the design of later treaty régimes. Whereas scientific assessments showed that in its original 1987 form the Montreal Protocol would not have halted an accelerating level of ozone depleting substances in the stratosphere, subsequent revisions evidence the dynamic and flexible way in which the régime has responded. Controls on ozone-depleting substances have been strengthened at successive meetings of the parties in 1990, 1992, 1995 and 1997. New substances have been added. The supervisory institutions have evolved. Problems submitted to the non-compliance procedure have largely been dealt with successfully, albeit at the price of some delay in implementation by a few states in Eastern Europe. Ultimate success in restoring the ozone layer may depend on many other factors, but at present international co-operation appears to be working.

Dr. Yoshida has written the most comprehensive contemporary study of the international ozone régime in English. He has explored both the negotiation of the relevant treaties and their operation in practice. His study addresses legal and institutional issues and gives important insights into some of the most novel features of the régime, including its non-compliance procedure. There is much in his work which will interest both lawyers and international relations specialists. Above all he shows that multilateral, negotiated, solutions to global environmental problems are possible, given sufficient political will. His conclusions deserve the wider appreciation which publication of this book will help to ensure.

Alan Boyle
Edinburgh

Editor's Preface

Protection of the environment—including the ozone layer and climate change—is an urgent concern in international law. Therefore, in the late 1980s, the Vienna Convention for the Protection of the Ozone Layer and the Montreal Protocol on Substances that Deplete the Ozone Layer were concluded, with the treaty as a whole being considered a model for subsequent climate change agreements and other environmental instruments.

This book is a revised second edition of Professor Yoshida's *International Legal Régime for the Protection of the Stratospheric Ozone Layer*, which was published in the *International Law in Japanese Perspective* series in 2001. Professor Yoshida thoroughly investigated the evolving ozone treaty practices, including non-compliance procedure operation and its possible implications on international law. This book is a valuable reference for international law on the ozone layer and climate change and makes a significant contribution to the study of international environmental law.

Yuji Iwasawa
Tokyo, May 2018

Preface to the Second Revised Edition

Nearly twenty-years have passed since the first edition of this book, *The International Legal Régime for the Protection of the Stratospheric Ozone Layer* (Kluwer Law International, 2001), based on my doctoral dissertation that I completed at Edinburgh Law School in 1998, was published.[1] It is a great honour that this book and related articles on the subject of the international ozone régime have been referred to and cited in many works in the field of international law.[2]

The main goal of this second edition is to inform the reader about the latest practice of dynamic environmental régime. I have again analysed the negotiation process of the ozone treaties and closely investigated new control measures for ozone-depleting substances (ODSs) under the Montreal Protocol, including the 2016 Kigali Amendments. The recent developments and important issues of the Non-Compliance Procedure (NCP) and the Financial Mechanisms of the Montreal Protocol will also be shown in this edition. However, it must be imphasised that this book, as a whole, is written to describe the gradual development of the system of general international law and international environmental law.

I am immensely obliged to the series editor, Professor Yuji Iwasawa, who kindly accepted my proposal to write this revised edition. Professor Iwasawa has been a wonderful mentor since I first met him in the United States as a doctoral student from Edinburgh Law School in 1997. I am also grateful to Professor Alan Boyle. Without his guidance and warm support in Edinburgh, the writing of this book itself would not have been possible.

Many distinguished scholars, practitioners and students of international law contributed to the completion of the work in various ways. In particular, I wish to express my thanks to Professor Yoshinori Abe, Professor Koji Teraya and Professor Yumiko Nakanishi, who kindly read some parts of the earlier

---

1 See a book review by Professor Nico Schrijver in 52 *Netherlands International Law Review* (2005), pp. 156–157.

2 See, for example, Ian Brownlie, *Principles of Public International Law* (7th ed. Oxford University Press, 2008); Patricia Birnie, Alan Boyle and Catherine Redgwell, *International Law and the Environment* (Third ed. Oxford University Press, 2009); Philippe Sands and Jacqueline Peel, *Principles of International Environmental Law* (3rd ed. Cambridge University Press, 2012); Pierr-Marie Dupuy and Jorge E. Viñuales, *International Environmental Law* (Cambridge University Press); Catherine Redgwell, 'International Environmental Law', in Malcolm D. Evans (ed.), *International Law* (4th ed. Oxford University Press, 2014); Patrick Daillier, Mathias Forteau and Alain Pellet, *Droit international public* (8th ed. L.G.D.J., 2009); Philippe Sands and Pierre Klein, *Bowett's Law of International Institutions* (6th ed. Sweet & Maxwell, 2009).

draft manuscript and provided insightful comments. Ms. Risa Saijo and Mr. Masami Tamura, both at the Ministry of Foreign Affairs of Japan, helped my research and gave me useful comments on practical aspects of the changing ozone treaties. Colleagues at the University of Tsukuba allowed me to devote considerable time to the writing of this project and I would like to thank, in particular, Professor Yoshihiko Takenaka and Professor Hisao Sekine. Professor Itsuro Nakamura taught me the importance of logical thinking as a responsible university researcher and I am grateful for his inspiring daily encouragement. I also want to thank Ms. Minami Kinjo, a research assistant at the University of Tsukuba from 2013 to 2014, now at Okinawa Prefectural Government, and my students and former students at Tsukuba for their warm assistance: Ms. Yu Suzuki, Mr. Takashi Mori, Ms. Ayako Tamura (Yamaguchi), Mr. Tatsuya Yamaguchi, Ms. Yuika Higashimura, Mr. Samon Fukasawa, Ms. Mio Iwai, Ms. Maria Poliakova and Mr. Ryotaro Sorimachi.

From 2008 to 2014, I was engaged in drafting principles of international law in the field of climate change, as a member of the ILA Committee on the Legal Principles Relating to Climate Change. Through intensive discussions with the ILA Committee members, I was able to learn a lot about the law of atmosphere. I am particularly grateful to Professor Shinya Murase (Chair), Professor Lavanya Rajamani (Rapporteur), Professor Alan Boyle, Professor Jutta Brunnée, Professor Marcel M.T.A. Brus, Professor Duncan French, Professor Maria Gavouneli, Dr Harald Hohmann, Professor Sandrine Maljean-Dubois, Professor Jacqueline Peel, Professor Akiho Shibata and Professor Yukari Takamura.

At Brill Academic Publishers (Martinus Nijhoff), I would like to thank Ms. Ingeborg van der Laan for her unfailing support during the long process of preparing this manuscript. Although I often felt it might be impossible to finish writing this new edition because of many unexpected difficulties I was faced with, Ms. van der Laan kept encouraging me to finalise the project. I can never adequately express my gratitude and respect for her professional advice.

Finally, I would like to dedicate this work to my family and daughters, Rino and Keika, with enduring love.

Osamu Yoshida
Tokyo, January 2018

About the Author

Osamu Yoshida, born in 1969, is Professor of International Law at the University of Tsukuba, Japan. He taught at the United Nations University and was a Member of the International Law Association's Committee on The Legal Principles relating to Climate Change, 2008–2014. From 1999 to 2000, he was a JSPS Research Fellow of International Law at Tokyo University and a Visiting Fellow at the Department of European, International and Comparative Law, University of Vienna (2003–2004). He received a doctoral degree (D.Phil) in Public International Law from Edinburgh University, School of Law, in 1998. Also, he was a Member of the Research Group on WTO Dispute Settlement Reports established in the Japan Ministry of Economy, Trade and Industry (METI), Trade Policy Bureau.

His publications in English include: *The International Legal Régime for the Protection of the Stratospheric Ozone Layer: International Law, International Regimes and Sustainable Development* (Kluwer Law International, 2001); 'Organising International Society? Legal Problems of International Régimes between Normative Claims and Political Realities', *Austrian Review of International and European Law*, Vol. 9 (Martinus Nijhoff Publishers, 2006), pp. 63–118; 'Procedural Aspects of the International Legal Regime for Climate Change: Early Operation of the Kyoto Protocol Compliance System', *Journal of East Asia and International Law*, Vol. 4 (2011), pp. 41–61: and 'Japan's Efforts in United Nations Peacekeeping Operations: From the Perspectives of International Law and Foreign Policy-Making', in Seowoo Lee and Hee Eun Lee (eds.), *Northeast Asian Perspectives on International Law: Contemporary Issues and Challenges* (Brill Nijhoff, 2013), pp. 113–130.

Abbreviations

AFDI	Annuaire Français de Droit International
AJIL	American Journal of International Law
ARIEL	Austrian Review of International and European Law
ASEAN	Association of South East Asian Nations
AUJILP	American University Journal of International Law and Politics
BISD	Basic Instruments and Selected Documents (GATT)
BCEALR	Boston College Environmental Affairs Law Review
BCICLR	Boston College International and Comparative Law Review
BYbkIL	British Year Book of International Law
CAAA	US Clean Air Act Amendment
CCAMLR	Convention on the Conservation of Antarctic Living Resources
CCl_4	Carbontetrachloride
CCM	Common Concern of (Hu)Mankind
CCOL	UNEP Coordinating Committee on the Ozone Layer
CEIT	Countries with Economies in Transition
CFCS	Chlorofluorocarbons
CH_3Br	Methylbromide
$C_2H_3Cl_3$	Methylchloroform
CHM	Common Heritage of Mankind
CIS	Commonwealth of Independent States
CITES	Convention on International Trade in Endangered Species of Wild Fauna and Flora
CMLR	Common Market Law Review
CMS	Common Market Studies
CTE	Committee on Trade and Environment (WTO)
CO_2	Carbondioxide
CYbkIL	Canadian Yearbook of International Law
DSB	Dispute Settlement Body
DSU	Dispute Settlement Understanding
EC/EU	European Community/European Union
ECJ	European Court of Justice
EEC	European Economic Community
EEZ	Exclusive Economic Zone
EIA	Environment Impact Assessment
EJIL	European Journal of International Law
EPA	Environment Protection Agency
EPL	Environmental Policy and Law

FAO	Food and Agriculture Organisation
GATS	General Agreement on Trade in Services
GATT	General Agreement on Tariffs and Trade
GEF	Global Environment Facility
GEMS	Global Environment Monitoring System
GYbkIL	German Yearbook of International Law
HBFCS	Hydrobromofluorocarbons
HCFCS	Hydrochlorofluorocarbons
HFCS	Hydrofluorocarbons
IAEA	International Atomic Energy Agency
IBRD	International Bank for Reconstruction and Development
ICAO	International Civil Aviation Organization
ICCPR	International Covenant on Civil and Political Rights
ICJ	International Court of Justice
ICLQ	International and Comparative Law Quarterly
ICOLP	Industry Co-operative for Ozone Layer Protection
IDI	Institut de Droit International
IGOS	Intergovernmental Organisations
IJECL	International Journal of Estuarine and Coastal Law
ILA	International Law Association
ILC	International Law Commission
ILJ	International Law Journal
ILM	International Legal Materials
ILO	International Labour Organisation
ILR	International Law Reports
IMO	International Maritime Organisation
IPCC	Intergovernmental Panel on Climate Change
ISBA	International Seabed Authority
ISO	International Organisation for Standardization
ITTO	International Tropical Timber Organization
IUCN	International Union for Conservation of Nature and Natural Resources
JAIL	Japanese Annual of International Law
JEL	Journal of Environmental Law
JIL	Journal of International Law
JTL	Journal of Transnational Law
JWT	Journal of World Trade
JWTL	Journal of World Trade Law
JYbkIL	Japanese Yearbook of International Law
LRTAP	Convention on Long-Range Transboundary Air Pollution
LJ	Law Journal

LNTS	League of Nations Treaty Series
LVCS	Low-Volume-ODS-Consuming Countries
MARPOL	International Convention for the Prevention of Pollution from Ships
MEA	Multilateral Environmental Agreement
MFN	most-favoured-nation treatment
MITI	Japan Ministry of International Trade and Industry
MLF	Montreal Protocol's Multilateral Fund
MOP	Meeting of the Parties
MP	Montreal Protocol
NAFTA	North American Free Trade Agreement
NCP	Non-Compliance Procedure
NGOS	Non-Governmental Organisations
NILR	Netherlands International Law Review
NRJ	Natural Resources Journal
NYbkIL	Netherlands Yearbook of International Law
OAS	Organisation of American States
OAU	Organisation of African Unity
OECD	Organisation for Economic Co-operation and Development
ODA	Overseas Development Aid
ODPS	Ozone Depleting Potentials
ODSS	Ozone Depleting Substances
OEWG	Open-Ended Working Group
OJ	Official Journal of the EC/EU
PCIJ	Permanent Court of International Justice
PFCS	Perfluorocarbons
POP	Persistent Organic Pollutant
PPM	Process and Production Method
Proc. ASIL	Proceedings of the American Society of International Law
QRs	Quantitative Restrictions
RGDIP	Revue Générale de Droit International Public
SOX	Oxides of Sulphur
SO_2	Sulphur Dioxides
TBT	Technical Barriers to Trade
TEAP	Technology and Economic Assessment Panel
TIAS	Treaties and Other International Acts
TREMS	Trade Related Environmental Measures
TRIPS	Trade Related Intellectual Property Rights
UNCLOS	UN Convention on the Law of the Sea
UNCTAD	UN Conference on Trade and Environment

ABBREVIATIONS

UNDP	UN Development Programme
UNCED	UN Conference on Environment and Development
UNECE	UN Economic Commission for Europe
UNEP	UN Environment Programme
UNEP (T)IE	UNEP Division of (Technology), Industry and Economics
UNESCO	United Nations Educational, Scientific and Cultural Organization
UNFCCC	United Nations Framework Convention on Climate Change
UNIDO	UN Industrial Development Organisation
UNTS	United Nations Treaty Series
WCED	World Commission on Environment & Development
WHO	World Health Organisation
WIPO	World Intellectual Property Organization
WMO	World Meteorological Organisation
WTO	World Trade Organisation
YbkEL	Yearbook of European Law
YbkIEL	Yearbook of International Environmental Law
ZaöRV	Zeitschrift für ausländisches und öffentliches Recht und Völkerrecht

List of Cases

Permanent Court of International Justice

Phosphates in Morocco Case (1938)   20n

International Court of Justice

Barcelona Traction Power and Light Co. Case (1970)   44, 73
Certain Expenses of the United Nations Case (1962)   33
Corfu Channel Case (1949)   19n, 77n
East Timor Case (1995)   44n
Fisheries Jurisdiction Case (1973)   20n, 276n
Gabcíkovo-Nagymaros Project Case (1997)   15, 29n, 276n
Libya-Malta Continental Shelf Case (1985)   24n
Nicaragua Case (1986)   24n, 94
North Sea Continental Shelf Case (1969)   24n
Nuclear Tests Cases (1974)   15
Nuclear Weapons Case (1996)   75n, 84n
Pulp Mills on the River Uruguay Case (2010)   20n
Reparation for Injuries Suffered in the Service of the United Nations
Case (1949)   33n
South West Africa, International Status of, Case (1950)   240n
South West Africa Cases (1966)   44n
Temple Case (1961)   20n
US Diplomatic and Consular Staff in Tehran Case (1980)   40n
Wall Case (2004)   44n
Whaling in the Antarctic Case (2014)   28n

International Arbitral Tribunals

Air Services Agreement Case (1978)   40n
Alabama Claims Arbitration Case (1872)   77n
Iron Rhine Railway Arbitration Case (2005)   29n

LIST OF CASES

Lac Lanoux Arbitration Case (1957) 19n, 20n
Trail Smelter Arbitration Case (1938, 1941) 18n, 74, 76

European Court of Justice

Case 232/78 Commission v. France (1979) 41n
Cases 90-91/63 Commission v. Luxembourg and Belgium (1964) 41n

WTO/GATT Decisions

Belgium – Family Allowances 177n
Brazil – Measures Affecting Imports of Retreaded Tyres 194
Canada – Measures Affecting Exports of Unprocessed Herring and Salmon 193n, 204
China – Measures Related to the Exportation of Various Raw Materials 205
EEC – Production Aids Granted on Canned Fruits and Dried Grapes 252n
EEC – Tariff Treatment on Imports of Citrus Products from Certain Countries in Mediterranean Region 252n
India – Measures Concerning the Importation of Certain Agricultural Products 189, 190n
Japan – Customs Duties, Taxes and Labelling Practices on Imported Wines and Alcoholic Beverages 173, 182, 251
Japan – Restrictions on Imports of Certain Agricultural Products 195
Thailand – Restrictions on Importation of and Internal Taxes on Cigarettes 180n, 189, 193n, 194n
United States – Final Anti-Dumping Measures on Stainless Steel from Mexico 182n
United States – Import of Prohibition of Certain Shrimp and Shrimp Products 193, 194n, 203, 204n, 205
United States – Prohibition of Imports of Tuna and Tuna Products from Canada 180n, 193n
United States – Restrictions on Imports of Tuna (Tuna Case I) 174n, 180n, 203n, 205n

United States – Restrictions on Imports of Tuna (Tuna Case II)   174n, 180n, 203n, 205

United States – Standards for Reformulated and Conventional Gasoline   180n, 183, 185n, 192n, 204

United States – Taxes on Petroleum and Certain Imported Substances   178n

International Case

Aaland Islands Case   13

Introduction

A growing phenomenon of this shrinking world is that the clear-cut distinction between national, transnational and global environmental problems is fast disappearing in the international legal community.[1] The depletion of the ozone layer is in this respect a typical example: no single State's activity will be responsible for potential adverse effects caused by ozone decreases, and most States have only a minimal role in both the production and the consumption of ozone-depleting chemicals (ozone depleters). The actions of those States that do produce or consume on a large scale potentially affect all States in the international community.

Ozone is an allotrope of Oxygen, made up of three atoms of Oxygen (O_3).[2] It is formed when the molecule of the stable form of Oxygen (O_2) is split by ultraviolet radiation or electrical discharge.[3] Ozone is mainly found in two regions of the atmosphere, the stratosphere (approximately from ten to fifty kilometres above the Earth's surface, with a peak concentration at twenty kilometres) and the troposphere[4] (which extends from the Earth's surface up to about ten kilometres). About ninety per cent of protective ozone – the blue, pungent-smelling gas – is concentrated in the stratospheric area (that is, ozone

---

1   On 'international environmental law', see, among others, Patricia Birnie, Alan Boyle and Catherine Redgwell, *International Law and the Environment* (Third ed. Oxford University Press, 2009); Philippe Sands and Jacqueline Peel, *Principles of International Environmental Law* (3rd ed. Cambridge University Press, 2012); Pierr-Marie Dupuy and Jorge E. Viñuales, *International Environmental Law* (Cambridge University Press); Alexandre Kiss and Jean-Pierre Beurier, *Droit international de l'environnement* (4th ed. A. Pedone, 2010); Ulrich Beyerlin and Thilo Marauhn, *International Environmental Law* (Hart Publishing/CH Beck, 2011); Günther Handl, 'Environmental Security and Global Change: The Challenge to International Law', 1 *YbkIEL* (1990), pp. 3–33; Peter H. Sand, *Transnational Environmental Law: Lessons in Global Change* (Kluwer Law International, 1999); Donald K. Anton, Jonathan I. Charney, Phillippe Sands, Thomas J. Schoenbaum and Michael K. Young, *International Environmental Law: Cases, Materials, Problems* (LexisNexis, 2007). As for policy and legal issues, see Andrew Hurrell and Benedict Kingsbury (eds.), *International Politics of the Environment* (Clarendon Press, 1992); Lynton Keith Caldwell, *International Environmental Policy: From the Twentieth to the Twenty-First Century* (3rd ed. Duke University Press 1996).
2   See Peter Fabian and Martin Dameris, *Ozone in the Atmosphere: Basic Principles, Natural and Human Impacts* (Springer, 2014), pp. 1–3.
3   See Michael Allaby, *Macmillan Dictionary of the Environment* (4th ed. Macmillan Press, 1994), p. 258.
4   At the ground level, ozone is simply 'bad': it can cause serious adverse effects in humans and animals, including eye, nose and respiratory problems, damage plants, field crops, and forests, and cause detrimental effects to many materials.

© KONINKLIJKE BRILL NV, LEIDEN, 2019 | DOI:10.1163/9789004290877_002

layer or ozone shield). The strong consensus of the international community is that certain man-made chemicals are destroying the stratospheric ozone layer, which protects the Earth from harmful UV-B rays from the sun (that is, ozone depletion),[5] though there still exists uncertainty on some issues.[6]

According to many experimental studies of plants and animals, and clinical studies of humans, health and environmental effects resulting from decreases in ozone include increased rates of skin cancer and eye cataracts; changes in the immune system in a dose and wavelength dependent fashion; damage to crops, such as soya beans; and decreases in phytoplankton in the marine food chain.[7] Further, it is well known that, as a result of damage to the stratospheric ozone layer, a continent-sized 'ozone hole' has formed over the Southern hemisphere (the Antarctic Ozone Hole).[8]

The leading cause of ozone depletion has proven to be Chlorofluorocarbons (CFCs), which were commonly used in air conditioners, refrigerators, foams, solvents and other CFC related products. CFCs were first invented in 1928 by E.I. du Pont de Nemours and Company (DuPont) and General Motors chemists who were looking for a non-toxic heat transfer fluid for refrigeration. Other ozone-depleting substances that are believed to be destroying the stratospheric ozone layer include Halons, Hydrochlorofluorocarbons (HCFCs), Carbontetrachloride (CCl_4), Methylchloroform or 1,1,1-trichloroethane

---

5 In 1974, Dr. Frank Sherwood Rowland and Dr. Mario J. Molina of California University published a scientific paper demonstrating how CFCs destroy ozone in the stratosphere. See Mario J. Molina and F. S. Rowland, 'Stratospheric Sink for Chlorofluoromethanes: Chlorine Atom-Catalysed Destruction of Ozone', 249 *Nature* (28 June 1974), pp. 810–812. It is said that their hypothesis first received a great deal of skepticism.

6 See Chapter 3(III.C.2.b) in this volume.

7 See, for example, UNEP, *Environmental Effects of Ozone Depletion: 1991 Update, Panel Report Pursuant to Article 6 of the Montreal Protocol on Substances that Deplete the Ozone Layer under the Auspices of UNEP* (November 1991); UNEP, *Environmental Effects of Ozone Depletion: 1998 Assessment, Persuant to Article 6 of the Montreal Protocol on Substances that Deplete the Ozone Layer under the Auspices of the United Nations Environment Programme* (November 1998); UNEP, *Synthesis of the Reports of the Scientific, Environmnetal Effects, and Technology and Economic Assessment Panels of the Montreal Protocol: A Decade of Assessment for Decision Makers Regarding the Protection of the Ozone Layer 1988–1999* (February 1999); Rumen D. Bojkov, *The Changing Ozone Layer* (UNEP/WMO, 1995), p. 19. See also Peter Fabian and Martin Dameris, *Ozone in the Atmosphere: Basic Principles, Natural and Human Impacts* (Springer, 2014), pp. 110–112; Lisa Elges, *Stratosphere Ozone Damage and Legal Liability* (Routledge, 2017), pp. 62 et seq.

8 See, for example, Rumen D. Bojkov, *The Changing Ozone Layer* (UNEP/WMO, 1995), pp. 11 et seq.; Neil R. P. Harris and Markus Rex, 'Ozone Loss in the Polar Stratosphere', in Rolf Müller (ed.), *Stratospheric Ozone Depletion and Climate Change* (RSC Publishing, 2012), pp. 149 et seq.

INTRODUCTION

($C_2H_3Cl_3$), Hydrobromofluorocarbons (HBFCs) and Methylbromide (CH_3Br). Chemicals such as CFCs, Halons and HCFCs can contribute to global warming.

As the title already indicates, this book is about international law for the protection of the ozone layer. It will analyse the international legal ozone régime established by the 1985 Vienna Convention on the Protection of the Ozone Layer and the 1987 Montreal Protocol on Substances That Deplete the Ozone Layer as amended and adjusted. The treaty régime – regulating the above-mentioned chemicals – is the first international institutional mechanism designed to address a global environmental problem.

In comparison to other MEA régimes such as the 1989 Basel Convention,[9] there is a relatively large amount of material, including articles[10] and several books,[11] devoted to studies of the ozone layer régime, particularly the earlier versions of the Montreal Ozone Layer Protocol. This book is indebted partly to these attempts made by the international legal and/or political scholars. However, to my knowledge, a comprehensive and detailed analysis of the international legal ozone régime still remains to be written. Moreover, some parts of the treaty régime have been strangely neglected. For example, (i) the 1985 Vienna Ozone Layer Convention – as a fundamental legal basis of the environmental régime – has not been fully examined;[12] (ii) the literature on the

---

9   See 28 *ILM* (1989), p. 657, in Patricia W. Birnie and Alan E. Boyle, *Basic Documents on International Law and the Environment* (Clarendon Press, 1995). See, in particular, Katharina Kummer, *International Management of Hazardous Wastes* (Oxford University Press, 1995).

10 There is a voluminous literature on the ozone negotiation. See, for example, Richard Benedick, *Ozone Diplomacy* (Harvard University Press, 1998); Edward A. Parson, *Protecting the Ozone Layer: Science and Strategy* (Oxford University Press, 2003); Thomas Gehring, *Dynamic International Regimes* (Peter Lang, 1994); Peter M. Haas, 'Banning Chlorofluorocarbons: Epistemic Community Efforts to Protect Stratospheric Ozone', 46 *International Organizations* (1992), pp. 187–224; Penelope Canan and Nancy Reichman, *Ozone Connections: Expert Networks in Global Environmental Governance* (Greenleaf, 2002).

11 See Richard Benedick, *Ozone Diplomacy* (Harvard University Press, 1998). The author is former United States' chief negotiator for the ozone treaties. From a political science perspective, see, for example, Karen T. Litfin, *Ozone Discourses: Science and Politics in Global Environmental Cooperation* (Columbia University Press, 1994); Ian H. Rowlands, *The Politics of Global Atmospheric Change* (Manchester University Press, 1995).

12 See, for example, Peter H. Sand, 'The Vienna Convention is Adopted', 27 *Environment* (June 1985), pp. 19–23; Iwona Rummel-Bulska, 'The Protection of the Ozone Layer under the Global Framework Convention', in Cees Flinterman, Barbara Kwiatkowska and Johan G. Lammers (eds.), *Transboundary Air Pollution* (Martinus Nijhoff, 1986), pp. 281–297; Rummel-Bulska, 'Recent Developments relating to the Vienna Convention for the Protection of the Ozone Layer', *Yearbook of the Association of Attenders and Alumni of the Hague Academy of International Law* (1984/85/86), pp. 115–125; Sylvia Maureen Williams, 'A Historical Background of the Chlorofluorocarbon Ozone Depletion Theory and

'dynamic' Montreal Protocol adjusted several times is already outdated;[13] (iii) few studies have so far made of the Montreal Protocol's Non-Compliance Procedure *in practice*[14] and (iv) the Montreal Protocol's Multilateral Fund has not been fully researched by international lawyers,[15] although this financial institution is deeply associated with compliance by a growing number of developing country parties under Article 5 of the Protocol. Finally and more fundamentally, (vi) the evolving concept of 'international legal régimes' – international régimes for the environment in the system of general international law – has not been clarified, despite the fact that the term is so frequently used in the literature of international law (for example, the ozone, climate chnage and LRTAP régimes). International environmental régimes, such as the technical ozone layer treaties,[16] must be analysed in their entireties as highly specialised legal systems in the sphere of international law.[17] Partial legal studies of international treaty régimes are often misleading, indeed.[18]

The structure of this book is as follows. Part I (Chapter 1), provides a useful introduction to the ozone régime and it analyses international legal régimes

---

      its Legal Implications' in Cees Flinterman, Barbara Kwiatkowska and Johan G. Lammers (eds.), *Transboundary Air Pollution* (Martinus Nijhoff, 1986), pp. 267–280.

13   See Jutta Brunnée, *Acid Rain and Ozone Layer Depletion: International Law and Regulation* (Transnational Publishers, 1988); Peter M. Lawrence, 'International Legal Regulation for Protection of the Ozone Layer', 2 *JEL* (1990), pp. 17–52; John W. Kindt and Samuel P. Menefee, 'The Vexing Problem of Ozone Depletion in International Environmental Law and Policy', 24 *Texas ILJ* (1989), pp. 261–293; Annette M. Capretta, 'The Future's So Bright, I Gotta Wear Shades: Future Impacts of the Montreal Protocol on Substances That Deplete the Ozone Layer', 29 *Virginia JIL* (1988), pp. 211–248; David Caron, 'La protection de la couche d'ozone stratosphérique et la structure de l'activité normative internationale en matière d'environnement', *AFDI* (1990), pp. 704–726; Dale S. Bryk, 'The Montreal Protocol and Recent Developments to Protect the Ozone Layer', 15 *Harvard ELR* (1991), pp. 275–298; J.T.B. Tripp, 'The UNEP Montreal Protocol: Industrial and Developing Countries Sharing the Responsibility for Protecting the Stratospheric Ozone Layer', 20 *NYUJILP* (1988), pp. 733–752.

14   See Chapter V in this volume.

15   See, for example, Elizabeth R. DeSombre and Joanne Kauffman, 'The Montreal Protocol Fund: Partial Success Story', in Robert O. Keohane and Marc A. Levy (eds.), *Institutions for Environmental Aid* (MIT Press, 1996), pp. 89–126.

16   For instance, the UNEP emphasised in its general report that the drafters of the ozone convention 'must include technical and scientific experts including modellers and persons with extensive knowledge of the socio-economic impacts of different strategies for reducing CFC production and use'. See UNEP/WG.69/3 ('Toward a Ozone Convention: A Look at Some Issue'), para. 55.

17   However, autonomous legal régimes do not necessarily deviate from established principles and rules of general international law. For a discussion of this point, see Chapter I in this volume.

18   See Richard Benedick, *Ozone Diplomacy* (Harvard University Press, 1998), p. xvi.

INTRODUCTION

for the environment, focusing on their relationship with law-making, international environmental cooperation, 'soft enforcement' of treaties by internal international organs, and, finally, non-governmental organisations. In this part, the international régime for ozone will be conceptually characterised as the 'self-contained' environmental régime, having *erga omnes* character in the field of general international law.

Part II (Chapters 2 and 3) is devoted to the detailed legal analysis of the international treaties for the protection of the ozone layer. Chapter 2 examines the 1985 Vienna Ozone Convention in the context of modern international law of the environment. It addressed, for example, the precautionary environmental 'principle' or approach and the common concern of humankind. Chapter 3 deals with (i) the gradual development or internationalisation of ODS regulatory measures under the 1987 Montreal Protocol. To understand the real operation of the ozone treaty régime, a great number of conference documents or reports prepared by the UNEP Secretariat will be used here.

Part III (Chapter 4) discusses extensively the relationship between Article 4 of the Montreal Protocol and the WTO/GATT trade law régime. It will be established that – viewed in its entirety the Montreal Protocol's Article 4 trade restrictions seem to be compatible with the stringent trade rules of the WTO/GATT principles and rules. Some issues in Part III are, of course, closely analysed by international trade lawyers.[19] This Chapter, however, includes detailed studies of Article 4 provisions as amended and the relationship between MEAs' dispute settlement mechanisms (Montreal NCP in particular) and the WTO/GATT dispute settlement system.

Part IV (Chapters 5 and 6) examines the compliance system of the international ozone régime, which can be considered as, to borrow A. Chayes and A.H. Chayes's phrase, 'a managerial model of compliance' relying on a co-operative approach, rather than as a traditional enforcement model'.[20] In Chapter 5, the dispute avoidance and settlement system of the Ozone Layer Protocol, that is, the Non-Compliance Procedure and the functions of the internal treaty organs are closely examined. Chapter 6 then investigates the Financial Mechanism of the Montreal Protocol, including the Multilateral Fund (MLF) that was

---

19   See, among others, James Cameron and Jonathan Robinson, 'The Use of Trade Provisions in International Agreements and Their Compatibility with the GATT', 2 *YbkIEL* (1991), pp. 3–30; Ernst-Ulrich Petersmann, 'International Trade and International Environmental Law: Prevention and Settlement of International Environmental Disputes in GATT', 27 *JWT* (1993), pp. 43–81; Rosalind Twum-Barima and Laura B. Campbell, *Protecting the Ozone Layer through Trade Measures* (United Nations Environment Programme, 1994).

20   See Abram Chayes and Antonia Handler Chayes, *The New Sovereignty* (Harvard University Press, 1995).

established in June 1990. The Financial Mechanism is indispensable for developing countries' 'capacity-building'.

Part V (Chapter 7) is intended as a provisional evaluation of the 'dynamic' international legal régime for the protection of the ozone layer. It may serve, at the same time, as a summary of this book.

PART 1

International Legal Régimes

∵

CHAPTER 1

International Environmental Régimes

I   Preliminary Examination of 'International Régimes'

In 1990, one German scholar, Thomas Gehring, concluded that:[1]

> ... international environmental régimes go far beyond treaty law as such. For a defined issue-area, they are international institutions comprising both an accepted body of normative prescriptions and an organised process for the making and application of these prescriptions. Given the successful integration of these two elements, international régimes turn out to be *comparatively autonomous sectoral legal systems.*

Perhaps the highly specialised environmental regime that has framed the legally-binding regulation of ozone-depleting chemicals will also be characterised as such a 'sectoral legal system' in international environmental relations. Yet, an often-voiced concern by international lawyers is that such a sectoral legal system in a given issue-area – founded on a multilateral treaty – may still coexist with the system of modern international law, even though its régime organs have successfully 'internalised' the making and application of law.[2]

I have much to say about the 'comparatively autonomous sectoral ozone régime' in the existing international legal system. The principal purpose of the present study is to contribute to a better understanding of the international ozone treaties through the study of the so-called normative 'régimes' within the discipline of public international law. More specifically, we are concerned with a close analysis of the treaty-based cooperative and regulatory ozone régime and its relatively 'self-contained' implementation mechanisms at the international level.

At present, the term 'international régimes' is frequently used in the literature of both international law and international relations.[3] For many of régime

---

1   See Thomas Gehring, 'International Environmental Régimes: Dynamic Sectoral Legal Systems', 1 *YbkIEL* (1990), p. 56 (emphasis added).
2   See Martti Koskenniemi, 'Breach of Treaty or Non-Compliance? Reflections on the Enforcement of the Montreal Protocol', 3 *YbkIEL* (1992), pp. 123–162.
3   With regard to differences between international law and international relations (political science), see, for example, Max Sørensen (ed.), *Manual of Public International Law* (St. Martin's Press, 1968), pp. 1–8; Yasuaki Onuma, 'International Law in and with International

---

© KONINKLIJKE BRILL NV, LEIDEN, 2019 | DOI:10.1163/9789004290877_003

theorists, international régimes – as legal norm-creating institutions – may normally be established not only by formal multilateral treaties but also by other non-binding legal instruments, including 'soft law'.[4] From this perspective, Professor Eckart Klein's traditional régime-definition that strictly requires, first of all, a formal treaty as positive law seems to be too narrow.[5]

In the political context of international relations studies, international régimes are generally defined as 'a set of implicit or explicit principles, norms, rules and decision-making procedures around which actors' expectations converge in a given area of international relations'.[6] In brief, they are 'international

---

Politics', 14 *EJIL* (2003), pp. 105–139; Koji Teraya, 'Kokusaihō ni okeru "Chikara (Power)"' ['Power' in the Science of International Law], in Yasuaki Onuma (ed.), *Law and Power in International Society* (Nihonhyoronsha, 2008), pp. 103–154; Otto Kimminich, 'Teaching International Law in an Interdisciplinary Context', 24 *Archiv des Völkerrechts* (1986), pp. 145 et seq.: Albert Bleckmann, *Völkerrecht* (Nomos, 2001), pp. 9–10; Robert Kolb, *Theory of International Law* (Hart Publishing, 2016), pp. 279 et seq.; Andrea Bianchi, *International Law Theories* (Oxford University Press, 2016), pp. 121–134; Andrew Hurrell, 'International Society and the Study of Regimes: A Reflective Approach', in Volker Rittberger (ed.), *Regime Theory and International Relations* (Claredon Press, 1992), pp. 54–57; Robert J. Beck, 'International Law and International Relations Scholarship', in David Armstrong (ed.), *Routledge Handbook of International Law* (Routledge, 2009), pp. 12–28; Bruno Simma, 'Völkerrechtswissenschfat und Lehre von den internationalen Beziehungen: Erste Überlegungen zur Interdependenz zweier Disziplinen' 23 *Österreichische Zeitschrift für öffentliches Recht* (1972), pp. 293–324.

4   In the latter case, it is particularly difficult to identify the precise moment when régime-formation occurs in international relations.

5   Defined as (i) a treaty between States or States and international organisations regulating the status of an area, such as the high seas or outer space, (ii) a general interest underlying the regulation and (iii) the régime which endows the area with the general status *erga omnes*. See Eckart Klein, 'International Régimes', in 9 *Encyclopedia of Public International Law* (North-Holland Pub. Co., 1986), pp. 202 et seq.; Klein, *Statusverträge im Völkerrecht* (Springer, 1980); Oscar Schachter, *International Law in Theory and Practice* (Martinus Nijhoff, 1991), pp. 74–76; L.F.E. Goldie, 'Special Régimes and Pre-emptive Activities in International Law', 11 *ICLQ* (1962), pp. 698–699, noting that régimes provide the 'ideal conditions for the early growth of the law'. For an extensive discussion, see also Winfried Lang, 'Regimes and Organizations in the Labyrinth of International Institutions', in Lang, *Völkerrecht in Zeitverantwortung – Ausgewählte Schriften zu Diplomatie, Umweltschutz, internationale Organisationen und Integration* (Heribert Franz Köck (ed.), NWV Verlag, 2006), pp. 171–182; Akira Kotera, 'Kokusai Regīmu no Ichi' [Position of International Régimes], in Masahiko Iwamura et al. (eds.), *Kokusai Shakai to Hō* [International Community and Law] (Iwanami-Koza Series, volume 2), (Iwanami Shoten, 1997), pp. 87–107 (in Japanese); Osamu Yoshida, 'Kokusaihō ni okeru "Kokusai Regīmu" no Shintenkai' [Developments of "International Régimes" in International Law], 99 *Kokusaihō Gaikō Zasshi* [Journal of International Law and Diplomacy] (2000), pp. 259–289; Yoshida, 'Organising International Society? Legal Problems of International Régimes between Normative Claims and Political Realities', 9 *ARIEL* (2006), pp. 63–118.

6   See Stephen D. Krasner, 'Structural Causes and Regime Consequences: Regimes as Intervening Variables', in idem (ed.), *International Regimes* (Cornell University Press, 1983), pp. 1–22;

institutions for the governance of limited issue-areas'.[7] International political cooperation fostered by international régimes within a given issue-area may eventually furnish the basis for international governance.

Although examples of such régimes in international political and economic relations may be multiplied indefinitely, the General Agreement on Tariffs and Trade (GATT)[8] – serviced by an *ad hoc* GATT Secretariat in Geneva having uncertain treaty status[9] – can be regarded as the prototype.[10] The GATT,

---

Amandine Orsini and Jean-Frédéric Morin, 'Regimes', in Jean-Frédéric and Amandine Orsini (eds.), *Essential Concepts of Global Environmental Governance* (Routledge, 2015), p. 171. For a critical argument of international relations theories, see Andrew Hurrell, 'International Society and the Study of Regimes: A Reflective Approach', in Volker Rittberger (ed.), *Regime Theory and International Relations* (Claredon Press, 1992), pp. 57–71; Shinya Murase, 'Perspectives from International Economic Law on Transnational Environmental Issues', 253 *Hague Recueil* (1995), pp. 299–300. See also Thomas Gehring, 'International Environmental Régimes: Dynamic Sectoral Legal Systems', 1 *YbkIEL* (1990), p. 37 (note 16), arguing that régime theorists do not fully deal with the impact of decision-making procedures and the relationship between normative and decision-making elements. In an attempt to improve the most frequently cited international régime definition provided by Krasner, some authors further argue, for instance, that régimes could be 'the organising concepts for softer, nonbinding agreements that embody cross-national intentions on particular issues', and that they are 'created and operated primarily through mechanisms of negotiation'. See Bertram I. Spector, Gunnar Sjöstedt and I. William Zartman (eds.), *Negotiating International Regimes: Lessons Learned from the United Nations Conference on Environment and Development* (UNCED) (Graham & Trotman/Martinus Nijhoff, 1994), pp. 3–4 (emphasis added). In addition, Osherenko and Young define international regimes as 'social institutions composed of agreed-upon principles, norms, and decision-making procedures that govern the interactions of actors in specific issue areas'. See Oran R. Young and Gail Osherenko, *Polar Politics: Creating International Environmental Regimes* (Cornell University Press, 1993), pp. 1 et seq.

7   See Thomas Gehring, *Dynamic International Regimes* (Peter Lang, 1994), p. 15. On the concept of 'governance', see Oran R. Young, 'Global Governance: Toward a Theory of Decentralised World Order', in idem (ed.), *Global Governance: Drawing Insights from the Environmental Experience* (MIT Press, 1997), pp. 273–299; Volker Rittberger (ed.), *Regime Theory and International Relations* (Claredon Press, 1992), pp. 392–94.

8   See Chapter 4(III) in this volume.

9   See William J. Davey, 'The WTO/GATT World Trading System: An Overview', in William J. Davey and Andreas F. Lowenfeld, *Handbook of WTO/GATT Dispute Settlement*, Vol.1 (1996), pp. 14–15. See also John H. Jackson, *The World Trading System* (2nd ed. MIT Press, 1997), p. 42, describing the Secretariat 'technically as a kind of a "leased group, whereby the GATT reimbursed" the ICITO for the costs of the secretariat'. See also Yuji Iwasawa, *WTO no Funsō Shori* [WTO Dispute Settlement] (Sanseido, 1995), pp. 5–6 (in Japanese).

10 See Thomas Gehring, *Dynamic International Regimes* (Peter Lang, 1994), pp. 29 et seq. The GATT contained no explicit provisions for setting up any institutions. On the legal status of the GATT, see Akira Kotera, 'GATT no Kokusaihō teki Chii' [International Legal Status of the GATT], 38 *Bōeki to Kanzei* [Trade Journal] (1990), pp. 39–45 (in Japanese).

which had been widely regarded as an international institution governing international trade relations, was originally intended to be only a provisional free-trade agreement until the establishment of the International Trade Organisation (ITO).[11] In other words, the GATT was applied through the Protocol of Provisional Application (PPA),[12] from 1 January 1948, essentially as a treaty obligation under public international law.[13] Although the WTO trade régime has taken over the old GATT régime, technically speaking, the original text of the GATT treaty still continues to exist as an international agreement.[14]

Certain types of treaties or special legal arrangements governing particular geographical areas often constitute 'objective régimes'[15] binding *erga mones* (affecting non-States) in public international law (see, for example, the 1856

---

11 The ITO Charter never entered into force. See Robert E. Hudec, *The GATT Legal System and World Trade Doplomacy* (2nd ed. Butterworth Legal Publishers, 1990), pp. 59–61.

12 The Protocol of Provisional Application to the General Agreement on Tariffs and Trade, 30 October 1947, *TIAS* No. 1700. See John H. Jackson, *The World Trading System* (2nd ed. MIT Press, 1997), pp. 39–41. The 23 members of the Preparatory Committee of the UNESC signed the General Agreement as an interim measure, and the GATT then entered into force in January 1948 with 23 founding contracting members, including China, France, the United Kingdom and the United States. The GATT 1994 does not include this Protocol (see Chapter 4(III) in this volume).

13 For further details, see Yuji Iwasawa, *WTO no Funsō Shori* [WTO Dispute Settlement] (Sanseido, 1995), Chapter 1(2) (in Japanese); Robert E. Hudec, *The GATT Legal System and World Trade Diplomacy* (Butterworth Legal Publishers, 2nd ed. 1990). See also D.W. Bowett, *The Law of International Institutions* (Stevens & Sons, 4th ed. 1982), p. 117, noting that 'This [GATT] is.... more an international treaty than an international organisation'. On the institutional structure of the WTO, see, for example, William J. Davey, 'The WTO/GATT World Trading System: An Overview' in William J. Davey and Andreas F. Lowenfeld, *Handbook of WTO/GATT Dispute Settlement*, Vol.1 (1996), pp. 12–16.

14 See Chapter 4(III.A) in this volume. In this respect, see also Ernst-Ulrich Petersmann, *The GATT/WTO Dispute Settlement System* (Kluwer Law International, 1997), pp. 50–51.

15 See 11 *YbkILC* (1964), pp. 26–34. For a discussion of 'objective régimes', see Akira Kotera, 'Kokusai Kiko no Hōteki Seikaku ni kansuru Ichikōsatsu' [Legal Nature of International Organisations, with Reference to the Agreements concluded by International Organisations], 93 *Kokka Gakkai Zasshi* [Journal of the Association of Political and Social Sciences] (1980), pp. 39 et seq. (in Japanese); Toshitaka Morikawa, 'Kokusai Seido no Taiseiteki Kōka' [International Régimes producing Effects *Erga Omnes*], 2 *Yokohama Kokusai Keizai Hōgaku* [Yokohama Journal of International Economic Law] (1993), pp. 1–26 (in Japanese); Hermann Mosler, *The International Society as a Legal Community* (Sijthoff & Noordhoff, 1980), Chapter 13; G.M. Danilenko, *Law-Making in the International Community* (Martinus Nijhoff, 1993), pp. 61–64; Richard A. Barnes, 'Objective Regimes Revisited', 9 *AYbkIL* (2000), pp. 97–145; Surya P. Subedi, *Land and Maritime Zones of Peace in International Law* (Clarendon Press, 1996), pp. 174–204; Francesco Salerno, 'Treaties Establishing Objective Regimes', in Enzo Cannizzaro (ed.), *The Law of Treaties Beyond the Vienna Convention* (Oxford University Press, 2011), pp. 225–243.

General Treaty of Peace demilitarising the Aaland Islands,[16] the 1888 Convention Respecting Free Navigation of the Suez Canal, the Mandate (Article 22 of the League of Nations Covenant) over South-West Africa (now Namibia), as 'an international institution with an international object' (that is, a 'sacred trust of civilisation')[17] and arguably, the 1959 Antarctic Treaty).[18] Analysing the 'objective régimes' is certainly important and interesting: just like international regulatory régimes for the environment, 'objective régimes' created by these inter-state treaties are concerned with a general interest of the international community as well as limited individual national interests. However, strictly speaking, 'objective régimes' of a traditional type are essentially connected with specified areas, zones or certain territories (that is, territorial régimes) and it cannot be denied therefore that they do not address newly emerging non-territorial and functional international régimes having administrative character, including the ozone treaty régime. In addition, unlike global commons régimes based on a framework-protocol approach,[19] 'objective régimes' do not necessarily focus attention on their régime-oriented compliance systems. From this perspective, it cannot be denied that some institutional and regulatory forms of international environmental cooperation are thus required.

In the international legal system that still lacks a centralised authority, the basic administrative function of régimes will be to organise partly 'unorganised international society',[20] consisting of sovereign States as territorially organised units. The building of such legal and political régimes has been taking place not only in the territorial dimension but also in non-territorial and functional areas, for example, global environmental protection such as ozone, human rights protection, arms control and the globalization of multilateral trade.

---

16   See the *Aaland Island* case, *LNOJ*, Special Supplement No. 3 (October 1920), p. 3; Arnold Duncan Mc Nair, 'Treaties Producing Effects «Erga Omnes»', in *Scritti di diritto internazionale in Onore di Tomaso Perassi*, Vol. 2 (Dott. A. Giuffrè, 1957), pp. 25–27.

17   See the *International Status of South-West Africa* case, *ICJ Report* (1950), p. 128.

18   See Bruno Simma, 'The Antarctic Treaty as a Treaty Providing for an "Objective Regime"', 19 *Cornell ILJ* (1986), pp. 189–209. See also Tomohito Usuki, 'Kankyō Hogo ni kansuru Nankyoku Jōyaku Sisutemu no Henyō' [Protection of the Antarctic Environment: From Resourcism to Earth-patriotism], 49 *Hokudai Hōgaku Ronshu* [Hokkaido Law Review] (1998), pp. 769–812 (in Japanese).

19   See Section III.A below.

20   On the concept of 'international society', see Georg Schwarzenberger, *A Manual of International Law* (5th ed. F.A. Praeger, 1967), pp. 8–15. See also Andrew Hurrell, 'International Society and the Study of Regimes: A Reflective Approach', in Volker Rittberger (ed.), *Regime Theory and International Relations* (Claredon Press, 1992), pp. 62 et seq.; Bruno Simma and Andreas L. Paulus, 'The "International Community": Facing the Challenge of Globalisation', 9 *EJIL* (1998), pp. 266–277.

14   CHAPTER 1

As far as environmental régimes are concerned, their crucial role would be to strictly regulate previously 'unregulated areas' of international environmental relations. These treaty régimes in various issue-areas have established an international or global network of legal obligations – whether reciprocal or non-reciprocal – through which both common interests of States and international community interests may be well preserved.

In many case studies of environmental régimes,[21] actors involved in the establishment and operation of (environmental) régimes are sovereign States or nations, international organisations, political organs of treaty régimes, non-governmental organisations, potentially affected industries, individuals and so forth. As we shall see, the role of non-State actors in building and sustaining international régimes cannot be ignored.

In order to understand the legal significance of the ozone régime, for the present purposes, we shall focus on international régimes formally based on multilateral treaties. Unlike a mere political régime (that is, non-binding instruments), the creation of a treaty régime can introduce more reliable rules and norms to legally regulate the activities and behaviour of State and non-State actors in need of internationally agreed regulations or standards in a given issue-area of international relations.

As Professor Shinya Murase argues, it is quite clear that international legal or treaty régimes are founded on the principle of good faith (*bona fides*),[22] which is the natural law concept of international law regarded as an 'implicit provision' of all treaty régimes.[23] The legal principle is politically important

---

21   See, for example, Oran R. Young and Gail Osherenko, 'Testing Theories of Regime Formation: Finding from a Large Collaborative Research Project', in Volker Rittberger (ed.), *Regime Theory and International Relations* (Claredon Press, 1992), pp. 223–251.

22   See Shinya Murase, 'Perspectives from International Economic Law on Transnational Environmental Issues', 253 *Hague Recueil* (1995), pp. 417–418; Murase, 'Kokusai Funsou ni okeru Singiseizitsu no Kinō', (Principle of Good Faith in the Implementation of International Obligations: The Function of Complaint Procedures in the Framework of International Regimes), 38 *Jochi Hogaku Ronshu* [Sophia University Law Review] (1995), pp. 189–221 (in Japanese). See also J.F. O'Connor, *Good Faith in International Law* (Dartmouth, 1991), p. 124, noting that the principle of good faith is a 'fundamental principle from which the rule *pacta sunt servanda* and other legal rules distinctively and directly related to honesty, fairness and reasonableness are derived, and the application of these rules is determined at any particular time by the compelling standards of honesty, fairness and reasonableness prevailing in the international community at that time' and: Robert Kolb, 'Principles as Sources of International Law (With Special Reference to Good Faith)', 53 *NILR* (2006), pp. 16–20.

23   See Markus Kotzur, 'Good Faith (Bona fides)', in Rüdiger Wolfrum (ed.), *Max Planck Encyclopedia of Public International Law*, Vol. I (Oxford University Press, 2012), pp. 508–509; Anthony D'Amato, 'Good Faith', 9 *Encyclopedia of Public International Law* (North-Holland

INTERNATIONAL ENVIRONMENTAL RÉGIMES

in securing international cooperation between States in the existing international system. In the *Nuclear Tests* case, the International Court of Justice (ICJ) held that:

One of the basic principles governing the creation and performance of legal obligations, whatever their sources, is the principle of good faith. Trust and confidence are inherent in international cooperation, in particular in an age when this cooperation in many fields becoming increasingly essential.[24]

In the *Gabcikovo-Nagymaros Project* case, the ICJ noted that:

Article 26 [of the 1969 Vienna Convention on the Law of Treaties] combines two elements, which are of equal importance. It provides that "Every Treaty in force is binding upon the parties to it and must be performed by them in good faith". This latter element, in the Court's view, implies that, in this case, it is the purpose of the Treaty, and the intentions of the parties in concluding it, which should prevail over its literal application. The principle of good faith obliges the Parties to apply it in a reasonable way and in such a manner that its purpose can be realised.[25]

Good faith is something more than a mere ethical or political principle.[26] These statements by the International Court of Justice are indicative of the philosophical view that the legal principle of good faith within international legal régimes will help maintain not 'blind' but mutual trust between régimes' State actors.[27] Under international treaty régimes, States are thus expected

---

Pub. Co., 1986), pp. 107–109; Alfred Verdross and Bruno Simma, *Universelles Völkerrecht* (3rd ed. Duncker & Humblot, 1984), pp. 46–48.

24 The *Nuclear Tests* cases (Australia v France and New Zealand v France), *ICJ Reports* (1974), p. 268, para. 46. For a discussion of the binding character of unilateral declaration, see, in particular, David Kennedy, 'The Sources of International Law', 2 *AUJILP* (1987), pp. 48 et seq.; Hiram E. Chodosh, 'Neither Treaty nor Custom: The Emergence of Declarative International Law', 26 *Texas ILJ* (1991), pp. 122–124.

25 See the *Gabcikovo-Nagymaros Project* case (Hungary/Slovakia), *ICJ Reports* (1997), pp. 75–76, para. 142. For a discussion, see Alan E. Boyle, 'The Gabcíkovo-Nagymaros Case', 8 *YbkIEL* (1997), pp. 13–20; Hugh Thirlway, *The Law and Procedure of the International Court of Justice*, Vol. II (Oxford University Press, 2013), p. 1230.

26 See Michel Virally, 'Good Faith in Public International Law', 77 *AJIL* (1983), pp. 130–134; Manfred Lachs, 'Some Thought on the Role of Good Faith in International Law', in Robert J. Akkerman, Peter J. van Krieken and Charles O. Pannenborg (eds.), *Declarations on Principles: A Quest for Universal Peace* (Sijthoff, 1977), pp. 47–54; Vladimir Paul, 'The Abuse of Rights and Bona Fides in International Law' 28 *Österreichische Zeitschrift für öffentliches Recht und Völkerrecht* (1977), pp. 121–125.

27 On the functions of the legal principle good faith in the WTO régime or international commercial law, see, in particular, Thomas Cottier and Krista Nadakavukaren Schefer,

to behave 'rationally' at least and this will come close to Kelsen's basic norm of international law (*Grundnorm des Völkerrechts*): 'States ought to behave as the others usually behave'[28]. Non-compliance in 'bad faith' with obligations of treaty régimes would lead to the collapse of their legal systems.[29]

Section II of this Chapter analyses in depth international environmental régimes in the field of international law. It first considers international legal régimes for the environment in general, and then discusses the link between these régimes and (i) law-making and the development of international cooperative or regulatory régimes for environmental regulation, (ii) the institutionalisation of international environmental cooperation, (iii) 'soft enforcement' of international environmental obligations and (iv) non-governmental organisations or institutions. Section III then examines the legal character of sectoral legal systems, or 'self-contained régimes', in international law.

II   International Régimes in International Environmental Relations

In the context of environmental protection, Professor Gehring defines international régimes as certain 'regulations' developed in a supreme organ of a treaty régime, governing a defined areas of international environmental relations.[30]

'Non-Violation Complaints in WTO/GATT Dispute Settlement: Past, Present and Future', in Ernst-Ulrich Petersmann (ed.), *International Trade Law and the GATT/WTO Dispute Settlement System* (Kluwer Law International, 1997), pp. 167–170; Robert Kolb, *Good Faith in International Law* (Hart Publishing, 2017), pp. 176–182.

28 See Hans Kelsen, *Reine Rechtslehre* (2nd ed. Franz Deuticke, 1960), pp. 221–223; Kelsen, *The Pure Theory of Law* (trans. by Max Knight, University of California Press, 1970), pp. 217–219; Joseph Raz, 'Kelsen's Theory of the Basic Norm', in Stanley L. Paulson and Bonnie Litschewski Paulson (eds.), *Normativity and Norms: Critical Perspectives on Kelsenian Themes* (Clarendon Press, 1998), pp. 47–67; Osamu Yoshida, 'Hans Keruzen no Konpon Kihan Ronkou' [Reflections on Hans Kelsen's Basic Norm in International Law], 44 *Tsukuba Hōsei* [Tsukuba University Journal of Law and Politics] (2008), pp. 103–125 (in Japanese).

29 See Michel Virally, 'Good Faith in Public International Law', 77 *AJIL* (1983), pp. 130–134; Antonio Cassese, *International Law in a Divided World* (Clarendon Press, 1986), p. 157; B.O. Iluyomade, 'The Scope and Content of a Complaint of Abuse of Right in International Law', 16 *Harvard ILJ* (1975), pp. 50–51. It is important to note that the principal source of non-compliance is not willful disobedience, but the result of a lack of capability, clarity or priority. See Abram Chayes and Antonia Handler Chayes, *The New Sovereignty* (Harvard University Press, 1995), pp. 13–15.

30 See Thomas Gehring, 'International Environmental Régimes: Dynamic Sectoral Legal Systems', 1 *YbkIEL* (1990), p. 36; Hermann E. Ott, *Umweltregime im Völkerrecht* (Nomos, 1998), pp. 37 et seq.

In a similar vein, Jurgielewicz identifies international environmental régimes as the development of legal regulations (normative expectations) by both State and non-State actors through collective decision-making, governing a specific issue area and creating a legal obligation among the actors.[31] Gehring lays special emphasis on the legislative function played by a Conference of the Parties or an equitable internal organ within a special treaty régime. Such a political organ often enjoys considerable independence and it is often only within the framework of international régimes that authoritative decisions are formally adopted.[32] On the other hand, Jurgielewicz's régime definition appears to come close to those of régime theorists of international relations studies.

The reason I first referred to these régime-definitions by two international lawyers is to show that international environmental régimes in many instances consist of legal regulations or standards. The standards or regulations established by regulatory régimes fall in the category of 'legal norms' having a relatively high degree of formality.[33] As Professor Birnie suggests, international regulations are meant to be a 'legal process since it implies an attempt to govern behaviour by the setting of rules and standards and the promulgation of principles'.[34] As far as very detailed legally-binding standards are concerned, however, it may be true that an environmental régime as a body of 'international environmental law' seems alien to general international law or

---

31 Lynne M. Jurgielewicz, *Global Environmental Change and International Law* (University Press of America, 1994) p. 105.

32 See Chapter 2(III.D.2) in this volume. It is noticeable in this context that the Consultative Meeting of the Parties to the Antarctic Treaty has steadily developed international treaties to regulate the conservation of marine living resources, mineral resources, and so forth. See the 1959 Antarctic Treaty (Article 9); the 1972 Antarctic Seals Convention; the 1980 Antarctic Marine Living Resources Convention (CCAMLR); the 1988 Antarctic Mineral Resources Convention (CRAMRA); the 1991 Antarctic Environment Protocol. See also Francesco Francioni, 'A Decade of Development in Antarctic International Law', in Francesco Francioni and Tullio Scovazzi (eds.), *International Law for Antarctica* (2nd ed. Kluwer Law International, 1996), pp. 1–12.

33 See Abram Chayes and Antonia Handler Chayes, *The New Sovereignty* (Harvard University Press, 1995), pp. 115–118. See also Rosalyn Higgins, 'The Role of Resolutions of International Organisations in the Process of Creating Norms in the International System', in W.E. Butler (ed.), *International Law and the International System* (Martinus Nijhoff, 1987), p. 21, defining a norm as 'an authoritative provision of law that continues to command significant community expectations as to its contemporary validity and which may be appropriately invoked and applied in the particular factual context': and Hermann E. Ott, *Umweltregime im Völkerrecht* (Nomos, 1998), p. 42.

34 See Patricia Birnie, 'International Environmental Law: Its Adequacy for Present and Future Needs', in Andrew Hurrell and Benedict Kingsbury (eds.), *International Politics of the Environment* (Clarendon Press, 1992), p. 51.

customary international law.[35] Such environmental regulations will include the so-called 'ecostandards', emission standards of NOx, consumption and production of CFCs and ODSs and other related instruments. They are generally annexed to the treaty texts and further adjusted by the highest treaty organ, in accordance with developments in related scientific and technical knowledge. Usually, these treaty-based international standards themselves are not capable of being customary international law for environmental protection.[36] For a number of reasons, they must therefore be supervised by internally specialised international agencies or institutions, rather than by formal judicial institutions for legal settlement.[37]

In this particular respect, these treaty régimes are correctly understood as international regulatory régimes for the environment (that is, international standard-setting treaties).[38] International regulatory régimes are designed to facilitate and consolidate the legal protection of international community interests as well as those of individual States. It is natural that such global regulatory régimes are based on international cooperation among developed and developing nations, international institutions, non-governmental and scientific institutions, industry and other non-State actors. In this way, they are defined as international cooperation régimes established specifically for the purposes of safeguarding the 'common interests'[39] of the international community as a whole.[40] The terminology is used here to accentuate the growing importance

---

35   See Ian Brownlie, 'A Survey of International Customary Rules of Environmental Protection, 13 *NRJ* (1979), pp. 179–189. See also Martti Koskenniemi, 'Breach of Treaty or Non-Compliance', 3 *YbkIEL* (1992), p. 161. Under the international case-law, the *Trail Smelter* arbitration still remains the only international adjudication in the field of air pollution. See *Trail Smelter Arbitration* (United States v. Canada), 33 *AJIL* (1939), p. 182 and 35 *AJIL* (1941), p. 648; J.E. Reid, 'The Trail Smelter Dispute', *CYbkIL* (1963), pp. 213–229.

36   See Patricia Birnie, Alan Boyle and Catherine Redgwell, *International Law and the Environment* (3rd ed. Oxford University Press, 2009), pp. 17–18; Martti Koskenniemi, 'Breach of Treaty or Non-Compliance', 3 *YbkIEL* (1992), arguing that detailed international standards have less than formal legal status.

37   See Section III(C) below and Chapters 3 and 5 in this volume.

38   See also Alan E. Boyle, 'Codification of International Environmental Law and the International Commission: Injurious Consequences Revisited', in Alan Boyle and David Freestone (eds.), *International Law and Sustainable Development: Past Achievements and Future Challenges* (Oxford University Press, 1999), p. 63.

39   On this point, see J.G. Merrills, *Anatomy of International Law: A Study of the Role of International Law in the Contemporary World* (Sweet & Maxwell, 1981), pp. 58–69.

40   In this respect, some international cooperation régimes would fall into the category of the régimes that 'endow the areas the general status *erga omnes*. It would be possible to argue that the ozone layer presently enjoys such a general status in general international law (see Chapter 2(III.B) in this volume).

of high levels of international cooperation between Northern industrialised and Southern industrialising countries in modern international environmental relations.[41]

International environmental regulations and legal rules can be defined as, in Professor W. Lang's phrase, 'primary elements' or substantive 'régimes' (or simply, provisions)[42] of multilateral environment treaties. For example, Articles 2 and 3 of the Montreal Ozone Protocol and Articles 3, 4 and Articles 7 and 8 of the 1989 Basel Convention[43] fall in this category. As we shall see later, international diplomatic negotiations on 'primary elements' of environmental treaties are usually protracted and difficult.[44] In addition, the legal dynamics of regulatory régimes will be characterised by further elaboration of precise binding international regulations and detailed rules or practices by internal treaty organs, such as the Conference or Meeting of the Parties.[45] Yet, this is only after the adoption of respective treaty régimes.[46]

The international regulatory and cooperative régimes would also, in many instances, need procedural provisions relating to (i) obligations of prior notification and consultation in the context of environmental hazard,[47] (ii) obligations to notify[48] and consult[49] in the case of accidents or emergencies

---

41 See Section III(B) below.

42 See Winfried Lang, 'Diplomacy and International Environmental Law-Making: Some Observations', 3 *YbkIEL* (1992), pp. 114–115.

43 See 28 *ILM* (1989), p. 657, in Patricia W. Birnie and Alan E. Boyle, *Basic Documents on International Law and the Environment* (Clarendon Press, 1995), p. 322. The Convention entered into force on 5 May 1992.

44 In the context of the ozone régime, see Chapter 2(II) and Chapter 3(II and IV) in this volume.

45 On the functions of the Conference of the Parties to MEAS, see Jacob Werksman, 'The Conference of the Parties to Environmental Treaties', in Jacob Werksman (ed.), *Greening International Institutions* (Earthscan, 1996), pp. 55–68.

46 See Jacob Werksman, 'The Conference of the Parties to Environmental Treaties', in Werksman (ed.), *Greening International Institutions* (Earthscan, 1996), pp. 56–57. In the context of the ozone régime, see Chapter 3(IV)) in this volume.

47 See the 1986 Early Notification Convention; the 1986 IAEA Assistance Convention; the 1983 Exchange of Notes between the United Kingdom and France Concerning Exchange of Information in the Event of Emergencies Occurring in One of the Two States which could have Radiological Consequences for the Other State. On this point, see also the following cases: the *Corfu Channel* case (United Kingdom v. Albania), *ICJ Reports* (1969), p. 4 and the *Lac Lanoux* arbitration (Spain v. France), 24 *ILR* (1957), p. 101.

48 For example, the 1982 UNCLOS (Article 198); the 1972 MARPOL Convention (Article 8(4)); the 1976 Barcelona Convention (Article 9(2)).

49 See, for example, the 1972 London Dumping Convention (Article V(2)); the 1974 Nordic Environmental Protection Convention (Article 11); the 1979 Geneva Convention (Articles 5 and 8); the 1978 UNEP Draft Principles (Principle 7); the 1986 WCED Legal Principles

20   CHAPTER 1

capable of causing transfrontier harm in general, (iii) environmental impact assessment (EIA)[50] and (iv) global environmental monitoring of treaty compliance[51] in general. They can be defined as 'secondary elements' of environment protection agreements. In logic and practice, such procedural 'régimes'[52] themselves are not necessarily dynamic in character, but they are absolutely indispensable for the development of substantive provisions of international legal régimes. In other words, procedural régimes contribute to the dynamics and maintenance of international cooperative and regulatory régimes in international law.

(Article 17); and the 1992 Rio Declaration (Principle 19). See also the *Lac Lanoux* Arbitration (France *v.* Spain), 24 *ILR* (1957), p. 101; the *Fisheries Jurisdiction* cases (United Kingdom v. Iceland), *ICJ Reports* (1974), p. 3. As to the continental shelf, see, for example, the 1989 Kuwait Protocol concerning Marine Pollution Resulting from Exploitation and Exploration and Exploitation of the Continental Shelf; the 1981 UNEP Principles Concerning the Environment Related to Offshore Drilling and Mining within the Limits of National Jurisdiction. In addition, the principle of 'prior informed consent' (PIC) would be included in this category.

50   Early examples include the 1978 UNEP Draft Principles of Conduct; the 1985 ASEAN Agreement (Article 14); the 1982 World Charter for Nature; the 1985 EC Environmental Assessment Directive; the 1982 UNEP Conclusions of the Study on the Legal Aspects Concerning the Environment related to Offshore Mining and Drilling within the Limits of National Jurisdiction; the 1982 UNCLOS (Article 206). On EIA, see, in particular, Philippe Sands and Jacob Werksman, 'Procedural Aspects of International Law in the Field of Sustainable Development: Citizen's Rights', in Konrad Ginther, Erik Denters and Paul J.I.M. de Waart (eds.), *Sustainable Development and Good Governance* (Martinus Nijhoff, 1995), pp. 187–196; Geoffrey Wandesforde-Smith, 'Environmental Impact Assessment', in Michael Bothe (ed.), *Trends in Environmental Policy and Law* (E. Schmidt, 1980), pp. 101–129; Nicholas A. Robinson, 'International Trends in Environmental Impact Assessment', 19 *Boston College Environmental Affairs Law Review* (1992), pp. 591–610; Akiko Okamatsu, 'Kokusaihō ni okeru Kankyō Eikyō Hyōka no Ichiduke' [Place of Environment Impact Assessment in International Law', in Junichi Eto (ed.), *Kokusaihō no TōTatsuten* [Achievements of International Law] (Shinzansha, 2015), pp. 711–725; Yuko Minami, 'Kokusai Kankyōhō no Hatten to Kankyō Asesumento' [The Development of International Environmental Law and Environment Assessment', 115 *Hitotsubashi Ronso* [*Hitotsubashi Law Review*] (1996), pp. 190–208 (in Japanese). See also *Pulp Mills on the River Uruguay* case, stating that 'neither the 1975 Statute nor general international law specify the scope and content of an environmental impact assessment' (*ICJ Reports* (2010), p. 73, para. 205).

51   See Section III(C) and Chapter 5 in this volume.

52   Yet, it must be noted that, as with the doctrine of 'estoppel' (by 'representation') as a general principle of international law (see, for example, the *Temple* case) or local remedies (see, for example, the *Phosphates in Morocco* case), the distinction between such 'procedural régimes' and 'substantive régimes' in international law is not necessarily clear-cut. See C.F. Amerasinghe, *Local Remedies in International Law* (Grotius Publications, 1990), pp. 347–350.

In the light of its environment-related purposes, the dynamics of the regulatory aspect of international environmental régimes (that is, the development of substantive provisions) is noteworthy. As Professor Gehring argues,[53] it is now undeniably one of the distinctive and unique characteristics of evolving régimes in international environmental relations. However, we as international lawyers must not forget that they nevertheless do co-exist with the system of general public international law and other specialised treaty régimes for various political and/or economic purposes (for example, the WTO/GATT régime),[54] even though such international environmental régimes often do have a comparatively autonomous 'self-contained' character in international law.

Further, we also need to take account of national implementation of environmental agreements, simply because it is crucial for the successful implementation of régimes.[55] In this respect, it is noteworthy that many environmental agreements, including the 1985 Vienna Ozone Convention,[56] required their parties to adopt necessary domestic measures and national implementation strategies.[57]

III International Environmental Régimes and International Law

A Law-Making in International Cooperation Régimes for Environmental Regulation

As stated earlier, international environmental régimes coming within the scope of the present legal study are created and maintained by formal multilateral treaties between States or international institutions (that is, conventions, treaties, accords, agreements, supplementing protocols and so forth). International law is generally regarded as deriving from the following sources, that is, the above-mentioned international conventions, whether general or

---

53 See Section I above.

54 On the compatibility of the WTO/GATT law and environmental treaty régimes, see Chapter 4 in this volume.

55 On this point, see Andrew Hurrell, 'International Society and the Study of Regimes: A Reflective Approach', in Volker Rittberger (ed.), *Regime Theory and International Relations* (Claredon Press, 1992), pp. 69–71.

56 Article 2(2).

57 In general, the parties enjoy broad discretion in taking such measures. Notable examples include the 1992 Climate Change Convention (Article 4(2.a)): the 1992 Biodiversity Convention (Article 6): the 1989 Basel Convention (Article 9(5)): the 1985 ASEAN Agreement on the Conservation of Nature and Natural Resources (Articles 1 and 2): the 1973 CITES (Articles VIII.1–2 and 7).

22

particular; international custom, general principles of law, and as a secondary source, judicial decisions and the teachings of the most highly qualified publicists.[58]

In the sphere of global environmental protection, as Gündling contends, international treaty law is of special importance, because it is by multilateral treaties that the necessary environmental obligations can be formulated in a sufficiently clear and systematic manner.[59] However, it is also very likely that, in view of the level of economic and political integration of the present international community, States would hesitate to adopt a comprehensive single agreement that will deal with all aspects of a given issue-area of international environmental relations.[60]

A growing number of environmental régimes are based on multilateral framework conventions and/or subsequent implementing protocols, including the 1985 Vienna Ozone Convention and its Montreal Protocol, the 1979 LRTAP Convention adopted under the auspices of the UN Economic Commission for Europe (UN/ECE) and its protocols,[61] the 1992 Climate Change

---

58   See Maarten Bos, *A Methodology of International Law* (North-Holland, 1984), pp. 48 et seq.; V.D. Degan, *Sources of International Law* (Martinus Nijhoff, 1997); David Kennedy, *International Legal Structures* (Nomos, 1987), pp. 11 et seq.; Alfred Verdross and Bruno Simma, *Universelles Völkerrecht* (3rd ed. Duncker & Humblot, 1984), pp. 321 et seq.; Yasuaki Onuma, *International Law in a Transcivilizational World* (Cambridge University Press, 2017), pp. 104 et seq.; Hugh Thirlway, *The Sources of International Law* (Oxford University Press, 2014); Patricia Birnie, Alan Boyle and Catherine Redgwell, *International Law and the Environment* (Third ed. Oxford University Press, 2009), pp. 14–42; Philippe Sands and Jacqueline Peel, *Principles of International Environmental Law* (3rd ed. Cambridge University Press, 2012), pp. 94 et seq.; Alexandre Kiss and Jean-Pierre Beurier, *Droit international de l'environnement* (4th ed. A. Pedone, 2010), pp. 61.

59   See Lothar Gündling, 'Environment, International Protection', 5 *Encyclopedia of Public International Law* (North-Holland Pub. Co., 1986), pp. 122 et seq. See also Paul C. Szasz, 'International Norm-Making', in Edith Brown Weiss (ed.), *Environmental Change and International Law: New Challenges and Dimensions* (United Nations University Press, 1992), pp. 41–62.

60   It is probably true that the existing environment treaty law is therefore fragmentary and unsystematic. Unlike the global 'Constitution for the Oceans' (UNCLOS), there exist no 'Convention on the Law of Global Air', as suggested at the 1989 Ottawa Meeting of Legal and Policy Experts on the Protection of the Atmosphere. See Peter H. Sand, 'UNCED and the Development of International Environmental Law', 3 *YbkIEL* (1992), p. 7.

61   See the 1979 Convention on Long-Range Transboundary Air Pollution, 18 *ILM* (1979), p. 1442; the 1984 Protocol on Long-term Financing of a Co-operative Programme for Monitoring and Evaluation of the Long-Range Transmission of Air Pollutants in Europe (EMEP), 27 *ILM* (1988), p. 701; the 1985 Protocol on the Reduction of Sulphur Emissions or Their Transboundary Fluxes, 27 *ILM* (1988), p. 707; the 1988 Protocol Concerning the Control of Emissions of Nitrogen Oxides or Their Transboundary Fluxes, 28 *ILM* (1989), p. 212; the 1991 Protocol Concerning the Control of Emissions of Volatile Organic Compounds or

Convention[62] and the 1997 Kyoto Protocol,[63] UNEP Regional Sea Conventions and their supplementing protocols,[64] and, arguably, the international waste régime of the 1989 Basel Convention.[65]

On many occasions, these régimes incorporated certain elements of non-binding 'soft law' instruments produced beforehand by negotiating State actors.[66] After the adoption of a treaty, the highest treaty institution within the respective régime would also generate not only 'hard law' but also internal soft law, such as decisions, resolutions or recommendations that lack formal binding force.[67]

Their Transboundary Fluxes, 31 *ILM* (1992), p. 573; the 1994 Protocol on Further Reduction of Sulphur Emissions, 33 *ILM* (1994), p. 1542 and: the 1998 Persistent Organic Pollutants Protocol (POPS Protocol), 37 *ILM* (1998), p. 505; the 1998 Protocol on Heavy Metals, 2237 *UNTS* (2005), p. 7; the 1999 Protocol to Abate Acidification, Eutrophication and Ground-level Ozone (Gothenburg Protocol), 2319 *UNTS* (2009), p. 81. On the effectiveness of the LRTAP régime, see J. Wettestad, 'Acid Lessons? LRTAP Implementation and Effectiveness', 7 *GEC* (1997), pp. 235–249.

62 1771 *UNTS* (2009), p. 107, in Patricia W. Birnie and Alan E. Boyle, *Basic Documents on International Law and the Environment* (Clarendon Press, 1995), p. 252.

63 37 *ILM* (1998), p. 22. For a general discussion, see Duncan French, '1997 Kyoto Protocol to the 1992 UN Framework Convention on Climate Change', 10 *JEL* (1998), pp. 227–239.

64 The UNEP Regional Sea Conventions include the 1976 Barcelona Convention for the Mediterranean and Protocols (15 *ILM* (1976), p. 290), supplemented by the 1980 Athens Protocol and the 1982 Geneva Protocol; the 1978 Kuwait Convention and Protocol (17 *ILM* (1978), p. 511) and the 1989/90 Protocols; the 1981 Abidjan Convention and Protocol (20 *ILM* (1981), p. 746), supplemented by the 1981 Protocol; the 1981 Lima Convention and Agreement supplemented by 1981/83/89 Protocols; the 1982 Jeddah Convention and the 1992 Protocol; the 1983 Cartagena Convention and Protocol (22 *ILM* (1983), p. 221) and the 1983/90 Protocols; the 1985 Nairobi Convention and Protocols; the 1986 Noumea Convention and Protocols (26 *ILM* (1987), p. 38). Many of these treaty texts can be found in Peter H. Sand, *Marine Environment Law in the United Nations Environment Programme: An Emergent Eco-Regime* (Cassell Tycooly, 1988).

65 See 28 *ILM* (1989) p. 657, in Patricia W. Birnie and Alan E. Boyle, *Basic Documents on International Law and the Environment* (Clarendon Press, 1995), p. 322.

66 Especially worthy of reference would be the 1972 Stockholm Declaration on Human Environment; the 1982 World Charter for Nature; the 1975 Mediterranean Action Plan (MAP); the 1985/87 Cairo Guidelines and Principles for the Environmentally Sound Management of Hazardous Wastes: and the 1989 Helsinki Declaration, which preceded the 1990 Revision of the Montreal Ozone Protocol (see Chapter 3(IV.B)) in this volume).

67 As described in the following chapters in this volume, internal 'soft law', adopted by the Ozone Meeting of the Parties ('Ozone Decisions'), has formed an important part of the international regulatory régime. Under the 1973 CITES régime, a total of 190 non-binding recommendations made by the Conference of the Parties – interpreting and elaborating its legal text – have shaped the international régime in a manner barely foreseeable at the time of its adoption. See Peter H. Sand, 'Whither CITES? The Evolution of a Treaty Regime in the Borderland of Trade and Environment', 8 *EJIL* (1997), p. 35.

One of the major reasons to rely on framework conventions-implementing protocols – and international soft law – is that their law-creating and developing techniques generally correspond to economic, political and social realities of the decentralised international legal community of nearly two hundred States.[68] In addition, even in a situation of scientific uncertainty, certain positive action must be taken by States to prevent serious or virtually irreversible environmental damage (for example, ozone depletion). In short, these legal instruments can provide a flexible law-creating process in international environmental relations. More concretely, by using these techniques, State actors can tackle controversial or complicated global environmental issues collectively at a time when they are in reality still hesitant in restricting their freedom of action.

In this respect, it cannot be denied that traditional customary international law rules and their law-making methods do not necessarily recognise the urgency of the need for efficient international cooperation and regulatory régimes for the environment. For example, customary law requires State practice in the international community combined with an *opinio juris*, and usually evolves over a relatively long period.[69] In a somewhat different context, a comprehensive set of rules and principles contained in the 1969 Vienna Convention on the Law of Treaties[70] by itself cannot provide flexible guidelines

---

68 See Atsuko Kanehara, 'Wakugumi Jōyaku' [Framework Convention], in Soji Yamamoto (Japan Energy Law Institute) (ed.), *Kokusaikankyōhō no Jūyō Kōmoku* [Basic Points of International Environmental Law] (Japan Energy Law Institute, 1995), pp. 1–7; Soji Yamamoto, *Kokusaihō* [International Law] (Revised ed. Yuhikaku, 1994), pp. 673–676.

69 But see, for example, the *North Sea Continental Shelf* cases (Federal Republic of Germany v. Denmark; Federal Republic of Germany v. the Netherlands), ICJ *Reports* (1969), p. 43, para. 73, noting that 'it might be that, even without the passage of any considerable period of time, a very widespread and representative participation in the convention might suffice of itself...'; the *Libya v. Malta* case, ICJ *Reports* (1985), pp. 29–30, paras. 26–27; the *Nicaragua* case (Merits: Nicaragua v. United States), ICJ Reports (1986), pp. 97–98, paras. 184–185. The ILA's London Statement of Principles Applicable to the Formation of General Customary International Law notes that: 'General customary international law is created by State practice which is uniform, extensive and representative in character.... Although normally some time will elapse before there is sufficient practice to satisfy these criteria, no precise account of time is required' (Section 12). See A.H.A. Soons and Christopher Ward (eds.), *Report of the Sixty-Ninth Conference Held in London, 25–29th July 2000* (2000), pp. 731–732. See also Bin Cheng, 'United Nations Resolutions on Outer Space: "Instant" International Customary Law?', *Indian JIL* (1965), pp. 23 et seq.; Paul C. Szasz, 'International Norm-Making', in Edith Brown Weiss (ed.), *Environmental Change and International Law: New Challenges and Dimensions* (United Nations University Press, 1992), pp. 66–69.

70 8 *ILM* (1969), p. 679; 63 *AJIL* (1969), p. 875, entered into force in 1980. See, in particular, I. Sinclair, *The Vienna Convention on the Law of Treaties* (2nd ed. Manchester University Press, 1984).

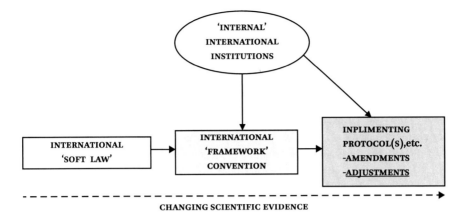

DIAGRAM 1: The framework conventions-protocol approach

to quickly reach international treaty régimes relating to global environmental protection. A new law-making technique is needed here.[71]

As illustrated in Diagram 1, in the first phase, framework conventions[72] lay down international substantive obligations in broad and general terms for hesitant States to take 'appropriate measures' or enact 'all practicable measures'. This, in effect, is the confirmation of the rule of international 'due diligence'.[73] However, as in the case of the 1985 Vienna Ozone Layer Convention (Articles 2–5) and the 1979 Geneva LRTAP Convention (Articles 3–9), framework convention régimes commonly furnish the institutional basis for future international environmental cooperation in scientific research, systematic observation, information exchange and so on.[74] Secretariats of environmental conventions

---

71   See Jonathan I. Charney, 'Universal International Law', *AJIL* 87(1993), p. 543: 'Rather than State practice and *opinio juris*, multilateral forums often play a central role in the creation and shaping of contemporary international law'. On the role of such 'multilateral forums' in the development of the ozone régime, see Chapters 2(II), 3(II), 5(II) and 6(II).

72   In a report entitled 'Towards an Ozone Convention', the UNEP Working Group defined a framework convention as 'an agreement by the signatories to a common objective; an agreement to co-operate in research, monitoring and exchange of information; and an expression of intent to effect future agreements for specific actions toward controls and other measures' (UNEP/WG.69/3, 31 December 1981, p. 10).

73   See Chapter 2(III.C(1)) in this volume. Unlike the 1985 Vienna Ozone Convention, the 1992 Climate Change Convention introduced certain emission reduction targets (Article 4(2.a-b)).

74   On this point, see Alan E. Boyle, 'The Principle of Co-operation: The Environment', in Vaughan Lowe and Colin Warbrick (eds.), *The United Nations and the Principles of International Law: Essays in Memory of Michael Akehurst* (Routledge, 1994), p. 131, suggesting

therefore typically provide important services, such as groups of technical experts.[75]

In the second phase, based on improved or changing scientific knowledge and technical data, protocols or subsequent treaties and/or annexes set detailed legally-binding international standards or regulations (for example, emission standards) that will give practical content to the vague rule of customary law, 'due diligence'. In the light of any newly emerging scientific evidence, if the need arises, Conferences/Meetings of the Contracting Parties established by convention/protocol régimes are to take further necessary measures on a regular basis.[76] As regards this point, a revolutionary simplified majority voting procedure established by the Montreal Protocol is particularly noteworthy.[77]

It should also be pointed out that, since the framework convention sets the fundamental basis on which supplementary protocols are built, no one may become a party to protocols unless they become a contracting party to the original convention régime.[78] In addition, any party which withdraws from the convention is therefore considered as also having withdrawn from any protocol to which it is a contracting party.[79] This cooperative and solid relationship between the convention and implementing protocols/annexes forms a united international regulatory régime, which will impose uniform international obligations of protocols on contracting parties. Additionally, this would also exclude different legal interpretations of its environmental treaty provisions.[80]

---

that 'the inability to agree cooperative solutions, unless evidence of bad faith, is not itself a breach of international law.

75   See Chapter 2(III.D.3) in this volume.

76   See Chapter 2(III.D.2) in this volume.

77   See Chapter 3(III.C) in this volume.

78   See, for example, the Vienna Ozone Convention (Article 16(1)). The close connection between a convention and subsequent protocols was emphasised throughout the Vienna Convention negotiation. See also the 1987 Montreal Protocol (Article 14); the Biodiversity Convention (Article 32(1)); the 1992 Framework Convention on Climate Change (Article 17(4)); the 1976 Barcelona Convention (Article 23). Article 32(2) of the Biodiversity Convention states that parties have the right to participate in the meetings of the parties to that protocol. Whether or not a party to an original convention ratifies the implementing agreements is its own decision.

79   See, for example, the 1985 Vienna Ozone Convention (Article 19(4)) and the 1997 Kyoto Protocol (Article 27(3)).

80   Article 31.2(a) of the Vienna Convention on the Law of Treaties provides that the 'context' for the purpose of the interpretation of a treaty includes 'any agreements relating to the treaty which was made between all the parties in connection with the conclusion of the treaty, added to its preamble and annexes'. See Mark E. Villiger, *Commentary on the 1969 Vienna Convention on the Law of Treaties* (Martinus Nijhoff, 2009), pp. 429–430; Oliver

Finally, it must be added that the eventual results of the framework convention approach are not necessarily always symbolic or 'lowest-common-denominator international agreements', as is often argued by some critical commentators.[81] Rather, a framework convention should be correctly understood as a necessary 'framework' of a solid legal régime for further international environmental cooperation. In many cases, subsequent scientific investigation prosecuted by 'internal' and/or 'external' régime institutions verifies further international cooperation in a given issue area, and new scientific discovery would help adopt future implementing protocols and/or annexes and other legal instruments.[82]

Turning to soft law,[83] the legal terminology is somewhat controversial, since the rules of law are considered in general only to be compulsory or legally binding: that is to say, such legal rules must always be 'hard law' as such. Strictly speaking, the term international 'soft law' may therefore be misleading. Soft law instruments can be considered, at best, as 'para-droit', 'per-droit' or 'pré-droit'.[84] In this study, I will use the legal term 'soft law' to refer to legally non-binding instruments which thus do not fall into the categories of sources referred to in Article 38(1)(c) of the ICJ Statute, namely, 'resolutions' or 'decisions' and 'declarations' by international organisations and conferences, non-binding international standards, code of conduct, standard of conduct,

---

Dörr and Kirsten Schmalenbach (eds.), *Vienna Convention on the Law of Treaties: A Commentary* (Springer, 2012), pp. 523 et seq.

81 See, for example, Lawrence E. Susskind, *Environmental Diplomacy: Negotiating More Effective International Agreements,* (Oxford University Press, 1992), p. 32.

82 In the context of the ozone régime, see Chapter 3(IV) in this volume.

83 For the analysis of 'soft law', see Patricia Birnie, Alan Boyle and Catherine Redgwell, *International Law and the Environment* (3rd ed. Oxford University Press, 2009), pp. 34–37; Alan Boyle, 'Soft law in International Law-Making', in Malcolm D. Evans (ed.), *International Law* (4th ed. Oxford University Press, 2014), pp. 118–133; Alan Boyle and Christine Chinkin, *The Making of International Law* (Oxford University Press, 2007), pp. 211–229; Pierre-Marie Dupuy, 'Soft law and International Law of the Environment', 12 *Michigan JIL* (1990), pp. 420–435; Tadeusz Gruchalla-Wesierski, 'A Framework for Understanding Soft Law', 30 *McGill LJ* (1984), pp. 37–88; C.M. Chinkin, 'The Challenge of Soft Law: Development and Change in International Law', 38 *ICLQ* (1989), pp. 850–866; Oscar Schachter, 'Recent Trends in International Law Making', 12 *Australian YbkIL* (1988–1989), pp. 11 et seq.; Patricia W. Birnie, 'Legal Techniques of Settling Disputes: The "Soft Settlement" Approach', in W.E. Butler, *Perestroika and International Law* (Martinus Nijhoff, 1990), pp. 183 et seq.; Akiho Shibata, 'International Environmental Lawmaking in the First Decade of the Twenty-First Century: The Form and Process', 54 *JYbkIL* (2011), pp. 37–39.

84 See Oscar Schacther, 'Recent Trends in International Law Making', 12 *Australian YbkIL* (1988–1989), p. 12.

gentlemen's agreement, and other non-binding agreements, including political principles and goals.

International soft law creates an expectation of future international environmental cooperation.[85] In political terms, international soft law instruments – less than formal legal status – could contribute to reinforcing certain 'expectations' shared by State actors and/or the international community. In addition, soft law can produce certain legal effects or norms without formal national ratification. In this sense, an international soft law approach possesses indirect but immediate practical value to the multilateral and global law-creating and developing process.

B   *The Institutionalisation of International Environmental Cooperation* The effectiveness of and compliance with international régimes for the environment depend on the corresponding degree of environmental cooperation among States, international organisations (IGOs), non-governmental and scientific organisations (NGOs), industry and individual citizens. The meaning of the term 'international cooperation' – that has never been defined by international treaties[86] – can be defined here as the internationally coordinated (collective) actions taken by governmental and non-governmental régime actors in a given issue-area of international environmental relations.[87] Thus, the concept of 'international cooperation' introduced here in the context of a régime analysis is much broader than the procedural obligations of notification, consultation and environmental impact assessment in international law. All of the governmental or non-governmental actors are involved in the creation and development of international environmental régimes.[88] A substantial number of environment-related treaties are adopted within the framework of international entities as 'catalysts' (for example, the UNEP and the International Maritime Organisation (IMO)). Scientific evidence readily piled up by individual scientists and their scientific institutions helps facilitate the further developments of highly technical régimes. In order to restrict economic

---

85   In the context of the ozone régime, see Chapter 2(II.B.1) in this volume.

86   See Rüdiger Wolfrum, 'International Law of Co-operation', 9 *Encyclopedia of Public International Law* (North-Holland Pub. Co., 1986), p. 193; Wolfrum, 'International Law', in idem, (ed.), *Max Planck Encyclopedia of Public International Law*, Vol. V (Oxford University Press, 2012), p. 828.

87   See Peter-Tobias Stoll, 'The International Environmental Law of Cooperation', in Rüdiger Wolfrum (ed.), *Enforcing Environmental Standards* (Springer, 1996), pp. 41–43, distinguishing between a 'law on cooperation' and a 'law of cooperation'. See also Helen Milner, 'International Theories of Co-operation Among Nations: Strengths and Weaknesses', 44 *World Politics* (1995), pp. 466–496.

88   On the significance of cooperation in treaty régimes, see *Whaling in the Antarctic* case, ICJ *Reports* (2014), p. 226.

activities that affect the environment, many governments have formed certain forms of partnership with their industries (for example, voluntary agreements and various economic instruments).[89] This means at the same time that the realisation of the so-called 'sustainable development'[90] will thus depend on their environmental efforts. The principle of 'sustainable development' has gained wide recognition in international law of the environment.[91] For the present purpose, however, we are concerned here with international cooperation among governmental actors.

In order to achieve their environmental objectives and purposes, depending on a specific issue area, international régimes must accommodate universal or wider participation from both developed and developing countries.[92] The growing role of developing State actors in establishing and maintaining régime institutions reflects the present importance of global environmental cooperation.[93] The following paragraphs will show that modern international treaty law for the environment has introduced relatively new legal and economic

---

89 In the context of the ozone régime, see Chapter 3(IV) in this volume.

90 The Brundtland Report defines the term as 'development that meets the needs of the present without compromising the ability of future generations to meet their own needs'. See World Commission on Environment and Development (WCED), *Our Common Future* (Oxford University Press, 1987), p. 43. See also Rio Principle 27, which states that 'State and people shall cooperate in good faith and in a spirit of partnership .... in the future development of international law in the field of sustainable development'; *Iron Rhine Railway Arbitration* case, XXVII *Reports of International Arbitral Awards* (2005), paras. 58–59, pp. 66–67. For an extensive discussion see, for example, Winfried Lang (ed.), *Sustainable Development and International Law* (Graham & Trotman/M. Nijhoff, 1995); Konrad Ginther, Erik Denters and Paul J.I.M. de Waart (eds.), *Sustainable Development and Good Governance* (Martinus Nijhoff, 1995); A.E. Boyle and D. Freestone (eds.), *International Law and Sustainable Development: Past Achievements and Future Challenges* (1999); Nico Schrijver, *The Evolution of Sustainable Development in International Law* (Martinus Nijhoff, 2008); Nico Schrijver and Friedl Weiss (eds.), *International Law and Sustainable Development: Principles and Practice* (Martinus Nijhoff, 2004).

91 See also separate opinion of Vice-President Weeramantry attached to the ICJ's *Gabčíkovo-Nagymaros Case,* (Hungary/Slovakia), reproduced in UNEP (ed.), *Compendium of Summaries of Judicial Decisions in Environment Related Cases* (1997), pp. 230–245.

92 For instance, due largely to a low number of ratifications and a shortage of funds, the 1979 Bonn Convention could not provide an effective international cooperative régime for the protection of endangered migratory species. See Patricia Birnie, Alan Boyle and Catherine Redgwell, *International Law and the Environment* (3rd ed. Oxford University Press, 2009), p. 681; Simon Lyster, 'The Convention on the Conservation of Migratory Species of Wild Animals (The 'Bonn Convention'), 29 *NRJ* (1989), pp. 979–1000.

93 However, for a variety of reasons, the interest of environmental protection collides with other societal interests – economic ones in particular – and the necessary decisions often involve 'value judgements' as such. See Lothar Gündling, 'Environment, International Protection', 9 *Encyclopedia of Public International Law* (North-Holland Pub. Co., 1986), p. 122.

instruments to foster global environmental cooperation in securing both participation and compliance.[94]

In the first place, as incentives for participation, international environmental régimes often contain 'economic sanctions' within their legal instruments.[95] Collective sanctions, having harmful effects on the economy of States, include restrictions of foreign trade with non-parties to a treaty and/or non-complying non-party States (for example, the Montreal Protocol (Article 4), the 1973 CITES (Article 5)[96] and the 1989 Basel Convention (Article 4(5)). For instance, as will be discussed in Chapter IV in this volume, Article 4 of the Montreal Ozone Protocol requires parties to strictly restrict international trade in ozone-depleting chemicals with non-complying non-parties to the Protocol.

It cannot be denied that these international trade mechanisms are virtually certain legal tools for promoting compulsory international cooperation in protecting the environment. Perhaps this is indicative of the political aspect of international environmental régimes that tends to reflect the economic and political interests of the powerful States, even though their environmental objectives would be adequately justified.[97] It is often said that the creation of the

---

94 Examples in this section are limited largely to legal instruments concerned directly with 'international environmental cooperation' (see Section II above). For a comprehensive review, see, in particular, Peter H. Sand, 'International Economic Instruments for Sustainable Development: Sticks, Carrots and Games', 26 *Indian JIL* (1996), pp. 1–16.

95 The term 'sanctions' is used here in a broad sense and is not limited to reactions to breaches of international obligations. See, in general, Alain Pellet and Alina Miron, 'Sanctions', in Rüdiger Wolfrum (ed.), *Max Planck Encyclopedia of Public International Law*, Vol. IX (Oxford University Press, 2012), pp. 1–12. For a critical analysis of sanctions in international law, see Kazuhiro Nakatani, 'Keizai Seisai no Kokusaihō jō no Kinō to sono Gōhōsei' [Functions and the Legality of Economic Sanctions under International Law: A Study of the Legal Consequences of International Wrongful Acts], 100–101 *Kokka Gakkai Zasshi* [Journal of the Association of Political and Social Sciences] (1987–1988) (in Japanese). In the context of environmental régimes, see generally Rüdiger Wolfrum (ed.), *Enforcing Environmental Standards* (Springer, 1996); Katharina Kummer, 'Providing Incentives to Comply with Multilateral Environmental Agreements: An Alternative to Sanctions?', 3 *European Environmental Law Review* (1994), pp. 256–263.

96 See 12 *ILM* (1973) p. 1055. The CITES entered into force in July 1975. For the text amended in 1979, see Patricia W. Birnie and Alan E. Boyle, *Basic Documents on International Law and the Environment* (Clarendon Press, 1995), p. 415.

97 See PRESS/TE019 (WTO Symposium on Trade, Environment and Sustainable Development, July 1997), noting that some participants (presumably, including delegations from developing States) felt that 'trade measures in MEAs were inappropriate, reflecting the power of industrialised countries over developing countries'. See also Ethan A. Nadelmann, 'Global Prohibition Regimes: The Evolution of Norms in International Society', 44 *International Organisations* (1990), pp. 480 and 511–524, arguing that the international drug control régime reflects the predominance of the United States and European States in creating norms regarding psychoactive substances. In other words, criminal laws of these dominant States have served as models for the drug control régime.

post-war regime for human rights depended fundamentally on the particular values and interests of the Western States, including the United States.[98]

International community pressure exercised by non-governmental institutions on a particular government, may in certain situations, encourage its universal participation in international cooperation régimes.[99] However, in most cases, these global sanctions are not sufficient to entice developing States into joining international regulatory régimes for the global environment.[100]

In the second place, international environmental régimes therefore commonly provide general or detailed provisions for capacity-building in developing countries.[101] The objective of capacity-building is to build up the long-term capacity of aid receiving countries to comply with legal obligations of particular environmental régimes. As will be described in Chapter VI in this volume, these provisions are designed especially for (i) bilateral, regional and/or international financial assistance, such as 'internal' treaty-based fund (for example, the Montreal Protocol's Multilateral Fund), (ii) international technology transfer, (iii) institutional strengthening and (iv) further development of aid-receiving States' environmental awareness. In this connection, the Global Environmental Facility (GEF),[102] which is jointly administered by the World Bank, the UNDP and the UNEP, will also strengthen the operation of

---

98   Andrew Hurrell, 'International Society and the Study of Regimes: A Reflective Approach' in Volker Rittberger (ed.), *Regime Theory and International Relations* (Claredon Press, 1992), p. 66.

99   'A major factor influencing the decision of many countries to become Party to CITES is the pressure that stems from adverse publicity about illegal or harmful wildlife trade and about the morality of animals in the large-scale pet trade'. See Malcolm J. Forster and Ralph U. Osterwoldt, 'Nature Conservation and Terrestrial Living Resources', in Peter H. Sand (ed.), *The Effectiveness of International Environmental Agreements: A Survey of Existing Legal Instruments* (Grotius Publications, 1992), p. 81.

100   It is worth noting that, before the adoption of the 1987 Montreal Ozone Protocol, only a few developing countries decided to become parties to the 1985 Vienna Ozone Convention. See Chapter 6(II.A) in this volume. See also Peter H. Sand (ed.), *The Effectiveness of International Environmental Agreements: A Survey of Existing Legal Instruments* (Grotius Publications, 1992), pp. 10–11.

101   See Alan E. Boyle, 'Comment on the Paper by Diana Ponce-Nava', in Winfried Lang (ed.), *Sustainable Development and International Law* (Graham & Trotman/Martinus Nijhoff, 1995), p. 138, suggesting that, at the present time, these special treaty provisions for developing countries are regarded as the 'price of participation'. See also Peter H. Sand, 'Trust for the Earth: New International Financial Mechanisms for Sustainable Development', in Winfried Lang (ed.), *Sustainable Development and International Law* (Graham & Trotman/Martinus Nijhoff, 1995), pp. 167–183.

102   For the text of the GEF restructured in 1994, see 33 *ILM* (1994) p. 1273, in Patricia W. Birnie and Alan E. Boyle, *Basic Documents on International Law and the Environment* (Clarendon Press, 1995), p. 666. On the GEF, see Chapter 6(III.B) in this volume.

environmental régimes in the fields of ozone protection, global warming, biodiversity and pollution of international waters.[103]

In the third place, just like the Montreal Ozone Protocol, international environmental régimes often contain special provisions for the sake of international equity. They will include 'grace periods' delaying implementation of treaty law,[104] the above-mentioned provisions for capacity-building and other compliance-related provisions peculiar to individual environmental régimes.[105] Their underlying philosophy will be the principle of common-but-differentiated responsibility that claims the common responsibility of developed and developing nations for the protection of the environment, while such responsibility should be equitably differentiated, in accordance with each State's contribution to the environmental damage and its level of economic development.[106] The 1992 UN Climate Change Convention (Article 3(1)) and the 1997 Kyoto Protocol (Article 10)) explicitly refer to this new 'principle' or approach. Furthermore, in some exceptional cases, régime organs' decision-making mechanisms are also designed for international equity considerations. Under the ozone régime, decisions on adjustments are to be taken by a two thirds majority vote of the contracting parties representing a majority of both developed and developing countries (Article 2(9)(c) of the Montreal Protocol).[107] The composition of the Executive Committee of the MLF also reflects the important role of international equity.[108]

C   'Soft Enforcement' of Treaties: Implementation of and Compliance
       with Legal Obligations of International Environmental Régimes

International environmental law is not a matter of either preventive rules or reparative rules. In many respects, both international legal instruments are needed as a united living organism. Yet, in this study, I would like to emphasise on the point that a growing number of international environmental régimes are founded to a lesser or greater extent on the principle of preventive action – represented by Stockholm Principle 21 (Rio Principle 2)[109] – and the precautionary 'principle' of international environmental law.

The precautionary environmental principle – that is, in my view, still closely related to the principle of preventive action – means, in short, that certain

---

103   See Chapter 6(III.B) in this volume.
104   See Chapter 3(III.E) in this volume.
105   This third category of provisions are not necessarily concerned with the special situation of developing countries. In the context of the ozone régime, see Chapter 3(III).
106   See Chapter 3(III.E.3) in this volume.
107   See Chapter 3(III.C) in this volume.
108   See Chapter 6(III.B.1) in this volume
109   For a discussion, see Chapter 2(III.C.1) in this volume.

preventive measures to protect the environment should be taken even, before a causal link has been established by absolutely clear scientific evidence.[110] The compelling reasons to rely on legal regulations of preventive character will be as follows: (i) some environmental damage (typically ozone depletion) might be irreversible; (ii) it would be less costly to prevent an environmental degradation than to restore the environment afterwards and (iii) it is difficult – though not impossible – to link environmental harm to a particular economic activity or a particular industrial installation. By relying on the comprehensive package of internationally coordinated preventive rules, régime members thus aim to protect the environment, and, at the same time, they could successfully avoid anticipated environmental disputes in a given issue-area of international environmental relations.

International supervision of treaty-based regulatory measures by internally specialised institutions[111] will be characterised as 'soft enforcement' of environmental treaties.[112] Unlike judicial tribunals that are essentially confrontational and bilateral, mechanisms for dispute avoidance and settlement within environmental régimes are multilateral in character. Instead of international adjudication based on existing rules and principles of international law, international supervision or control – such as environmental reporting/monitoring, fact-finding and research, data or information collection and inspection – is increasingly used for compliance control of treaty régime rules.[113] In this context, it should be emphasised, as Professor Alan Boyle says, that:

---

110 See further Chapter 2(III.C) in this volume.

111 For present purpose, treaty organs or agencies, such as the Meetings of the Parties, treaty Secretariat and technical Committees, may also be called 'internal international institutions'. In a strict sense, they are different from international organisations of universal character, such as the United Nations and its various specialised agencies. See the 1975 Vienna Convention on the Relationship of States in Their Relations with International Organisations of a Universal Character (Article 1(2)). Unlike these internal treaty organs, it is established that the United Nations has certain international legal personality. See the *Reparation for Injuries Suffered in the Service of the United Nations* case (Advisory Opinion), *ICJ Reports* (1949), p. 174; *Certain Expenses of the United Nations Case, ICJ Reports* (1962), p. 151.

112 See Osamu Yoshida, '"Soft Enforcement" of Treaties: The Montreal Non-Compliance Procedure and the Functions of the Internal International Institutions', 9 *Colorado JIELP* (1999), pp. 95–141.

113 See, for example, Patricia Birnie, Alan Boyle and Catherine Redgwell, *International Law and the Environment* (3rd ed. Oxford University Press, 2009), pp. 242–245. See also Akio Morita, 'Kokusai Kontorōru (contrôl international) Riron no Rekishiteki Tenkai' [The Historical Development of the Theory of International Supervision: Focusing on the Legal Concept based on its Functions', 95 *Kokusaiho Gaiko Zasshi* [*Journal of International Law and Diplomacy*] (1996), p. 313–355 (in Japanese); Morita, *International Control: Theory and Practice* (University of Tokyo Press, 2000) (in Japanese).

The absence of any provision for institutional supervision or regulation is .... often a sign that the treaty in question is ineffective and leads to obsolescence.[114]

Because of strict limitations of State sovereignty, international environmental régimes rely mainly on intergovernmental compliance monitoring[115] through some forms of data collection, including statistics indicating the extent of government and private activity in a given issue-area of international environmental relations, notification of adoption of relevant domestic legislation, and detailed regulations and national specific programmes.[116] Yet, self-reporting or its data-analysis is the only first step toward successful international supervision, simply because it is a kind of 'early warning system'[117] for non-compliance problems. Under the 1973 CITES régime, the Standing Committee has frequently recommended all parties to collectively apply sanctions against non-complying States and in a point of fact, that procedure was used regarding several non-compliance cases.[118] In the sense that such dispute avoidance and settlement systems are operated by internal treaty organs consisting of government representatives, 'soft enforcement' of régime rules is rather political in nature. However, it should not be forgotten that impartial technical experts of internal régime organs (for example, the UNEP Secretariat) are also involved in the multilateral enforcement process.[119]

---

114 See Alan E. Boyle, 'Saving the World? Implementation and Enforcement of International Environmental Law Through International Institutions', 3 *JEL* (1991), p. 232. But see also Boyle, 'Remedying Harm to International Common Spaces and Resources: Compensation and Other Approaches', in Peter Wetterstein (ed.), *Harm to the Environment* (Clarendon Press, 1997), pp. 84–100.

115 See Abram Chayes and Antonia Handler Chayes, *The New Sovereignty* (Harvard University Press, 1995), Chapter 7. See also Günther Handl, 'Controlling Implementation of and Compliance with International Environmental Commitments: The Rocky Road from Rio', 5 *Colorado JIELP* (1994), pp. 305–331; Kamen Sachariew, 'Promoting Compliance with International Environmental Legal Standards: Reflections on Monitoring and Reporting Mechanisms', 2 *YbkIEL* (1991), pp. 31–52.

116 M.J. Peterson, 'International Organisations and the Implementation of Environmental Regimes', in Oran Young (ed.), *Global Governance: Drawing Insights from the Environmental Experience* (MIT Press, 1997), pp. 125–126. See also Chapter 5(VII.A.1) in this volume.

117 See Abram Chayes and Antonia Handler Chayes, *The New Sovereignty* (Harvard University Press, 1995), p. 155.

118 See Article XIV(1). See also Peter H. Sand, 'Whither CITES? The Evolution of a Treaty Regime in the Borderland of Trade and Environment', 8 *EJIL* (1997), pp. 38–40.

119 However, secretariats of treaty régimes are not necessarily free from political influence. See Sikina Jinnah, *Post-Treaty Politics: Secretariat Influence in Global Environmental Governance* (MIT Press, 2014), pp. 21 et seq.

A conspicuous example of highly institutionalised negotiation for an environmental dispute avoidance and settlement system is a formal non-compliance procedure (NCP) of the Montreal Protocol, which comes close to international conciliation.[120] Initially, the breach of binding but detailed legal regulations (for example, Article 2 control measures for ODSs) and other disputes arising under the treaty régime are to be dealt with by internal technical organs of the NCP. Ultimately, hardened non-compliance cases would be addressed by the highest treaty organ, the Meeting of the Parties to the Protocol. The Montreal Protocol type of the NCP is revolutionary in the sense that many international régimes for the environment had no provisions that explicitly promote further compliance and also penalise intentional non-compliance arising from 'bad faith'. However, it must be added that non-compliance should be best addressed on a case-by-case basis, depending on its nature, reasons and length. In a case that a party still remains non-compliant with treaty obligations after the NCP had been used, there is a slight possibility that traditional mechanisms for dispute settlement would be invoked by the parties to a treaty régime.[121] For instance, breach of the treaty obligations under Article 4 of the Montreal Protocol (TREMs) may be dealt with by traditional dispute settlement procedures. This opens up the possibility of making the 'comparatively autonomous' ozone régime a less 'self-contained' legal system in general public international law.[122]

D *Non-Governmental Organizations as Actors of International Legal Régimes*

There is a general recognition that international cooperation between government actors would not be sufficient to protect the global environment.[123]

---

120 See Chapter 5(VI) in this volume.

121 In most cases, dispute settlement procedures within international cooperative régimes of the environment are only optional for contracting parties and are therefore not implemented on a compulsory basis. For instance, the 1985 Vienna Ozone Convention provides for optional use of the ICJ or arbitration over a dispute regarding treaty interpretation and application. In a case where the parties have accepted no procedure (or a different one), they are obliged to submit the dispute to international conciliation (see Chapter 2(III.D.4) in this volume).

122 See Section IV below.

123 See, for example, Alan Boyle and Christine Chinkin, *The Making of International Law* (Oxford University Press, 2007), pp. 41 et seq.: Ulrich Beyerlin and Thilo Marauhn, *International Environmental Law* (Hart Publishing/CH Beck, 2011), pp. 300–301; Mark A. Drumbl, 'Actors and Law-Making in International Environmental Law', in Malgosia Fitzmaurice, David M. Ong and Panos Merkouris (eds.), *Research Handbook on International Environmental Law* (Edward Elgar, 2010), pp. 11–13; Pierr-Marie Dupuy and Jorge E. Viñuales, *International Environmental Law* (Cambridge University Press), pp. 32–33; Philippe Sands and Jacqueline Peel, *Principles of International Environmental Law* (3rd ed. Cambridge

Not only UN-based international organs but also internal treaty organs within international régimes are mostly political meeting places in which traditional State actors still play dominant roles. As a marked trend, however, non-governmental organisations (NGOs) – that are not endowed with international legal personality[124] – are now involved in the process of international environmental régime-building and maintenance.[125] Environmental NGOs aim to advance their particular purposes in defined issue-areas of international environmental relations through the means available to them. Of course, it is not necessary for NGOs that are in principle free from governmental control to look after, or safeguard, narrowly defined 'national interests', whether political, economic or social. Their influence over régime State actors will depends on the available financial and human resources and technical skills required (for example, bargaining, legal or scientific) on the particular occasion.

NGOs generally include public interest and private voluntary organisations, professional associations, academic institutions, industry or trade associations, private companies, and so forth.[126] According to Tolbert, 'environmental NGOs' can be divided into three categories, namely, (i) public interests NGOs (for example, Greenpeace International, World Wide Fund for Nature), (ii) scientific NGOs (for example, the International Union for Conservation of Nature and Natural Resources (IUCN)) and (iii) the so-called 'think tanks' (for example, the International Law Association (ILA) and the World Committee

---

University Press, 2012), pp. 86–93; Hilary French, 'The Role of Non-State Actors', in Jacob Werksman (ed.), *Greening International Institutions* (Earthscan, 1996), pp. 251–258.

124 This may be defined as the capacity to bear rights and duties under international law. However, NGOs often do have legal personality in national legal systems and regional legal systems (for example, in the EU and the Nordic community). See Philippe Sands, 'The Environment, Community and International Law', 30 *Harvard ILJ* (1989), pp. 412–415.

125 See Patricia Birnie, Alan Boyle and Catherine Redgwell, *International Law and the Environment* (3rd ed. Oxford University Press, 2009), pp. 100–101; P.J. Sands, 'The Role of Non-Governmental Organisations in Enforcing International Environmental Law', in W.E. Butler (ed.), *Perestroika and International Law* (Martinus Nijhoff, 1990), pp. 61–81; S. Bilderbeek, *Biodiversity and International Law* (IOS Press, 1992), pp. 162 et seq. See also M.J. Peterson, 'Politics and Law in International Environmental Governance', in Wayne Sandholtz and Christopher A. Whytock (eds.), *Research Handbook on the Politics of International Law* (E. Elgar, 2017), pp. 446–450.

126 See Lee A. Kimball, 'The Role of NGOs in the Implementation of the 1982 LOS Convention', in Alfred H.A. Soons (ed.), *Implementation of the Law of the Sea Convention Through International Institutions* (Law of the Sea Institute, William S. Richardson School of Law, University of Hawaii, 1990), p. 141; Anna-Karin Lindblom, *Non-Governmental Organisations in International Law* (Cambridge University Press, 2005), pp. 36–46.

on Environment and Development (WCED)).[127] The principal functions of environmental NGOs include:

(i) identifying and choosing environmental problems which they are going to support;

(ii) mobilising and organising international public opinions by formulating and disseminating information on the environment to the public and governments;

(iii) monitoring compliance with international obligation at national and/or international level;

(iv) participating in international environmental negotiations: in many cases, NGOs enjoy access to meetings of supreme organs or committees (and subsidiary agencies) of treaty régimes in international law as official 'observers'[128] or 'advisory experts', or under another equivalent status:[129] and

(v) participating in the drafting of international environmental treaties and the setting of international standards or norms.[130]

It is worth mentioning that there are many cases where NGOs are allowed to participate as observers in institutions within environmental treaty régimes: the 1971 Ramsar Convention (Article 7(1)),[131] the 1972 World Heritage Convention (Article 8(3)),[132] the 1973 CITES (Article 11(7)) and the 1979 Bonn Convention (Article 7(9)).[133] Added to these, the 1992 Convention for the

---

127 See David Tolbert, 'Global Climate Change and the Role of International Non-Governmental Organisations', in Robin Churchill and David Freestone (eds.), *International Law and Global Climate Change* (Graham & Trotman, 1991), pp. 96–97.

128 For the definition of 'observers' and their roles, see Henry G. Schermers, 'International Organisations, Observer Status', 5 *Encyclopedia of Public International Law* (North-Holland Pub. Co., 1983), pp. 151–152; Henry G. Schermers and Niels M. Blokker, *International Institutional Law* (5th. rev. ed. Martinus Nijhoff, 2011), pp. 131–136.

129 See, for example, Michael Bothe, 'Compliance Control beyond Diplomacy: The Role of Non-Governmental Actors', 27/4 *EPL* (1997), pp. 293–297.

130 See David Tolbert, 'Global Climate Change and the Role of International Environmental Organisations', in Robin Churchill and David Freestone (eds.), *International Law and Global Climate Change* (Graham & Trotman, 1991), p. 98. It is well-known that the International Union for the Conservation of Nature (IUCN) framed early draft articles for the 1971 Ramsar Convention, the 1973 CITES and the 1992 Biodiversity Convention.

131 See 11 *ILM* (1972) p. 963. The Convention entered into force on 21 December 1975. The amended text is reproduced in Patricia W. Birnie and Alan E. Boyle, *Basic Documents on International Law and the Environment* (Clarendon Press, 1995), p. 447.

132 See 11 *ILM* (1972), p. 1358, in Patricia W. Birnie and Alan E. Boyle, *Basic Documents on International Law and the Environment* (Clarendon Press, 1995), p. 375.

133 See 19 *ILM* (1980), p. 15. The Convention entered into force on 1 November 1983. The text is reproduced in Patricia W. Birnie and Alan E. Boyle, *Basic Documents on International Law and the Environment* (Clarendon Press, 1995), p. 433.

Protection of the Marine Environment of the North-East Atlantic[134] inserted provisions that do not discriminate against NGOs and other IGOs (Article 11(1–3)). Yet most MEAs and their rules of procedure usually do not provide for a specific role of NGOs.[135] Provided they have a really expert knowledge and could represent community interests, in my view, they should be allowed to participate in decision-making processes through treaty régimes' specialised internal organs.[136]

In addition, brief mention should be made of NGOs' role in securing compliance with international environmental régimes. Under the CITES régime, environmental NGOs, such as the Wildlife Trade Monitoring Unit in Cambridge (WTMU) and the Trade Records Analysis of Flora and Fauna in Commerce (TRAFFIC), considerably help the CITES Secretariat in monitoring compliance with the treaty.[137] In the case of the international waste régime of the 1989 Basel Convention, NGOs, such as Greenpeace International, have assumed important roles as 'watchdogs' in tracking hazardous wastes exports and alerting possible importing countries.[138] Furthermore, under the 1992 Biodiversity Convention, supplementary information by environmental NGOs would be important, since the legal régime still does not have any treaty provision for independent monitoring and inspection.[139]

In the present case of the Montreal Ozone Protocol, NGOs are allowed to participate in the regular Meeting of the Parties,[140] meetings of the Executive Committee of the Multilateral Fund[141] and meetings of the Open-Ended

---

134 See 32 *ILM* (1993), p. 1068.

135 See Kamen Sachariew, 'Promoting Compliance with International Environmental Legal Standards: Reflections on Monitoring and Reporting Mechanisms', 2 *YbkIEL* (1991), p. 49.

136 On the role of industry in the process of negotiating treaty régimes, see Michael Bothe, 'The Evaluation of Enforcement Mechanisms in International Environmental Law', in Rüdiger Wolfrum (ed.), *Enforcing Environmental Standards: Economic Mechanisms as Viable Means?* (Springer, 1996), p. 18.

137 See Patricia Birnie, Alan Boyle and Catherine Redgwell, *International Law and the Environment* (3rd ed. Oxford University Press, 2009), pp. 687–688. In the United Kingdom, the Royal Society for the Protection of Birds (RSPB) plays an important role in the prosecution process. See M.J. Bowman, 'International Treaties and the Protection of Birds: Part I', 11 *JEL* (1999), p. 103.

138 See Günther Handl, 'Environmental Security and Global Change: The Challenge to International Law', 1 *YbkIEL* (1990), p. 18.

139 See Alan E. Boyle, 'The Convention on Biodiversity', in Luigi Campiglio (eds.), *Environment after Rio* (Graham & Trotman/M. Nijhoff, 1994), p. 125.

140 See Article 11(5). At the Ninth Meeting of the Parties, Greenpeace International and the Alliance for Responsible CFC Policy were granted the 1997 Ozone Awards among other 21 other individuals and organisations. See UNEP.OzL.Pro.9/12, para. 24.

141 See Rules 6 and 7 of the Rules of Procedure of the Executive Committee. For a discussion, see Chapter 6(III(1)) in this volume.

Working Group established by Decision I/5 of the Meeting of the Parties.[142] Though NGOs are not currently allowed to participate in meetings of the Implementation Committee of the NCP, under the Montreal NCP, NGOs could potentially play active roles as international and domestic pressure groups to help enforce international legal rules.[143]

IV   The Emergence of the 'Self-Contained' Régime for Obligations *Erga Omnes*: Ensuring Universal Compliance

Any international régime established by bilateral or multilateral treaty law is based to a greater or lesser extent on the existing system of general international law. In this restricted sense, the term 'self-contained régimes' in international law incurs a certain contradiction in terms.[144] Nonetheless, the reason I dare to discuss the legal concept of 'self-contained régimes' is that it seems to indicate the distinctive character of the international legal régime for the protection of the ozone layer.

In the practice of international jurisprudence after the establishment of the International Court of Justice, the term 'self-contained régime' was first used by the Court in the *Teheran Hostages* case.[145] In this case, after referring to the possibility of sending government notification *persona non grata*, the International Court of Justice stated that:

> [t]he rules of diplomatic law, in short, constitute a self-contained regime, which, one the one hand, lays down the receiving States' obligations regarding the facilities, privileges and immunities to be accorded to diplomatic missions and, on the other, foresees their possible abuse by members of the mission and specifies the means at the disposal of

---

142   See Articles 6 and 11 of the Montreal Protocol.

143   See Chapter 5(IV.B(2)(b)) in this volume. For an extensive discussion, see Akira Sakota and Osamu Yoshida, 'Kokusai Ozonsou Hogo Jōyaku Rejīmu ni okeru NGO no Yakuwari' [The Role of NGOs in the International Legal Régime for the Protection of the Ozone Layer], in *Kankyo Sisaku ni okeru Jūmin Sanka, NGO Katsudō ni kansuru Hōgaku oyobi Gyōseigaku teki Kenkyū* [Legal and Administrative Studies on Public Participation and NGO Activities in Environmental Measures] (Japan Environment Protection Agency, October 1998).

144   *Collins Cobuild English Dictionary* (1987) defines 'self-contained' as 'something complete and separate and does not need help or resources from outside'.

145   See the *United States Diplomatic and Consular Staff in Tehran* case, *ICJ Reports* (1980), p. 40, para. 86. See also Eckart Klein, 'Self-Contained Regime', in Rüdiger Wolfrum (ed.), *Max Planck Encyclopedia of Public International Law*, Vol. IX (Oxford University Press, 2012), p. 98.

the receiving States to counter any such abuse.... the principle of the inviolability of the persons of diplomatic agents and the premises of diplomatic missions is one of the very foundations of this long-established regime, to the evolution of which the traditions of Islam made a substantial contribution.[146]

Subsequently, Special Rapporteur Riphagen developed this concept in the ILC Draft Articles on State Responsibility,[147] but he did not intend the term to have a different meaning from that given by the ICJ.[148] Self-contained international régimes have so far been discussed specifically in the context of the law of State responsibility.[149] Special treaty régimes of self-contained character often preclude legal recourse to normal countermeasures – not including belligerent reprisals[150]– in general international law. In principle, these treaty régimes are self-contained legal systems that, in practice, apply their own legal remedies available.

In the final section of his article 'Self-Contained Régimes', Professor Simma concludes: 'the adoption of "self-contained régimes" is to be welcomed if these *leges speciales* increase the effectiveness of the primary rules concerned and introduce procedures and collective decisions'.[151] This is an important point

---

146   See the *United States Diplomatic and Consular Staff in Tehran* case, *ICJ Reports* (1980), p. 40, para. 86.

147   See 'Content, Forms and Degrees of International Responsibility (Part 2 of the Draft Articles), Draft Articles submitted by the Special Rapporteur', in *Yearbook of the International Law Commission 1982, Volume I, Summary Records of the Meetings of the Thirty-Fourth Session, 3 May-23 July 1982* (United Nations, New York, 1983), pp. 199–202; Arnold Pronto and Michael Wood, *The International Law Commission 1999–2009*, Volume IV (Oxford University Press, 2010), pp. 679–681.

148   See L.A.N.M. Barnhoorn, 'Diplomatic Law and Unilateral Remedies', 25 *NYbkIL* (1994), p 69.

149   See, for example, Bruno Simma and Dirk Pulkowski, 'Leges Speciales and Self-Contained Régimes', in James Crawford, Alain Pellet and Simon Olleson (eds.), *The Law of International Responsibility* (Oxford University Press, 2010), pp. 139–162.

150   The legal term 'countermeasure', which was first used in the *Air Services Agreement* case of 27 March 1946, generally refers to an illegal act that is rendered lawful as a response to a prior illegal act. For a comprehensive review, see Yoshiro Matsui, 'Countermeasures in International Legal Order', 37 *Japanese Annual of International Law* (1994). On the concept of armed reprisals, see Osamu Yoshida, 'Buryoku Kisei Hō no Kihan teki Kōzō to Senji Fukkyu no Shosō' [Normative Structure of the Law Regulating Force and Belligerent Reprisals], 33 *Tsukuba Hōsei* [Tsukuba University Journal of Law and Politics] (2002), pp. 1–69 (in Japanese).

151   See Bruno Simma, 'Self-Contained Régimes', 16 *NYbkIL* (1985), p. 135.

INTERNATIONAL ENVIRONMENTAL RÉGIMES

to note, because there are many international law instruments that are well drafted, but in reality are never put into operation ('sleeping treaties', such as the 1940 Western Hemisphere Convention).[152] Professor Simma provides three major examples of such self-contained régimes:[153] (i) diplomatic law, (ii) the law of the European Community[154] and (iii) human rights treaties.

Professor Kuyper argues that the WTO/GATT trade law régime also has certain aspects of such a self-contained legal system, which could be observed in, for example, treaty interpretation, the exhaustion of local remedies, State responsibility and the law of remedies.[155] Under the WTO/GATT system, as Professor Iwasawa suggests, it is generally agreed that the parties must first use the WTO/GATT dispute settlement system as a special settlement régime in international law; only if the legal mechanism proves ineffective, WTO/GATT members then may take appropriate countermeasures in accordance with general international law – which must, however, be properly authorised by the WTO/GATT members.[156]

The Montreal Protocol – which contains an internal quasi-judicial system of the non-compliance procedure (NCP) – is the first multilateral environmental treaty that is labelled as a 'self-contained' legal system in the primary sense that the dispute settlement régime noticeably deviates from established principles and rules of general law.[157] As was already mentioned in Section I above, in a different context, Professor Gehring called the ozone régime a 'comparatively autonomous sectoral legal system'.

If self-contained treaty régimes mean special régimes which maintain their legal rules totally separate from established principles and rules of general

---

152 See Patricia Birnie, Alan Boyle and Catherine Redgwell, *International Law and the Environment* (3rd ed. Oxford University Press, 2009), p. 240.

153 See Bruno Simma, 'Self-Contained Regimes', 16 *NYbkIL* (1985), pp. 111–136.

154 See Cases 90–91/63 Commission v. Grand Duchy of Luxembourg and Kingdom of Belgium, ECR (1964), p. 631; Case 232/78 Commission v. French Republic ('Mutton and Lamb'), ECR (1979–1978), p. 2379. See also Math Noortmann, *Enforcing International Law: From Self-help to Self-contained Regimes* (Ashgate, 2005), Chapter 9, pp. 149 et seq.

155 See P.J. Kuyper, 'The Law of GATT as a Special Field of International Law', 25 *NYbkIL* (1994), pp. 227–257; Eckart Klein, 'Self-Contained Regime', in Rüdiger Wolfrum (ed.), *Max Planck Encyclopedia of Public International Law*, Vol. IX (Oxford University Press, 2012), pp. 100–101. For supporting evidence, see also Yuji Iwasawa, *WTO no Funsō Shori* [WTO Dispute Settlement] (Sanseido, 1995), Chapter 3, pp. 54–55, its notes 89–90 and pp. 158 et seq. (in Japanese).

156 See, for example, Yuji Iwasawa, *WTO no Funsō Shori* [WTO Dispute Settlement] (Sanseido, 1995), pp. 159 et seq. (in Japanese).

157 See Martti Koskenniemi, 'Breach of Treaty or Non-Compliance?', 3 *YbkIEL* (1992), pp. 123–162.

international law or the law of State responsibility, in a strict sense, the international régime for the ozone layer is by no means 'self-contained' as such. The point to observe is that the international ozone régime has certain substantive and/or procedural rules that are relatively independent of – or deviate to some extent from – such principles and rules of general international law or traditional and long-established customary law. There is no categorical answer to such a debatable question whether the international ozone régime is self-contained or not. Rather, this should be decided on a case-by-case basis, depending on a specific situation. As the subsequent chapters will show, such legal deviation of the ozone régime must be correctly measured not only by general international law, including the law of State responsibility, but also by evolving principles of international environmental law, including the precautionary environmental principle or approach.

It is tentatively suggested that the self-contained legal character of the international legal régime for the protection of the ozone layer can be characterised by the following four points. In the first place, the law of State responsibility or international liability in the context of ozone layer depletion seems to be only of doubtful utility. Since no single State's activities are responsible for adverse effects caused by ozone loss, and most of the States have only a minimal role in both the production and the consumption of ODSs, it is therefore impossible to establish a sufficient link of causation or causality between stratospheric ozone-depleting activities of particular States or private individuals and companies (that is, a culpable act) and potential direct injury to individual States (for example, deteriorating human health or economic loss) that might have been caused potentially by ozone loss or depletion.[158] This clearly means that, since such 'injured States' – if any – cannot acquire standing to bring international claims, individual States cannot have recourse to such inter-State claims even against one of the largest producers and consumers of ODSs. In this respect, the legal character of the international regulatory régime for the ozone layer is essentially different from that of other environmental régimes, including, for example, the international waste régime of the 1989 Basel Convention – because breaches of legal rules regarding the international control of transboundary movements of hazardous wastes normally affect only two or three States, not only the compensation for the victims, but also the

---

158 See, for example, Alexandre Kiss, *Droit international de l'environnement* (A. Pedone, 1989), pp. 106 et seq. The same may be said of acid rain problems. See, for example, Douglas M. Johnston and Peter Finkle, 'Acid Precipitation in North America: The Case for Transboundary Co-operation', 14 *Vanderbilt JTL* (1981), p. 796.

application of the 'polluter pays principle'[159] developed by the OECD would be presumably possible.[160]

An alternative approach, the notion of *'actio popularis'* (or *'actio communis'*) – which is often controversial even in national legal systems – has not, however, been recognised by general international law,[161] excluding limited treaty régimes (for example, the frequently cited Article 259 of the Treaty establishing the European Community).[162] Since third parties (such as environmental NGOs) do not have such standing before international tribunals, they cannot seek preventive relief, even if it is scientifically considered that actual damage or harm to the global environment has been taking place.

Of course, it is also important to consider that under the former Article 19(3.d) of the ILC Draft Articles on State Responsibility,[163] massive pollution of the atmosphere or sea was categorised as a 'international crime'.[164] In this context, all States are 'injured States' with standing and the depletion of the

---

159   On the polluter pays principle, see, in particular, Alan E. Boyle, 'Economic Growth and Protection of the Environment: The Impact of International Law and Policy', in Boyle (ed.), *Environmental Regulation and Economic Growth* (Clarendon Press, 1994), pp. 179 et seq.; Alan E. Boyle, 'Making the Polluter Pay? Alternative to State Responsibility in the Allocation of Transboundary Environmental Costs', in Francesco Francioni and Tullio Scovazzi (eds.), *International Responsibility for Environmental Harm* (Graham & Trotman/Kluwer Academic Publishers, 1991), pp. 363–379.; Sanford E. Gaines, 'The Polluter-pays Principle: From Economic Equity to Environmental Ethos', 26 *Texas ILJ* (1991), pp. 436–496.

160   See Katharina Kummer, *International Management of Hazardous Wastes* (Oxford University Press, 1995), p. 36.

161   In the *South West Africa* cases (second phase), the ICJ decided that 'although a right of this kind may be known to certain municipal systems of law, it is not known to international law as it stands at present: nor is the Court able to regard it as imposed by "general principles of law" referred to in Article 38, paragraph 1(c), of its Statute'. See *ICJ Reports* (1966), p. 47, para. 88; Christine D. Gray, *Judicial Remedies in International Law* (Clarendon Press, 1987), pp. 212–214; Brigitte Bollecker-Stern, *Le préjudice dans la theorie de la responsabilité internationale* (A. Pedone, 1973), pp. 21–22.

162   See, for example, Christian J. Tams, 'Individual States as Guardians of Community Interests', in Ulrich Fastenrath, Rudolf Geiger, Daniel-Erasmus Khan, Andreas Paulus, Sabine von Schorlemer, and Christoph Vedder (eds.), *From Bilateralism to Community Interest: Essays in Honour of Bruno Simma* (Oxford University Press, 2011), p. 384.

163   See Draft Articles on State Responsibility, 37 *ILM* (1998), p. 440. See also 'Draft Articles proposed by the Drafting Committee: Article 18 (International crimes and international delicts [wrongs])', in *Yearbook of the International Law Commission 1976, Volume I, Summary Records of the Twenty-Eighth Session, 3 May–23 July 1976* (United Nations, 1977), pp. 239 et seq.

164   See James Crawford, 'International Crimes of States', in James Crawford, Alain Pellet and Simon Olleson (eds.), *The Law of International Responsibility* (Oxford University Press, 2010), pp. 407–409.

44   CHAPTER 1

ozone layer as the 'common concern of mankind'[165] would be one of the strong
candidates. However, as a practical matter, it is still difficult to see what kind
of legal value such a designation would have in the present international legal
community.[166] Obviously, normal judicial remedies, such as compensation, are
largely unthinkable.[167]

Arguably, as Schachter suggests, the global protection of the ozone layer
would be included in the general category of international obligations *erga
omnes*.[168] In its judgement on the *Barcelona Traction* case delivered in February 1970, the ICJ stated that:[169]

> ... an essential distinction should be drawn between the obligations of
> a State towards the international community as a whole, and those aris-
> ing vis-à-vis another State in the field of diplomatic protection. By their
> nature the former are the concern of all States. In view of *the importance
> of the rights involved,* all States can be held to have a legal interest in their
> protection; they are obligations *erga omnes.* ...Such obligations derive,
> for example, in contemporary international law, from the outlawing of
> acts of aggression, and of genocide, as also from the principles and rules
> concerning the basic rights of the human person, including protection
> from slavery and racial discrimination. Some of the corresponding rights
> of protection have entered into the body of general international law ....;

---

165   See Chapter 2(III.B) in this volume.
166   See Patricia Birnie, 'International Environmental Law: Its Adequacy for Present and Fu-
      ture Needs', in Andrew Hurrell and Benedict Kingsbury (eds.), *International Politics of
      the Environment* (Clarendon Press, 1992), pp. 81–82. See also Jutta Brunnée, '"Common
      Interest" – Echoes from an Empty Shell?', 49 *ZaöRV* (1989), pp. 803–805.
167   See Alan E. Boyle, 'Remedying Harm to International Common Spaces and Resources:
      Compensation and Other Approaches', in Peter Wetterstein (ed.), *Harm to the Environ-
      ment* (Clarendon Press, 1997), pp. 93–94: Patricia Birnie, 'International Environmental
      Law: Its Adequacy for Present and Future Needs', in Andrew Hurrell and Benedict Kings-
      bury (eds.), *International Politics of the Environment* (Clarendon Press, 1992), pp. 81–82.
168   See Oscar Schachter, *International Law in Theory and Practice* (Martinus Nijhoff, 1991),
      p. 381. See also Alfred Rest, 'State Responsibility/Liability: *Erga Omnes* Obligations and
      Judicial Control', 40/6 *EPL* (2010), pp. 301–302.
169   See *Barcelona Traction* case (Belgium *v* Spain, second phase), *ICJ Reports* (1970), p. 32,
      paras. 33–34 (italics added); and the ICJ's controversial *South West Africa* decision of 1966,
      ICJ Reports (1966), p. 6. See also the *East Timor* case, 34 *ILM* (1995), para. 29, saying that
      in the ICJ's opinion, 'Portugal's view that the right of peoples to self-determination, as it
      evolved from the Charter and from United Nations practice, has an *erga omnes* character
      is irreproachable.... it is one of the essential principles of contemporary international
      law': and *Legal Consequences of the Construction of a Wall in the Occupied Territory* (Advi-
      sory Opinion), *ICJ Reports* (2004), pp. 199–200, paras. 155–160.

others are conferred by international instruments of a universal or quasi-universal character.

Such 'importance of the rights involved' will reflect the basic values of the international community as a whole and it also 'explains the concern that all States are considered to have in the protection of those rights, and hence in compliance with the corresponding obligations'.[170]

As we shall see, the international ozone régime has gradually assumed the *erga omnes* character in international law. As of January 2018, nearly 197 States are now parties to the Vienna Ozone Convention and the Montreal Protocol[171] and these environmental treaty instruments are therefore universally accepted. Although the Montreal Protocol's Article 4 trade restrictions seem to run against the traditional maxim *pacta tertiis nec nocent nec prosunt*,[172] these

---

170 Giorgio Gaja (Rapporteur), 'Second Report' (Obligations *Erga Omnes* in International Law), in *Yearbook of the Institute of International Law*, Volume 71-I, Session of Kracow (Pologne), Preparatory Work, 2005 (2005), p. 190; Giorgio Gaja, 'Obligations *Erga Omnes*, International Crimes and *Jus Cogens*: A Tentative Analysis of Three Related Concepts', in Joseph H.H. Weiler, Antonio Cassese and Marina Spinedi (eds.), *International Crimes of State: A Critical Analysis of the ILC's Draft Article 19 on State Responsibility* (Walter de Gruyter, 1989), pp. 151–160. See also Yuji Iwasawa, 'Kokusai Gimu no Tayōsei' [Diversity of International Obligations: Focusing on Obligations *Erga Omnes*], in Junji Nakagawa and Koji Teraya (eds.), *Kokusaihōgaku no Chihei* [Horizon of International Law: Essays in Honour of Yasuaki Onuma] (Toshindo, 2008), pp. 123–162; Hugh Thirlway, *The Sources of International Law* (Oxford University Press, 2014), pp. 145–153; Santiago Villapando, 'Some Archeological Explorations on the Birth of Obligations *Erga Omnes*', in *Liber Amicorum Raymond Ranjeva: l'Afrique et le droit international : variations sur l'organisation internationale* (A. Pedone, 2013), pp. 623–637; Jochen Abr. Frowein, 'Die Verpflichtungen erga omnes im Völkerrecht und ihre Durchsetzung', in Rudolf Bernhardt, Wilhelm Karl Geck, Günther Jaenicke and Helmut Steinberger (eds.), *Völkerrecht als Rechtsordnung, internationale Gerichtsbarkeit, Menschenrechte: Festschrift für Hermann Mosler* (Springer, 1983), pp. 241–262; Frowein, 'Obligations *Erga Omnes*', in Rüdiger Wolfrum (ed.), *Max Planck Encyclopedia of Public International Law*, Vol. VII (Oxford University Press, 2012), pp. 916–919; Claudia Annacker, 'The Legal Régime of *Erga Omnes* Obligations in International Law', 46 *Austrian Journal of Public and International Law* (1994), pp. 131–166; Christian J. Tam, *Enforcing Obligations Erga Omnes in International Law* (Cambridge University Press, 2005); Maurizio Ragazzi, *The Concept of International Obligations Erga Omnes* (Clarendon Press, 1997).

171 Information provided by the UNEP Ozone Secretariat. See at: <http://ozone.unep.org/sites/ozone/modules/unep/ozone_treaties/inc/datasheet.php> (last visited on 31 January 2018).

172 'Third States cannot be bound by treaty obligations without their consent'. See Articles 34–38 of the 1969 Vienna Convention on the Law of Treaties. See also Rüdiger Wolfrum, 'Purposes and Principles of International Environmental Law', 33 *GYbkIL* (1990), p. 329; Mark E. Villiger, *Commentary on the 1969 Vienna Convention on the Law of Treaties*

trade provisions have never been formally challenged by any States, including the parties to the WTO/GATT law régime. Moreover, even non-parties to the Protocol regularly submit required technical data on ODSS to the UNEP Ozone Secretariat,[173] and the ozone layer is now given the evolving legal status of common concern of mankind (CCM).[174] It may safely be assumed that both parties and non-parties – that is, virtually all States – are acting in the interests of the humankind, towards the international protection of the ozone layer.[175] As Professor Charney says, it will be true that 'If the community responds strongly in favour of universal application, no obstacle to such a choice can be found in the constitutional foundation of the international legal system'.[176] However, even if the ozone treaty régime has created intended general legal effects of an *erga omnes* nature as regards ozone-depleting activities, the remedies available in case of their breach would be, again, severely limited.[177]

Secondly, with regard to dispute avoidance and settlement procedure of the Montreal NCP, as Professor Koskenniemi argued, 'non-compliance' – thus implying that the violated international obligation (detailed ODS control measures) is not necessarily legally binding – can ultimately result in (collective) suspension of rights and privileges under the Ozone Layer Protocol, 'in accordance with the applicable rules of international law concerning the suspension of the operation of a Treaty'. This cannot be taken for granted, because the

---

(Martinus Nijhoff, 2009), pp. 467 et seq.; Oliver Dörr and Kirsten Schmalenbach (eds.), *Vienna Convention on the Law of Treaties: A Commentary* (Springer, 2012), pp. 605 et seq.

173 See Chapter 5(VII.A(1)) in this volume. See, for example, Decision IV/17C, Decisions III/16 and IV/17(1) regarding data reports on Article 4 of the Montreal Protocol. It is suggested that, because of the fear that Article 4 trade measures may conflict with the GATT law, data-reporting requirements on that Article were not included in the 1987 original text of the Protocol. See further Chapter 5(VII.A(3)) in this volume.

174 One possible interpretation of the CCM is that it creates international obligations *erga omnes*. See Alan E. Boyle, 'International Law and the Protection of the Global Atmosphere: Concepts, Categories and Principles', in Robin Churchill and David Freestone (eds.), *International Law and Global Climate Change* (Graham & Trotman, 1991), p. 12.

175 In this respect, see Rene Jean Dupuy, 'Humanity and the Environment', 2 *Colorado JIELP* (1991), p. 2, arguing that international obligations *erga omnes* are especially concerned with respect for the rights of man and the environment.

176 See Jonathan I. Charney 'Universal International Law', 87 *AJIL* (1993), p. 550. It is also important to note that the Montreal Protocol introduced a revolutionary simplified majority voting procedure under Article 2(9): adjustments are binding on all parties (see Chapter 3(III.C) in this volume).

177 See Patricia Birnie, Alan Boyle and Catherine Redgwell, *International Law and the Environment* (3rd ed. Oxford University Press, 2009), pp. 234–235.

procedure seems to eliminate the determination of breach of treaty or wrongful act from the beginning.[178]

It is important to note, however, that the commencement of the NCP operation is not founded on the traditional system of State responsibility for environmental damage or the establishment of standing to bring inter-State claims. In this respect, the Montreal NCP – as an internally instituted dispute settlement system consistent with the 'consensus building of communication within an international régime'[179] – can be characterised as an unprecedented procedural mechanism that is designed to effectively operate or enforce *erga omnes* obligations (that is, the global protection of the ozone layer).[180] Paradoxically speaking, the ozone régime needed a 'self-contained' dispute avoidance and settlement system to implement international obligations *erga omnes*. In this limited sense, the ozone régime will be a self-contained régime for international obligations *erga omnes*.

Under the Montreal NCP, the legal rules of binding control measures in Articles 2, 4 and 5 are supervised by special and internal implementation mechanisms.[181] As for ozone treaty disputes on highly technical issues, traditional settlement mechanisms seem out of place.[182] On most occasions, it will be only after the NCP is 'exhausted' that traditional dispute settlement mechanisms provided for in Article 11 of the Vienna Ozone Convention (that is, the use of the international tribunals, such as the ICJ and arbitration) would be invoked by the contracting parties to the Montreal Protocol. Yet, such 'soft enforcement' of treaty obligations[183] should be correctly understood as supplementary to these traditional legal settlement procedures. In other words, international supervision or control by political treaty organs is not meant to readily supplant or replace the final resort still available to the parties to the Montreal Protocol.[184]

---

178 The exact meaning of 'non-compliance' may be seen as a grey area in the ozone régime. See Chapter 5(III) in this volume.

179 See Thomas Gehring, 'International Environmental Regimes', 1 *YbkIEL* (1990), p. 37. See also Chapter 5 in this volume.

180 See Tomohito Usuki, 'Chikyu Kankyō Hogo Jōyaku ni okeru Funsō Kaiketsu Tetsuduki no Hatten [Development of Dispute Settlement Procedures in Global Environmental Conventions], in Takane Sugihara (ed.), *Funsō Kaiketsu no Kokusaihō* [International Law for Dispute Settlement: Essays in Celebration of Judge Shigeru Oda's Seventieth Birthday] (Sanseido, 1997), pp. 182–183 (in Japanese).

181 See Chapters 5 and 6 in this volume.

182 On the Montreal NCP in practice, see Chapter 5(VII) in this volume.

183 See Section III(C) above. See also Chapter 5(VII) in this volume.

184 On the relationship between Article 11 dispute settlement mechanisms and the Montreal NCP, see Chapter 5(III.B) in this volume.

Thirdly, after the adoption of the 1987 Montreal Protocol, internal organs established by the regulatory treaty régime (that is, the Meeting of the Parties to the Montreal Protocol in particular)[185] has successfully 'internalised' the making and application of the ozone treaty rules. At present, the international ozone régime, whose highest treaty organs have adopted over 800 decisions,[186] appears to have its own jurisprudence. In relation to treaty interpretation, the 1991 Third Ozone Meeting of the Parties decided that it could make and interpret its legal ozone rules as it prefers: 'the responsibility for legal interpretation of the Protocol ultimately rests with the Parties themselves'.[187] Furthermore, it must be noted that the legal character of ozone-oriented Decisions adopted by the Meeting of the Parties has often caused legal conflicts with established principles and rules of public or private international law and other generally accepted treaty rules, such as those contained in WTO/GATT trade law.[188]

It must be added, however, that if the need arises, the ozone régime reaffirms established principles of general international law. To take a simple example, in its Thirteenth Meeting, the Implementation Committee of the Montreal NCP requested the UNEP Ozone Secretariat to seek clarification from the Legal Counsel of the United Nations on the status of new States emerging out of the former Soviet Union and their succession to international treaties like the Montreal Protocol.[189]

Finally, the Montreal Ozone Protocol has somewhat controversial trade-related provisions within its Article 4 that have caused some legal conflicts with another 'self-contained' legal system of the WTO/GATT trade law.[190] However, it is interesting that dispute settlement systems of both the international ozone régime and the WTO/GATT have not been invoked by contracting parties to these multilateral agreements.[191] In the following chapters, these 'self-contained' aspects of the international régime for the ozone layer will be

---

185   As with its Protocol, the 1985 Vienna Ozone Layer Convention has its own supreme organ, that is, the Conference of the Parties. See Chapter 3(III.D(2)) in this volume.

186   See UNEP, *Handbook for the Montreal Protocol on Substances That Deplete the Ozone Layer* (11th ed. 2017), pp. 50 et seq.

187   Decision IV/5(5). See Chapter 5(IV.B(3)(b)) in this volume.

188   See Chapter 4 in this volume.

189   See UNEP/OzL.Pro/ImpCom/13/3, para. 8(b). In the Seventh Ozone Layer Meeting held in 1995, the Russian Federation argued, in violation of the Montreal Protocol, that the collapse of the former Soviet Union constituted a fundamental change in circumstances. For a discussion of this point, see Chapter 5(VII.B(1)) in this volume.

190   See Chapter 4 in this volume.

191   In this respect, see reports of meetings of the WTO Committee on Trade and Environment (CTE), for example, PRESS/TE021 (19 December 1997). See also Chapter 4(IV.B) in this volume.

INTERNATIONAL ENVIRONMENTAL RÉGIMES 49

extensively discussed in the broad context of the system of general international law.

v   Conclusions

A supranational law-making and developing institution for the global environment (that is, supranational government) is unlikely to emerge from the existing international system. International environmental regimes within specific issue-areas of environmental relations are practical alternatives to the 'highest human institution' for the environment, political, legal and social.

An individual international régime for the environment acquires, depending on the issue-area and subject matter, its own characteristics. As discussed in the previous section, the international legal régime for the protection of the ozone layer has several 'self-contained' aspects or autonomous character in the system of international law. In any case, the creation of international legal régimes by itself is not an ultimate goal, and it is a means employed by IGOs – and non-governmental entities - to achieve their environmental, economic, social and/or political objectives. This might mean that, in certain exceptional cases, the stated purposes and objectives of international environmental régimes might be achieved at the sacrifice of 'strict consistency'[192] in general international law.

It is important to bear in mind that any international legal régime is commonly founded on generally accepted guiding principles of international law, including the legal principle of good faith (*bona fides*). Many modern treaty régimes for the environment – some of which are established by the framework-implementing protocol approach – now specifically endorse not only customary rules of the environment but also the evolving precautionary principle or approach of international environmental law. In addition, international regulatory régimes also have internal organs for coordinated effective environmental actions. As a strategy for ensuring close cooperation and greater compliance, these régimes contain, within their legal frameworks, collective economic sanctions, capacity-building instruments and international equity considerations.

The effective combination of the fragmented sectoral régimes consisting of these legal 'sticks' and 'carrots' would ultimately help establish a mass of international environmental régimes for the promotion of sustainable development,

---

192   Certainly, it should be the law-makers of the legal régimes (for example, States and highest treaty organs) who must ensure such consistency.

although this will depend on efforts made by States and non-State actors in the international community. Needless to say, international legal régimes are only limited guarantees of environmental protection: the same thing could be true of the present global ozone régime. However, it is still necessary to ask to what extent international régimes, in a given issue-area of environmental relations, can legally guarantee protection of the environment, such as in the case of the ozone layer.

PART 2

The International Treaties for the Protection of the Ozone Layer

∵

CHAPTER 2

The 1985 Vienna Convention for the Protection of the Ozone Layer and Principles of Modern International Environmental Law

I   Introduction

The 1985 Vienna Convention for the Protection of the Ozone Layer (hereafter, the 'Vienna Ozone Convention')[1] is a 'framework' law-making treaty[2] that contains no specific legal standards or regulations for CFCs at the international level. Since the adoption, in 1987, of the Montreal Ozone Protocol that contains not only control provisions for CFCs/ODSs but also strong supervisory and implementation mechanisms, the 'umbrella' Convention has been given only a secondary role.[3] Despite its evident weaknesses, however, it is still important to remember that the 1985 Vienna Ozone Convention has been one of the first international environmental agreements to give an indication of the precautionary environmental 'principle' or approach,[4] and at the same time the treaty laid the legal basis for the Montreal Protocol. In a period of grave scientific uncertainty about ozone depletion, the Vienna Convention was a politically acceptable international cooperation régime for participating States in the context of CFC regulation and further scientific research.

In Chapter II, we are concerned with the framework Ozone Convention. Section II first describes briefly national regulatory measures prior to the adoption of the 1985 Convention, focusing on the States that belonged to the so-called 'Toronto Group' (that is, the United States, Canada, Sweden, Norway, Finland, Denmark, New Zealand, Australia and Switzerland)[5] and the European Community (EC). Then, by using conference documents, it analyses the

---

1   Convention for the Protection of the Ozone Layer, Vienna, 22 March 1985. Reprinted in 26 *ILM* (1987), p. 1529; Patricia W. Birnie and Alan E. Boyle, *Basic Documents on International Law and the Environment* (Clarendon Press, 1995), p. 211.
2   On this concept, see Chapter I(III.A) in this volume.
3   But see Decision I/3 of the Conference of the Parties saying that 'the Convention is the most appropriate instrument for harmonizing the policies and strategies on research'.
4   For a discussion, see Section III(C) below.
5   Named after the group's first meeting in Toronto. See Richard Benedick, *Ozone Diplomacy* (Harvard University Press, 1998), p. 42. However, the Group called itself the 'Friends of the Protocol'. See Edaward A. Parson, 'Protecting the Ozone Layer', in Peter M. Haas, Robert O. Keohane and Marc A. Levy (eds.), *Institutions for the Earth* (MIT Press, 1993), note 31, p. 38.

© KONINKLIJKE BRILL NV, LEIDEN, 2019 | DOI:10.1163/9789004290877_004

protracted Convention negotiation, that is, the first stage of the international régime building.[6] Section III, which is devoted to the detailed analysis of the Vienna Ozone Convention, considers the meaning of 'adverse effects'(Section A), the legal status of the ozone layer (Section B); the relationship between the evolving precautionary 'principle' or approach and the international ozone régime (Section C) and basic provisions of the Convention (Section D), including 'General Obligations'(Article 2), the role of the Conference of the Parties (Article 6) and the dispute settlement procedures (Article 11).

II   The Negotiation of the 1985 Vienna Ozone Convention

The negotiation of the Vienna Convention formally started in January 1982 within the framework of the United Nations Environment Programme (UNEP).[7] Under the meetings of the *Ad Hoc* Working Group of Legal and Technical Experts for the Elaboration of a Global Framework Convention for the Protection of the Ozone Layer established by the UNEP Governing Council in May 1981,[8] participating States considered proposals not only on a global framework ozone convention but also a supplementary (separate) protocol of a highly technical nature, containing specific control measures for specified CFCs.[9] The 1985 Convention negotiation process was rather tedious and laborious because of a divisive confrontation between the Toronto Group and the EC. Moreover, a number of scientific uncertainties about ozone depletion (that is, its cause and effects) continued throughout the Vienna Convention negotiation. Therefore, the drafting of the Convention and its annexes/protocols turned out to be very difficult. However, the UNEP and its former Executive Director, Dr. Mostafa Tolba (1922–2016),[10] did what could be done to cope with such a challenging situation, and participating governmental and non-governmental actors succeeded in agreeing on international environmental efforts for the protection of the ozone layer.

---

6   The second and third phases are (ii) from Vienna to Montreal (1986–1987) and (iii) the post-Montreal period (1988–1997). For a discussion, see Chapter III(II) in this volume.

7   See also Edward A. Parson, *Protecting the Ozone Layer: Science and Strategy* (Oxford University Press, 2003), pp. 114 et seq.

8   See Decision 9/13B, adopted on 26 May 1981.

9   However, from its Third Session, the Working Group decided to focus on discussions on an expected framework ozone convention.

10   See Donald W. Kaniaru, 'Mostafa Tolba of UNEP: The Not-so-well-known Goodness of a Great Scientist and Leader', 46 EPL (2016), pp. 205–208; Penelope Canan and Nancy Reichman, *Ozone Connections: Expert Networks in Global Environmental Governance* (Greenleaf, 2002), pp. 48–52.

The 1985 Vienna Convention for the Protection of the Ozone Layer was signed on 22 March 1985 by twenty States and the EC Commission. It entered into force on 22 September 1988.[11] By January 2018, 197 countries had ratified the Vienna Ozone Convention, including most of the major CFC/ODS producers and consumers in the international community.

A   *National and Regional Regulation of Major Chlorofluorocarbons (CFCs)*

Before discussing the Vienna Convention negotiation, it may be helpful to describe briefly earlier ozone regulations at the national and regional levels. In negotiating specific contents of expected ozone treaties, including annexes and protocols, participating States naturally supported regulatory measures that would reflect their own domestic or regional ozone legislation.

The United States, which was the largest producer/consumer of CFCs, held about forty per cent of the international market share of CFCs in 1976. Thus it was only natural that such a manufacturing country took an initiative in legally restricting the use of CFCs at the domestic level. In January 1975, the Council on Environmental Quality and the Federal Council for Science and Technology jointly established the Federal Interagency Task Force on Inadvertent Modification of the Stratosphere (IMOS). In addition, a special Federal Action was undertaken to restrict uses of CFC-11 and CFC-12.[12] Further, in August 1977, the United States' Clean Air Act Amendment (CAAA) relating to the protection of the stratospheric ozone layer was passed by Congress.[13] In 1978, it also unilaterally banned CFC use as a propellant in non-essential aerosols (for example, deodorants, polishes, hair lacquer and paint). By that time, adequate substitutes for most propellant uses of CFCs were already securable. The domestic market for spray cans containing CFCs had dramatically fallen by almost two-thirds owing to American citizens' consideration of the potential environmental impact of these ozone-depleting substances.[14] At the time of the adoption of the Ozone Convention, the United States, backed by its industries, aimed to internationalise such domestic regulations that limited the aerosol use of CFCs only.

Mention should also be made of the fact that the United States' Environment Protection Agency (EPA) was sued in 1984 by an environmental NGO,

---

11   Seven States and governmental and non-governmental organizations participated in the meeting as observers. See Final Act of the Conference, paras 4–5.

12   See UNEP/WG.69/8, para. 14 and note 14.

13   See also Elizabeth Cook, 'Wrapping it up', in Cook (ed.), *Ozone Protection in the United States: Elements of Success* (World Resources Institute, 1996), p. 23; Edward A. Parson, *Protecting the Ozone Layer: Science and Strategy* (Oxford University Press, 2003), pp. 89–91.

14   See Richard Benedick, *Ozone Diplomacy* (Harvard University Press, 1998), pp. 27–28.

56   CHAPTER 2

the Natural Resources Defence Council (NRDC).[15] The plaintiff organisation insisted in the suit that the EPA had not fully implemented its legal obligations based on Section 157(b) of the CAAA. The NRDC further demanded that a schedule be established for a decision on the control of CFCs[16] It may be argued that the prominent leadership of the United States during the formation of the international ozone régime was strengthened by such environmental movement at the domestic level.

Following the example of the United States, Sweden (in 1979) and Norway (in 1980) formed similar domestic ozone regulations and policies in order to implement bans on cans containing CFCs.[17] In 1980, Canada banned three main CFC products: hair spray, deodorant and antiperspirant. In addition, the Netherlands imposed labelling requirements for CFC aerosol containers upon its industry. However, the attitude of the EC – which in 1976 was responsible for thirty-four per cent of the international sales of CFCs – contrasted remarkably with that of the United States and other countries belonging to the Toronto Group.

The position of the EC was substantially influenced by the European chemical industry that relied heavily on CFC technologies (for example, the United Kingdom-based Imperial Chemical Industries).[18] For instance, the European industry had insisted that CFC substitutes were unthinkable and the regulation of the use of CFCs – as seen in the United States – might create unemployment among its workers.[19] Although in 1977 Holland proposed a measure requiring the labelling of spray cans containing CFCs, the EC emphatically rejected this proposal.[20] Likewise, a Community-wide CFC aerosol ban led by former West Germany was rejected in 1979 by other Member States.[21]

With regard to its regional CFC regulation, the EC adopted a Council Resolution on the use of CFCs in 1978.[22] The regulation required the Member States 'to present the research which they had carried out into the effects of CFCs on

---

15   See Edward A. Parson, *Protecting the Ozone Layer: Science and Strategy* (Oxford University Press, 2003), p. 122. The NRDC participated in the First, Second and Fourth Ozone Meetings of the Parties.

16   See Brenda M. Seaver, 'Stratospheric Ozone Protection: IR Theory and the Montreal Protocol on Substances That Deplete the Ozone Layer', 6 *Environmental Politics* (1997), p. 55.

17   These two countries did not produce, but imported, CFCs.

18   See Nigel Heigh, 'The European Community and International Environmental Policy', 3 *International Environmental Affairs* (1991), pp. 160–178.

19   See Richard Benedick, *Ozone Diplomacy* (Harvard University Press, 1998), p. 25.

20   See ibid.

21   See further ibid., p. 24.

22   See Council Regulation of 30 May 1978 on Chlorofluorocarbons in the Environment, *Official Journal*, No. C133 (7 June), p. 1.

THE VIENNA CONVENTION AND INTERNATIONAL ENVIRONMENTAL LAW 57

man and the environment, and to co-operate on a Community basis so that the research could be planned and the results made available'. In 1980, the Council of the EC adopted Decision 80/372,[23] which set an immediate freeze on production 'capacity' – that is, not to enlarge but maintain CFC-11 and CFC-12 production facilities, without restricting the actual production of CFCs, and a provision for a thirty per cent reduction compared to the 1976 level of the use of CFCs in aerosols by the end of 1981.[24] The Decision also required the EC to develop 'the best practicable technologies' in order to limit emissions in refrigeration, solvent and foam plastics sectors. Furthermore, in 1982 the Council adopted the Decision in order to consolidate the previous measures already taken in 1980. The decision required the Member States to apply precautionary measures to the other sectors using CFCs, such as synthetic foam, refrigeration and solvents as well as aerosol use of CFCs.[25]

Finally, in 1980, Japan – whose negotiating position was largely similar to that of the EC – publicly declared in the OECD its readiness to control CFC production (CFC-11 and CFC-12 in particular) and aerosol uses.[26] Since then, the Japanese Ministry of International Trade and Industry (MITI) has provided its industry with related administrative guidance.[27]

B   *The Vienna Convention Negotiation within the UNEP as a Law-Making Forum*

(1)   The International Ozone Régime-Building from 1977 to 1980

The creation of the 1985 Vienna Convention régime – and the adoption of the Montreal Protocol in 1987 – was a major test of the UNEP's effectiveness in its catalytic role in the progressive development of international environmental law. As we shall see, we may say that the UNEP succeeded in passing this painstaking test.[28]

---

23   See Decision 80/372 of 26 March 1980 Concerning Chlorofluorocarbons in the Environment, *Official Journal*, No. 90 (3 April), p. 45.

24   But this reduction level had already been achieved by the beginning of 1980.

25   See Decision 82/795 of 15 November 1982 on the Consolidation of Precautionary Measures Concerning Chlorofluocarbons in the Environment, in *Official Journal*, No. 329 (25 November), p. 29.

26   See Hirotoshi Goto, 'Seisouken Ozon no Hogo' [The Protection of the Stratospheric Ozone Layer], 69 *Kikan Kankyō Kenkyū* [Environmental Research Quarterly] (1988), pp. 25–26 (in Japanese).

27   On national ozone laws and regulations in Japan, see Chapter III(V.B) in this volume.

28   See also Richard Benedick, *Ozone Diplomacy* (Harvard University Press, 1998), p. 6, noting that 'UNEP went far beyond a traditional secretariat function: it was a model for effective multilateral action'.

At the international level, in 1977, the UNEP first convened an international meeting of scientists, with representatives from thirty-three States and the EC to draft 'the World Plan of Action on the Ozone Layer'.[29] The Ozone Layer Action Plan was to be implemented by international institutions such as the World Meteorological Organisation (WMO)[30] and the World Health Organisation (WHO),[31] along with the UNEP as a catalyst, national governments and non-governmental organisations. At the same time, the UNEP Co-ordinating Committee on the Ozone Layer (UNEP/CCOL) was established to make periodic scientific assessments relating to the state of potential ozone depletion.[32] This newly established scientific institute undertook most of the research on ozone depletion.[33] The UNEP/CCOL was independent of governments, and mainly funded by the UNEP and environmental NGOs.[34] Yet the Committee was not given any power to provide policy recommendations.

In April 1980, at its Eighth Session, the UNEP Governing Council adopted the WMO/UNEP Principles that called for reductions in the production of two major CFCs (that is, CFC-11 and CFC-12), as well as a production capacity cap.[35]

---

29   See Decision 65/IV of the UNEP Governing Council. See also proceedings, UNEP/WG.7/25, in Asit K. Biswas (ed.), *The Ozone Layer: Proceedings of the Meeting of Experts Designated by Governments, International Nongovernmental Organizations on the Ozone Layer Organised by the United Nations Environmental Programme in Washington DC, 1–9 March 1977* (Pergamon Press, 1979).

30   The WMO, a successor to the International Meteorogical Organisation which was established in 1873, formally came into existence in 1950 and became a UN specialised agency in 1951. See, in general, D. W. Bowett, *The Law of International Institutions* (4th ed. Sweet & Maxwell, 1982), pp. 115–116.

31   Established in 1948, became a UN specialised agency the same year. See generally D. W. Bowett, *The Law of International Institutions* (4th ed. Sweet & Maxwell, 1982), p. 114.

32   See UNEP Governing Council Decision 84/C(V) of 25 May 1977 (A/32/25); Mostafa K. Tolba et al. (eds.), *The World Environment 1972–1992: Two Decades of Challenge* (Chapman & Hall, 1992), p. 51.

33   On the CCOL, see UNEP/WG. 7/25/Rev.1; UNEP/WG.69/5, paras. 6–7. The CCOL was annually convened until 1985.

34   On the other hand, the Intergovernmental Negotiating Committee for the Framework Convention on the Climate Change (INC) – which was the main body carrying out research on climate change – consisted chiefly of government representatives. In the end, the UNEP and the WMO were forced to give up their control over the Climate Change Convention negotiation (see UN General Assembly Resolution 45/212, 21 December 1990). On the INC, see Stern Nilsson and David Pitt, *Protecting the Atmosphere: The Climate Change Convention and its Context* (Earthscan, 1994), pp. 15–17. See also Ian H. Rowlands, *The Politics of Global Atmospheric Change* (Manchester University Press, 1995), p. 91, saying that 'the decision of "where" to conduct the science was political, and it had implications for the subsequent international political'.

35   Decision 8/7B of 29 April 1980 (A/35/25). The Nordic countries took the initiative in adopting the decision. See Peter H. Sand, 'The Vienna Convention is Adopted', 27 *Environment* (1985), p. 40.

THE VIENNA CONVENTION AND INTERNATIONAL ENVIRONMENTAL LAW   59

The Principles also called for the development of scientific research and techniques in order to avoid further ozone depletion.[36] Subsequently, the UNEP Governing Council adopted Decision 9/13B of 26 May 1981 that argued for 'the desirability of initiating work aimed at the elaboration of a global framework convention which would cover monitoring, scientific research and the development of best available and economically feasible technologies'.[37] Following this decision, the UNEP Governing Council established an *Ad Hoc* Working Group of Legal and Technical Experts for the Elaboration of a Framework Convention. The decision also asked the UNEP Executive Director 'to ensure that in the work so initiated, all relevant information and related work under way in other forums, as well as the results of any discussions on this subject at the *Ad Hoc* Meeting of Senior Government Officials Experts in Environmental Law are taken into account' and to 'invite the Co-ordinating Committee on the Ozone Layer, as part of its activities under its mandate'.[38]

The 'Montevideo Meeting' held in Uruguay in November 1981 endorsed Decision 9/13B and selected the protection of the ozone layer as a 'major subject area' for which guidelines, principles or agreements should be developed.[39] The meeting also adopted an objective, a strategy and elements of strategy and specific recommendations for initial action concerning this subject matter. The recommendations suggested – highlighting the need for the catalytic role of the UNEP – that the environmental institution 'should continue to strengthen its coordinating role as regards research, monitoring and assessment of the ozone layer, in particular through the CCOL mechanism, and expand the dissemination of information on the problems of the stratospheric ozone layer'.

In this meeting, the delegations of Finland, Sweden and Switzerland tabled 'Draft Recommendations' on an expected framework convention for the protection of the ozone layer.[40] The Draft Recommendation stated that the legal

---

36   See 'Selected Documents' in 6/2 EPL (1980), p. 101. Principle VI of the Weather Modification Provisions embodies Principle 21 of the 1972 Stockholm Declaration.

37   See Decision 9/13B(a) and (b) in UNEP/WG.69/10, para. 1.

38   Additionally, the Executive Director was also requested (i) to contribute to the work of the *ad hoc* working group and (ii) to compile all relevant information, including statistical and technical data, on implementation of the recommendations contained in decision 8/7B of 29th April 1980, in particular data relating to the reduction in the use of Chlorofluorocarbons 11 and 12, as well as to production capacity on the basis of an agreed definition.

39   For further details of the Montevideo Programme, see Alexandre S. Timoshenko, 'Development and Periodic Review of Environmental Law in the 1990s: UNEP Programmatic Approach', in Alexandre Kiss and Françoise Burhenne-Guilmin (eds.), *A Law for the Environment: Essays in Honour of Wolfgang E. Burhenne* (IUCN, 1994), pp. 17–20.

40   See 'Draft Recommendations on Legal Aspects and Elements of a Global Framework Convention for the Protection of the Stratospheric Ozone Layer', in *Report of the Ad*

framework should 'be sufficiently flexible to be easily adaptable to changing circumstances as new scientific evidence becomes available'.[41] The Recommendations also suggested that (i) the framework should be provided by an original convention and (ii) that the specific measures – which are internationally agreed and shall be nationally enforced – should be laid out in the annex(es) that may be amended whenever need be without disturbing the functioning of the basic structure.[42] This early proposal text gave an important indication of a flexible approach adopted later in the 1985 Vienna Ozone Layer Convention.[43] However, the 1981 Montevideo Meeting did not adopt the Nordic Recommendation.[44]

(2)   The Discussions at the *Ad Hoc* Working Group (1982–1985)
From 1982 to 1985, the *Ad Hoc* Working Group held a total of four sessions consisting of seven meetings among the fifty participants and eleven intergovernmental and non-governmental organisations.[45] It was quite difficult to agree on the specific contents of the framework ozone convention, detailed annexes and implementing technical protocols.[46] During the negotiations leading up to the adoption of the 1985 Vienna Convention, the Toronto Group insisted on the need for CFC emission reductions focused on non-essential uses of these chemicals in spray cans with a possible capacity cap (the 'multi-option approach'). On the other hand, the EC preferred CFC production capacity limitation (the 'single-option approach'). Because of the different strategic positions,

---

Hoc Meeting of Senior Government Officials Expert in Environmental Law, UNEP/GC.10/3, Appendix II.

41   See UNEP/GC.10/5/Add.2/Annex/Appendix II, para. 2, cited in Thomas Gehring, *Dynamic International Regimes* (Peter Lang, 1994), p. 202.

42   These are based on the Nordic proposal and statements made at the First Session of the Working Group held in Stockholm in January 1982 (UNEP/WG.69/CPR.2).

43   In this respect, see Thomas Gehring, *Dynamic International Regimes* (Peter Lang, 1994), p. 202.

44   See UNEP/GC.10/5/Add.2, para. 38, cited in Thomas Gehring, *Dynamic International Regimes* (Peter Lang, 1994), p. 202.

45   See UNEP/IG.53/4. First Session (20–28 January 1982, Stockholm); Second Session (first part: 10–17 December 1982, Geneva), (second part: 11–15 April 1983, Geneva); Third Session, (first part: 17–21 October 1983, Geneva), (second part: 16–20 January 1984, Vienna) and; Fourth Session, (first part: 22–26 October 1984, Geneva), (second part: 21–25 January 1985, Geneva). See UNEP/IG.53/4 para. 10, noting that the following governments provided financial support and/or meeting facilities for the sessions: Austria, Canada, Finland, Netherlands, Norway, Sweden, Switzerland and the United States.

46   See, among others, Richard Benedick, *Ozone Diplomacy* (Harvard University Press, 1998), Chapters 4–8.

THE VIENNA CONVENTION AND INTERNATIONAL ENVIRONMENTAL LAW 61

participating States finally decided to adopt a framework ozone convention only.

In January 1982, the UNEP convened the First Session of the Working Group in Stockholm at the invitation of the Swedish government.[47] All members of the United Nations were invited to the meeting of this Session indicating that ozone depletion was truly regarded as global in nature.

For the First Session, the delegations of Finland, Norway and Sweden[48] and the UNEP Secretariat[49] prepared draft texts of a global ozone convention. The Nordic countries' ambitious proposal – whose contents are largely similar to the previous text submitted at the 1981 Montevideo Meeting – addressed several important aspects, including fundamental obligations (article 1),[50] cooperation (article 2), information exchange (article 3), national report (article 4), technology transfer (article 5), institutional structures (articles 7–9), dispute settlement (article 10) and a simplified amendment procedure (articles 12 and 13). In short, the Nordic proposal already reflected the fundamental structure of the 1985 Vienna Ozone Convention. Its flexible approach, combining a framework convention with annexes and/or protocols, was generally supported by the Toronto Group and the EC.[51] However, the debatable issues on the relationship between the convention and annexes and/or protocols was not settled yet (in the Nordic proposal, annexes containing CFC controls were to form integral parts of the ozone convention). In addition, at this session, there was agreement that there should be internal régime organs, such as the Conference of the Parties as a major decision-maker and a treaty secretariat (provided by the UNEP) having administrative functions,[52] and some provisions on dispute settlement.[53]

The Working Group considered that such a flexible approach would be necessary 'in order to allow the accommodation of changing scientific knowledge

---

47 See UNEP/WG.69/10.

48 'Draft International Convention for the Protection of the Stratospheric Ozone Layer: Text submitted by the Delegations of Finland, Norway and Sweden' (UNEP/WG.69/3).

49 See 'Draft International Convention for the Protection of the Stratospheric Ozone Layer', (UNEP/WG.69/3/Add.1, containing a preamble only).

50 'The parties shall limit, reduce and prevent activities under their jurisdiction or control which have or are likely to have adverse effects upon the stratospheric ozone layer'. See also comments by participating experts in UNEP/WG.69/10, para. 20.

51 See Thomas Gehring, *Dynamic International Regimes* (Peter Lang, 1994), p. 206.

52 See UNEP/WG.69/10, paras 21, 24 and 25.

53 For a discussion, see UNEP/WG.69/10, para. 25. The 1979 Geneva Convention (Article 13), the draft Convention on the Law of the Sea (Article 279), the UN Charter (Article 33), the 1972 London Dumping Convention (Article 10) were mentioned as possible models in the context of ozone layer protection.

and policy alternatives as they became available'.[54] The Working Group agreed to draw up a framework convention to be supplemented by annexes and/or protocols that would contain provisions aimed at controlling specific types of actions or substances. It also recommended that the UNEP Secretariat should prepare a new draft text for its Second Session.[55] This preparation proceeded on the basis of the analysis of the following international treaties: the UN Charter, the 1969 Vienna Convention on the Law of Treaties, the 1972 Stockholm Declaration; the 1982 UNCLOS, the framework conventions/protocols of UNEP Regional Seas Programmes,[56] the 1973 MARPOL, the 1979 Geneva LRTAP Convention; the 1973 CITES, Principles on Shared Natural Resources (UNEP/IG.12/2), the draft convention submitted by Finland, Norway and Sweden (UNEP/WG.69/3) and other relevant treaties.[57]

Subsequently, in the first part of the Second Session held in January 1983, a number of delegations – influenced by scientific uncertainties – cautioned against 'moving too rapidly', since that would eventually lead to an 'ill-conceived convention'.[58] There was also disagreement as to whether technical annexes or protocols should be developed simultaneously with the convention.[59]

In the second part of the Second Session held in April 1983, Sweden, on behalf of the Nordic countries, introduced a revised new text, namely, a proposal annex concerning measures to control/limit/reduce CFC emission and use (the 'Nordic Annex').[60] In response to this ambiguous proposal, a number of delegations, including the EC, Japan and the former Soviet Union, suggested that such a proposal could only be regarded as one of the options for an expected *protocol*, since its contents were of a regulatory nature.[61] In this respect,

---

54   See UNEP/WG.69/10, para. 10.

55   For the draft convention, see UNEP/WG.78/2.

56   The most successful example is seen in the Mediterranean. The 1976 Barcelona Convention and its Protocols were signed and ratified by many countries in this region. The 1980 Athen Protocol addresses land-based and airborne sources pollution, but most of the agreements related to marine environment avoid these problems. See Peter H. Sand, *Marine Environment Law in the United Nations Environment Programme: An Emergent Eco-Regime* (Cassell Tycooly, 1988), pp. ix–xxvi; Patricia Birnie, Alan Boyle and Catherine Redgwell, *International Law and the Environment* (3rd ed. Oxford University Press, 2009), pp. 395–396.

57   See UNEP/WG.78/2, para. 8.

58   See UNEP/WG.78/8, para. 9.

59   See ibid., para. 10.

60   See UNEP/WG.78/11. See also relevant statements in UNEP/WG.78/13, paras. 17–22.

61   See UNEP/WG.94/4/Add.1. But see also comments concerning developing countries that are generally supportive of this Nordic proposal (Central African Republic, Djibouti, Kenya and Sri Lanka) in UNEP/WG.94/4/Add.2.

the United Kingdom expert made a general reservation regarding the need for annexes and/or protocols.[62]

In the first part of the Third Session of the Working Group, Sweden noted that the proposed draft annex might be discussed as a proposal for a future ozone protocol.[63] In this context, the United States, which was initially critical of this Nordic proposal text, indicated support for an integral protocol to the convention concerning non-essential aerosol uses of CFCs.[64] In addition, though the number itself was very small, several developing countries participated in this meeting. They insisted on the need for transfer of environmentally sound technology in order to ease anticipated serious economic burdens.[65] It was stressed at the first part of the Third Session that more extensive participation from developing countries was desirable to ensure that the ozone convention was universal in scope.[66]

In the heated confrontation between the United States, Canada, and the Scandinavian countries and the EC, the second revised draft convention[67] and protocols[68] were discussed in 1983, the third draft convention in January 1984,[69] the revised second draft protocol in January 1984,[70] the fourth revised convention containing draft technical annexes[71] and the fourth revised draft protocol in March 1985.[72] By the beginning of the first part of the Fourth Session of the Working Group held in January 1984, the draft ozone convention had been virtually finalised.[73]

(3)   Negotiating an Ozone Protocol for Controlling CFCs

In respect of the much disputed protocol(s) to the convention, at the second meeting of the Fourth Session of the Working Group held in January 1985, the Toronto Group introduced a flexible 'multi-option approach' consisting of four options from which each party to the convention might select the option it

---

62   See UNEP/WG.78/13, para. 16. The United Kingdom later withdrew this reservation. See UNEP/WG.94/5, para. 8.
63   See the draft text in UNEP/WG.94/4 and UNEP/WG.78/13, Annex III.
64   See UNEP/WG.94/5, para 9.
65   See 'Selected Documents' in 10/2 EPL (1983), p. 35.
66   See 'United Nations Activities', 11/3 EPL (1983), p. 58.
67   See UNEP/WG.94/3.
68   See UNEP/WG.94/9.
69   See UNEP/WG.94/8.
70   See UNEP.WG.94/12.
71   See UNEP/WG.94/11.
72   See UNEP/IG.53/4, Annex III.
73   Most articles in the fourth draft convention (UNEP/WG.94/11) remained unchanged.

preferred.[74] It was argued, for example, that the approach would 'enable countries in widely differing circumstances to accept the protocol and would also reward past action by governments to reduce CFC use'.[75] An uncompromising response from the EC was, however, that the 'so-called multi-option approach would still amount to a ban on use of CFCs in aerosols and did not imply any effort on the part of those countries to limit CFC production'. The EC thus concluded that 'his proposal constituted a truly global approach to the problem of protecting the ozone layer, since it proved not only for limitations on production but also for reductions in the use of CFCs in the aerosol sector and for measures in the non-aerosol sector'.[76]

As one expert pointed out in this meeting held at the last stage, both of the major approaches had some shortcomings and future elaboration was required: 'All CFC emissions, and not only those originating from aerosols, should be reduced'.[77] The underlying problem of this expected Article 2 on control measures is expressed best by Lammers: 'neither proposal embodied a set of interrelated rules covering all elements which are vital for effective CFCs control mechanism, i.e. production, use, import, export and emission of all CFCs'.[78]

(4)   'The Vienna Ozone Layer Convention is Adopted'

After the Fourth Session of the Working Group, the draft convention was finally adopted and signed on 22 March 1985 by twenty States and the EEC. In the end, the fifth draft protocol on CFCs prepared by the Working Group[79] was not adopted, in spite of diplomatic missions and an informal meeting at the absolute edge of the Vienna Conference.

Under Article 1(6) of the Vienna Ozone Convention, for the first time, the EC was allowed to become party to a 'mixed international agreement' (that

---

74   See UNEP/IG.53/4, Annex II, paras. 17 et seq. Options (1) and (2) were concerned only with a staged reduction of the total annual use/exports of CFCs in aerosols. Option (3) addressed total production capacity for CFCs, regardless of their use, which did not exceed the total production capacity at the entry into force of the protocol. Option IV addressed a reduction of the total annual use of CFCs of only twenty per cent. See in detail Johan G. Lammers, 'Efforts to Develop a Protocol on Chlorofluorocarbons to the Vienna Convention for the Protection of the Ozone Layer', 1 *Hague YbkIL* (1988), pp. 227–230.

75   See UNEP/IG.53/4, Annex II, para. 17.

76   See UNEP/IG.53/4, Annex II, para. 31. See also discussions during the first part of the Fourth Session in UNEP/WG.110/4, Section V.

77   See UNEP/IG.53/4, Annex II, para. 25.

78   Johan G. Lammers, 'Efforts to Develop a Protocol on Chlorofluorocarbons to the Vienna Convention of the Ozone Layer, 1 *Hague YbkIL* (1988), p. 231 (emphasis added).

79   See Fifth Revised Draft Protocol on Chlorofluorocarbons (UNEP/IG.53/3).

is, both the Community and its Member States are party to it) as a 'regional economic integration organisation' without any of its Member States being required to do so.[80] It is pointed out that this was the EC Commission's legal and political strategy to gain greater competence within the EC. Such an international treaty clause potentially allows the EC Commission to propose Community legislation to implement the framework ozone convention and expected protocols on a regional basis.[81]

The Vienna Conference for the Protection of the Ozone Layer adopted a Resolution that urged 'all States and regional integration organisations, pending entry into force of a protocol, to control their emissions of CFCs, inter alia in aerosols, by any means at their disposal, including controls on production or use, to the maximum extent possible'.[82] The Resolution also required the Working Group to continue work on a protocol that would address 'both short and long term strategies to control equitably global production, emissions and use of CFCs', taking into account the special situation of developing countries and new scientific evidence.[83] A series of negotiations of the protocol to the Vienna Ozone Convention formally started in December 1986, again within the framework of the UNEP as a law-making forum.[84]

III   The 1985 Vienna Convention for the Protection of the Ozone Layer

We can now turn to the basic provisions of the 1985 Vienna Ozone Convention. As is the case with the 1979 LRTAP Convention, the operational parts of the 'framework' Convention are specifically designed for facilitating international environmental cooperation in scientific research and the exchange of information. However, the Ozone Convention also contains several important rules and principles of international environmental law. As with its Montreal Ozone

---

80 Defined as 'an organization constituted by sovereign States of a given region which has competence in respect of matters governed by the Convention or its protocols and has been duly authorised, in accordance with its internal procedures, to sign, ratify, accept, approve or accede to the instruments concerned'. On the procedures, see Article 13(2). This definition is based on earlier relevant provisions regarding signature, ratification, acceptance or approval and accession by such an organization, including Article 1 of Annex IX of the UNCLOS. See 'Texts Relating to Final Clause', in UNEP/WG.94/5/Add.1. See also Article 2(8) of the Montreal Ozone Protocol and Chapter III(III.D) in this volume.
81 See Markus Jachtenfuchs, 'The European Community and the Protection of the Ozone Layer', 28 *CMS* (1990), p. 263.
82 Resolution 2(6).
83 Resolution 2(1).
84 See Chapter III(II) in this volume.

66   CHAPTER 2

Protocol (Article 18), the Vienna Convention totally excludes reservations with
a view to maintaining the universality of the international ozone régime (Article 18).[85]

A   *The Definition of 'Adverse Effects' Caused by Ozone Depletion*
(1)   The Limited Scope of the Term 'Air Pollution' in Regional
           Environmental Treaties

According to the textbooks of environmental science, ozone depletion is
generally included in the category of air pollution, such as global warming
caused by CO_2 emissions.[86] Yet, as seemingly a minor difference in wording,
the term 'pollution'[87] – contained in the 1979 LRTAP Convention (Article 1)
or the 1991 Canada-United States Air Quality Agreement (Article 1(1–2))[88] –
cannot fully explain the global nature of potential 'adverse effects' posed by
ozone depletion. To take an example of acid rain, the most obvious pollutants
of the atmosphere (for example, sulphur dioxide and oxides of nitrogen) are
being transported over long distances and, as a result, these substances cause
transboundary adverse effects on the environment. In this general context, the
term 'transboundary pollution' illustrates short range, regional or bilateral environmental harm or damage. Under the Statement of 'The Rules of International Law Applicable to Transboundary Pollution' (Montreal Rules), prepared
by the ILA International Committee on Legal Aspects of the Conservation of
the Environment', 'transboundary pollution' is defined as 'pollution of which

---

85   However, it should be noted that even if reservations are completely excluded from treaties, States can still enter 'political statements' or 'interpretative declarations'. For the definition of interpretative declarations, see *ILC Yearbook* (1966–II), pp. 189–190; D. M. McRae,
      'The Legal Effect of Interpretative Declarations', 49 *BYbkIL* (1978), p. 155.
86   See, for example, Derek M. Elsom, *Atmospheric Pollution* (Blackwell, 1992), Chapter 1.
87   The concepts of 'pollution' is controversial one. Its meaning depends largely on each treaty's context. A full study of the definition of 'pollution' lies outside the scope of this thesis.
      For a discussion, see Patricia Birnie, Alan Boyle and Catherine Redgwell, *International
      Law and the Environment* (3rd ed. Oxford University Press, 2009), pp. 188–189; Pierr-Marie
      Dupuy and Jorge E. Viñuales, *International Environmental Law* (Cambridge University
      Press), pp. 123–124; Catherine Redgwell, 'Transboundary Pollution: Principles, Policy and
      Practice', in Tommy Koh, Robert Beckman, Hao Duy Phan and S. Jayakumar (eds.), *Transboundary Pollution: Evolving Issues of International Law and Policy* (Edward Elgar, 2015),
      pp. 11–35. See also Allen L. Springer, *The International Law of Pollution* (Quorum Books,
      1983), pp. 63–88, defining 'pollution' mainly as 'a particular level of environmental change
      that is legally significant because of the nature and degree of injury that does or can result
      to important human interests'.
88   See 30 *ILM* (1991), p. 676. See also the 1982 UNCLOS (Article 1(4)).

the physical origin is wholly or in part situated within the territory of one State and which has deleterious effects in the territory of another State'.[89]

On the other hand, ozone depletion shows the emergence of a different kind of 'pollution' *within* the ecosystem as a whole: the 'adverse effects' in the context of ozone depletion cannot be clearly divided according to national territorial boundaries.[90] Just as the concept of 'pollution' cannot address environmental disasters happening within an individual State, it cannot deal adequately with 'pollution' within the global environment. But the definitions of both 'pollution' and 'adverse effects' contained in environmental agreements are helpful in determining the 'threshold' beyond which environmental damage might entail State responsibility.[91]

(2)   Adverse Effects Caused by Ozone Depletion

The technical term 'adverse effects' is defined in the Convention text as, *inter alia,* 'changes in the physical environment or biota, including changes in climate, which have significant deleterious effects on human health or on the composition, resilience and productivity of natural and managed ecosystems, or on materials useful to mankind'[92] This definition – which is based on a text prepared by technical experts[93] – is used here to accurately define negative impacts of ozone depletion that must be mitigated by international environmental cooperation.[94] As indicated in the *Introduction* to this volume, ozone loss may lead to increases in solar ultraviolet radiation (UV-B) with detrimental biological effects such as additional cases of skin cancer and eye cataracts, reduced growth of crop plants sensitive to UV-B and other commercially

---

89   Article 2(2). See *Report of the Sixtieth Conference held at Montreal 1982, August 29th, 1982, to September 4th, 1982* (Canada: 1983), pp. 2 and 159–160 (Comments on Article 2).

90   See Introduction and Chapter I(IV) in this volume.

91   See Philippe Sands and Jacqueline Peel, *Principles of International Environmental Law* (3rd ed. Cambridge University Press, 2012), p. 707.

92   Article 1. The relevant draft provision, as proposed by the UNEP Secretariat, read as follows; "'Adverse effects" means changes in the physical environment or biota, including changes in climate, which are, taken over-all, deleterious to human health or to the composition, resilience and productivity of natural and managed ecosystems' (UNEP/WG.78/2), p. 8. See also Article 7(d) of the 1979 LRTAP, which defines the environment as 'agriculture, forestry, materials, aquatic and other natural ecosystems and visibility'; the 1992 Climate Change Convention (Article 1(1)), which emphasises effects on 'the operation of socio-economic systems or on human health' after deleterious effects on the environment, and inserting the term 'human (health and) welfare'.

93   See UNEP/78/2, p. 8.

94   See UNEP/WG.69/10, para. 20, noting that the need to precisely define the term was stressed during the First Session.

important materials. Moreover, although its environmental adverse effects are long-term and only cumulatively harmful, and not immediate or apparent, the depletion of the ozone layer is virtually irreparable. The definition further recognises that some CFCs/ODSs could probably contribute to global atmospheric warming.[95] It is also important to notice that its broad wording is capable of covering human rights protection (that is, the right to life and a healthy environment).[96]

B   *The Legal Status of the Ozone Layer in General International Law*

'The ozone layer is located in the atmosphere at an attitude ranging between 1- and 50 km. The question arises of what its legal status is'.[97]

At the outset it must be noticed that in the present case of ozone depletion – unlike the utilisation of the living resources of the High Seas or the deep seabed – what matters in the international community has been not 'equal access' or 'freedom' of the stratospheric ozone layer as an internationalised public territory, but potential 'adverse effects' that would be produced by gradual ozone loss. It can easily be assumed that there will be few customary international law based on State practice concerning the possible 'utilisation' of the ozone layer as 'physical' *res communis omnium* for any specific commercial purposes. However, it is strange to think that the stratospheric ozone layer – which States formally decided to protect by using international legal instruments does not have any specific legal status in international law.

(1)   National Jurisdiction over the Ozone Layer
As a matter of an academic legal argument, it is possible to geographically divide State jurisdiction over the ozone layer.[98] In theory, national jurisdiction

---

95   In this respect, in 1998, the Meeting of the Parties adopted Decision X/16 (Implementation of the Montreal Protocol in the light of the Kyoto Protocol). On the Kigali Amendments, see Chapter III in this volume.

96   On the role of human rights law in environmental protection, see Alan E. Boyle and Michael R. Anderson (eds.), *Human Rights Approaches to Environmental Protection* (Oxford University Press, 1996).

97   Statements by the UNEP Secretariat in its report: 'Some Observations on the Preparation of a Global Framework Convention for the Protection of the Stratospheric Ozone Layer' (UNEP/WG.69/8), para. 29. The UNEP Secretariat did not define the legal status of the ozone layer. By referring to the 1979 LRTAP Convention, the Secretariat simply emphasised the importance of scientific and technological co-operation. See UNEP/WG.69/8, para. 35.

98   See Peter M. Lawrence, 'International Legal Regulation for Protection of the Ozone Layer', 2 *JEL* (1990), pp. 21–22.

THE VIENNA CONVENTION AND INTERNATIONAL ENVIRONMENTAL LAW 69

extends only to the portion of the ozone layer that lies directly above the territory and territorial sea of any particular State.[99] In this respect, the 1944 Chicago Convention on International Civil Aviation illustrates the established legal principle of exclusive State sovereignty over (i) the airspace above its territory and (ii) the 'territorial sea'.[100] Yet air space above (i) the High Sea,[101] (ii) the continental shelf,[102] (iii) the Exclusive Economic Zone (EEZ)[103] and (iv) Antarctica[104] must be considered as outside of the sovereignty of any individual State – that is to say, must be considered as 'common property' under international law.

However, even if the concept of State jurisdiction is clarified to some extent, as a practical matter, such an academic argument appears to be utterly fruitless. Firstly, in a strict sense, the ozone layer is by no means 'exploitable shared natural resources'[105] (such as an international river, fish, and other aquatic life), and is not subject to the obligation of equitable utilisation that seen as a rule of customary international law.[106] Secondly, ozone depletion simply ignores the traditional notion of artificial geographic boundaries between sovereign States.[107] Hence, it cannot be denied that the legal concept of 'shared natural

---

99   See the 1944 Chicago Convention on International Civil Aviation (Articles 1 and 15), 15 UNTS, p. 295; the 1958 Convention on Territorial Sea and the Contiguous Zone (Article 2); the 1982 UNCLOS (Article 2).

100   Articles 1 and 2; the 1982 UNCLOS (Article 2(2)). See also the 1919 Convention on the Regulation of Aerial Navigation, 11 LNTS, p. 173.

101   See the 1982 UNCLOS (Article 87).

102   See the 1982 UNCLOS (Article 78(2)).

103   See the 1982 UNCLOS (Articles 55 and 58).

104   See the 1959 Antarctic Treaty (Article 4 in particular). In the context of environmental protection, see Tomohito Usuki, 'Kankyō Hoho ni kansuru Nankyoku Jōyaku Sisutemu no Henyō' [Protection of the Antarctic Environment: From Resourcism to Earth-patriotism], 49 Hokkaido Hōgaku Ronshū [Hokkaido Law Review] (1998), pp. 769–812 (in Japanese).

105   See Nico Schrijver, Sovereignty over Natural Resources: Balancing Rights and Duties (Cambridge University Press, 1997), defining the term 'natural resources' as 'supplies drawn from natural wealth which may be either renewable or non-renewable and which can be used to satisfy the needs of human beings and other living species'. In this respect, under the Draft Principles on the Protection of the Atmosphere prepared by the Environmental Law Committee of the ILA Australian Branch, the atmosphere is defined as 'a shared natural resource and in its natural state is not capable of being the subject of ownership by anyone, State or individual'. See Report of the Fifty-Ninth Conference held at Belgrade, August 17th, 1980 to August 23rd, 1980 (1982), pp. 550–563.

106   However, see Patricia Birnie, Alan Boyle and Catherine Redgwell, International Law and the Environment (3rd ed. Oxford University Press, 2009), p. 344, pointing out that under the LRTAP Convention, the parties seem to treat the European air mass as a shared resource.

107   See Introduction to this volume and Section A above.

resources'[108] – which is embodied in bilateral or regional environmental treaty agreements such as the 1979 LRTAP Convention, UNEP Regional Sea Agreements and international 'soft law' instruments[109] – would not be particularly applicable in the present international regulatory régime for the ozone layer.

In a somewhat different context the same can be said of the more ambitious but controversial legal concept of the 'common heritage of mankind' (CHM)[110] employed in the 1979 Moon Treaty and in the 1982 UNCLOS. The concept of the CHM is concerned with the international 'management' of certain (shared) natural resources or areas, including (i) the deep sea-bed and ocean floor beyond the limits of the present national jurisdiction,[111] (ii) outer space[112] and arguably, (iii) Antarctica.[113] For instance, the creation of the International Sea Bed Authority (ISBA) – as a means of achieving 'distributive justice' – is a form of international marine cooperation in the exploration, conservation and use of the area concerned.[114]

Ozone cannot be described as the CHM for the following reasons: (i) areas to which the notion of the CHM can be applied seem rather limited; (ii) the CHM is associated with 'conservation',[115] but in the context of resources;[116] (iii) the idea of the CHM is originally intended to *internationalise* ownership

---

108   On this concept, see Alan E. Boyle, 'International Law and the Protection of the Global Atmosphere: Concepts, Categories and Principles', in Robin Churchill and David Freestone (eds.), *International Law and Global Climate Change* (Graham & Trotman, 1991), p. 8.

109   See, for example, the 1988 Toronto Conference on the Changing Atmosphere, Conference Statement; and the 1989 Ottawa Conference of Legal and Policy Experts, Statement of the Meeting of Legal and Policy Experts, in 5 *AUJILP* (1990), pp. 515 et seq. and p. 528.

110   On this concept, see Kemal Baslar, *The Concept of the Common Heritage of Mankind in International Law* (Martinus Nijhoff, 1998).

111   See the UNCLOS (Articles 133, 136 and 137).

112   See UN General Assembly Resolution 1962 (XVIII) of 13 December 1963; the 1967 Outer Space Treaty (Article 1); the 1979 Moon Treaty (Article 1(1), Article 3(1), Article 4(1) and Article 11).

113   See the Preamble of the 1991 Protocol to the Antarctic Treaty, stating that 'the development of a comprehensive regime for the protection of the Antarctic environment and dependent and associated ecosystems is in the interest of mankind as a whole'. See also Joe Verhoeven, Philippe Sands and Maxwell Bruce (eds.), *The Antarctic Environment and International Law* (Graham & Trotman, 1992), Chapters 12–13.

114   On the ISA, see Michael Wood, 'International Seabed Authority', in Rüdiger Wolfrum (ed.), *Max Planck Encyclopedia of Public International Law*, Vol. VI (Oxford University Press, 2012), pp. 146–155.

115   The 1980 CCAMLR (Article 11(3)); the 1958 High Seas Conservation Convention (Article 2). See also 1986 WCED Principles (para. (i)).

116   Jutta Brunnée, 'A Conceptual Framework for an International Forests Convention', in Canadian Council on International Law (ed.), *Global Forests and International Environmental Law* (Kluwer Law International, 1996), p. 56.

of natural resources (that is, 'international management'):[117] and (iv) the CHM was employed neither in the Ozone Convention nor modern environmental treaties, including the 1992 Climate Change Convention and the 1992 Biodiversity Convention.[118]

(2)   The Ozone Layer as 'Common Concern of Mankind'

Under the text of the Vienna Ozone Convention, the 'ozone layer' is defined as the 'layer of atmospheric ozone above the planetary boundary layer' (that is, ozone in the upper troposphere and the stratosphere that acts to filter out UV-B).[119] This definition is based on a report by an informal technical working group suggesting that it is consistent with the definition by the UNEP/CCOL and, moreover, avoids possible conflicts with the 1979 LRTAP Convention that concerns boundary layer pollution.[120] It indicates that 'ozone' in this environmental treaty refers to the planet's only natural sun screen 'stratospheric ozone layer' or 'ozone shield', and thus not 'ground-level ozone'.[121] We may say, therefore, that this definition of the ozone treaty régime seems to treat the protective ozone layer as a global unit having no national boundaries.[122] As Shaw says, the area defined thus constitutes 'a distinctive unit with an identity of its own irrespective of national sovereignty or shared resources claims'.[123]

In the light of the recent development of international environmental régimes, though the legal texts of neither the Ozone Convention nor the Montreal Protocol refers to this new legal term,[124] it will be logical to treat the ozone

---

117   See Alan E. Boyle, 'The Rio Convention on Biological Diversity', in Michael Bowman and Catherine Redgwell (eds.), *International Law and the Conservation of Biological Diversity* (Kluwer Law International, 1995), p. 40. For instance, Article 4 of the Moon Treaty emphasises cooperation in enterprises concerning the moon and other celestial bodies. See Peter Malanczuk, 'Space Law as a Branch of International Law', 25 *BYbkIL* (1994), p. 172.

118   See Patricia Birnie, Alan Boyle and Catherine Redgwell, *International Law and the Environment* (3rd ed. Oxford University Press, 2009), pp. 130 and 338.

119   Article 1(1) (emphasis added). Thus, the 'ozone layer' does not necessarily belong to a particular part of the atmosphere. See the discussion at the Second Session of the Working Group, in UNEP/WG.78/13, para. 24. Correspondingly, Article 1 in an earlier draft convention reads that the ozone layer means 'the total ozone above the earth's surface, most of which is found in the stratosphere' (UNEP/WG.78/8, Annex I).

120   See UNEP/WG.78/13, Annex IV, para. 2.

121   See Introduction to this volume.

122   See Patricia Birnie, Alan Boyle and Catherine Redgwell, *International Law and the Environment* (3rd ed. Oxford University Press, 2009), p. 338.

123   See Malcolm N. Shaw, *International Law* (7th ed. Cambridge University Press, 2014), pp. 635–636.

124   On this point, see Jutta Brunnée, 'A Conceptual Framework for an International Forests Convention: Customary Law and Emerging Principles', in Canadian Council of

72   CHAPTER 2

layer as having the international legal status of the 'common concern of (hu) mankind' (CCM). The CCM should be rightly observed as something more than a vague political principle or declaration. According to Boyle, a common concern (of (hu)mankind) implies that 'the international community has both a legitimate interest in resources of global significance and a common responsibility to assist in their protection'.[125] Similar to the concept of the CHM, the CCM is also intended to conserve the environment (for example, the ozone layer) for the interests of future generations.

The legal concept of the CCM was first used by UN General Assembly Resolution 43/53.[126] It was then incorporated into two modern multilateral environmental agreements, namely, the 1992 Climate Change Convention and the 1992 Biodiversity Convention. For instance, the Preamble of the Climate Change Convention states that 'change in the Earth's climate and its adverse effects are a common concern of mankind'.[127] This seems to favour the idea that all States in the international community – irrespective of whether injured or not – share equally the international common legal interests in preventing potential adverse effects caused by global climate change. In this respect, it seems possible to argue that this comparatively new legal concept, the CCM, is to an important extent concerned with the notion of international obligations *erga omnes* – that is, 'obligations owed to the international community

---

International Law (ed.), *Global Forests and International Environmental Law* (Kluwer Law International, 1996), p. 57 (note 98), saying that '[i]t may be speculated that, were the convention [the 1985 Vienna Convention] to be adopted today, it would declare the depletion of the ozone layer a "common concern of humankind"'.

125   See Alan E. Boyle, 'Remedying Harm to International Common Spaces and Resources: Compensation and Other Approaches', in Peter Wetterstein (ed.), *Harm to the Environment* (Clarendon Press, 1997), p. 86. On this legal concept, see also Boyle, 'International Law and Protection of the Global Atmosphere: Concepts, Categories and Principles', in Robin Churchill and David Freestone (eds.), *International Law and Global Climate Change* (1991); Jacob Werksman, 'Consolidating Governance of the Global Commons: Insights from the Global Environmental Facility', 6 *YbkIEL* (1995), pp. 40–44; Alexandre Kiss, 'La notion de patrimoine commun de l'humanité', 175 *Hague Recueil* (1982–II), Chapter I; Alexandre Kiss, 'Common Concern of Mankind', 27 *EPL* (1997), pp. 244–247; Ellen Hey, *Advanced Introduction to International Environmental Law* (Edward Elgar, 1996), pp. 62–64.

126   For the text, see Patricia W. Birnie and Alan E. Boyle, *Basic Documents on International Law and the Environment* (Clarendon Press, 1995), p. 248.

127   See the 1959 Antarctic Treaty (Preamble); the 1946 International Convention for the Regulation of Whaling (Preamble). In the context of climate change, see Friedrich Soltau, 'Common Concern of Humankind', in Cinnamon P. Carlarne, Kevin R. Gray and Richard G. Tarasofsky (eds.), *The Oxford Handbook of International Climate Change Law* (Oxford University Press, 2016), pp. 202–212.

as a whole' – introduced by the International Court of Justice in its judgement on the *Barcelona Traction* case.[128] As Shelton says, '[b]oth concept [common concern and *erga omnes* obligations] related to matters which touch the interests of people throughout the world. It may very well be that one of the consequences of denoting a subject a common concern of mankind is that it gives rise to *erga omnes* obligations that may be pursued by any party'.[129] It is also important that, under the ILC's draft guidelines on the protection of the atmosphere, the protection of the atmosphere, which is defined as 'the envelope of gases surrounding the Earth',[130] is regarded as 'a pressing concern of the international community as a whole'.[131] Yet, as previously discussed, the legal consequences that would flow from the concept of international obligations *erga omnes* in the context of ozone protection are undeniably unclear.[132]

In summary, the ozone layer as 'common concern of mankind' therefore belongs to all States and to mankind *as a whole*. This means that all States now have a legal duty to protect the ozone layer adequately from ozone-depleting economic activities. Yet it must be emphasised at the same time that this norm-creating legal concept in international law is still premature and its future implications for the international community and for individual States have yet to be developed.[133]

---

128 The *Barcelona Traction, Light and Power Company Limited* case (Belgium *v* Spain: Second Phase), *ICJ Reports* (1970), p. 3. See Frederic L. Kirgis, 'Standing to Challenge Human Endeavours that Could Change the Climate', 84 *AJIL* (1990), p. 527; Patricia Birnie, Alan Boyle and Catherine Redgwell, *International Law and the Environment* (3rd ed. Oxford University Press, 2009), pp. 129–132. See also Chapter I(IV) in this volume.

129 See Dinah Shelton, 'Common Concern of Humanity', 39/2 *EPL* (2009), p. 86.

130 See Guideline 1(1) of the draft guidelines on the protection of the atmosphere.

131 See Preamble. See *Report of the International Law Commission, Sixty-Eighth Session* (2 May-10 June and 4 July-12 August 2016), Supplement No. 10 (UN Doc. A/71/10), p. 283. See also *Second Report on the Protection of the Atmosphere by Shinya Murase, Special Rapporteur*, UN Doc. A/CN.4/681 (2 March 2015), pp. 6–12.

132 See Chapter I(IV) in this volume.

133 See Jacob Werksman, 'Consolidating Governance of the Global Commons: Insights from the Global Environmental Facility', 6 *YbkIEL* (1995), p. 41, observing that '[s]uch designation [the common concern of humankind] alone does not change the nature of legal rights and duties associated with the designated area or resource'; Frank Biermann, *Saving the Atmosphere: International Law, Developing Countries and Air Pollution* (Peter Lang, 1995), p. 15; Wolfgang Benedek, Koen De Feyter, Matthias C. Kettemann and Christina Voigt, 'Introduction', in idem, *The Common Interest in International Law* (Intersentia, 2014), pp. 20–23.

74   CHAPTER 2

C   *The Vienna Ozone Convention and the 'Principle' of the*
        Precautionary Approach in Modern International Law
        of the Environment

'If and when a global convention for the protection of the ozone layer came
into force, it would represent a major break-through in international environmental co-operation, in the sense that the world community would have declared its determination to take action *before* a serious global environmental
threat materialized, i.e. preventive global action instead of the remedial action
taken hitherto'.[134]

The international ozone régime is based on the precautionary environmental 'principle' or approach,[135] regarded as a gradual and marked development,
or an effective modification, of Principle 21 of the 1972 Stockholm Declaration.
The concept of 'precautionary approach' would not have emerged as a 'new
legal principle' without the existence or elaboration of this customary international law norm developed from the *Trail Smelter* Arbitration.

(1)   The Vienna Ozone Convention and Principle 21 of the 1972
         Stockholm Declaration on the Human Environment

The Vienna Ozone Convention, just like the 1982 UNCLOS (Article 194(2)), the
1979 LRTAP (Preamble), the 1992 Biodiversity Convention (Article 3) and the 1992
Climate Change Convention (Preamble), contains a specific reference to Principle 21 of the 1972 Stockholm Declaration on the Human Environment:[136]

States have, in accordance with the Charter of the United Nations and principles of international law, the sovereign right to exploit their own resources
pursuant to their own environment policies, and the responsibility to ensure that activities within their jurisdiction or control do not cause damage
to the environment of other States or areas beyond the limits of national
jurisdiction.[137]

---

134   Opening statement by the Swedish Minister for Agriculture and the Environment at the
      First Session of the Working Group, in UNEP/WG.69/10, para. 3 (emphasis original).
135   See UNEP/OzL.Pro.7/12 para. 60, noting that '[a] number of representatives said that the
      precautionary principle, which had been a cornerstone of the ozone regime from the out-
      set, should continue to be applied as Parties addressed ongoing threat to the ozone layer.
      For a discussion, see also Section C(2.b) below.
136   For a discussion of Principle 21, see among others Patricia Birnie, Alan Boyle and Cath-
      erine Redgwell, *International Law and the Environment* (3rd ed. Oxford University Press,
      2009), pp. 143 et seq.; Philippe Sands and Jacqueline Peel, *Principles of International Envi-
      ronmental Law* (3rd ed. Cambridge University Press, 2012), pp. 190 et seq.; Nico Schrijver,
      Sovereignty over Natural Resources: Balancing Rights and Duties (Cambridge University
      Press, 1997), pp. 125–128.
137   The first draft convention also addresses this principle. See UNEP/WG.69/3/Add.1. See
      also the commentary of a draft convention, saying that 'obligation to protect the ozone

Principle 21 (that is, Principle 2 of the Rio Declaration)[138] is an expression of the 'principle of preventive action' or *sic utere tuo ut alienum non laedas*. In general, it requires States to take certain positive and preventive action and, at the same time, it fixes a 'threshold'[139] of transboundary environmental harm that will be unacceptable. Although Principle 21 is widely regarded as a rule of customary international law,[140] in the view of some authors such as Kosken-niemi, it is often seen as a 'process-definition' that indicates relevant values but leaves the determination of their normative impact into further process.[141]

However, it should be noted that the essential element of this Principle is that States have the 'responsibility'[142] to take certain preventive measures in order to protect the 'environment' (not 'territory' of a State). In this sense, Principle 21 is something more than a mere principle of good neighbourliness or *bon voisinage*,[143] and is concerned to some extent with the ozone layer having

---

layer is indirectly embodies in principle 21 of the Stockholm Declaration' (UNEP/WG.78/2, p. 7).

138   But Stockholm Principle 21 was slightly modified by Rio Principle 21 containing the words 'and developmental [policies]'. See Phillipe Sands, 'International Law in the Field of Sustainable Development', 66 *BYbkIL* (1995), pp. 342–343, suggesting such modification 'does not materially change its meaning and effect'.

139   On its definition, see Kamen Sachariew, 'The Definition of Thresholds of Tolerance for Transboundary Environment Injury under International Law: Development and Present Status', 37 *NILR* (1990), pp. 193–206.

140   See, for example, Patricia Birnie, Alan Boyle and Catherine Redgwell, *International Law and the Environment* (3rd ed. Oxford University Press, 2009), pp. 143 et seq.; Alexandre Kiss, *Droit international de l'environment* (Pedone, 1989), pp. 80 et seq.; Philippe Sands and Jacqueline Peel, *Principles of International Environmental Law* (3rd ed. Cambridge University Press, 2012), pp. 190 et seq.; Rene-Jean Dupuy, 'Humanity and the Environment', 2 *Colorado JIELP* (1991), p. 203; Yoshiro Matsui, *Kokusai Kankyōhō no Kihon Gensoku* [International Law of the Environment: Its Fundamental Principles] (Toshindo, 2010), pp. 62 et seq. See also *Nuclear Weapons Advisory Opinion, ICJ Reports* (1996), pp. 241–242, paras. 29–30. See Oscar Schachter, *International Law in Theory and Practice* (Martinus Nijhoff, 1991), p. 364, arguing that Principle 21 has not become a customary law; Pierr-Marie Dupuy and Jorge E. Viñuales, *International Environmental Law* (Cambridge University Press), p. 58, suggesting that 'the content of Principle 21 was both a reflection of general international law (re-affirming the no harm principle) and an attempt at progressive development of this area of law (introducing the responsibility of States not to cause damage to areas outside of State jurisdiction'.

141   See Martti Koskenniemi, 'Peaceful Settlement of Environmental Disputes', 60 *Nordic JIL* (1991), p. 76.

142   In the context of Principles 21 and 22 and the 1982 UNCLOS (Article 235), 'responsibility' refers to the obligation to protect and conserve the environment, while 'liability' suggests the obligation to compensate for environmental damage. See also Alan E. Boyle, 'State Responsibility and International Liability for Injurious Consequences of Acts not Prohibited by International law: A Necessary Distinction?', 39 *ICLQ* (1990), pp. 8–10.

143   For further details regarding this principle, see, for example, Maria Gavouneli, *Pollution from Offshore Installations* (Graham & Trotman/Martinus Nijhoff, 1995), pp. 82–84.

a CCM character. At present, it is regarded as including the high seas and the airspace above them, the deep seabed, outer space, the Moon and other celestial bodies, and Antarctica.[144]

Principle 21, which appears in the Preamble of the Convention, was originally inserted both in Article 1 of the draft ozone convention submitted by the delegations of Finland, Norway and Sweden,[145] and Article 2 of the draft conventions prepared by the UNEP Secretariat.[146] Those earlier proposals lacked adequate support from some States because they were likely to entail obligations that might exceed their capacities.[147] Unlike its operative treaty provisions, the Preamble itself does not establish binding legal obligations and therefore the Principle must therefore be seen as an informative guide not only to determining the object and purpose of the Convention but also to interpreting the meaning of these particular provisions.[148] However, Principle 21 is supported by Article 2(2)(b) of 'General Obligations' of the Vienna Ozone Convention.[149]

This wide support of Principle 21 is unlikely by itself to provide a workable legal approach to address the depletion of the ozone layer. To begin with, it is important to notice that the origin of the rule is derived from or based on the frequently cited *Trail Smelter* Arbitration. There, the tribunal directly addressed State liability for transboundary air pollution and it supported responsibility for wrongful acts that breached such obligations, but not for lawful acts.[150] In this context, as Handl rightly observed, it may not be denied that 'Principle 21 can only be understood as referring to *material damage alone*, and

---

144   See Patricia Birnie, Alan Boyle and Catherine Redgwell, *International Law and the Environment* (3rd ed. Oxford University Press, 2009), pp. 144 et seq.; Riccardo-Pisillo-Mazzeschi, 'Form of International Responsibility for Environmental Harm', in Francesco Francioni and Tullio Scovazzi (eds.), *International Responsibility for Environmental Harm* (Graham & Trotman/Martinus Nijhoff, 1991), pp. 28 et seq.; Günther Handl, 'State Liability for Accidental Transboundary Environmental Damage by Private Persons', 74 *AJIL* (1980), pp. 528–529.

145   See 'Fundamental Obligation' (Article 1), in *Draft International Convention for the Protection of the Stratospheric Ozone Layer* (UNEP/WG.69/3).

146   See Alternatives 1 and 2 of Article 2, 'General Obligation', in UNEP/WG.78/2.

147   See UNEP/WG.78/8, para. 8, reporting that a number of delegations expressed a strong preference for the weaker Alternative 3.

148   See Ian Sinclair, *The Vienna Convention on the Law of Treaties* (2nd ed. Manchester University Press, 1984), pp. 127 et seq.

149   See Section D(1) below.

150   In the *Trail Smelter case,* the tribunal declared that: '.... no State has a right to use or permit the use of its territory in such a manner as to cause injury by fumes in or to the territory of another or the properties or persons therein, when the case is of serious consequences and the injury is established by *clear and convincing evidence*' (emphasis added).

THE VIENNA CONVENTION AND INTERNATIONAL ENVIRONMENTAL LAW 77

that it thus confirms that material damage is the precondition for a state's responsibility arising out of an activity lawful per se'.[151] This remark can be borne out by the fact that many delegates, in the preparatory works for Stockholm Principle 21, endorsed the view that responsibility for environmental harm should be solely based on a State's negligence, but not on the forms of liability for lawful acts.[152] Therefore, it may be assumed that States' responsibility in the context of customary international law arises only if the breach of specific primary obligation exists. Principle 22 of the Stockholm Declaration recognised this crucial point[153] – nevertheless liability schemes for lawful acts have been poorly developed over the past three decades. The same thing may be said of the concept of objective responsibility for wrongful acts.[154]

The above review will show that, although many international environmental treaties, including the Vienna Ozone Convention, have incorporated Principle 21, it ultimately proved that in a sense their primary aim was to establish obligations of prevention limited by the rule of 'due diligence'.[155] The legal

---

151   See Günther Handl, 'Territorial Sovereignty and the Problem of Transnational Pollution', 69 *AJIL* (1975), p. 67 and note 103 (emphasis added); Handl, 'Balancing of Interests and International Liability for the Pollution of International Watercourses: Customary Principles of Law Revisited', 13 *CYbkIL* (1975), pp. 160 et seq.; Handl, 'State Liability for Accidental Transboundary Environmental Damage by Private Persons', 74 *AJIL* (1980), pp. 535 et seq.

152   See UN Doc. A/CONF.48/PC. 12, Annex II, p. 15. See also Riccardo Pisillo-Mazzeschi, 'The Due Diligence Rule and the Nature of the International Responsibility of States', 35 *GYbkIL* (1992), p. 38; Günther Handl, 'Balancing Interests and International Liability for Pollution of International Watercourses: Customary Principles of Law Revised', 13 *CYbkIL* (1975), pp. 160 et seq.

153   Principle 22 reads as follows: 'States shall co-operate to develop further the international law regarding liability and compensation for the victims of pollution and other environmental damage caused by activities within the jurisdiction or control of such States to areas beyond their jurisdiction'.

154   But see Katharina Kummer, *International Management of Hazardous Wastes* (Clarendon Press, 1995), pp. 215–216. See also Patricia Birnie, Alan Boyle and Catherine Redgwell, *International Law and the Environment* (3rd ed. Oxford University Press, 2009), pp. 216 et seq.; L. F. E. Goldie, 'Liability for Damage and the Progressive Development of International Law', 14 *ICLQ* (1965), pp. 1189–1264.

155   See the *Alabama Claims* Arbitration, 1872, John Bassett Moore, *History and Digest of the International Arbitrations to Which the United States has been a party* (Government Printing Office, 1898), vol. 1, pp. 495–682; the *Hostages in Iran* case, *ICJ Reports* (1980), pp. 29–33, paras. 57–68; the *Corfu Channel* case, *ICJ Reports* (1949), p. 3. Riccardo Pisillo-Mazzeschi, 'The Due Diligence Rule and the Nature of the International Responsibility of States', 35 *GYbkIL* (1992), pp. 9–51; idem, 'Forms of International Responsibility for Environmental Harm', in Francesco Francioni and Tullio Scovazzi (eds.), *International Responsibility for Environmental Harm* (Graham & Trotman/Martinus Nijhoff, 1991), pp. 15–35; Alan E. Boyle, 'Nuclear Energy and International Law: An Environmental Perspective', 50 *BYbkIL* (1989), pp. 272–273.

78 CHAPTER 2

terminology of due diligence can be generally defined as 'necessary and practicable measures', that is, an expression of good environmental conduct.[156] It is commonly accepted that States are not responsible for environmental damage, unless it results from a lack of international due diligence.[157] Perhaps its advantages – or its flexibility – are reflected in the following three points:

(i) the effectiveness of different environmental control measures concerning the severity of the threat;

(ii) considerations for the various levels of national economic developments (for example, resources available to developed/developing countries)[158] and:

(iii) approaches toward the different nature of the specific activity.[159]

The flexibility of the legal terminology of due diligence means at the same time that it has serious disadvantages, for example, the lack of 'clear' and 'reliable' guidance for State actors and its industries in relation to specific environmental legislation and administrative controls. Accordingly, under these conditions, it is very likely that States or industries should naturally follow 'agreed-upon *minimum* international environmental standards' (for example, those contained in the International Standards Organisation (ISO),[160] the World Health

---

156   See Patricia Birnie, Alan Boyle and Catherine Redgwell, *International Law and the Environment* (3rd ed. Oxford University Press, 2009), pp. 147 et seq.: Alan E. Boyle, 'Nuclear Energy and International Law: An Environmental Perspective', in 50 *BYbkIL* (1989), pp. 272 et seq.; Malcolm N. Shaw, *International Law* (7th edn. Cambridge University Press, 2014), pp. 620–621.

157   The rule of 'due diligence' has been applied in particular to (i) the security of aliens and representatives of foreign States, (ii) the security of foreign States and (iii) the conservation of the environment. See Riccardo Pisillo-Mazzeschi, 'The Due Diligence and the Nature of the International Responsibility of States', 35 *GYbkIL* (1992), pp. 22 et seq. For an extensive discussion, see also Kimio Yakushiji, 'Ekkyo Songai to Kokka no Tekihō Kōi Sekinin' [Transboundary Harm and State Liability for International "Lawful Act"], 93 *Kokusaihō Gaikō Zassi* [Journal of International Law and Diplomacy] (1994), pp. 383 et seq. [in Japanese].

158   As far as the resources available to the States are concerned, considerable controversy could arise as to the question of the standard of national treatment and an 'international minimum standard' or 'a moral standard for civilised states'. For a discussion, see, for example, Ian Brownlie, *Principles of Public International Law* (4th ed. Clarendon Press, 1990) pp. 523–528; D. J. Harris, *Cases and Materials on International Law* (4th edn. Sweet & Maxwell, 1991), pp. 493 et seq. Disagreement on this subject partly led to the failure of the 1930 Hague Codification Conference and García Amador's attack on the ILC on the subject of State responsibility (1956–1961).

159   See UNEP, 'International Due Diligence', informal note for the Executive Director's Advisory Group on Banking and the Environment (October 1993) [on file with the author].

160   On the functions of standards and rules, see Naomi Roht-Arriaza, 'Private Voluntary Standard-Setting, the International Organisation for Standardisation, and International

Organisation (WHO) and the International Maritime Organisation (IMO)).[161] Further, in the field of environmental protection, scientific uncertainty some-times makes the concept of due diligence more complicated and difficult for States and industries to apply on a particular occasion.

In the context of ozone layer protection, the customary law rule of inter-national due diligence cannot form dependable standards for production and consumption of ozone-depleting chemicals such as CFCs. This point is illus-trated in the Chernobyl disaster of 1986. Although it may be assumed that Prin-ciple 21 could be applicable to this type of transboundary environmental harm, it was difficult to show a failure of due diligence in the absence of binding international standards that regulate national nuclear activities.[162]

In summary, the customary rule of due diligence only requires States to take appropriate measures or make every effort in accordance with the means at their disposal and capabilities. In other words, it cannot be denied that the rule leaves too much discretion and offers no clear guideline or specific standards.[163]

(2)   The Vienna Ozone Convention and the Precautionary
        Environmental 'Principle': the Emergence of a New Approach

(a)   *International Environmental Cooperation: Developments Subsequent
        to the Adoption of Principle 21 of the 1972 Stockholm Declaration*

As was discussed above, Principle 21 suggests that States have the responsibility to take certain preventive measures to protect the environment, even though the meaning of 'responsibility' is not necessarily clear. In addition, even if this rule is seen only as a 'process-definition' of environmental treaties, it is likely

---

Environmental Lawmaking', 6 *YbkIEL* (1995), pp. 107–163.

161   See UNEP, 'International Due Diligence', information note for the Executive Director's Ad-visory Group on Banking and the Environment (October 1993) [on file with the author]. See also Alan E. Boyle, 'Nuclear Energy and International Law: An Environmental Per-spective', 50 *BYbkIL* (1989), pp. 272–273.

162   But this could have be done in the above-mentioned *Trail Smelter* case. The former Soviet Union was not a party to the 1960 Paris Convention or the 1963 Vienna Convention. See also Alan E. Boyle, 'Nuclear Energy and International Law: An Environmental Perspec-tive', 50 *BYbkIL* (1989), pp. 272–273; Boyle, 'Chernobyl and the Development of Interna-tional Environmental Law', in W. E. Butler, *Control Over Compliance with International Law* (Martinus Nijhoff, 1991), pp. 203 et seq.; Philippe Sands, 'The Environment, Commu-nity and International Law', 30 *Harv. ILJ* (1989), pp. 401 et seq.

163   Seen in this way, it is quite understandable that Principle 24 of the Stockholm Declaration provides that '[c]o-operation through multilateral or bilateral arrangements or other ap-propriate means is essential to effectively control, prevent, reduce and eliminate adverse environmental effects'.

that such a general legal norm could have facilitated further international co-operation on various aspects of environmental protection and developments of its application.[164]

It should be noted that early references to 'preventive measures' can be seen in many legal instruments, including several principles of the Final Declaration of the 1972 Stockholm Declaration,[165] the 1975 Final Act of the Conference on Security and Cooperation in Europe, the 1982 Nairobi Declaration adopted by the UNEP Governing Council (No. 9) and the 1982 World Charter for Nature.[166] Moreover, it may be argued that, in certain cases, the customary rule has inevitably entailed procedural obligations to cooperate in protecting the human environment.[167] Examples of this include (i) obligations of prior notification and consultation in the context of environmental hazard;[168] (ii) obligations to notify and consult[169] in the case of accidents or emergencies capable of causing transfrontier harm in general: and (iii) environmental impact assessment (EIA).[170] This means that the so-called 'Principle 20' of the 1972 Stockholm Declaration prepared by the Working Group – which could not get final approval, however –[171] is now widely supported by modern international environment treaties containing these procedural obligations.

---

164   See Riccardo Pisillo-Mazzeschi, 'Forms of International Responsibility for Environmental Harm', in Francesco Francioni and Tullio Scovazzi (eds.), *International Responsibility for Environmental Harm* (Graham & Trotman/Martinus Nijhoff, 1991), pp. 28–29.

165   For example, conservation of natural resources for present and future generations (Principle 2); maintenance of the capacity of the earth to produce vital renewable resources (Principle 3); non-exhaustion of non-renewable resources (Principle 5).

166   See UN General Assembly Resolution 37/7. The Charter provides that '[a]ctivities which are likely to cause irreversible damage to nature shall be avoided' (No. 11(a)), and '[a]ctivities which are likely to pose a significant risk to nature shall be preceded by an exhaustive examination' (No. 11(b)).

167   See Alan E. Boyle, 'Nuclear Energy and International Law: An Environmental Perspective', 50 *BYbkIL* (1989), pp. 278–287; Alexandre Kiss, 'Nouvelles tendances en droit international de l'environnement', 16 *GYbkIL* (1973), p. 246; Albert E. Utton, 'International Environmental Law and Consultation Mechanisms', 12 *Columbia JTL* (1973), pp. 56–72; Phoebe N. Okowa, 'Procedural Obligations in International Environmental Agreements', 67 *BYbkIL* (1996), pp. 275–336.

168   Examples include the 1986 Early Notification Convention and the 1986 IAEA Assistance Convention.

169   See, for example, the 1972 London Dumping Convention (Article V(2)); the 1974 Nordic Environmental Protection Convention (Article 11); the 1979 Geneva Convention (Article 5 and 8). See further Chapter I in this volume.

170   See, for example, the 1978 UNEP Draft Principles of Conduct; the 1985 ASEAN Agreement (Article 14); the 1982 UNCLOS (Article 206).

171   It reads '[e]ach State has the duty to undertake international consultations before proceeding with activities which may damage to the environment of another State or to the

In so far as environmental impact assessment shows a foreseeable risk, the problems of the rule of due diligence will be partly mitigated. However, we should note that it is usually difficult to build up consensual scientific knowledge in most environmental problems. This is an important fact to stress: during the formation of scientific consensus in the international community, the environment is increasingly polluted, and sometimes we may be going 'beyond the limits' of the physical environment, although not intending to do so.[172]

(b)   *The Precautionary Environmental 'Principle' or Approach*
Under the condition that the customary international law rule of 'due diligence' secures little promise for environmental protection, a radical idea has gradually emerged from the customary rule of Principle 21: even when there is a lack of scientific proof of the cause and effect relationship, certain preventive measures to protect the environment should be taken. This is the so-called precautionary (environmental) 'principle' or approach.[173]

It is widely agreed that the 1987 Ministerial Declaration of the Second International Conference on the Protection of the North Sea (London Declaration) is the first agreement that *explicitly* formulated the precautionary principle. It reads:

---

environment of areas beyond the limits of national jurisdiction. A State having reason to believe that the activities of another State may cause damage to its environment or to the environment of area beyond the limits of national jurisdiction, may request international consultations concerning the envisaged activities'. See UN Doc.A/CONF.48/PC/WG.I (11)/CRP.4(1972), p. 2, cited in L. B. Sohn, 'The Stockholm Declaration on the Human Environment', 14 *Harvard ILJ* (1973), p. 497.

172   See Donella H. Meadows, Dennis L. Meadows and Jørgen Randers, *Beyond the Limits: Global Collapse or a Sustainable Future* (Earthscan, 1992), dealing with potential 'overshoot' caused by human society.

173   Regarding this 'principle', see David Freestone and Ellen Hey, 'Origins and Development of the Precautionary Principle', in David Freestone and Ellen Hey (eds.), *Precautionary Principle and International Law* (Kluwer Law International, 1996), pp. 3–15; James Cameron, 'The Status of the Precautionary Principle in International Law', in Tim O'Riordan and James Cameron (eds.), *Interpreting the Precautionary Principle* (Cameron May, 1994), pp. 276 et seq.: Patricia Birnie, Alan Boyle and Catherine Redgwell, *International Law and the Environment* (3rd ed. Oxford University Press, 2009), pp. 159–164; Günther Handl, 'Environmental Security and Global Change: The Challenge to International Law', 1 *YbkIEL* (1990), pp. 20–24. It may also be argued that the principle was deprived from a German legal concept of *Vorsorgeprinzip*. See David Freestone, 'The Precautionary Principle', in Robin Churchill and David Freestone, *International Law and Global Climate Change* (Graham & Trotman, 1991), p. 21.

.... in order to protect the North Sea from possibly damaging effects of the most dangerous substances, a precautionary approach is necessary which may require action to control inputs of such substances even before a causal link has been established by absolutely clear scientific evidence.[174]

The Vienna Ozone Convention, for the first time, made reference to the term 'precautionary measures' taken at national and international level for the protection of the ozone layer.[175] Although there was already general agreement at the First Session of the Working Group held in 1982 in Stockholm that 'precautionary action is necessary for the sake of man and the environment',[176] perhaps not surprisingly, the wording 'precautionary' was cautiously bracketed in earlier draft framework conventions.

The introduction of 'precautionary measures' is a remarkable development in international environmental law-making. International environmental treaties adopted before the 1985 Ozone Layer Convention – for instance, the 1979 LRTAP – only claimed the recognition of the existence of 'possible adverse effects' of transboundary air pollution in the short or long term.[177] As Birnie and Boyle say, the Ozone Convention is therefore one of the first international treaties that perceived the need for precautionary action without full scientific certainty.[178] In the middle of 1980, serious scientific difficulties concerning the theory of ozone-depletion remained unsolved, and there was not sufficient scientific consensus. Until 1985, no scientific observation of the actual ozone-loss was published and the Rowland-Molia hypothesis suggested in 1974[179] was not confirmed until 1988.

---

174 Paragraph VII. See Yves van der Mensbrugghe, 'Legal Status of International North Sea Conference Declarations', 5 *IJECL* (1990), pp. 15–22; Takeo Horiguchi, 'Kokusai Kankyōhō ni okeru Yobō Gensoku no Kigen' [The Origin of the Precautionary Principle in International Environmental Law], 15 *Kokusaikankeiron Kenkyū* [Studies on International Relations] (2000), pp. 29–50.

175 See Preamble. This terminology is first found in the Alternative 1 of 'General Obligations', in the second revised draft convention. See 'Second Revised Draft Convention for the Protection of the Ozone Layer', in UNEP/WG.94/3.

176 See UNEP/WG.69/10, para. 9.

177 See Preamble. In this respect, it is probable that this pre-1980 position was influenced not only by the political will of Member States but also by scientific uncertainty on the causes and effects of acid rain. See, for example, Lothar Gündling, 'Multilateral Co-operation of States under the ECE Convention on Long-Range Transboundary Air Pollution', in Cees Flinterman, Barbara Kwiatkowska and Johan G. Lammers (eds.), *Transboundary Air Pollution* (Martinus Nijhoff, 1986), p. 20.

178 See Patricia Birnie, Alan Boyle and Catherine Redgwell, *International Law and the Environment* (3rd ed. Oxford University Press, 2009), p. 351.

179 See Introduction to this volume.

As we shall see in later chapters, it was the Montreal Ozone Protocol that actually achieved the precautionary 'principle' or approach, by introducing specific control measures for specified eight CFCs/ODSs contained in its Annexes.[180] The Preamble of the Montreal Protocol provides that the parties are 'determined to protect the ozone layer by taking precautionary measures to control total emissions of substances that deplete it'.

At present, there is enough cogent scientific evidence to support the control measures of Articles 2 and 5 under the Montreal Protocol.[181] In a more restricted sense, this regulatory ozone régime may no longer be a 'precautionary' treaty régime.[182] However, it should be emphasised that scientific information for the shaping of global environmental policy on ozone depletion will never be perfect or accurate.[183] In other words, it must continue to be strengthened. It should be noted, for example, that skin cancer is still the only expected impact for which sufficient data and information are available to make quantitative predictions.[184]

The precautionary environmental 'principle' or approach is now widely incorporated into a number of environmental law instruments, including Principle 15 of the 1992 Rio Declaration, the 1996 Protocol to the London Dumping

---

180 See in detail Chapter III(III.B.1) in this volume

181 See, for example, F. Sherwood Rowland, 'Stratospheric Ozone Depletion', in Christos Zerefos, G. Contopoulos and Gregory Skalkeas (eds.), *Twenty Years of Ozone Decline – Proceedings of the Symposium for the 20th Anniversary of the Montreal Protocol* (Springer, 2009), pp. 23–63.

182 On this point, see Jutta Brunnée, 'Conceptual Framework for an International Forests Convention: Customary Law and Emerging Principles', in Canadian Council on International Law (ed.), *Global Forests and International Environmental Law* (Kluwer Law International, 1996), p. 72 (note 175), noting that 'only after compelling evidence that depletion was in fact occurring emerged, were concrete measures agreed to in the *Montreal Protocol*' (emphasis original).

183 For a discussion of the relationship between science and policy-making, see, in particular, John M. Stonehouse and John D. Mumford, *Science, Risk Analysis and Environmental Decisions* (United Nations Environment Programme, 1994); Jacqueline Peel, *Science and Risk Regulation in International Law* (Cambridge University Press, 2010), pp. 73 et seq.

184 See statement by Dr. J. C. Van der Lean (Co-Chair of the Panel on Environmental Effects of Ozone Depletion) at the 1997 Ninth Ozone Meeting of the Parties in UNEP/OzL.Pro.9/12, para. 32. See also statement by Co-Chair of the TEAP in UNEP/OzL.Pro.9/12, para. 29, suggesting the need of financial resources for monitoring and further research of ozone depletion; See Peter Fabian and Martin Dameris, *Ozone in the Atmosphere: Basic Principles, Natural and Human Impacts* (Springer, 2014), p. 112. As for the emergence of revisionism against ozone science, see Richard Benedick, *Ozone Diplomacy* (Harvard University Press, 1998), pp. 226–228; Fred Singer, 'Swedish Academy's Choice of Honourees Signals That Ozone Politics Played a Role', *The Scientist* (4 March 1996), p. 9, cited in Benedick, op. cit., p. 228.

Convention (Articles 2, 3 and 4), the 1995 Straddling Fish Stocks Convention (Article 6/Annex II),[185] the Treaty for the Functioning of the European Union (Article 191(2)), the Convention for the Protection of the Marine Environment of the North-East Atlantic (the OSPAR Convention: Preamble and Article 2(2)(a)), the 1992 Convention on the Protection of the Marine Environment of the Baltic Sea Area (Baltic Sea Convention (Article 3(2)), the 1992 Helsinki Convention on the Protection and Use of Transboundary Watercourses and Lakes (Article 2(5)(a)), the 1992 Bamako Convention (Article 4(3)(f)), the 1992 Climate Change Convention (Preamble), and perhaps arguably, Article 6 of the 1989 Basel Convention (the Prior Informed Consent Procedure (PIC)).[186]

As noted by many commentators, though these multilateral environmental treaties seem to accept this new approach, defining the international law 'principle' is not an easy task.[187] Although I have space for no more than an indication, the international legal status of this 'principle' in international law still remains undeniably ambiguous.[188] As some authors have suggested, there may be some cogent evidence to show that the precautionary 'principle' has already become part of customary international law of the environment, but it must be said that the authenticity for that argument still remains uncertain.[189]

In my view, this is hardly surprising, however.[190] Firstly, it should be noticed that, despite a marked difference between the precautionary 'principle' or

---

185 See David A. Balton, 'Strengthening the Law of the Sea: The New Agreement on Straddling Fish Stocks and Highly Migratory Stocks', 27 *ODIL* (1996), pp. 125–151.

186 Other examples include the 1988 CRAMRA (Article 4); the 1992 Biodiversity Convention (Preamble); the 1992 Baltic Sea Convention (Article 3(2)); the 1992 Transboundary Watercourses Convention (Article 2(5)(a)); the 1992 OSPAR Convention (Article 2(2)(a)); the 1992 Maastricht Treaty (Article 130f). See also ICJ's *Nuclear Weapons Advisory Opinion,* 35 *ILM* (1996), paras. 29–30.

187 For an extensive discussion, see Philippe Sands and Jacqueline Peel, *Principles of International Environmental Law* (3rd ed. Cambridge University Press, 2012), pp. 217–228; David Freestone, 'The Precautionary Principle', in David Freestone and Robin Churchill (eds.), *International Law and Global Climate Change* (Graham & Trotman, 1992); David Freestone and Ellen Hey, 'Origins and Development of the Precautionary Principle', in David Freestone and Ellen Hey, *Precautionary Principle and International Law* (Kluwer Law International, 1996), pp. 3–15; Lothar Gündling, 'The Status in International Law of the Principle of Precautionary Action', 5 *IJECL* (1990), pp. 25 et seq.

188 For a discussion see, for example, Lothar Gündling, 'The Status in International Law of the Principle of Precautionary Action', 5 *IJECJ* (1990), pp. 23–30.

189 See James Cameron and Juli Abouchar, 'The Precautionary Principle: A Fundamental Principle of Law and Policy for the Protection of the Global Environment', 14 *BCICLR* (1991), pp. 34–52.

190 For similar arguments, see David Freestone and Zen Makuch, 'The New International Environmental Law of Fishries: The 1995 United Nations Straddling Stocks Agreement',

approach and the Stockholm Principle 21/Rio Principle 2, as far as the former new approach is inherently based on the latter customary rule, these two principles are still closely inter-related. Secondly, and perhaps more importantly, what the precautionary approach actually means will significantly depend on context, objective and the nature of each environmental problem. For instance, the legal character of the precautionary approach in the ozone convention intrinsically differs from that of oceans and sea, water resources or hazardous activities that are more closely concerned with the 'threshold' of environmental damage.

Regardless of its formal legal status in positive international law, in the present international community of over 190 developed and developing States, this evolving 'principle' or approach within modern environmental treaty régimes would not be maintained by participating States unless supported, to a greater or less extent, by additional legal instruments for international environmental co-operation and global capacity-building.[191]

D   *The Provisions of the Vienna Ozone Convention*
(1)   The General Obligations: Legal Basis of the Montreal
        Ozone Protocol

The so-called 'General Obligations', 'Fundamental Principles' or equivalent articles – which are central to any international environmental treaties – contain contracting parties' legitimate expectations for the development and maintenance of the international treaty régimes. In general, they express the guiding rules of such regime instruments that address the rational behaviour of participating States. Some general provisions in this kind of article may be regarded as confirmation of the legal rule of 'international due diligence'[192] to take appropriate measures at least.[193] This means that, on most occasions, these provisions may not gain clear or objective meaning unless supported by other substantial treaty provisions and specific environmental regulations for successful implementation of the respective regimes.

Although the contents of such provisions depend on the character of each environmental régime, they generally cover (i) the control over activities

---

        7 *YbkIEL* (1996), p. 13, saying that 'the precautionary principle may not be such a radical departure from existing international principle'.

191   See Chapter I(III.B) in this volume.

192   See Sachiko Kuwabara, *The Legal Regime of the Protection of the Mediterranean against Pollution from Land-Based Sources* (Tycooly International, 1984), p. 71.

193   See, for example, Article 192 of the 1982 UNCLOS, providing that 'States have the obligation to protect and preserve the marine environment' and Article 194 requiring them to use the 'best practicable means at their disposal and in accordance with their capabilities'.

within (and outside) national jurisdiction, (ii) exchange of information relating to scientific and technical information and data, (iii) financial/technical assistance and international transfer of technology, and (iv) the general obligations to internationally cooperate.[194] Good examples that include some or most of the above-mentioned obligations are the 1979 LRTAP Convention (Article 2); the 1989 Basel Convention (Article 4); the 1991 Bamako Convention on the Transboundary Movement and Management of Hazardous Wastes within Africa (Article 4);[195] the 1992 Biodiversity Convention (Article 3)[196]; the 1992 Climate Change Convention (Article 3); the 1985 ASEAN Agreement (Article 1); and the 1994 UN Convention to Combat Desertification in Those Countries Experiencing Serious Drought and/or Desertification, Particularly in Africa (Article 4).

The following content of 'General Obligations' of the Vienna Ozone Convention (Article 2) is a product of long constructive discussions, selected from many 'Alternatives' in its draft texts revised several times.

Responding to 'preventive measures' in the Preamble, Article 2 provides that the parties are to take appropriate measures to protect human health and the environment against adverse effects resulting from related human activities (Article 2(1)). The phrase 'appropriate measures' accurately reflects the nature of this framework environmental treaty.[197] Such measures must be based on relevant scientific and technical considerations (Article 2(4)).[198] In accordance with the means at their disposal and capabilities (Article 2(2)), the parties are to 'adopt appropriate legislative or administrative measures' and to 'co-operate in harmonising appropriate policies to control, limit, reduce or

---

194   For a discussion of environmental cooperation, see Alan E. Boyle, 'The Principle of Co-operation: the Environment', in Vaughan Lowe and Colin Warbrick (eds.), *The United Nations and the Principles of International Law: Essays in Memory of Michael Akehurst* (Routledge, 1994), pp. 129–132.

195   See 30 *ILM* (1991), p. 775.

196   But note that most of important principles seen in draft Article 3 were moved up to its 'Preamble' during the final stage of the negotiation.

197   See Harald Hohmann (ed.), *Basic Documents of International Environmental Law*, Vol. II (Graham & Trotman, 1992), p. 668, saying that Article 2(2) is a loophole for all – especially for economically weaker States. The corresponding Article of the 1974 Paris Convention provides that the parties 'pledge themselves to take all possible steps to prevent pollution of the sea' (Article 1) – this wording is comparatively stronger than that of the Vienna Ozone Convention.

198   During the Session of the Working Group, one expert argued that it was possible to interpret the phrase 'in accordance with the means at their disposal and their capabilities' (Article 2(2)) as suggesting that the Member States would not necessarily enact any legislation in their implementation of the Convention. See UNEP/WG.94/10, p. 10.

prevent human activities under their jurisdiction or control', if these activities have or are likely to have adverse environmental effects concerned with ozone depletion (Article 2(2.b)). The parties may adopt domestic measures 'additional' to measures mentioned above in accordance with international law (Article 2(3)).[199] Yet, 'General Obligations' of the Ozone Convention do not specifically deal with the special treatment of developing countries, although Article 4(2) addresses such matters in the context of transfer of environmentally sound technology. In this respect, unlike the Vienna Convention, the Montreal Protocol as amended/adjusted contains strong provisions for the so-called 'Article 5 developing country' and moreover it established the Multilateral Fund within the ozone régime.[200]

Article 2(2.a) requires the parties to cooperate through systematic observations, research and information exchange to understand and assess the relationship between human activities and ozone depletion. Such obligations to globally cooperate are absolutely indispensable for environmental framework conventions facing scientific uncertainty, since it would help to achieve relevant scientific breakthroughs.[201] Article 2(2.a) should be read together with Article 3 ('Research and Systematic Observation') and Article 4 ('Cooperation in the Legal, Scientific and Technical Field'). Article 4(1) provides that the parties are to facilitate and encourage the exchange of scientific, technical, socio-economic, commercial and legal information relevant to the Convention as elaborated in Annex II.[202] In this respect, at its Sixth Meeting held in 2002, the Conference of the Parties to the Vienna Ozone Convention adopted Decision VI/2 'Ozone-related Monitoring and Research Activities for the Vienna Convention' and in 2003, it established an extrabudgetary fund for receiving voluntary contributions from the Parties and international organizations for the purpose of funding certain research and observation activities related to the

---

199   In the third revised draft convention, the term 'stricter' was used instead of 'additional'. See UNEP/WG.94/8, p. 2.

200   See Chapter III(III.E) and Chapter VI in this volume.

201   The 1979 LRTAP Convention also laid a basis for further cooperation in scientific research, and it established a 'Cooperative Programme for the Monitoring and Evaluation of the Long-Range Transmission of Air Pollutants in Europe (Article 9).

202   See Annex 2(2), providing that '[t]he Parties to the Convention, in deciding what information is to be collected and exchanged, should take account the usefulness of the information and the costs of obtaining it. The Parties further recognise that co-operation under this annex has to be consistent with national laws, regulations practice regarding patents, trade secrets, and protection of confidential and proprietary information'. The view of the developed countries is that patents and intellectual property concerned with the protection of the ozone layer should be guarded.

Vienna Convention.[203] The primary aim of this Fund is to provide complementary support for the continued maintenance and calibration of the World Meteorological Organization Global Atmospheric Watch ground-based stations for monitoring column ozone, ozone profiles and ultra-violet radiation in the developing countries and in the countries with economies in transition.[204] It is reported that, as of 31 December 2013, the Trust Fund received $274,454 from Andorra, the Czech Republic, Estonia, Finland, France, Kazakhstan, South Africa, Spain, Switzerland and the United Kingdom of Great Britain and Northern Ireland, together with in-kind contributions in conjunction with activities undertaken under the Fund.[205]

In order to adopt supplementing protocols/annexes, the parties are required to cooperate in the formulation of agreed measures, procedures and standards for the implementation of the Convention (Article 2(2.c)).[206]

(2)   The Conference of the Parties to the Vienna Ozone Convention

In many cases, just like other treaty régimes, modern international environmental agreements establish independent intergovernmental organs to ensure effective implementations of and compliance with their legal commitments.[207] These highest treaty organs – which provide forums for continuous multilateral environmental negotiations – are called by a variety of names such as the 'Conference of the Parties', the 'Meetings of the Parties', the 'Executive Body', and so forth.[208] They are usually empowered to adopt amendments to conventions, implementing protocols and/or related technical annexes, and additional international treaties, technical annexes and legally non-binding

---

203 See Decision VI/2 in UNEP, *Handbook for the Vienna Convention for the Protection of the Ozone Layer* (10th ed. 2016), p. 31.

204 Decision VI/2, para. 4.

205 See UNEP/OzL.Conv.10/7, para. 176.

206 At the Third Session of the Working Group, it was agreed that protocols should be adopted by the Conference of the Parties, rather than diplomatic conference. See also UNEP/WG.94/3, commentary on article 9, saying protocols should be adopted at an 'extraordinary' meeting.

207 See Jacob Werksman, 'The Conference of Parties to Environmental Treaties' in Werksman (ed.), *Greening International Institutions* (Earthscan, 1996), pp. 55–68; Alan E. Boyle, 'Saving the World? Implementation and Enforcement of International Environmental Law through International Institutions', 3 *JEL* (1991), pp. 229–245.

208 Examples include the 'Conference of Parties' (the 1985 Vienna Ozone Convention, the 1992 Climate Change Convention), the 'Executive Body' (the 1979 LRTAP Convention), and so forth. However, the supreme organs of international organisations are called: 'Assembly' (ICAO, IMO, WHO, OAU), 'General Conference' (IAEA, ILO, UNESCO), 'Conference' (FAO, OAS), or 'Congress' (WMO, UPU).

recommendations or resolutions. These treaty bodies as main sources of régime-dynamics thus often enjoy considerable legislative autonomy.[209] Further, they also provide forums for dispute avoidance and settlement by discussion and negotiation or consultation.[210] As was mentioned in Chapter I in this volume, NGOs are widely allowed to participate in the institutions' regular meetings.

The Conference of the Parties to the Vienna Ozone Convention as a legislative body is empowered to adopt (i) amendments to the Convention, protocols and their annexes, (ii) protocols to the Convention, and (iii) additional annexes to the Convention (Article 6(e-h)).[211] With regard to amendments of the Convention, only if all efforts at consensus proved unsuccessful, adoption by a two-thirds majority vote is then allowed as a last resort (Article 9(3)). This procedure applies to amendments to any protocol, although in this case a two-thirds majority of the parties to the protocol present and voting at the meeting is required (Article 9(4)).[212] This procedure is also applicable to the adoption and amendment of annexes to the Convention and protocols (Article 10(2)). Amendments adopted in accordance with Article 9(3/4) mentioned above shall enter into force between parties having accepted them (Article 9(5)).[213]

---

209 See, for example, Alan Boyle and Christine Chinkin, *The Making of International Law* (Oxford University Press, 2007), pp. 151–154. See also Jacob Werksman, 'The Conference of Parties to Environmental Treaties' in Werksman (ed.), *Greening International Institutions* (Earthscan, 1996), p. 60, suggesting that these organs' decision-making procedures are shaped by Stockholm Principle 21.

210 See Alan E. Boyle, 'Saving the World? Implementation and Enforcement of International Environmental Law Through International Institutions', 3 *JEL* (1991), pp. 232–233. In the context of the NCP, see Chapter V(IV.B.3 and VII.B.2) in this volume.

211 Annexes to the Convention or to any protocols are strictly restricted to scientific, technical and administrative matters, but form an integral part of the Convention or of such protocols. The amendment procedure mentioned above was a compromise reached by mutual concession – many experts supported a two-third majority vote in both cases, but others insisted on the necessity of a large majority vote or consensus. See UNEP/WG.94/10, para 24; 'United Nations Activities: Draft Convention not Finalised', 12/1–2 *EPL* (1984), p. 10.

212 See the Montreal Protocol (Article 2(9)(c-d)). Under the Montreal Ozone Protocol, both developed and developing countries have 'veto power', and further amendments can be easier to achieve than in the case of the Convention (see Chapter III in this volume). See also the 1992 Framework Convention on Climate Change (Articles 15 and 17) and its Protocol (Articles 20(3) and 21(4)).

213 In contrast, the Conference of the Parties of the 1992 Biodiversity Convention does not have the power to adopt binding amendments to annexes by majority decision-making (Article 29(4)). See Alan E. Boyle, 'The Convention on Biodiversity', in Luigi Campiglio et al. (eds.), *The Environment after Rio: International Law and Economics* (Graham & Trotman/Martinus Nijhoff, 1994), p. 126.

As for the Rules of Procedure for the Conference of the Parties,[214] they are substantially the same as those for the Meeting of the Parties to the Montreal Protocol, except for Rules 1 and 2.[215]

The Conference of the Parties is also designed to fulfil many other institutional functions: it reviews the scientific information concerned with the destruction of the ozone layer (Article 6(4.b)),[216] promotes the harmonisation of policies, strategies and measures to minimise the omissions of ozone-depleting substances and make recommendations on any other measures relating to the Convention (Article 6(4.c)), and adopts programmes for research, systematic observations, scientific and technological cooperation, the exchange of information and transfer of technology and knowledge (Article 6(4.d)).[217]

In relation to cooperation with other international organisations, the Conference of the Parties may ask for the services of the WMO, the WHO, and the UNEP/CCOL relating to scientific and systematic observation (Article 6(4.j)). Lastly, in accordance with paragraph 4(i) of Article 6, the Conference of the Parties has established internal treaty institutions, such as the Trust Fund of the Vienna Convention[218] and the Bureau of the Conference of the Parties.[219]

(3)   The UNEP Ozone Secretariat for the Vienna Convention and the Montreal Protocol

The basic function of Secretariats for environment treaties is to help implement multilateral agreements by coordinating and facilitating data collection and information exchange and by giving certain technical assistance for State parties (developing countries in particular). Secretariats are usually required to compile information submitted by the parties and prepare and distribute periodic summary reports.[220] Generally speaking, their authority is strictly

---

214 Rules of procedure for meetings of the Conference of the Parties to the Vienna Convention and Meetings of the Parties to the Montreal Protocol, reproduced in UNEP, *Handbook for the Vienna Convention for the Protection of the Ozone Layer* (10th ed. 2016), p. 59.

215 See Decision VCI/1 (Rules of Procedures for the Conference of the Parties); Article 6(3) of the Vienna Ozone Convention.

216 See also Article 5 of the Vienna Ozone Convention and Decision VCI/2 of the Conference of the Parties (Reporting of Measures taken by Parties).

217 The basis of these provisions can be found in *Institutional Arrangements for a Convention for the Protection of the Ozone Layer* (UNEP/WG.78/4).

218 See Decision VCI/9 of the Conference of the Parties (Financial Arrangements), in UNEP, *Handbook for the Vienna Convention for the Protection of the Ozone Layer* (10th ed. 2016), p. 40.

219 See Decision VCI/6 of the Conference of the Parties (Subsidiary Bodies).

220 See US General Accounting Office (GAO), *International Environmental Agreements are not Well Monitored* (January 1992), p. 29.

limited, and they are not expected to verify the information received by the parties.[221]

Initially, the UNEP Ozone Secretariat had carried out this function on an interim basis (Article 7(2)), but it currently serves as a permanent basis.[222] The UNEP disseminates a great deal of information concerning the international ozone treaties, the science and technologies, government policies, industry news, meetings and workshops, and training programmes.[223] The reason the UNEP in Nairobi (Kenya) is designated to this post is that it possesses assessment programmes such as the Global Environmental Monitoring System (GEMS)[224] for monitoring the effectiveness of the provisions of the global convention and coordinating international mechanisms, such as the UNEP's Coordinating Committee on the Ozone Layer, and an Environmental Law Unit.[225] Of course, another advantage of the treaty secretariat co-located with this UN organ will be that the creation of a new organ will not be necessary (in other words, those advantages include economy of staff and so forth).[226] The Trust Fund of the Vienna Ozone Convention (and the Montreal Protocol), which provides financial support to the Convention, is administered by the Executive Director of the UNEP.[227]

The UNEP Ozone Secretariat exercises some influence over the compliance of the parties with the Ozone Convention and the Montreal Protocol. In general, the Ozone Secretariat arranges or services the Conference of the Parties, the Meeting of the Parties, their Committees, Bureaux, Working Groups and Assessment Panels. It also arranges the implementation of the decisions taken by these meetings. The Secretariat prepares reports based on information received in accordance with treaty provisions, and ensure the necessary coordination with other relevant international agencies (Article 7(1)). In this

---

221　See ibid., pp. 29–30. But see also Chapter V(IV.B.1) in this volume.

222　See Decision VCI/8 of the Conference of the Parties (Designation of Secretariat).

223　See Richard Benedick, *Ozone Diplomacy* (Harvard University Press, 1998), p. 253; "'Ozone-Friendly" Computer Programme Updated', *Envirolink Environment News Service* (24 April 1997).

224　The GEMS was one of the first programmes established by the UNEP in 1970s. See in detail Mostafa K. Tolba et al. (eds.), *The World Environment 1972–1992: Two Decades of Challenge* (Chapman & Hall, 1992), pp. 614–615.

225　See UNEP/WG.78/4, para. 11–13.

226　See UNEP/WG.78/4, para. 11–12.

227　See Decision VCI/9 (Financial Arrangements) and the Terms of Reference for the Administration of the Trust Fund for the Vienna Convention for the Protection of the Ozone Layer, in UNEP, *Handbook for the Vienna Convention for the Protection of the Ozone Layer* (10th ed. 2016), pp. 40–42. See also Gilbert M. Bankobeza, *Ozone Protection* (Eleven International, 2005), pp. 184 et seq.

respect, the Ozone Secretariat often represents the Convention or Protocol in the relevant international bodies (for example, the WTO Committee on Trade and Environment).[228] As a subsidiary institution, the Secretariat also performs other functions determined by the Conference of the Parties (Article 7(f)). As we shall see, under the Montreal Protocol, the Ozone Secretariat has expanded its functions (Article 12) and it is now empowered to trigger the Protocol's Non-Compliance Procedure.[229]

Lastly, it should be noted that the Ozone Secretariat communicates proposed amendments not only to the contracting parties but also to the 'signatories' to the Convention for information (Article 9(2)). Although this procedure was – as discussed in the Third Session of the Working Group – contrary to common treaty practice as embodied, for example, in the 1982 UNCLOS,[230] recent environmental treaties widely follow such a trend.[231] As a result of this practice of the UNEP Ozone Secretariat, some signatories – which are pending ratification – might decide to become new contracting parties to the ozone régime.

(4)   The Dispute Settlement Procedures under the Vienna
        Ozone Convention[232]

Dispute settlement mechanisms of international treaty régimes usually include (i) diplomatic means of dispute settlement – namely, negotiation or consultation, mediation, and international conciliation, and/or (ii) legally binding methods – namely, recourse to arbitration and tribunals at the international level.[233] Dispute settlement procedures within environmental régimes are important for a variety of reasons, including the interpretation or application of the treaty and preservation of the integrity of the treaty thereof.[234] In most cases, however, dispute settlement procedures within international

---

228   See Chapter IV(I.B) in this volume.

229   See Chapter V(IV.B.1) in this volume.

230   See UNEP/WG.94/10, para. 25. See also 'United Nations Activities: Draft Convention not Finalised', 12/1–2 EPL (1984), p. 10.

231   See the 1989 Basel Convention, (Article 17(2)), the 1992 Framework Convention on Climate Change (Article 15 (2)) and the 1992 Biodiversity Convention (Article 29(2)).

232   For a discussion of dispute settlement in an environmental context, see Chapter V in this volume.

233   For a detailed analysis of dispute settlement procedures, see, for example, United Nations Office of Legal Affairs Codification Division, *Handbook on the Peaceful Settlement of Disputes between States* (United Nations, 1992), Chapter II.

234   See Alan E. Boyle 'Settlement of Disputes Relating to the Law of the Sea and the Environment', 26 *Thesaurus Acroasium* (1997), pp. 301–305.

THE VIENNA CONVENTION AND INTERNATIONAL ENVIRONMENTAL LAW   93

environmental régimes are only optional for contracting parties and are not implemented on a compulsory basis.

The Vienna Ozone Convention follows the classical model of providing a wide range of techniques to settle environmental disputes arising between the parties. It provides for optional use of the International Court of Justice or arbitration over a dispute regarding treaty interpretation and application; in a case where the parties have accepted no procedure (or a different one), they are then obliged to submit the dispute to international conciliation.[235] It may be argued that the mere existence of such settlement mechanisms is important.[236] Yet, not surprisingly, the procedures under the Vienna Ozone Convention have never so far been invoked or used.

Article 11 of the Convention (Settlement of Disputes) firstly states that the parties concerned are to seek a solution through diplomatic channels, that is, negotiation (Article 11(1)). This is consistent with the view that negotiation in general should be considered as the preferred option, as expressed in Article 33 of the United Nations Charter. Needless to say, its primary objective is, first of all, to identify an existing problem and moreover to define the issues.[237] It is also widely recognised that the essence of negotiation is to demonstrate considerable flexibility toward political and economic problems. However, it must be added that such an outcome often reflects power-relations between the States concerned.[238]

If negotiation proves ineffective, the parties concerned can seek mediation through the intervention of a third party (Article 11(2)). If a party has not accepted such compulsory dispute settlement procedures as arbitration[239] or/ and the International Court of Justice (as a rule, most of the parties reject such a compulsory jurisdiction), the Convention formally endorses conciliation, which contains elements of both inquiry and mediation (Article 11(4)). Based on the request of one of the parties concerned, a conciliation commission is established, and the commission decides a final and recommendatory award

---

235 See Article 11 of the Vienna Ozone Convention.

236 See Ian Sinclair, *The Vienna Convention on the Law of Treaties* (2nd ed. Manchester University Press, 1984), p. 235. It is still necessary to appreciate the deterrence effects of third party judicial mechanisms. See further Chapter V in this volume.

237 See Oscar Schachter, *International Law in Theory and Practice* (Martinus Nijhoff, 1991), pp. 214–217.

238 See, for example, J. G. Merrils, *International Dispute Settlement* (2nd ed. Grotius Publications, 1991), p. 24. In the context of the GATT, see, in particular, Yuji Iwasawa, *WTO no Funsō Shori* [WTO Dispute Settlement] (Sanseido, 1995), pp. 36–38 (in Japanese).

239 In its First Meeting, the Conference of the Parties adopted the Arbitration Procedure. See Decision I/7: Annex II of the Report of the First Meeting, reprinted in UNEP, *Handbook for the Vienna Convention for the Protection of the Ozone Layer* (10th ed. 2016), p. 51.

(Article 11(5)). As in the case of mediation, this is not legally binding and thus will be considered only in good faith.

These dispute settlement procedures in general apply to the Protocol(s) concluded under the Convention (Article 11(6)). In this respect, there exist some legal questions on the relationship between the dispute settlement procedure of the Vienna Ozone Convention and the Non-Compliance Procedure of the Montreal Protocol.[240] Theoretically speaking, the institutional mechanisms of both ozone treaties might clash over how to respond to 'ozone disputes' among the parties.[241]

Though there is no need to go into great details about this political issue, despite the fact that during the Convention negotiation many Western countries advocated procedures for the compulsory jurisdiction of the International Court of Justice, the United States firmly rejected this idea because of the ICJ's judgement in 1984 against the United States in the *Nicaragua* Case. In the Final Act, the sixteen countries officially stated that it was a truly regrettable decision.[242]

IV   Assessment of the Vienna Ozone Convention

Weaknesses of the key provisions of the 1985 Vienna Ozone Layer Convention are the reflection of customary international law relating to preventive actions, unsolved scientific uncertainty concerning ozone depletion, and contracting parties' political will influenced by economic considerations. Consequently, it is not surprising that the Convention did not mention anything specific about reducing the use of CFCs or ODSs, but merely listed in its Annex I(4) specific substances only 'thought' to have the potential to modify the ozone layer. The analysis above therefore verifies the inevitable conclusion that the Vienna Ozone Convention provided in effect a far from perfect solution to the depletion of the ozone layer.

However, the framework ozone treaty, which now includes major ODS producing or consuming nations, proved to be an initial step toward creating a much stronger Montreal Ozone Protocol, containing in its Article 2 (and Article 5) strong control measures for ODSs. It has therefore formed the legal

---

240   Martti Koskenniemi, 'Breach of Treaty or Non-Compliance?', 3 *YbkIEL* (1992), pp. 155–161.
241   See Chapter V(III.B) in this volume.
242   See the Final Act to the Vienna Convention for the Protection of the Ozone Layer, in 14/2–3 *EPL* (1985), p. 71. See also Peter H. Sand, 'The Vienna Convention is Adopted', 27 *Environment* (1985), p. 42.

basis for the 'dynamic' international régime for the protection of the ozone layer.[243]

The following four points were given explicit emphasis in this Chapter. Firstly, under the initial Convention régime, the ozone layer – 'above the planetary boundary layer', that is, not belonging to any particular part of the global atmosphere – can be regarded as the 'common concern of mankind' (CCM), having *erga omnes* character. In this context, *all States* in the international community have a legal duty to adequately protect the 'ozone shield'.

Secondly, the Ozone Convention claimed to implement Principle 21 of the 1972 Stockholm Declaration and, for the first time, it made reference to the term 'precautionary measures' in binding international environmental instruments. As we have seen, a number of scientific uncertainties regarding ozone depletion remained unresolved throughout the Convention negotiations. Viewed against this background, we may say that the Vienna Ozone Convention illustrated the precautionary approach or 'principle' and may have influenced to some extent subsequent treaty making in the sphere of environmental protection.

Thirdly, the Ozone Convention established a relatively strong institutional machinery for international supervision and control, that is, the Conference of the Parties. The Conference of the Parties to the Convention is designed to ensure sound implementation of the international environmental régime. Under Article 6, the highest internal organ within the ozone régime enjoys considerable legislative autonomy. The Convention also created the UNEP Ozone Secretariat as a group of technical experts in the field of ozone protection.

Finally, as with the 1979 LRTAP Convention, the Vienna Convention has provided a framework for strengthening international environmental cooperation in scientific research on ozone depletion and other related problems. The Ozone Convention's stated purpose has been to promote the exchange of information, research, and data on monitoring to protect human health and the environment against activities that have an adverse effect on the ozone layer. In this respect, the contracting parties are specifically required to internationally cooperate, through systematic observations, research and information exchange to understand and assess the link between human activities and ozone depletion. As I emphasised, such legal obligations to internationally cooperate

---

243   See UNEP, 'Vienna plus Ten – The Vienna Convention: 10 Years of Achievement', *OzonAction* (Special Supplement, no. 3, November 1995).

are absolutely indispensable for evolving environmental régimes faced with scientific uncertainty.[244]

Having observed the Vienna Ozone Convention, we are now ready to consider how the Montreal Ozone Protocol has remedied the deficiencies of the framework or umbrella Convention. Chapters III–VI will examine the significance of the global environmental treaty.

---

244 See Chapter I(III.A) in this volume.

CHAPTER 3

The Montreal Protocol: the Evolution of the International Regulatory Régime for the Protection of the Ozone Layer

I Introduction

Absolutely indispensable for the precautionary ozone régime have been, as addressed in Chapter 2 in this volume, internationally accepted binding standards and regulations to control chemicals which potentially deplete the ozone layer in the stratosphere. In relation to this point, we have already observed that customary law rules of the environment cannot provide such satisfactory international legal instruments for the preservation of the ozone layer, even though this does not necessarily mean, however, that they have no part to play.

A series of meetings and negotiations of the Protocol to the 1985 Vienna Ozone Convention – conducted in an *ad hoc* forum within the framework of the UNEP[1] – formally started in December 1986, and concluded, in a remarkably brief period of time, in September 1987. Perhaps not surprisingly, it was thus prior to the entry into force of the 1985 Vienna Ozone Convention.[2]

It is often said that the global ozone régime and the subsequent implementing Protocol have supplied a working model for multilateral negotiation of future environmental régimes, including climate change régime.[3] As Ambassador Richard Elliot Benedick (the chief United States negotiator for the ozone treaties) correctly observed, the Montreal Ozone Protocol is regarded as a prototype for an 'evolving new form of international cooperation', particularly in its treatment of (i) scientific uncertainty, (ii) commercial rivalries, (iii) economic incentives to non-parties and (iv) North-South relations.[4] To borrow Gehring's

---

1   For the role of the UNEP in the development of environment treaties, see Chapter 1(III.A) in this volume. See also Steffen Bauer, 'The Secretariat of the United Nations Environment Programme: Tangled Up in Blue', Frank Biermann and Bernd Siebenhüner (eds.), *Managers of Global Change: the Influence of International Environmental Bureaucracies* (MIT Press, 2009), pp. 169–192.

2   As stated earlier, the 1985 Vienna Ozone Convention entered into force on 22 September 1988.

3   See, for example, Winfried Lang, 'Is the Ozone Depletion Regime a Model for an Emerging Regime on Global Warming?', in Heribert Franz Köck (ed.), *Völkerrecht in Zeitverantwortung: Ausgewählte Schriften zu Diplomatie, Umweltschutz, internationalen Organisationen und Integration* (NXV Verlag, 2006), pp. 440–450.

4   Richard Benedick, *Ozone Diplomacy* (Harvard University Press, 1998), pp. 3 et seq. (emphasis added).

© KONINKLIJKE BRILL NV, LEIDEN, 2019 | DOI:10.1163/9789004290877_005

98   CHAPTER 3

phrase, the Ozone Protocol may also be characterised as a 'comparatively autonomous sectoral legal system' in general public international law.[5]

At present, in non-Article 5 developed countries, the most dangerous specified ODSS (namely, CFCS, Halons, Carbontetrachloride and Methylchloroform) have been phased out, and ODSS-related industry and governments have established certain forms of cooperation or partnership – such as binding or non-binding 'voluntary agreements' – for mitigating ozone depletion. Added to this, some Article 5 developing countries that had been given a ten-year grace period are phasing out major ODSS faster than legally required under the Montreal Protocol,[6] while in some Article 5 nations 'consumption' of ODSS is, in fact, still increasing. In the light of strong control provisions and actual State practice, we may safely say that the Montreal Protocol has clearly established the precautionary environmental 'principle',[7] which was only illustrated in the framework Ozone Convention.

Chapter 3 is concerned with the discussions on the substantive provisions for international control measures for specified ODSS under the Montreal Ozone Protocol. Sections I, II and III of this chapter provides a legal, sociological and political analysis of the historical evolution of the regulatory treaty, focusing on the development of its control measures based on a percentage reduction approach. However, since numerous attempts have already been made by many commentators to explain the negotiation process of the Montreal Protocol,[8] for the present purposes, only basic points in the history of the

---

5   See Thomas Gehring, 'International Environmental Régimes', 1 *YbkIEL* (1990), pp. 35–56. For a discussion, see also Chapter 1(IV). It has been pointed out that the basis of such a régime is the so-called ecological epistemic community', defined as 'a knowledge-based network of specialists who shared beliefs in cause-and-effect relations, validity tests, and underlying principles values and pursued common policy goals'. See Peter M. Haas, 'Banning Chlorofluorocarbons: Epistemic Community Efforts to Protect Stratospheric Ozone', 46 *International Organizations* (1992), pp. 187–224.

6   At the Ninth Meeting of the Parties, the UNEP Executive Director granted awards to the following twelve parties for making 'exceptional efforts' to implement the Protocol. The countries were Burkina Faso, Egypt, Ghana, Islamic Republic of Iran, Malaysia, Peru, Philippines, Singapore, Tunisia, Turkey, Uruguay and Venezuela. See UNEP/OzL.Pro.9/12, para. 7.

7   On this point, see Chapter 2(III.C(2)(b)) in this volume, dealing with the relationship between the Montreal Protocol and the precautionary 'principle' or approach.

8   For a more detailed account of the ozone negotiations, see among others, Richard Benedick, *Ozone Diplomacy* (Harvard University Press, 1998); Thomas Gehring, *Dynamic International Regimes* (Peter Lang, 1994), Chapters 5–7; Karen T. Litfin, *Ozone Discourses* (Columbia University Press, 1994); Patrick Széll, 'Negotiations on the Ozone Layer', in Gunnar Sjöstedt (ed.), *International Environmental Negotiation* (Sage Publications, 1994), pp. 31–47; Edward A. Parson, 'Protecting the Ozone Layer', in Peter M. Pass, Robert O. Keohane and Marc A. Levy (eds.), *Institutions for the Earth* (MIT Press, 1993), pp. 27–73; Edward A. Parson, *Protecting*

treaty will be underlined. Section IV then deals with national implementation of the ozone treaties, focusing on Japan's domestic measures taken since its adoption of the both ozone treaties in 1988. Obviously, as in other fields of international law, effective national implementation of treaty norms is crucial for the successful implementation of the international environmental régime.

Concretely, Chapter 3 analyses the second and third phases of ozone régime building, which are divided into two parts, negotiations from Vienna to Montreal and the post-Montreal period.[9] The second phase considers law-making within the framework of the UNEP, that is, key Sessions of the *Ad Hoc* Working Group of Legal and Technical Experts (the so-called 'Vienna Group'): the First Session of the Working Group (December 1986), the Second Session (February 1987) and the Third Session (April 1987). Next, the final international agreement adopted in Montreal regarding control measures for ODSs will be analysed. The third phase briefly examines law-making within the institutional structure of the international ozone régime. As will be argued below, the Montreal Protocol will be regarded as a constructively flexible environmental instrument. Owing to a revolutionary decision-making procedure for adjustments, the regulatory measures of the environmental régime could be periodically updated by the Meeting of the Parties to the Protocol, as the scientific evidence concerned strengthens, without having to be completely re-negotiated. In this respect, it is important that, unlike the ozone treaty régime, the parties to the 1992 UNFCCC had to renegotiate a new environmental treaty to update the contents of the 1997 Kyoto Protocol, that is, the adoption of the Paris Agreement of 2015. Section IV deals with subsequent decisions and revisions taken by the Ozone Meeting, including the 1989 Helsinki Declaration, the 1990 London Amendments and Adjustments, the 1992 Copenhagen Amendments and Adjustments, the 1995 Vienna Adjustments and the 1997 Montreal Amendments and Adjustments, the 1999 Beijing Amendments and Adjustments, the 2007 Montreal Adjustments, and the 2016 Kigali Amendments. Reference will be made to other substantive issues relating to the Montreal Protocol, including trade with non-parties (Article 4), the Non-Compliance Procedure (Article 8/ Decisions) and the Montreal Protocol's Financial Mechanism, including the

---

the Ozone Layer: Science and Strategy (Oxford University Press, 2003); Reiner Grundmann, *Transnational Environmental Policy: Reconstructing Ozone* (Routledge, 2001); Brian J. Gareau, From *Precaution to Profit: Contemporary Challenges to Environmental Protection in the Montreal Protocol* (Yale University Press, 2013). For a discussion of the Sessions of the Working Group, see Johan G. Lammers, 'Efforts to Develop a Protocol on Chlorofluorocarbons to the Vienna Convention for the Protection of the Ozone Layer', 1 *Hague YbkIL* (1988), pp. 225–269.

9   The Vienna Convention negotiation forms the first stage of the ozone layer régime-building. See Chapter 2(II.B) in this volume.

Multilateral Fund and the transfer of ozone-friendly technologies (Articles 10 and 10A). These issues will be analysed in depth in the subsequent chapters.

II The Montreal Protocol Negotiation: Preparation of the Protocol on the Protection of the Ozone Layer within the UNEP

As with the case of the Vienna Convention, the main actors of the negotiations of the Montreal Protocol were, again, the two blocs of industrialised States – namely, the Toronto Group (that is, the United States, Canada, Sweden, Norway, Finland, New Zealand, Australia and Switzerland), and the European Community, whose negotiating position was generally supported by some other States, including Japan and the former Soviet Union.[10] The Toronto Group supported a regulatory approach based on a reduction of CFCs consumption (strictly speaking, 'adjusted production') while the European Community preferred to control their CFCs production only.

A *The First Session of the Working Group*

Six months after the conclusion of the 1985 Vienna Conference, the UNEP decided to convene two informal workshops, in Rome in May 1986,[11] and in Leesburg, Virginia in September 1986.[12] At the Leesburg workshop, for the first time, the representatives of Japan and the former Soviet Union acknowledged that they would accept the need for international ozone regulation.[13] Also for the first time, environmental NGOs participated in an international ozone negotiation as observers.[14]

Yet, 'conclusive scientific evidence' of ozone modification – an unimpeachable source of legitimacy in any environmental régime – was not readily provided. Scientific uncertainty continued to exist after the adoption of the 1987

---

10 See Patrick Széll, 'Negotiations on the Ozone Layer', in Gunnar Sjöstedt (ed.), *International Environmental Negotiation* (Sage Publications, 1994), p. 45, saying that '[i]n general, countries that operated individually did not make a significant impact on the texts of the ozone agreements' with an exception of the former Soviet Union.

11 See UNEP/WG.148/2. It has been said that the meeting was a grave disappointment and dominated by European industries. See Richard Benedick, *Ozone Diplomacy* (Harvard University Press, 1998), pp. 47–48.

12 See UNEP/WG.148/2 Corr. 4 and UNEP/WG.148/3.

13 See Richard Benedick, *Ozone Diplomacy* (Harvard University Press, 1998), p. 49.

14 These NGOs include the World Resources Institute, the Sierra Club, Environmental Defence Fund, the NRDC and the USEPA. See *Report of the Second Part of the Workshop on the Control of CFCs*, 8–12 September 1986, UNEP/WG.151/Background 2, Annex III.

THE MONTREAL PROTOCOL   101

Montreal Protocol. Thus, the European Community, Japan and their industries decided to emphasise this crucial point.

Nevertheless, Ambassador Benedick recalls that there was already 'a growing general belief that some kind of international regime was required, that past national positions would have to be modified, and that every country would have to make concessions'.[15] In fact, as will be discussed below, the final text of the Protocol included certain special environment treaty provisions for the European Community,[16] Japan,[17] the former USSR[18] and Article 5 developing countries.[19]

In December 1986, at the First Session of the *Ad Hoc* Working Group of Legal and Technical Experts for the Preparation of the Protocol on Chlorofluorocarbons to the Vienna Convention for the Protection of the Ozone Layer, which was held in Geneva, Switzerland, in accordance with Decision 13/18 of the UNEP Governing Council,[20] the United States, Canada, the European Community and the Nordic countries put forward a number of different proposals. The United States – which initially focused on aerosol restrictions[21] – proposed a near complete ban of ODSS, including major CFCs and Halons. The United States' proposal envisaged that emissions of these chemicals, calculated on the basis of 1986 levels, were to be reduced in three steps, that is, by twenty per cent, fifty per cent and ninety-five per cent in accordance with each target year.[22] Because such aggregate annual emissions or consumption of a country would be in reality difficult to estimate, this proposal depended on the so-called 'adjusted production' approach (that is, production, plus bulk imports, minus bulk exports to parties, minus amount destroyed).[23] In other words, the

---

15   *Ibid.*, p. 49.
16   See Section III(D) below.
17   See Section III(B.3) below.
18   See Section III(B.4) below.
19   See Section III(E.2) below.
20   See UNEP/WG.151/L.4. (1–5 December 1986). The *Ad Hoc* Working Group was divided into two groups: (i) an *ad hoc* scientific working group that determines which ozone depleting substances should be included in the protocol for regulation and (ii) an *ad hoc* working group on legal and institutional matters that considers the legal, institutional and financial aspects of the protocol. The second *ad hoc* working group was to discuss on the Fifth Revised Draft Protocol on Chlorofluorocarbons which had been prepared by the *Ad Hoc* Working Group.
21   See Chapter 2 in this volume.
22   See UNEP/WG.151/L.4, para. 8.
23   See the US proposal, UNEP/WG.151/L2, Article 3; UNEP/WG.167/2:11. For example, if a country imported 6 kilograms of CFC-11, produced 100 kilograms of CFC-11, and exported 20 kilograms of CFC-11, its 'adjusted production' would be 86 kilograms. See UNEP/WG.167/CPR.4.

United States' proposal addressed annual national emissions or consumption levels of parties whose data would be readily obtainable. Of course, it was clear that the proposal focused on the world's biggest ODSS exporter, the European Community.[24] The United States argued that this legal formulation would (i) allow for free trade among the parties,[25] (ii) provide a more equitable allocation (than control measures based strictly on production)[26] and (iii) address the issues of shared responsibility.[27]

The United States' proposal also contained provisions for an economic incentive, that is, international trade with non-parties that is designed to ensure maximum participation in the expected protocol.[28] Similarly to the existing provisions of Article 4, the United States' proposal called for trade restrictions on imports of controlled substances from non-parties, unless they do not comply with the control measures and periodically offer information about their compliance with the ozone treaty.[29] However, these proposals for trade restrictions were, as expected, bitterly denounced by the United Kingdom and the European Commission through the ozone negotiations.[30] The proposal also had a provision for the regular assessment and adjustments of ODSS control measures, which later developed into a revolutionary procedure for future adjustments.[31] Prior to this meeting, the United States had already started its political strategies to mobilise support for this proposal by other States.[32]

Canada, which also favoured a strong regulatory régime,[33] took an entirely different approach, however. In short, Canada advocated a proposal that each State should be equally granted an entitlement to emit within the 'global

---

24 See Thomas Gehring, *Dynamic International Regimes* (Peter Lang, 1994), p. 237.

25 The United States argued that, by not penalising producer nations for exports to other parties, it facilitated free trade and access to these chemicals consistent with the responsibilities identified under the Protocol. See UNEP/WG.167/CPR.4, p. 3.

26 UNEP/WG.167/CPR.1, p. 2. Adjusted production 'allocates an annual quota to both producer and consumer nations, thus substantially broadening the number of nations with access to CFCs and Halons'. See UNEP/WG.167/CPR.4, p. 3.

27 'By increasing the number of nations to include both producers and users, this definition encourages more nations to be part of a unified effort to reduce the risks of global pollution'. See UNEP/WG.167/CPR.4, p. 3.

28 See UNEP/WG.151/L.2, Article V; UNEP/WG.167/CPR.1.

29 See, for example, UNEP/WG.167/CPR.7.

30 It was at Montreal in 1987 that compromises were finally reached. See Richard Benedick, *Ozone Diplomacy* (Harvard University Press, 1998), p. 92.

31 See Section II(C) below.

32 See Richard Benedick, *Ozone Diplomacy* (Harvard University Press, 1998), p. 55.

33 See Chapter 2(II.B) in this volume.

THE MONTREAL PROTOCOL 103

emission limit' (GEL)[34] in accordance with the so-called 'national emission limits' (NELS).[35] This proposal was based on the ground that there would be a safe margin for the distribution of emissions without causing irreversible harm to the ozone layer. As Gehring pointed out, it thus structured a 'pollution rights approach' based on 'maximum sustainable pollution',[36] rather than placing the burden directly on producers and emitters of ODSs. Although this proposal could not find favour with the United States and the European Community, it addressed all potential 'ozone-modifying substances' (OMSs). In this limited sense, the Canadian proposal went beyond the control measures devised by the United States.

On the other hand, the European Community – strongly influenced by its industry[37] – countered these two elaborate proposals with its own control measures based on a limitation of CFC production. However, since the European Community was one of the biggest net exporters of ODSs, it was virtually essential to put certain restrictions on the consumption of CFCs and foreign trade in CFCs.

Having rejected the control measures based on both emissions of and use of CFCs, the European Community offered a proposal based on a 'staged approach' under which the future protocol would initially control CFCs 11 and 12 – and possibly CFCs 113 and 114 – after which a definite time-table should be set down for a comprehensive review of the control measures.[38] This meant

---

34   Defined as the total quantity of ozone modifying substances (OMSs) weighed in accordance with their ozone depleting potential, whose release did not cause irreversible harm to the ozone layer. See Article I, *Draft Protocol on Chlorofluorocarbons or Other Ozone-Depleting Substances*, Proposal submitted by Canada (UNEP/WG.151/L.1, 29 October 1986). See also UNEP/WG.167/CPR.3.

35   The emission limit calculated using the GEL and in accordance with certain procedural mechanism.

36   See Thomas Gehring, *Dynamic International Regimes* (Peter Lang, 1994), p. 238. Canada once stated its approach recognises 'the uncertainties which continues to exist regarding the ozone depletion issue, for example smaller, less stringent, steps than are now contemplated might be appropriate if the science does not continue to offer convincing evidence of harm' (UNEP/WG.167/CRP.3, cited in *ibid.*, p. 243).

37   The position of the European Community represented the opinions of France, Italy and the United Kingdom under considerable industry influence. The companies in question were Atochem (a subsidiary of Elf-Aquitaine, France), ICI, Europe's largest producer (United Kingdom), and Hoechst (Denmark). See Nigel Heigh, 'The European Community and International Environmental Policy', 3 *International Environmental Affairs* (1991), p. 177. See also Chapter 2(II.B) in this volume. Within the European Community, however, the former West Germany, the Netherlands, Denmark and Belgium supported a strong regulatory régime and therefore the positions of the governments were not necessarily similar. See also Chapter 2(II.A) in this volume.

38   See UNEP/WG.151/L.4, para. 16.

that, theoretically, the European Community would reduce exports in order to maintain consumption of ODSs in its domestic market, and a number of developing countries would then encourage their own manufacture of CFCs, without joining in an expected regulatory régime.[39] As to foreign trade issues, the European Community merely suggested that parties should study the feasibility of restrictions on importation of the regulated substances from non-parties to the protocol.[40]

As illustrated above, it was clear that, in comparison to those proposals by the United States and Canada, the proposal(s) made by the European Community were in reality severely weaker in (i) the contents of chemicals to be controlled, (ii) the gradual reduction schedule, (iii) the procedure for adjustments and (iv) an economic incentive.

It was natural that the Nordic countries – which were net CFCs importing countries – supported a regulatory approach based on a reduction of CFC emissions.[41] It can be easily assumed that, if a reduction scheme based on the production approach were finally adopted, those CFCs importing countries might potentially be discriminated against by major CFCs producers. Consequently, the Nordic countries followed the United States' proposal, and they even offered stronger control measures for CFCs.[42]

Finally, the former Soviet Union, for the first time, presented its draft.[43] The USSR generally supported the above-mentioned Canadian proposals that were based on the 'global emission limit'.[44] Some other participating countries, such as Australia, and developing countries – represented by Argentina, Brazil, Egypt, Kenya and Venezuela – were initially neutral, but they later moved closer to the strong United States position.[45] At the time of the adoption of the Protocol, less enthusiastic developing countries did not dispute the validity of the scientific evidence.[46]

---

39   For further details, see Richard Benedick, *Ozone Diplomacy* (Harvard University Press, 1998), pp. 79–82.

40   See UNEP/151/CRP.5, cited in Thomas Gehring, *Dynamic International Regimes* (Peter Lang, 1994), p. 240. Without restrictions on trade with non-parties, it can be deduced that, in the light of European scheme based on production, European CFC industries could externalise their production capacity in the territory of non-parties to the protocol.

41   See UNEP/WG.151/L.4, paras. 9 and 11.

42   See UNEP/WG.151/CPR.2.

43   Other Eastern European countries did not regularly join the ozone negotiations.

44   See UNEP/WG.151/CRP.10.

45   See Richard Benedick, *Ozone Diplomacy* (Harvard University Press, 1998), p. 69.

46   See Karen T. Litfin, *Ozone Discourses* (Columbia University Press, 1994), p. 118.

B   *The Second Session of the Working Group*

The Second Session of the Working Group was held in Vienna in February 1987. At this session, four informal *ad hoc* working groups were established;[47] those *ad hoc* working groups addressed:

(i)   the periodic review process and hierarchy of ozone-depleting substances

(ii)   the special needs of developing countries in respect of regulatory measures

(iii)   control measures of Article II of the future protocol, and

(iv)   trade issues.

However, the core subject of this session was still regulatory measures of ODSs. Nevertheless, no agreement was reached on whether the 'adjusted production' formula or the production approach should be regulated, nor on the drawing up of a specific time schedule for gradual reductions of ODSs. As to the question of the hierarchy of ozone-depleting substances, the scientific working group listed CFC-11, CFC-12, CFC-22, CFC-113, CFC-114, CFC-115, Halon-1211, Halon-1301, Methylchloroform ($CH_2H_3Cl_3$) and Carbontetrachloride (CCl_4). Although it was generally agreed that CFC-11 and CFC-12 should be subject to future international regulation, opinions were divided on the question of other ozone-depleting chemicals.

By this stage in the negotiations, the United States' proposal based on its 'adjusted production' approach had attracted considerable support from the majority of participating States. Accordingly, Canada and the Nordic countries finally decided to withdraw their own regulatory proposals mentioned above.[48]

The European Community – just as in the First Session – sought to control ODSs production only on the grounds of simplification of procedures.[49] In its discussion paper, the European Community said that the concept of 'adjusted production' is 'too complicated to be implemented effectively and adds nothing to the protection of the environment'.[50] It further argued that some CFCs reduction could be a precautionary measure, provided that industry has

---

47   See UNEP/WG.167/2, paras. 9–10.

48   Yet negotiating positions of Japan and the former USSR were still 'enigmatic'. See Richard Benedick, *Ozone Diplomacy* (Harvard University Press, 1998), p. 70.

49   See *ibid.*, p. 11. A representative of the Commission of EC suggested that Article 9 of the Vienna Ozone Convention could justify its regulatory approach. See also discussion paper by the Commission, in UNEP/WG.167/CPR.6.

50   UNEP/WG.167/CPR.6, para. 4.

106   CHAPTER 3

a suitable time in which to adjust.[51] However, this opposing argument was in practice unsound, simply because, as the United States suggested, all three fundamental components of the 'adjusted production' approach (that is, (i) production, (ii) imports and (iii) exports) were not necessarily difficult to analyse.

The United States and its allies brushed off the European Community's negative suggestion. These countries insisted that controlling production of ODSs would only invalidate the effectiveness of the future regulatory ozone protocol, because, as stated above, production control alone would fail to cover a number of countries that do not produce CFCs but consume these chemicals. What is more, as the Toronto Group pointed out, it was also obvious that the European Community was likely to make unreasonable profits and hold advantages over CFC-importing countries (developing States in particular).[52]

Though the Second Session of the Working Group could not settle much controversy between the big two groups, it seemed apparent that considerable pressure was eventually brought to bear on the European Community to change its isolated position in the protocol negotiation process.[53] Nevertheless, it was still true that ozone disputes as to scientific knowledge were not yet resolved.

As regards preferential treatment of developing countries whose contribution toward the potential threat to the ozone was only slight, the Working Group on developing countries noted that the 'element of equity" in the context of regulatory measures would encourage more such countries to adhere to the Protocol régime, and it would also facilitate implementation of the ozone treaty obligations.[54] However, since the special needs of these countries in themselves could not be clearly identified, at this phase, the Working Group could only provide rather broad possible options on this issue to be subsequently analysed.[55]

In relation to economic 'sanctions' to be applied to non-cooperating nations, most experts emphasised the need to restrict imports from non-parties

---

51   See *ibid.*, para. 7. In addition, it is worth mentioning that the European Community suggested that it did 'not believe that scientific information available today justifies the total phasing out of CFCs.

52   See Richard Benedick, *Ozone Diplomacy* (Harvard University Press, 1998), p. 81.

53   See Thomas Gehring, *Dynamic International Regimes* (Peter Lang, 1994), p. 246 and its note 162.

54   See UNEP/WG.167/2, p. 25.

55   See UNEP/WG.167/2, p. 29.

THE MONTREAL PROTOCOL

and to discourage movement of capital and facilities outside the regulatory protocol area.[56]

C   *Toward a Final Decision in Montreal in September 1987*

In early April 1987, the UNEP Secretariat, led by Dr. M. Tolba, an Egyptian scientist who is seen as 'a father of the Montreal Protocol',[57] convened a scientific meeting of five modelling teams in Würzburg, then in West Germany, known as the *Ad Hoc* Meeting to Compare Model Assessment of the Ozone Layer.[58] The results and findings of the Würzburg meeting had a 'decisive impact' on the subsequent negotiations of the regulatory régime.[59] In spite of the fact that participating scientists used different computer models to compare the predictable results of CFCs control strategies or measures, those computer models clearly showed striking similarities. This meant that serious ozone loss would continue to happen under the regulatory measures proposed by the ozone negotiators. In addition, participating scientists envisaged the need for controlling the main ODSs, namely, CFC-11, CFC-12, CFC-113, CFC-114 and CFC-115, and Halon-1301 and Halon-1211.[60] The conclusions of the UNEP report on the Würzburgh meeting were endorsed by an informal scientific group at the Third Session of the Working Group.[61]

By the time of the Third Session, scientific certainty about ozone decreases was thus finally confirmed.[62] As the Executive Director stated, 'it was no longer possible to oppose action to regulate CFC releases on the grounds of scientific dissent'.[63] The Third Session of the Working Group was held in April 1987 in

---

56   UNEP/WG.167/2, p. 14. See also a report of the Working Group on Trade Issues, in *ibid.*, p. 22.

57   See Donald W. Kaniaru, 'Mostafa Tolba of UNEP: The Not-so-well-known Goodness of a Great Scientist and Leader', 46/3–4 EPL (2016), pp. 205–208; Martin Weil, 'Mostafa K. Tolba, U.N. Environmental Official, Dies at 93', *The Washington Post* (Washington, D.C.), 29 Mar 2016.

58   See UNEP/WG.167/INF.1; UNEP/WG.167/INF.1/Add.1; UNEP/WG.172/2, pp. 2–3.

59   See Richard Benedick, *Ozone Diplomacy* (Harvard University Press, 1998), p. 71.

60   See UNEP/WG.167/INF.1. See also Richard Benedick, *Ozone Diplomacy* (Harvard University Press, 1998), p. 78 et seq.

61   See UNEP/WG.172/2, para. 10. However, the representative of Japan publicly stated that 'it was regrettable that Japan had not been invited to the *Ad Hoc* scientific meeting at Würzburg', and thus still emphasised scientific uncertainty. See UNEP/WG.172/2, para. 13.

62   However, this did not mean that such ozone decreases were concerned with man-made CFC emissions or human activities. See Section IV(A) below.

63   See UNEP/WG.172/2, p. 2 (emphasis added).

Geneva.[64] During this session Dr. Tolba, for the first time, convened informal meetings of chief delegations[65] to address control measures for ODSs.[66] As a result, the Executive Director produced the so-called 'Chairman's Personal Text',[67] which subsequently came to serve as the basis for subsequent ozone negotiations. The proposed text dealt with major ODSs (CFC-11, -12, -113, -114, -115 and possibly Halons) and was similar to the proposal made by the United States.

The European Community decided to re-examine its strategic position.[68] Although the European Community still favoured the above-mentioned production approach as the appropriate basis for simple calculation, it tentatively accepted a freeze on imports, provided that European Community members were treated as a 'single unit'.[69] This was an important fact to stress, because such a trade restriction on imports implies that the European Community was ready to accept compromise with the United States supported by many other countries.

In this meeting, as to the special treatment of developing countries, Canada suggested that industrialising States be exempt from the provisions of any agreement for a period of five years, or until their annual use of CFCs reached 0.1 kg per capita.[70]

In the *Revised Proposal for Reduction Formula,* which was produced as a result of the Third Meeting, the United States' 'adjusted production' approach was labelled as 'consumption', which is to be measured therefore as 'production, plus imports, minus exports and minus quantities of the substances destroyed by techniques approved by the Parties'. As we shall see, this definition of consumption has been incorporated in the Montreal Ozone Protocol.[71]

---

64   See UNEP/WG.172/2. Out of thirty-three participating governments, eleven were governments of developing countries.

65   The chief delegation heads who participated in the meetings were from Canada, Japan, New Zealand, Norway, the former Soviet Union, the United States, the European Commission, and Belgium, Denmark and the United Kingdom. The Executive Director served as the representative of the developing countries. See Richard Benedick, *Ozone Diplomacy* (Harvard University Press, 1998), p. 72.

66   See Richard Benedick, *Ozone Diplomacy* (Harvard University Press, 1998), p. 72.

67   See 'Text Prepared by the Executive Director After Consultation With A Small Sub-Working Group of Heads of Delegations', in UNEP/WG.172/2, Article II, Control Measures in Annex.

68   See UNEP/WG.172/2, p. 5. See also a proposal of the European Community, in UNEP/WG.172/CRP.2.

69   See UNEP/WG.172/2, para. 11. See also Richard Benedick, *Ozone Diplomacy* (Harvard University Press, 1998), pp. 94–97. The European Community was allowed to implement control measures under Article 2 jointly. See further Section III(D) below.

70   See UNEP/WG.172/2, p. 20 and its Annex. See also Section B(2) below.

71   See Article 1(6).

THE MONTREAL PROTOCOL   109

In June 1987, the Informal Consultations toward the Elaboration of a Proto-col on the Control of CFCs to the Vienna Convention was held in Brussels, and the European Environmental Bureau invited NGOs from Europe and the United States to the meetings. As a result of these meetings, some progress was made on the reduction schedule for CFCs. In addition, immediately after the meet-ings, the Environmental Committee of the European Parliament announced an eighty-five per cent reduction of CFCs production and consumption by 1997.[72]

In the light of the arguments developed in the Informal Consultations, the Working Group drew up the Seventh Revised Draft Protocol.[73] Though the draft text still had to evade some questions that should have been thrashed out long ago, at this final stage, it envisaged the following regulatory measures:

(i)   CFC-11, CFC-12, CFC-113, CFC-114, CFC-115, Halon-1211, Halon-1301 should be regulated;

(ii)   a freeze at 1986 levels of production and consumption within one year after the protocol entered into force;

(iii) An eighty per cent reduction of production and consumption at 1986 lev-els within four years, and:

(iv)   A fifty per cent reduction of production and consumption at 1986 levels within eight or ten years.

III   International Legal Regulation of Specified ODSs under the Montreal Protocol

A   *The Final Agreement: Provisions of the Montreal Protocol*

The diplomatic 'Conference of Plenipotentiaries on the Protocol on Chloro-fluorocarbons to the Vienna Convention for the Protection of the Ozone Layer' was convened at the invitation of the Canadian government, from 14 to 16 Sep-tember 1987 in Montreal. Fifty-eight States, the European Community and five States in an observer status participated in the conference, and the Montreal Protocol on Substances That Deplete the Ozone Layer was finally adopted on 16 September 1987.[74] The Protocol was signed by twenty-six parties[75] and then entered into force on 1 January 1989.

The 1987 version of the Protocol was adjusted and amended by the 1990 Sec-ond Meeting of the Parties, adjusted and amended by the 1992 Fourth Meeting

---

72   See Markus Jachtenfuchs, 'The European Community and Protection of the Ozone Layer', 28 *CMS* (1990), p. 266.

73   See UNEP/IG.79/3/Rev.1.

74   See 26 *ILM* (1987), p. 1550; 'Selected Documents', in 17/6 *EPL* (1987), p. 256.

75   Out of the twenty-four signatories, only seven were developing countries.

of the Parties, adjusted by the 1995 Seventh Meeting of the Parties, adjusted and amended by the 1997 Ninth Meeting of the Parties, adjusted and amended by the 1999 Eleventh Meeting of the Parties, adjusted by the 2007 Nineteenth Meeting of the Parties, and amended by the 2016 Twenty-Eighth Meeting of the Parties.[76] At present the Protocol includes all major developed countries and most developing countries, including China and India.

Unlike the 1985 Vienna Convention that demonstrated only certain general principles, the 1987 Montreal Protocol (and its subsequent Amendments and Adjustments) contains specific targets in the substantive provisions of Article 2. On the basis of a 'percentage reduction approach', the Protocol sets specific quantitative limits both on the production and on consumption of the so-called specified 'controlled ozone-depleting substances'.[77]

In addition, Article 7 requires contracting parties to supply statistical data on each of the controlled ODSs in technical Annexes to the Protocol.[78] Article 4, based on the United States' proposals, controls foreign trade in ODSs with non-parties to the Protocol.[79] Article 5 relates to the special situation of developing countries.[80] Article 9 calls for international cooperation in the promotion of scientific research, development issues, public awareness and exchange of scientific and technical information.[81] Article 10 requires parties to promote technical assistance to the developing countries to facilitate their implementation of the control measures of ODSs. In this content, the 1990 Ozone Meeting decided to establish the Financial Mechanism that includes the Multilateral Fund.[82] Though the question of the Non-Compliance Procedure was not fully addressed during the Montreal negotiations,[83] the 1992 Copenhagen Ozone

---

76 See Section IV below.

77 'Controlled substances' refers to a substance in Annexes to the Protocol, whether existing alone or in a mixture. It includes the isomers of any such substances, but excludes any controlled substances or mixture in a manufactured product other than container used for the transportation or storage of that substance. On the definition of the 'controlled substances', see further Decisions I/12A and IV/12.

78 See also Decision I/11. Non-compliance with reporting requirements has been a serious problem. See Chapter 5 in this volume.

79 See in detail Chapter 4(II.B) in this volume.

80 See Section E and Chapter 6(III-IV) in this volume.

81 Parties must also submit reports on summaries of such activities to the Ozone Secretariat, every two years (Article 9(3)). See Chapter 5(VII.A.1) in this volume.

82 In accordance with the London Amendments, Article 10 of the original Protocol was then replaced by new Articles 10 and 10A. See further Chapter 6 in this volume.

83 See Richard Benedick, *Ozone Diplomacy* (Harvard University Press, 1998), p. 270, noting that '[a]s the negotiator who introduced article 8, I can attest that it was consciously intended as a laconic but important maker, not as a tactic'. See further Chapter 5(II) in this volume.

Meeting formally adopted the new dispute avoidance and settlement procedure as Annexes to the Protocol.[84] Finally, in line with the Ozone Convention,
parties to the Protocol may not make any reservations to the Protocol's requirements.[85] However, four years after a party's obligation to comply becomes operative, a party can withdraw from the Protocol at any time.[86] The Montreal
Protocol operates a number of specialised treaty institutions: (i) the Meeting
of the Parties to the Protocol as the highest treaty organ, (ii) the Implementation Committee of the NCP, (iii) the Executive Committee of the Multilateral
Fund, (iv) the UNEP Ozone Secretariat in Nairobi and the Multilateral Fund
Secretariat in Montreal and (v) technical sub-committees such as the Technology and Environment Assessment Panel (TEAP).[87] In addition, other international institutions, such as the International Civil Aviation (ICAO)[88] and the
World Meteorological Organisation (WMO),[89] also work with the UNEP.

B   *International Control Measures for ODSS*

Article 2 of the Montreal Protocol specifies precisely what level of reduction is
required for each ODS over a specific time period.[90] In addition, the Montreal
Protocol does not prevent parties from taking stronger regulatory action if they
wish to do so.[91]

(1)   The Substances Covered by the Montreal Ozone Protocol

In Montreal, it was decided to control five principal CFCs (that is, CFC-11,
CFC-12, CFC-113, CFC-114 and CFC-115: Group I of Annex A) and three Halons (that is, Halon-1211, Halon-1301 and Halon-2402: Group II of Annex A).
These chemicals are widely considered to have high ozone-depleting potential and are simultaneously of the largest commercial significance. It cannot

---

84 See further Chapter 5 in this volume.

85 See Article 18.

86 See Article 19 and Decision II/6.

87 See Figure 15.1 in Richard Benedick, *Ozone Diplomacy* (Harvard University Press, 1998), p.
     221; Figure 2.1 in Duncan Brack, *International Trade and the Montreal Protocol* (Earthscan,
     1996), p. 24. On the TEAP, see Chapter 5(IV.B.2.a) in this volume. On the role of MEAs' sub-
     sidiary bodies, see Jacob Werksman, 'The Conference of Parties to Environmental Trea-
     ties', in *idem* (ed.), *Greening International Institutions* (Earthscan, 1996), pp. 58–59.

88 See generally D. W. Bowett, *The Law of International Institutions,* (4th ed. Sweet & Maxwell,
     1982), pp. 130–131. On the impact of aircraft engine emissions on ozone, see UNEP/WMO,
     Scientific Assessment of Ozone Depletion 1994 (WMO Global Ozone Research and Monitor-
     ing Project – Report no. 37), p. 15.

89 See Chapter 2(II.B.1) in this volume.

90 See Tables 1 and 2 below.

91 See Article 2(11).

be denied that the now out-dated Protocol addresses only limited numbers of ODSs, though it paved the way for the negotiations of further amendments and adjustments.[92]

As a result of subsequent treaty amendments introduced by the regular Meeting of the Parties,[93] the following substances were added to the original text: other fully halogenated Chlorofluorocarbons (CFCs) (Article 2C and Group I of Annex B), Carbontetrachloride (CCl_4: Article 2D and Group II of Annex B), Methylchloroform or 1,1,1-trichloroethane ($C_2H_3Cl_3$: Article 2E and Group III of Annex B), HCFCs (Article 2F and Group I of Annex C), Hydrobromofluoro carbons (HBFCs: Article 2G and Group II of Annex C) and Methylbromide (CH_3Br: Article 2H and Annex E).[94]

As we shall see, reduction schedules for these newly added substances have also been adjusted periodically by the Meeting of the Parties.[95] For example, the 1997 Meeting of the Parties adopted a decision regarding new substances having the potential to deplete the ozone layer, which are not listed under Article 2 of the Protocol.[96]

(2)   The Percentage Reduction Approach: Consumption
        and Production

The Montreal Protocol has adopted a percentage reduction approach (employing a calculated level of production and consumption of controlled ODSs).[97] At the regional level, this reduction approach was first formally included in the out-dated 1985 Sulphur Protocol to the 1979 Geneva Convention (the Helsinki Protocol).[98] Yet, unlike the reduction rates of Montreal Protocol, the reduction rates of the Sulphur Protocols related exclusively to 'emissions' of possible pollutants.[99]

---

92   See in detail Section IV(A) below.

93   See Section IV(C, D and F) below.

94   See Section IV and Tables below.

95   See in detail Section IV(C, D, E and F) below.

96   See Decision IX/24 (Control of New Substances with Ozone-Depleting Potential), in UNEP/OzL.Pro.9/12.

97   See Tables 1 and 2 below.

98   See 'Protocol on the Reduction of Sulphur Emissions or Their Transboundary Fluxes by at least Thirty Per Cent', 27 ILM (1988), p. 707. See Jonas Ebbesson, *Compatibility of International and National Environmental Law* (Kluwer Law International, 1996), p. 138. The Montreal Protocol establishes uniform percentage reduction targets for the two categories of the parties, that is, Article 5 and non-Article 5 countries.

99   In addition, the 1994 Sulphur Protocol – which is regional in scope – fixes specific reduction rates for each contracting party.

THE MONTREAL PROTOCOL

As regards 'consumption',[100] Article 2 of the Protocol as adopted in Montreal required the parties to reduce the 1986 CFCs consumption level by fifty per cent by 1999, and to freeze the consumption of Halons at the 1986 level by 1992. The production[101] of CFCs also follows the same reduction scheme, except for the allowance of a ten or fifty per cent increase for the purpose of 'industrial rationalisation'[102] between parties and/or for satisfying the 'basic domestic needs'[103] of developing countries. In this respect, the 1998 Tenth Meeting of the Parties adopted Decision X/15, which requested the TEAP to make an assessment of the quantities of ODSs in Annexes A and B that need to be produced and exported by non-Article 5 countries to meet Article 5 countries' 'basic domestic needs', during the period from 1999 to 2010. The concept of 'basic domestic needs' turned out to be one of the elements of ODSs illegal trade,[104] and the subsequent Meeting of the Parties to the Protocol has adopted additional decisions on reporting requirements and other compliance issues.

By enabling such 'industrial rationalisation', under paragraph (5) of Article 2, non-Article 5 developed countries still may exceed their decided production quotas – even after domestic phaseout – as long as such excess goes to Article 5 low-volume-consuming countries. This represents a transfer of ODS

---

100   For the purposes of the Montreal Protocol, Consumption = Production + Imports – Exports (of controlled substances): Production = Production (of controlled substances) – the amount destroyed by technologies – the amount used as feedback in the manufacture of other chemicals. The amount recycled and reused is not be considered (Article 1(5)). The definitions of both 'production' and 'consumption' are to be discussed further in subsequent ozone meetings. On the definition of 'production', see, for example, Decisions I/12B; VI/10; VII/10; VII/30. Regarding calculation of control levels, see Section 3 below.

101   Defined as: 'the amount of controlled substances produced minus the amount destroyed by technologies to be approved by the Parties and minus the amount entirely used as feedstock in the manufacture of other chemicals. The amount recycled and reused is not to be considered as 'production".

102   According to Article 1(8), 'industrial rationalisation' is defined as 'the transfer of all or a portion of the calculated level of production of one party to another, for the purpose of achieving economic efficiencies or responding to anticipated shortfalls in supply as a result of plant closures'. See also Decision I/12D 'Clarification of Terms and Definitions: Industrial Rationalization', adopted at the First Meeting of the Parties to the Montreal Protocol.

103   See also Section III(E) below.

104   See also Joanna Depledge, 'Vienna Convention/COP-7, Montreal Protocol/MOP-17: The Ozone Meetings', 36/1 EPL (2006), p. 24; Decision XVII/12: Minimizing Production of Chlorofluorocarbons by Parties not Operating under Paragraph 1 of Article 5 of the Montreal Protocol to Meet the Basic Domestic Needs of Parties Operating under Paragraph 1 of Article 5.

production, which may be seen as a limited form of 'joint implementation'.[105] This treaty provision, proposed by the Canadian government in Montreal, is also designed partly to prevent Article 5 industrialising nations from putting up new manufacturing facilities for ODSs in these regions.[106]

The international base level (in this case, the level as it stood in 1986) for calculating the level of the freeze and subsequent ODS reductions is important in order to facilitate detailed comparison of the technical and scientific data in question.[107] The 1985/1994 Sulphur Protocols to the 1979 Geneva Convention also refers to the year of reference (in the case of the 1994 Sulphur Protocol, the base year is 1980).

Although Article 2 of the Executive Directors' text prescribed an 'ultimate objective of .... elimination' of ODSs, at the request of the EC Commission, this ambitious clause was then transferred to the 'less authoritative' Preamble of the Protocol text.[108] Further, the three-year delayed freeze on the Halons mentioned above was also the result of the European Community's partial success in the multilateral ozone diplomacy.[109]

(3)   The Ozone-Depleting Potentials (ODPs)

The chemicals in Annexes A-C and E-F of the Protocol are weighted in accordance with their ozone-depleting potentials (ODPs) to calculate the international base levels of both production and consumption. In common with the control measures, the ODPs are official estimates based on existing knowledge and, therefore, they must be reviewed and revised periodically. Article 3 provides detailed methods for calculating production and consumption levels (for example, production equals multiplying annual production of each ODS by ODP, and adding together, for each such group, the resulting figures). It is important to notice that, by calculating in this way, parties can organise a highly flexible reduction schedule within each of the classes of

---

105   See Farhana Yamin, 'The Use of Joint Implementation to Increase Compliance with the Climate Change Convention', in James Cameron, Jacob Werksman and Peter Roderick (eds.), *Improving Compliance with International Environmental Law* (Earthscan, 1996), p. 229, note 1. In the context of the European Community, see also Section D below.

106   Alfred C. Aman, Jr., 'The Montreal Protocol on Substances that Deplete the Ozone Layer', in Francesco Francioni and Tullio Scovazzi (eds.), *International Responsibility for Environmental Harm* (Graham & Trotman, 1991), pp. 203–204.

107   See Article 3. Regarding the negotiation on the base year, see Richard Benedick, *Ozone Diplomacy* (Harvard University Press, 1998), pp. 82–83.

108   See Richard Benedick, *Ozone Diplomacy* (Harvard University Press, 1998), p. 87.

109   See *ibid.*, p. 79.

THE MONTREAL PROTOCOL

substances, for example, CFCs, Halons and HCFCs. As far as they do not exceed an ODP limit, parties can use whatever combinations of CFCs or ODSs they choose. It is said that these provisions were inserted partly to accommodate Japan's concern about controlling CFC-113, that is used for cleaning electronic components.[110]

(4)   The Special Situation of the Former USSR

Regarding the special situation of the former USSR, it was also decided that paragraph (6) of Article 2 – which allows parties that had facilities under construction prior to signing of the Protocol (16 September 1987) to add the production of such facilities to its 1986 production level – should be inserted to accommodate the concerns of the former Soviet Union, that had a five-year plan for new CFCs-related plants. It is argued that this concession created a potential loophole for the former USSR.[111]

(5)   Non-Compliance with the ODS Control Measures:
         Compliance Control[112]

International ozone disputes, having a 'group aspect', are essentially global in character and therefore they would affect all States, rather than a limited number of States.[113] In early stages, anticipated non-compliance with these detailed legal standards or regulations to control ODSs should be dealt with by the specialised internal treaty institutions, that is, the UNEP Ozone Secretariat and the standing Implementation Committee of the NCP – and ultimately, the Ozone Meeting of the Parties as the highest treaty organ within the régime.[114] By using various compliance-management techniques,[115] they can

---

110   See Richard Benedick, *Ozone Diplomacy* (Harvard University Press, 1998), pp. 78–79. See also Brenda M. Seaver, 'Stratospheric Ozone Protection: IR Theory and the Montreal Protocol on Substances that Deplete the Ozone Layer', 6 *Environmental Politics* (1997), p. 39.

111   See Christine B. Davidson, 'The Montreal Protocol: The First Step toward Protecting the Global Ozone Layer', 20 *NYJILP* (1988), pp. 814–815; Richard Benedick, *Ozone Diplomacy* (Harvard University Press, 1998), p. 83. The 1989 Ozone Meeting decided that this clause did not allow an increase in production to be exported to non-parties. See Decision 12 G(b), in UNEP/OzL.Pro.1/5, p. 19.

112   On 'compliance monitoring', see Chapter 1(III.C) in this volume.

113   See Chapters 1(IV) and 5(I) in this volume.

114   See Chapter 1(III.C) and Chapter 5 in this volume. Unlike judicial tribunals, their dispute settling and avoiding functions are of conciliatory rather than adjudicative in character. See further Chapter 5(V.A) in this volume.

115   See Chapter 1(III.C) in this volume; Abram Chayes and Antonia Handler Chayes, *The New Sovereignty* (Harvard University Press, 1995).

organise community pressure on non-complying countries. In this respect, the decision-making process of Decision VII/18 as to Russia's non-compliance may illustrate the 'group aspect' of the NCP régime.[116]

However, it is also right to say that, depending upon the nature of issues involved and reasons for such treaty non-compliance, non-compliance with the Protocol obligations should be best addressed on a case-by-case basis.[117]

C   *The Internal Mechanisms for Amendments and Adjustments: Strengthening the System of the International Control Measures*

Just like the control measures for CFCs, the adoption of a procedure for the expected adjustments of ODSs was also subject to disagreement during the negotiations of the international ozone régime.[118] As a result of the negotiations, however, the following agreement about the procedure – which is unprecedented in international environmental treaty law – was finally reached between the two groups, that is, the Toronto Group countries and the European Community, supported by the former Soviet Union.

As an initial step, paragraph 9(c) of Article 2 encourages parties to make every effort to reach agreement by consensus. Yet, if all efforts at consensus have been exhausted, decisions in question are then to be adopted by a two-thirds majority vote of the parties present and voting representing a majority of both industrialised non-Article 5 and industrialising Article 5 countries.[119]

It is important to note that such decisions on adjustments are binding on all State parties to the Protocol, even though their contents may in reality be

---

116   As we shall see in Chapter 5(VII.B) in this volume, the Montreal NCP was first invoked in 1995 by several countries of CEITs, which were in non-compliance with ODS control measures of the Montreal Protocol.

117   Factors affecting non-compliance may include, for example, economic ability to comply, careless mistakes, ambiguity of texts and even wilful treaty violations. See further Chapter 5 in this volume.

118   See Thomas Gehring, *Dynamic International Regimes* (Peter Lang, 1994), p. 225.

119   According to the 1990 London Amendment, the words 'representing at least fifty per cent of the total consumption of the controlled substances of the Parties' were thus deleted from paragraph 9(c) of Article 2 of the 1987 original version. On double majority, see Patrick Széll, 'Decision Making under Multilateral Environmental Agreements', 26/5 EPL (1996), p. 213. Under the 1994 Sulphur Protocol, 'adjustments' must be adopted by consensus and thus, unlike the Ozone Protocol, not by majority voting (Article 11(6)).

THE MONTREAL PROTOCOL

unacceptable to up to one-third of the régime members.[120] This provision may thus indicate one of the essential features of the international ozone layer régime having *erga omnes* character, that is, a changing direction from individual sovereignty to global multilateralism.[121] ODSS, which are newly incorporated into the regulatory Protocol text, are then subject to this simplified voting procedure under Article 2(9).

As to assessment and review of control measures, Article 6 of the Protocol requires parties to assess, at least every four years, the substantive regulatory measures for ODSS on the basis of 'available scientific, environmental, technical and economic information'.[122] In the light of such subsequent assessments, parties are to consider proposals for future adjustments.

In practice, however, the 1990 London Adjustments, the 1992 Copenhagen Adjustments, the 1995 Vienna Adjustments, 1997 Montreal Adjustments, the 1999 Beijing Amendments and Adjustments, the 2007 Montreal Adjustments, and the 2016 Kigali Amendments to the Protocol have all been adopted by consensus among the parties and thus without resort to the above-mentioned revolutionary simplified majority voting process. Yet this does not necessarily mean that this procedure has no impact on the development of the ozone layer régime. As Werksman says, it is possible that, 'the majority voting provisions

---

120 See Article 2(9)(d). An international committee of legal experts hailed this procedure as a 'great novelty in international environmental law' (cited in Richard Benedick, *Ozone Diplomacy* (Harvard University Press, 1998), p. 90). See the 1994 Sulphur Protocol (Article 11), calling for consensus only; the 1989 Basel Convention (Article 17(3)), calling for consensus and a three-fourth majority vote; the 1992 Climate Change Convention (Article 15(3)), calling for consensus and a three-fourth majority vote. See also Gilbert M. Bankobeza, *Ozone Protection* (Eleven, 2005), pp. 114–117; Johan Lammers, 'The Mechanism of Decision-making under the Vienna Convention and the Montreal Protocol for the Protection of the Ozone Layer', in Gerard Kreijen *et al.* (eds.), *Sovereignty, and International Governance* (Oxford University Press, 2002), pp. 412–413.

121 See Jacob Werksman, 'The Conference of the Parties to Environmental Treaties', in Werksman (ed.), *Greening International Institutions* (Earthscan, 1996), pp. 60–61. But see also Patrick Széll, 'Decision Making under Multilateral Environmental Agreements', 26/5 EPL (1996), p. 213, noting that 'the circumstances of the Montreal Protocol were unusual'. It is important that, at the adoption of the 1987 Protocol, ozone negotiators anticipated eventual total elimination of all ODSS.

122 See UNEP/WMO, *Scientific Assessment of Ozone Depletion 1994* (WMO Global Ozone Research and Monitoring Project, Report no. 37); UNEP, *Environmental Effects of Ozone Depletion: 1994 Assessment* (November 1994). On the importance of periodic assessments, see Environment Canada, *10th Anniversary Colloquium: 'Lessons from the Montreal Protocol* (13 September 1997).

help to set the parameters of the Parties expectations'.[123] Such shared 'expectations' may be included in the general category of 'régime-rules' we have considered in Chapter 1(I) in this volume.[124]

Finally, it must be noted that, unlike 'adjustments' of control measures, further 'amendments' to the Montreal Protocol text must be adopted in accordance with Articles 9 and 10 of the 1985 framework Ozone Convention. Amendments are thus subject to domestic treaty-acceptance procedures.[125] The London, Copenhagen, Montreal and Beijing Amendments entered into force with the ratification of twenty parties to the Protocol, while Article 9(5) of the Vienna Convention requires a two-third majority vote.[126] The Kigali Amendment will also enter into force in the same way, on 1 January 2019.[127] Just like the Protocol's dynamic control measures, these decisions may also contribute to the dynamics of the international ozone régime as a whole.

D The European Community as the 'Regional Economic Integration Organisation': the Joint Implementation of the ODS Control Measures

With regard to the much-disputed question of a 'regional economic integration organisation',[128] the parties could also reach the following agreement at a very late stage in the ozone régime negotiations.

The European Community, as a 'single unit',[129] was allowed to jointly fulfil its reduction obligations, provided that (i) the combined levels of consumption of the individual States did not exceed the determined levels and (ii) all

---

123 See Jacob Werksman, 'The Conference of Parties to Environmental Treaties', in *idem* (ed.), *Greening International Institutions* (Earthscan, 1996), p. 61.

124 'A set of implicit or explicit principles, norms, rules and decision-making procedures around which actors' expectations converge in a given area of international relations'.

125 See Chapter 2(III.D.2) in this volume. See also Jacob Werksman, 'The Conference of the Parties to Environmental Treaties', in *idem* (ed.), *Greening International Institutions* (Earthscan, 1996), p. 61.

126 See *ibid.*, p. 61. See Article 2(1) of the 1990 Amendments and Article 3(1) of the 1992 Amendments.

127 See Article IV. HFC trade controls under Article 4 of the Montreal Protocol will enter into force on 1 January 2033, provided that seventy parties ratified the Amendment.

128 As was suggested, the definition provided for in Article 1(6) of the Ozone Convention was taken from the 1982 UNCLOS. See in detail Chapter 2(II.B(4)) in this volume.

129 See Section II(C) above.

THE MONTREAL PROTOCOL 119

States of the European Community became parties.[130] This 'joint implementation' mechanism[131] is not applicable to production obligations, however.[132]

To date, the European Community is the only regional economic integration organisation under the international ozone régime. This legally 'differentiated' treatment under the Protocol will also be regarded as the partial success of the European Community's ozone diplomacy.[133] The European Community is also treated as an organisation having a special status, for example, in the 1992 Climate Change Convention,[134] the 1992 Biodiversity Convention,[135] and the 1989 Basel Convention.[136] Similarly, the 1994 Sulphur Protocol provides that the Executive Body may decide to allow two or more parties jointly to implement treaty obligations to reduce emissions.[137]

---

130 See Article 2(8.a). Since the European Community can exchange consumption quota, it was possible for some Member States to evade the treaty obligation concerning reductions on CFC production and consumption. See Richard Benedick, *Ozone Diplomacy* (Harvard University Press, 1998), pp. 94–97.

131 Yamin claims that a limited form of joint implementation has been adopted in the Montreal Protocol (that is, Articles 2(5) and 2(8.a)). See Farhana Yamin, 'The Use of Joint Implementation to Increase Compliance with the Climate Change Convention', in James Cameron, Jacob Werksman and Peter Roderick (eds.), *Improving Compliance with International Environmental Law* (Earthscan, 1996), p. 229, note 1; Phoebe N. Okowa, 'The European Community and International Environmental Agreements', 15 *YbkEL* (1995), p. 180; Onno Kuik, Paul Peters and Nico Schrijver (eds.), *Joint Implementation to Curb Climate Change* (Kluwer Academic Publishers, 1994), pp. 9–11. Regarding Article 2(5), see Section III(B.2) above. In the context of the Kyoto Protocol, see Duncan French, '1997 Kyoto Protocol to the 1992 UN Framework Convention on Climate Change', 10 *JEL* (1998), pp. 236–237.

132 See Patrick Széll, 'Ozone Layer and Climate Change', in Winfried Lang, Hanspeter Neuhold and Karl Zemanek (eds.), *Environmental Protection and International Law* (Graham & Trotman/Martinus Nijhoff, 1992), p. 171 and its note 12, noting that the European Community tried to achieve such a concession for itself.

133 'The Community is prepared to support the idea that there should be a freeze on production together with a limitation of imports of CFCs by non-producing countries, provided that for this purpose the Community itself is treated as *a single producing unit*' (emphasis added). See UNEP/WG.167/CPR.6, para. 3.

134 See Article 1(6). See Farhana Yamin, 'The Use of Joint Implementation to Increase Compliance with the Climate Change Convention', in James Cameron, Jacob Werksman and Peter Roderick (eds.), *Improving Compliance with International Environmental Law* (Earthscan, 1996), pp. 229–242; Sten Nilsson and David Pitt, *Protecting the Atmosphere* (Earthscan, 1994), pp. 48–49, 141–143.

135 See Article 2.

136 The European Community is regarded as a 'political and/or economic integration organisation'. See Article 2(20).

137 See Article 2(7).

Such special treatment may be potentially beneficial for the régime members of the Community and their industry. In the case of the Montreal Protocol, the special status of the organisation enables members of the Community to exchange consumption quotas, thus allowing European industry to re-distribute production among CFC manufacturers in different countries to secure the 'maximum efficiency'.[138] Corresponding Article 14 of EC Regulation 1005/2009 of the European Parliament and of the Council of 16 September 2009 on substances that deplete the ozone layer allows trading in production rights between EU members. However, as the United States argued during the Montreal negotiation process, this would imply that over-fulfilment of environmental obligations by some ambitious members (for example, Germany) might be potentially exploited by others (for example, the United Kingdom and France).[139] Finally, it should be noted that the members of the Community still individually report technical data to the UNEP Ozone Secretariat.[140]

E   *Special Situation of Developing Countries: the 'Grace Period' for Article 5 Countries*

Participation by developing countries – as large potential sources of ODS emissions – has been essential to both establishing and sustaining the regulatory Protocol. As will be addressed in Chapter 4(II.A) in this volume, a substantial number of industrialising nations decided to participate in the ozone régime, due partly to possible economic 'sanctions' provided for in Article 4 of the Montreal Protocol. However, is the universal and immediate application of Article 2 control measures acceptable for newly industrialising nations?

(1)   The Justification for the Grace Period

In the first place, it should not be forgotten that the contribution to ozone modification by developing nations had been relatively modest.[141] On the other hand, industrialised nations as major polluters have substantively benefited from almost unrestrained use of ozone-depleting CFCs or ODSs for the past forty years or more. For this historical reason, it can be said that differentiated environmental standards should apply to these countries defined as 'low-volume-consuming countries'.

---

138   See Karen T. Litfin, *Ozone Discourses* (Columbia University Press, 1994), p. 114.

139   See Thomas Gehring, *Dynamic International Regimes* (Peter Lang, 1994), p. 254.

140   Non-compliance with data reporting has been observed in some Member States. See Chapter 5(VII.A(1)) in this volume.

141   While in 1986 developing countries accounted for 15 per cent of the total usage of ODSs, by 1991, the figure had risen to 21 per cent.

In the second place, many of developing countries do not currently have the capability to comply fully with the control measures for CFCs and ODSs.[142] In other words, they still suffer financial, structural and administrative difficulties in meeting their legal obligations under the Ozone Protocol. Technically speaking, their treaty compliance is likely to depend on the availability of financial resources or CFC-free replacements, including HFCs and not-in-kind technologies (NIK), the extent of ODS recycling and its technological feasibility, and environmental acceptability.[143]

Therefore, it would seem apparent that, under the evolving international co-operation régime, non-Article 5 industrialised nations should take on greater international responsibility regarding a decrease of stratospheric ozone layer.

| (2) | The Grace and Phaseout Period for Article 5 |
| | Developing Countries |

The Montreal Protocol shows international equity considerations for industrialising countries (or 'low-volume-consuming' countries: LVCs). A special treaty provision under Article 5 allows 'developing countries' to delay their compliance with the international regulations under Article 2 for ten years, provided that their annual consumption of Annex A substances is less than 0.3 kilograms per capita and 0.2 kilograms per capita for Annex B controlled substances. As a result, they were allowed to produce and consume specified CFCs and Halons until 2010 (that is, reduce by fifty per cent by 2005, eighty-five per cent by 2007 and finally phase out by 2010),[144] though they must put an immediate freeze on their consumption by 1 July 1999. In other words, these Article 5 developing countries are not allowed to consume more than 0.3 or 0.2 kilograms per capita on the date of entry into force of the Protocol and ten years thereafter. Parties in non-compliance with these requirements (and potentially reporting requirements under Articles 7 and 9 of the Protocol) would not be classified as 'developing countries' under the Montreal Protocol. Such a situation whereby Article 5 countries exceed that limit should be first dealt with by – just like

---

142 See Principle 23 of the 1972 Stockholm Declaration, concerning 'the extent of the applicability of standards which are valid for the most advanced countries but which may be inappropriate and of unwarranted social cost for the developing countries'.

143 See further Chapter 6(IV.B) in this volume.

144 See Article 5(1) and 8*bis*, in UNEP/OzL.Pro.7/12, Annexes I–II; Section IV(F) below. Yet, as Bales says, it must be noted that developing countries are not necessarily allowed unlimited pollution of the environment through ODS use. This argument may be further developed in the context of the concept of international obligations *erga omnes*. See Jennifer S. Bales, 'Transnational Responsibility and Recourse for Ozone Depletion', 19 *Boston CICLJ* (1996), pp. 285–286.

non-compliance with Article 2 control measures[145] – the Ozone Secretariat and the Implementation Committee, on a case-by-case basis.[146] An average of each Article 5 country's consumption between 1995 and 1997 is used as the reference base level for the staged reductions, which took effect in 1999 (that is, freeze of CFC consumption). In this respect, in 2001, the Ozone Meeting of the Parties identified potential non-compliance with the Protocol's control measures by fourteen Article 5 parties – Bangladesh, Chad, Comoros, Dominican Republic, Honduras, Kenya, Mongolia, Morocco, Niger, Nigeria, Oman, Papua New Guinea, Paraguay, Samoa and Solomon Islands – that did not reported data on CFC consumption for either the year 1999 and/or 2000 that was above their individual baselines.[147] These Article 5 parties in non-compliance stated that 'phase-out activities had been hampered by unanticipated delays in the preparation of projects for the Multilateral Fund or in their approval, or in the disbursement of funding by the implementing agencies' and thus referred to the need of sufficient financial and technical assistance.[148] Faced with Article 5 parties' non-compliance, in accordance with recommendations by the Implementation Committee, the succeeding Meetings of the Parties has continued to adopt similar decisions.[149]

At the final stage of the negotiations, Canada's proposal advocating a five year delay in compliance was rejected by developing countries as 'too restrictive'.[150] The grace period of ten years, as part of a package deal, is a product of political compromise, and thus not necessarily based on detailed scientific or economic considerations or reliable technical data.[151] It appears that the ozone negotiators were not necessarily clear about the long-term consequences of this unprecedented environmental provision.[152] What was certain was that, during

---

145 See III(B.5) above.
146 See Decision IV/15 and discussion at the Open-Ended Working Group, in UNEP/OzL. Pro/WG.I/7/4, para. 135.
147 See Decision XIII/16 on potential non-compliance with the freeze on CFC consumption in Article 5 Parties in the control period 1999–2000, in UNEP/OzL.Pro.13/10, pp. 41–42.
148 See UNEP/OzL.Pro.13/10, para. 98.
149 See, for example, Decision XIV/17, in UNEP/OzL.Pro.14/9, p. 49; Decision XV/21, in UNEP/OzL.Pro.15/9, p. 55. See further Chapter 5 in this volume.
150 See Section II(C) above and Richard Benedick, *Ozone Diplomacy* (Harvard University Press, 1998), p. 93.
151 In the case of the 1985 Sulphur Protocol, the figure 30 per cent was chosen as an 'achievable first step'. Thus, similarly, this reduction rate was also not founded on reliable technical data. See Robin R. Churchill, Gabriela Kütting and Lynda M Warren, 'The 1994 UN ECE Sulphur Protocol', 9 *JEL* (1995), p. 179.
152 See *ibid.*, pp. 92–94.

THE MONTREAL PROTOCOL 123

this specified period of 'capacity-building',[153] they would have to develop capabilities to fully comply with the detailed binding controls under the Protocol with the help of Non-Article 5 industrialised nations.

(3)   The Principle of Common-But-Differentiated Responsibility

This 'differentiated' legal obligation, the grace period, could be labelled as a so-called 'mutual but differentiated' duty or a 'common-but-differentiated' responsibility (or responsibilities) in the field of international law for sustainable development.[154]

The principle of common-but-differentiated responsibility claims the common responsibility of developed and developing nations for the protection of the environment, whilst such responsibility should be equitably differentiated in accordance with (i) each State's contribution to environmental damage and (ii) its level of economic development. In short, this therefore means that industrialised nations may be required to shoulder immediate heavier burdens of environmental protection in a given issue-area of international environmental relations. International environmental régimes, containing this newly developing legal principle, may be called 'concentric régimes' for the environment.[155]

Not surprisingly, this principle has recently attained significant recognition in environmental legal instruments.[156] The Preambles of the 1985 Vienna Convention and its Protocol seem to endorse the evolving new principle. In addition, Principle 7 of the Rio Declaration provides that 'States shall co-operate

---

153   See Chapter 1(III) and Chapter 6 in this volume.

154   For an extensive discussion, see Philippe Sands and Jacqueline Peel, *Principles of International Environmental Law* (3rd ed. Cambridge University Press, 2012), pp. 233–236; Jacob Werksman, 'The Conference of the Parties to Environmental Treaties', in Werksman (ed.), *Greening International Institutions* (Earthscan, 1996), pp. 64–68; Peter H. Sand, *Lessons Learned in Global Environmental Governance* (World Resources Institute, 1990), pp. 6–14; Gilbert M. Bankobeza, *Ozone Protection* (Eleven, 2005), pp. 61–72; Takeo Horiguchi, 'Chikyuondanka Mondai ni okeru 'Kyōtsū daga Sai no aru Sekinin" ['Common-But-Differentiated Responsibility' in the Problems of Global Warming], in Fumikazu Yoshida *et al.* (eds.), *Jizokukano na Teisansoshakai* [Sustainable Low Oxygen Society] (Hokkaido University Press, 2010), pp. 85–103. In the context of the ozone régime, see Richard Benedick, *Ozone Diplomacy* (Harvard University Press, 1998), Chapter 16.

155   See Jacob Werksman, 'The Conference of the Parties to Environmental Treaties', in Werksman (ed.), *Greening International Institutions* (Earthscan, 1996), pp. 65–67. See also Duncan French, 'Developing States and International Environmental Law: The Importance of Differentiated Responsibilities', 49 *ICLQ* (2000), p. 46 ff.

156   Legal instruments advocating this 'principle' include the 1992 Climate Change Convention and the 1997 Kyoto Protocol (Preamble, Articles 3(1) and 4) and the 1992 Biodiversity Convention (Preamble).

in a spirit of global partnership to conserve, protect and restore the health and integrity of the Earth's ecosystem. In view of the different contributions to global environmental degradation, States have common but differentiated responsibilities'. In the 1994 Sulphur Protocol, differentiated target years 2000/2005/2010 were introduced in order to accommodate participation from Central/Eastern European States.[157]

Yet, it is right to say that the terminology in the sphere of international law at present has no definite meaning, and therefore it may be regarded as a policy-oriented concept in the international legal system.[158] Perhaps we can only say that, as in the present case of the international ozone layer régime, its potential flexibility as a concept can be of some practical use in the law-making process of environmental treaties.[159] It is easily assumed that, without this grace period, the regulatory ozone layer régime would remain merely a rich club of industrialised nations located in the northern hemisphere.[160]

Essential ingredients of the principle of common-but-differentiated responsibility would be (i) time required for compliance (for example, a grace period of a limited time span), (ii) money (financial and technical assistance) and (iii) other compliance-related factors peculiar to each environmental agreement. In the present case of the ozone régime, major contents of the principle will be (i) the ten years' grace period, (ii) the creation of the Multilateral Fund and technology transfer[161] and (iii) the provisions for 'basic domestic needs' in Article 5.[162]

---

157   See Appendix II of the Sulphur Protocol.

158   See also Christopher D. Stone, 'Common but Differentiated Responsibilities in International Law', 98 *AJIL* (2004), p. 299, stating that '[t]he practice of differentiated responsibilities has not, despite occasional claims by its proponents, been elevated to the status of a customary principle of international law'; Ellen Hey, 'Common but Differentiated Responsibilities', in Rüdiger Wolfrum (ed.), *Max Planck Encyclopedia of Public International Law*, Vol. II (Oxford University Press, 2012), p. 447. This term is loosely and generally used in many Meetings of the Parties. See, for example, UNEP/OzL.Pro9/12, para. 48. See also Richard Benedick, *Ozone Diplomacy* (Harvard University Press, 1998), p. 241, noting that 'the principle was never precisely defined and was subject to *differentiated interpretations* (emphasis added). The 'polluter pays principle' is also used in the same way. See, for example, UNEP/OzL.Pro.8/12, para. 4.

159   See Chapter 1(III.B) in this volume.

160   In spite of such special treatment under Article 5(1), developing countries, including India and China, were reluctant to participate in the international regulatory ozone régime. In reality, most industrialising nations decided to participate in the legal régime after the creation of the Montreal Protocol's Multilateral Fund.

161   Article 5(5) provides that the ability of Article 5 countries to comply with the Protocol 'will depend upon the effective implementation of the financial co-operation .... and the transfer of technology' clauses. See further Chapter 6 in this volume.

162   See Section IV(E) below.

THE MONTREAL PROTOCOL

(4)   The Consequences of the Grace Period

Apart from its expected utility to secure universal participation from developing nations, the real value of the compliance-delay clause in maintaining (that is, not 'establishing') the global ozone régime remains uncertain. It must be pointed out that the Article 5 grace period has created the danger of weakening the precautionary environmental 'principle' that formed the core of the international environmental régime.

First, rapid increase in CFCs and other ODSs consumption in Article 5 nations is likely to eventually undermine non-Article 5 countries' earlier phaseout efforts. Undeniably, it will retard, rather than expedite, the possible recovery of the ozone layer.[163] Second, it is often pointed out that this first introduction of the grace period in environmental treaties has become a potential source of illegal international trade in controlled CFCs.[164] Perhaps the same may be true of the term 'basic domestic needs' that was deliberately left undefined by the original ozone negotiators.[165]

It could be tentatively suggested that having only one category of 'developing countries' with a uniform grace period seems to be too broad. Ideally, parties to the Protocol should have introduced two or three categories of 'developing countries' whose grace or phase-out period should also be differentiated, depending on the amount of their ODS consumption and/or the state of economic growth (for example, Gross Domestic Product, and so forth).[166]

Having said this, attention should be drawn to the fact that during the phaseout period, Article 5 industrialising countries have already received financial and technical assistance from the Montreal Protocol's Multilateral Fund established in 1990. Indeed, faster phaseout of the major ODSs depends on the political will of Article 5 developing nations as well as strong commitments by non-Article 5 countries, including available financial resources and technological alternatives as provided by Articles 10 and 10A of the Protocol.[167]

---

163   It is said that if they keep on increasing their consumption of ODSs at current growth rate, their use will double every seven years. See UNEP, 'Press Release', at: <http://www.unep .ch/iuc/submenu/press/ozone/pr9-97a.htm>.

164   See, for example, Ning Liu, Vira Somboon and Carl Middleton, 'Illegal Trade in Ozone Depleting Substances', Lorraine Elliott and William H. Schaedla (eds.), *Handbook of Transnational Environmental Crime* (Edward Elgar, 2016), p. 215. See also Armin Rosencranz and Siddharth Johar, 'Illegal Smuggling of Ozone-depleting Substances', 45/2 EPL (2015), pp. 73–76.

165   See Section IV(E).

166   Under the Climate Change Convention, countries 'undergoing the process of transition to a market economy' are to enjoy 'a certain degree of flexibility' in the implementation of their commitments, only if it is so allowed by the Conference of the Parties (Article 4(6)).

167   See Chapter 6(IV) in this volume.

126   CHAPTER 3

IV   The Development of the International Cooperative and Regulatory
        Ozone Régime: the Evolution of International Control Measures
        and Other ODSs-Related Issues

The following is a brief overview of régime-developments subsequent to the
adoption of the 1987 Montreal Ozone Protocol.

A   *The Need for Revisions of the 1987 version of the Protocol:*
        New Scientific Knowledge on the State of the Ozone Layer
Shortly after the signing of the 1987 Montreal Protocol, the environmental
treaty was accused of not going far enough to protect the global ozone layer.[168]
Dramatic scientific advances on ozone modification suggested that even full
global compliance with the existing regulatory measures under the 1987 Protocol would not be sufficient to protect the severely damaged ozone layer.[169]

Only two weeks after signing the text of the Protocol, scientists of the second international expedition in Antarctica announced that the Antarctic
'ozone hole' in the stratosphere could be attributed to anthropogenic chemicals containing chlorine and bromide.[170] It must be noted therefore that, until
this 'post-Montreal period', the existence of the Antarctic ozone hole could not
be decisively linked to man-made CFC emissions.[171]

This means at the same time that, because of this localised 'hole', countries
such as Argentina and Australia are at a high risk due to increased solar UV-B
radiation, although the majority of ODSs are released by developed countries
located in the northern hemisphere. Furthermore, measurements over the
Arctic indicated that real reductions of ozone were occurring over the Arctic

---

168   See, for example, Caroline Thomas, *The Environment in International Relations* (Royal In-
      stitute of International Affairs, 1992), pp. 225–227.
169   See UNEP/OzL.Pro.Asmt.1/2.
170   See Caroline Thomas, *The Environment in International Relations* (Royal Institute of Inter-
      national Affairs, 1992), pp. 202 et seq.
171   Though the ozone hole had already been discovered before the adoption of the Montreal
      Protocol, the cause for the hole was not been established during the treaty negotiations.
      See, for example, Richard Benedick, 'Protecting the Ozone Layer: New Directions in Di-
      plomacy' in Jessica Tuchman Mathews (ed.), *Preserving the Global Environment* (W.W.
      Norton, 1991), p. 133; Brenda M. Seaver, 'Stratospheric Ozone Protection: IR Theory and
      the Montreal Protocol on Substances that Deplete the Ozone Layer', 6 *Environmental Poli-
      tics* (1997), pp. 33–34; Lori B. Talbot, 'Recent Development in the Montreal Protocol on
      Substances that Deplete the Ozone Layer: The June 1990 Meeting and Beyond', 26 *The
      International Lawyer* (1992), p. 14.

THE MONTREAL PROTOCOL

as well.[172] The 1989 UNEP Scientific Meeting, therefore, reported that; 'one ramification of our conclusion is that even if the Montreal Protocol with its present control measures, was ratified by all nations the Antarctic ozone hole would remain forever'.[173]

One of the early criticisms of the Protocol was that the CFC and Halon reduction targets were not substantial enough to protect the damaged ozone layer. In addition to this point, the Protocol was severely accused of not covering all CFCs and other important ODSs and HCFCs. They had become popular among the CFC-producing companies in the late 1980s as a substitute and turned out to have an ozone depleting potential of from two to ten per cent of the CFCs regulated under the Protocol. Moreover, it was emphasised that not only CFCs but the next best substitutes, HCFCs, have global warming potential. Methylchloroform (CH_3CCl_3), which is the fifth biggest destroyer of the stratospheric ozone layer, contributes more to chlorine loading in the atmosphere than CFC-113, but the chemical was not covered under the 1987 version of the Montreal Protocol. Similarly, carbon tetrachloride (CCl_4) was also not covered until the 1990 amended Protocol.

Since as early as 2000s, the parties to the international ozone régime were also required by the scientific community to take specific actions for regulating HFCs,[174] which have high global warming potentials (GWP), but with zero

---

172   UNEP/OzL.1/5, para. 17; *Scientific Assessment of Ozone Depletion 1994: Executive Summary*, World Meteorological Organisation Global Ozone Research and Monitoring Project – Report No. 37, WMO and UNEP. In April 1997, the WMO reported that the ozone layer was from fifteen to twenty-five per cent thinner over the Arctic in March 1997 than in March 1996 and that the worst-affected area was over the North pole region and north-central Siberia. See also Rumen D. Bojkov and Dimitris S. Balis, 'The History of Total Ozone Measurements: the Early Search for Signs of a Trend and an Update', Christos Zerefos, Georgios Contopoulos and Gregory Skalkeas, *Twenty Years of Ozone Decline: Proceedings of the Symposium for the 20th Anniversary of the Montreal Protocol* (Springer, 2009), pp. 98–99; Rolf Müller, 'Introduction', in Müller (ed.), *Stratospheric Ozone Depletion and Climate Change* (RSC Publishing, 2012), pp. 16–18.

173   UNEP/OzL.Sc.1/14, p. 2. It is worth noting that a 1989 scientific report to the parties of the Protocol reviewed new scientific findings: the dilution effect on ozone over southern populated latitudes caused by the recurring Antarctic ozone hole; unexpectedly large ozone losses over northern latitudes; the potential for serious ozone loss over Arctic; a hypothesis that a large volcano eruption could propel minute sulfate particles into the stratosphere, which could intensify chlorine's ozone-destroying effect over heavily populated regions.

174   See Stephen O. Andersen, K. Madhava Sarma and Kristen N. Taddonio, *Technology Transfer for the Ozone Layer* (Earthscan 2007), p. 111, suggesting that HFCs were 'a global issue already commented upon by scientists and in the preliminary stages of consideration by the governments for a solution'.

ozone-depletion potentials. HFCS are critical replacements for some ODSS, such as health and safety aerosol products, specialised fire protection, military applications and solvents,[175] and emissions of HFCS have been regulated by another environmental treaty, that is, the Kyoto Protocol as 'greenhouse gases' under its Annex A.[176] In 2014, the WMO/UNEP's assessment report, *Scientific Assessment of Ozone Depletion* suggested that the GWP-weighted emissions from HFCS and HCFCS were equal to those from the CFCS.[177]

Apart from these international ozone regulations, the special treatment of Article 5 developing countries and the establishment and operation of the Financial Mechanism for the implementation of the Protocol – which were not pressing central concerns until 1987 – has also become one of the substantive issues in the international cooperation régime.[178] Thus, as we shall see, after the Montreal-period, developing countries (that is, Article 5 countries) have also become key ozone régime actors.

B   *The 1989 Helsinki Ozone Meeting and its International Soft Law*
Following an International Conference on Saving the Ozone Layer, organised by the British government and the UNEP,[179] the First Meeting of the Conference of the Parties to the Vienna Convention and the First Meeting of the Parties to the Protocol took place in Helsinki from 26 to 28 April 1989 and from

---

175   See Stephen O. Andersen, K. Madhava Sarma and Kristen N. Taddonio, *Technology Transfer for the Ozone Layer* (Earthscan, 2007), pp. 217–218; Durwood Zaelke, Stephen O. Andersen and Nathan Borgford-Parnell, 'Strengthening Ambition for Climate Mitigation: The Role of the Montreal Protocol in Reducing Short-lived Climate Pollutants', 21 *RECIEL* (2012), p. 236; David W. Fahey, 'The Montreal Protocol Protection of Ozone and Climate', 14 *Theoretical Inquiries in Law* (2013), pp. 33–34.

176   Unlike the 2016 Kigali Amendment to the Montreal Protocol, the Kyoto Protocol does not regulate production and consumption of HFCS. See Durwood Zaelke, Stephen O. Andersen and Nathan Borgford-Parnell, 'Strengthening Ambition for Climate Mitigation: The Role of the Montreal Protocol in Reducing Short-lived Climate Pollutants', 21 *RECIEL* (2012), pp. 237–238; Daniel Bodansky, Jutta Brunnée and Lavanya Rajamani, *International Climate Change Law* (Oxford University Press, 2017), pp. 164–165.

177   See World Meteorological Organization, United Nations Environment Programme, National Oceanic and Atmospheric Administration, National Aeronautics and Space Administration and European Commission, *Assessment for Decision-Makers: Scientific Assessment of Ozone Depletion 2014*, WMO Global Ozone Research and Monitoring Project, Report No. 56 (2014), p. 12.

178   See further Chapter 6 in this volume.

179   The Conference was attended by 123 countries. See UNEP/OzL.Pro.1/5, p. 5; 'Other International Developments', 19/2 *EPL* (1989), pp. 45–46; Richard Benedick, *Ozone Diplomacy* (Harvard University Press, 1998), pp. 123–124.

THE MONTREAL PROTOCOL   129

2 to 5 May 1989, respectively.[180] The Vienna Ozone Convention had already entered into force on 22 September 1988, and the 1987 Montreal Protocol on 1 January 1989.

We may say that, at this development stage, the international ozone régime had largely been based on the Montreal Protocol and therefore, the 1985 Vienna Ozone Layer Convention and its treaty institution (that is, the Conference of the Parties) were given only a secondary role in ozone diplomacy.[181] Yet it was decided that (i) the Convention was the most appropriate instrument for harmonising the policies and strategies on research, and (ii) the Protocol was the appropriate instrument for achieving the harmonisation of policies, strategies and measures for minimising the release of ODSs.[182]

Although the Protocol in itself was not legally revised due mainly to notice requirements,[183] the First Meeting of the Parties produced an important international 'soft law' instrument that influenced strong decisions in London in 1990 – the Helsinki Declaration on the Protection of the Ozone Layer.[184]

Concretely, under the Helsinki Declaration, it was declared that a phase-out of CFCs would be necessary no later than the year 2000,[185] and Halons should eventually be phased out completely.[186] In addition, it was further agreed that controls should be introduced for HCFCs, Methylchloroform (CH_3CCl_3) and Carbontetrachloride (CCl_4), as soon as feasible. The Helsinki Declaration also addressed developing-country issues, including the disputable interpretation of 'basic domestic needs' and the creation of an international fund for financial and technical assistance for such States.

It is worth mentioning that the First Meeting decided to create four 'assessment panels' consisting of internationally recognised experts in the respective field, that is to say, (i) the Panel for Ozone Scientific Assessment, (ii) the Panel for Environment Assessment, (iii) the Panel for Economic Assessment and (iv) the Panel for Technical Assessment.[187] Yet the Panels for Economic and

---

180   See UNEP/OzL.Conv.1/5 and UNEP/OzL.Pro.1/5.

181   See also Thomas Gehring, *Dynamic International Regimes* (Peter Lang, 1994), pp. 268–269.

182   See Decision I/3 by the Conference of the Parties to the Convention.

183   The Vienna Ozone Convention and the Montreal Protocol provide that any proposed amendments and adjustments of the Protocol must be submitted to the UNEP for communication to all parties at least six months before the meeting of the parties which would consider them.

184   See UNEP/OzL.Pro.1/5: Appendix 1; 'Selected Documents', in 19/3–4 *EPL* (1989), p. 137.

185   However, this was subject to the special situation of developing countries.

186   'Helsinki Declaration on the Protection of the Ozone Layer', reproduced in 28 *ILM* (1989), p. 1335.

187   See UNEP/OzL.Pro.1/5, Annex VI. On Terms of Reference of the TEAP, see 'Terms of Reference of the Technology and Economic Assessment Panel and its Technical Options

130   CHAPTER 3

Technical Assessment have been merged into the Technology and Economic Assessment Panel (TEAP).

Lastly, the First Ozone Meeting decided to establish an Open-ended Working Group, which is a comparatively less formal régime group open to all parties, *inter alia* to prepare draft proposals for any amendments to the Montreal Protocol.[188]

c   *The 1990 London Ozone Meeting: Strengthening the Control*
       Measures and the Establishment of the Multilateral Fund
The Second Meeting of the Parties to the Montreal Protocol, which was hosted by the British government, was held in London from 27 to 29 June 1990.[189] The primary goals of the London Ozone Meeting of the Parties were (i) to further expedite the total phaseout of CFCs and ODSs and (ii) to establish a Funding Mechanism for assistance to developing countries, with a view to securing wide participation by major ODSs-producing and consuming States (that is, India and China, together accounting for forty per cent of the world's population).[190] The 1990 London Amendments entered into force on 10 August 1992 in accordance with Article 2(1) of the Amendment.[191]

With regard to the control measures for ODSs, by updating the 1987 text, the London Ozone Meeting could adopt a comprehensive regulatory régime. Besides the political will of the parties, this was due partly to the astonishing speed of technological advances (for example, the availability of CFC substitutes and alternatives in virtually all sectors) and growing domestic and international pressures for ozone protection, which are generated by the alarming scientific evidence described above.

In respect of contents of ODSs, unlike the original 1987 regulatory régime, the 1990 London Amendments addressed five Groups of controlled ODSs under the Protocol: (i) the original five CFCs and (ii) three important Halons in Annex A, (iii) ten CFCs, (iv) Carbontetrachloride (CCl_4) and (v) Methylchloroform

---

           Committees and Temporary Subsidiary Bodies' (Annex to Decision XXIV/8), in UNEP, *Handbook for the Montreal Protocol on Substances That Deplete the Ozone Layer* (11th ed. 2017), p. 619.
188   See Decision I/5.
189   The Conference was attended by 54 parties to the Protocol and 42 non-parties. See UNEP/ OzL.Pro.2/3; 'United Nations Activities', 20/4–5 *EPL* (1990), pp. 134–135.
190   By the time of the Meeting, 58 countries plus the European Community, representing 99 per cent of estimated CFCs in the world production and 90 per cent of the consumption had ratified or acceded to the Protocol.
191   As of 31 January 2018, it had 197 parties. The Adjustments entered into force on 1 March 1991.

THE MONTREAL PROTOCOL   131

(CH_3CCl_3) in Annex B.[192] In addition, the Meeting of the Parties also adopted a non-binding resolution that addressed other Halons and 'transitional substances', namely, Hydrochlorofluorocarbons (HCFCs).[193]

As regards the reduction schedules, the 1990 London Adjustments introduced the gradual phaseout of both consumption and production of the five original CFCs and three Halons by the year 2000,[194] which is subject to the ten-year period of grace for Article 5 developing countries and an allowance of 15 per cent on production, based on 1986 levels. Other newly added controlled substances were scheduled for various interim reductions and/or phase out in ten to fifteen years. For the most part, however, industrialising countries were not actively involved in the discussion on the control measures for ODSs.

Apart from these control measures, the parties could also agree to establish the Financial Mechanism that includes the Multilateral Fund of $160 million for assisting Article 5 developing countries in meeting their legal obligations under the Protocol.[195] It is particularly important to notice here that Article 5(5) States that the capacity of Article 5 developing countries to fulfil their obligations will depend on the effective implementation of the international financial cooperation relating to technology transfer.[196] In addition, the procedure for voting on adjustments has also changed based on the principle of international equity.[197]

Furthermore, at this stage, the 'interim' Montreal NCP was adopted, and its Implementation Committee as a standing governmental institution thus began its early operations.[198]

D   *The 1992 Copenhagen Ozone Meeting: Strengthening the Control Measures of HCFCs and the Establishment of the Montreal NCP*

The Fourth Meeting of Parties was convened in Copenhagen from 23 to 25 November 1992. The Copenhagen Amendments entered into force on 1 June 1994

---

192 See Thomas Gehring, *Dynamic Environmental Regimes* (Peter Lang, 1994), p. 285, pointing out that the reduction schedule for methyl chloroform was the only major surprise.

193 See UNEP/OzL.Pro.2/3. para. 51 and its Annex VII.

194 Many of the Parties favoured a total phaseout of CFCs by 1997, though, as a matter of fact, UNEP's technology assessment panel had not concluded that a complete phaseout was technically feasible before 2000. See Richard Benedick, *Ozone Diplomacy* (Harvard University Press, 1998), pp. 171–172.

195 See Chapter 6(III.A) in this volume.

196 But there exists conditionality between the MLF funding and compliance with the Protocol. See Chapter 6(III.D.4) in this volume.

197 See Section III(C) above.

198 See further Chapter 6(VII.A) in this volume.

132   CHAPTER 3

in accordance with Article 3(1) of the Amendments.[199] According to Decision III/12, the Panels established by the First Ozone Meeting had produced a 'synthesis document'.[200] Scientific and technical finding in the paper influenced the sequences of the negotiations which led to Copenhagen.

In general, the new package of ODS control provisions under Article 2 may be considered as an amicable agreement based on political and economic considerations. The reduction schedules of ODSs were, again, re-negotiated by the parties and then significantly accelerated.[201]

In relation to the reduction schedules, the Meeting agreed on a seventy-five per cent reduction of consumption and production of five major CFCs by 1994 with a total phaseout by 1996. The Meeting also decided on the total elimination of an additional ten CFCs to January 1996, with the possible exception of certain necessary 'essential uses', which have to be agreed by the parties.[202] Though the most serious exception in the 1990 London Amendments was the treatment of HCFCs as 'transitional substances' (that is, not subject to a reduction schedule), the consumption of HCFCs in Group I of Annex C was to be capped at 1989 levels with a total elimination by 2030.[203] HCFCs were to be selected for use in a manner that minimises ozone depletion and that also meets other environmental, safety and economic considerations.[204] Moreover, the 1992 Copenhagen Adjustments introduced the total phaseout of Halons to take effect from January 1994. The 'essential use' exception is still valid, and definitions of 'essential use' were adopted by Decision IV/25 of the Adjustment.[205]

---

199   As of 31 March 2017, it has 197 parties. The Adjustments entered into force on 22 September 1993. See also Section III(C) above.

200   See UNEP/OzL.Pro/WG.1/6/3.

201   For details, see Richard Benedick, *Ozone Diplomacy* (Harvard University Press, 1998), pp. 202–209; Karen T. Litfin, *Ozone Discourses* (Columbia University Press, 1994), p. 174; Thomas Gehring, 'The Copenhagen Meeting', 23/1 EPL (1993), pp 6–12.

202   See the 1992 Adjustment, Article 2A, Article 2C(1), (2) and (3).

203   The Article also requires parties to endeavour to ensure that the use of HCFCs is limited to applications where alternatives are not available, and that such use is not outside the areas of application currently met by substances in Annex A, B and C, except in rare cases for the protection of human life or human health.

204   See the1992 Amendments, Article 2F(7) (a), (b) and (c).

205   Use will only be 'essential' if it is necessary for health and safety or critical for the functioning of society and there are no technically and economically feasible alternatives or substitutes which are acceptable from a health and environment standpoint. Furthermore, 'essential use' will only be permitted if all economically feasible steps have been taken to minimise the essential use and associated emissions, and the controlled substance is not available in sufficient quantity and quality from existing stocks or banked or recycled controlled substances. See also Decisions V/14; V/18; VI/8; VI/9; VII/28; VII/11; IX/17; X/19; XI/15; XV/8; XVI/16; XVII/10; XVII/13; XVIII/15; XIX/17; XXI; XXII/7; XXIII/6;

THE MONTREAL PROTOCOL

The Meeting also agreed on a prohibition on the consumption of 'new' ODSS not covered by the 1987/1990 text, that is, Hydrobromofluorocarbons (HBFCS) in Group II of Annex C after January 1996, except for 'essential uses'. Similarly, under Article 2H, annual consumption of Methylbromide (CH_3BR) in Group I of Annex E[206] is to be limited to 1991 levels for 1995 and hereafter. In addition, the 1992 Copenhagen Adjustments brought forward the total phase-out of Carbontetrachloride (CCl_4) in Group II of Annex B and Methylchloroform (CH_3CCl_3) in Annex E to January 1996.[207]

It is true that previous Ozone Meetings did not pay much attention to the problems of recycling or reclamation of ODSS to prevent their release into the atmosphere. In this context, the Copenhagen Ozone Meeting adopted Decision IV/24 that is followed by Decision VI/19. The parties agreed, for instance, that the import and export of recycled and used ODSS should not be taken into account in calculating consumption, provided that parties report relevant data to the Ozone Secretariat.[208] However, Decision VI/24(2) became a source of the illegal 'grey' market in CFCs that are disguised (or mislabelled) as 'recycled substances'. It is reported that the availability of recycled materials for maintaining ODSS-using equipment, and the potential to trade in these chemicals for non-Article 5 nations phasing out such equipment, will be an important factor in minimising the so-called 'adaptation costs'.[209]

Finally, the 1992 Copenhagen Ozone Meeting further strengthened the Financial Mechanism, including the Multilateral Fund.[210] The 1992 Meeting could also adopt the formal Montreal NCP as 'Annexes' to the Protocol text. The Montreal NCP is to be given a first case in the 1995 Seventh Meeting of the Parties.[211]

XXVI/4; XXVI/5; XXVII/2; XXVIII/6 (exemption for laboratory and analytical uses). Some environmental NGOs consider 'essential uses' as potential loopholes. For a discussion, see Richard Benedick, *Ozone Diplomacy* (Harvard University Press, 1998), pp. 236–240.

206 Methylbromide is an economically important chemical that is used for fumigating commodities and soils for crops. Some 70,000 tonnes are produced every year and developing countries account for nearly eighty per cent of its use. On the negotiations on methyl bromide, see Richard Benedick, *Ozone Diplomacy* (Harvard University Press, 1998), pp. 207–209.

207 See the 1992 Adjustments, Article 2D(1) and (2); Article 2E(1), (2) and (3).

208 See also Decision VI/19 stating that 'only used controlled substances may be excluded from the calculated level of consumption of countries importing or exporting such substances'. See also discussions at the Open-Ended Working Group, in UNEP/OzL. Pro/WG.I/7/4, para. 79.

209 See UNEP/OzL.Pro/WG.12/2/Add.1, cited in Duncan Brack, *International Trade and the Montreal Protocol* (Earthscan, 1996), p. 42.

210 See Chapter 6 in this volume.

211 See Chapter 5 in this volume.

E   *The 1995 Vienna Ozone Meeting: the Control Measures for HCFCs and*
Methylbromide, and the Extension of the Grace Period

In 1995 the Seventh Meeting of the Parties was held in Vienna, immediately after an unofficial ceremonial event – the tenth anniversary of the 1985 Vienna Ozone Convention.[212] The Vienna Adjustments entered into force on 7 August 1996.

In the meantime, the 1993 Fifth Ozone Meeting decided not to allow any production of Halons for 'essential uses'[213] and further extended the funding of the Financial Mechanism.[214] The 1994 Sixth Ozone Meeting then decided to allow production of certain ODSS to continue at a low level after January 1996 for certain defined 'essential uses'.[215] At this stage, non-Article 5 nations had already concentrated their efforts on control measures for HCFCs and Methylbromide in Annexes C and E, rather than on CFCs in Annexes A and B. At the Vienna Meeting, only after arduous negotiations, the parties could have agreed on new – but rather tentative – reduction schedules for some ODSS.

In accordance with EC Regulation 3093/94, the European Community had already agreed in 1994 to completely phase out HCFCs by the year 2015, that is, fifteen years earlier than the Copenhagen decision of 2030. However, the United States, whose industries had already heavily invested in HCFCs, were resolutely opposed to the restrictions of these chemicals.[216] As a result, the Ozone Meeting could not adopt a new reduction schedule for HCFCs.[217] However, a number of parties delivered harsh criticisms of control measures for HCFCs and Methylbromide. Twenty-four parties thus officially signed the 'Vienna Declaration on HCFCs'[218] and the 'Declaration on Methyl Bromide',[219] respectively. One representative of the NGO even professed concern that 'many of

---

212   See UNEP/OzL.Pro.7/12; 'The Vienna Meeting', 26/2–3 EPL (1996), pp. 66–71; Richard Benedick, *Ozone Diplomacy* (Harvard University Press, 1998), pp. 287 et seq.; Winfried Lang, 'Ozone Layer', 6 *YbkIEL* (1995), pp. 220–223. See also UNEP, 'Vienna Plus Ten: The Vienna Convention: 10 Years of Achievement' (OzonAction Special Supplement, November 1995).

213   See Decision V/14.

214   See UNEP/OzL.Pro.5/12; 'United Nations Activities', 24/2–3 EPL (1994), pp. 67–68.

215   Decision VI/9. See UNEP/OzL.Pro.6/7; 'United Nations Activities', 25/1–2 EPL (1995), pp. 21–23; Winfried Lang, 'Ozone Layer', 5 *YbkIEL* (1994), pp. 162–163.

216   See also Richard Benedick, *Ozone Diplomacy* (Harvard University Press, 1998), pp. 292–293.

217   Yet it was decided that the calculated baseline level of consumption had been changed and consumption of HCFCs before its phaseout was to be restricted to the servicing of refrigeration and air conditioning equipment (Article 2F(1)(a) and (5)). See Annex III of UNEP/OzL.Pro.7/12.

218   See UNEP/OzL.Pro.7/12, p. 80.

219   See *ibid.*, p. 81.

THE MONTREAL PROTOCOL

those positions [on the control measures for HCFCs and Methylbromide] represented a retreat from commitments at London and Copenhagen'.[220]

In addition, the Vienna Ozone Meeting clarified requirements of the regulatory Protocol on Article 5 developing countries. According to the 1992 Copenhagen Adjustments, developing countries are eventually to phase out CFCs by the year 2006 and Halons by 2004. However, at the Meeting, these Article 5 nations insisted that the Copenhagen Adjustments should not apply to these nations.[221] As a result, it was finally agreed that, in order to meet their 'domestic needs', Article 5 countries are thus entitled to delay for ten-years compliance with the control measures for CFCs and Halons, adopted by the 1990 London Meeting, thus not by the 1992 Copenhagen Meeting.[222] This means that they are entitled to consume and produce the specified CFCs and Halons until the year 2010 (in case of Methylchloroform, until 2015).

The meaning of the term 'basic domestic needs' was not defined in the 1987 Protocol, due partly to a lack of time.[223] Thus subsequent Meetings of the Parties had to clarify the ambiguity of the text.[224] In this respect, the 1989 First Ozone Meeting had decided only that 'basic domestic needs' should be understood as not to allow production of products containing ODSs to expand for the purpose of export.[225]

The 1995 Vienna Ozone Meeting adopted Decision VII/9, which recognises the 'need of Article 5 countries for adequate and quality supplies of ozone-depleting substances at fair and equitable price' and the need to avoid monopolies of supply. It was thus decided that until July 1999, Article 5 countries could supply controlled ODSs to meet the 'basic domestic needs' of other Article 5

---

220 See *ibid.*, p. 22.

221 See Article 5(1) and 8*bis*, in UNEP/OzL.Pro.7/12, Annexes I–II; Richard Benedick, *Ozone Diplomacy* (Harvard University Press, 1998), pp. 212–213. The developing countries made an abortive effort to weaken the 1990 London Agreement by demanding a 'service tail' after the year 2010. On this point, see 'United Nations Activities', 26/2–3 EPL (1996), p. 67.

222 See Article 5(8 *bis* a).

223 See Patrick Széll, 'Negotiations on the Ozone Layer', in Gunnar Sjöstedt (ed.), *International Environmental Negotiation* (Sage Publications, 1994), p. 46, noting that the key term was deliberately left undefined.

224 For an extensive discussion of 'basic domestic needs', see Duncan Brack, *International Trade and the Montreal Protocol* (Earthscan, 1996), pp. 90–94. It is important to bear in mind that the ambiguity of treaty texts – which could often provide certain flexibility – would become a potential source of environmental disputes; in this context, this will be defined as 'treaty disputes'.

225 Decision I/12C. Other Decisions relating to the term are: Decision IV/29, Decision V/16, Decision V/25 and Decision VI/14A; Decision VI/14B; Decision VII/9; Decision X/15; Decision XI/28; Decision XV/2; Decision XVII/12; Decision XIX/28 (see UNEP, *Handbook for the Montreal Protocol on Substances That Deplete the Ozone Layer* (11th ed. 2017), pp. 294–300).

industrialising nations.[226] At the same time, Decision VII/9(7) prohibit new production capacity for ODSs in Annexes A and B after December 1995. They have to monitor and regulate such ODS-related trade by means of a new licensing system, which was instituted by the 1997 Montreal Ozone Meeting.

Lastly, the Non-Compliance Procedure (NCP) of the Montreal Protocol was invoked for the first time regarding the implementation of treaty obligations in the Russian Federation, Belarus, Bulgaria, Poland and Ukraine.[227]

F   *The 1997 Montreal Ozone Meeting: Control Measures of*
      Methylbromide and Illegal Trade in CFCs and ODSs

The Ninth Meeting of the Ozone Parties, which reached the tenth anniversary of the Montreal Ozone Protocol, took place in Montreal from 15 to 17 September 1997. In the previous year, the 1996 Meeting of the Parties discussed issues concerning the replenishment of the Multilateral Fund and illegal trade in CFCs and adopted Decisions about these issues.[228]

In respect of ODSs, the Montreal Ozone Meeting of the Parties decided to take more strict measures on Methylbromide in Annex E of the Protocol. Article 2H decided, with regard to non-Article 5 countries, on the interim reductions of twenty-five per cent by 1999, fifty per cent by 2001, seventy per cent by 2003 and a total phaseout by 2005, with exemptions for emergency and critical uses, and quarantine and pre-shipment.[229]

Regarding Article 5 countries that were committed only to a freeze by 2002, the Meeting decided on a twenty per cent reduction by 2005 and a phaseout by 2015.[230] A four-year average from 1995 to 1998 will be used as the reference year (period) for calculating the ODS phaseout.[231] Yet the interim reduction schedule must be reviewed in 2003.[232] The Multilateral Fund would make available $25 million per year for activities in both 1998 and 1999 to phase out methyl bromide in Article 5 developing nations.[233]

The proposals by the European Community and Switzerland to strengthen the consumption controls for HCFCs and to add controls on its production[234]

---

226   Decision I/12C(2).
227   See further Chapter 5(VII.B) in this volume.
228   See UNEP/OzL.Pro.8/12; 'United Nations Activities', *EPL* 27/2 (1997), pp. 86–88.
229   See Decisions IX/3, IX/6 and IX/7; Article 2H, Annex III in UNEP/OzL.Pro.9/12.
230   See Article 5(8)(*ter*)(d)(ii)-(iii). See also Decision IX/5.
231   See Article 5(8)(*ter*)(d)(ii).
232   Decision IX/5(e).
233   See Decision IX/5(b).
234   See the proposal by the European Community, in UNEP/OzL.Pro/WG.1/15/2/Add.3. See proposals by the United States in UNEP/OzL.Pro/WG.1/15/2/Add.2; Canada in UNEP/OzL.

THE MONTREAL PROTOCOL

were eventually withdrawn due to widespread rejections mainly by the Group of 77 and China.[235] Yet the European Community, supported by other parties, adopted a declaration that at the Eleventh Meeting in Egypt the parties should decide further steps to control HCFCS.[236]

As indicated above, it must also be noted that, as the date of the 1996 phaseout of ODS production and its use by non-Article 5 industrialised countries came around, a black market for ODSs had emerged in the international community. Consequently, the ozone régime's developmental process and effectiveness has been impaired.[237] In relation to this point, it should be remembered that, due to their delayed compliance, Article 5 developing countries may continue to produce large amounts of ODSS at relatively cheap prices. Consequently, these chemicals are illegally imported from Article 5 industrialising countries to non-Article 5 industrialised countries, such as the rich OECD nations.[238] As in the case of India, by using the international financial aid, the country had built new industrial plants capable of producing or using CFCs that are in fact unnecessary for meeting its 'basic domestic needs'.[239] This non-compliance matter is thus not necessarily concerned with Article 4 trade restriction provisions imposed on non-parties, which are designed to plug possible loopholes in the global ozone régime.

In an attempt to remedy the situation, in 1995, the Meeting of the Parties adopted Decision VII/33 that requests additional reports on dumping, illegal imports and exports from the UNEP Secretariat.[240] In the next year, Decision VIII/20 that is based on the United States' proposal[241] was adopted by the Eight Meeting of the Parties and it urged non-Article 5 countries to establish a system for validation and approval of imports of any used, recycled or reclaimed ODSs before they are imported. Afterward, the 1997 Montreal Ozone Meeting

---

Pro/ WG.1/15/2/Add.5; Switzerland in UNEP/OzL.Pro/WG.1/15/2/Add.6.

235   See UNEP/OzL.Pro.9/12, para. 87.

236   Annex XI in UNEP/OzL.Pro.9/12.

237   See Decision IX/23 on continuing availability of CFCs. See also Frederick P. Landers, Jr., 'The Black Market Trade in Chlorofluorocarbons: The Montreal Protocol Makes Banned Refrigerants a Hot Commodity', 26 *Georgia JICL* (1997), pp. 457–485; Duncan Brack, *International Trade and the Montreal Protocol* (Earthscan, 1996), Chapter 6; Richard Benedick, *Ozone Diplomacy* (Harvard University Press, 1998), pp. 273–276.

238   This means that the demand for CFCs or ODSs from industrised countries was still likely to continue. See UNEP, *Illegal Trade in Ozone Depleting Substances: Asia and Pacific Region* (2007).

239   On the basic domestic needs, see Section E above.

240   This decision is based on a proposal by the United States. See Richard Benedick, *Ozone Diplomacy* (Harvard University Press, 1998), p. 276.

241   See Richard Benedick, *Ozone Diplomacy* (Harvard University Press, 1998), p. 276.

138   CHAPTER 3

amended the text of Article 4 of the Protocol and instituted a new licensing system to help national governments track international trade in ODSs and discourage unlicensed black/grey market trade.[242] New Article 4B requires the parties to establish and implement a system for licensing the import/export of new/recycled/reclaimed ODSs in Annexes A, B, C and E.[243] However, it is said that implementation of this new ODS licensing system across the parties has only been 'patchy', at best.[244] Because of large-scale installed capacity of equipment dependent on CFCs or ODSs, demand in developed countries such as the United States and European Union remains unchanged, and CFC production was increasing in developing countries, particularly China and India.[245] For example, in the United States, more than 100 individuals were condemned for crimes regarding CFCs between 1995 and 2000.[246] Studies show that typical methods for smuggling ODSs include false labelling, mis-declaration of documents, concealment, fake recycled materials and transhipment fraud.[247] Unfortunately, after its Twelfth meeting (2000), the Ozone Meeting of the Parties has come to adopt many decisions regarding illegal trade in ODSs.[248]

---

242   See Article 4B of the Protocol and Decisions IX/8 and IX/9.

243   The 1997 Montreal Amendment entered into force on 10 November 1999.

244   Joanna Depledge, 'Montreal Protocol/MOP-18: Looking to the Future?', 36/6 *EPL* (2006), p. 253.

245   See United Nations Office on Drugs and Crime (UNODC), *Transnational Organized Crime in East Asia and the Pacific: A Threat Assessment* (2013), p. 115, available at: <https://www.unodc.org/toc/en/reports/TOCTA-EA-Pacific.html>. See also UNEP, *Illegal Trade in Ozone Depleting Substances: Asia and Pacific Region* (2007), p. 7.

246   See Armin Rosencranz and Siddharth Johar, 'Illegal Smuggling of Ozone-depleting Substances', 45/2 *EPL* (2015), p. 73.

247   See Environmental Investigation Agency, *Update on the Illegal Trade in Ozone-Depleting Substances: EIA Briefing to the 38th Meeting of the Open-Ended Working Group of the Parties to the Montreal Protocol July 18–21 2016, Vienna, Austria* (July 2016), pp. 3–4, available at: <https://eia-international.org/report/update-illegal-trade-ozone-depleting-substances>; United Nations Office on Drugs and Crime (UNODC), *Transnational Organized Crime in East Asia and the Pacific: A Threat Assessment* (2013), pp. 116–118; Armin Rosencranz and Siddharth Johar, 'Illegal Smuggling of Ozone-depleting Substances', 45/2 *EPL* (2015), p. 76.

248   See, for example, Decision XII/10 (Monitoring of international trade and prevention of illegal trade in ozone-depleting substances, mixtures and products containing ozone-depleting substances), Decision XIII/12 (Monitoring of international trade and prevention of illegal trade in ozone-depleting substances, mixtures and products containing ozone-depleting substances), Decision XIV/7 (Monitoring of trade in ozone-depleting substances and preventing illegal trade in ozone-depleting substances), Decision XVI/33 (Illegal trade in ozone-depleting substances), Decision XVII/16 (Preventing illegal trade in controlled ozone-depleting substances), Decision XVIII/18 (Preventing illegal trade in ozone-depleting substances through systems for monitoring their transboundary movement between Parties) and Decision XIX/12 (Preventing illegal trade in ozone-depleting

THE MONTREAL PROTOCOL 139

G   *The 1999 Beijing Ozone Meeting: a Freeze in HCFCs Production and the Control of a New ODS – Bromochloromethane*

The EU, which was initially regarded as reluctant to control HCFCS as CFC sub-stitutes, has gradually emerged as a 'champion of much more severe limits' of the ODSs.[249] As described above, because the 1992 Copenhagen Amendment has already introduced controls on HCFCS consumption in developed coun-tries, the EU's next pressing concern was that 'HCFCS were the only ozone-de-pleting substances listed in the Montreal Protocol whose production remained entirely uncontrolled and for which trade with non-Parties was permitted'.[250] Against this background, the EU proposed the following three changes re-garding HCFCS: (i) controls on HCFC production in non-Article 5 countries to achieve a freeze on HCFC production from a specified base year with phase-out by 2025,[251] (ii) tighter controls on HCFC consumption in non-Article 5 countries to reduce the HCFC cap from 2.8 per cent to 2.0 per cent with effect from 1 Janu-ary 2001; and an adjustment to paragraphs 2 and 3 of Article 2F to accelerate the phase-down schedule, and (iii) ban on trade in HCFCS with non-parties.[252] However, it is said that the EU's proposals was hailed with 'little enthusiasm' and met with 'outright objection' by other parties.[253] During the Beijing Meet-ing, some representatives argued that 'HCFCS were the most viable alternative to CFCs for the developing countries' and many delegations pointed out that consumption was approaching the cap and thus they were not able to support the EU's proposals.[254] As a result, although the parties could not agree on such tighter controls on HCFC consumption in non-Article 5 countries, they could adopt an amendment to freeze HCFC production from 1 January 2004 for non-Article 5 countries and from 2016 for Article 5 countries.[255] In addition, the

---

     substances), in UNEP, *Handbook for the Montreal Protocol on Substances That Deplete the Ozone Layer* (11th ed. 2017), pp. 277–284.

249   See Richard Benedick, *Ozone Diplomacy* (Harvard University Press, 1998), p. 205.

250   See UNEP/OzL.Pro.11/10, para. 36 (emphasis added).

251   For Article 5 countries, HCFC production controls should apply with levels and dates identical to the existing consumption controls. See UNEP/OzL.Pro.11/10, para. 36(a).

252   See UNEP/OzL.Pro.11/10, para. 36. See also Sebastian Oberthür, 'Ozone Layer Protection at the Turn of the Century: The Eleventh Meeting of the Parties', 30/1–2 *EPL* (2000), p. 36.

253   See Sebastian Oberthür, 'Ozone Layer Protection at the Turn of the Century: The Eleventh Meeting of the Parties', 30/1–2 *EPL* (2000), p. 36.

254   See UNEP/OzL.Pro.11/10, paras. 43–44.

255   See Decision XI/5, in UNEP/OzL.Pro.11/10, para. 112, and Annex V in *ibid.*, p. 38. In concrete, parties shall ensure that their calculated level of production does not exceed the average of (i) the sum of HCFC consumption in 1989 and 2.8 per cent of their calculated level of consumption in 1989 of the controlled substances in Group I of Annex A and (ii) the sum of HCFC production in 1989 and 2.8 per cent of their calculated level of production in 1989 of the controlled substances in Group I of Annex A (Amendment, Article 1(C)). In order

140 CHAPTER 3

parties to the Beijing Amendment had to ban the import of the controlled substances in Group I of Annex C from any State not party to this Protocol from January 2004 (Article 4, paragraphs 1 quin. and 1 sex.).

The second important aspect of the Beijing Amendment is the introduction of additional control measures for a new ODS, namely, Bromochloromethane (CH₂BrCl), which is to be completely phased out in all contracting parties to the Amendment by January 2002. Bromochloromethane was developed by Germany as an alternative to Methylbromide during World War II[256] and historically, the substance was used as a fire-extinguisher fluid in aircraft and portable fire extinguishers.[257] It had been feared that Bromochloromethane might be widely used as a solvent and it could have a significant market potential.[258] As a result, the number of ODSS covered by the Montreal Protocol was increased to ninety-five.[259]

Furthermore, an amendment was made for providing to the Ozone Secretariat statistical data on the annual amount of Methylbromide used for quarantine and pre-shipment applications.[260] Decision XI/12 specifies that such pre-shipment applications are those non-quarantine applications applied within twenty-one days prior to export to meet the official requirements of the importing country or existing official requirements of the exporting country. During the Meeting, the European Community stated that the exemption for quarantine and pre-shipment under Article 2H of the Protocol represented a potential loophole in the instrument's control measures which could delay the recovery of the ozone layer.[261]

---

to satisfy the basic domestic needs of the Article 5 countries, their HCFC production may exceed that limit by up to fifteen per cent of their calculated level of production of the controlled substances in Group I of Annex C (*ibid.*). As of 1 January 2016, Article 5 countries shall comply with the control measures for HCFCs and, as the basis, it shall use the average of their calculated levels of production and consumption in 2015 (Amendment, Article 1(L)).

256 See Stephen O. Andersen, K. Madhava Sarma and Kristen N. Taddonio, *Technology Transfer for the Ozone Layer* (Earthscan 2007), p. 74.

257 See National Industrial Chemicals Notification and Assessment Scheme (Australia), 'EnvironmentTierIIAssessmentforMethane,Bromochloro-'(21March2017),availableat:<https://www.nicnas.gov.au/chemical-information/imap-assessments/imap-assessments/tier-ii-environment-assessments/bromochloromethane#_ENREF_24>.

258 See Sebastian Oberthür, 'Ozone Layer Protection at the Turn of the Century: The Eleventh Meeting of the Parties', 30/1–2 EPL (2000), p. 39.

259 See Scott Barrett, *Environment and Statecraft* (Oxford University Press, 2003), pp. 238–239.

260 Annex V, Article 1: Amendment, O: Article 7, para. 3, in UNEP/OzL.Pro.11/10.

261 See UNEP/OzL.Pro.11/10, para. 38. See also Sebastian Oberthür, 'Ozone Layer Protection at the Turn of the Century: The Eleventh Meeting of the Parties', 30/1–2 EPL (2000), pp. 38–39.

THE MONTREAL PROTOCOL   141

The Beijing Ozone Meeting also adopted three decisions on further adjustments[262] concerning, respectively, the Montreal Protocol's Annexes A (Article 2A: CFCs and Article 2B: Halons), B (Article 2C: Other fully halogenated CFCs) and E (Article 2H: Methylbromide) and thus it introduced a freeze on CFCs production by 2004 in non-Article 5 parties, with a fifteen per cent allowance for basic domestic needs of Article 5 countries.[263] These adjustments were also based on proposals by the European Community, which considered that 'while Article 5 Parties had to freeze their CFC production in 1999 and halve it in 2005, non-Article 5 Parties could continue indefinitely to produce and export up to 15 per cent of their 1986 CFC baseline to meet the basic domestic needs of Article 5 Parties and it therefore feared that those Parties' phase-out efforts might be undermined by the continued and unrestricted availability of CFCs and other controlled substances on the world market'.[264] In this respect, Oberthür suggests that in 1997, the EU was responsible for virtually all global CFC production for export to non-Article 5 parties.[265]

In addition, the removal of the following uses from the global exemption for laboratory and analytical uses for controlled substances was decided: (i) testing of oil, grease and total petroleum hydrocarbons in water, (ii) testing of tar in road-paving materials and (iii) forensic finger-printing.[266]

H   *The 2007 Montreal Ozone Meeting: Adjustments for Accelerating HCFCs Phaseout*

After the entry into force of the Kyoto Protocol on 16 February 2005, issues regarding the interlinkage between the ozone treaty régime and the climate change treaty régime have come to be frequently discussed in various environmental forums.[267] This is only natural because many parties to the Montreal Protocol are also parties to the Kyoto Protocol of the UNFCCC régime – although, for example, the United States is not included, they are forced to consider the overall effectiveness of both régimes' binding obligations for damaged global atmosphere as a whole. At the Eighteenth Ozone Meeting of the Parties held in 2006, one government representative referred to the need to consider the interaction of the ozone and climate change régimes more

---

262   Decision XI/2, Decision XI/3 and Decision XI/4, in UNEP/OzL.Pro.11/10, para. 112.
263   See Article 2A(2).
264   See UNEP/OzL.Pro.11/10, para. 41.
265   See Sebastian Oberthür, 'Ozone Layer Protection at the Turn of the Century: The Eleventh Meeting of the Parties', 30/1–2 EPL (2000), p. 38.
266   Decision XI/15, in UNEP/OzL.Pro.11/10, para. 112.
267   See, for example, Joanna Depledge, 'Montreal Protocol/MOP-18: Looking to the Future?', 36/6 EPL (2006), p. 253.

closely, and stressed the need to consider the impact of ongoing projects under the Kyoto Protocol's Clean Development Mechanism on the production of HCFC-22 and HFC-23.[268] In addition, a representative from an environmental NGO called on parties to enact mandatory controls to restrict banked CFC and HCFC emissions, and to work with the Kyoto Protocol for establishing mandatory controls to restrict emissions of banked HCFCs and accelerate the phase-out of HCFCs.[269] Next year in 2007, during the Montreal Ozone Meeting of the Parties, most speakers regarded the continued use of HCFCs as a major challenge to be dealt with, and many representatives expressed their commitment to phasing out HCFCs ahead of their relatively longer schedule, 'stressing that that would not only benefit the ozone layer but also contribute to combating climate change'.[270] However, it should be noted, at the same time, that there were also several countries, such as China, Japan and the Russian Federation, which are not necessarily supportive for such more stringent control measures, due to the problems of expected costs and the availability of HCFC substitutes.[271]

In accordance with Decision XIX/6, the Nineteenth Meeting of the Parties determined to accelerate the phase-out of both production and consumption of HCFCs, by way of an adjustment in accordance with Article 2(9) of the Montreal Protocol and as contained in Annex III to the report of the Meeting of the Parties, which modifies Articles 2F and 5. Consequently, Article 5 parties are obliged to limit the production and consumption of HCFCs in 2013, at the average level of 2009–2010, and to reduce HCFCs by ten per cent in 2015, thirty-five per cent in 2020, 67. per cent in 2025, 97.5 per cent by 2030, with 2.5 per cent allowed for the servicing of refrigeration and air-conditioning equipment, until 1 January 2040.[272] Non-Article 5 parties are to phase-out seventy-five per cent of production by 2010, with a 99.5 per cent phase-out by 2020, and 0.5 per cent allowed for the servicing of refrigeration and air-conditioning equipment, until 1 January 2030.[273]

---

268 See UNEP/OzL.Pro.18/10, para. 48. See also Decision XVIII/12: Future work following the Ozone Secretariat workshop on the Intergovernmental Panel on Climate Change/Technology and Economic Assessment Panel special report, in UNEP/OzL.Pro.18/10, para. 221.
269 See UNEP/OzL.Pro.18/10, para. 47.
270 See UNEP/OzL.Pro.19/7, para. 46.
271 See Joanna Depledge, 'Adjustments: A Double Hit for Ozone and Climate', 37/6 EPL (2007), p. 451. For background on China's position over ozone treaties, see Xiangqian Gong, 'Undertaking the Common but Differentiated Responsibilities: China's Decision to Accept the Two Amendments to the Montreal Protocol on Substances that Deplete the Ozone Layer', 4 Journal of East Asia and International Law (2011), pp. 515–518.
272 See Article 5(8 ter) in Annex III, UNEP/OzL.Pro.19/7, p. 63.
273 See Article 2F in Annex III, UNEP/OzL.Pro.19/7, p. 62.

THE MONTREAL PROTOCOL   143

Also, celebrating the Montreal Protocol's twentieth anniversary, the Nineteenth Meeting of the Parties adopted the 'Montreal Declaration' as Annex to its report.[274] In line with the new adjustments of control measures for HCFCs, the Declaration emphasizes the interlinkage between the ozone régime and the climate change régime, by stating that 'actions taken to protect the ozone layer have resulted in significant beneficial impacts on global atmospheric issues, including climate change'. The 2007 Montreal Adjustments entered into force on 14 May 2008.

With regard to illegal trade in ODSs, Decision XIX/12 recommended the parties to take the following measures on a voluntary basis: (i) sharing information with other Parties, such as by participating in an informal prior informed consent procedure or similar system, (ii) establishing quantitative restrictions, for example import and/or export quotas, (iii) establishing permits for each shipment and obliging importers and exporters to report domestically on the use of such permits, (iv) monitoring transit movements (trans-shipments) of ozone-depleting substances, including those passing through duty-free zones, for instance by identifying each shipment with a unique consignment reference number, (v) banning or controlling the use of non-refillable containers, (vi) establishing appropriate minimum requirements for labelling and documentation to assist in the monitoring of trade of ozone-depleting substances, (vii) cross-checking trade information, including through private-public partnerships and (viii) including any other relevant recommendations from the ozone-depleting substances tracking study.[275]

I   *The 2016 Kigali Ozone Meeting: Phasing Down of*
        Hydrofluorocarbons (HFCs)
As was suggested above, particularly after the entry into force of the Kyoto Protocol, although issues regarding the interlinkage between the ozone régime and the climate change régime, including control measures of HFCs having high global warming potentials, have come to be frequently discussed in various environmental forums, perhaps not surprisingly, 'in most cases, this relationship was not clearly stated'[276] within the Meeting of the Parties to the Montreal Protocol. For example, at the Doha Ozone Meeting of the Parties held in 2008, while numerous representatives emphasised the relationship between the ozone treaties and related environmental agreements, such as the

---

274   See Annex IV, in UNEP/OzL.Pro.19/7, pp. 64–65.
275   See Decision XIX/12 in UNEP/OzL.Pro.19/7, p. 39.
276   See 'Montreal Protocol/MOP-22: "Universal' Agreement Makes Limited Progress', 41/1 *EPL* (2011), p. 25.

144   CHAPTER 3

Climate Change Convention and its Kyoto Protocol, and also suggested that
the synergies between them should be developed, in a formal sense, there was
no agenda on this controversial matter and the Ozone Meeting of the Parties
only adopted a decision that requests the UNEP Ozone Secretariat to convene
a workshop among parties and seek the participation of the secretariats of
other multilateral environmental agreements and experts from funding institutions for the discussion of technical, financial and policy issues related to the
management and destruction of ozone-depleting substance banks and their
implications for climate change'.[277] It was obvious that there was serious disagreement among the parties to the ozone régime on whether HFCs, alternative to CFCs or HCFCs, should be considered as additional ODSs under the text
of the Montreal Protocol.

However, after the Twenty-First Meeting of the Parties, issues on HFCs have
come to be considered under specific agenda items,[278] and some parties, such as
Canada, Mexico, the United States and the Federal States of Micronesia, began
to submit proposals to amend the Montreal Protocol for the purpose of incor-
porating HFCs as new controlled substances.[279] Although some parties argued
that HFCs did not fall within the scope of the Montreal Protocol or the ozone
régime because HFCs emissions were not associated with ozone depletion,[280]

---

277   See Decision XX/8 on workshop for a dialogue on high-global warming potential alterna-
      tives for ozone-depleting substances, in UNEP/OzL.Pro.20/9, p. 40. See also Hugo-Maria
      Schally, 'Ozone Layer', 19 *YbkIEL* (2008), p. 231.

278   It was suggested that '[t]his was clearly the most sensitive item on the agenda of MOP-
      21'. See Hugo-Maria Schally, 'Ozone Layer', 20 *YbkIEL* (2009), p. 270. See also Joanna De-
      pledge, 'Montreal Protocol/MOP-21: The "Climate MOP"', 39/6 *EPL* (2009), pp. 274–281. At
      the Twenty-Third Meeting of the Parties held in 2011, the parties argued whether issues on
      HFCs should be included as the agenda of the meetings under the Montreal Protocol. See
      UNEP/OzL.Pro.23/11, paras. 15–18.

279   For example, at the Twenty-First Meeting of the Parties, the representatives of Cana-
      da, Mexico and the United States jointly presented a proposal that included 'a 'phase-
      down', or gradual reduction, of HFC production and consumption'. See UNEP/OzL.
      Pro.21/8, para. 36; Communication submitted by the Government of the United States
      of America with regard to a proposed amendment to the Montreal Protocol, in UNEP/
      OzL.Pro.WG.1/29/INF/2 (20 May 2009). See also a joint proposal to amend the Montreal
      Protocol submitted by the Federated States of Micronesia and Mauritius, in UNEP/OzL.
      Pro.WG.1/29/8 (4 May 2009); Tomiloa Akanle, Impact of Ozone Layer Protection on the
      Avoidance of Climate Change: Legal Issues and Proposals to Address the Problem', 19(2)
      RECIEL (2010), p. 242.

280   See, for example, UNEP/OzL.Pro.22/9, para. 49; UNEP/OzL.Pro.23/11, para. 111; UNEP/OzL.
      Pro.25/9, para. 124; UNEP/OzL.Pro.26/10, para. 132. Opponent States of the amendment
      proposals were developing countries, such as Brazil, China, India, Malaysia and Paki-
      stan, including those reliant on air-conditioning, that is, Saudi Arabia, Kuwait and other
      Gulf States. See Joanna Depledge, 'Montreal Protocol/MOP-21: The "Climate MOP"', 39/6

THE MONTREAL PROTOCOL

TABLE 1 Control Schedule for Main ODSs under the Montreal Protocol[a]

Ozone depleting substance	Control schedules	
	Non-Article 5 countries	Article 5 countries
Annex A – Group I:Chlorofluorocarbons (CFCs)	Total phase-out by 1/1/1996	Freeze at average 1995–1997 level on 1/7/199950% reduction by 1/1/2005 85% reduction by 1/1/2007 Total phase-out by 1/1/2010
Annex A – Group II: Halons	Total phase-out by 1/1/1994	Freeze at average 1995–1997 level on 1/1/200250% reduction by 1/1/2005 Total phase-out by 1/1/2010
Annex B – Group II: Carbon tetrachloride	Total phase-out by 1/1/1996	85% reduction at average 1998–2000 on 1/1/2005Total phase-out by 2010
Annex B – Group III: Methyl chloroform (TCA)	Total phase-out by 1/1/1996	Freeze at average 1998–2000 level on 1/1/200330% reduction by 1/1/2005 70% reduction by 1/1/2010 Total phase-out by 1/1/2015
Annex C – Group I: Hydrochlorofluorocarbons (HCFCS)	Freeze from beginning of 199635% reduction by 1/1/2004 75% reduction by 1/1/2010 90% reduction by 1/1/2015 99.5% reduction by 1/1/2020* Total phase-out by 1/1/2030 *0.5% is restricted to the servicing of refrigeration and air-conditioning equipment existing during the period 2020–2030 and subject to review in 2015	The HCFC baseline for compliance is the average of2009 and 2010 production and consumption Freeze at average 2009–2010 level on 1/1/2013 10% reduction by 1/1/2015 35% reduction by 1/1/2020 67.5% reduction by 1/1/2025 97.5% reduction by 1/1/2030** Total phase-out by 1/1/2040 **The annual average of 2.5% is restricted to the servicing of refrigeration and air-conditioning equipment existing during the period 2030–2040 and subject to review in 2025.
Annex C – Group II: HBFC	Total phase-out by 1/1/1996	Total phase-out by 1/1/1996
Annex C – Group III: Bromochloromethane (BCM)	Total phase-out by 1/1/2002	Total phase-out by 1/1/2002
Annex E: Methyl bromide (horticultural uses)	Freeze in 1995 at 1991 baseline level25% reduction by 1/1/1999 50% reduction by 1/1/2001 70% reduction by 1/1/2003 Total phase-out by 1/1/2005 (with possible critical use exemptions)	Freeze at average 1995–1998 level on 1/1/200220% reduction by 1/1/2005 Total phase-out by 1/1/2015

a See *Executive Committee Primer – 2016 An introduction to the Executive Committee of the Multilateral Fund for the Implementation of the Montreal Protocol* (2016), Appendix 1, p. 4.

146   CHAPTER 3

Canada, Mexico and the United States had presented, jointly and continuous-
ly, their ambitious proposals, what they called a 'North American Proposal', at
the Twenty-Second Meeting of the Parties (2010),[281] the Twenty-Third Meeting
of the Parties (2011),[282] the Twenty-Fourth Meeting of the Parties (2012),[283] the
Twenty-Fifth Meeting of the Parties (2013),[284] the Twenty-Sixth Meeting of the
Parties (2014),[285] and the Twenty-Seventh Meeting of the Parties (2015).[286] At
the same time, the Open-ended Working Group of the Parties to the Montreal
Protocol began to consider their proposals to amend the Protocol to include
HFCs, and at its meetings, the representatives of the United States, Canada and
Mexico argued repeatedly that Article 2.2(b) of the Vienna Ozone Convention
specified that parties should harmonize atmospheric policies to limit adverse
effects resulting from the phaseout of ODSS and hence it was legally and logi-
cally possible to cover HFCs under the Montreal Protocol.[287] At the Twenty-
Fifth Meeting of the Parties, supporting the amendment to the Protocol, one
representative referred to the scientific finding that the unusually high level of
depletion of the ozone layer over the Arctic in 2011[288] was due to the increasing
concentration of greenhouse gases in the atmosphere and, under Article 2(1)
of the Vienna Ozone Convention, the parties were obliged to take appropriate measures to protect human health and the environment against adverse

---

EPL (2009), p. 275; Durwood Zaelke, Stephen O. Andersen and Nathan Borgford-Parnell,
'Strengthening Ambition for Climate Mitigation: The Role of the Montreal Protocol in
Reducing Short-lived Climate Pollutants', 21 RECIEL (2012), p. 241. It is reported that Brazil said that 'it would be premature to consider addressing HFCs unless and until new
additional funding is provided or concretely promised to the Protocol to address these
maters'. See 'Montreal Protocol/OEWG-33: Exemptions, Guidelines and Amendments
Considered', 43/4–5 EPL (2013), pp. 191–192.

281   See UNEP/OzL.Pro.22/9, para. 49.
282   See UNEP/OzL.Pro.23/11, paras. 105–109. See also 'Montreal Protocol: Difficult Negotia-
       tions as Inter-Linkages Expand', 42/1 EPL (2012), pp. 26–27.
283   See UNEP/OzL.Pro.24/10, paras. 126–131; 'Montreal Protocol/MOP-24: Governance, Proce-
       dure, Finance and Compliance, 42/6 EPL (2012), p. 326.
284   See UNEP/OzL.Pro.25/9, paras. 113–115.
285   See UNEP/OzL.Pro.26/10, paras. 114–115, 117; 'Montreal Protocol/MOP-26: Challenging Dis-
       cussions on Next Steps', 45/2 EPL (2015), pp. 59–60.
286   See UNEP/OzL.Pro.27/13, paras. 60–62. See also 'Montreal Protocol/MOP-27: Ozone Pro-
       tection: Continued Progress', 46/1 EPL (2016), pp. 40–41.
287   See, for example, UNEP/OzL.Pro.WG.1/32/7, para. 111; 'Montreal Protocol/OEWG-32: Prep-
       arations for 25th Anniversary MOP', 42/4–5 EPL (2012), pp. 253–254. See also 'Montreal
       Protocol/OEWG-33: Exemptions, Guidelines and Amendments Considered', 43/4–5 EPL
       (2013), pp. 191–192.
288   It is said that the largest chemical ozone loss in the Arctic occurred in spring 2011. See
       Peter Fabian and Martin Dameris, *Ozone in the Atmosphere: Basic Principles, Natural and
       Human Impacts* (Springer, 2014), p. 92.

THE MONTREAL PROTOCOL   147

effects resulting from human activities that modified or were likely to modify the ozone layer.[289] In the meantime, the WMO/UNEP's assessment report, *Scientific Assessment of Ozone Depletion* states that 'replacements with low GWPS or alternate technologies are becoming commercially available'.[290] The following statements by the representative of the United States well explain the situation the parties to the ozone régime was faced:

> It was clear that global awareness of the threat posed to the climate system by HFCs was growing. The outcome document of the United Nations Conference on Sustainable Development had included a commitment to support a gradual phase-down in the consumption and production of HFCs, language that clearly referred to the Protocol. In September 2013, the Group of 20 had agreed to support complementary initiatives through multilateral approaches that included using the expertise and the institutions of the Protocol to phase down the production and consumption of HFCs, based on the examination of economically viable and technically feasible alternatives. Similar support for action using the institutions and expertise of the Protocol had been expressed in bilateral meetings, including that between the President of the United States, Barack Obama, and the President of China, Xi Jinping, in September 2013, which had called for the establishment of an open-ended contact group to consider all relevant issues, including financial and technological support to developing countries, cost-effectiveness, safety of substitutes, environmental benefits and an amendment to the Protocol. Against that backdrop, it was becoming increasingly difficult to explain why the parties to the Protocol were not moving forward.[291]

Based on such recognition, on 15 October 2016, the Ozone Meeting of the Parties unanimously adopted the Kigali Amendment to the Montreal Protocol as Annex I to the report of its Twenty-Eighth Meeting, which consists of five

---

289   See UNEP/OzL.Pro.25/9, paras. 131.
290   See World Meteorological Organization, United Nations Environment Programme, National Oceanic and Atmospheric Administration, National Aeronautics and Space Administration and European Commission, *Assessment for Decision-Makers: Scientific Assessment of Ozone Depletion 2014*, WMO Global Ozone Research and Monitoring Project, Report No. 56 (2014), p. 18; Durwood Zaelke, Stephen O. Andersen and Nathan Borgford-Parnell, 'Strengthening Ambition for Climate Mitigation: The Role of the Montreal Protocol in Reducing Short-lived Climate Pollutants', 21 *RECIEL* (2012), pp. 240–241.
291   UNEP/OzL.Pro.25/9, para. 115.

articles.[292] A new Annex F[293] was added to the Montreal Protocol after Annex E and it covers all types of HFCs (Group I), except for HFC-23 Hydrofluoroolefins (HFOs)[294] and HFC-23[295] (Group II). Under the Kigali Amendment, its parties, which are divided into three categories,[296] are obliged to gradually reduce HFCs use by eighty or eight-five per cent by the late 2040. In concrete, in accordance with Article 2J newly added, most non-Article 5 parties are to achieve ten per cent reduction in 2019; forty per cent in 2024; seventy per cent in 2029; eighty per cent in 2034, and finally, eighty-five percent in 2036.[297] Belarus, Kazakhstan, Russian Federation, Tajikistan and Uzbekistan are permitted to delay the first two steps of the phasedown, beginning in 2020 with a five per cent reduction, and thirty-five per cent reduction in 2025.[298] The baseline agreed is based on the average of the party's calculated levels of HFCs consumption for the years 2011, 2012 and 2013, plus fifteen per cent of its HFCs production/consumption to account for a transitional period in which conversion from HCFCs to HFCs may have occurred.[299] The majority of Article 5 parties ('Group 1') will freeze HFCs consumption in 2024, based on 2020–2022 levels, and ultimately achieve an eighty per cent reduction by 2045.[300] Other ten Article 5 parties ('Group 2'), namely, Bahrain, India, the Islamic Republic of Iran, Iraq, Kuwait, Oman, Pakistan, Qatar, Saudi Arabia and the United Arab Emirates, are allowed to delay a freeze of HCFs consumption for four years and

---

292   See UNEP/OzL.Pro.28/12, p. 46. See also Decision XXVIII/1 and Decision XXVIII/2, in ibid., pp. 31–36. As to comments made during the adoption of the Kigali Amendment, see UNEP/OzL.Pro.28/12, paras. 194–207. See also Daniel Bodansky, Jutta Brunnée and Lavanya Rajamani, *International Climate Change Law* (Oxford University Press, 2017), pp. 274–275.

293   See UNEP/OzL.Pro.28/12, pp. 52–53.

294   HFOs are one of the HFC replacements, which have relatively lower GWPs. See, for example, 'HFOs: The New Generation of F-Gases', Greenpeace Position Paper (July 2016), available at: http://www.greenpeace.org/international/Global/international/documents/climate/HFOs-the-new-generation-of-f-gases.pdf.

295   HFC-23 is a by-product of HCFC-22 production and has a high GWP. See UNEP, Technology and Economic Assessment Panel, *Supplement to the IPCC/TEAP Report* (November 2005), p. 7; Durwood Zaelke, Stephen O. Andersen and Nathan Borgford-Parnell, 'Strengthening Ambition for Climate Mitigation: The Role of the Montreal Protocol in Reducing Short-lived Climate Pollutants', 21 *RECIEL* (2012), p. 236; David W. Fahey, 'The Montreal Protocol Protection of Ozone and Climate', 14 *Theoretical Inquiries in Law* (2013), pp. 36–37.

296   See Table 2 below.

297   See Article 2J, in Annex I, UNEP/OzL.Pro.28/12, p. 46.

298   See Decision XXVIII/2 (Decision related to the amendment phasing down hydrofluorocarbons), in UNEP/OzL.Pro.28/12, para. 211.

299   See Keith Ripley and Cleo VerKuijl, "Ozone Family' delivers Landmark Deal for the Climate', 46/6 *EPL* (2016), p. 372.

300   See Article 5, in Annex I, UNEP/OzL.Pro.28/12, p. 49.

THE MONTREAL PROTOCOL   149

a differentiated baseline is to be applied to those countries.[301] The final phase-down dates are the same for all Non-Article 5 countries.

In accordance with Decision XXVIII/2, 'high-ambient-temperature parties', defined as 'parties with an average of at least two months per year over ten consecutive years with a peak monthly average temperature above 35 degrees Celsius',[302] are eligible for exemption, provided that suitable alternatives do not exist for the specific sub-sectors, (i) multi-split air conditioners (commercial and residential), (ii) split ducted air conditioners (commercial and residential) and (iii) ducted commercial packaged (self-contained) air-conditioners.[303] The high-ambient-temperature parties are allowed to delay compliance for four years[304] and it can be regarded as one of the reflections of 'common but differentiated responsibilities' among the parties to the ozone régime.[305] As for 2025 and 2026, the Implementation Committee and the Meeting of the Parties are to defer consideration of the HCFC compliance by high-ambient-temperature parties where they have exceeded their allowable consumption or production levels owing to its HCFC-22 consumption or production for the sub-sectors listed in Appendix I to Decision XXVIII/2, on the condition that the party concerned is following the phase-out schedule for HCFCs for other sectors and has formally requested a deferral through the Ozone Secretariat.[306]

The Kigali Amendment will enter into force on 1 January 2019, provided that it is ratified by at least twenty parties to the Protocol[307] and the changes to its Article 4, control of trade with non-parties under Article I of this Amendment, will take effect on 1 January 2033.[308]

---

301 See Decision XXVIII/2 (Decision related to the amendment phasing down hydrofluoro-carbons). in UNEP/OzL.Pro.28/12, para. 211.

302 See paragraph 29 of Decision XXVIII/2, in UNEP/OzL.Pro.28/12, p. 35. Those parties include Algeria, Bahrain, Benin, Burkina Faso, Central African Republic, Chad, Côte d'Ivoire, Djibouti, Egypt, Eritrea, Gambia, Ghana, Guinea, Guinea-Bissau, Islamic Republic of Iran, Iraq, Jordan, Kuwait, Libya, Mali, Mauritania, Niger, Nigeria, Oman, Pakistan, Qatar, Saudi Arabia, Senegal, Sudan, Syrian Arab Republic, Togo, Tunisia, Turkmenistan, United Arab Emirates. See Appendix II of Decision XXVIII/2, in UNEP/OzL.Pro.28/12, p. 36.

303 See Appendix I of Decision XXVIII/2, in UNEP/OzL.Pro.28/12, p. 36.

304 See paragraph 28 of Decision XXVIII/2, in UNEP/OzL.Pro.28/12, p. 35.

305 At the Twenty-Second Meeting of the Parties held in 2010, one representative said that 'consideration of HFCs under the Montreal Protocol would thus entail clear disrespect of the principle of common but differentiated responsibilities'. See UNEP/OzL.Pro.22/9, para. 57.

306 See paragraphs 36 and 37 of Decision XXVIII/2, in UNEP/OzL.Pro.28/12, p. 35.

307 Article IV(1) of the Kigali Amendment. On 17 November 2017, the number of ratifications reached 20. See UNEP, 'Press Release: Montreal Protocol celebrates another milestone as agreement to reduce climate-warming gases is set to enter into force in 2019', at: <https://www.unenvironment.org/news-and-stories/press-release/montreal-protocol-celebrates-another-milestone-agreement-reduce> [last visited on 31 January 2018].

308 Article IV(2) of the Kigali Amendment.

TABLE 2 Phase-down Schedule for HFCs in Article 5 and Non-Article 5 Parties[a]

	A5 parties (developing countries) Group 1	A5 parties (developing countries) Group 2	Non-A5 parties (developed countries)
Baseline formula	Average HFC consumption levels for 2020–2022 + 65% of hydrochlorofluorocarbon (HFC) baseline	Average HFC consumption levels for 2024–2026 + 65% of HFC baseline	Average HFC consumption levels for 2011–2013 + 15% of HFC baseline
Freeze	2024	2028	–
1st step	2029–10%	2032–10%	2019–10%
2nd step	2035–30%	2037–20%	2024–40%
3rd step	2040–50%	2042–30%	2029–70%
4th step	–	–	2034–80%
Plateau	2045–80%	2047–85%	2036–85%

For Belarus, Russian Federation, Kazakhstan, Tajikistan and Uzbekistan, 25% HCFC component of baseline and different initial two steps (1) 5% reduction in 2020 and (2) 35% reduction in 2025.

Notes:

1. Group 1: Article 5 parties not party of Group 2
2. Group 2: Bahrain, India, the Islamic Republic of Iran, Iraq, Kuwait, Oman, Pakistan, Qatar, Saudi Arabia and the United Arab Emirates
3. Technology review in 2022 and every five years
4. Technology review four to five years before 2028 to consider the compliance deferral of two years from the freeze of 2028 of Article 5 Group 2 to address growth in relevant sectors above certain threshold.

a UNEP, *Ozonews*, Vol. XVI (15 November 2016), p. 3, available at: <http://www.unep.fr/ozonaction/information/nonmmcfiles/OzoNews-VolXVI-15%20November%202016.pd>.

V The Domestic Implementation of the International Treaties for the Protection of the Ozone Layer

A *Introduction*

In Sections II, III and IV of the present chapter, the historical evolution of the Montreal Protocol was examined through its dynamic development of the regulatory measures taken by the Meeting of the Parties to the Protocol. Yet, in the international community consisting of individual nation States, measures for implementing the international ozone treaties are to be undertaken by domestic means of each party that formally decided to accept the international environmental commitments to global ozone protection.[309] In this regard, it must be recalled that the Vienna Ozone Convention specifically requires its parties to adopt 'appropriate legislative or administrative measures and co-operate in harmonising appropriate policies'.[310] Although the regulatory Protocol does not require parties to adopt any definite form of ozone protection laws at the national level,[311] the obvious lack of such legislative, administrative or executive measures would therefore imply a possible violation of the binding instrument.

As was described in the first edition of this work, the parties to the Montreal Protocol have progressively taken creative approaches, including domestic percentage reductions, taxes on ODSs, voluntary agreements between government and industry, labelling requirements, economic incentives/disincentives, and so forth.[312] This section deals with domestic implementation of the ozone treaties and, as one of the important cases among non-Article 5 parties,[313] we will focus on Japan's implementation measures and also refer to other parties' legislative actions.

---

309   For an extensive discussion of the relationship between international and national law, see, in particular, Yuji Iwasawa, 'Domestic Application of International Law', 378 *Recueil des cours* (2015), pp. 21–249; Jonas Ebbesson, *Compatibility of International and National Environmental Law* (Kluwer Law International, 1996); Kazuya Hirobe and Tadashi Tanaka (eds.), *Kokusaihō to Kokunaihō: Kokusai Kōeki no Tenkai* [International Law and National Law: Development of International Public Good] (Keisoshobo, 1991) (in Japanese).

310   Article 2(2). See the 1973 CITES (Articles VIII.1–2 and 7) and the 1989 Basel Convention (Article 9(5)).

311   In other words, they are thus required to achieve specified results.

312   See Osamu Yoshida, *The International Legal Régime for the Protection of the Stratospheric Ozone Layer* (Kluwer Law International, 2001), pp. 119–129.

313   For a comprehensive review of US Clean Air Act regarding ozone protection, see David R. Wooley and Elizabeth M. Morss (eds.), *Clean Air Act Handbook: A Practical Guide to Compliance* (26th ed. Thomson Reuters, 2016), pp. 561–588. On EU's regulations for ODSs, see, for example, David Langlet and Said Mahmoudi, *EU Environmental Law and Policy* (Oxford University Press, 2016), pp. 217–219; Ludwig Krämer, *EU Environmental Law* (8th ed., Sweet & Maxwell, 2016), pp. 352–353; Raphaël Romi, *Droit international et européen de l'environnement* (3rd ed. LGDJ, 2017), pp. 227–229; Suzanne Kingston, Veerle Heyvaert and Aleksandra Čavoški, *European Environmental Law* (Cambridge University Press, 2017), pp. 303–305.

B   *Domestic Implementation of the Ozone Treaties in Japan*

Japan ratified the Vienna Ozone Convention and the Montreal Protocol on 30 September 1988 and succeeding amendments to the Protocol,[314] except for the 2016 Kigali Amendment. In May 1988, Japan enacted the Act on the Protection of the Ozone Layer Through the Control of Specified Substances and Other Measures,[315] which aims to protect the ozone layer through international cooperation, to set in place measures, for controlling the manufacture, reducing the emissions, and rationalizing the use of specified substances, in order to ensure the appropriate and smooth implementation of the Vienna Ozone Convention and the Montreal Protocol, thereby contributing to protecting people's health and conserving the living environment[316]. Based on the Ozone Act, since 1989, regulations on the production and importation of specified CFCs and ODSS have been enforced by the Ministry of Economy, Trade and Industry (METI).[317] A person who seeks to manufacture specified substances must, for each kind of substance and for each control year, receive permission from the METI for the quantity of the specified substance the person seeks to manufacture during said control year.[318] The kinds of specified substance under this Act are to be specified by Cabinet Order[319] and a corresponding Ordinance on the Protection of the Ozone Layer Through Regulation of Specified Substances and Other Measures of 26 September 1994 provides for a detailed list of ODSS[320]. The

---

314   The London Amendment on 4 September 1991, the Copenhagen Amendment on 20 December 1994, the Montreal Amendment on 30 August 2002, and the Beijin Amendment on 30 August 2002. For a discussion of environmental law in Japan in general, see, for example, A. Morishima, 'Environmental Law of Japan', J. Andrew Schlickman, Thomas M. McMahon, Nicoline Van Reil (eds.), *International Environmental Law and Regulation* (Butterworth Legal Publishers, 1991), Jpn-4 et seq.

315   See Tokuteibussitsu no Kisei tō ni yoru Ozonsō no Hoho ni kansuru Hōritsu [Act on the Protection of the Ozone Layer Through the Control of Specified Substances and Other Measures], Law No. 53 of 1988. A text of unofficial and tentative translation by the Ministry of Justice is available at: <http://www.japaneselawtranslation. go.jp/law/detail/?vm=04&re=01&id=2140> [Japanese Law Translation] [last visited on 31 January 2018]. See also Tsūshōsangyōshō Kisosangyōkyoku Kagakuhinanzenka Ozonsōhogotaisakusitsu [Management Office for Ozone Layer Protection, Ministry of International Trade and Industry] (ed.), *Kaisei Ozonsōhogohō* [Ozone Protection Act as Amended] (Gyosei, 1991) (in Japanese).

316   See Article 1 of the Ozone Act.

317   In January 2001, the Ministry of International Trade and Industry (MITI) was transformed into the Ministry of Economy, Trade and Industry (METI) with some institutional changes.

318   See Article 4 of the Ozone Act.

319   See Article 2 of the Ozone Act.

320   Tokuteibussitsu no Kisei tō ni yoru Ozonsō no Hoho ni kansuru Hōritsu Sekōrei [Ordinance on the Protection of the Ozone Layer Through Regulation of Specified Substances

THE MONTREAL PROTOCOL   153

controls on production and import of ODSs are governed by Chapter 2 of the
Ozone Act and Article 52 of the Foreign Exchange and Foreign Trade Control
Law.[321] In accordance with the Foreign Exchange and Trade Control Law, trade
with non-parties in ODSs and products containing or made with these specified
chemicals has been prohibited. In addition, sanctions against violation of the
regulations under the Ozone Act include fines and jail.[322] In concrete, a person
who manufactures a specified substance in violation of the provisions of Article 4(1) or Article 5(4) is sentenced to imprisonment with work for not more
than three years, a fine of not more than one million yen, or both.[323] In the past,
Japan reported seven ODS smuggling cases to the Meeting of the Parties of the
Protocol and Japan Customs reported eleven ODS cases to the Customs Enforcement Network (CEN).[324] With regard to financial and other assistance, it
is provided that Japan shall make efforts to take necessary measures with a view
to facilitating the development and use of substitutes for ODSs and of equipment for controlling emissions of specialised substances.[325]

Furthermore, in 2001, Japan enacted Law for Ensuring the Implementation
of the Recovery and Destruction of Fluorocarbons Contained in Specified
Products (Law Concerning the Recovery and Destruction of Fluorocarbons).[326]

---

and Other Measures], Enforcement Order No. 308 of 26 September 1994. Tentative translation of this Ordinance by the Ministry of Justice is available at: <https://www.env.go.jp/
en/earth/ozone/laws.html> [last visited on 31 January 2018]. See also Tokuteibussitsu no
Kisei tō ni yoru Ozonsō no Hoho ni kansuru Hōritsu Sekōkisoku [Enforcement Regulations on the Protection of the Ozone Layer Through Regulation of Specified Substances
and Other Measures], Order No. 80 of 24 December 1988 (as amended).

321   Gaikokukawase oyobi Gaikokubōeki Kanrihō [Foreign Exchange and Foreign Trade Control Law], Act No. 228 of 1 December 1949. A text of unofficial translation by the Ministry of Justice is available at: <http://www.japaneselawtranslation.go.jp/law/detail/
?vm=04&re=01&id=21> [Japanese Law Translation] [last visited on 31 January 2018].

322   See Chapter 6 of the Ozone Act, that is, Articles 30–34, and Article 70 of the Japanese Foreign Exchange and Foreign Trade Control Law. For commentaries, see Tsūshōsangyōshō
Kisosangyōkyoku Kagakuhinanzenka Ozonsōhogotaisakusitsu [Management Office
for Ozone Layer Protection, Ministry of International Trade and Industry] (ed.), *Kaisei
Ozonsōhogohō* [Ozone Protection Act as Amended] (Gyosei, 1991), pp. 195–197. In Japan
there are many ODSs smuggling cases and criminal judgments of conviction have often
been given.in national courts. See, for example, 'Furon wo Mitsuyu, Fukuokachisai-
Kokurashibu [Judgments of Conviction for CFC-12 smuggling, Fukuoka District Court
(Kokura Branch)], *Asahi Shinbun*, 11 January 2002, p. 30.

323   See Article 30 of the Ozone Act.

324   See UNEP, *Illegal Trade in Ozone Depleting Substances: Asia and Pacific Region* (2007),
p. 26.

325   See Article 21 of the Ozone Act.

326   Tokuteiseihin ni kakaru Furonrui no Kaishū oyobi Hakai no Jisshi no Kakuho tō ni kansuru Hōritsu [Law for Ensuring the Implementation of the Recovery and Destruction of

Under this law, ODSs had been recovered from commercial refrigerators and air conditioners at the time of maintenance and disposal of equipment and recycled or destroyed to prevent fluorocarbons from being released into the air.[327] Thereafter, in June 2013, Japan amended the Law Concerning the Recovery and Destruction of Fluorocarbons in order to implement comprehensive measures throughout the life cycle of fluorocarbons[328] and it was renamed as the Act on Rational Use and Proper Management of Fluorocarbons[329], which came into force on 1 April 2015.[330] The term 'rational use' means reducing the

---

Fluorocarbons Contained in Specified Products], Law No. 64 of 22 June 2001. For an overview of this law, see Ministry of the Environment, Government of Japan, 'Summary of Japan's Law concerning the Recovery and Destruction of Fluorocarbons (Fluorocarbons Recovery and Destruction Law) (promulgated in June 2001)', available at: <http://www .env.go.jp/en/earth/ozone/laws.html> [last visited on 31 January 2018].

327 See Ministry of the Environment, Government of Japan, *Let's Protect the Ozone Layer*, 2016 edition, available at: <http://www.env.go.jp/en/focus/docs/04_ge/index.html> [last visited on 31 January 2018].

328 This amendment is based on the recognition that 'HFCs emissions have been increasing rapidly and are expected to double in 2020 as compared to the emissions in 2011 from refrigeration and air conditioning equipment. The recovery rate of fluorocarbons from end-of-life commercial refrigerators and air conditioners remained low (about 30%) and it was found out that refrigerant leakage from the equipment in use was much higher than expected due to poor maintenance, aging, etc'. See Ministry of the Environment, Government of Japan, *Act on Rational Use and Proper Management of Fluorocarbons* (March 2016), available at: <https://www.env.go.jp/en/earth/ozone/laws/ozone4.pdf> [last visited on 31 January 2018]; Keizaisangyōshō Seizōsangyōkyoku Kagakubussitsukanrika Ozonsōhogotousuisinsitsu, Kankyōshō Chikyūkankyōkyoku Chikyūondankasaisakuka Furontaisakusitsu [Fluoride Gases Management Office, Chemicals Management Office, Manufacturing Industries Bureau, METI / Office of Fluorocarbons Control Policy, Global Environment Bureau, Ministry of the Environment] (eds.), *Yokuwakaru Furonhaishutsuyokuseihō* [Undersatnding the Act on Rational Use and Proper Management of Fluorocarbons] (Chūohhōki, 2017), p. i. See also Motoyuki Kumakura, 'Revision of the Fluorocarbons Law', 9 *Japan Environment Quarterly* (March 2015), available at: <https://www.env.go.jp/en/focus/jeq/issue/vol09/feature.html> [last visited on 31 January 2018].

329 Furonrui no Shiyō no Gōrika oyobi Kanri no Tekiseika ni kansuru Hōritsu [Act on Rational Use and Proper Management of Fluorocarbons], Law No. 39 of 12 June 2013. A text of unofficial translation by the Ministry of Justice is available at: <http://www .japaneselawtranslation.go.jp/law/detail/?id=2848&vm=04&re=01> [Japanese Law Translation] [last visited on 31 January 2018].

330 See Ministry of the Environment, Government of Japan, *Act on Rational Use and Proper Management of Fluorocarbons* (March 2016), available at: <https://www.env.go.jp/en/ earth/ozone/laws/ozone4.pdf>. According to the Ministry of the Environment, in Japan, there are more than 40 home-appliance recycling plants, more than 20 fluorocarbons gas recycling facilities and more than 60 fluorocarbons gas destruction facilities in commercial operation, using various technologies.

THE MONTREAL PROTOCOL 155

use of Fluorocarbons by such measures as manufacture, etc. of substances which serve as an alternative to Fluorocarbons, which will not deplete the ozone layer and will not have a serious impact on global warming, or reducing the amount of Fluorocarbons used in products using Fluorocarbons.[331] 'Proper management' means making efforts to reduce emissions of Fluorocarbons by properly conducting confirmation of amounts of emissions of, filling specified products with, and recovery, recycling and destruction of Fluorocarbons, or any other acts in connection with the use, etc. of specified products.[332] Major stakeholders engaging in the rational use or proper management of Fluorocarbons are divided into five categories, namely, (i) Fluorocarbons producers,[333] (ii) designated product manufacturers,[334] (iii) users, maintenance operators and disposal operators of specified products,[335] (iv) registered fluorocarbons filling and recovery operators[336] and (v) approved fluorocarbons recycling and destruction operators.[337] For example, the first category of the stakeholders, that is, producers and importers of Fluorocarbons, must endeavour to take necessary measures for the development of substances alternative to Fluorocarbons and other rational use of Fluorocarbons, and shall cooperate with the policies implemented by the national and local governments for the rational use of Fluorocarbons and the proper management of Fluorocarbons used in specified products.[338] The manufacturers of 'designated products' in the second category shall endeavour to take necessary measures for the development of products which use substances alternative to Fluorocarbons, reduction in the impact on depletion of the ozone layer and global warming caused by Fluorocarbons emitted upon the use of the designated Products and other rational use of Fluorocarbons, and cooperate with the policies implemented by the national and local governments for the rational use of Fluorocarbons.[339] Users of specified products, which belong to the third category, are obliged to carry out inspection of the equipment in accordance with the evaluation

---

331 See Article 2(6) of the Act on Rational Use and Proper Management of Fluorocarbons.
332 See Article 2(9) of the Act on Rational Use and Proper Management of Fluorocarbons.
333 See Article 2(7) of the Act on Rational Use and Proper Management of Fluorocarbons.
334 See *ibid.*
335 See Article 2(8) of the Act on Rational Use and Proper Management of Fluorocarbons.
336 See Article 2(10) of the Act on Rational Use and Proper Management of Fluorocarbons.
337 See Articles 2(11) and 2(12) of the Act on Rational Use and Proper Management of Fluorocarbons.
338 See, for example, Article 4(1) of the Act on Rational Use and Proper Management of Fluorocarbons.
339 See, for example, Article 4(2) of the Act on Rational Use and Proper Management of Fluorocarbons.

criteria for initiatives by users[340] and report calculated leakage amount to the national government if there is leakage of a certain amount or more of fluorocarbons.[341] Some details concerning Law Concerning the Recovery and Destruction of Fluorocarbons are set out in the Ordinance on the Recovery and Destruction of Fluorocarbons[342] and the Enforcement Regulations on the Recovery and Destruction of Fluorocarbons.[343] Although their roles are rather limited, local governments, which are delegated administrative functions by the national government, have also taken necessary measures regarding ozone protection, including enlightenment of the public through lectures on ozone laws and other educational activities.[344]

At present, the Japanese government is trying to find ways to achieve eighty-five per cent HFCs reduction before 2036, earlier than the deadline under the Kigali Amendment (Article 2J).[345]

---

340 See Articles 16–18 of the Act on Rational Use and Proper Management of Fluorocarbons. See also Daiisshutokuteiseihin no Kanrisha no Handan no Kizyun to narubeki Jikō [Standards of Judgment for Managers of Class I Specified Products], Kokuji No. 13 of 10 December 2015 (Ministry of Economy, Trade and Industry/Ministry of the Environment), reproduced in Keizaisangyōshō Seizōsangyōkyoku Kagakubussitsukanrika Ozonsōhogotousuisinsitsu, Kankyōshō Chikyūkankyōkyoku Chikyūondankasaisakuka Furontaisakusitu [Fluoride Gases Management Office, Chemicals Management Office, Manufacturing Industries Bureau, METI / Office of Fluorocarbons Control Policy, Global Environment Bureau, Ministry of the Environment] (eds.), *Yokuwakaru Furonhaishutsuyokuseihō* [Understanding the Act on Rational Use and Proper Management of Fluorocarbons] (Chuohhoki, 2017), at p. 290 (in Japanese).

341 See Article 19 of the Act on Rational Use and Proper Management of Fluorocarbons. See also Furonrui Santei Rōeiryōtou no Hōkokutou ni kansuru Meirei [Regulation for Reporting on an Amount of Leakage of Fluorocarbons Calculated], 10 December 2015, reproduced in Keizaisangyōshō Seizōsangyōkyoku Kagakubussitsukanrika Ozonsōhogotousuisinsitsu, *supra* note, at p. 133.

342 See Furonrui no Shiyō no Gōrika oyobi Kanri no Tekiseika ni kansuru Hōritsu Sekōrei [Ordinance on the Recovery and Destruction of Fluorocarbons], Enforcement Order No. 396 of 12 December 2002 [Enforcement Order No. 114 of 27 March 2016, amended], available at: <http://www.env.go.jp/earth/ozone/cfc/law/kaisei_h27/index.html> [last visited on 31 January 2018].

343 See Furonrui no Shiyō no Gōrika oyobi Kanri no Tekiseika ni kansuru Hōritsu Sekōkisoku [Enforcement Regulations on the Recovery and Destruction of Fluorocarbons], Order No. 7 of 10 December 2015 (Ministry of Economy, Trade and Industry/Ministry of the Environment) [Order No. 2 of 29 March 2016, amended], available at: <http://www.env.go.jp/earth/ozone/cfc/law/kaisei_h27/index.html> [last visited on 31 January 2018].

344 See information on related activities of a local public body, provided by the Ministry of the Environment, at: <http://www.env.go.jp/press/102917.html> (in Japanese) [last visited on 31 January 2018].

345 See a report prepared by a committee on Fluorocarbons, 'Furonrui Taisaku no Kongo no Arikata ni kansuru Kentōkai Hōkokusho' [Report of the Committee on Future Measures for Fluorocarbons], available at: <http://www.env.go.jp/earth/ozone/conf.html> (in Japanese) [last visited on 31 January 2018].

THE MONTREAL PROTOCOL

TABLE 3   DESIGNATED PRODUCT MANUFACTURES[a]

Designated products[b]	Refrigerant currently in use (GWP)	Target value (GWP)	Target year
Room air-conditioning	HFC-410A (2090)	750	2018
	HFC-32 (675)		
Commercial air-conditioning(for offices and stores)	HFC-410A (2090)	750	2020
Mobile air-conditioning (for passenger cars of passenger capacity less than 11 people)	R134a (1430)	150	2023
Condensing unit and refrigerating unit(except equipment of the rated capacity of the compressor 1.5kw or |lower.)	HFC-404A (3920)	1500	2025
	HFC-410A (2090)		
	HFC-407C (1774)		
	CO2 (1)		
Cold storage warehouse(for more than 50,000 m³ new facilities)	HFC-404A (3920)	100	2019
	Ammonia (lower than 10)		
Rigid urethane foam insulation (for spray foam for house building materials)	HFC-245fa (1030)	100	2020
	HFC-365mfc (795)		
Dust blowers (except for applications that require a non-flammable)	HFC-134a (1430)	10	2019
	HFC-152a (124)		
	CO2 (1), DME (1)		

a   See Ministry of the Environment, Government of Japan, *Act on Rational Use and Proper Management of Fluorocarbons* (March 2016), p. 4.

b   Other types of product will be added to the designated products, depending on the availability of alternatives.

VI   Conclusions

The overall success of the Montreal Protocol will be characterised by international environmental cooperation in protecting the ozone layer among its régime actors, namely, non-Article 5 and Article 5 countries, international agencies such as the UNEP and the TEAP, scientists, industry, and environmental NGOs. Most contracting parties, both non-Article 5 and Article 5 countries, have dedicated considerable efforts to meet the legal requirements of the Montreal Protocol. As Benedick says, it is true that '[i]n the world of ambiguity and imperfect knowledge, the Montreal Protocol will hopefully prove to be the forerunner of an evolving partnership between scientists and policy makers, as sovereign nations seek ways to deal with uncertain dangers while accepting common responsibility for stewardship of planet Earth'.[346] Attention should also be directed at the régime's specialised internal organs – namely, the Meeting of the Parties to the Protocol, the Executive Committee of the Multilateral Fund, the Implementation Committee of the NCP and their subsidiary bodies – that have been playing important roles in long sustaining the cooperative and regulatory régime.[347] In addition, OzonAction in the UNEP and its partners has organised a number of meetings for achieving objectives of the Montreal Protocol.[348]

However, it should be noted that, even with full compliance with the amended Protocol obligations, the ultimate objective of the international environmental régime, that is, complete recovery of the ozone layer, would not occur until the middle of the next century: peak ozone decreases are expected to occur during the next several years.[349] Furthermore, according to recent scientific research, it is said that a chemical called 'dichloromethane', not regulated under the Montreal Protocol, may contribute to ozone depletion.[350] Though this was not discussed in the present chapter, greater financial resources for

---

346   Richard E. Benedick, 'Science Inspiring Diplomacy: The Improbable Montreal Protocol', Christos Zerefos, Georgios Contopoulos and Gregory Skalkeas, *Twenty Years of Ozone Decline: Proceedings of the Symposium for the 20th Anniversary of the Montreal Protocol* (Springer, 2009), p. 18.

347   See Chapters 5–6 in this volume.

348   See, for example, 'Thematic Meeting on Implementation of HCFC Phase-out Management Plans (HPMPs), Chisinau, Republic of Moldova, 8–10 November 2016', XVI *OzoNews*, 15 November 2016; 'OzonAction Special University Course for Future Engineers', XVI *OzoNews*, 30 November 2016, available at: <http://www.unep.org/ozonaction/resources/ozonews-e-news-service>. It is said that methods to raise and develop awareness includes (i) organising seminars and workshops; (ii) promoting environmentally-friendly government and private enterprise efforts; (iii) encouraging industry pledges to adopt alternatives and substitutes; (iv) giving awards to recognise contributions from public and private sectors; (v) delivering environmentally-friendly messages via banners, posters etc., (vi) holding competitions and field activities; (vii) celebrating the International Day for the Protection of the Ozone Layer (that is, 16 September); (viii) disseminating information through various information media. See K. Madhava Sarma, Stephen O. Andersen and Kristen N. Taddonio, 'Lessons from the Success of the Montreal Protocol', Donald Kaniaru (ed.), *The Montreal Protocol: Celebrating 20 Years of Environmental Progress: Ozone Layer and Climate Protection* (Cameron May, 2007), pp. 141–142; Stephen O. Andersen and K. Madhava Sarma, *Protecting the Ozone Layer: The United Nations Story*, edited by Lani Sinclair (Earthsacn, 2002), pp. 333–336.

349   See Jason Samenow, 'Ozone Layer is Healing, Expected to Recover by Around 2050, Major Report Finds', *The Washington Post*, Washington, D.C., 11 Sep 2014. See also 'Ozone Hole Gets Bigger, Earth to Bear More UV Damage', *IANS English* (New Delhi), 30 Oct 2015.

350   See 'Ozone Layer Recovery Could Be Delayed by a Rise in a Gas Commonly Used in Paint Strippers', *Targeted News Service* (Washington, D.C.), 28 June 2017.

THE MONTREAL PROTOCOL

monitoring, research and analysis of the state of the ozone layer should be allocated to internal and external scientific régime institutions, such as the TEAP and its sub-committees and the WMO.[351] As in the past, it will be new scientific findings and technological and economic assessments that can encourage further developments of the international control measures for ODSs.[352]

For purposes of assessing and judging the effectiveness of the regulatory measures for ODSs, data reporting under Articles 7 and 9 of the Montreal Protocol must be improved substantially. It has been pointed out that both non-Article and Article 5 country parties are submitting incomplete data.[353]

The following chapters will examine Article 4 trade restrictions (Chapter 4), the Montreal NCP (Chapter 5), and the Financial Mechanism of the Protocol, including the Multilateral Fund (Chapter 6). These treaty provisions and institutions all help toward securing full compliance with the above-mentioned substantive provisions of Articles 2, 2A to 2J – and corresponding control measures contained in Article 5.

---

351 See statements by Co-Chair of the TEAP, in UNEP/OzL.Pro.9/12, para. 29.

352 It is suggested that, although most ODSs are declining, other source gases, such as N_2O, CH_4 and water vapour, are also important for understanding ozone change. See UNEP, 'Press Release: Increased Research and Observation Crucial to Efforts to Continue to Protect the Ozone Layer and Climate', at: <https://www.unenvironment.org/news-and -stories/press-release/increased-research-and-observation-crucial-efforts-continue-protect> [last visited on 31 January 2018].

353 See 20/18 *International Environment Reporter* (3 September 1997) p. 820. See further Chapter 5(VII.A.1) in this volume.

PART 3

The Ozone Régime and the WTO/GATT Régime

∴

CHAPTER 4

The Montreal Protocol and the International Trade Law Régime of the WTO/GATT

I Introduction

A *Multilateral Environmental Agreements and WTO/GATT Law*

One of the vexing problems of global environmental protection is the complicated relations between multilateral environmental agreements (MEAs) and trade-oriented rules and principles of WTO/GATT law. Although the relentless pursuit of economic growth or free capital mobility – which is likely to have adverse environmental impacts – is frequently subject to certain treaty obligations under MEAS, WTO/GATT trade law does not specifically address current issues relating to environmental protection.[1]

Consequently, the legal status of trade-related provisions of MEAs within the framework of the WTO/GATT law régime remain, to a greater or lesser extent, controversial.[2] International trade restrictions of ODSs contained in Article 4 of the Montreal Ozone Protocol provide an archetypal and striking example of the conflicts that exist between MEAs and the WTO/GATT in the context of developing international environmental law.[3] To begin with, it will be helpful to consider MEAs briefly, before moving to the main exacting task in this Chapter.

---

1 See Alan Boyle, 'Relationship between International Environmental Law and Other Branches of International Law', in Daniel Bodansky, Juta Brunnée and Ellen Hey (eds.), *The Oxford Handbook of International Environmental Law* (Oxford University Press, 2007), pp. 125–145.

2 See Peter-Tobias Stoll, 'World Trade Organization', in Rüdiger Wolfrum (ed.), *Max Planck Encyclopedia of Public International Law*, Vol. x (Oxford University Press, 2012), p. 986, stating that 'it has not been clarified how the provisions of an international environmental agreement might be taken into consideration in a case where a measure at hand is based on such instrument'; Christiane R. Conrad, *Processes and Production Methods (PPMs) in WTO Law* (Cambridge University Press, 2011), p. 436, suggesting that 'the application of MEAs as sources of law in WTO agreement is currently problematic'.

3 See, in general, James Cameron and Jonathan Robinson, 'The Use of Trade Provisions in International Agreements and Their Compatibility with the GATT', 2 *YbkIEL* (1991), pp. 3–30; Ernst-Ulrich Petersmann, 'International Trade and International Environmental Law: Prevention and Settlement of International Environmental Disputes in GATT', 27 *JWT* (1993), pp. 43–81; Halina Ward, 'Trade and Environment in The Round - and After', 6 *JEL* (1994), pp. 263–295; 'Trade and the Environment: A Report Prepared by the GATT Secretariat (1992)', reprinted in John H. Jackson, William J. Davey and Alan O. Sykes, *Legal Problems of International Economic Relations* (3rd ed. West, 1995), pp. 561–567.

© KONINKLIJKE BRILL NV, LEIDEN, 2019 | DOI:10.1163/9789004290877_006

B *Multilateral Environmental Agreements (MEAS)*

The newly-coined term 'MEAS' – which is now widely accepted in international legal literature – implies that the environmental treaties contain some kinds of trade-related provisions or international economic rules.[4] It is said that at present there exist several hundreds of MEAS[5] and some twenty of them contain certain kinds of trade-related environmental measures (TREMS), laying down quantitative restrictions on foreign trade, at least.[6] As was described in

---

4　Regarding the basic features of MEAS, see, for example, Jacob Werksman, 'The Conference of Parties to Environmental Treaties', in Werksman (ed.), *Greening International Institutions* (Earthscan, 1996), pp. 55–68; Vinod Rege, 'GATT Law and Environment-Related Issues Affecting the Trade of Developing Countries', 28 *JWT* (1994), p. 126; Thomas J. Schoenbaum, 'International Trade and Protection of the Environment: the Continuing Search for Reconciliation', 91 *AJIL* (1997), pp. 281–284; Jutta Brunnée, 'Environment, Multilateral Agreements', in Rüdiger Wolfrum (ed.), *Max Planck Encyclopedia of Public International Law*, Vol. III (Oxford University Press, 2012), pp. 484–497.

5　See Ronald B. Mitchell, 'International Environmental Agreements: A Survey of Their Features, Formation, and Effects', 28 *Annual Review of Environment and Resources* (2003), pp. 430 et seq.

6　The 1933 Convention Relative to the Preservation of Fauna/Flora in Their Natural State (Article 9), 172 *LNTS* 241; the 1940 Western Hemisphere Convention (Article 9), 161 *UNTS* 193; the 1950 Birds Convention (Article 6), 638 *UNTS* 185; the 1956 FAO Plant Protection Agreement for South-East Asia and the Pacific Region (Article III), 247 *UNTS* 400; the 1957 Interim Convention on Conservation of North Pacific Fur Seals (Article VIII), 314 *UNTS* 105; the 1959 Agreement Concerning the Co-operation in the Quarantine of Plants and Their Protection against Pests and Diseases (Article 4), 1 *SMTE* 153; the 1967 Phyto-sanitary Convention for Africa; the 1968 African Nature Convention (Article IX); the 1968 European Convention for the Protection of Animals During International Transport (Article I), *IELMT*; the 1970 Benelux Birds Convention (Articles 6 and 9), 847 *UNTS* 255; the 1973 Polar Bears Agreement, 13 *ILM* (1974), p. 13; the 1980 Convention for the Conservation/Management of the Vicuña (Article 4); the 1985 ASEAN Agreement; the 1985 FAO Code of Conduct on the Distribution/Use of Pesticides; the 1989 Amended London Guidelines for the Exchange of Information on Chemicals in International Trade; the 1989 Wellington Convention (Article 3(2.c), 29 *ILM* (1990), p. 1449; the 1989 Basel Convention on the Control of Transboundary Movement of Hazardous Wastes and Their Disposal (Article 4), 28 *ILM* (1989), p. 657; the 1992 UN Climate Change Convention, 31 *ILM* (1992), p. 849; the 1992 Biodiversity Convention (Article 16), 31 *ILM* (1992), p. 822; the 1994 Oslo Sulphur Protocol (Preamble); the 1994 International Tropical Timber Agreement (Article 36); the 1997 Kyoto Protocol (Articles 2, 6, 12 and 17), 37 *ILM* (1998), p. 22; the Cartagena Protocol on Biosafety to Biodiversity Convention (Articles 4 and 6), 39 *ILM* (2000), p. 1027; Stockholm Convention on Persistent Organic Pollutants (Article 3), 40 *ILM* (2001), p. 532; the Minamata Convention on Mercury (Article 3), 55 *ILM* (2016), p. 582. See Ernst-Ulrich Petersmann, *International and European Trade and Environmental Law after the Uruguay Round*, (Kluwer Law International, 1996) Annex VIII; Junji Nakagawa, Akira Shimizu, Satoru Taira and Isamu Mamiya, *Kokusai Keizai Hō* [International Economic Law] (2nd ed. Yuhikaku, 2012), p. 309 (in Japanese). The WTO Secretariat's list of MEAS includes recent environmental instruments employing trade measures, including the Minamata Convention on Mercury. See Committee on Trade and Environment, Committee on Trade and

Chapter 3 in this volume, the Montreal Ozone Protocol places quantitative limits on production and consumption of specified controlled substances in its Article 2 and technical Annexes.[7]

MEAs are generally classified in three broad categories: (i) agreements for the protection of wildlife, for example, the 1973 CITES,[8] (ii) agreements for the protection of the environment of the importing states from harmful organisms and products – for example, the 1989 Basel Convention,[9] and (iii) agreements for the protection of the so-called 'global commons'.[10] It is argued that at present the Montreal Ozone Layer Protocol is the only MEA which addresses the third category in considerable detail.[11]

It is interesting to note here that the North American Free Trade Agreement (NAFTA) specifically referred to the Montreal Ozone Layer Protocol, the 1973 CITES and the 1989 Basel Convention. Under Article 104 (Relation to Environmental and Conservation Agreements), the trade-related environmental provisions of these MEAs, such as provided for in the Ozone Protocol's Article 4, may prevail over the NAFTA general exceptions 'to the extent of their consistency [with the NAFTA], provided that where a Party chooses among equally

---

Environment in Special Session, *Matrix on Trade-Related Measures Pursuant to Selected Multilateral Environmental Agreements, Note by the Secretariat, Revision*, WT/CTE/W/160/Rev.7 TN/TE/S/5/Rev.5 (4 September 2015).

7   The original text of the 1987 Montreal Protocol intended to adopt restrictions on the methods used in the production or processing of products (see Section II(B) below). The legal strategies of the ozone régime are not based on domestic production and consumption taxes, labelling, etc.

8   Articles III, IV and V. See further Michael Bowman, Peter Davies and Catherine Redgwell, *Lyster's International Wildlife Law* (Cambridge University Press, 2010), Chapter 15; Timothy M. Swanson, 'The Evolving Trade Mechanisms in CITES', 1 *RECIEL* (1992), pp. 57–63.

9   Article 4(5), arguably, the most controversial MEA in the context of GATT law. See the 1991 Bamako Convention (Article 4); the 1989 Lomé Convention (Article 39). For a comprehensive review, see Katharina Kummer, *Transboundary Movements of Hazardous Wastes at the Interface of Environment and Trade* (United Nations Environment Programme, 1994).

10   See James O. Cameron, Thobeka Mjolo-Thamage and Jonathan C. Robinson, 'Relationship between Environmental Agreements and Instruments Related to Trade and Development', in Peter H. Sand (ed.), *The Effectiveness of International Environmental Agreements: A Survey of Existing Legal Instruments* (Grotius Publications, 1992), Chapter 13, pp. 475 et seq. See also Pierr-Marie Dupuy and Jorge E. Viñuales, *International Environmental Law* (Cambridge University Press, 2015), pp. 398–399, referring to two categories of MEAs, namely, 'treaties the main purpose of which is to impose trade restrictions and those in which trade restrictions are one implementation tool among others'.

11   See James O. Cameron, Thobeka Mjolo-Thamage and Jonathan C. Robinson, 'Relationship between Environmental Agreements and Instruments Related to Trade and Development', in Peter H. Sand (ed.), *The Effectiveness of International Environmental Agreements: A Survey of Existing Legal Instruments* (Grotius Publications, 1992), pp. 487 et seq.

166 CHAPTER 4

effective and reasonably available means of complying with such obligations, the Party chooses the alternative that is the *least inconsistent* with the other provisions of the Agreement'.[12]

On the other hand, WTO/GATT trade law does not contain such a provision designed specifically for clarifying the complicated relationship between any of these major MEAs and the international trade law régime. It is only in the Preamble that the WTO refers to an environmental principle of international environmental law, namely, the principle of sustainable development.[13] In this respect, however, the WTO Committee on Trade and Environment (CTE) – which is established in accordance with the Decision of 14 April 1994[14] – has played an active role within the framework of the WTO.[15] In 2001, the WTO Ministerial Declaration decided to reorganise the CTE and created two thematic clusters, that is, the regular Committee on Trade and Environment ('regular' CTE) and the committee's negotiating sessions, 'special sessions' (CTESS).[16]

---

12   Article 104 also states that parties may add to an Annex additional agreements to which the consistency provisions of Article 104 apply ('The Parties may agree in writing to modify Annex 104.1 to include any amendment to an agreement referred to in paragraph 1, and any other environmental or conservation agreement'). See also Article 904 (Basic Rights and Obligations) regarding scientific justification for strict environmental regulations; Article 2015 (Scientific Review Boards) as to the possibility of some environmental expertise in the dispute settlement Procedures; Article 1106(6) regarding investment incentives. See John H. Knox, 'The Judicial Resolution of Conflicts between Trade and Environment', 28 *Harvard Environmental Law Review* (2004), saying that 'in fact it [Article 104] is ineffective at best, and may actually worsen the problem it purports to solve'.

13   It reads 'allowing for the optimal use of the world's resources in accordance with the objective of *sustainable development*, seeking both to protect and preserve the environment and enhance the means of doing so in a manner consistent with their respective needs and concerns at different levels of economic development' (emphasis added). On the meaning of 'sustainable development' in the context of the WTO, see Wolfgang Benedek, 'Implications of the Principle of Sustainable Development, Human Rights and Good Governance for the GATT/WTO', Konrad Ginther, Erik Denters and Paul J.I.M. de Waart (eds.), *Sustainable Development and Good Governance* (Martinus Nijhoff, 1995), pp. 274–288; Christina Voigt, *Sustainable Development as a Principle of International Law: Resolving Conflicts between Climate Measures and WTO Law* (Martinus Nijhoff, 2009), Chapters 5–6.

14   See Doc. MTN.TNC/MIN(94)/1/Rev.1, reproduced in Philippe Cullet and Alix Gowlland-Gualtieri (eds.), *Key Materials in International Environmental Law* (Ashgate, 2004), p. 500.

15   See, for example, Jennifer Schult, 'The GATT/WTO Committee on Trade and the Environment: Toward Environmental Reform', 89 *AJIL* (1995), pp. 423–439. For a discussion, see Richard G. Tarasofsky, 'Ensuring Compatibility between MEAs and GATT/WTO', 7 *YbkIEL* (1996), pp. 58–62.

16   See further Manisha Sinha, 'An Evaluation of the WTO Committee on Trade and Environment', 47 *JWT* (2013), pp. 1291 et seq.

It is the latter sessions which are mandated to specifically consider the relationship between MEAS and trade rules.[17]

At the Meeting of the CTE held in July 1996, on behalf of ASEAN countries, Singapore put forward an *expost* or *ex ante* proposal for creating a 'multi-year' and 'case-by-case' waiver for trade measures of MEAS, based on non-binding guidelines for measures that might be eligible for such treatment.[18] ASEAN pointed out that trade measures that are specifically to be used in MEAS could be recognised on a case-by-case basis as exceptional circumstances qualifying for a WTO Article IX waiver, subject to them meeting conditions and criteria including 'necessity', 'least trade restrictiveness', 'effectiveness', 'proportionality' and the 'degree of scientific evidence'.[19] Thereafter, in the sixteenth meeting of the CTESS held in 2006, the EC presented a submission aiming to 'have a formal WTO reconfirmation of the basic principles governing relations between MEAS and the WTO'[20] and to 'ensure the WTO did not act in clinical isolation from international environmental law'.[21] However, many delegations opposed to this proposal and, for example, the United States stated that 'the EC proposal went well beyond the limited scope of the mandate and even more disturbing, it appeared to mischaracterize WTO rules and other concepts related to MEAS. The EC proposal also failed to reflect the factual, experience-based discussions the CTESS had had most recently under Paragraph 31(i) [of the Ministerial Declaration]'.[22]

The purpose of this Chapter is to explore in depth the trade related aspects of the international ozone régime. Section II analyses trade measures against

---

17   According to paragraph 31 of the Ministerial Declaration, the CTESS is required to consider (i) the relationship between WTO rules and specific trade obligations in MEAS (the negotiations shall be limited in scope to the applicability of such existing WTO rules as among parties to the MEA in question); (ii) procedures for regular information exchange between MEA Secretariats and the relevant WTO committees, and the criteria for the granting of observer status and: (iii) the reduction or, as appropriate, elimination of tariff and non-tariff barriers to environmental goods and services. For recent CTE activities on MEAS matters, see WTO, *Annual Report 2016* (2016), p. 82.

18   See WTO, *Trade and Environment*, PRESS/TE013 (27 September 1996).

19   See ibid. Yet some WTO Members such as the United States, Switzerland and Canada suggested that the waiver approach would be inappropriate to resolve legal conflicts of MEAS and the WTO/GATT. On this point, see Ernst-Ulrich Petersmann, *International and European Trade and Environmental Law after the Uruguay Round* (Kluwer Law International, 1996), p. 43.

20   See *Summary Report on the Sixteenth Meeting of the Committee on Trade and Environment in Special Session, 6–7 July 2006, Note by the Secretariat*, TN/TE/R/16 (22 December 2006), p. 2, para. 6.

21   See ibid., p. 2, para. 9.

22   See ibid., p. 8, para. 43.

non-parties under Article 4 of the Montreal Protocol. Section III briefly discusses international trade rules governing the WTO/GATT régime, although limitations of space do not permit a detailed discussion on that issue. We will focus rather on the relationship between the well-known Article XX exceptions in GATT trade law and Article 4 trade controls of the Montreal Ozone Protocol. Section IV focuses on the possible legal conflicts between MEAs and the WTO/GATT, including the relationship between dispute settlement procedures of MEAs – the Montreal NCP in particular – and the WTO dispute settlement system. In deciding which international treaty obligations should be given priority, it is desirable to consider briefly the principles and rules of the 1969 Vienna Convention on the Law of Treaties (Section IV(A)). Section V is devoted to the main analysis of the relationship between GATT Article XX and the global protection of the ozone layer under the Montreal Protocol.

II   The International Régime for Trade Restrictions of ODSs

A   *The Background of Article 4 of the Montreal Protocol: Resolving the Problem of Non-Participation in the MEA Régime*

It is no exaggeration to say that most transboundary or global – or even purely domestic – environmental problems assume, to a greater or lesser extent, trade-related aspects. In other words, nowadays the modern nation State and its contemporary life-style could not eliminate direct or indirect dependence on the growing world trade system (that is, 'interdependence').[23]

Yet, unlike the above-mentioned cases of species extinction (the 1973 CITES) or illegal hazardous waste disposal (the 1989 Basel Convention), the ultimate cause of ozone depletion is not necessarily trade transactions in themselves at the bilateral, regional or international levels. CFCs or ODSs in themselves are neither directly harmful to human health nor natural resources shared by countries. More correctly, it may be said that the consumption and production of CFCs or other ODSs within each State – whether developed or developing – could be considered as the central and obvious cause of the stratospheric ozone depletion.[24]

---

23   'The World has become increasingly interdependent'. See John H. Jackson, *The World Trading System: Law and Policy of International Economic Relations* (2nd. ed. MIT Press, 1996), Chapter 1; John H. Jackson, William J. Davey and Alan O. Sykes, *Legal Problems of International Economic Relations* (6th ed. West, 2013), Chapter 1.
24   For a discussion see, Section V(D.1) below.

Nonetheless, it is only natural that, in order to control or limit the proliferation of ODSs, members of the international ozone treaty régime needed some kind of trade restrictions on them commonly used in the import and export of industrial products. In other words, they therefore needed legally effective global strategies to surmount knotty problems of the so-called 'free-rider'.[25] In this respect, R. Snape refers to the undeniable fact that 'trade measures are not ideal instruments of environmental policy, but they may often be the only policy options available' to environmentally motivated countries.[26]

Thus, it can be said that, without such trade restrictions, non-parties would simply increase their production as ozone parties gradually phase down their ODS production, and it is possible that unrestricted imports from non-parties would impair the further development of CFC/ODS substitutes. Furthermore, if industries using ODSs simply move to non-parties and then manufacture such products for export to the parties, this would eventually nullify the environmental benefits of the Montreal Protocol.[27] During the negotiation leading up to the 1987 Montreal Protocol, the United States therefore argued that '[w]ithout restrictions on imports of ozone-depleting chemicals from non-parties, there would be a strong incentive for the development of 'pollution heavens'.[28]

It cannot be emphasised too strongly that the Protocol's Article 4 TREMS are therefore likely to help accommodate much wider participation by sovereign States. The incorporation of the tough export and import restrictions in the Montreal Protocol is designed to prevent CFC-producing countries and

---

25 In general, it means 'to try to make individual gains without contributing to the collective control of the resource'. See Alice Enders and Amelia Porges, 'Successful Conventions and Conventional Success: Saving the Ozone Layer', in Kym Anderson and Richard Blackhurst (eds.), *The Greening of World Trade Issues* (Prentice-Hall, 1992), pp. 135 et seq.; R. Kerry Turner, David Pearce and Ian Bateman, *Environmental Economics* (Johns Hopkins University Press, 1994), pp. 215–216; Alfred C. Aman, 'The Montreal Protocol on Substances that Deplete the Ozone Layer: Providing Prospective Remedies Relief for Potential Damage to the Environmental Commons', in Francesco Francioni and Tullio Scovazzi (eds.), *International Responsibility for Environmental Harm* (Graham & Trotman/Kluwer Academic Publishers Group, 1991), p. 192.

26 Richard H. Snape, 'The Environment, International Trade and Competitiveness', in Kym Anderson and Richard Blackhurst (eds.), *The Greening of World Trade Issues* (Prentice-Hall, 1992), pp. 73–92 (emphasis added).

27 See Rosalind Twum-Barima and Laura B. Campbell, *Protecting the Ozone Layer through Trade Measures* (United Nations Environment Programme, 1994), pp. 51–54; Discussion Paper submitted by the United States, GATT *Considerations and the Ozone Protocol* (4 September 1987).

28 Discussion Paper submitted by the United States, GATT *Considerations and the Ozone Protocol* (4 September 1987), p. 1. See further Chapter 3(II.A) in this volume.

potential producers (in particular, developing States that remained outside the international régime for ozone) to gain market shares left behind by the parties to the Protocol.[29] Under the Montreal Protocol, possible 'free-riding' non-parties are wholly denied access to international markets for CFCs/ODSs, although many of these controlled chemicals could be indispensable for high-technology industries, etc. Moreover, it is also worth mentioning that non-parties are also denied access to the 'best available, environmentally safe substitute and related technologies' in the context of the Protocol's Financial Mechanism.[30] In one view, Article 4 trade restrictions employed for the purposes of global ozone layer protection can be seen as environmental 'sanctions', in a broad sense, against non-parties to the international legal régime for ozone.[31]

For the reasons stated above, it seems right to say that Article 4 of the Montreal Protocol does not necessarily conform to the maxim *pacta tertiis nec nocent nec prosunt*. Nevertheless, because 'a treaty does not create either obligations or rights for a third State [that is, a non-party] without its consent',[32] it is also true, in theory, the Montreal Protocol régime cannot entirely prevent non-parties from legally producing any ozone-depleting chemicals.[33]

B   *Article 4 of the Montreal Protocol: Process and Production Method-Related Arguments*

Such trade provisions had been contemplated since the first discussions on an expected protocol to the Vienna Ozone Convention. The fundamental structure

---

29   It is pointed out, for instance, that the threat of economic 'sanctions' by ozone régime members (such as the United States and the United Kingdom) against Korean exports seems to have influenced South Korea's decision in 1992 to become a party to the Montreal Protocol. See Duncan Brack, *International Trade and the Montreal Protocol* (Earthscan, 1996), pp. 55–56; Benedict Kingsbury, 'The Tuna-Dolphin Controversy, The World Trade Organisation, and the Liberal Project to Reconceptualize International Law', 6 *YbkIEL* (1995), p. 29; Richard Benedick, *Ozone Diplomacy* (Harvard University Press, 1998), p. 244.

30   As for the Multilateral Ozone Fund, see Chapter 6 in this volume.

31   On this point, see Ethan A. Nadelmann, 'Global Prohibition Regime: The Evolution of Norms in International Society', 44 *International Organizations* (1990), suggesting that political aspects of international régimes tend to reflect the economic/political interests of the powerful States, for example, the US. For a discussion, see also Chapters 1(III.B) and 5(VI) in this volume.

32   Article 34 of the Vienna Convention on the Law of Treaties. See Mark E. Villiger, *Commentary on the 1969 Vienna Convention on the Law of Treaties* (Martinus Nijhoff, 2009), pp. 467 et seq.: Ian Sinclair, *The Vienna Convention on the Law of Treaties* (Manchester University Press, 1984), pp. 98 et seq.

33   But, in reality, most newly developing countries (Article 5 LVCs) — which do not have necessary technologies to produce CFCs/ODS related industrial products — have decided to join the international ozone régime.

of this Article can be seen in a proposal by the United States of America.[34] The GATT Secretariat – participating in the 1987 Montreal Protocol's negotiation[35] – rather favourably commented upon the expected inclusion of Article 4 trade provisions in the ozone agreement.[36]

The Montreal Ozone Protocol contains no restrictions on foreign trade between contracting parties, although it seems to conflict with the terms of the 1989 Basel Convention, about the shipment of controlled ODSs, such as CFCs and Halons.[37]

Article 4 of the Protocol, however, requires contracting parties to prohibit international trade of ODSs with non-parties and/or non-treaty-compliers. The global strategies prescribed by the Ozone Protocol are:

(i) trade in controlled substances by parties with States that are not parties to the Protocol;

(ii) trade in products containing controlled substances;

(iii) trade in products produced with but not containing controlled substances: and

(iv) the export of relevant technologies.

It is said that Article 4 'constitutes a highly sophisticated and well graduated scheme': that is, from ODSs themselves to products containing ODSs or products produced with ODSs.[38]

The Montreal Ozone Layer Protocol (as amended in London, Copenhagen, Vienna, Montreal, Beijing, and Kigali) envisages that, after January 1990, the import of major ODSs in Groups I and II of Annex A (that is, CFCs and Halons) from non-parties would to be totally banned (Article 4(1)), and import of ODSs in Annex B was also banned from January 1993 (Article 4(1bis)). Within one year of the date of entry into force of the 1992 Copenhagen Amendment (that is, June 1994), imports of any controlled substances in Group II of Annex C,

---

34 See UNEP/WG.167/CPR.7; Discussion paper by the United States, *GATT Considerations and the Ozone Protocol* (4 September 1987).

35 See Chapter 3(II) in this volume.

36 See Section V(D) below. See also Rosalind Twum-Barima and Laura B. Campbell, *Protecting the Ozone Layer through Trade Measures* (United Nations Environment Programme, 1994), p. 113 (note 113).

37 See Decision V/24 and Decision VII/31. It is agreed, however, that recycled CFCs and Halons meeting usable purity specifications prescribed by appropriate institutions (such as International Standards Organisation (ISO)) are not considered as 'wastes' under the Basel Convention.

38 See Winfried Lang, 'Trade Restrictions as a Means of Enforcing Compliance with International Environmental Law' in Rüdiger Wolfrum (ed.), *Enforcing Environmental Standards: Economic Mechanisms as Viable Means?* (Springer, 1996), p. 270. In this respect, Lang argues that drafters of Article 4 were aware of the so-called GATT 'necessity' argument.

172   CHAPTER 4

such as Hydrobromofluorocarbons, from non-parties must be banned (Article 4(1ter)). Similarly, the import of the ODSS in Annex E (that is, Methylbromide) was to be prohibited within one year of the entry into force of the 1997 Montreal Amendment (November 1999).

Article 4 of the Montreal Protocol also requires parties to ban the export of the ODSS in Annex A (from January 1993); ODSS in Annex B (from August 1993); ODSS in Group II of Annex C (from June 1995); ODSS in Annex E (one year after the entry into force of the 1997 Montreal Amendment); ODSS in Group III of Annex C (from February 2002) and: ODSS in Group I of Annex C (from January 2004).[39] In addition, the parties which ratify the Kigali Amendment of 2016 are to ban the export of HFCs in Annex F. With regard to restrictions on products containing ODSS in Annex A, as required by Article 4(3), the 1991 Third Ozone Meeting of the Parties adopted a list as Annex D to the Protocol.[40]

Furthermore, it is important to note that Article 4(4) of the Protocol provides that the parties shall determine the feasibility of banning or restricting the import of products produced with, but not containing, controlled ODSS from non-parties to the Protocol.[41] The 1993 Fifth Meeting of the Parties in Bangkok adopted in this respect a decision which states 'it is not feasible to impose a ban or restriction on the import of such products [that is, products produced with, but not containing, controlled substances] under the Protocol at this stage'.[42] This means that the risk of a complaint as to the use of PPMs as

---

39   See Article 4(2).
40   Products contain (i) automobile and truck air conditioning units, (ii) domestic and commercial refrigeration and air conditioning/heat pump equipment, (iii) aerosol products, except medical aerosols, (iv) portable fire extinguisher, (v) insulation boards, panels and pipe covers and (vi) pre-polymers. Regarding this issue, the 1985 Vienna Ozone Meeting adopted Decision VII/32 ('Control of Export and Import of Products and Equipment Containing Substances Listed in Annexes A and B of the Montreal Protocol', in UNEP/OzL.7/12, p. 43). For a comprehensive analysis, see Duncan Brack, *International Trade and the Montreal Protocol* (Earthscan, 1996), pp. 46–47.
41   See also Articles (4bis) and (4ter), as amended in London and Copenhagen. Ozone-depleting substances such as CFC-11 and CFC-113, used as solvents for cleaning semiconductor chips, are related to such environmental PPMs. During the Montreal Protocol's negotiation, Japan initially insisted that CFC-113 should be excluded from the list of controlled substances, since it is indispensable for the technology of manufacturing computers. However, as it was finally decided through the Montreal negotiations that parties can organise flexible reduction schedule within each of the two classes of controlled substances (CFCs and Halons), Japan's objection was resolved (see Chapter 3(III.B(3)) in this volume). Enders and Porges noted that products produced with, but not containing, CFCs amounted to 16 per cent of world trade. See Alice Enders and Amelia Porges, 'Successful Conventions and Conventional Success: Saving the Ozone Layer', in Kym Anderson and Richard Blackhurst (eds.), *The Greening of World Trade Issues* (Prentice-Hall, 1992), p. 132.
42   See Decision V/17 in UNEP/OzL.Pro.5/12. See also Duncan Brack, *International Trade and the Montreal Protocol* (Earthscan, 1996), pp. 48–49; Ernst-Ulrich Petersmann, *International*

THE MONTREAL PROTOCOL AND THE INTERNATIONAL TRADE LAW RÉGIME   173

trade barriers has therefore been greatly diminished – or even vanished.[43] Yet some developed countries such as Finland had banned the import of certain products containing or made with CFCs (Decree no. 891 of 24 September 1992). Finland gave notification of this decision in accordance with GATT rules.[44]

GATT Article XX environmental exceptions are generally applicable to 'like products'[45] that directly address characteristics of products, and not the production or processing of products (PPM)[46] in the exporting countries. This argument is primarily based on GATT Article III, which imposes the national treatment obligation on domestic taxes or standards applied to imports. Article III(4) reads:

> The products of the territory of any contracting party imported into the territory of any other contracting party shall be accorded treatment no less favourable than that accorded to like products of national origin in respect of all laws, regulations and requirements affecting their internal sale, offering for sale, purchase, transportation, distribution or use.[47]

---

and European Trade and Environmental Law after the Uruguay Round (Kluwer Law International, 1996), p. 43.

43 See Winfried Lang, 'Trade Restrictions as a Means of Enforcing Compliance with International Environmental Law', in Rüdiger Wolfrum (ed.), *Enforcing Environmental Standards* (Springer, 1996), p. 273.

44 See Rosalind Twum-Barima and Laura B. Campbell, *Protecting the Ozone Layer through Trade Measures: Reconciling the Trade Provisions of the Montreal Protocol and the Rules of the GATT* (United Nations Environment Programme, 1994), p. 104. However, Finland's Decree no. 891 was abated and harmonized with the EU Regulation 1005/2009.

45 In GATT law, there is no precise definition of this term. The meaning of the word 'like product' would be clarified only in a concrete context. See John H. Jackson, *World Trade and the Law of GATT* (Bobbs-Merrill, 1969), pp. 259 et seq.; Vinod Rege, 'GATT Law and Environment-Related Issues affecting the Trade of Developing Countries', 28 *JWT* (1994), pp. 159–162; GATT, *Guide to GATT Law and Practice* (6th ed. 1994), p. 35 (online edition at <https://www.wto.org/english/res_e/booksp_e/gatt_ai_e/gatt_ai_e.htm>). See also the Panel Report on *Japan - Custom Duties, Taxes and Labelling Practices on Imported Wine and Alcoholic Beverages*, BISD 34S/83 (10 November 1987), para. 5.6.

46 On this theme, see, in particular, Markus Schlagenhof, 'Trade Measures based on Environmental Processes and Production Methods', 30 *JWT* (1995), pp. 123–155; Thomas J. Schoenbaum, 'International Trade and Protection of the Environment', 91 *AJIL* (1997), pp. 288–301; Shinya Murase, 'Perspectives from International Economic Law on Transnational Environmental Issues', 253 *Recueil des cours* (1995), pp. 336 et seq.; Satoru Taira, 'Live with a Quiet but Uneasy Status Quo?: An Evolutionary Role the Appellate Body can play in Resolution of 'Trade and Environment' Disputes', in Harald Hohmann (ed.), *Agreeing and Implementing the Doha Round of the WTO* (Cambridge University Press, 2008), pp. 420–437.

47 GATT Panels frequently offers interpretations of GATT Article III. See, for example, *Italy-Discrimination Against Imported Agricultural Machinery*, BISD 7S/60 (23 October 1958); *United States-Section 337 of the Tariff Act of 1930*, BISD 36S/345 (7 November 1989).

In the view of some legal authors, since Article 4(4) of the Montreal Ozone Layer Protocol is closely related not only to the characteristics of products but also to the methods used in PPMs, such measures are therefore in breach of the related GATT obligations.[48] Assuming that products which use CFCs in the production process are not distinguishable from products using other 'ozone safe' PPMs, we could say that they would fall in the 'like products' concept of the GATT.[49] With regard to GATT case law, it is worth noting that the *Tuna* Panels distinguished between a regulation regarding product characteristics and a regulation related to a production process. Significantly, the Panels held that Article III covered the former, but not the latter.[50] Supporters of the GATT Panel decisions may argue that restrictions on international trade of products produced with, but not containing, controlled substances are by no means 'necessary' trade-related environmental measures.

Under paragraph 5 of Article 4 of the Montreal Protocol (as amended in 2016), each party undertakes to the 'fullest practicable extent' to discourage the export of technology for producing and utilising controlled substances in Annexes A, B, C, E and F to any non-parties to the Protocol. Article 4 also requires parties to refrain from providing new subsidies, aid, credits, guarantees or insurance for the export to non-parties of products, equipment, plants or technology which would facilitate the production of controlled substances in

---

48 See, for example, Markus Schlagenhoff, 'Trade Measures Based on Environmental Process and Production Methods', 30 *JWT* (1995), pp. 147 et seq.

49 See ibid., pp. 148 et seq.; Alice Enders and Amelia Porges, 'Successful Conventions and Conventional Success: Saving the Ozone Layer', in Kym Anderson and Richard Blackhurst (eds.), *Greening World Trade Issues* (Prentice-Hall, 1992), pp. 134 et seq. It can be also assumed that such PPMs might invite discrimination in certain elements of trade competitiveness, such as low labour costs. See James O. Cameron, Thobeka Mjolo-Thamage and Jonathan C. Robinson, 'Relationship between Environmental Agreements and Instruments Related to Trade and Development', in Peter H. Sand (ed.), *The Effectiveness of International Environmental Agreements: A Survey of Existing Legal Instruments* (Grotius Publications, 1992), pp. 488–499.

50 See *United States-Restrictions on Imports of Tuna (Tuna case II)*, 16 June 1994, unadopted, DS29/R444, reproduced in 30 *ILM* (1991), p. 1594, paras. 5.8–5.9; *United States-Restrictions on Imports of Tuna (Tuna case I)*, 3 September 1991, unadopted, BISD 39S/155, reproduced in 33 *ILM* (1994), p. 839, paras. 5.11–5.15. Provided tuna imports from Mexico were polluted, unsafe, or harmed humans or animals, there is little question that the United States could impose a regulation that was practically equal to that imposed on their own products. However, the United States' prohibition of imports of tuna and its product caught by vessels of Mexico was based on humanitarian considerations, that is, incidental killing of dolphins caused by the use of 'purse sein nets' in fishing for tuna. The Panel said that such incidental taking of dolphin could not possibly affect tuna as a product.

Annexes A, B, C, E and F.[51] However, it should be noticed that certain exceptions are allowed for products, equipment, plants or technology that could improve the containment, recovery, recycling or destruction of controlled substances, promote the development of alternative substances, or otherwise contribute to the reduction of emissions of these controlled substances.[52]

Article 4A of the Montreal Amendment provides that where a party is unable to cease production of ODSs for domestic consumption, it shall ban the export of used, recycled and reclaimed quantities of the ODSs, other than for the purpose of destruction: this paragraph applies 'without prejudice to the operation of Article 11 of the Convention and the non-compliance procedure developed under Article 8 of the Protocol'.[53] It is important that Article 4B of the 1997 Montreal Amendment introduced a new system for licensing the import and export of new, used, recycled and reclaimed ODSs. As the MOP's decisions reiterate, licensing systems are useful for the monitoring of imports and exports of ODSs (data collection) and will help to prevent illegal ODSs trade.[54] According to Decision XXIII/31, 182 of the 185 parties to the Montreal Amendment established such licensing systems and 174 of those submitted disaggregated information on their licensing systems.[55] However, both some parties – such as Korea and Thailand – and non-parties to the Montreal Amendment, which failed to provide disaggregated information on their licensing systems, were required, 'as a matter of urgency', to submit such date to the UNEP Ozone Secretariat.[56]

III WTO/GATT Trade Law

WTO/GATT trade law, consisting of substantive, procedural and institutional rules, is the specialised branch of international economic law, which is part of public international law.[57] It is often argued in legal literature that the

---

51   See Article 4(6).

52   See Article 4(7).

53   See Article 4A(2).

54   See, for example, Decisions XX/14, XXI/12 and XXII/19.

55   Decision XXIII/31, reproduced in Ozone Secretariat, UNEP, *Handbook for the Montreal Protocol on Substances that Deplete the Ozone Layer* (10th ed. 2016), pp. 259–260.

56   See ibid.

57   See Yuji Iwasawa, *WTO no Funsō Shori* [WTO Dispute Settlement] (Sanseido, 1995), p. 16 (in Japanese), noting the so-called 'constitutional functions' of 'International Economic Law' within nation States. On the autonomous functions of the WTO/GATT régime in general international law, see Akira Kotera, *Paradigm Kokusaihō* [Basic Structure of International Law] (Yuhikaku, 2004), pp. 3–12 (in Japanese); Kotera, *WTO Taisei no Hō Kōzō* [Legal

176   CHAPTER 4

WTO/GATT has its own flexible 'jurisprudence', and in a certain sense, the trade
law régime may be seen as a 'self-contained system' in the context of general international law.[58] However, strictly speaking, the question whether the
WTO/GATT is self-contained or not depends largely on the particular context in
which the term 'self-contained' is used.[59] It is important to note that reports
by the panels and the WTO Dispute Settlement Body frequently refer to the
customary international law rules codified in the 1969 Vienna Convention on
the Law of Treaties.[60]

A   *WTO/GATT Law*

To put it plainly, the central aim of the WTO/GATT law is to encourage the
world trading system.[61] In this regard, the WTO/GATT is vitally important
in creating a degree of certainty for international traders. The GATT[62] is the

---

Structure of the WTO Regime] (University of Tokyo Press, 2000) (in Japanese); Kotera,
'Kokusai Rejiimu no Ichi' [The Position of International Régimes], in Masahiko Iwamura
et al. (eds.) *Gendai no Hō* [Modern Law], Vol. 2 (Iwanami Shoten, 1997), pp. 87–107 (in
Japanese).

58   See P.J. Kuyper, 'The Law of GATT as a Special Field of International Law', 25 *NYbkIL*
(1994), pp. 227–257. On the concept of 'self-contained' régimes, see Chapter 1(IV) in this
volume.

59   See Yuji Iwasawa, *WTO no Funsō Shori* [WTO Dispute Settlement] (Sanseido, 1995), Chapter 6, p. 161 and its endnote 355 (in Japanese). See also the DSU (Article 3(2)), saying that
'the Members recognise that it [the WTO's dispute settlement system] serves .... to clarify
the existing provisions of those agreements in accordance with *customary rules of interpretation of public international law*' (emphasis added).

60   See Section IV(A) below.

61   See Peter-Tobias Stoll, 'World Trade Organization', in Rüdiger Wolfrum (ed.), *Max Planck
Encyclopedia of Public International Law*, Vol. x (Oxford University Press, 2012), p. 987, saying that the WTO 'embodies a trade system which should not be burdened with other international concerns, just like the future implementation of social standards and human
rights, which require action by other and more appropriate international institutions'.

62   The 1994 Uruguay Round Agreement established the World Trade Organisation (WTO)
as a successor to the GATT. The WTO thus incorporates the GATT 1947. The GATT 1994
is legally distinct from GATT 1947 (General Agreement on Tariffs and Trade, opened for
signature 30 October 1947). To be precise, once all contracting parties to the GATT 1947
have become Members of the WTO Agreement, the GATT 1947 may be considered as
terminated and States will be governed exclusively by the WTO Agreement (a country
joining the WTO is to adhere to all and not just one or some of its agreements). Even if
one argues that the GATT 1947 would not be terminated, it will remain applicable only
to the extent that it is compatible with the WTO Agreement. However, a country which
is a signatory of the GATT 1947 and which chooses not to join the WTO would remain a
contracting party of the GATT 1947. See Article II(4) of the Agreement Establishing the
WTO. See also Akira Kotera, 'Sekaibōekikikan Setsuritsu no Hōteki Igi' [Legal Significance
of the World Trade Organisation], 3 *Nihon Kokusaikeizaihōgakkai Nenpō* [International

principal multilateral treaty for trade in goods supported by a series of over two hundred agreements, protocols, process-verbaux and statements. It is often said that 'only ten people in the world understand it [that is, GATT], and they are not telling anybody'.[63]

It is certain that environmental protection was not regarded as a serious 'international' issue when GATT trade law was drafted in the post-war periods. Therefore, as with the United Nations Charter,[64] it contains no explicit reference to environmental issues. Rather, the original negotiators were concerned largely with free trade law instruments that are designed to promote 'better relations among nations', that is, world peace that is based on economic well-being.[65]

B   *The Governing Economic Principles of* GATT *Law*

GATT law is designed to regulate multilateral trade, mainly by reducing tariffs and other barriers to trade and by using the principle of the (unconditional) 'most-favoured-nation treatment' (MFN).[66] GATT trade law therefore obliges contracting parties to treat other GATT members at least as well as they treat any other country with regard to imports or exports. In other words, GATT contracting parties are to accord non-discriminatory treatment to goods coming

---

Economic Law] (1994), pp. 55–68 (in Japanese); Gabrielle Zoe Marceau, 'Transition from GATT to WTO: A Most Pragmatic Operation', 29 *JWT* (1995), pp. 150–151.

63   Statement by an American jurist, Gardner, cited in Antonio Cassese, *International Law in a Divided World* (Clarendon Press, 1986), p. 340. In this respect, see also Yuji Iwasawa, *WTO no Funsō Shori* [WTO Dispute Settlement] (Sanseido, 1995), Chapter 1, p. 2 and its notes 8–9 (in Japanese). As to the complexities of GATT Articles, see, in particular, John H. Jackson, *World Trade and the Law of* GATT (Bobbs-Merrill, 1969), Chapter 1.

64   On this issue, see Patricia Birnie 'Environmental Protection and Development', 20 *Melbourne ULR* (1995), pp. 66–67.

65   See William J. Davey, 'The WTO/GATT World Trading System: An Overview', in Pierre Pescatore, William J. Davey and Andreas F. Lowenfeld, *Handbook of* WTO/GATT *Dispute Settlement*, Vol.1 (1996), pp. 10–11.

66   'Any advantage, favour, privilege or immunity granted by any contracting party to any product originating in or destined for any other country shall be accorded immediately and unconditionally to the like product originating in or destined for the territories of all other contracting parties' (Article I(1), emphasis added). See, for example, Georg Schwarzenberger, *The Frontiers of International Law* (Stevens, 1962), pp. 225–226: Schwarzenberger, 'The Most-Favoured-Nation Standard in British State Practice', 22 *BYbkIL* (1945), pp. 96–121: John H. Jackson, *The World Trading System* (2nd ed. MIT Press, 1997), Chapter 6; MITI Industrial Structure Council, *1999 Report on the* WTO *Consistency of Trade Policies by Major Trading Partners* (1999), Chapter 1. See also *Belgium-Family Allowances*, BISD 1S/59 (7 November 1952).

from the territories of other contracting parties. In addition, the principle of legal 'reciprocity' forms the basis of this MFN treatment.[67]

It is interesting to note that the International Law Commission (ILC) once observed that the legal principle of the MFN, which has existed over several centuries,[68] is not an established rule of customary international law.[69] This means that the principle of the MFN must be based specifically on bilateral or multilateral economic treaty law.[70] In this respect, Georg Schwarzenberger and John H. Jackson take a similar view.[71]

To take a short-sighted and surface view of the Montreal Ozone Protocol, the restrictions on international trade with 'free-riding' non-parties under Article 4 seem to be in breach of the principle of the 'multilateral' MFN, simply because it provides that trade with non-parties must be banned or more severely restricted than trade between State parties.[72]

GATT trade law further provides that imports shall be treated no worse than domestically produced goods under internal taxation or regulatory measures (Article III: National Treatment on Internal Taxation and Regulation).[73] Its general purpose is to ensure that taxes and regulations are not imposed to afford protection to the domestic industries of the importing country. The import and export ban of the 1973 CITES based on a finding of detriment may

---

67   There are two types of reciprocity, namely, discriminatory and non-discriminatory. The former relates chiefly to bilateral agreements.

68   See Georg Schwarzenberger, 'The Most-Favoured-Nation Standard in British Practice', 22 *BYbkIL* (1945), pp. 96–121.

69   See Stephen Zamora, 'Is There Customary Economic Law?', 32 *GYbkIL* (1989), p. 29 and note 97. See also the ILC Final Draft Articles and Commentary on most favoured nations clauses (1978), reproduced in Arthur Watts, *The International Law Commission 1949–1998*, Vol. III (1999), p. 1807, suggesting that '[whether a given treaty provision falls within the purview of a most-favoured nations clause is a matter of interpretation. Most-favoured nations clauses can be drafted in the most diverse ways, ...'.

70   See also Meinhard Hilf and Robin Geiß, 'Most-Favoured-Nation Clause', in Rüdiger Wolfrum (ed.), *Max Planck Encyclopedia of Public International Law*, Vol. VII (Oxford University Press, 2012), pp. 384–385, 389.

71   See, for example, Georg Schwarzenberger, 'Equality and Discrimination in International Economic Law', 25 *Yearbook of World Affairs* (1971), p. 163: John H. Jackson, *The World Trading System* (2nd ed. MIT Press, 1997), p. 158.

72   See, for example, Robert Housman et al. (eds.), *The Use of Trade Measures in Selected Multilateral Environmental Agreements* (United Nations Environment Programme, 1995), p. 79.

73   See William J. Davey, 'The WTO/GATT World Trading System: An Overview', in William J. Davey and Andreas F. Lowenfeld, *Handbook of WTO/GATT Dispute Settlement*, Vol.1 (1996), pp. 28–35; GATT, *Guide to GATT Law and Practice* (6th ed. 1994), pp. 116 et seq. See also *United States-Taxes on Petroleum and Certain Imported Substances*, BISD 34S/136 (17 June 1987).

be regarded as a violation of both the MFN principle and the principle of national treatment, provided that the parties fail to regulate domestic or internal consumption.

In the context of environmental protection, it should be noted is that GATT Article XI provides for the general elimination of quantitative restrictions (QRs).[74] It has been suggested that this provision is the subject of more GATT dispute panel reports than any other.[75] Many international trade lawyers have pointed out that MEAs with global trade controls that distinguish between parties to the agreements and non-parties, such as the Montreal Ozone Protocol, the 1989 Basel Convention and the 1973 CITES, might violate the general prohibition against quantitative restrictions provided in GATT Article XI: this is a point to which we shall return later.

GATT Article XVI deals with subsidies which are tolerated if they do not harm the export interests of other countries.[76] Some commentators point out that the Montreal Multilateral Fund,[77] which provides 'environmental subsidies' for developing country parties, may be in violation of a basic GATT principle that aims to eliminate subsidies as undesirable barriers to international trade.[78]

Generally speaking, the WTO as a successor of the GATT deals with not only tariff barriers but non-tariff barriers to foreign trade, subsidies, trade in services, intellectual property and other trade policies. WTO trade law includes: (i) the Agreements on Trade in Goods (this includes GATT 1994), (ii) the Agreement on Trade in Services (GATS), (iii) the Agreement on Trade-related Aspects

---

74 See Section V(A) below. On this theme see, for example, GATT, *Guide to GATT Law and Practice* (6th ed. 1994), pp. 287 et seq.; John H. Jackson, *World Trade and the Law of GATT* (Bobbs-Merrill, 1969), Chapter 13; Tracy Murray and Ingo Walter, 'Quantitative Restrictions, Developing Countries, and GATT', 11 *JWT* (1977), pp. 391–421.

75 See William J. Davey, 'The WTO/GATT World Trading System: An Overview', in William J. Davey and Andreas F. Lowenfeld, *Handbook of WTO/GATT Dispute Settlement*, Vol.1 (1996), pp. 41–42.

76 See, in general, William J. Davey, 'The WTO/GATT World Trading System: An Overview', in William J. Davey and Andreas F. Lowenfeld, *Handbook of WTO/GATT Dispute Settlement*, Vol.1 (1996), pp. 59–62; John H. Jackson, William J. Davey and Alan O. Sykes, *Legal Problems of International Economic Relations* (6th ed. West, 2013), pp. 941 et seq.

77 See Chapter 6 in this volume.

78 See Scott N. Carlson, 'The Montreal Protocol's Environmental Subsidies and GATT: A Needed Reconciliation', 29 *Texas ILJ* (1994), p. 211; Anupam Goyal, 'Do Environmental Subsidies under Montreal Protocol Offend SCM Agreement of WTO? An Analysis', 44 *Indian JIL* (2004), pp. 521–531. See also Rosalind Twum-Barima and Laura B. Campbell, *Protecting the Ozone Layer through Trade Measures* (United Nations Environment Programme, 1994), pp. 77–79.

180 CHAPTER 4

of Intellectual Property Rights including trade in counterfeit goods (TRIPS),[79] (iv) the Understanding on Rules and Procedures Governing the Settlement of Disputes (1994 WTO DSU) and (v) the Trade Policy Review Mechanism.[80]

However, these WTO obligations are subject to many exceptions. WTO/GATT members could justify the possible breach of the principles of WTO/GATT trade law by relying on them.[81] Examples of those exceptions include: (i) the waiver authority of Article XXV(5), (ii) the escape clause of Article XIX that specifies conditions of emergency action on imports of particular products, (iii) Articles XII-XIV addressing balance of payments problems, (iv) Article XXIV relating to customs unions and free trade areas and (v) Article XX and Article XXI dealing mainly with general exceptions for national health and safety regulations and national security.

The point to observe here is that some of these GATT exceptions are directly or indirectly related to the protection of the ozone layer. For reasons that we shall go into later, it seems reasonable to suppose that, as far as the Montreal Ozone Protocol is concerned, its TREMs for CFCs or ODSs could be justified on the grounds of GATT Article XX exceptions.

C   *GATT Case-Law*[82]

With regard to GATT case-law, Professor Murase has observed that '[I]n studying an instrument such as GATT, we should take "common law approach"

---

79 The TRIPS (Article 27(2)) is concerned with the Biodiversity Convention (Article 16). See, for example, Mara Ntona, 'Technology Transfer', in Elisa Morgera and Jona Razzaque (eds.), *Biodiversity and Nature Protection Law* (Edward Elgar, 2017), pp. 358–368

80 See GATT, *The Results of the Uruguay Round of Multilateral Trade Negotiations: The Legal Texts* (1994); Ernst-Ulrich Petersmann, *The GATT/WTO Dispute Settlement System* (Kluwer Law International, 1997), pp. 44 et seq.; John H. Jackson, William J. Davey and Alan O. Sykes, *Legal Problems of International Economic Relations* (6th ed. West, 2013), pp. 227 et seq.

81 See John H. Jackson, *World Trade and the Law of GATT* (Bobbs-Merrill, 1969), Chapters 21 and 28; Benedict Kingsbury, 'Environment and Trade: The GATT/WTO Regime in the International Legal System', in Alan Boyle (ed.), *Environmental Regulation and Economic Growth* (Oxford University Press, 1994), pp. 217–219.

82 The GATT case law regarding environmental matters include, for example, *United States-Restrictions on Imports of Tuna (Tuna case I)*, 3 September 1991, unadopted, BISD 39S/155, reproduced in 33 *ILM* (1994), p. 839; *United States-Restrictions on Imports of Tuna (Tuna case II)*, 16 June 1994, unadopted, DS29/R444, reproduced in 30 *ILM* (1991), p. 1594; *Thailand-Restrictions on Importation of and Internal Taxes on Cigarettes*, BISD 37S/200 (7 November 1990); *United States-Prohibition of Imports of Tuna and Tuna Products from Canada*, BISD 29S/91 (22 February 1982); *Canada-Measures Affecting Exports of Unprocessed Herring and Salmon*, BISD 35S/98 (22 March 1988); *United States-Standards for Reformulated and Conventional Gasoline*, WT/DS2/29 (20 May 1996); *United States-Import of*

rather than "legalist" or "management" approaches, as was once mentioned by Dr. Frieder Roessler, then Director of the GATT Legal Office. The reality of the GATT law cannot be well understood by simply reading the statutes. [....] Rather, the GATT law is largely an accumulation of panel findings that leads to the continuous development of substantive GATT law'.[83] In a sense, WTO/GATT panel decisions that have evolved within the unique treaty system of the WTO/GATT may be regarded as 'subsequent practice in the treaty which establishes the agreement of the parties regarding its interpretation', as stated in the 1969 Vienna Convention on the Law of Treaties.[84]

In addition, it should be pointed out that the reasoning advanced by reports of the WTO/GATT dispute settlement panels or the DSB does not necessarily apply to future transnational disputes concerning the WTO/GATT, simply because, in principle, these precedents do not produce a legally binding effect. Yet, just like other national and international tribunals, WTO/GATT panels frequently refer to the previous panel decisions with a view to resolving trade disputes.[85]

It is interesting to note that, in the *Japan Alcohol Taxes* case of 4 October 1996, by rejecting the view of the panel that adopted panel reports 'constituting subsequent practice in the *specific* case', the Appellate Body described panel reports as 'an important part of the GATT *acquis*', creating 'legitimate

---

     Prohibition of Certain Shrimp and Shrimp Products, WT/DS58/R (6 November 1998) and WT/DS58/AB/R (21 November 2001). These cases, except for the *Shrimp-Turtle* case, are briefly summarised in Ernst-Ulrich Petersmann, *The GATT/WTO Dispute Settlement System* (Kluwer Law International, 1997), Chapter 3.

83   See Shinya Murase, 'Perspectives from International Economic Law on Transnational Environmental Issues', 253 *Recueil des cours* (1995), p. 329. See also Yuji Iwasawa, *WTO no Funsō Shori* [WTO Dispute Settlement] (Sanseido, 1995), pp. 3 and 18 (in Japanese).

84   See further Yuji Iwasawa, *WTO no Funsō Shori* [WTO Dispute Settlement] (Sanseido, 1995), pp. 138–139 (in Japanese); Alexander M. Feldman, 'Evolving Treaty Obligations: A Proposal for Analyzing Subsequent Practice Derived from WTO Dispute Settlement', 41 *NYJILP* (2009), pp. 676 et seq. Recently, Nolte considers effects of decisions adopted between WTO members in the context of subsequent agreements. See Georg Nolte, Special Rapporteur, *Third Report on Subsequent Agreements and Subsequent Practice in Relation to the Interpretation of Treaties*, International Law Commission Sixty-Seventh Session, Geneva, 4 May-5 June and 6 July-7 August 2015, A/CN.4/683 (7 April 2015), paras. 63–67, pp. 22–25; Georg Nolte (ed.), *Treaties and Subsequent Practice* (Oxford University Press, 2013), pp. 215 et seq.

85   See John H. Jackson, *The World Trading System* (2nd ed. MIT Press, 1997) p. 122, noting that 'A common-law lawyer would find himself very much at home in GATT legal discussions!'. Davey notes in this respect that reports by the new Appellate Body will often be relied upon by future panels and effectively constitute 'fairly stable body of precedent'. William J. Davey, 'The WTO/GATT World Trading System', in William J. Davey and Andreas F. Lowenfeld, *Handbook of WTO/GATT Dispute Settlement*, Vol.1 (1996), pp. 19–20.

182   CHAPTER 4

expectations among WTO members'.[86] And more recently, the Appellate Body suggests that ensuring "security and predictability" in the WTO dispute settlement system implies that an adjudicatory body will resolve the same legal question in the same way in a subsequent case.[87] This seems to fall short of the 'subsequent practice' principle and thus indicates that the Body may wish to retain some flexibility in GATT case law.[88] Lastly, it should be noted that the 1994 Agreement provides that 'The Ministerial Conference and the General Council shall have the exclusive authority to adopt interpretations of this Agreement and of the Multilateral Trade Agreement'.[89]

IV   The Legal Conflicts between MEAS and WTO/GATT Trade Law

In Chapter 1(IV) in this volume, it is argued that, in theory, the international régime for the protection of the ozone layer is a multilateral treaty of a unique *erga omnes* character. However, does this mean that contracting parties to the ozone layer régime – that are also, for the most part, contracting parties to the WTO/GATT régime – can completely ignore WTO/GATT trade law obligations that are also widely accepted in the international community? In order to effectively 'operate' the international norms of *erga omnes* character, such parties have to minimise (at least) expected legal conflicts in the 'practice' of public international law of the environment. This balancing between environment and trade law régimes is known as 'bridge-building'.[90] It is also important to note that, apart from the ozone layer régime, most MEAS do not assume such distinctive and normative character *erga omnes*.[91]

---

86   See the discussion in *Japan-Taxes on Alcoholic Beverages*, WT/DS8/AB/R, WT/DS10/AB/R, WT/DS11/AB/R (1 November 1996).

87   See *United States – Final Anti-Dumping Measures on Stainless Steel from Mexico*, WT/DS344/AB/R (30 April 2008), para. 160.

88   Thus, its decision disagreed with the above-mentioned view of Murase. See William J. Davey, 'The WTO/GATT World Trading System: An Overview', in William J. Davey and Andreas F. Lowenfeld, *Handbook of WTO/GATT Dispute Settlement*, Vol.1 (1996), p. 20. See also Ernst-Ulrich Petersmann, *The GATT/WTO Dispute Settlement System* (Kluwer Law International, 1997), pp. 111–117.

89   Article Ix(2).

90   See Winfried Lang, 'Is the Protection of the Environment a Challenge to the International Trading System?', 7 *Georgetown IELR* (1995), pp. 463–483.

91   See Winfried Lang, 'International Environmental Agreements and the GATT: The Case of the Montreal Protocol', 3–4 *Wirtschaftspolitische Blatter* (1993), p. 371, noting that 'drafters of environmental treaties should be invited to consider/reconsider the trade impact of certain measures written into the respective instruments'.

A *The Legal Conflicts between MEAS and WTO/GATT Trade Law*

In the 1996 panel report on *US Standards for Gasoline,* the WTO Appellate Body noted that Article 31 of the 1969 Vienna Convention on the Law of Treaties 'forms part of the "customary rules of interpretation of public international law"' and that GATT law 'is not to be read in clinical isolation from public international law'.[92] The Vienna Convention on the Law of Treaties has thereby proven its relevance in practice regarding international trade law of a highly technical character.[93]

Legal principles and rules provided for in the Vienna Convention on the Law of Treaties supply basic guidelines on problems posed by successive treaties or incompatible treaties concerned with the same subject matter. It may be said that the TREMs provided for in the Montreal Ozone Protocol and the GATT deal with such 'same subject matter' of international trade restrictions of certain goods (that is, controlled CFCs and ODSs).

Article 30 of the 1969 Vienna Convention lays down a hierarchical principle, as well as the principles of *lex prior* and *lex posterior*:[94]

1) Subject to Article 103 of the Charter of the United Nations, the rights and obligations of States parties to successive treaties relating to the same subject-matter shall be determined in accordance with the following paragraphs.

2) When a treaty specifies that it is subject to, or that it is not to be considered as incompatible with, an earlier or later treaty, the provision of that other treaty prevail;

3) When the parties to the later treaty do not include all the parties to the earlier one;

   (a) as between States parties to both treaties the same rule applies as in paragraph 3 [that is, the earlier treaty applies only to the extent that its provisions are compatible with those of the later treaty];

   (b) as between a State party to both treaties and a State party to only one of the treaties, the treaty to which both States are parties governs their mutual rights and obligations.

---

92 See the discussion in *United States-Standards for Reformulated and Conventional Gasoline* (the *Venezuela Gas* case), WT/DS2/AB/R (20 May 1996), Section B.

93 In this respect, see also Yuji Iwasawa, *WTO no Funsō Shori* [WTO Dispute Settlement] (Sanseido, 1995), p. 117; Ernst-Ulrich Petersmann, *The GATT/WTO Dispute Settlement* (Kluwer Law International, 1997), pp. 111 et seq.; John H. Jackson, *The World Trading System* (2nd ed. MIT Press, 1997), p. 127.

94 See Ian Sinclair, *The Vienna Convention on the Law of Treaties* (Manchester University Press, 1984), pp. 96–98.

184   CHAPTER 4

TABLE 1 Relationship between MEAs and WTO/GATT trade law

		Country 'A' is a Party to:			
		MEAS	WTO	MEAS+WTO	[Non-Party]
Country	MEAS	X1	X2	X3	-
'B' is a	WTO	X4	X5	X6	-
Party to:	MEAS+WTO	X7	X8	X9	-
	[Non-Party]	-	-	-	-

The principle of *lex specialis*, that is, the principle of more specific treaties taking priority over earlier ones, is also important and a well-established conflict
rule of international law, although it is not provided for in Article 30.[95] In addition, it should be noted here that the decision as to which treaty is the earlier
depends on the date of adoption, and not that of its entry into force.

As Table 1 above illustrates, types of potential trade-environmental disputes
multiply enormously.[96] Furthermore, the number of both MEAs and independent sovereign States is likely to grow in the international community. With
regard to the Montreal Ozone Protocol, since most of the members of the
ozone régime are also parties to the WTO/GATT régime, it may safely be assumed that the potential legal conflicts are likely to happen in the case of X9,
rather than X2 or X4.[97] In this connection, Ernst-Ulrich Petersmann submits
the following three legal situations: (i) disputes between WTO members over
the WTO consistency of MEA trade measures accepted by both parties to the
disputes, (ii) disputes between WTO members over the WTO consistency of

---

95   See ibid., p. 96; Oliver Dörr and Kirsten Schmalenbach (eds.), *Vienna Convention on the
      Law of Treaties: A Commentary* (Springer, 2012), p. 116.
96   See Nobuto Iwata, 'WTO Taisei ni okeru Kankyō Mondai to Bōeki Funsō' [Environmen-
      tal Problems and Trade Disputes in the WTO System], 6 *Bōeki to Kanzei* [Trade Journal],
      (1996), p. 50 (in Japanese). It assumed that the countries are parties to both GATT 1994 and
      the WTO Agreement. In X1, X3 and X7, parties should refer to MEAs. In X5, X6 and X8, par-
      ties can settle disputes by referring to WTO/GATT law. In X2 and X4, it is actually difficult
      to rely on either MEAs or WTO/GATT law. See Article 30 (4) of the Vienna Convention on
      the Law of Treaties.
97   Yet it may be true that, as Canada pointed out in a meeting of the WTO Committee on
      Trade and Environment, disputes between parties and non-parties had the potential to
      become a more important issue. See WTO, *Trade and Environment*, PRESS/TE008 (29
      April 1996).

MEA trade measures accepted by only one party, and (iii) disputes between WTO members over trade measures not specifically regulated in MEAs.[98]

Before the establishment of the WTO, under Article 30 of the Vienna Convention on the Law of Treaties, the international ozone treaties were given priority over GATT 1947 obligations for those States that were parties to both agreements. Therefore, those treaty provisions that were likely to violate related GATT principles generally formed exceptions to the rules (see Table: X2, X7 and X9). It thus meant that only if the GATT parties were not parties to the 1985 Vienna Convention and the Montreal Ozone Protocol (see Table: X4, X5, X8 or 'Non-Party'), they were allowed to hold prior rights to the GATT incompatible provisions.

However, in 1994, the WTO formally incorporated the GATT 1947.[99] The GATT 1994 was thus established and 'CONTRACTING PARTIES' (not 'Members' as such) effectively withdraw from the original GATT 1947. They formally became members of the GATT 1994. It would therefore be possible to argue that the situation has been completely reversed. This means that the 1994 WTO/GATT law now prevails over all earlier MEAs in accordance with the principle of *lex posterior* (see Table: X6, X8 and X9).

Nevertheless, it should also be noted, as I have strongly emphasised in this book, that international environmental treaty régimes have a dynamic and flexible character – just like the international ozone régime and the climate change régime, they are in many cases subject to periodic review, future amendments and adjustments that may be often extensive.[100] It is for this reason that Conferences or Meetings of the Parties have played a central role in the development of international environmental régimes.

In conclusion, it is not to be denied that conflicts between the WTO/GATT legal régime and MEA régimes cannot be easily solved by traditional legal principles such as *lex prosterior* or *lex specialis*, as mentioned above.[101] For example, while MEA provisions allowing trade restrictions are certainly more 'specific' and 'technical' than GATT Article XX environmental exceptions, it is also certain that these environment-related exceptions must be read together with other relevant rules of the WTO/GATT trade law régime.[102] In addition,

---

98   See Ernst-Ulrich Petersmann, *The GATT/WTO Dispute Settlement System* (Kluwer Law International, 1997), pp. 132–134.

99   See Section III(A) above.

100 See Chapter 1 and Chapter 3(IV) in this volume.

101 The same opinion is expressed in Richard G. Tarasofsky, 'Ensuring Compatibility between MEAs and GATT/WTO', 7 *YbkIEL* (1996), p. 65.

102 On this point see, for example, *United States-Standards for Reformulated and Conventional Gasoline*, WT/DS/AB/R (20 May 1996), Section B ('relating to the conservation of exhaustible natural resources').

certain treaty rules, as contained, for example, in the Agreement on Technical Barriers to Trade (TBT) or other WTO/GATT law instruments could be more specific than the TERMS contained in MEAS. As Professor Lang once observes, it will be true that:

> [T]rade and environment disputes in general would probably need some special kind of overarching jurisdiction in which the different legal regimes [that is, ozone and GATT régimes] could be considered together and applied in a balanced way.[103]

B   *The Relationship between MEA Dispute Settlement Procedures and the WTO Dispute Settlement System: the Montreal NCP or the WTO Dispute Settlement Procedures?*

(1)   General Discussions

There exist many problems regarding the legal hierarchy of MEA dispute settlement procedures and the WTO dispute settlement system.[104] Some commentators argue, for instance, that legal conflicts between MEAS and the WTO/GATT should be decided in their entirety by an authoritative international tribunal, for example, the International Court of Justice (ICJ).[105] It has been suggested that seeking an Advisory Opinion from the ICJ would be 'attractive especially as regards systematic problems'.[106] However, the WTO Committee on Trade and Environment seems to believe that environment-related trade disputes between an MEA party and an MEA non-party that is a member of the WTO should be addressed by a WTO dispute settlement panel.[107] When the parties

---

103   Winfried Lang, 'Trade Restrictions as a Means of Enforcing Compliance with International Environmental Law', in Rüdiger Wolfrum (ed.), *Enforcing Environmental Standards* (Springer, 1996), p. 282.

104   For a comprehensive discussion of the WTO/GATT settlement system, see among others, Yuji Iwasawa, *WTO no Funsō Shori* [WTO Dispute Settlement] (Sanseido, 1995) (in Japanese); Ernst-Ulrich Petersmann, *The GATT/WTO System* (Kluwer Law International, 1997); Kati Kulovesi, *The WTO Dispute Settlement* (Wolters Kluwer, 2011).

105   As in the cases of MEAS, however, disputes involving WTO/GATT law has so far never been brought to the ICJ. See John H. Jackson, *The World Trading System* (2nd ed. MIT Press, 1997), p. 124; Yuji Iwasawa, *WTO no Funsō Shori* [WTO Dispute Settlement] (Sanseido, 1995), Chapter 3, p. 55 and notes 95–97 (in Japanese). On the analysis of the WTO dispute settlement in comparison with other systems of 'second-order' compliance in international law, see Yoshinori Abe, 'Implementation System of the WTO Dispute Settlement Body: A Comparative Approach', 6 *JEAIL* (2013), pp. 7–28.

106   See Richard G. Tarasofsky, 'Ensuring Compatibility between MEAS and GATT/WTO', 7 *YbkIEL* (1996), p. 71.

107   See WTO, *Trade and Environment Bulletin*, No. 3 (22 May 1995).

to a WTO trade dispute are also MEA parties, their right to the WTO dispute settlement system cannot be denied.[108] However, it is important to note that a number of countries have argued in the CTE that the WTO settlement procedures should not be overburdened, and the MEA dispute settlement process should be 'exhausted' before a dispute is brought to the WTO's settlement mechanism.[109]

(2)   The NCP or the WTO Dispute Settlement Procedures?

To discuss all the questions submitted by Professor Petersmann is certainly beyond the scope of this volume, having as it does the limited purposes stated in the *Introduction*.[110] However, as many delegations at the WTO's CTE meetings suggested, it might be better for environment-related disputes (for example, between WTO members which are MEA parties or non-parties) to be dealt with first by MEA dispute settlement procedures, and not by the more 'judicialised' WTO settlement mechanism,[111] particularly if the MEA contains a flexible dispute settlement procedure, such as a non-compliance procedure (NCP).

Two points are noted here in the context of the non-compliance régime of the Montreal Protocol type.[112] In the first place, it is possible to argue that the settlement of MEA/WTO-related trade disputes by the formal non-compliance procedure would be 'politically' feasible.[113] In the Montreal NCP model, non-parties to the MEA[114] – particularly non-parties in non-compliance with the TREMS – are likely to be allowed to participate in the meetings of the standing

---

108 In this context, at the Third Meeting of the WTO's CTE, some delegations - such as Columbia - suggested that WTO Members had to maintain their right of submitting to the WTO dispute settlement mechanism any conflicts which might arise as a result of an environmental measure (see WTO, *Trade and Environment*, PRESS/TE008 (29 April 1996)). See also Ernst-Ulrich Petersmann, *The GATT/WTO Dispute Settlement System* (Kluwer Law International, 1997), pp. 132–133.

109 In this connection, the delegations of Norway rightly observed that the issue of non-parties could be problematic, especially if dispute settlement procedures of MEAS were inadequate. Efficient dispute settlement mechanisms should be developed within MEA régimes. See WTO, *Trade and Environment*, PRESS/TE008 (29 April 1996).

110 See Ernst-Ulrich Petersmann, *The GATT/WTO Dispute Settlement System* (Kluwer Law International, 1997), pp. 132–134.

111 This means that the formal NCP presently has many political aspects, rather than judicial ones. See Russia's non-compliance case in Chapter 5(VII.B) in this volume.

112 See further Chapter 5 in this volume.

113 See also Richard G. Tarasofsky, 'Ensuring Compatibility between MEA and GATT/WTO', 7 *YbkIEL* (1996), pp. 70–71.

114 Even in the case of disputes between WTO members over the WTO consistency of a particular MEA's provisions for trade accepted by only one party.

188   CHAPTER 4

Implementation Committee.[115] Constructive discussions within this international 'conciliation' body could potentially contribute to amicably settling/
avoiding this kind of TREM-related dispute.

As a precondition, in order to supply the internally specialised institutions
of the ozone régime with impartial and workable advice, the UNEP Ozone Secretariat – as a group of technical experts – should cooperate with the WTO
Secretariat and other secretariats of international institutions in various fields.
Undeniably, the Ozone Secretariat is not necessarily expert in questions of international economic law rules, such as WTO/GATT trade law.[116] In this connection, Switzerland suggested at the CTE that '[m]any conflicts between
MEAS and WTO rules could be prevented if cooperation existed between trade
and environment officials at the national and international level, and a cooperation mechanism should be concluded between the WTO and competent
MEA bodies, based on reciprocity which applied, *inter alia*, to observer status
and information exchange'.[117] Several countries, including Japan, take a similar
view.[118]

In the second place, although this point may be arguable, the law of the
WTO/GATT is still ill-equipped for 'amicably' settling today's increasing global
environmental problems. It is true that WTO/GATT panels are primarily designed to apply WTO/GATT rules only and not necessarily 'international law'
as a whole.[119] In this sense, the legal tools that a WTO dispute settlement panel may employ to approach environmental matters are still severely limited,
although it may refer to 'other relevant rules of international law' through

---

115   In case of the Montreal NCP, although observers (for example, environmental NGOs) are
      currently not allowed to participate in the meetings of the Implementation Committee
      (see Chapter 5(IV.B(2)(b)), non-parties to the Protocol (for example, Czech and Slovak
      Federal Republic) in reality participated in such political forums (see UNEP/OzL.Pro/
      ImpCom/3/3, para. 4) [Czech Republic ratified the Montreal Protocol in 1993].

116   It is important that the UNEP Secretariat has been invited as an observer to meetings of
      the WTO Committee on Trade and Environment. See, for example, *Summary Report on
      the Seventeenth Meeting of the Committee on Trade and Environment in Special Session, 1–2
      March 2007, Note by the Secretariat*, TN/TE/R/17 (18 April 2009), p. 1.

117   WTO, *Trade and Environment*, PRESS/TE010 (8 July 1996), Item 1. See also WTO *Trade and
      Environment Bulletin*, no. 3 (22 May 1995). The topic concerning information exchange be-
      tween the WTO and MEAS is dealt with in the CTESS meetings. See, for example, *Summary
      Report on the Sixteenth Meeting of the Committee on Trade and Environment in Special Ses-
      sion, 6–7 July 2006, Note by the Secretariat*, TN/TE/R/16 (22 December 2006), pp. 23–31,
      paras. 128–170.

118   See 'The Relationship between Trade Measures Pursuant to MEAS and the WTO Agree-
      ment', WT/CTE/W/31 (May 1996), proposal by the Japanese government.

119   See Paragraphs 1–2 of Article 7 of the DSU. See also Yuji Iwasawa, WTO *no Funsō Shori*
      [WTO Dispute Settlement] (Sanseido, 1995), p. 99.

Article 31(3)(c) of the Vienna Convention on the Law of Treaties.[120] Certainly, the basic sources of WTO/GATT law are formed by the General Agreement, the 1994 Uruguay Understandings on the General Agreement and Side Agreements.[121] In a meeting of the CTE, the United States argued the 'necessity'[122] of trade measures in MEAs was best determined by MEA negotiators themselves, and the WTO did not have the technical competence to determine whether other measures that are 'reasonably available' to achieve the same objectives of MEAs meet MEA objectives.[123]

However, it must be noted at the same time that provisions for trade-related environmental disputes to be dealt by the WTO Expert Review Groups, which is provided for in Appendix 4 of the 1994 WTO Understanding (DSU, Annex 2), would contribute greatly to the resolution of such technical questions.[124] Moreover, Article 13 of the WTO Understanding states that WTO panels shall have the right to seek useful information and technical advice from any individual or body – which might be environmental experts (for example, MEA Secretariats)[125] and they may also seek information from any relevant source (for example, NGOs). In 1990, in the *Thailand-Restrictions on Importation of and Internal Taxes on Cigarettes* case, the Panel sought specialist advise from the WHO on the health risks of smoking on the effectiveness of non-discriminatory tobacco-control strategies.[126] In the *India – Measures Concerning The Importation Of Certain Agricultural Products* case, the Panel sought advice from experts and international organizations, that is, a written consultation with the OIE on the interpretation of the OIE"s Terrestrial Animal Health Code and a written and oral consultation with two individual experts on the avian

---

120 On this point, see Joost Pauwelyn, *Conflict of Norms in Public International Law* (Cambridge University Press, 2003), pp. 253 et seq.; Anja Lindroos and Michael Mehling, 'From Autonomy to Integration? International Law, Free Trade and the Environment', 77 *Nordic Journal of International Law* (2008), pp. 267–271.

121 See William J. Davey, 'The WTO/GATT World Trading System: An Overview', in William J. Davey and Andreas F. Lowenfeld, *Handbook of WTO/GATT Dispute Settlement*, Vol.1 (1996), pp. 18–21.

122 See Section V(A) below.

123 See WTO, *Trade and Environment*, PRESS/TE008 (29 April 1996).

124 It is provided that '[p]articipation in expert review groups shall be restricted to persons of *professional standing and experience* in the field in question' (Appendix 4(3), emphasis added).

125 On the role of the MEA Secretariat, see Chapter 2(III.D(3)) in this volume; Bharat H. Desai, *Multilateral Environmental Agreements: Legal Status of the Secretariats* (Cambridge University Press, 2010), pp. 93 et seq.

126 See Ernst-Ulrich Petersmann, *International and European Trade and Environmental Law after the Uruguay Round* (Kluwer Law International, 1996), p. 39.

influenza surveillance regime with particular respect to India's domestic measures and its disease situation.[127]

To summarise, as a matter of judicial policy, it is my opinion that the NCP would be a reasonable starting point. Based on the above, however, it still cannot be denied that possible conflicts between MEAs and the WTO/GATT (for example, trade measures applied against non-parties) should be addressed on a case-by-case basis (through dispute settlement of MEAs, including the NCP and/or the WTO).[128] Moreover, in the present case of the international ozone treaties, if the Montreal NCP proves to be too 'soft' or ineffective, it is still possible that traditional dispute settlement procedures under Article 11 of the 1985 Vienna Ozone Convention, including arbitration,[129] could also be applied to Article 4-related environmental disputes.

V GATT Article XX and the Global Protection of the Ozone Layer under the Montreal Protocol

A   *The Exceptions under GATT Articles XI(1) and XX*

GATT law exceptions, which were usually provided for in bilateral trade agreements,[130] are largely based on a proposal made by the United States of America. The *travaux préparatoris* of Article XX are not necessarily helpful in clarifying the exact meaning of these GATT exceptions.[131] Yet, it must be emphasised at the outset that treaty drafting history or preparatory work is only a

---

127 See *India – Measures Concerning the Importation of Certain Agricultural Products*, WT/DS430/R (14 October 2014), paras. 1.20–1.23.

128 See also Cinnamon Carlarne, 'The Kyoto Protocol and the WTO: Reconciling Tensions between Free Trade and Environmental Objectives', 17 *Colorado JIELP* (2005/2006), pp. 84–85.

129 See Chapter 2(III.D(4)).

130 In this respect, see Thomas J. Schoenbaum, 'Free International Trade and Protection of the Environment: Irreconcilable Conflicts?', 86 *AJIL* (1992), p. 711, pointing out that '[t]he text apparently derived from the kinds of exceptions traditionally written into bilateral treaties of friendship, commerce and navigation'.

131 For a discussion of the drafting history of GATT Article XX, see GATT, *Guide to GATT Law and Practice* (6th ed. 1994), pp. 519 et seq.: Steve Charonvitz, 'Exploring the Environmental Exceptions in GATT Article XX', 25 *JWT* (1991), pp. 38–47; John H. Jackson, *World Trade and the Law of GATT* (Bobbs-Merrill, 1969), pp. 742–745; Rüdiger Wolfrum, Peter-Tobias Stoll and Anja Seibert-Fohr (eds.), *WTO – Technical Barriers and SPS Measures* (Martinus Nijhoff, 2007), pp. 67–68.

THE MONTREAL PROTOCOL AND THE INTERNATIONAL TRADE LAW RÉGIME   191

'supplementary means of interpretation' and they cannot be used unless 'primary sources' turns out to be unreliable for interpretative questions.[132]

In order to eliminate trade barriers between parties to the international economic régime, GATT Article XI(1) prohibits the use of quotas or other quantitative limitations on exported or imported products in general. Article XI(1) provides:

> [N]o prohibitions or restrictions *other than duties, taxes or other charges*, whether made effective through quotas, import or export licences or other measures shall be instituted or maintained by any contracting party on the importation of any product of the territory of any other contracting party or on the exportation or sale for export of any product destined for the territory of any other contracting party.[133]

However, exceptions are permitted under GATT Article XI(2), *inter alia,* for temporary prohibitions or restrictions applied to prevent or relieve critical shortages of other products essential to the exporting contracting parties. We can find here striking similarities in Articles 34 and 35 of the Treaty on the Functioning of the European Union that generally prohibit quantitative restrictions and all measures having equivalent effects on imports.[134]

Article XX contains general exceptions to the GATT trade law régime. As we will see, Article XX exceptions are closely related to the possible 'adverse effects'[135] that may result from the depletion of the ozone layer. Article XX states that:

> Subject to the requirement that such measures are not applied in a manner which would constitute a means of arbitrary or unjustifiable discrimination between countries where the same conditions prevail, or a disguised restriction on international trade, nothing in this Agreement shall be construed to prevent the adoption or enforcement by any contracting party of measures: ...

---

132   See John H. Jackson, *The World Trading System* (2nd ed. MIT Press, 1997), p. 122. On Article 32 of the Vienna Convention on the Law of Treaties, see, for example, Oliver Dörr and Kirsten Schmalenbach (eds.), *Vienna Convention on the Law of Treaties: A Commentary* (Springer, 2012), pp. 571 et seq.

133   Emphasis added.

134   For a discussion, see Ernst-Ulrich Petersmann, *International and European Trade and Environmental Law after the Uruguay Round* (Kluwer Law International,1996), pp. 64–71.

135   See Chapter 2(III.A) in this volume.

(b) necessary to protect human, animal or plant life or health; ...

(f) imposed for the protection of national treasures of artistic, historic or archaeological value;

(g) relating to the conservation of exhaustible natural resources if such measures are made effective in conjunction with restrictions on domestic production or consumption.[136]

Any such restrictions, if they are to be permitted under Article XX, must not be applied in a manner which would constitute (i) arbitrary discrimination (between countries where the same conditions prevail), (ii) unjustifiable discrimination (with the same qualifier), or (iii) a disguised restriction on international trade.[137] It has been suggested that the introductory paragraph of Article XX – 'whose legal meaning had never before been convincingly and precisely clarified in GATT panel practice'[138] – was inserted in order to prevent abuse of such general exceptions to Article XX. At present, it is customary interpretative practice for the Appellate Body to first examine whether the measure in question falls within the terms under Article XX and if it is met, to consider it in the context of the *chapeau*.[139]

136　See *United States-Standards for Reformulated and Conventional Gasoline*, WT/DS/R (20 May 1996), Sections D and G. The *Tuna* Panel II stated that Article XX (b) and (g) adjudication should follow a three step process: (i) whether the policy underlying the trade measure at issue fit within the range of policies meant to conserve exhaustible natural resources and whether the policy was made effective in conjunction with domestic restrictions, (ii) whether the trade measure was "related to" the conservation of exhaustible natural resources, and (iii) whether the measure conformed to the Article XX headstone.

137　See the Preamble (*Chapeau*). See also *United States-Standards for Reformulated and Conventional Gasoline*, WT/DS2/AB/R (20 May 1996), Section IV; GATT, *Guide to GATT Law and Practice* (6th ed. 1994), pp. 519–521; John H. Jackson, *World Trade and the Law of GATT* (Bobbs-Merrill, 1969), p. 743. Likewise, Principle 12 of the 1992 Rio Declaration states that: 'States should cooperate to promote a supportive and open international economic system that would lead to economic growth and sustainable development in all countries, to better address the problems of environmental degradation. Trade policy measures for environmental purposes should not constitute a means of arbitrary or unjustifiable discrimination or a disguised restriction on international trade'.

138　See Ernst-Ulrich Petersmann, *The GATT/WTO Dispute Settlement System* (Kluwer Law International, 1997), pp. 114 et seq.; Thomas J. Schoenbaum, 'International Trade and Protection of the Environment', 91 *AJIL* (1997), p. 274. See also *United States-Standards for Reformulated/Conventional Gasoline*, WT/DS2/AB/R (20 May 1996), Section IV, noting that 'the text of the chapeau is not without ambiguity, including one relating to the field of application of the standards its contains'.

139　See William J. Davey, *Non-discrimination in the World Trade Organization: The Rules and Exceptions* (Martinus Nijhoff, 2012), pp. 249–250, 306–307; Erich Vranes, *Trade and Environment* (Oxford University Press, 2009), pp. 276–278.

THE MONTREAL PROTOCOL AND THE INTERNATIONAL TRADE LAW RÉGIME   193

In this respect, it is worth noting that, in its report on the *Shrimp-Turtle* case, the Appellate Body argued that the *chapeau* of Article xx was one expression of the principle of good faith[140] and that 'our task here is to interpret the language of the *chapeau*, seeking *additional interpretative guidance*, as appropriate, from the general principles of international law' (that is, Article 31(3)(c) of the Vienna Convention on the Law of Treaties).[141] In short, the Appellate Body therefore emphasised the importance of such general principles and the preamble of the wto Agreement in interpreting the *chapeau* of Article xx.[142]

It is generally observed that Article xx(b) focuses on the use of sanitary measures to safeguard the life or health of humans, animals or plants within the jurisdiction of the importing States.[143] It is interesting to note here that during the Geneva Session of the Preparatory Committee it was agreed to delete from the New York draft of paragraph (b) the phrase 'if corresponding domestic safeguards under similar conditions exist in the importing country'.[144] The term 'necessary' under GATT Article xx(b) has been strictly interpreted, and parties invoking Article xx are therefore faced with a number of hurdles before their claims of exception to the GATT obligations will be accepted.[145] For a treaty provision to be 'necessary', there must be 'no alternative measure consistent with the General Agreement, or less inconsistent with it, which

---

140 See WT/DS58/AB/R (6 November 1998), para. 158. The Body refers to Professor Cheng's *General Principles of Law as Applied by the International Courts and Tribunals* (1953), *Oppenheim's International Law* (Jennings and Watts eds., 1992), and the following cases: *Border and Transborder Armed Actions* case, *Rights of Nationals of the US in Morocco* case and *Anglo-Norwegian Fisheries* case.

141 See WT/DS58/AB/R (6 November 1998), para. 158 (emphasis added).

142 See further WT/DS58/AB/R (6 November 1998), paras. 152–153 and 158.

143 See the *Tuna* Panel II, para. 5.27. See further Section D below. In this respect, we may recall that Article 36 of the Treaty on the Functioning of the European Union allows Member State to adopt measures restricting the free movement of goods for the purpose of protecting a series of non-economic values such as public morality, public policy, public security and protection of human health, animals and plants. See, for example, Robin Griffith, 'International Trade Treaties and Environmental Protection Measures', 1 *RECIEL* (1992) pp. 26–27; David Langlet and Said Mahmoudi, *EU Environmental Law and Policy* (Oxford University Press, 2016), pp. 77 et seq.

144 See further GATT, *Guide to GATT Law and Practice* (6th ed. 1994), p. 521. See also the interpretation of Article xx(d) in *United States-Section 337 of the Tariff Act of 1930*, BISD 36S/345 (7 November 1989), para. 5.26.

145 GATT cases have defined this term to mean 'least GATT-inconsistent'. See *Thailand-Restrictions on Importation of and Internal Taxes on Cigarettes*, BISD 37S/200 (7 November 1990); *United States-Prohibition of Imports of Tuna and Tuna Products from Canada*, BISD 29S/91 (22 February 1982); *Canada-Measures Affecting Exports of Unprocessed Herring and Salmon*, BISD 35S/98 (22 March 1988).

194

CHAPTER 4

[a country] could reasonably be expected to employ to achieve its health policy objectives'.[146]

Article xx thus generally establishes the following legal requirements:[147]

i. Trade measures must avoid arbitrary or unjustifiable discrimination between countries where the same conditions prevail;

ii. Trade measures must not be a disguised restriction on international trade;

iii. The purpose of the import or export bans must be for one of the purposes listed in GATT Article xx; and

iv. The measures invoking an Article xx exception must be necessary for the purpose in question.

In the past, most panels, as well as the Appellate Body, have considered the specific paragraphs of Article xx (that is, paragraphs iii and iv), before reviewing the applicability of the conditions in the introductory provision (paragraphs i and ii).[148] Furthermore, in the *Brazil – Measures Affecting Imports of Retreaded Tyres* case, the Appellate Body suggests:[149]

.... in order to determine whether a measure is "necessary" within the meaning of Article xx(b) of the GATT 1994, a panel must consider the relevant factors, particularly the importance of the interests or values at stake, the extent of the contribution to the achievement of the measure's objective, and its trade restrictiveness. If this analysis yields a preliminary conclusion that the measure is necessary, this result must be confirmed by comparing the measure with possible alternatives, which may be less trade restrictive while providing an equivalent contribution to the

---

146 See *Thailand-Restrictions on Importation of and Internal Taxes on Cigarettes*, BISD 37S/200 (7 November 1990), para. 75 (emphasis added). In this respect, however, it is said that, in recent cases, the Appellate Body seemed to have relaxed the necessity requirement and tries to apply a 'multi-factored balancing test'. See Yoshiko Naiki, GATT Dai 20 Jō ni okeru Hitsuyōsei Yōken [Necessary Requirements under GATT Article 20], 15 *Nihon Kokusaikeizaihōgakkai Nenpō* [International Economic Law] (1994), pp. 217–256 (in Japanese); Daniel Bodansky and Jessica C. Lawrence, 'Trade and Environment', in Daniel Bethlehem, Isabelle Van Damme, Donald McRae and Rodney Neufeld (eds.), *The Oxford Handbook of International Trade Law* (Oxford University Press, 2009), pp. 516–517; Appellate Body Report, *Brazil – Measures Affecting Imports of Retreaded Tyres*, WT/DS332/AB/R (3 December 2007), para. 151, stating that '[w]e recognize that certain complex public health or environmental problems may be tackled only with a comprehensive policy comprising a multiplicity of interacting measures'.

147 See also Sections B to E.

148 See, for example, the *Shrimp-Turtle* case, WT/DS58/AB/R (21 November 2001), paras. 117–120.

149 *Brazil – Measures Affecting Imports of Retreaded Tyres*, WT/DS332/AB/R (3 December 2007), para. 178.

achievement of the objective. This comparison should be carried out in the light of the importance of the interests or values at stake. It is through this process that a panel determines whether a measure is necessary.

Next, we will examine whether the trade restrictions against non-parties under the Montreal Protocol comply with these stringent requirements.

B   *GATT Article XI(2) Exceptions and the Montreal Protocol*

As has been suggested, although certain exceptions are permitted under GATT Article XI, they are not particularly applicable to the trade controls of ozone-depleting substances. As in the *Japanese Agricultural Restriction* case,[150] the Article XI(2) exceptions – which are designed essentially for agricultural products – have been very strictly construed.[151] First, trade measures under Article 4 of the Montreal Protocol are by no means 'temporary prohibitions' in the context of Article XI(2.a). Secondly, ODSS are not 'foodstuffs'. In addition, controlled substances (for example, CFCs and specified Halons) are not be 'essential', since there already exist some substitutes available for these chemicals.[152] Thirdly, the ozone layer as a common concern of humankind (CCM)[153] does not fall under the category of tradable products.[154] Further, the Montreal Protocol's trade measures are not 'necessary to the application of standards or regulations for the classification, grading or marketing of commodities in international trade' (GATT Article XI(2.b)).

C   *The Preamble Conditions for GATT Article XX Exceptions and Article 4 of the Montreal Protocol: Compliance with the Terms of the Chapeau*

As to the question whether trade measures discriminate on justifiable and nonarbitrary bases, it can be argued that the Montreal Protocol's TREMs do not

---

150   See *Japan-Restrictions on Imports of Certain Agricultural Products*, BISD35S/163 (22 March 1988).

151   See John H. Jackson, William J. Davey and Alan O. Sykes, *Legal Problems of International Economic Relations* (3rd ed. West, 1995), p. 423; William J. Davey 'The WTO/GATT World Trading System: An Overview', in William J. Davey and Andreas F. Lowenfeld, *Handbook of WTO/GATT Dispute Settlement*, Vol.1 (1996), pp. 44–45.

152   See, for example, UNEP, *1991 Assessment Report of the Technology and Economic Assessment Panel* (December 1991); Chapter 1 in this volume.

153   See Chapter 2(III.B) in this volume.

154   See Betsy Baker, 'Protection, Not Protectionism: Multilateral Environmental Agreements and the GATT', 26 *Vanderbilt JTL* (1993), p. 449, arguing that 'the ban is certainly being applied to prevent a critical shortage of an item, ozone, that is essential to the CFC exporting country'.

constitute arbitrary discrimination and, at the same time, have not disguised trade restrictions on international trade. The ozone régime commonly set up guiding purposes in their legal texts and the foreign trade restrictions of controlled ODSs are by no means unpredictable.[155] In addition, just as the United States suggested during the negotiation of Article 4, terms of the TREMS are clear, open and environmentally-motivated.[156] If the country applying the import ban was acting with the intention of protecting human health or other related causes as listed in GATT Article XX(b) – and not seeking to protect its own ODS production – this cannot be treated as disguised restrictions.[157] The same logic also applies to the cases of the 1973 CITES and the 1989 Basel Convention.[158]

Further, we can be certain that cogent scientific evidence contributes to eliminating such arbitrary or unjustifiable discrimination between countries. It is also important to notice that a precautionary environmental 'principle' or approach[159] approved by a number of environmental agreements is in many cases subject to careful periodic reviews of trustworthy data produced by scientists and their scientific institutions.

A question arises, however, as to the application of the environmental measures, namely TREMS. The Montreal Ozone Protocol once encountered judicious criticism from the GATT Secretariat for claiming a clear distinction between parties and non-parties.[160] However, it is nevertheless possible to argue that under GATT Article XX, trade discrimination would be legally permissible provided it does not take place between countries 'where the same conditions prevail'.[161] The ozone drafters therefore inserted the following provision to ensure compatibility between Article 4 of the Montreal Protocol (as amended in 2016) and the GATT rule:

---

155   See Robert Housman et al. (eds.), *The Use of Trade Measures in Selected Multilateral Environmental Agreements* (United Nations Environment Programme, 1995), p. 83. Such legitimate environmental purposes can be observed in 'General Obligations' or 'Fundamental Principles' of these international treaties. See Chapter 2(III.D.1) in this volume.

156   See Discussion Paper by the United States, *GATT Considerations and the Ozone Protocol* (4 September 1987).

157   See Peter M. Lawrence, 'International Legal Regulation for Protection of the Ozone Layer: Some Problems of Implementation', 2 *JEL* (1990), p. 39.

158   See Robert Housman et al. (eds.), *The Use of Trade Measures in Selected Multilateral Environmental Agreements* (United Nations Environment Programme, 1995), Chapters 5 and 6

159   See Chapter 2(III.C) in this volume.

160   For the same reason, the 1973 CITES and the 1989 Basel Convention were also criticised as discriminatory. See Article 4(5) of the Basel Convention.

161   See UNEP/WG.167/2, p. 22.

Notwithstanding the provisions of this Article, imports and exports referred to in paragraphs 1 to 4 ter of this Article may be permitted from, or to, any State not party to this Protocol, if that State is determined, by a meeting of the Parties, to be in full compliance with Article 2, Articles 2A to 2J and this Article, and have submitted data to that effect as specified in Article 7.[162]

It must be noted that this provision allows export to non-parties and thus tactfully suggests that the Montreal Ozone Protocol draws a distinction between treaty compliers – regardless of whether they are parties to the Protocol or not – and noncompliers, rather than parties and non-parties.[163] In other words, a State's membership or formal status is not the ozone régime's paramount concern. Of course, non-parties to the Ozone Protocol can avoid this discrimination in so far as they would apply the Article 2 production/consumption restrictions provided by the Montreal Protocol. In light of the fact that non-parties, which seek special permission for exportation or importation, are required to submit to the UNEP Ozone Secretariat scientific and technical data on their ODS production[164] imports and exports of ODSs, it seems reasonable to suppose that they may wisely decide to ratify the Montreal Protocol in order to regain lost markets.

Unlike the Montreal Protocol, the 1989 Basel Convention has adopted trade measures that clearly distinguish between parties and non-parties, rather than treaty-compliers and non-compliers, such a restriction is not fully compatible with the one Preamble condition of GATT Article XX.[165]

In addition, it could be pointed out that the differences between production costs in countries accepting and not accepting reductions in production

---

162 See Article 4(8) of the Montreal Protocol (emphasis added). Likewise, trade provisions of the 1973 CITES would be justified unless non-parties to the treaty substantially conform to the CITES and supply comparable documentation (Article X). However, it was pointed out during the negotiation of the Montreal Protocol that 'if the Protocol were to provide for such a year-by-year escape . . . this would be a powerful incentive for states not to join the Protocol. The Protocol would be weakened from an institutional standpoint, and its environmental benefits would be nullified or impaired'. See Discussion Paper by the United States, GATT Considerations and the Ozone Protocol (4 September 1987).

163 See also UNEP/Trade/IEA/1/7, para. 13, cited in Winfried Lang, 'Trade Restrictions as a Mean of Enforcing Compliance with International Environmental Law', in Rüdiger Wolfrum (ed.), Enforcing Environmental Standards (Springer, 1996), p. 281.

164 See the discussion on compliance of non-parties in Chapter 5(VII) in this volume.

165 While the trade restrictions of the Basel Convention raise a number of serious WTO/GATT issues, in practice, parties to the treaty would appear more likely to conclude appropriate bilateral agreements under Article 11 than to initiate a WTO/GATT challenge.

and use of ODSS could make them countries where the 'same conditions' do not prevail.[166] Moreover, it would be possible to argue that, unlike the parties to the Ozone Protocol, non-parties are not subject to the NCP of the Montreal Protocol. This would also support the argument that the same conditions do not prevail between parties and non-parties.[167] Yet, as the UNEP Ozone Secretariat suggests, if the Meeting of the Parties decides to take a 'countermeasure' as listed in the NCP – that is, suspension of Protocol privileges[168] then the 'same condition' would prevail.[169]

With regard to the 1973 CITES, Professor Wold plausibly argues that restrictions on trade with non-parties under the CITES régime would not discriminate between countries where the same conditions prevail, in so far as parties to the environmental treaty, which comply with substantive provisions of the CITES, operate under a strict régime affecting their economy and trade.[170]

D   *GATT Article XX(b) and the Protection of the Ozone Layer*
It must be noted at the outset that during the negotiation of the 1987 version of the Montreal Ozone Protocol, the GATT Secretariat said that 'such an article on control of trade would be in order in accordance with article XX paragraph (b) of the GATT concerning the protection of human, animal or plant life or

---

166 Such differences in production costs, boosted by MEA compliance, would be a matter of foreign trade competition. However, it should be noted that 'it is impossible to distinguish between the sort of cost difference... and that caused, for example, by differences in the minimum wage'. It is also interesting to note that if 'different conditions' under GATT Article XX contain environmental law in different countries, the 'internationalisation of environmental costs' would grow. This does not require an amendment of Article XX. See Ralf Buckley, 'International Trade, Investment and Environmental Regulation: An Environmental Perspective', 27 JWT (1993), p. 132.

167 See Robert Housman et al. (eds.), *The Use of Trade Measures in Selected Multilateral Environmental Agreements* (United Nations Environment Programme, 1995), pp. 81–82.

168 See Chapter 5(IV.B(3)(a)) in this volume.

169 In this respect, see Benedict Kingsbury, 'Environment and Trade: The GATT/WTO Regime in the International Legal System', in Alan E. Boyle (ed.), *Environmental Regulation and Economic Growth* (Oxford University Press, 1994), p. 207, noting that the 'question as to whether the same conditions exist and, if so, what forms of discrimination would be arbitrary or unjustified, are potentially problematic, particularly as in some cases the onus of demonstrating that a measure is justified under Article XX appears to rest on the party relying on it'.

170 See Chris Wold, 'The Conservation on International Trade in Endangered Species of Wild Fauna and Flora', in Robert Housman et al. (eds.), *The Use of Trade Measures in Selected Multilateral Environmental Agreements* (United Nations Environment Programme, 1995), pp. 178–180 and 190–192.

health'.[171] Added to this, there is fairly general agreement that Article 4 TREMS of the Montreal Protocol seem to qualify for the exception under Article xx(b) due to growing threats to human, animal and plant life and health from the severe depletion of the stratospheric ozone layer.

(1) Article 4 of the Montreal Protocol is 'Necessary' to Protect Human Health and the Environment: GATT Article xx(b) and International Environmental Law

As we have seen in Chapter 2(III.A) and the Introduction to this volume, degradation of the ozone layer would result in injury not only to the health of human beings but also to the ecosystem as a whole.[172] The global protection of the ozone layer is indispensable for maintenance of human health. In this connection, it is worth noting that, as the 1994 Final Report of the Sub-Commission (the so-called 'Ksentini Report') asserts '[a]ll persons have the right to freedom from pollution, environmental degradation and activities that adversely affect the environment, threaten life, health, livelihood, well-being or sustainable development within, across or outside national boundaries'.[173]

As was described earlier, scientific uncertainty regarding ozone observations was already settled after the adoption of the 1987 Montreal Protocol.[174] Surely, this will lessen to a great extent the ozone régime members' burden of proof that GATT Article xx exceptions would apply to their environmental legal régime. The 'principle' of sound scientific evidence would not be used as opposed to the ozone régime's precautionary approach for the protection of the environment.[175] In addition, it is particularly important to note that – as Professor Petersmann rightly observes[176] – since all GATT contracting parties

---

171 It should be noted that the GATT Secretariat stressed that the final judgement as to whether the action proposed satisfied Article xx lay with the GATT contracting parties themselves. See UNEP/WG.172/2, p. 18. See also UNEP/167/2, p. 22; Ernst-Ulrich Petersmann, 'International Trade Law and International Environmental Law: Prevention and Settlement of International Environmental Disputes in GATT', 27 JWT (1993), pp. 74 et seq.

172 See Chapter 2(III.A) in this volume.

173 UN Document, E/CN.4/Sub.2/1994/9 (6 July 1994), reprinted in Alan E. Boyle, 'The Role of International Human Rights Law in the Protection of the Environment', in Alan E. Boyle and Michael R. Anderson (eds.), *Human Rights Approaches to Environmental Protection* (Clarendon Press, 1996), pp. 65–69.

174 See Chapter 3(IV.A) in this volume.

175 In the meeting of the CTE, one WTO member suggested that the principle of a sound scientific basis, rather than the precautionary principle should be used for environmental measures. See WTO, *Trade and Environment*, PRESS/TE010 (8 July 1996), Item 2. On the precautionary 'principle' or approach, see Chapter 2(III.C.2.b) in this volume.

176 See Ernst-Ulrich Petersmann, 'The Settlement of International Environmental Disputes in GATT and EEC' (FIELD London Conference, 23 April 1993), p. 12 and note 19.

have recognised the customary law rule of Stockholm Principle 21 and Rio Principle 2,[177] this established rule of international environmental law must be taken into account in interpreting the GATT trade law rules. Viewed from this perspective, the parties to the Montreal Protocol could argue collectively or individually that Article 4 trade restrictions would protect human, animal and plant life at the domestic levels. The global protection of the stratospheric ozone layer is a matter of no small concern to each country in the international community and therefore the unique trade control system is 'necessary' to protect parties' own environments.

Article 4 TREMS of the Montreal Protocol could therefore be justified or exempted under GATT Article XX(b) as 'necessary' environment-related trade measures that are consistent with GATT trade law. Likewise, it is also possible to argue that trade restrictions of endangered species of wildlife under the 1973 CITES are also 'necessary' in order to protect the life and health of animals and plants listed in the Appendixes. These measures would fall within the category of GATT Article XX(b).

An expected opposing argument is that, as Schoenbaum argued,[178] the principal purpose of Article 4 TREMS of the Montreal Protocol is only to encourage non-parties to join the ozone regime and therefore this could be done by other available means, including financial and technical assistance through the Protocol's Financial Mechanism. While the ozone regime's stated purpose has been 'to protect human health and the environment against adverse effects',[179] it seems difficult to deny, however, that Article 4 trade provisions as certain kind of collective 'sanctions' specifically aim to secure States' participation.[180]

---

177 See Chapter 2(III.C(1)) in this volume.

178 See Thomas J. Schoenbaum, 'Free International Trade and Protection of the Environment: Irreconcilable Conflicts?', 86 *AJIL* (1992), p. 720; Markus Schlagenhof, 'Trade Measures based on Environmental Processes and Production Methods', 30 *JWT* (1995), p. 149; Duncan Brack, 'The Shrimp-Turtle Case: Implications for the Multilateral Environmental Agreement – World Trade Organization Debate', 9 *YbkIEL* (1998), p. 17, stating that '[t]he entire point of the trade measures directed against non-parties to the Montreal Protocol is to compel them to change their policies, to phase out the production and consumption of ozone-depleting substances in the same way as parties, or, at least, to make market access to parties conditional on this phase-out policy. It is intentionally discriminatory between parties and non-parties or, to be more accurate, between countries in compliance with the protocol (whether they are formally parties or not) and those not in compliance. It is difficult to believe that the panel and the Appellate Body could maintain their lines of reasoning and still find in favour of this kind of trade measures'. See also Ernst-Ulrich Petersmann, 'International Trade and International Environmental Law: Prevention and Settlement of International Environmental Disputes in GATT', 27 *JWT* (1993), p. 76.

179 See Chapter 2(III) in this volume.

180 See Section II(A) above.

In this similar vein, the 1990–91 GATT Report on International Trade suggests that 'the parties to the Montreal Protocol on Chlorofluorocarbons (CFCs) could have structured the Protocol in such a way that it reduced consumption of CFCs in the participating countries by the target amount, without the necessity of including provisions for special restrictions on trade with non-parties'.[181]

It is still unlikely, however, that these economic measures constitute 'reasonably available alternatives' to the Protocol's Article 4 restrictions, which are, as we have seen, skilfully drafted so as to prevent potential 'free-riders' in the international community of over 190 States. Though seen as less inconsistent with the GATT, they cannot be arguably 'alternative measures' in the context of ozone protection: 'all options reasonably available' to the parties to the Protocol having been exhausting, ozone would be completely depleted and all States would then be subject to cumulative and serious adverse effects.

(2)   Environmental Objectives of the International Ozone Régime Are Widely Recognised by the International Community

It is also important to note that nearly two hundred States are contracting parties to both the Montreal Protocol and the 1985 Vienna Ozone Layer Convention. This could mean that the environmental objectives of the international ozone régime have been widely accepted in the international legal community as a whole. Indeed, as the GATT Secretariat states:

> GATT rules could never block the adoption of environmental policies which have broad support in the world community .... What the rules do constrain is attempts by one or a small number of countries to influence environmental policies in other countries not by persuasion and negotiation, but by unilateral reductions in access to their markets.[182]

---

181   The GATT Report advocates, for instance, a proposal to impose taxes on the consumption of CFCs. '[O]ne way would be to impose taxes on the consumption of CFCs, or quota on domestic consumption, implemented by a system of auctioned domestic sales licences which permitted the licence holder to buy from all potential suppliers, regardless of whether they are in a participating country. In either case, the scarcity value of the reduced amount of CFCs would accrue to the government (in the form of tax or auction receipts). Production of CFCs in participating countries could then be regulated by quotas set at the projected level of consumption in those countries' (cited in Vinod Rege, 'GATT Law and Environment-Related Issues Affecting the Trade of Developing Countries', 28 JWT (1994), p. 124). See also Alice Enders and Amelia Porges, 'Successful Conventions and Conventional Success: Saving the Ozone Layer', in Kym Anderson and Richard Blackhurst (eds.), *The Greening of World Trade Issues* (Prentice-Hall, 1992), pp. 133 et seq.

182   'Trade and the Environment: A Report Prepared by the GATT Secretariat (1992)', reprinted in John H. Jackson, William J. Davey and Alan O. Sykes, *Legal Problems of International*

Perhaps one may notice here that this point is in line with Principle 12 of the 1992 Rio Declaration on Environment and Development, which states:

> Environmental measures addressing transboundary or global environmental problems should, as far as possible, be based on an international consensus.[183]

It may be suggested that a failure to attempt to reach international consensus may establish arbitrary discrimination.[184] Similarly, the 1994 TBT Agreement provides that technical regulations that are prepared, adopted, or applied in accordance with relevant international standards are rebuttably presumed not to create an unnecessary barrier to international trade.[185]

In contrast, in the *Tuna* cases,[186] the United States adopted a unilateral trade policy (that is, an embargo against Mexican tuna) based on the Marine Mammal Protection Act (MMPA), which is national act based on PPM[187] standards (harvesting techniques), still lacking in widely obtained international support. Consequently, the GATT Panels decided that such a trade embargo could not be justified under the exceptions in GATT Article XX(b) or XX(g).

It is assumed that, should the United States apply the trade measure under the authority of a related international environmental agreement, the GATT Panels might approve the GATT Article XX exception(s).[188] In this regard, at the meetings of the WTO's CTE, many government delegations repeatedly warned against the use of unilateral trade measures for environmental purposes, and indicated a general preference for multilateral approaches over any form of unilateral measures.[189]

     Economic Relations (3rd ed. West, 1995), p. 566. The final judgement of a bilateral dispute would depend on the decision of contracting parties to the WTO/GATT, however.

183   UN Doc. A/CONF.151/5/Rev.1, reprinted in 31 *ILM* (1992), p. 878.

184   See Margaret A. Young, 'Principle 12: The Environment and Trade', in Jorge E. Viñuales (ed.), *The Rio Declaration on Environment and Development: A Commentary* (Oxford University Press, 2015), p. 341.

185   See Article 2. On the legal validity of the 'dolphin-safe' label introduced by the US, see *United States – Measures concerning the Importation, Marketing and Sale of Tuna and Tuna Products*, WT/DS381/AB/R (16 May 2012); Armin Rosencranz and Aditya Vora, 'Two Decades of the Tuna-Dolphin Dispute: A New Wrinkle', 46/3–4 *EPL* (2016), pp. 213–217.

186   See panel reports on the *Tuna* cases I and II, reproduced in 30 *ILM* (1991), p. 1594 and 33 *ILM* (1994), p. 839.

187   See Section E below.

188   See *Tuna* Panel I, para. 5.28. See also Wen-Chen Shih, 'Multilateralism and the Case of Taiwan in the Trade Environment Nexus', 30 *JWT* (1996), p. 131.

189   In the CTE, several delegations cautioned that the 'only appropriate and effective manner with which to address transboundary environmental problems at the international

E   *GATT Article XX(g) and the Protection of the Ozone Layer*

As regards Article XX(g), since GATT Article XX does not make reference to the term 'environment' itself – neither do the WTO Agreements provide the definition of this term – it is debatable whether the protection of the ozone layer falls into the category of 'exhaustible natural resources' in the context of the GATT trade law.[190]

It is said that, in light of the drafting history of Article XX(g), that the 'natural resources' in question can be generally considered as 'resources of certain economic value rather than resources not exploitable economically in any shape or form'.[191] Presumably, they include renewable flow resources (for example, animals, plants and fisheries) as well as stock resources (for example, minerals).[192] Given that, we may say that the protection of life and health of listed animals and plants under the 1973 CITES is directly concerned with the 'exhaustible natural resources', and trade measures under the environmental treaty might cover the meaning of GATT Article XX(g) exceptions.[193] In the *Shrimp/Turtle* case, the Appellate Body held that sea turtles, listed in Appendix I of the CITES, constituted resources for the purposes of GATT Article XX(g)[194] and stated that '[t]hey [words of Article XX(g), "exhaustible natural resources"] must be read by a treaty interpreter in the light of contemporary concerns of the community of nations about the protection and conservation of the environment. While Article XX was not modified in the Uruguay Round, the preamble attached to the WTO Agreement shows that the signatories to that Agreement were, in 1994, fully aware of the importance and legitimacy of environmental protection as a goal of national and international policy. The preamble of the WTO Agreement [....] explicitly acknowledges "the objective

---

       level was through MEAS' (WTO, *Trade and Environment News Bulletin*, TE006 (8 December 1995)). On unilateralism in the context of environmental protection, see, for example, Ilona Cheyne, 'Environmental Unilateralism and the WTO/GATT System', 24 *Georgia JICL* (1995), pp. 433–465.

190   See Peter M. Lawrence, 'International Legal Regulation for Protection of the Ozone Layer: Some Problems of Implementation', 2 *JEL* (1990), p. 39.

191   See ibid.

192   See Ernst-Ulrich Petersmann, 'International Trade Law and International Environmental Law', 27 *JWT* (1993), p. 70, note 55. See also Steve Charnoviz, 'Exploring the Environmental Exceptions in GATT Article XX', 25 *JWT* (1991), pp. 45–47. The *Tuna* case I (para. 5.26) and the *Tuna* case II (para. 5.13); the *Shrimp-Turtle* case (paras. 128–131).

193   See Robert Housman et al. (eds.), *The Use of Trade Measures in Selected Multilateral Environmental Agreements* (United Nations Environment Programme, 1995), pp. 181–182.

194   See WT/DS58/AB/R, paras. 128–134. See also Mitsuo Matsushita, Thomas J. Schoenbaum and Petros C. Mavroidis, *The World Trade Organization: Law, Practice, and Policy* (2nd ed. Oxford University Press, 2006), p. 797.

of *sustainable development*".[195] Further, in the panel report on *United States' Standards for Gasoline*, the WTO/GATT panel observed that clean air was an 'exhaustible natural resource' in the context of Article XX(g).[196]

In the context of the ozone layer, we should take into account that the cumulative effects of stratospheric ozone loss on plants (including crops), animals and global climate could hinder the world's food production.[197] Theoretically speaking, the 'complete destruction' of the ozone layer, as Dotto and Schiff suggested with some emphasis, would result in 'the end of all life on earth'.[198] In this respect, although the stratospheric ozone in itself is free from any economic value, it may be possible to argue that 'policy' for ozone conservation would fall within the range of laws or policies regarding the conservation of 'exhaustible natural resources'. Article 4 restrictions would thus seem to qualify under Article XX(g).[199] In this connection, one knowledgeable commentator on GATT trade law observes that the wording of the Article XX exceptions seems to address most trade-related environmental objectives.[200]

Added to the above-mentioned requirement for an Article XX(g) environmental exception was previously – as stated in a panel report on *Canada's Restrictions on Exports of Unprocessed Herring and Salmon* – that a trade measure as to the conservation of natural resources must primarily be aimed at rendering effective restrictions on domestic production or consumption (that is, effectiveness requirement).[201] Nevertheless, the 90 per cent of the protective

---

195   See WT/DS58/AB/R, para. 129 (emphasis original).

196   See WT/DS2/AB/R, para. 6.37, noting that 'a *policy* to reduce the depletion of clean air was a *policy* to conserve a natural resource within the meaning of Article Xx(g)' (emphasis added). See also WT/DS2/AB/R, Section B.

197   See Introduction to this volume.

198   See Lydia Dott and Harald Schiff, *The Ozone War* (Doubleday, 1978), p. 2.

199   The same opinion is expressed in Rosalind Twum-Barima and Laura B. Campbell, *Protecting the Ozone Layer through Trade Measures* (United Nations Environment Programme, 1994), p. 71; Alex Bree, *Harmonization of the Dispute Settlement Mechanisms of the Multilateral Environmental Agreements and the World Trade Agreements* (Erich Schmidt, 2003), p. 47.

200   See Ernst-Ulrich Petersmann, 'International Trade Law and International Environmental Law: Prevention and Settlement of International Environmental Disputes in GATT', 27 *JWT* (1993), p. 72.

201   See BISD 35S/98 (22 March 1988), p. 114. See also *Tuna* Panel I, para. 5.31; *United States- Standards for Reformulated and Conventional Gasoline*, WT/DS2/R, paras. 6.39–6.40; the *Shrimp-Turtle* case, WT/DS58/AB/R, paras. 135–141: and Ernst-Ulrich Petersmann, *The GATT/WTO Dispute Settlement System* (Kluwer Law International, 1997), p. 116, noting that 'the term "relating to" need no longer be interpreted as "primarily aimed at"'.

ozone layer (stratospheric ozone shield) is located in the upper atmosphere area. More recently, in the *China – Measures Related to the Exportation of Various Raw Materials* case, the Appellate Body suggests that:[202]

> it did not consider that, in order to be justified under Article xx(g), measures "relating to the conservation of exhaustible natural resources" must be primarily aimed at rendering effective restrictions on domestic production or consumption. Instead, the Appellate Body read the terms "in conjunction with", "quite plainly", as "together with" or "jointly with", and found no additional requirement that the conservation measure be primarily aimed at making effective certain restrictions on domestic production or consumption.

With regard to jurisdictional issues, the Panel in the *Tuna* I case decided that GATT Article xx(b) and (g) had no application to natural resources located outside the jurisdiction of the trade-restricting state.[203] In this context, one commentator has observed that the CITES régime violates GATT Article XI(1) due to trade restrictions applied to natural resources outside the jurisdiction of a party.[204] However, the next Panel in the *Tuna* case II suggested that the text of environmental exceptions does not explicitly provide any jurisdictional limitation as far as public international law permits governments to exercise jurisdiction over their nationals and vessels outside their territory.[205] Likewise, Professor David Pearce points out, the legal text of the GATT does not strongly indicate the 'location' of the environmental damage done relevant to an exception.[206] In the *Shrimp-Turtle* case, the Appellate Body stated that 'there is a sufficient nexus between the migratory and endangered marine populations involved and the United States for the purposes of Article xx(g)', and it purposely avoided the issues of jurisdiction.[207] In the context of the global protection of the ozone layer, it must be emphasised that, since the depletion of the

---

202 *China – Measures Related to the Exportation of Various Raw Materials*, WT/DS394/395/398 (30 January 2012), para. 358.

203 See the *Tuna* case I, paras. 5.26 and 5.31–5.32.

204 See Thomas J. Schoenbaum, 'Tree International Trade and Protection of the Environment', 86 *AJIL* (1992), p. 720.

205 See the *Tuna* case II, paras. 5.15–5.20, 5.31–5.33.

206 See David Pearce, 'The Greening of the GATT: Some Economic Considerations', in James Cameron, Paul Demaret and Damien Geradin (eds.), *Trade and the Environment*, Vol. 1 (Cameron, 1994), p. 25.

207 See WT/DS58/AB/R, para. 133 (emphasis added).

ozone will not respect territorial boundaries, the above-mentioned argument presented by the *Tuna* Panel II cannot not be overemphasised.

VI   Conclusions

It should be concluded, from what has been observed above, that we can broadly accept the coexistence of the TREMs in the Montreal Protocol (Article 4) with the free-market principles or rules governing the WTO/GATT trade law régime. At the very least, the Montreal Ozone Protocol's Article 4 could be seen as compatible with Article XX(b) of the GATT trade rules. Viewed in its entirety, Article 4 of the Montreal Ozone Protocol thus seems to be a 'non-discriminatory' trade measures for the protection of the ozone layer. Hence, the Montreal Protocol seems to form an important environmental exception to the international free trade principles and rules of WTO/GATT law.

However, apart from the above-mentioned problems of Article 4 of the Ozone Protocol, there will be further points which need to be clarified regarding the relationship between the WTO/GATT régime and other existing MEAs, such as the 1989 Basel Convention, the 1973 CITES, the climate change régime and the Biodiversity Convention. In addition, the potential tension or conflicts may exist between future international environmental régimes which decide to use trade restrictions and the existing WTO/GATT régime. TREMs provided for in these MEAs must be applied and enforced in practice for their environmental objectives.

Although the potential amendments to GATT law for environmental protection have not been discussed here, it might still be desirable or advisable for members to partly amend the GATT Article XX and other environment-related provisions, so as not to retard the evolving concept of 'sustainable development' in international law.[208] This assumption seemed to have been widely accepted in legal writing:[209] as one commentator says, generally speaking, the

---

208   See Richard G. Tarasofsky, 'Ensuring Compatibility between Multilateral Environmental Agreements and GATT/WTO', 7 *YbkIEL* (1996), p. 54, noting the legal uncertainty and 'the chill effect' on elaborating TERMs in future MEAs.

209   See, for example, James Cameron and Jonathan Robinson, 'The Use of Trade Provisions in International Agreements and Their Compatibility with the GATT', 2 *YbkIEL* (1991), pp. 18 et seq.; Mitsuo Matsushita, Thomas J. Schoenbaum and Petros C. Mavroidis, *The World Trade Organization: Law, Practice, and Policy* (2nd ed. Oxford University Press, 2006), pp. 804–805; Shinya Murase, 'Perspectives from International Economic Law on Transnational Environmental Issue', 253 *Recueil des cours* (1995), pp. 347–348; Murase, 'Trade

WTO is reluctant to allow environmental requirements on the basis of the existing framework of GATT Article XX.[210] However, it is also true that adding amendments to GATT trade law depends on the strong political will of the contracting parties of the trade law régime and, in practice, this will be extremely difficult.[211] It has been suggested that at the CTE circle, developing States are generally opposed to making any modification to the WTO trade rules in favour of MEAs.[212] Or alternatively, as Philippe Sands and Jacqueline Peel argue, given that 'the WTO Appellate Body has been inspired by rules of international arising outside the WTO', the amendments of the GATT instruments may not be necessary any more.[213] A second-best option could be the adoption of authoritative interpretation by the Ministerial Conference and by the General

---

and the Environment: With Particular Reference to Climate Change Issues', in Harald Hohmann (ed.), *Agreeing and Implementing the Doha Round of the WTO* (Cambridge University Press, 2008), pp. 401–402; Thomas J. Schoenbaum, 'International Trade and Protection of the Environment', 91 *AJIL* (1997), pp. 268–313; Daniel Bodansky and Jessica C. Lawrence, 'Trade and Environment', in Daniel Bethlehem, Isabelle Van Damme, Donald McRae and Rodney Neufeld (eds.), *The Oxford Handbook of International Trade Law* (Oxford University Press, 2009), pp. 535–536; Cinnamon Carlarne, 'The Kyoto Protocol and the WTO: Reconciling Tensions between Free Trade and Environmental Objectives', 17 *Colorado JIELP* (2005/2006), p. 86. However, see also GATT, *Trade and the Environment: News and Views from the GATT,* TE004 (26 November 1993), p. 3; Ernst-Ulrich Petersmann, 'International Trade Law and International Environmental Law', 27 *JWT* (1993), p. 72.

210 See Shawkat Alam, 'Trade and the Environment: Perspectives from the Global South', in Shawkat Alam, Sumudu Atapattu, Carmen G. Gonzalez, and Jona Razzaque (eds.), *International Environmental Law and the Global South* (Oxford University Press, 2015), p. 305.

211 Amendment of GATT Article XX requires two-thirds majority of the Members (Article X of the WTO Agreement), but forced votes will be rare. See Yuji Iwasawa, *WTO no Funsō Shori* [WTO Dispute Settlement] (Sanseido, 1995), p. 9 (in Japanese); Shinya Murase, 'Perspectives from International Economic Law on Transnational Environmental Issues', 253 *Recueil des cours* (1995), pp. 346–348. See also John H. Jackson, *The World Trading System* (2nd ed. MIT Press, 1997), p. 343, noting that the difficulty of amending the texts could lead to a host of 'ad hoc or other "end-run" type measures'.

212 See Richard G. Tarasofsky, 'Ensuring Compatibility between MEAs and GATT/WTO', 7 *YbkIEL* (1996), p. 61 and note 49

213 Philippe Sands and Jacqueline Peel, *Principles of International Environmental Law* (3rd ed. Cambridge University Press, 2012), p. 867. See also William J. Davey, *Non-discrimination in the World Trade Organization: The Rules and Exceptions* (Martinus Nijhoff, 2012), p. 278, stating that 'the scope of the Article XX (b) exception has been interpreted quite broadly. Thus, the concerns that existed in the late 1980s and 1990s that GATT Article XX (b) was inadequate to allow Governments to adopt appropriate health measures .... seem overblown today'.

Council,[214] or the adopting of a new WTO side agreement.[215] It is hoped that the CTE, in cooperation with MEA secretariats, would contribute to settling the question as to the disputed legal status of trade provisions of MEAs,[216] such as those in the Montreal Ozone Layer Protocol within the WTO/GATT régime.

---

214 See Christiane R. Conrad, *Processes and Production Methods (PPMs) in WTO Law* (Cambridge University Press, 2011), p. 438.

215 See Duncan Brack, 'The Shrimp-Turtle Case: Implications for the Multilateral Environmental Agreement – World Trade Organization Debate', 9 *YbkIEL* (1998), p. 19.

216 See Steve Charnovitz, 'The WTO's Environmental Progress', in William J. Davey and John Jackson (eds.), *The Future of International Economic Law* (Oxford University Press, 2008), p. 252, stating that '[t]he value of such mutual socialization should not be underestimated'. At a flagship event on trade and environment marking the 20th anniversary of the WTO, Director-General Roberto Azevêdo mentioned that '[i]n the 20 years since then, the connections between trade and the environment have grown significantly. We must therefore do more to ensure that trade and environmental policies work better together, both at national and international levels. Today we have taken an important step forward to improve multilateral cooperation and dialogue on these issues'. WTO, Press Release, PRESS/741 (28 April 2015), p. 1.

PART 4

The Compliance System of the Montreal Protocol

∵

CHAPTER 5

The Montreal Non-Compliance Procedure and the Functions of the Internal International Organs

I   The Montreal Non-Compliance Procedure (NCP)

A   *The Judicial Settlement of International Environmental Disputes*
International environmental disputes do arise on sundry occasions, and corresponding means of settling these disputes often vary widely in accordance with the type of issues involved, the type of natural resources, the parties concerned, geographical scope, the source of pollution or adverse effects, and the nature of the harm done, its potential remedies, and so forth.[1] In order to fully guarantee treaty compliance with their environment-related obligations, the dispute settlement mechanisms of international environmental régimes must be designed properly and flexibly to enable these régimes to settle, or ideally avoid, such various kinds of environmental disputes.

In actual practice, however, it is disappointing that a number of environmental agreements contain inadequate dispute settlement clauses in their legal instruments. In addition, traditional and legally binding methods of dispute settlement procedures – such as those envisaged in Article 33 of the United Nations Charter – are not necessarily preferred approaches to settling environmental disputes at the international level, because of their highly complex procedures, a lack of confidence, time-consuming legal processes with considerable expense, and long-pending problems as to the principles of State responsibility.[2] Consequently, States do not usually resort to these strictly judicial procedures, even though several environmental agreements provide the widest possible choice of legal devices for the settlement of disputes, for example, the dispute 'settlement' procedures under Article 11 of the Ozone

---

*   An earlier version of this chapter appeared in 10 *Colorado Journal of International Environmental Law and Policy* (1999), pp. 95–141.

1   For a further discussion of 'international' or 'transnational' environmental disputes, see Richard B. Bilder, 'The Settlement of Disputes in the Field of the International Law of the Environment', 144 *Recueil des cours* (1973), pp. 153–236.

2   See ibid., pp. 225–227; Patricia Birnie, Alan Boyle and Catherine Redgwell, *International Law and the Environment* (3rd ed. Oxford University Press, 2009), pp. 211 et seq. See also Chapter 2(III.C) in this volume.

© KONINKLIJKE BRILL NV, LEIDEN, 2019 | DOI:10.1163/9789004290877_007

Convention.[3] In most cases, States are more inclined to retain their freedom of action relying on the principle of State sovereignty.[4]

Naturally, where an appropriate or reliable dispute avoidance or settlement mechanism or system still does not exist for the purpose of ensuring treaty performance, it would often be much easier for régime Member States to ignore their established treaty obligations. Analysing these real-life situations, Professor Palmer thus observed in the early 1990s that 'nearly twenty years after the Stockholm Declaration, we still lack the institutional and legal mechanisms to deal effectively with transboundary and biosphere environmental degradation'.[5]

B   *The Avoidance and Quasi-Judicial Settlement of Multilateral Environmental Disputes: the Non-Compliance Procedure (NCP)*

It is possible to argue that 'ozone disputes' can arise from non-compliance relating to 'compatibility with the objectives of international régimes',[6] for non-performance of ozone treaty obligations would affect the international community as a whole, rather than being geographically limited to particular sovereign States or individuals under State jurisdictions. In this sense, potential ozone disputes differ radically from environmental disputes or conflicts concerning transboundary air pollution or conservation of living and non-living natural resources.[7] Judging from the above, we may say therefore that 'there is undoubtedly need for regime-specific legal compliance mechanisms'.[8]

With this background in mind, drafters of the Montreal Protocol's dispute avoidance and settlement system have become more concerned with the crucial question of ensuring greater compliance with the ozone treaties' obligations that generally deal with the application and interpretation of complex

---

3   In this respect, see Yuji Iwasawa, *WTO no Funsō Shori* [WTO Dispute Settlement] (Sanseido, 1995), p. 55 (in Japanese). Professor Iwasawa suggests that the role of the ICJ in 'settling' economic disputes (of a highly technical nature) is rather limited and treaty instruments regarding international economy do not usually include resort to the international tribunal.

4   Indeed, it is true that the most frequently used mechanism for settling international and transnational environmental disputes is, without doubt, direct discussion of a dispute between States concerned, that is, official and/or unofficial diplomatic negotiation and consultations.

5   See Geoffrey Palmer, 'New Ways to Make International Environmental Law', 86 *AJIL* (1992), p. 259.

6   See Shinya Murase, 'Perspectives from International Economic Law on Transnational Environmental Issues', 253 *Recueil des cours* (1995), p. 415.

7   See Chapter 3(III.A) in this volume.

8   See Günther Handl, 'Controlling Implementation of and Compliance with International Environmental Commitments: The Rocky Road from Rio', 5 *Colorado JIELP* (1994), p. 327.

THE MONTREAL NON-COMPLIANCE PROCEDURE 213

and detailed environment-related obligations and standards – for example, ODS emission reductions (Articles 2 and 5), trade controls of CFCs/ODSs (Article 4) and national and regional reporting requirements (Articles 7 and 9) – than with purely legalistic and political issues in the branch of customary international law or international human rights law. As a result of their pioneering endeavours,[9] a flexible arrangement for environmental dispute avoidance and settlement – that is, a 'non-compliance procedure' (NCP)[10] has been added as an integral part to the Montreal Ozone Protocol (Article 8/Decisions). It is said that the creation of the Implementation Committee in particular constituted a 'real breakthrough' in international environmental law.[11]

At present, NCPs are incorporated in many multilateral environmental agreements (MEAS).[12] Some examples of these MEAS include the following: the NCP under the 1979 Convention on Long-Range Transboundary Air Pollution and its Protocols;[13] the Mechanism for Promoting Implementation and

---

9   On the negotiation of the NCP, see Section II below.

10   An 'internal' compliance-monitoring or dispute avoidance and settlement mechanism based on Article 8 of the Montreal Protocol. Some authors, such as Patrick Széll, describe the NCP as a 'régime'. See, for example, Patrick Széll, 'Compliance Regimes for Multilateral Environmental Agreements', 27/4 *EPL* (1997), pp. 304–307.

11   See Alexander-Charles Kiss, 'Compliance with International and European Environmental Obligations', *Hague YbkIL* (1996) p. 51; Lakshman D. Guruswamy, Geoffrey W.R. Palmer and Burns H. Weston (eds.), *International Environmental Law and World Order* (West Pub. Co. 1994), p. 1120.

12   See, for example, Pierr-Marie Dupuy and Jorge E. Viñuales, *International Environmental Law* (Cambridge University Press), pp. 285–292; Susana Borràs, 'Comparative Analysis of Selected Compliance Procedures under Multilateral Environmental Agreements', in Sandrine Maljean-Dubois and Lavanya Rajamani (eds.), *Implementation of International Environmental Law* (Martinus Nijhoff, 2011), pp. 319–371; Osamu Yoshida, 'Procedural Aspects of the International Legal Regime for Climate Change: Early Operation of the Kyoto Protocol Compliance System', 4 *JEAIL* (2011), pp. 42–44.

13   See Doc. EB.AIR/WG.5/CPR.13; Decision 2012/25 on improving the Functioning of the Implementation Committee, Annex: Implementation Committee, Its Structure and Functions and Procedures for Review, in ECE/EB.AIR/113/Add.1, available at: <http://www.unece.org/fileadmin/DAM/env/documents/2012/EB/Decision_2012_25.pdf> (last visited on 31 January 2018). For a recent development of the NCP, see Enrico Milano, 'Procedures and Mechanisms for Review of Compliance under the 1979 Long-Range Transboundary Air Pollution Convention and Its Protocols', in Tullio Treves et al. (eds.), *Non-Compliance Procedures and Mechanisms and the Effectiveness of International Environmental Agreements* (T.M.C. Asser Press, 2009), pp. 169–180; 'Practice of the Implementation Committee under the Convention on Long-Range Transboundary Air Pollution', in Ulrich Beyerlin, Peter-Tobias Stoll and Rüdiger Wolfrum (eds.), *Ensuring Compliance with Multilateral Environmental Agreements* (Martinus Nijhoff, 2006), pp. 39–48; Tuomas Kuokkanen, 'The Convention on Long-Range Transboundary Air Pollution', in Geir Ulfstein (ed.), *Making Treaties Work* (Cambridge University Press, 2007), pp. 166–175.

Compliance with the 1989 Basel Convention;[14] the Compliance Procedures and Mechanisms of the Protocol to the 1972 Convention on the Prevention of Marine Pollution by Dumping of Wastes and Other Matter (1996 Protocol);[15] the Procedures and Mechanisms on Compliance under the 2000 Cartagena Protocol on Biosafety to the 1992 Convention on Biological Diversity (2000 Cartagena Protocol);[16] and the Procedures and Mechanisms established under the Kyoto Protocol:[17] and the Review of Compliance under the 1998 Aarhus Convention on Access to Information, Public Participation in Decision-making

14   See 'Mechanism for Promoting Implementation and Compliance of the Basel Convention on the Transboundary Movements of Hazardous Wastes and Their Disposal', Decision VI/12, Sixth Conference of the Parties, 9–13 December 2002, UNEP/CHW.6/40, reproduced in Philippe Cullet and Alix Gowlland-Gualtieri (eds.), *Key Materials in International Environmental Law* (Ashgate, 2004), p. 628. For an analysis of the NCP, see Akiho Shibata, 'Ensuring Compliance with the Basel Convention – Its Unique Features', in Ulrich Beyerlin, Peter-Tobias Stoll and Rüdiger Wolfrum (eds.), *Ensuring Compliance with Multilateral Environmental Agreements* (Martinus Nijhoff, 2006), pp. 69–87.

15   Article 11. See 'Compliance Procedures and Mechanisms Pursuant to Article 11 of the 1996 Protocol to the London Convention 1972, adopted in 2007, LC 29/17, Annex 7; Seline Trevisanut, 'The Compliance Procedures and Mechanisms of the 1996 Protocol to the 1972 London Convention on the Prevention of Marine Pollution by Dumping of Wastes and other Matter', Tullio Treves et al. (eds.), *Non-Compliance Procedures and Mechanisms and the Effectiveness of International Environmental Agreements* (T.M.C. Asser Press, 2009), pp. 49–61.

16   Article 34. See Decision BS-I/7 (Establishment of Procedures and Mechanisms on Compliance under the Cartagena Protocol on Biosafety), UNEP/CBD/BS/COP-MOP/1/15, Annex, available at: <https://www.cbd.int/decision/mop/default.shtml?id=8289> (last visited on 31 January 2018); Elas Tsioumani, 'Nagoya Protocol CoP/MoP-1: Entry Into Force and Compliance Procedures', 44/6 *EPL* (2014), pp. 513–516; Chiara Ragni, 'Procedures and Mechanisms on Compliance under the 2000 Cartagem Protocol on Biosafety to the 1992 Convention on Biological Diversity', Tullio Treves et al. (eds.), *Non-Compliance Procedures and Mechanisms and the Effectiveness of International Environmental Agreements* (T.M.C. Asser Press, 2009), pp. 101–120.

17   Article 18. See 'Procedures and Mechanisms Relating to Compliance under the Kyoto Protocol', Decision 27/CMP.1, in FCCC/KP/CMP/2005/8/Add.3; 'Compliance Committee', Decision 4/CMP.4, in FCCC/KP/CMP/2008/11/Add.1; 'Compliance Committee', Decision 4/CMP.2, in FCCC/KP/CMP/2006/10/Add.1, 'Compliance Committee', Decision 8/CMP.9, in FCCC/KP/CMP/2013/9/Add.1. These texts are available at: < http://unfccc.int/kyoto_protocol/compliance/items/2875.php> (last visited on 31 January 2018). See also Farhana Yamin and Joanna Depledge, *The International Climate Change Regime: A Guide to Rules, Institutions and Procedures* (Cambridge University Press, 2004), pp. 386 et seq.; Osamu Yoshida, 'Procedural Aspects of the International Legal Regime for Climate Change: Early Operation of the Kyoto Protocol Compliance System', 4 *JEAIL* (2011), pp. 41–61; René Lefeber and Sebastian Oberthür, 'Key Features of the Kyoto Protocol's Compliance System', in Jutta Brunnée, Meinhard Doelle and Lavanya Rajamani (eds.), *Promoting Compliance in an Evolving Climate Regime* (Cambridge University Press, 2012), pp. 77–101.

and Access to Justice in Environmental Matters.[18] The NCP under the Kyoto Protocol seems to be based on lessons learned from the Montreal Protocol model,[19] whose enforcement branch is empowered to take more stringent measures of a 'punitive' character. In addition, the Paris Agreement on climate change is to establish a new mechanism to facilitate implementation of and promote compliance with the provisions of the Agreement, and it will consist of a committee that is expert-based and facilitative in nature, and function in a manner that is transparent, non-adversarial and non-punitive.[20]

Under the international régime for the protection of the ozone layer, as we have already seen, the only legal 'remedy' at present is collective treaty compliance – monetary fines for sovereign States consuming ODSs or for transnational corporations (TNCs) producing ODSs is not available.[21] It cannot be emphasised too strongly that, under the Montreal NCP, both any Member State and the UNEP Ozone Secretariat can initiate this procedural mechanism to ensure the implementation of the ozone layer treaties, without any question of its own legal interests being involved. Therefore, needless to say, these international NCP initiators do not have to exhaust any domestic legal remedies as a precondition. In this way, the Montreal NCP can be characterised as an

---

18 Article 15. See Decision I/7 on 'Review of Compliance', in ECE/MP.PP/2/Add.8. For the recent practice of the Committee, see, for example, Elsa Tsioumani, 'Aarhus Convention: Compliance Committee – 40th Meeting', 43/4–5 EPL (2013), pp. 207–211; Veit Koester, 'The Compliance Committee of Aarhus Convention: An Overview of Procedures and Jurisprudence', 37/2–3 EPL (2007), pp. 83–93.

19 On this point, see Jacob Werksman, 'Compliance and the Kyoto Protocol: Building a Backbone into a "Flexible" Regime', 9 YbkIEL (1999), pp. 70–74: Sebastian Oberthür and Hermann E. Ott, The Kyoto Protocol: International Climate Policy for the 21st Century (Springer, 1999), pp. 219–222; Gilbert M. Bankobeza, 'The Ozone Protection Non-Compliance Mechanism: A Model for Implementation of Climate Change Convention and the Kyoto Protocol', in R. K. Dixit and C. Jayaraj (eds.), Dynamics of International Law in the New Millennium (Indian Society of International Law in association with Manak Publications, 2004), p. 346; Jane Blumer, 'Compliance Regimes in Multilateral Environmental Agreements', in Jutta Brunnée, Meinhard Doelle and Lavanya Rajamani (eds.), Promoting Compliance in an Evolving Climate Regime (Cambridge University Press, 2012), p. 57; Pierr-Marie Dupuy and Jorge E. Viñuales, International Environmental Law (Cambridge University Press), p. 285.

20 Article 15(1)(2). Dagnet and Northrop suggest that whether the new mechanism is designed to focus on 'softer measures' or 'stronger measures' is uncertain. See Daniel Klein, Maria Pia Carazo, Meinhard Doelle, Jane Bulmer, and Andrew Higham (eds.), The Paris Agreement on Climate Change: Analysis and Commentary (Oxford University Press, 2017), p. 342; Daniel Bodansky, Jutta Brunnée and Lavanya Rajamani, International Climate Change Law (Oxford University Press, 2017), p. 246.

21 See Chapters 1(IV) and 3(III.C) in this volume.

unprecedented procedural mechanism that is designed to effectively operate or enforce obligations *erga omnes*.[22]

It should be noted that this new dispute avoidance and settlement differs essentially from pre-existing or historical rights conciliation committees, such as those of the First Optional Protocol to the International Covenant on Civil and Political Rights (ICCPR), or the European Convention for the Protection of Human Rights and Fundamental Freedoms (European Human Rights Convention) that strictly require the exhaustion of local remedies.[23]

Although we still should not make any easy generalisations about the Montreal NCP, on the basis of its early operation, the NCP – in which the internal treaty agencies exercise regulatory and supervisory functions – can be regarded as a compliance-monitoring[24] or quasi-judicial settlement mechanism based on a 'collective reaction' or 'multilateralism', but not on confrontational bilateralism common to formal dispute settlement mechanisms. The multilateralism is concerned with traditional collective non-sanctions, such as 'informal persuasion' and the 'mobilisation of shame' applied by global institutions.[25] What is more, compared with formal judicial settlement that usually require time-consuming processes, the NCP seems to be much more flexible, simple and rapid. We may also say at the same time that, in the light of step-by-step negotiation processes of the NCP, this mechanism shows, by seeking feasible and amicable solutions, a scrupulous respect for the sovereignty of ozone régime Member States.

Apart from these four characteristics – that is, multilateralism, flexibility, simplicity and rapidity, it is also important to note that the Montreal NCP has gradually established a close link with international financial mechanisms, namely, the Multilateral Fund of the Montreal Protocol and the Global

---

22   See Chapter 1(IV) in this volume.

23   See the 1966 ICCPR (Article 5.2(b)); the ECHR (Article 35). The Committee against Torture under the Convention against Torture and Cruel, Inhuman or Degrading Treatment or Punishment has a similar provision. Yet these interstate complaints procedures (that is, Committee jurisdiction) must be formally accepted by States concerned. As to the burden of proof in relation to human rights protection, see Chittharanjan Felix Amerssinghe, *Local Remedies in International Law* (Grotius Publications, 1990), pp. 291–297. The 1962 UNESCO Protocol provides that 'The Commission shall deal with a matter referred to ... only after it has ascertained that all available domestic remedies have been invoked and exhausted in the case, in conformity with the generally recognised principles of international law' (Article 14). See further Jean-Pierre Cot, *International Conciliation* (Europa Publications, 1972), pp. 311–312.

24   See Chapter 1(3.C).

25   See Frederic L. Kirgis, *International Organizations in Their Legal Setting* (2nd ed. West Pub. Co., 1993), pp. 524 et seq.

THE MONTREAL NON-COMPLIANCE PROCEDURE   217

Environment Facility.[26] This will certainly strengthen 'soft enforcement' of environmental régime rules.

The organisation of this Chapter is as follows. Section II provides a brief summary of the Montreal NCP negotiation process. Section III then clarifies, to some extent, the meaning of the legal term 'non-compliance' within the Montreal Protocol and the Ozone Convention. It also addresses the relationship between the Montreal NCP and the settlement procedures under Article 11 of the Vienna Convention. Section IV deals with the mechanics of the operation of the Montreal NCP, pointing out the important functions played by the specialised NCP organs – that is, the UNEP Ozone Secretariat, the Implementation Committee and the Meeting of the Parties. Section V then attempts a comparison between the Montreal NCP and other dispute settlement procedures, (i) the WTO/GATT Violation Procedure and (ii) the Complaints Procedure in the ILO Supervisory Machinery. It also characterises the NCP as a multilateral conciliation mechanism. Section VI discusses the unique relationship which exists between the Montreal NCP and the evolving principle of international environmental law, that is, the precautionary environmental principle or approach. Section VII is devoted to the Montreal NCP in practice. It analyses the effectiveness of the specific treaty requirements, including technical data reporting, control measures of ODSs and trade controls. This Section also gives a case study of the Russian Federation's non-compliance with Article 2 control measures.

II   The Negotiation of the Montreal NCP

While the 1987 version of the Montreal Protocol succeeded in introducing specific control measures of ODSs to prevent steady ozone depletion,[27] negotiators of the ozone régime could not conclusively establish the non-compliance procedure in time for its adoption.[28] As a result, it was provided in Article 8 of the Protocol that:

---

26   See further Chapter 6 in this volume.
27   See Chapter 3(II–III) in this volume.
28   See David G. Victor, *The Early Operation and Effectiveness of the Montreal Protocol's Non-Compliance Procedure* (International Institute for Applied Systems Analysis, 1996), p. 4, pointing out that, although the United States offered a detailed non-compliance procedure in the final stages of the negotiation, some negotiators of the European Community considered it as a 'strategy to clutter the agenda at the last minutes'. See also Richard Benedick, *Ozone Diplomacy* (Harvard University Press, 1998), p. 270, noting that 'I can

218   CHAPTER 5

> The Parties, at their first meeting, shall consider and approve procedures
> and institutional mechanisms for determining non-compliance with the
> provisions of this Protocol and for treatment of Parties found to be in
> non-compliance.

It then took several years of preparations, however, to establish the Montreal NCP.

The 1989 Helsinki Meeting of the Parties[29] established an *Ad Hoc* Working Group of Legal Experts,[30] which was to develop three different proposals for a non-compliance procedure submitted by the United States,[31] the Netherlands,[32] and Austria.[33] At this stage, some developed States – the United States and Nordic countries, in particular – strongly supported a 'more stringent and punitive approach' rather than an 'encouragement-based approach' that was recommended by the Working Group of Legal Experts.[34] Industrialising countries and the European Community supported the encouragement-based approach.

The First Meeting of the *Ad Hoc* Working Group was held in Geneva in 1989.[35] The United States' new proposal, unlike its initial proposal, addressed a conciliation procedure for non-compliance under the 1985 Vienna Ozone Convention, which could ultimately lead to recommendations and/or further punitive measures approved by the Meeting of the Parties. Under an Australian proposal, the Secretariat was to be given stronger powers to match its role as the 'guardian of the Protocol', including regular reporting regarding compliance and non-compliance.[36] After an extensive discussion about the non-compliance procedure, it was agreed that:[37]

---

        attest that it was consciously intended as a laconic but important maker, not as a tactic'.
        On the United States' proposal, see UNEP/OzL.WG.Data.2/3/Rev.2/Annex VII.
29   See Chapter 3(IV.B) in this volume.
30   See Decision I/8.
31   See UNEP/OzL.Pro.LG.1/2/Annex II.
32   See UNEP/OzL.Pro.LG.1/CRP.1.
33   See UNEP/OzL.Pro.LG.1/CRP.4.
34   See UNEP/OzL.Pro.WG.IV/3, para. 4; Richard Benedick, *Ozone Diplomacy* (Harvard University Press, 1998), pp. 182–183.
35   UNEP/OzL.Pro.LG.1/3; 19/5 EPL (1989), pp. 147–148.
36   The proposal also stated that 'the determination of compliance or non-compliance should be as far as possible a time-bound, non-political process, producing a legal and technical decision'. See Thomas Gehring, *Dynamic International Regimes* (Peter Lang, 1994), p. 315.
37   UNEP/OzL.Pro.LG.1/3, para. 9. The ideas propounded were all shaped into the existing Montreal NCP.

THE MONTREAL NON-COMPLIANCE PROCEDURE

(i) it was important to avoid drawing up an unnecessarily complex and duplicative system;

(ii) the procedure should not be confrontational;

(iii) action under the non-compliance procedure could be commenced by either one or a number of Parties or the Parties collectively registering concern with the Secretariat;

(iv) the procedure proposed should not alter or weaken in any way article 11 of the Vienna Convention on the Protection of the Ozone Layer;

(v) confidentiality must be respected and specific reference to this should be made in the procedures proposed;

(vi) the Secretariat's role should be that of a servicing, administrative body rather than a judicial one;

(vii) the Secretariat should compile the necessary data and other information;

(viii) early indications of possible non-compliance might be resolved through administrative action by the Secretariat and through diplomatic contacts between Parties: and

(ix) decisions on non-compliance should be recommendatory rather than mandatory.

In addition to these matters, the Working Group also agreed that there should be a supervisory body that was called the 'Implementation Committee'.[38] Since many delegations demanded that the Implementation Committee not have a judicial function, the *Ad Hoc* Working Group agreed that any decisions concerning non-compliance would be made by the régime's supreme entity, the Meeting of the Parties.[39] The Working Group also approved a 'Draft Non-Compliance Procedure', which specified basic functions of the Ozone Secretariat, the Implementation Committee and the Meeting of the Parties.[40] The 1990 London Meeting of the Parties[41] adopted this draft NCP as prepared by the Working Group on an interim basis, and it established the standing Implementation Committee.[42]

In the Second Meeting of the Working Group held in 1991, the European Community offered the most sweeping proposal. That proposal included in its draft text 'Indicative Lists of Steps to Bring about Full Compliance with

---

38 Ibid., para. 10.

39 Ibid., paras. 11 and 17.

40 Ibid., Annex.

41 See Chapter 3(IV.C) in this volume.

42 Decision II/5. This Decision also extended the mandate of the *Ad Hoc* Working Group to elaborate the NCP itself and the terms of reference for the Committee. The Decision III/2, adopted by the Third Ozone Meeting, also extended the mandate of the Working Group with regard to the development of an Indicative List of Measures.

the Protocol' that dealt with three types of non-compliance, that is, (i) reporting requirements, (ii) control measures of ODSs and (iii) trade restrictions.[43] Under the European Community's proposal, the functions of internal international organs, including the Ozone Secretariat and the Committee, were essentially similar in many respects to the existing Montreal NCP. Apart from draft proposals submitted, it is worth noting that many experts at this Meeting communicated the view that dispute settlement procedures under the 1985 Vienna Ozone Convention and the Montreal NCP were 'two distinct and separate procedures which could well exist in parallel'.[44] The formal NCP, as improved by the Third Meeting of the *Ad Hoc* Working Group, was finally adopted at the 1992 Copenhagen Ozone Meeting.[45] The decision is legally binding because of the enabling provisions of Articles 8 and 11(3.d).[46]

Subsequently, the 1997 Montreal Meeting of the Parties[47] decided to review and strengthen the NCP 1992 and it established an *Ad Hoc* Working Group of Legal and Technical Experts on the NCP, which was composed of fourteen members from both developed (Article 5) and developing (non-Article 5) countries, namely, Australia, Canada, European Community, Russian Federation, Slovakia, Switzerland, United Kingdom, Argentina, Botswana, China, Georgia, Morocco, Sri Lanka and St. Lucia.[48] In November 1998, the Cairo Meeting of the Parties[49] adopted the revised NCP as prepared by the Working Group.[50] Under the NCP 1998, the functions of the internal organs, including the Secretariat

---

43   UNEP/OzL.Pro/WG.3/2/3/Annex; Thomas Gehring, *Dynamic International Régimes* (Peter Lang, 1994), pp. 316–317.

44   UNEP/OzL.Pro/WG.3/2/3, para. 18. See Section IV. A(3).

45   See Decision IV/5 and Chapter 3(IV.D) in this volume.

46   See also Michael Bothe, 'The Evaluation of Enforcement Mechanisms in International Environmental Law', in Rüdiger Wolfrum (ed.), *Enforcing Environmental Standards* (Springer, 1996), p. 31.

47   See Chapter 3(IV.F) in this volume.

48   See Decision IX/35(5) in UNEP/OzL.Pro.9/12. The newly established *Ad Hoc* Working Group of Legal and Technical Experts on the NCP was to consider (i) any proposals by parties for strengthening the NCP, including how repeated instances of major significance of non-compliance could trigger the adoption of measures under the Indicative List of Measures with a view to ensuring prompt compliance with the Protocol and (ii) any proposals for improving the effectiveness of the functioning of the Implementation Committee, including with respect to data-reporting and the conduct of its work. The Working Group composed of fourteen members. See the following reports by the *Ad Hoc* Working Group: UNEP/OzL.Pro/WG/1/1/Add.1 (14 April 1998); UNEP/OzL.Pro/WG.4/1/1/Add.2 (18 May 1998); UNEP/OzL.Pro/WG/1/1/Add.1 (15 April 1998).

49   See UNEP/OzL.Pro.10/9; 29/1 *EPL* (1999) p. 9.

50   See Annex II, UNEP/OzL.Pro.10/9.

and the Implementation Committee, are clarified to some extent.[51] The 1998 Meeting of the Parties decided to consider the operation of the NCP, no later than the end of 2003.[52] Consequently, at the Fourteenth Meeting of the Parties in 2002, the United States submitted a conference room paper containing a draft decision on the NCP, aiming to 'enable the Implementation Committee to meet its obligations to the Parties in a more timely and effective manner than in the past'.[53] However, many government representatives considered that the proposed amendments to the terms of office of members of the Implementation Committee could jeopardize the principles of equitable geographic distribution and rotation, and they would impose an additional burden on Article 5 developing countries concerning reporting requirements.[54] As a result, owing to the lack of agreement on all elements of the proposal, the United States withdrew its proposed decision.[55]

III   The Meaning of 'Non-Compliance' in the Montreal Protocol:
        a Grey Area of the International Ozone Régime

A   *The Meaning of 'Non-Compliance' in the Evolving Ozone Régime*
In general, the term 'compliance' refers a 'desired state of conformity with the law, a regulation, or a demand'. Its working definition will not be static. Unlike the term 'enforcement', 'compliance' implies that régime Member States are technically induced to comply, rather than being coerced to do so.[56] In this sense, the use of the legal terminology '(non-) compliance' in the Montreal

---

51   See Annex II(2), (3), (5) and (7.d).
52   See Decision X/10(5).
53   See UNEP/OzL.Pro.14/9, para. 84.
54   See ibid., para. 86.
55   See ibid., para. 88.
56   See Bridget M. Hutter, *Compliance: Regulation and Environment* (Oxford University Press, 1997), Chapters 1–4. Generally speaking, 'compliance' in English, (non-conformité/Nichtbefolgung) refers to 'obedience' or 'conformance'. See Edith Brown Weiss and Harold Karan Jacobson, 'Strengthening Compliance with International Environmental Accords: Preliminary Observations from a Collaborative Project', 1 *Global Governance* (1995), pp. 123 et seq., defining compliance as 'whether countries in fact adhere to the provisions of the accord and to the implementing measures that they have instituted' — 'compliance' should be thus distinguished from 'effectiveness'. The term 'violation' can be defined as 'breach of right, duty or law' and 'enforcement' as the execution of a law. 'Enforcement' implies rather positive coercion, such as 'countermeasures', 'reprisals' and 'police force and courts'. These terms are often used interchangeably, however. See *Black's Law Dictionary* (6th ed. West, 1990); Louis Henkin, 'General Course on Public International Law', 216 *Recueil des cours* (1989), pp. 67 et seq.; Laurence Boisson de Chazournes, 'La mise en

Protocol seems to be particularly appropriate for its global regulatory rules on ODS controls. It should be noticed here that, in case of developing 'Article 5 countries'[57] in particular, compliance with these legally binding treaty obligations (in this case, administrative standards) depends largely on financial and technical assistance, as we shall see in the next chapter. It is questionable, however, that the concept of non-compliance in the emerging global environmental régimes, including the ozone régime, still exists as a specific and distinct legal category in the realm of public international law.

Naturally, States' 'non-compliance' can be defined as the breach of obligations owed under general international law, that is, the determination of internationally wrongful acts. It may be true that, as the ILC says, 'Every internationally wrongful act of a State entails the responsibility of that State'.[58] However, it is also true that possible non-compliance with the ozone treaty provisions is not necessarily concerned with States' responsibility or liability in the context of the payment of compensation for environmental damage.[59] In addition, as has already been pointed out, the legal character of the detailed treaty-based obligations under Articles 2 and 5 of the Montreal Protocol, in particular, is not necessarily understood in the context of traditional legal obligations undertaken by State entities. ODS/CFC control provisions – but not including Article 4 TREMS – are in effect alien to customary law and the law of State responsibility.

It is very likely that 'non-compliance', including a breach of obligations, may be judged by political criteria other than strictly legal ones. Seen in this light, non-compliance may be generally regarded as a 'treaty-specific political process'.[60] However, as will be argued below, it will be in the interests of the parties to the Montreal Protocol to adopt a régime-oriented procedure for collective environmental management. Undeniably, such a special mechanism, though effective in accomplishing the treaty régime's environmental objectives, would not, however, be completely appropriate to breach of treaty.

The definition of the term non-compliance is not provided for in the legal text of the Montreal Protocol or in that of the 1985 Vienna Ozone Convention. The reason for this is that the 1992 Copenhagen Ozone Meeting was not ready to adopt an 'Indicative List of Possible Situations of Non-compliance with

---

œuvre du droit international dans le domaine de la protection de l'environnement: enjeux et défis', 99 *Revue générale de droit international public* (1995), pp. 62 et seq.

57 On the definition of Article 5 countries, see Chapter 3(III.E(2)) in this volume.

58 Article 1 of the ILC's Draft Articles on State Responsibility. See James Crawford, *The International Law Commission's Articles on State Responsibility* (Cambridge University Press, 2002), pp. 77–80.

59 See Chapter 1(IV) in this volume and Section I above.

60 See Martti Koskenniemi, 'Breach of Treaty or Non-Compliance', 3 *YbkIEL* (1992), p. 145.

the Protocol', as prepared by the *Ad Hoc* Working Group of Legal Experts.[61] In the absence of such a helpful list of potential non-compliance, as a matter of fact, the risk of non-compliance is likely to increase. As Professor Bothe says, 'compliance is furthered by the possibility of obtaining a clear determination of the content of a norm in relation to a given case'.[62] Yet, in the light of the flexible nature of the NCP, it is also possible to argue in response that formal and strictly legal determination of non-compliance could be merely counterproductive.[63]

Taking account of the draft Indicative List, we may safely assume that non-compliance with regard to the following four ozone treaty obligations would first be determined by the Montreal NCP:

(i)   non-compliance with treaty provisions relating to ODS control measures (Articles 2, 2A-2J);
(ii) non-compliance with treaty provisions relating to restrictions on trade with non-parties (Articles 4, 4A-4B);
(iii) non-compliance with time schedules reporting of data (Article 7): and
(iv) non-compliance with reporting of a summary of national ozone activities (Article 9).[64]

It is arguable, however, that non-payment of contributions to the financial mechanism, namely, the Montreal Multilateral Fund, could be also regarded as possible non-compliance with the ozone layer treaty. Whereas most donor countries consider the obligation to contribute to the MLF as legally binding,

---

61   See UNEP/OzL.Pro/WG.3/3/3/Annex II. paras. 32–43; K. Madhava Sarma, 'Compliance with the Multilateral Environmental Agreements to Protect the Ozone Layer', in Ulrich Beyerlin, Peter-Tobias Stoll and Rüdiger Wolfrum (eds.), *Ensuring Compliance with Multilateral Environmental Agreements* (Martinus Nijhoff, 2006), p. 29.

62   See Michael Bothe, 'International Obligations, Means to Secure Performance', 1 *Encyclopedia of Public International Law* (North-Holland Pub. Co., 1982), p. 102.

63   See Martti Koskenniemi, 'New Institutions and Procedures for Implementation Control and Reaction', in James Cameron, Jacob Werksman and Peter Roderick (eds.), *Improving Compliance with International Environmental Law* (Earthscan, 1996), p. 246 and its endnotes.

64   Other forms include: non-provision of the contributions referred to in Article 10, paragraph 1, for the purpose of financing on a grant or concessional basis the incremental costs agreed upon in its paragraph 3, as well as what is provided for in Article 10 A concerning substitute substances and the transfer of technology; failure to take every practicable step consistent with the programmes supported by the financial mechanism, for transfer of technology: and non-compliance with the obligations in decisions of the Parties to the Protocol. The Working Group noted, however, that 'the above list is without prejudice to the generally accepted rules of international law related to the interpretation and application of treaties'. See UNEP/OzL.Pro/WG.3/3/3 (Annex II: Indicative Lists).

224   CHAPTER 5

the United States, for instance, interprets it as merely 'voluntary compliance'.[65] The legal text of the MLF is silent on this contentious matter, and the Implementation Committee has never decided the issue. Consequently, the legal status of these monetary contributions is still left intentionally ambiguous.[66]

B   *Depoliticising Multilateral Environmental Disputes? The Relationship between the NCP and the Dispute Settlement Mechanisms in the Vienna Ozone Convention*

The above analysis implies that the confirmation of non-compliance with ozone treaty obligations is likely to depend to some extent on the practical decisions of the Implementation Committee, the Meeting of the Parties, as the supreme treaty organ, and/or the Contracting Parties themselves.

In relation to this, Professor Koskenniemi points out that 'a dispute about whether some particular type of non-compliance is wrongful act is another dispute about interpretation or application of the treaty and capable of being resolved only within the procedures under Article 11 of the Vienna Ozone Convention', and ultimately, 'the question of wrongfulness is one of general international law, and *not* a question that can be solved, or indeed even approached, from within the special regime of the Vienna Ozone Convention

---

65   See UNEP/OzL.Pro/WG.3/3/3, paras. 37–38, noting that developing countries disputed the view that Article 10 (Financial Mechanism), after entry into force, did not contain an obligation to contribute to the financial mechanism. This disruptive issue among ozone régime members is often raised in the Ozone Meeting of the Parties (see, for example, UNEP/OzL.Pro.5/12, para. 22; UNEP/OzL.Pro.7/12). While the 1992 Climate Change Convention and the 1992 Biodiversity Convention require industrised State parties to provide new and additional financial resources to newly industrising State parties, monetary contributions under these two environmental agreements could be regarded as only voluntary. See Alan E. Boyle, 'The Rio Convention on Biological Diversity', in Michael Bowman and Catherine Redgwell (eds.), *International Law and the Conservation of Biological Diversity* (Kluwer Law International, 1995), pp. 46–47. See also Gilbert M. Bankobeza, *Ozone Protection* (Eleven International, 2005), pp. 188–190; Chapter 6 in this volume.

66   The Implementation Committee has never discussed this issue. See Richard Benedick, *Ozone Diplomacy* (Harvard University Press, 1998), pp. 262 and 271, saying that 'the contributions are, from a strictly legal perspective, voluntary' and that 'arranges of payment were never formally deplored by the parties but never labelled as non-compliance with the protocol'. See also David G. Victor, 'The Montreal Protocol's Non-Compliance Procedure: Lessons for Making Other International Environmental Régimes More Effective', in Winfried Lang (ed.), *The Ozone Treaties and Their Influence on the Building of Environmental Régimes* (Austrian Ministry of Foreign Affairs, Vienna, Austria), pp. 67 et seq.

THE MONTREAL NON-COMPLIANCE PROCEDURE 225

and the Protocol at all'.[67] In order to be a judicial organ, the Meeting of the Parties may only suspend the rights of an allegedly defaulting party, only if there exist non-compliance or breach of treaty, as an internationally wrongful act by that State party.[68]

With regard to the relationship between Article 11 of the Convention and the Montreal NCP, the Convention provides that 'the provisions of Article 11 of the Vienna Convention shall apply with respect to any protocol except as provided in the protocol concerned'.[69] This means that the operation of the Montreal NCP is not necessarily stipulated as condition precedent to the settlement mechanisms enumerated in the Vienna Ozone Convention.[70] Moreover, since under the ozone treaty régime (and under general international law) there does not exist a hierarchy – except for the full use of diplomatic negotiations as a departure point – in settling disputes, no ozone régime member could or would eliminate the possibility of invoking binding procedures under the Ozone Convention.[71] For instance, the allegedly defaulting party (for example, Article 5 country parties and the CEITS) – which considers that it has not committed an internationally wrongful act entailing State responsibility – can invoke, as a means of avoiding collective suspension of rights or countermeasures, the traditional settlement mechanisms under the Convention. At this later stage, the Montreal NCP may not be seen as 'self-contained' environmental system. The NCP of the Protocol provides only that:

(i) the special procedural régime (that is, the NCP) shall apply 'without prejudice to the operation of the settlement of disputes procedure laid down in Article 11 of the Vienna [Ozone] Convention' (Preamble);

(ii) the Meeting of the Parties may issue an interim call and/or recommendations, pending completion of these proceedings (Annex IV(13)): and

---

67 See Martti Koskenniemi, 'Breach of Treaty or Non-Compliance?', 3 *YbkIEL* (1992), p. 144, saying that 'The *travaux préparatoires* of the NCP as well as the composition and functions of the Implementation Committee and, *a foriori*, the Meeting of the Parties, make it clear that neither can, or is expected to, work as a judicial body, assessing the performance of the parties' obligations with a view of determining whether or not there has been a wrongful act triggering state responsibility'. See also UNEP/OzL.Pro/WG.3/3/3, para. 46.

68 See Martti Koskenniemi, 'Breach of Treaty or Non-Compliance?', 3 *YbkIEL* (1992), p. 145.

69 Article 11(6). See also Article 14 of the Montreal Protocol.

70 The Implementation Committee once noted that the parallel exercise might even be conductive to the functioning of the NCP. See Winfried Lang, 'Ozone Layer', 2 *YbkIEL* (1991), p. 109.

71 In cases of disputes involving TREMS, parties to the Protocol may first use the WTO/GATT dispute settlement system, rather than the NCP (see Chapter 4(IV.B) in this volume).

(iii) the Contracting Parties that decide to use a dispute settlement mechanism described in Article 11 of the Vienna Ozone Convention must inform the Meeting of the Parties through Ozone Secretariat (Annex IV(12)).

These three points will not radically change the above-mentioned controversial relationship between the traditional settlement mechanisms Article 11 of the Ozone Convention and the Montreal NCP.[72]

It should be noted that the 1991 Nairobi Meeting of the Parties decided, as has already been pointed out, that these two types of processes for dealing with parties' non-compliance were distinct and separate procedures.[73] Furthermore, at the 1992 Copenhagen Ozone Meeting of the Parties, it was also decided that 'the responsibility for legal interpretation of the Protocol rests ultimately with the Parties themselves'.[74]

Perhaps one acceptable explanation for this situation would be that the internally specialised treaty bodies, as legal advisers to the régime-practitioners, still have to take account of the existing principles and rules of international law as a whole, in deciding what is 'non-compliance' or 'breach of treaty' and which measure (assistance and countermeasure) should then be taken.[75] This solution makes sense even if members of these bodies are, in reality, unwilling to clarify such a nagging question and, in the quest for flexibility, would allow it to remain a grey area of the international legal ozone régime.

Though this view is not necessarily confirmed in practice,[76] it is likely that the international institutional supervision of compliance through the Montreal NCP would simply be powerless or too weak to resolve certain ozone disputes. Hence, as a rule, should failure by the NCP to settle ozone disputes occur, an allegedly defaulting party could still be taken to the formal dispute settlement procedure under Article 11 of the Vienna Ozone Convention that includes binding third party settlement.[77]

---

72 For a comprehensive discussion, see Martti Koskenniemi, 'Breach of Treaty or Non-Compliance?', 3 *YbkIEL* (1992), pp. 157–161.

73 See Decision III/2; UNEP/OzL.Pro.3/L.4.

74 See Decision IV 5(5). See also Section IV. B(3) below.

75 See also Section V below.

76 See Section VII below. It has been often pointed out, however, that the NCP of the Montreal type is 'too soft' (For example, by Jo Elizabeth Butler at *the 91st Annual Meeting of the American Society of International Law*, 'The Establishment of a Dispute Resolution/Non-Compliance Mechanism in the Climate Change Convention', 11 April 1997, Washington DC).

77 See Martti Koskenniemi, 'Breach of Treaty or Non-Compliance?', 3 *YbkIEL*(1992), p. 160.

IV The Mechanics of the Operation of the Montreal NCP: the Function of the Specialised Internal Treaty Bodies

A *The Structure of the Montreal NCP*

(1) The Actors of the NCP

The main actors of the Montreal NCP, apart from the State Parties, are three specialised internal treaty organs, namely, (i) the UNEP Ozone Secretariat, (ii) the Implementation Committee, and (iii) the Meeting of the Parties. All three entities are 'functional' and 'sectional' organs in the field of international ozone layer protection. The NCP can be triggered in the three régime actors by (i) one party against another party, (ii) a party itself which is/would be in non-compliance, and (iii) the UNEP Ozone Secretariat.

The role of régime-supporting actors of international financial mechanisms (that is, the Executive Committee, the Multilateral Fund Secretariat, the World Bank and other UN institutions, such as the UNDP and the UNIDO) will be considered in Chapter 6 in this volume. Unlike NGOs in the field of international human rights protection law – such as Amnesty International[78] – environmental NGOs are given only a minor role in releasing informal information about anticipated non-compliance.[79]

(2) The Principle of Good Faith (Bona Fides)

In the light of its reliance on voluntary political cooperation in ensuring implementation of various technical obligations, it is noteworthy that the fundamental basis of the NCP is the principle of good faith – that which has also formed the foundation of the international ozone régime itself.[80] The principle of good faith is originally based on the principle of reciprocity: Member States of the ozone régime, that is, mainly Non-Article 5 developed countries,

---

78   As regards human rights law régimes, under the European Convention for the Protection of Human Rights and Fundamental Freedoms, individuals and NGOs can submit applications against States that have accepted the right of individual petition (Article 34); entered into force on 3 September 1953). The Inter-American Commission, likewise, receives complaints from individuals and other non-state entities (American Convention on Human Rights, Article 44). See also Article 87(b) of the Charter of the United Nations.

79   For details, see Akira Sakota and Osamu Yoshida, 'Kokusai Ozonsou Hogo Jōyaku Rejīmu ni okeru NGO no Yakuwari' [The Role of NGOs in the International Legal Régime for the Protection of the Ozone Layer], in *Kankyo Sisaku ni okeru Jūmin Sanka, NGO Katsudō ni kansuru Hōgaku oyobi Gyōseigaku teki Kenkyū* [Legal and Administrative Studies on Public Participation and NGO Activities in Environmental Measures] (Japan Environment Protection Agency, October 1998).

80   See Chapter 1(I) in this volume.

which already have the capacity to fully comply with ozone treaty obligations, entertain the rational expectation that other majority group members – namely Article 5 developing States – will also try to comply with stringent but differentiated ozone treaty obligations and other related principles and rules of international environmental law.

Despite the difficulties in enforcing multilateral environmental treaty rules, international reputations have some political significance. As Professor Henkin observed, it may be said with some exaggeration that 'States recognise that stability, law and order, reliability (and a warranted reputation for reliability) are in their national interest, and therefore that they have a more-or-less enlightened self-interest in compliance'.[81]

As we shall see, under the NCP, if a non-complying party fails to respond within fixed periods, or if the matter cannot be settled by diplomatic means, the Secretariat then includes that information in its report of the Meeting of the Parties and informs the standing Implementation Committee regarding the situation.[82] It is possible that this 'sociological sanction' might, to some extent, have some effect.[83]

B   *The Functions of the Internal International Agencies in the Montreal Non-Compliance Procedure*

(1)   The UNEP Ozone Secretariat

The Vienna Ozone Convention established the UNEP Ozone Secretariat on an interim basis. At present, the Secretariat serves on a permanent basis.[84] Whereas the Secretariat also carries out similar secondary functions in its routine, as provided for in Article 12 of the Montreal Protocol, it has expanded its role as a régime-supporter in the NCP. The UNEP Ozone Secretariat acts at an early stage to monitor compliance with detailed technical ozone regulations, and then identify the points at issue.[85]

The Montreal NCP may be invoked through or by the UNEP Ozone Secretariat in the following three cases, regardless of whether or not there exists material damage or breach of treaty under general international law.[86] The mechanics

---

81   See Louis Henkin, 'General Course on Public International Law', 216 *Recueil des cours* (1989), p. 72.
82   The NCP 1998, Annex II(3).
83   See also Section VII(A.1) below.
84   See Chapter 2(III.D(3)) in this volume.
85   For details, see Section VII(A) below.
86   See also Gilbert M. Bankobeza, *Ozone Protection* (Eleven International, 2005), pp. 267–268 and 271.

of the operation of the Montreal NCP are not based on the establishment of standing to bring inter-State claims.[87]

Case I: One Party against Another Party

The UNEP Secretariat, in this event, (i) receives a report presented by any contracting parties that have reservations as to another party's implementation of its treaty obligations under the Protocol,[88] (ii) sends that submission made by party/parties to the party whose implementation is at issue, and send a reminder to the party, if the Secretariat do not receive a reply from it three months,[89] and (iii) transmits the submission provided by parties, including reply and information, to the standing Implementation Committee, not later than six months after receiving the submission.[90] The submission must be supported by 'corroborating information', which might include informal information offered by non-state international actors such as environmental NGOs.[91]

Case II: Self-Reporting

The UNEP Secretariat, in this case, (i) obtains a written explanation given by the party with regard to the particular circumstances of the causes for non-compliance,[92] and (ii) transmits the submission to the Implementation Committee.[93] It is interesting to note that this self-reporting system was instituted into the NCP based on the proposal made by the former Soviet Union,[94] several of whose successors, that is, the CEITs, for the first time, initiated the Montreal NCP.[95]

87　See also Pierr-Marie Dupuy and Jorge E. Viñuales, *International Environmental Law* (Cambridge University Press), pp. 289.

88　Annex II(1).

89　Annex II(2). See the NCP 1992, Annex IV(2).

90　See ibid.

91　For details, see Akira Sakota and Osamu Yoshida, 'Kokusai Ozonsou Hogo Jōyaku Rejīmu ni okeru NGO no Yakuwari' [The Role of NGOs in the International Legal Régime for the Protection of the Ozone Layer], in *Kankyo Sisaku ni okeru Jūmin Sanka, NGO Katsudō ni kansuru Hōgaku oyobi Gyōseigaku teki Kenkyū* [Legal and Administrative Studies on Public Participation and NGO Activities in Environmental Measures] (Japan Environment Protection Agency, October 1998) (in Japanese).

92　See Annex IV(4).

93　See ibid.

94　See Patrick Széll, 'The Development of Multilateral Mechanisms for Monitoring Compliance, in Winfried Lang (ed.), *Sustainable Development and International Law* (Graham & Trotman/ Martinus Nijhoff, 1995), p. 100.

95　See Section VII(B) below. Subsequently, at the Eighteenth Meeting of the Parties in 2006, the President of the Implementation Committee stated that 'Bangladesh had been the

Case III: The UNEP Ozone Secretariat

The UNEP Secretariat can also invoke the NCP by itself, where it becomes aware of possible non-compliance 'during the course of preparing its reports'. The Ozone Secretariat can request any party to provide necessary information in connection with its possible non-compliance, invoking, among others, reporting requirements, control measures and trade restrictions.[96] If the party does not respond within a fixed period, or if the matter cannot be settled by diplomatic means, the Secretariat includes the matter in its report of the Meeting of the Parties, and also informs the Implementation Committee.[97] This is the first instance in which the Secretariat has been empowered to invoke a formal MEA dispute avoidance and settlement procedure. In comparison, the Secretariat under the 1979 Convention on Long-Range Transboundary Air Pollution appears to have been given relatively stronger powers.[98]

This third scenario shows how it would be possible for information derived from individuals and environmental NGOs reach the Montreal NCP without any governmental support.[99] Although government officials tend to regard NGOs as long-haired radicals with no understanding of the complexity of the

---

first Party for ten years to use self-nomination to trigger the non-compliance procedure and had notified the Secretariat that it might fall into non-compliance in the years 2007 to 2009 due to difficulties in phasing out CFCs used in the manufacture of metered-dose inhalers'. See UNEP/OzL.Pro.18/10, para. 137. In October 2006, Bangladesh notified the Implementation Committee that, despite having made its best bona fide efforts, the party anticipated non-compliance with its phase-out schedule for the years 2007–2009 for CFCs. See UNEP/OzL.Pro/ImPCom/43/5, para. 25; UNEP/OzL.Pro/ImPCom/39/7, para. 59; UNEP/OzL.Pro/ImPCom/37/7, para. 3.

96   See Annex II(3); Article 7.

97   See Annex II(3). The Committee shall consider the matter as soon as practicable (NCP 1998). See also the NCP 1992, Annex II(3).

98   The text of the NCP provides that 'Where the secretariat, *in particular upon reviewing the reports* .... become aware of possible non-compliance by any Party.... it may request the Party concerned to furnish necessary information about the matter' (emphasis added). See Decision 2012/25 on improving the functioning of the Implementation Committee, Annex: Implementation Committee, Its Structure and Functions and Procedures for Review, in ECE/EB.AIR/113/Add.1, Section VI.

99   See Alan E. Boyle, 'Settlement of Disputes Relating to the Law of the Sea and the Environment', 26 *Thesaurus Acroasium* (1996), p. 259; Thomas Gehring, *Dynamic International Regimes* (Peter Lang, 1994), p. 318. The same thing can be said of the NCP under the 1994 Protocol on Further Reduction of Sulphur. See David G. Victor, *The Early Operation and Effectiveness of the Montreal Protocol's Non-Compliance Procedure* (International Institute for Applied Systems Analysis, 1996), p. 7, suggesting that though an NGO appealed for its participation in the meeting of the Committee in 1992, it was denied on the ground that 'confidential, delicate, and sensitive information might be discussed and the presence of an NGO could limit frank discussion'.

issues, the detailed information provided by NGOs regarding illegal trade in CFCs seems particularly reliable and helpful.[100] NGOs, including industrial NGOs, have demonstrated a commitment to working toward implementation of the Protocol. It therefore may be good idea to increase NGO input in the existing NCP process.[101] Until now, however, the UNEP Ozone Secretariat has been rather reluctant to invoke the NCP in this way.[102]

(2)   The Implementation Committee of the Montreal NCP

(a)   *The Structure of the Implementation Committee*

Some commentators view the creation of the Implementation Committee as a real breakthrough in international environmental law.[103] The standing Implementation Committee – as the 'legitimate first stop' in any formal discussion'[104] – has examined and decided most of the debatable non-compliance issues. However, more vexed questions, such as non-compliance by the CEITs, may have to be ultimately referred to the Meeting of the Parties (and other appropriate settlement procedures).

It is widely agreed that the Implementation Committee is not a judicial organ.[105] Rather, the Committee can be regarded as a conciliatory body within the specialised environmental régime. As we noted, the 1990 London Meeting of the Parties established the Implementation Committee under the interim NCP as a standing governmental committee, which originally consisted of five members in accordance with Decision 11/5.[106] The Implementation Committee meets at least twice a year, and its meetings are organised by the UNEP Ozone Secretariat.

---

100   See, for example, Jim Vallette, 'Allied Signal, Quimobasicos and Frio Banditos: A Case Study of the Black Market in CFCs', *Ozone Action Report* (November 1996).

101   For a similar argument, see Michael Bothe, 'Compliance Control beyond Diplomacy: The Role of Non-Governmental Actors', 27/4 EPL (1997), p. 296. Yet the *Ad Hoc* Working Group established by the Ninth Meeting of the Parties decided to deny a proposal to enable the NCP to be triggered by NGOs on the ground that this was adequately covered in paragraph 3 of the existing procedure. See UNEP/OzL.Pro/WG.1/17/3, para. 85.

102   The Working Group on the NCP has discussed the fact that the mandate of the Secretariat to receive information from any source should be clarified. See UNEP/OzL.Pro/WG.4/1/1, para. 17.

103   See Alexandre Kiss, 'Compliance with International and European Environmental Obligations', *Hague YbkIL* (1996), pp. 50–51.

104   See David G. Victor, *The Early Operation and Effectiveness of the Montreal Protocol's Non-Compliance Procedure* (International Institute for Applied Systems Analysis, 1996), p. 36.

105   See UNEP/OzL.Pro/7/12, para. 39, noting that 'the Committee had operated in a co-operative, non-judicial and non-confrontational atmosphere'.

106   See UNEP/OzL.Pro.2/3, para. 47. The first parties elected were Japan, Norway, Trinidad and Tobago, Hungary and Uganda.

At present, the Implementation Committee consists of ten representatives from State Parties elected to two-year terms by the Meeting of the Parties to the Protocol. At the Twenty-Eighth Meeting of the Parties to the Protocol, committee members are selected from the following States: Bangladesh, Canada, Haiti, Kenya, Romania, the Congo, Georgia, Jordan, Paraguay and the United Kingdom.[107] The amended NCP 1998 requires each party elected to the Committee (i) to notify the Secretariat, within two months of its election, of the name of the individual and (ii) to endeavour to ensure that the same individual remains its representative throughout the entire term.[108]

As is often pointed out, sovereign States are usually reluctant to entrust independent experts with strong decision-making powers. On this particular point, Professor Alexandre-Charles Kiss argues that 'the existence of independent elements inside a commission may be considered as fundamental criterion for deciding whether it really may be called an international institution'.[109]

While the members of the Implementation Committee do not necessarily have either technical and scientific expertise and skills or any special legal competence, they still have to deal with not only political or diplomatic matters, but with all matters pertaining to technical or scientific non-compliance issues.[110] In this respect, the importance of the role of the UNEP Ozone Secretariat as a highly experienced body of technical and scientific experts cannot be overemphasised. In addition, in order to improve the immediate situation, a subsidiary agency of the UNEP, the Technical and Economic Assessment Panel (TEAP), has also contributed toward selecting, organising and supplying information concerning the expected non-compliance of parties.[111]

---

107   See Decision XXVIII/13 in UNEP/OzL.Pro.28/12.

108   See Annex II(5) (emphasis added). See also Gilbert M. Bankobeza, *Ozone Protection* (Eleven International, 2005), p. 261.

109   See Alexandre Kiss, 'Mechanisms of Supervision of International Environmental Rules', in Frits Kalshoven, Pieter Jan Kuyper and Johan G. Lammers (eds.), *Essays on the Development of the International Legal Order* (Sijthoff & Noordhoff, 1980), p. 103 (emphasis added).

110   See Patrick Széll, 'The Development of Multilateral Mechanisms for Monitoring Compliance', in Winfried Lang (ed.), *Sustainable Development and International Law* (Graham & Trotman/ Martinus Nijhoff, 1995), p. 108.

111   The TEAP has reported on the anticipated non-compliance by the Countries with Economic in Transition (CEITs), such as the Russian Federation and Ukraine. Yet, it is natural that powers delegated to the agency are no more than those of the Implementation Committee. See UNEP, *Assessment of Basic Problems Confronting Countries with Economies in Transition in Complying with the Montreal Protocol: Report of the TEAP Ad-Hoc Working Group on CEIT Aspects* (November 1995). See also Decision VII/34 in UNEP/OzL.Pro.7/12, pp. 43–46.

Like many other international conciliation commissions, the composition of the Implementation Committee is based on the principle of equitable geographical distribution designed to ensure a political equilibrium in which common interests of the international community are represented.[112] Unlike the Implementation Committee, however, the Executive Committee of the Montreal Multilateral Fund consists of seven representatives from both developed country parties and developing county parties (the 7 plus 7 formula).[113]

(b)   *The Functions of the Committee in the Montreal NCP*
Under the Montreal NCP, the Implementation Committee performs the following four prominent functions 'with a view to securing an amicable solution of the matter on the basis of respect for the provisions of the Protocol'.[114] These conciliatory functions are not necessarily in conflicts with the dispute settlement procedures of the Vienna Ozone Convention, if in fact these procedures are utilised at all.[115]

First of all, the Implementation Committee receives, considers and reports on:

(i)   a report from a party/parties in another party's implementation of its treaty obligations under the Protocol;[116]

(ii)   the submission provided by a party that considers itself unable to comply fully with its obligations;[117]

---

112   Parties of the Montreal NCP may be re-elected for one immediate consecutive terms (Annex IV(5)). The Implementation Committee elects its own President and Vice-President who serve for one year. In the Third Meeting of the Parties, it was decided that the number of Parties should be increased by five to ten. See Decision III/21, UNEP/OzL. Pro.3/L.4. The NCP Committee of the 1979 Convention on Long-Range Transboundary Air Pollution consists of nine parties. See Decision 2012/25 on improving the functioning of the Implementation Committee, Annex: Implementation Committee, Its Structure and Functions and Procedures for Review, in ECE/EB.AIR/113/Add.1, Section I.

113   See Decision II/20. Importantly, the United States holds a permanent seat on the Executive Committee. See Chapter 6(III.B(1)) in this volume.

114   See Annex IV(8). The NCP of the 1979 Convention on Long-Range Transboundary Air Pollution employs the phrase, 'securing a constructive solutions'. See Decision 2012/25 on improving the functioning of the Implementation Committee, Annex: Implementation Committee, Its Structure and Functions and Procedures for Review, in ECE/EB.AIR/113/Add.1, Section IV.3(b); Patrick Széll, 'The Development of Multilateral Mechanisms for Monitoring Compliance', in Winfried Lang (ed.), *Sustainable Development and International Law* (Graham & Trotman/ Martinus Nijhoff, 1995), p. 106.

115   See Martti Koskenniemi, 'Breach of Treaty or Non-Compliance?', 3 *YbkIEL* (1992), p. 159.

116   See Annex IV(7-a).

117   See ibid.

(iii) other relevant submissions, replies and information concerned:[118] and

(iv) any information or observations with regard to compliance or production, import and export of controlled substances received and forwarded by the UNEP Secretariat.[119]

When analysing these reports and submissions, and in order to make appropriate recommendations, the Implementation Committee must identify the reasons underlying a party's anticipated non-compliance. The amended NCP of 1998 contains a new paragraph, saying that the Committee 'identify the facts and possible causes relating to individual cases of non-compliance'.[120] In the light of national data reporting from parties, the Implementation Committee also 'amicably' arranges the (re-)classification of 'developing countries'[121] that are entitled to receive funding from the Montreal Multilateral Fund.

In addition, the Implementation Committee may request further information through the UNEP Ozone Secretariat, when it considers it to be necessary.[122] The Committee's initial four years were occupied with discussions on information obtained from reported data, though, since late 1993, it has also examined substantial non-compliance issues, such as trade controls.[123]

The Committee also considers confidential information regarding treaty performance contained in such data reports. Its reports, however, must not include such delicate matters[124] and the members of the Committee and any party involved in its NCP processes must protect the confidentiality of information. Due partly to the fear that such confidential data might be publicly disclosed,[125] environmental NGOs are, at present, totally excluded from the

---

118 See ibid. The UNEP Ozone Secretariat, as we noted, is assigned the role to transmit such information on possible non-compliance.

119 See Annex IV(7-b).

120 See Annex II(7.d).

121 The Implementation Committee often submits corrections to the data reports of State parties.

122 See Annex II(7-c).

123 See Section VII(A) below. See also David G. Victor, *The Early Operation and Effectiveness of the Montreal Protocol's Non-Compliance Procedure* (International Institute for Applied Systems Analysis, 1996), Chapter 6.

124 See Annex II (15–16). It is worth noting that the Third Meeting of the Parties decided that data submitted to the Secretariat on the production of controlled substances would be confidential, while data on the consumption of these substances would not. It follows that environmental NGOs alone could not compile exact data regarding global trade in ODSs. At the Twenty-Fifth Meeting of the Implementation Committee, the Ozone Secretariat stated that 'a confidential communication from the Russian Federation had been circulated to Committee members'. See UNEP/OzL.Pro/ImpCom/25/2, para. 9.

125 See Patrick Széll, 'The Development of Multilateral Mechanisms for Monitoring Compliance', in Winfried Lang (ed.), *Sustainable Development and International Law* (Graham & Trotman/Martinus Nijhoff, 1995), p. 102.

THE MONTREAL NON-COMPLIANCE PROCEDURE

Implementation Committee meetings.[126] Yet it is important that NGOs are free to send written submissions on any matter they consider important to the Implementation Committee.[127]

By contrast, it is noticeable that a number of committees and commissions in the field of international humanitarian law rely, to an appreciable extent, on unofficial information supplied by human rights NGOs at national and international levels, whereas their complaints procedures are undertaken in closed meetings.[128] The Basel Convention compliance régime also depends in part on NGOs' active informal monitoring regarding trading in illegal hazardous wastes at national and international levels.[129] It is also interesting to note that under the dispute settlement mechanisms of the NAFTA, environmental NGOs are allowed to file complaints with its Commission.[130]

Secondly, the Implementation Committee submits a report, including any recommendations on individual non-compliance cases, to the Meeting of the Parties.[131] The Implementation Committee may also make recommendations where it considers them appropriate, though the parties concerned cannot participate in the decision-making process.[132] In other words, parties, including non-complying countries, are not normally invited to attend the meetings of the Implementation Committee on the first occasion that their status is

---

126 See also Gilbert M. Bankobeza, *Ozone Protection* (Eleven International, 2005), p. 244.

127 Information provided by Mr. G. Bankobeza of the Ozone Secretariat (11 March 1998). Environmental NGOs are allowed to attend the Meetings of the Parties as observers and may circulate documents at such ozone meetings. They also participate in meetings of the Executive Committee of the Montreal Multilateral Fund.

128 The legal texts, however, do not assign this role to NGOs. See, for example, Henry J. Steiner and Philip Alston, *International Human Rights in Context* (Clarendon Press, 1996), Chapter 8. See also Martin Scheinin, 'The International Covenant on Civil and Political Rights', in Geir Ulfstein (ed.), *Making Treaties Work* (Cambridge University Press, 2007), p. 59.

129 See Günther Handl, 'Environmental Security and Global Change: The Challenge to International Law', 1 *YbkIEL* (1990), p. 18. On the role of NGOs in the 1973 CITES, see Kamen Sachariew, 'Promoting Compliance with International Environmental Legal Standards', 2 *YbkIEL* (1991), p. 39; Michael J. Bowman, 'International Treaties and the Global Protection of Birds: Part I', 11 *JEL* (1999), p. 104; Rosalind Reeve, *Policing International Trade in Endangered Species: the CITES Treaty and Compliance* (Royal Institute of International Affairs and Earthscan, 2002), pp. 43 et seq.

130 See, for example, Norma S. Munguía Aldaraca, 'The North American Agreement on Environmental Cooperation', 2 *RECIEL* (1994), pp. 98–104; Philippe Sands and Jacqueline Peel, *Principles of International Environmental Law* (3rd ed. Cambridge University Press, 2012), pp. 850–860.

131 See Annex II(7-d) and Annex II(8). Under the early NCP, the Committee was not empowered to make such recommendations.

132 See Annex II(9). See also the statement by the President of the Implementation Committee, Mr. Schally, who stresses the importance of confidentiality (UNEP/OzL.Pro.7/INF.1, paras. 38 and 41).

considered.[133] In making such recommendations, the Implementation Committee as a subsidiary body of the Meeting of the Parties must conform to the Rules of Procedure adopted by the 1989 Ozone Meeting, by applying *mutatis mutandis,* however.[134]

It should be noted that, under international law, the Committee is not necessarily restricted to basing its recommendations on the ozone treaties, but that it can also provide recommendations *ex aequo et bono* by taking all the relevant circumstances into account.[135] While such recommendations themselves are legally non-binding on ozone régime members, they do carry political weight[136] and, in general, they are widely followed. This voluntary acceptance of the Committee's recommendations has contributed to its favourable reputation on anticipated treaty non-compliance.

Thirdly, the Implementation Committee undertakes consensual information-gathering in the territory of a party for achieving its functions based on the consent of the party. These are so-called 'on-the-spot investigations', or a kind of 'verification' mission, in a limited sense.[137] During the negotiation of

---

133 See UNEP/Ozl.Pro.14/9, para. 138. At later stages of non-compliance, parties are invited to attend meetings of the Implementation Committee. See, for example, UNEP/OzL.Pro/ImpCom/34/6, para. 66 (Bangladesh); UNEP/OzL.Pro/ImpCom/58/4, paras. 59–63 (Israel and Kazakhstan); UNEP/OzL.Pro/ImpCom/25/2, para. 7 (Israel and the Russian Federation). See also Gilbert M. Bankobeza, *Ozone Protection* (Eleven International, 2005), p. 279.

134 See the Rules of Procedures, in UNEP/Ozl.Pro.1/5. See UNEP, *Handbook for the Montreal Protocol on Substances That Deplete the Ozone Layer* (11th ed. 2017), pp. 548–549 and 697. In principle, they would apply to meetings of any subsidiary committees and panels. See UNEP/OzL.Pro.1/5, para. 7; See also Gilbert M. Bankobeza, *Ozone Protection* (Eleven International, 2005), p. 275. It may be assumed, however, that the Committee usually makes its recommendations by unanimous vote or by consensus. The Executive Committee has its own rules of procedure.

135 See Rudolf L. Bindschedler, 'Conciliation and Mediation', 1 *Encyclopedia of Public International Law* (North-Holland Pub. Co., 1982), pp. 47 et seq. See also Section V(A) below.

136 See also Rudolf L. Bindschedler, 'International Organizations, General Aspects', 5 *Encyclopedia of Public International Law* (North-Holland, 1982), p. 133.

137 See Annex II(7-e). This provision also appears in the NCP of the 1979 Long-Range Transboundary Air Pollution Convention. Decision 2012/25 on improving the functioning of the Implementation Committee, Annex: Implementation Committee, Its Structure and Functions and Procedures for Review, in ECE/EB.AIR/113/Add.1, Section VIII.6(b). See also the 1991 Protocol to the Antarctic Treaty on Environmental Protection (Article 14); the 1971 Nuclear Weapons Treaty (Article III(6)). For instance, the IAEA has its own inspectors who carry out on-site inspections and then report to the institution. For further details on inspection, see Alan E. Boyle, 'Saving the World? Implementation and Enforcement in International Environmental Law Through International Institutions', 3 *JEL* (1991), pp. 236 et seq.; W. Fischer, *The Verification of International Convention on Protection of the Environment and Common Resources* (Forschungszentrum Jülich GmbH, 1992).

the Montreal NCP, developing countries regarded as unacceptable the consideration by the Implementation Committee of information from on-site inspections that were undertaken on the Committee's initiative, as well as information from NGOs, industries, the media and individuals.[138] A workable compromise – consensual information-gathering – was finally reached by mutual concession.

Finally, since financial and/or technical assistance are, in practice, closely related to a party's capability to comply with obligations, the Implementation Committee maintains an exchange of information with the Executive Committee of the MLF concerning this assistance.[139]

(3)   The Meeting of the Parties to the Montreal Protocol
(a)   *The Functions of the Meeting of the Parties in the NCP*
As already pointed out, the Meeting of the Parties serves as the final decision-maker under the Montreal NCP.[140] Hence the highest organ of the ozone régime retains, to the very end, direct control over multilateral ozone disputes raised among Member States. It should not be denied that this decision-making arrangement reveals parties' intentions to conserve their various economic and political national interests in environmental organisations rather than turning over such power to representative subgroups or other institutions. The same may be said of other non-compliance mechanisms of international environmental régimes.

After receiving the reports from the standing Implementation Committee, the Meeting of the Parties considers the circumstances of the matter, decide upon and call for steps to bring about full compliance with the Protocol, including measures to assist the parties' compliance with the Protocol, and to further the Protocol's objectives.[141]

The 'Indicative List of Measures' lists actions that might be taken by the Meeting of the Parties in response to non-compliance with the treaty obligations:

(i)   providing appropriate assistance with the collection and reporting of data, technical assistance, technology transfer and financial assistance, information transfer and training.

(ii)   issuing cautions.

---

138   See UNEP/OzL.Pro/WG.3/3/3, para. 23.

139   See Annex II(7-f). Since 1992, the Implementation Committee has invited representatives from the Secretariat of the Montreal Multilateral Fund and its implementing agencies to its meetings.

140   See Sections III(A) and IV(B) above.

141   See Annex II(9).

238   CHAPTER 5

(iii) suspending, in accordance with the applicable rules of international
       law concerning the suspension of the operation of a treaty, of specific
       rights and privileges under the Protocol, whether or not to time limits,
       including those concerned with industrial rationalisation, production,
       consumption, trade, transfer of technology, financial mechanism and in-
       stitutional arrangements.

The Meeting of the Parties may also make an interim call and/or recommendations.[142] Moreover, it can request the standing Implementation Committee
to make recommendations to assist the Meeting's consideration of matters of
treaty non-compliance.[143] Those decisions and recommendations made by the
Meeting of the Parties with a view to implementation must be fully effective in
accordance with the objectives of the international ozone régime.

It is worth pointing out, in passing, other basic but vital functions of the
Meeting of the Parties that will help enhance its efficiency in deciding which
measure(s) should be taken for a Member State's anticipated non-compliance
with treaty obligations. The Meeting of the Parties can:

(a) decide on any adjustments/reductions;[144]
(b) decide on any addition to/insertion in/removal from any annex of sub-
     stances and on related control measures;[145]
(c) establish guidelines or procedures for reporting of information;[146]
(d) review requests for technical assistance submitted;[147]
(e) review reports prepared by the Secretariat;
(f) assess and review control measures;[148]
(g) consider and adopt proposals for amendment of the Protocol or any an-
     nex and for any new annex;[149]
(h) consider and adopt the budget for implementing the Protocol:[150] and
(i) consider and undertake any additional action that may be required for
     the achievement of the purposes of the Protocol.[151]

---

142   See Annex II(13); Section VII below.
143   See Annex II(14); Section VII below.
144   See Chapter 3(IV) in this volume.
145   See ibid.
146   See ibid.
147   See Chapter 6 in this volume.
148   See Chapter 3(IV) in this volume.
149   See ibid.
150   See Chapter 6 in this volume.
151   See Section IV.B(b) below. It is worth noting that, in order to analyse destruction technol-
      ogies, the 1990 London Meeting of the Parties established an *Ad Hoc* Technical Advisory
      Committee on Destruction Technologies. 'The members shall be experts on destruction

(b)   *The Legal Nature of the Decisions of the Meeting of the Parties*

Here we shall focus on some of the important features of the binding quality of decisions adopted by the Meeting of the Parties to the Montreal Ozone Protocol.

By October 2016, the Meeting of the Parties to the Protocol alone had adopted over 800 decisions in accordance with the Rules of Procedure.[152] Many of them are, directly or indirectly, related to non-compliance issues concerning international regulation of ODSS, trade controls of ODSS and data reporting. They usually stipulate that régime members should take further necessary measures for the achievement of the purposes of the dynamic regulatory régime, or they often reiterate obligations already laid down in the articles of the ozone treaties.

However, the legal status of the decisions of the Meeting remains unsettled[153] – although, presumably, 'ordinary decisions' are non-binding,[154] and it is not necessarily clear that non-compliance with the commitments contained in the decisions of the Parties to the Protocol (and to the Vienna Ozone Convention) can be regarded as non-compliance or breach of treaty.[155] In addition, the decisions are often vague and open to a variety of interpretations – their vagueness may often be the result of workable political compromise within the environmental régime.[156]

---

technologies and selected with due reference to equitable geographical distribution' (UNEP/OzL.Pro.2/3, pp. 15–16 and para. 48).

152   The processes to adopt these decisions are rather complicated. See 'Rules of Procedures for the Meeting of the Parties' in UNEP/OzL.Pro.1/5/Annex I; Cf. Article 11.4(j) of the Montreal Protocol. Cf. the Rules of Procedure for Meetings of the Executive Committee in UNEP/OzL.Pro.3/11/Annex VI. On Rules of Procedure in MEAS, see Patrick Széll, 'Decision Making under Multilateral Environmental Agreements', 26/5 *EPL* (1996), p. 211.

153   See also Susana Borràs, 'Comparative Analysis of Selected Compliance Procedures under Multilateral Environmental Agreements', in Sandrine Maljean-Dubois and Lavanya Rajamani (eds.), *Implementation of International Environmental Law* (Martinus Nijhoff, 2011), pp. 351 et seq.

154   See Hugh Adsett, Anne Daniel, Masud Husain and Ted L. McDorman, 'Compliance Committees and Recent Multilateral Environmental Agreements: The Canadian Experience with Their Negotiation and Operation', 42 *CYbkIL* (2005), p. 103.

155   In August 2006, the United States Court of Appeals for the District of Columbia Circuit held that decisions of the Meeting of the Parties to the Montreal Protocol were political commitments, not enforceable in the domestic courts. See 'D.C. Court of Appeals Finds Decisions under Montreal Protocol Lack Domestic Legal Effect Source', 101 *AJIL* (2007), pp. 208–209; John H. Knox, 'Natural Resources Defense Council v. Environmental Protection Agency. 464 F.3d 1', 101 *AJIL* (2007), pp. 471–477.

156   See, for example, Decision VII/8 regarding Russia's non-compliance with Article 2 control measures.

240   CHAPTER 5

It is interesting to note that, during the negotiations of the Montreal NCP, many government representatives suggested that such decisions made by the Meeting of the Parties to the Protocol were distinct from Articles of the Montreal Protocol's text. Likewise, some States were of the opinion that not all decisions were binding on the State Parties.[157] Yet some other representatives stated that such decisions were always legally binding, if they related to 'matters of substance'.[158] In this regard, China made a formal reservation.[159] Consequently, as stated earlier, the 1992 Copenhagen Meeting failed to adopt the 'Indicative List of Possible Situations of Non-Compliance' that includes 'non-compliance with the obligations in decisions of the Parties'. Until now, this matter has not been formally discussed in the Meeting of the Parties and in meetings of the Conference of the Parties to the Vienna Ozone Convention.

One may notice that, in contrast to State entities that have established fully independent legal personality in international law,[160] the functional capacity or 'implied powers' of the Meeting of the Parties – as the product of the multilateral ozone treaty – are strictly limited to their 'objectives' and 'functions', and, generally speaking, they are not well defined by customary international law or general international law, but based primarily on the Montreal Ozone Protocol. While the regular Meeting of the Parties has some supranational aspects, it is not a 'super-State' organization. As Professor Birnie and Professor Boyle shrewdly pointed out, 'the supervisory body, whether a meeting of the parties or a Commission, is in substance no more than a diplomatic conference of States, and the existence ... of a separate legal personality does not alter the reality that the membership of these institutions is in no sense independent of

---

157 See UNEP/OzL.Pro/WG.3/3/3, para. 41 and 'Indicative List of Possible Situations of Non-Compliance with the Protocol' (in Annex II). See also comments made at the time of adoption of Decision IV/17 C (Application of Trade Measures Under Article 4 to Non-Parties to the Protocol), in UNEP/OzL.Pro.4/15, paras. 73–74.

158 See ibid.

159 See ibid.

160 Regarding international legal personality, see *Reparation for Injuries Suffered in the Service of the United Nations Case, ICJ Reports* (1949), p. 180; *The International Status of South West Africa Case, ICJ Reports* (1950), pp. 136–138. Ian Brownlie, *Principles of Public International Law* (4th ed. Oxford University Press, 1990), Chapter 3; D. W. Bowett, *The Law of International Institutions* (4th ed. Sweet & Maxwell, 1982), Chapter 11; N. D. White, *The Law of International Organisations* (Manchester University Press, 1996), Chapter 2; Rosalyn Higgins, *Problems and Process: International Law and How We Use It* (Clarendon Press, 1994), pp. 46 et seq.

THE MONTREAL NON-COMPLIANCE PROCEDURE   241

the States they represent'.[161] In this connection, it is also possible to argue that 'any additional action',[162] required for the achievement of the purposes of the Montreal Protocol, should be defined in terms of its limited functional capacity or its 'implied powers' in general international law.[163]

In addition, it is important to note that 'internal' international law and the procedural rules of the Meeting of the Parties are subject to customary international law and rules governing the principles of State sovereignty and equality of States.[164] In theory, the decisions adopted according to the internal legal rules of the Ozone Meeting are – in a formal sense, at least – of secondary importance for the ozone régime, unless declared with an expressed intention to be bound. Hence, ozone régime members may dispute the validity of a decision adopted by the Ozone Meeting on the grounds that it violates the Rules of Procedure.[165]

In the light of the above considerations, we may say that an ozone decision cannot impose on régime Member States a legal obligation to adopt measures which conflict with the objectives of the international ozone régime. Needless to say, however, certain specific decisions adopted through formal procedures provided in advance in the ozone treaties (for example, adjustments and amendments[166]) are legally binding on Member States.[167] In this context, they are properly regarded as 'hard' international law.

---

161 See Patricia Birnie and Alan E. Boyle, *International Law and the Environment* (Clarendon Press, 1992), p. 165.

162 See Article 11(f). See Section IV(B.a) above.

163 See also Susana Borràs, 'Comparative Analysis of Selected Compliance Procedures under Multilateral Environmental Agreements', in Sandrine Maljean-Dubois and Lavanya Rajamani (eds.), *Implementation of International Environmental Law* (Martinus Nijhoff, 2011), p. 333. It is noteworthy, however, that a key feature of the doctrine of 'implied powers' is its flexibility, and such powers must be defined in the light of specific circumstances. See Henry G. Schermers and Niels M. Blokker, *International Institutional Law* (5th. rev. ed. Martinus Nijhoff, 2011), p. 188; Robert Jennings and Arthur Watts (eds.), *Oppenheim's International Law* (9th ed. Longman, 1992), pp. 16–22.

164 See Georg Schwarzenberger, *A Manual of International Law* (5th edn. Stevens & Sons Limited/Frederick A. Praeger, 1967), pp. 32–33 and 268–269. Article 38 of the Statute of International Court of Justice does not necessarily refer to the legal status of 'internal' international law of institutions.

165 For a discussion of non-compliance with rules of procedure, see, for instance, Benedetto Conforti, 'The Legal Effect of Non-Compliance with Rules of Procedure in the U.N. General Assembly and Security Council', 63 *AJIL* (1969), pp. 479–489.

166 See Chapter 3(IV.C-H) in this volume.

167 See also Pierr-Marie Dupuy and Jorge E. Viñuales, *International Environmental Law* (Cambridge University Press), pp. 287–288.

At the same time, it may be argued that this controversial issue presents a key factor toward the understanding of the 'self-contained' ozone régime that now assumes a dynamic character.[168] Indeed, one of the primary functions of the Meeting of the Parties as a quasi-legislative body is to change 'constantly' the international law of ozone layer protection. Numerous decisions – whether adopted as 'soft' or 'hard' law instruments[169] – have created certain legal norms, expectations and elements that form part of the international legal system of the developing regulatory régime. As this question is taken up in Chapter 6 in this volume, it is worth noting that, as with the NCP, the 'Interim' Multilateral Fund of the Montreal Protocol – which is seen as a prototype for financial mechanisms in protecting the global environment – was established on the basis of Decision 11/18 of the Ozone Meeting of the Parties, rather than by amendment.[170] Therefore, it is mistake to think that they have no legal effects.[171] On the contrary, in the same manner that decisions of international organisations have contributed to customary international institutional law, many decisions of the Meeting of the Parties show 'immediate' evidence of consensus among régime actors.[172] At the same time, they provide essential indicators for a proper understanding of the developing ozone regulatory régime.

Finally, we should not overlook the fact that the current rapid pace of environmental degradation has produced a situation in which customary international law obviously does not keep pace with the immediate need to find solutions for new environmental problems, such as ozone depletion, global climate change and the depletion of living and non-living natural resources.[173]

Another important legal issue to be taken account in the present discussion is the power of the Meeting of the Parties to interpret the ozone treaties. At the 1995 Vienna Meeting, the Russian Federation insisted that the Meeting of the Parties should have applied 'appropriate measures' in accordance with the Indicative List in an ascending order of importance, that is, from assistance,

---

168   See Alan E. Boyle, 'State Responsibility for Breach of Obligations to Protect the Global Environment', in W. E. Butler (ed.), *Control over Compliance with International Law* (Martinus Nijhoff, 1991), pp. 75–77.

169   See Chapter 1(III.A) in this volume.

170   It is also important to note that, subsequently, the Ozone Meeting adopted Decision VII/16 regarding judicial personality, privileges and immunities of the Multilateral Fund. See UNEP/OzL.Pro.6/7, p. 22; Chapter 6 in this volume.

171   See also Pierr-Marie Dupuy and Jorge E. Viñuales, *International Environmental Law* (Cambridge University Press), pp. 288.

172   See Jonathan I. Charney, 'Universal International Law', 87 *AJIL* (1993), pp. 529–551.

173   See Chapter 1(III.A) in this volume, on the framework-protocol and 'soft law' approaches.

THE MONTREAL NON-COMPLIANCE PROCEDURE 243

caution to sanctions.[174] At present, there does not exist, in a legal sense, a clear preference among the measures listed. Such an 'appropriate measure' – Decision VII/18, which Russia would not describe in such mild terms – was, as we shall see, adopted according to the Rules of Procedure of the Meeting of the Parties, but with the help of the Ozone Secretariat's own practical interpretation. Based on Article 31 of the Vienna Convention on the Law of Treaties,[175] it is possible to argue that the *travaux préparatoires* of the Montreal NCP would partly defend Russia's position. Furthermore, as a last resort, dispute relating to treaty interpretation might be resolved through traditional settlement procedures under Article 11 of the Vienna Ozone Convention. Yet, as we noted, the Meeting of the Parties to the Protocol decided in its Third Meeting that 'the responsibility for legal interpretation of the Protocol ultimately rests with the Parties themselves' (that is, the 'control' of the interpretation of the ozone treaty texts).

Given that this debatable statement implies that the quasi-judicial interpretative organ of the ozone régime is not be entirely bound by the principles or rules of general international law, such decisions (or rules of behaviour) adopted by the Meeting of the Parties, as a result of the inter-State bargaining process, may not conceal their political orientations in existing international environmental relations. Such outcomes might be criticised by some for lack of 'legitimacy',[176] or as mere declarations of international environmental politics. So, to what extent must such decisions take account of general international law? Is the Ozone Meeting's real intention declared, ultimately, to interpret and apply the provisions of the ozone treaties in the light of multi-faceted national interests of the ozone régime Member States? These are difficult questions.

174　In this context, the 1969 Vienna Convention on the Law of Treaties provides 'A treaty shall be interpreted in good faith in accordance with the ordinary meaning to be given to the terms of treaty in their context and in the light of its object and purpose' (Article 31). However, the subsequent conduct of the Meeting of the Parties (or the Implementation Committee) may determine this issue (see Article 31(3)).

175　See Article 32. See, for example, Ian Sinclair, *The Vienna Convention on the Law of Treaties* (2nd ed. Manchester University Press, 1984), pp. 115–117. It is also important that the régime member's original intentions are clarified in terms of the purposes of the ozone treaties.

176　In the widest sense, the term legitimacy can be defined as the quality of a rule which derives from a perception on the part of those whom it is applied that it has come into being in accordance with a fair process, that is, one based on valid sources, but also encompasses literary, socio-anthropological and philosophical insights. See Thomas Frank, 'Legitimacy in the International System', 82 *AJIL* (1988), pp. 705–759: Oscar Schachter, 'United Nations Law', 88 *AJIL* (1994), pp. 9–16.

244   CHAPTER 5

It may be suggested tentatively that internal international régime organs within the system of the ozone treaties are more suitable for interpretations and settlement of disputes than judicial organs external to them. For instance, interpretation of IMF rules are always made by the Executive Board, the Board of Governors or/and a Committee on Interpretation.[177] In addition, it has been argued in the legal literature that governmental representation in one environmental legal régime can be often regarded as a certain 'guarantee' for a consistent diplomatic policy in another international legal régime or international organisation.[178] This may partly explain why Member States of the WTO/GATT law régime have never formally disputed the validity of Article 4 TREMS of the Montreal Protocol, the Multilateral Fund's environmental subsidies[179] and other MEA trade restrictions.

V   The Principal Features of the NCP: the Montreal NCP, International
        Conciliation and Other Dispute Settlement Procedures

What I seek to show in this Section is that dispute settlement under the NCP can be viewed as a mixture of diplomatic and quasi-judicial efforts in resolving treaty disputes at the multilateral level. It consists of a new set of institutionalised global negotiation processes that decrease the likelihood of international confrontation.[180] Among other settlement techniques,[181] international conciliation[182] is chosen here as a candidate somewhat similar to the Montreal

---

177   See Henry G. Schermers and Niels M. Blokker, *International Institutional Law* (5th. rev. ed. Martinus Nijhoff, 2011), p. 856.
178   For arguments against composing independent technical bodies, see Henry G. Schermers and Niels M. Blokker, *International Institutional Law* (5th. rev. ed. Martinus Nijhoff, 2011), pp. 214 et seq.
179   For details of the relationship between the Fund's environmental subsidies and the GATT, see Scott N. Carlson, 'The Montreal Protocol's Environmental Subsidies and GATT: A Needed Reconciliation', 29 *TEXAS ILJ* (1994), pp. 211–230.
180   It is also probable that such an institutionalised negotiation procedure would reduce the impact of power relations between the parties to the dispute which are inherent in negotiation process.
181   Methods of peaceful settlement of disputes are generally classified into seven broad categories: (i) negotiations, (ii) good offices, (iii) enquiry and fact-finding, (iv) mediation, (v) conciliation, (vi) arbitration and (vii) formal judicial settlement. For details, see Office of Legal Affairs, Codification Division (United Nations), *Handbook on the Peaceful Settlement of Disputes between States* (United Nations, 1992).
182   See, for example, J. G. Merrills, *International Dispute Settlement* (6th ed. Cambridge University Press, 2017), Chapter 4; D. W. Bowett, 'Development in the Settlement of Disputes', 180 *Recueil des cours* (1983), pp. 185 et seq.; Jean-Pierre Cot, *International Conciliation*

NCP model.[183] In addition, dispute settlement procedures in (i) the 'old' system in the European Human Rights Convention, prior to the entry into force of Protocol 11 in 1998 (that is, the role of the Committee of Ministers), (ii) the WTO/GATT dispute settlement system and (iii) the ILO will be briefly considered in comparison to the Montreal NCP.

A *The Montreal NCP as a Multilateral Conciliation Mechanism*

(1) International Conciliation and the NCP

In conciliation, a friendly third party or an international institution such as a conciliation commission works out an amicable, but not necessarily an authoritative, solution and produces a report with recommendations for the parties concerned, based on hearings, findings and evidence. In contrast to an arbitral award, its advantages are that 'the parties retain control over the outcome and remain free to negotiate a politically acceptable settlement of their differences without being bound to adhere to treaty provisions of international law'.[184]

The text of the Montreal NCP does not employ the term 'conciliation', although it refers to an amicable solution.[185] Yet, as far as the functions of the standing Implementation Committee as an 'international conciliation body'[186] (and of the Secretariat as a group of technical experts[187]) are concerned, the NCP comes close to international conciliation as a formal method of settling various treaty disputes. Such treaty disputes are, as described above, concerned with reporting of data (Articles 7 and 9), ODS control measures (Articles 2 and 5),

---

(trans. by R. Myers, Europa Publications, 1972), pp. 8–13. See the 1928 General Act for the Pacific Settlement of International Disputes, revised on April 28 1949, (Articles 1–16); the 1957 European Convention for the Peaceful Settlement of Disputes; the 1969 Vienna Convention on the Law of Treaties (Article 66 and Annex); the 1971 Convention on International Liability for Damage caused by Space Objects (Article XIX); the United Nations Rules of the Conciliation of Disputes between States (Chapter 7 regarding rules applicable to conciliation by commission); the 1992 Decision on Peaceful Settlement of Disputes including the Convention on Conciliation and Arbitration Within the CSCE (Annex III).

183 Merrills suggest that environmental compliance procedures constitute a special form of conciliation. See J. G. Merrills, *International Dispute Settlement* (6th ed. Cambridge University Press, 2017), p. 83.

184 See Alan E. Boyle, 'Settlement of Disputes Relating to the Law of the Sea and the Environment', 26 *Thesaurus Acroasium* (1996), p. 259. See also James Leslie Brierly, *The Law of Nations* (6th ed. by Sir Humphrey Waldock, Clarendon Press, 1963), pp. 373–376.

185 Article 28 of the European Human Rights Convention reads: 'it shall at the same time place itself at the disposal of the parties concerned with a view to securing *a friendly settlement of a matter on the basis of respect for Human Rights* as defined in this Convention' (emphasis added).

186 See Section IV(B.2) above.

187 See Chapter 2(III.D(3)) in this volume and Section IV(B.1) above.

trade matters (Article 4) and the classification of Article 5 country parties. Under the Montreal NCP, the Implementation Committee plays a similar role to a conciliator who is given the task of investigating the dispute in its various aspects and of helping parties reach an amicable but non-binding agreement.[188] The Ozone Secretariat and subsidiary treaty bodies are to provide the NCP Committee with relevant expert information.

However, the NCP is not a conciliatory dispute settlement procedure in a true sense of the term.[189] Strictly speaking, therefore, this means therefore that the NCP falls into the category of 'other peaceful means' of settling disputes provided for in Article 33 of the United Nations Charter.[190] There are at least two differences between normal conciliation procedures and the NCP of the Montreal Protocol type.

In the first place, international conciliation – and formal judicial proceedings – is more applicable in the case of bilateral, rather than multilateral disputes or agreements.[191] Strictly speaking, as Professor Bindschedler says, the primary objective of conciliation is not to establish a 'uniform legal order'.[192] As noted above, a non-compliance dispute regarding the ozone treaties is not a bilateral dispute between two or more parties but a multilateral dispute between one party and all other parties.[193] It is important in this respect that non-compliance complaints may be initiated by both any party and the Secretariat. Those NCP initiators by themselves may determine the 'right timing' to trigger the dispute avoidance and settlement procedure.[194] Unlike normal international conciliation procedures, the NCP as a multilateral conciliation

---

188 See Section VII(A) below.

189 The Vienna Ozone Layer Convention contain a good international conciliation procedure. See in detail Chapter 2(III.D(4)) in this volume.

190 Regarding 'other peaceful means', see Office of Legal Affairs, Codification Division (United Nations), *Handbook on the Peaceful Settlement of Disputes between States* (United Nations, 1992), paras. 288–312.

191 However, a number of multilateral treaties do contain detailed conciliation procedures. See Office of Legal Affairs, Codification Division (United Nations), *Handbook on the Peaceful Settlement of Disputes between States* (United Nations, 1992), para. 143.

192 See, for example, Rudolf L. Bindschedler, 'Conciliation and Mediation', 1 *Encyclopedia of Public International Law* (North-Holland Pub. Co., 1982), p. 49.

193 See also Michael Bothe, 'The Evaluation of Enforcement Mechanisms in International Environmental Law', in Rüdiger Wolfrum (ed.), *Enforcing Environmental Standards* (Springer, 1996), pp. 32–33.

194 See Section VII(B.2) below. See also Richard Benedick, *Ozone Diplomacy* (Harvard University Press, 1998), p. 281.

mechanism thus inspires a collective reaction taken by the parties in cases of non-compliance.[195]

In the second place, the NCP Committee is not an independent third party but is composed of government representatives.[196] This partly reflects one of the noteworthy political aspects of the Montreal NCP. It may be assumed that the Committee is likely to decide what measures should be taken on non-compliance cases at its broad discretion. Under the NCP, the members of the Committee are strictly required to protect the confidentiality of information from the parties and, moreover, NGOs are not allowed to participate in the Committee's meetings.[197] In this respect, Professor Palmer argues that the Committee could 'ignore certain rules of international law whose application might not be considered desirable and it may draw upon the body of *normative expectations* developed within the [ozone] regime regardless of the formal legal status of any particular rule'.[198]

Yet under the Montreal NCP – unlike under both an *ad hoc* conciliation or arbitration commission and the so-called 'panels' in the field of international economic law – the question at issue will be addressed by the permanent Committee that meets several times a year, and not, therefore, by a temporary *ad hoc* third party commission. The Committee is a treaty organ created specifically for the settlement of treaty disputes concerning the global protection of the ozone layer. In political terms, this pre-constituted international system may foster a 'basic set of ideas relating to societal values'[199] shared by the ozone régime members.

(2)   From Conciliation to the Political Organ of the MEA

The role and capability of the Implementation Committee are strictly limited to the adoption of non-binding recommendations and the Committee is not granted comprehensive, but only conciliatory powers. Should the standing Committee not succeed in settling an ozone dispute, however, the supreme organ of the ozone régime, that is, the Meeting of the Parties, is then to take

---

195   See Laurence Boisson de Chazournes, 'Mise en œuvre du droit international dans le domaine de la protection de l'environnement: enjeux et défis', 99 *Revue générale de droit international public* (1995), p. 63; Thomas Gehring, *Dynamic International Régimes* (Peter Lang, 1994), pp. 318–319.

196   For details, see Section IV(B.2) below.

197   See Section IV(B.2.a) above.

198   Lakshman D. Guruswamy, Geoffrey W. R. Palmer and Burns H. Weston (eds.), *International Environmental Law and World Order* (West Pub. Co., 1994), p. 1120 (emphasis added).

199   See William D. Coplin, *The Functions of International Law: An Introduction to the Role of International Law in the Contemporary World* (Rand McNally, 1966), Chapter 5.

'quasi-judicial' decisions regarding treaty non-compliance by a régime member in accordance with the Indicative List of Measures in Annex V.[200]

As in the case of Russia's non-compliance, this dynamic 'quasi-legislative' activity of the international political organ often far exceeds the conciliatory role of the Implementation Committee, and its decisive power may be comparable to that of the Committee of Ministers under the European Human Rights Convention, prior to the entry into force of the Eleventh Protocol in 1998.[201] In exceptional circumstances involving cases which have not been referred to the European Court of Human Rights, the Committee of Ministers – which consists of State representatives, usually the foreign ministers of Member States – is empowered to make a binding determination, whether or not there has been a violation of the Convention. Its deliberations on certain cases were confidential and the individual applicant was totally excluded from the Committee's procedure.[202] In short, as is the case with decisions of the Meeting of the Parties,[203] it was likely that the Committee of Ministers might also 'politicise' disputes that remain unsolved to a not inconsiderable extent.

In addition, it is worth noting that there have been many cases in which the Committee of Ministers failed to achieve the required two-thirds majority, and, in fact, the Committee had taken no decision at all.[204] In such cases, in a sense, this lack of decisions might be viewed as non-compliance of the Committee under Article 32(1) in deciding whether or not there had been a violation of

---

200 It should be noted, however, that even if a régime member refuses to accept compliance-related recommendations by the Implementation Committee, the whole procedure for settling ozone disputes does not have to be restarted before the Meeting of the Parties. International ozone negotiations within the Meeting of the Parties will continue, based on evidence and factual, technical data provided by the Committee, the Ozone Secretariat and other technical bodies such as temporary sub-committees.

201 It is said that, in the 'old' system of human right protection, the use of a political organ was a compromise to ensure that all applications resulted in a final determination. See Bernadette Rainey, Elizabeth Wicks and Clare Ovey, *Jacobs, White, and Ovey, The European Convention on Human Rights* (6th ed. 2014, Oxford University Press), p. 9; Henry G. Schermers, 'The Eleventh Protocol to the European Convention on Human Rights', 19 *European Law Review* (1994), pp. 367 et seq.; Andrew Drzemczewski, 'A Major Overhaul of the European Human Rights Convention Control Mechanism: Protocol No. 11', 6/2 *Collected Courses of the Academy of European Law* (Kluwer Law International, 1997), pp. 132–134.

202 See Francis G. Jacobs and Robin C. A. White, *The European Convention on Human Rights* (2nd ed. Clarendon Press, 1996), p. 395.

203 See Decision VIII/26(1), discussed in Section VII(B.2) below.

204 See Francis G. Jacobs and Robin C. A. White, *The European Convention on Human Rights* (2nd ed. Clarendon Press, 1996), p. 396.

the European Human Rights Convention.[205] This fact clearly shows the inherent limitations of such political treaty bodies, when dealing with controversial issues.

Accordingly, while the Committee of Ministers acted in a quasi-judicial capacity, it was probable that the Committee took account of considerations of political expediency and in certain cases, such decisions made by the diplomatic institution were thus not necessarily consistent with general international law.

B *The Dispute Settlement Mechanisms Used by Other International Institutions*

Let us, for a moment, consider dispute settlement procedures of the WTO/GATT legal system and of the International Labour Organisation (ILO). There are some similarities between the Montreal NCP, on the one hand, and the WTO/GATT non-violation procedure and the complaints procedure in the ILO, on the other hand.

(1) The WTO/GATT Non-Violation Procedure in International Economic Law[206]

The GATT dispute settlement procedure – though formally based on GATT Articles XXII and XXIII (and a few other provisions) – has been built over time through the progressive development of subsequent customary practice.[207] It is important that the principal purpose of the WTO/GATT dispute settlement procedure is not to sanction breaches of a treaty rule, but to ensure

---

205 See D. J. Harris, M. O'Boyle and C. Warbrick, *Law of the European Convention on Human Rights* (Butterworths, 1995), p. 695.

206 On the WTO/GATT dispute settlement system, see, among others, Yuji Iwasawa, *WTO no Funsō Shori* [WTO Dispute Settlement] (Sanseido, 1995) (in Japanese); Ernst-Ulrich Petersmann, *The GATT/WTO Dispute Settlement System* (Kluwer Law International, 1997). With regard to the non-violation complaints, see Ernst-Ulrich Petersmann, 'Violation and Non-Violation Complaints in Public International Trade Law', 34 *GYbkIL* (1991), p. 192; Thomas Cottier and Krista Nadakavukaren Schefer, 'Non-Violation Complaints in WTO/GATT Dispute Settlement: Past, Present and Future', in Ernst-Ulrich Petersmann (ed.), *International Trade Law and the GATT/WTO Dispute Settlement System* (Kluwer Law International, 1997), Chapter 3; Armin von Bogdandy, 'The Non-Violation Procedure of Article XXIII:2, GATT: Its Operational Rationale', 26 *JWT* (1992), pp. 95–111; P. J. Kuyper, 'The Law of GATT As a Special Field of International law', 25 *Netherlands YbkIL* (1994), pp. 245–249.

207 See Yuji Iwasawa, *WTO no Funsō Shori* [WTO Dispute Settlement] (Sanseido, 1995), Chapter 2; (in Japanese); Ernst-Ulrich Petersmann, *The GATT/WTO Dispute Settlement System* (Kluwer Law International, 1997), Chapter 2; John H. Jackson, *The World Trading System* (2nd ed. MIT Press, 1997), pp. 112–120.

predictability and the maintenance of the balance of advantages in the changing circumstances of international economic relations.[208]

The dispute settlement system of WTO/GATT trade law is now clearly described in the 1994 WTO Understanding on Rules and Procedures Governing the Settlement of Disputes (the DSU/Annex II) that prescribes considerable changes.[209] Article 3(1) of the DSU provides that the Members affirm their adherence to the principles for the management of disputes heretofore applied under GATT Articles XXII and XXIII, and the procedures further elaborated and modified. Furthermore, Article 3(2) of the DSU states that the WTO settlement system is 'a central element in providing security and predictability to the multilateral trading system and it serves to 'clarify the existing provision of [the] agreements in accordance with customary rules of interpretation of public international law'.

One of the distinguishing features of the WTO/GATT dispute settlement procedures has been the introduction of the panel system (Articles 6–16 and 18–19 of the 1994 DSU),[210] which incorporates certain elements of international conciliation with a marked (quasi-)judicial character.[211] The WTO Secretariat must suggest the names of three panelists for the dispute. If the parties cannot agree on them within twenty days, the Director General appoints the panelists he considers most appropriate. The members of a panel perform their duties

---

208 See the General Provisions contained in Article 3 of the 1994 DSU (paras. 2, 3, 7 and 10).

209 It applies to all multilateral trade agreements in the Annexes to the 1994 WTO Agreements. For a brief summary of these improvements, see John H. Jackson, *The World Trading System* (2nd ed. MIT Press, 1997), pp. 125–126.

210 The WTO/GATT dispute settlement procedure commences with bilateral consultations, however (see GATT Articles XXII(1) and XXIII(1); Article 4 of the DSU). The member concerned must reply within ten days to a request for consultations and should enter into consultations within thirty days from the date of request. If these consultations prove unsuccessful, and if both parties so agree, the case may be brought to the WTO General, acting *ex officio*, may offer his good office. If the party concerned does not respond to the request for consultations within ten days, or if the consultations fail to arrive at a solution after sixty days, the other party may request that a panel be set up by the Dispute Settlement Body (DSB). It is interesting to note that a panel is established unless there is a consensus not to do so (it is almost 'automatic'). The WTO dispute settlement system contains mandatory consultations (Article 4), arbitration procedures (Article 25), and optional procedures for good offices (Articles 5 and 24), conciliation and mediation (Articles 5 and 24). There are also several special dispute settlement bodies, such as the Textile Monitoring Body (TMB).

211 For a comprehensive discussion, see Yuji Iwasawa, *WTO no Funsō Shori* [WTO Dispute Settlement] (Sanseido, 1995), Chapters 3–4 and 7 (in Japanese). See also panel reports on the cases referred to in Chapter 4 in this volume.

THE MONTREAL NON-COMPLIANCE PROCEDURE   251

in an individual capacity and may not receive instructions from their governments (Article 8(9) of the DSU).

The panels examine the dispute, consider the various questions of fact and
law involved, record their findings and recommendations, and finally, send
their report to the Dispute Settlement Body (DSB) for a decision. In accordance
with Article 11 of the DSU, this report must include 'an objective assessment of
the matter before it', and present such findings and recommendations as will
assist the Dispute Settlement Body (DSB) in making its recommendations or
rulings (Article 7 of the DSU).[212] The panel report itself has no legal force and is
therefore treated as an advisory opinion by the DSB. In contrast to the situation
under the procedures of the GATT 1947, panel reports are now automatically
adopted by the political body of the DSB, unless otherwise decided by consensus (Article 16(4) of the DSU). Of course, this essentially differs from the NCP of
the Montreal Protocol. In addition, the 1994 DSU instituted an appellate review
system (Articles 17–19).[213]

It is interesting that, in support of its request for a panel, a party does not
necessarily have to invoke an actual breach of a rule of the agreements in question, including the GATT, GATS and TRIPs. A party need only claim that (i) a
benefit accruing to it under the agreements in question has been nullified or
impaired,[214] or that (ii) the attainment of any objective of the agreements in
question is impeded, as a result of the following three situations:

(a) the failure of another Contracting Party to carry out its obligations under
     this Agreement ('violation complaints')
(b) the application by another Contracting Party of any measure, whether
     or not it conflicts with the provisions of this Agreement ('non-violation
     complaints')
(c) the existence of any other situation ('situation complaints').

If the breach of a rule is invoked, adverse effects on the balance of benefits
are presumed. Only two of the six different kinds of complaints – claims (i) or
(ii) in conjunction with situations (a), (b) or (c) – have been so far used by the
parties, namely (i-(a)) 'violation complaints' over 'nullification or impairment'

---

212 See also Yuji Iwasawa, *WTO no Funsō Shori* [WTO Dispute Settlement] (Sanseido, 1995), pp.
     117–118 (in Japanese).
213 For a discussion, see for example, Ernst-Ulrich Petersmann, *The GATT/WTO Dispute Settle-
     ment System* (Kluwer Law International, 1997), pp. 186–191; Yuji Iwasawa, *WTO no Funsō
     Shori* [WTO Dispute Settlement] (Sanseido, 1995), pp. 133–135 (in Japanese). See reports
     on 'United States-Standards for Reformulated and Conventional Gasoline', adopted on 20
     May 1996, WT/DS2/AB/R (discussed in Chapter 4 in this volume); 'Japan-Taxes on Alco-
     holic Beverages', adopted on 1 November 1996, WT/DS8, 10 and 11 AB/R.
214 See John H. Jackson, *The World Trading System* (2nd ed. MIT Press, 1997), p. 115.

252   CHAPTER 5

(over ninety per cent) and (i-(b)) 'non-violation complaints' over 'nullification or impairment' (less than ten per cent).[215] Complaints by the GATT parties involving claims of type (ii) have been extremely rare.[216] This means, therefore, that parties and GATT panels have chosen to place the greatest emphasis on normal violation complaints.[217] Article XXIII(2) provides for three types of remedies: (i) 'appropriate' recommendations; (ii) 'appropriate' rulings and (iii) suspension of obligations.[218]

Parties can bring complaints under the non-violation procedure (Article XXIII(1.b)), regardless of the existence of an actual breach of the WTO/GATT trade rules in or material damage. It may be argued that the non-violation procedure is related to the concept of 'international liability for injurious consequences arising out of acts not prohibited by international law'.[219] In the past, the non-violation procedure, as a supplement to GATT Article XXVIII, appeared to be useful particularly in protecting tariff concession,[220] although panels reports regarding the non-violation procedure on *EEC Production Aid on Canned Fruit* [221] and *EEC Tariff Treatment* [222] have not been adopted.[223] The non-violation provision of the specialised trade régime such as the WTO may be useful for handling the increase in international economic transactions, but

---

215   See Ernst-Ulrich Petersmann, *The GATT/WTO Dispute Settlement System* (Kluwer Law International, 1997), p. 136.

216   Complaints regarding this case (two) are indicative of the notion of *actio popularis*. See Yuji Iwasawa, *WTO no Funsō Shori* [WTO Dispute Settlement] (Sanseido, 1995), p. 76 (in Japanese).

217   See Edmond McGovern, 'Dispute Settlement in the GATT – Adjudication or Negotiation?', in Meinhard Hilf, Francis G.Jacobs and Ernst-Ulrich Petersmann (eds.), *The European Community and GATT* (Kluwer, 1986), p. 77.

218   See the 1994 DSU (Articles 19, 21 and 22). For a discussion, see for example, P. J. Kuyper, 'The Law of GATT as a Special Field of International Law', 25 *NYbkIL* (1994), Section 5.

219   See Ernst-Ulrich Petersmann, 'Violation-Complaints and Non-Violation Complaints in Public International Trade Law', 34 *GYbkIL* (1991), pp. 175–177; Yuji Iwasawa, *WTO no Funsō Shori* [WTO Dispute Settlement] (Sanseido, 1995), pp. 77–78 (in Japanese). See P. J. Kuyper, 'The Law of GATT as a Special Field of International Law', 25 *NYbkIL* (1994), pp. 246–247.

220   See summary of cases concerning non-violation complaints summarised in Ernst-Ulrich Petersmann, 'Violation-Complaints and Non-Violation Complaints in Public International Trade Law', 34 *GYbkIL* (1991), pp. 200–220; Yuji Iwasawa, *WTO no Funsō Shori* [WTO Dispute Settlement] (Sanseido, 1995), pp. 82–84 (in Japanese).

221   'EEC-Production Aids Granted on Canned Fruits and Dried Grapes', L/5778 (1985).

222   'EEC Tariff Treatment on Imports of Citrus Products from Certain Countries in Mediterranean Region', L/5776 (1985).

223   See Armin von Bodandy, 'The Non-Violation Procedure of Article XXIII:2, GATT: Its Operation and Rationale', 26 *JWT* (1992), pp. 98–99.

only if it is to be properly used on a case-by-case basis.[224] Professor Armin von Bogdandy made several important statements on the non-violation procedure:

> it is sensitive to have a procedure in which any trade related concern can be brought up, irrespective of the lawfulness of the measure in question. The non-violation procedure is important as it allows .... the closing-up of a loophole in substantive law. It offers the possibility of maintaining the balance of interests even in cases where the substantive law does not cover the issues at hand.[225]

Finally, it should be mentioned that the 1994 DSU brought about significant improvements. For example, it established the requirement that a complaining party that triggers the non-violation procedure must submit a 'detailed justification in support of any complaint relating to a measure which does not conflict with the relevant covered agreement'. This requirement constitutes the introduction of a reversal of the burden of proof (Article 26(1.a) of the DSU).[226] It also indicates the growing trend towards 'legalisation' or 'judicialisation' of the WTO/GATT dispute settlement rules and procedures and its development 'from power-oriented diplomatic to rule-oriented legal methods of dispute settlement'.[227] In addition to this, the 1994 DSU only requires a panel/Appellate Body to make rulings or recommendations regarding such 'non-violation complaints' (Article 26(1.b) of the DSU). It follows that there is actually no obligation to withdraw the measure discussed, even though they

---

224   See Thomas Cottier and Krista Nadakavukaren Schefer, 'Non-Violation Complaints in WTO/GATT Dispute Settlement: Past, Present and Future', in Ernst-Ulrich Petersmann (ed.), *International Trade Law and the GATT/WTO Dispute Settlement System* (Kluwer Law International, 1997), p. 182, noting that 'the political agenda of trade policy must remain separated from the legal debate if the non-violation provision is not to develop into the all-encompassing – and therefore meaningless – tool for harassment and *ex aequo et bono* decisions'. See also Dae-Won Kim, *Non-Violation Complaints in WTO Law* (Peter Lang, 2006), pp. 16–19.

225   See Armin von Bogdandy, 'The Non-Violation Procedure of Article XXIII:2, GATT: Its Operational Rationale', 26 *JWT* (1992), p. 110.

226   See Thomas Cottier and Krista Nadakavukaren Schefer, 'Non-Violation Complaints in WTO/GATT Dispute Settlement: Past, Present and Future', in Ernst-Ulrich Petersmann (ed.), *International Trade Law and the GATT/WTO Dispute Settlement System* (Kluwer Law International, 1997), p. 154, suggesting that it is meant to clarify the principle of GATT case-law. With regard to subparagraph (c) situation complaints, similarly, a complaining party must present a 'detailed justification in support of any argument made with respect to issues covered under this paragraph' (Article 26(2.a)).

227   See Ernst-Ulrich Petersmann, 'The Dispute Settlement System of the WTO and the Evolution of the GATT Dispute Settlement System Since 1948', 31 *CMLR* (1994), p. 1169.

254   CHAPTER 5

are regarded as inconsistent with objectives and purposes of the WTO/GATT legal system. Furthermore, the TRIPS agreement also limits the use of the non-violation procedure (Article 64).[228]

(2)   The ILO Complaints Procedure

The International Labour Organisation (ILO), which is one of the specialised agencies of the United Nations, basically aims to improve conditions of labour.[229] In order to fulfil this particular purpose, the ILO advocates two guiding principles: (i) 'the interdependence of human rights and social policy' and (ii) 'the interdependence of social policy and policies of an economic character and the primacy of the social objective'.[230]

It is interesting to note that, as in the case of the ozone régime, the founders of the ILO recognised that non-compliance behaviour of one Member State would undermine the stability of the established legal system of the ILO. The ILO Constitution declares that 'the failure of any nation to adopt humane conditions of labour is an obstacle in the way of other nations which desire to improve the conditions in their own countries'.[231] The ILO is unique in that it included representation of workers and employers, as well as governments (in accordance with the principle of 'tripartism'), and it consists of three permanent treaty institutions: the General Conference of Representatives of the Member States (International Labour Conference), the Governing Body and

---

228   See further Thomas Cottier and Krista Nadakavukaren Schefer, 'Non-Violation Complaints in WTO/GATT Dispute Settlement: Past, Present and Future', in Ernst-Ulrich Petersmann (ed.), *International Trade Law and the GATT/WTO Dispute Settlement System* (Kluwer Law International, 1997), p. 156.

229   The ILO was established in 1919 as a part of the League of Nations. Since then, the 1946 Montreal Amendments to the ILO Constitution greatly expanded its roles in protecting human rights regarding labour conditions. For detailed arguments for the historical background of the institution, see, for example, Victor-Yves Ghebali, Roberto Ago and Nicolas Valticos (eds.), *The International Labour Organisation: A Study on the Evolution of U.N. Specialised Agencies* (Martinus Nijhoff, 1988), pp. 1–24; Klaus Theodor Samson, 'International Labour Organisation', 5 *Encyclopedia of Public International Law* (North-Holland Pub. Co., 1983), pp. 87–88.

230   See Felice Morgenstern, 'Wilferd Jenks in the ILO', 46 *BYbkIL* (1972–1973), pp. xxii-xxiii.

231   See the Preamble of the Constitution of the International Labour Organisation, (adopted on 9 October 1946), 15 UNTS, p. 35. Regarding South Africa's apartheid régime, Wilfred Jenks observed that 'the universality and performance of the world community preclude recourse to expulsion as an effective sanction for violation of its standards; such problems must be solved within its membership by insistence on the obligations of membership, not by measures of expulsion or exclusion the practical effect of which is to release the offender from those obligations'. See *Universality and Ideology in the ILO* (Geneva, 1969), p. 7; Felice Morgenstern, 'Wilfred Jenks in the ILO', 46 *BYbkIL* (1972–1973), p. xviii.

the International Labour Office.[232] These organs have played important functions in ensuring the effective application of international labour standards.

The ILO supervision or compliance system may be roughly divided into three categories: (i) examinations of periodic reports from Member States by the Committee of Experts on the Application of Conventions and Recommendations (the Committee of Experts) and the Conference Committee on the Application of Standards (the Conference Committee),[233] (ii) the ILO Representation Procedure[234] and (iii) the ILO Complaints Procedure. These ILO supervision procedures are widely seen as instructive and sophisticated precedents for other international institutions and multilateral treaty régimes.[235]

---

232 See Articles 2–13.

233 See Articles 19, 22 and 23. Article 22 requires a ratifying State to report regularly to the International Labour Office 'on measures which it has taken to give effect to the provisions of the Convention to which it is a party'. Complaints may be raised with regard to the examinations of reports. See David G. Victor, *The ILO System of Supervision and Compliance Control: A Review and Lessons for Multilateral Environmental Agreements* (International Institute for Applied Systems Analysis, 1996), p. 4 et seq.; Heiko Sauer, 'International Labour Organization (ILO)', in Rüdiger Wolfrum (ed.), *Max Planck Encyclopedia of Public International Law*, Vol. V (Oxford University Press, 2012), p. 815. See also Yozo Yokota, 'The Role of the Committee of Experts in the ILO's Supervisory Mechanism: Reflections on Ten Years' Experience as a Member', in Rüdiger Wolfrum, Maja Seršić and Trpimir M. Šošić (eds.), *Contemporary Developments in International Law: Essays in Honour of Budislav Vukas* (Brill/Martinus Nijhoff, 2016), pp. 652–674; Francis Maupain, 'ILO Normative Action in Its Second Century: Escaping the Double Bind?', Adelle Blackett and Anne Trebilcock (eds.), *Research Handbook on Transnational Labour Law* (Edward Elgar Pub., 2015), pp. 310 et seq.

234 Article 24 of the ILO Constitution provides for representations by employers/workers associations, alleging failure to secure the observance of ratified Conventions. The Governing Body may establish an Examination Committee in order to examine the representation and publish its findings. See further David G. Victor, *The ILO System of Supervision and Compliance Control: A Review and Lessons for Multilateral Environmental Agreements* (International Institute for Applied Systems Analysis, 1996), pp. 10–11; Heiko Sauer, 'International Labour Organization (ILO)', in Rüdiger Wolfrum (ed.), *Max Planck Encyclopedia of Public International Law*, Vol. V (Oxford University Press, 2012), pp. 815–816.

235 See, for example, D. W. Bowett, *The Law of International Institutions* (4th ed. Stevens & Sons, 1982), p. 152; *Consideration of the Establishment of a Multilateral Consultative Process for the Resolution of Questions Regarding Implementation* (Conference of the Parties of the 1992 Climate Change Convention, 22 March 1995), in James Cameron, Jacob Werksman and Peter Roderick (eds.), *Improving Compliance with International Environmental Law* (Earthscan, 1996), pp. 138–139; David G. Victor, *The ILO System of Supervision and Compliance Control: A Review and Lessons for Multilateral Environmental Agreements* (International Institute for Applied Systems Analysis, 1996), pp. 3–4.

However, at present, we will concentrate on the third category of the ILO supervision techniques. Under Article 26 of the ILO Constitution, any member – including employees and employers – that is dissatisfied with the adherence of other ratifying members, can invoke *ad hoc* dispute settlement procedure by filing a complaint with the International Labour Office. This is the so-called ILO Complaints Procedure.[236] The Governing Body can also trigger this procedure either of its own accord or on receipt of a complaint from a delegate to the Conference.[237] Unlike the Montreal NCP, the ILO Secretariat does not possess the power to invoke this procedure on its own initiative. Nevertheless, as in the case of Montreal NCP complaints, formal complaints made by ILO plaintiffs, including States and their nationals, do not necessarily have to be based on any direct injury to them, provided that they are much concerned with common purposes of ILO Member States.

After prior communication to the government in question,[238] the Governing Body can appoint *ad hoc* Commissions of Inquiry to consider and report on the complaint.[239] The Commissions are normally composed of three highly qualified individuals who serve in their personal capacity (for example, university professors)[240] and may carry out on-the-spot investigations, though this is subject to the consent of the government involved.[241]

In the initial stages, the Commission of Inquiry investigates the charges in question. It considers not only information offered by the parties concerned, but also that provided by other governments, international institutions,

---

236 For useful information on the Commissions of Inquiry, see Nicolos Valticos, 'Les commissions d'enquête de l'Organisation internationale du travail', 91 *Revue générale de droit international public* (1987), pp. 847–879. See also Victor-Yves Ghebali, Roberto Ago and Nicolas Valticos (eds.), *The International Labour Organisation: A Study on the Evolution of U.N. Specialised Agencies* (Martinus Nijhoff, 1988), pp. 233–234.

237 See Article 26(4). See, for example, E. A. Landy, *The Effectiveness of International Supervision: Thirty Years of I.L.O. Experience* (Stevens, 1966), pp. 173 et seq.

238 See Article 26(2).

239 See Article 26(3).

240 See Nicolos Valticos, 'Les commissions d'enquête de l'Organisation internationale du travail', 91 *Revue générale de droit international public* (1987), pp. 855–856. They are appointed by the Governing Body on the recommendation of the Director-General.

241 In the past, Commissions investigated situations in Chile, the Dominican Republic, the Federal Republic of Germany, Haiti, Nicaragua, Portugal, Romania and South Africa. See Nicolos Valticos, 'Les commissions d'enquête de l'Organisation internationale du travail', 91 *Revue générale de droit international public* (1987), pp. 873 et seq.; David C. Victor, *The ILO System of Supervision and Compliance Control: A Review and Lessons for Multilateral Environmental Agreements* (International Institute for Applied Systems Analysis, 1996), p. 12.

THE MONTREAL NON-COMPLIANCE PROCEDURE   257

workers/employers agencies and NGOs.[242] Provided it discovers a breach of
the ILO Convention, the Commission then incorporates its findings and recommendations in a published report. The reports of these Commissions are
not legally binding, however. In this respect, the ILO Commission of Inquiry
may be regarded, like the Montreal Implementation Committee, as a quasi-
judicial body, rather than a judicial one.[243]

In contrast to the Montreal NCP, however, a government that declines to
accept these recommendations can refer the complaint to the International
Court of Justice (ICJ),[244] which 'may affirm, vary or reserve any of findings and
recommendations of the Commission of Inquiry'.[245] In the event that a member fails to implement the recommendations made by the Commission (or the
decision of the Court), the Governing Body 'may recommend to the Conference such action as it may deem wise and expedient to secure compliance
therewith'.[246] In practice, in the majority of cases, the governments concerned
have accepted reports presented by the Commission of Inquiry. Consequently,
the ICJ has never participated in the legal processes of the ILO Complaints
Procedure. In fact, under the ILO's machinery of supervision, complaints, in
themselves, have been infrequent.

VI   The Montreal NCP Theory: Soft Enforcement of International
        Environmental Law

Before examining the Montreal NCP in practice, an understanding of the philosophical foundation of this dispute avoidance and settlement procedure in
the sphere of international environment protection law is necessary to place
the régime in context.[247] The distinctive characteristics of the Montreal NCP
must be viewed against a background of the nature of the technical Protocol's
specific obligations – which requires international environmental cooperation

---

242   See David G. Victor, *The ILO System of Supervision and Compliance control: A Review and
      Lessons for Multilateral Environmental Agreements* (International Institute for Applied
      Systems Analysis, 1996), p. 12.
243   See ibid., pp. 11 et seq.
244   See Article 29(2).
245   See Article 32.
246   See Article 33. However, it should be noted that the defaulting party may at any time
      inform the Governing Body that it has taken the steps necessary to comply with the rec-
      ommendations of the Commission or the decisions of the ICJ. In addition, the party may
      require the Governing Body to constitute a Commission of Inquiry to verify its contention
      (Article 34).
247   On the role of the principle of good faith in the Montreal NCP, see Section IV(A.2) above.

in facilitating the capability of Article 5 industrialising countries to comply with their obligations, and of the evolving principles and rules of public international law of the environment.

It is true that certain issues of law enforcement arise whenever States fail to comply with their legally binding obligations under environmental treaties or customary international law. It is also right to say that most countermeasures, including the suspension of certain rights and privileges, are often presented as direct responses to the consequences of such violations of international rules and obligations. In early 1990, Professor Koskenniemi therefore brought forward the argument that 'from the perspective of state responsibility, the Montreal NCP appears as a mechanism for collective countermeasures (or reprisals) in case of non-performance'.[248] His detailed analysis on the Montreal NCP may be true, though within certain limitations.

It would be nearer the truth to say that, in theory, resorting to the NCP reflects both limitations of existing principles and customary rules of environmental protection or of State responsibility, and the growing roles of international supervisory institutions.[249] Since customary international law cannot react quickly enough to deal with environmental problems, the existence of an international institution that can establish new international environmental law norms at short notice may be the only effective way to deal with global environmental problems. In the author's view, Professor Koskenniemi's speculative legal argument, founded on traditional international rules on law 'enforcement', obscures the fact that the NCP – within a 'self-contained' ozone régime – must be based on the precautionary approach to environmental destruction and that the NCP's redeeming characteristic feature may be its adaptability to changing circumstances. The NCP may have both merits and limitations in complicated international relations, but it is not a consequence of ignorance of the traditional principles and rules of general international law.

To begin with, the nature and contents of the ozone treaty régime must be recalled here in examining the NCP. In the first place, it is important to note that many developing countries, including Article 5 LVCs, decided rather reluctantly to join in the international regulatory régime, mainly because of Article

---

248 Martti Koskenniemi, 'Breach of Treaty or Non-Compliance', 3 *YbkIEL*(1992), p. 142; Section III(B) above. Koskenniemi also criticised the character of the amicable solution, the nature of decisions by the Meeting of the Parties, and the relationship between the NCP and the dispute settlement procedures under the 1985 Vienna Ozone Convention. See also Martti Koskenniemi, 'New Institutions and Procedures for Control and Reaction', in James Cameron, Jacob Werksman and Peter Roderick (eds.), *Improving Compliance with International Environmental Law* (Earthscan, 1996), pp. 236–248.

249 See Chapters 1 and 2(III.C) in this volume.

4 trade restrictions, in spite of the fact that they were not quite sure, in reality, how to comply with the substantial and technical treaty obligations, including reporting procedures, control measures of CFCs/ODSs and trade controls. With a few exceptions, States usually decide to participate in international legal régimes only when they think they will comply with the treaty obligations.[250] Hence, we may say that, in a certain sense, considerable 'collective economic countermeasures' (in a broad sense),[251] which would make it possible to ensure not only treaty compliance but the necessary universal participation, were therefore employed beforehand through the Article 4 TREMs of the Montreal Protocol.[252]

In the second place, it is also important that, despite the objection of State Parties, adjustments of control measures of ODSs to the Protocol are binding on all the parties on the basis of the revolutionary simplified majority decision-making.[253] Assuming that there would be some dissenting minority States that unsuccessfully oppose time-targeted adjustments adopted in such a simplified procedure, on account of their recognised low capacity to comply, we may say that this departure from the traditional principle of unanimity might become a potential cause of multilateral ozone disputes.[254]

In the third place, in order to ensure strict consistency in the international obligations of all the State Parties to the ozone régime, no reservation is allowed under the Vienna Ozone Convention and its Protocol.[255] Nevertheless, in reality, most Non-Article 5 developed State Parties have duly come to recognise that a number of Article 5 developing State Parties, unlike developed States, do not necessarily have the capacities to comply fully with the technical treaty obligations, including the national reporting requirement.[256]

In practice, as we shall see, the Implementation Committee under the Montreal NCP has been overloaded with routine administrative work, such as locating missing baseline and annual data, the correction of such data reports

---

250 See Michael Bothe, 'The Evaluation of Enforcement Mechanisms in International Environmental Law', in Rüdiger Wolfrum (ed.), *Enforcing Environmental Standards* (Springer, 1996), p. 14.

251 On the theoretical aspects of 'countermeasures', see, in particular, Yoshiro Matsui, 'Countermeasures in the International Legal Order', 37 *Japanese Annual of International Law* (1994), pp. 1–37.

252 See Chapter 4 in this volume.

253 Article 2(9). See also Chapter 3(III.B-C) in this volume.

254 However, the 1990 London Adjustments, 1992 Copenhagen Adjustments, the 1995 Vienna Adjustments, the 1997 Montreal Adjustments, the 1999 Beijing Adjustments and 2007 Montreal Adjustments were adopted by consensus, not by a unanimous vote.

255 Article 18 (Vienna Ozone Convention) and Article 18 (Montreal Ozone Protocol).

256 See Chapter 6 in this volume.

from parties, and a detailed classification and reclassification of Article 5 developing countries. Obviously, apart from purely bureaucratic matters, such non-compliance with national and regional reporting requirements has stemmed from a lack of Member States' capacities to comply, and it cannot be denied that, in most cases, non-complying States within the regulatory ozone régime are at present Article 5 developing country parties under the Montreal Protocol, and the CEITs such as the Russian Federation, Baltic States and Eastern European States. This view is entirely confirmed in practice.[257]

Given the aforementioned problems, one can understand why the basic mechanics of the Montreal NCP for dealing with possible non-compliance would be to encourage the party that is willing to – but occasionally unlikely to – fulfil its treaty obligations by providing 'appropriate' financial and technical assistance.

Patrick Széll, who was the chairman of the NCP negotiations, noted that 'a régime should be based on the recognition that non-compliance was frequently the consequence, not of malice or greed, but rather of technical, administrative or economic difficulties'.[258] In addition, as was described earlier, the *travaux préparatoires* of the Montreal NCP support the idea that the new procedure should follow an encouragement-based approach, or one based on the friendly settlement of environmental disputes:[259] 'All possible assistance measures encouraging Parties to comply with the Protocol should be exhausted before stronger measures were considered'.[260]

We may say, at the same time, that the primary functions of both the standing Committee and the Ozone Meeting of the Parties are to control effectively the fulfilment by Member States of their international obligations derived from the international ozone régime (that is, compliance monitoring), rather than to decide what sources of international law should be applied in cases of treaty non-compliance (breach of treaty) or non-performance:[261] There is now some validity to this concept, though it should not be pushed too far.[262]

In summary, countermeasures as seen in the paragraph © of the Indicative List of the Montreal NCP could or would be merely counterproductive. One of

---

257 See Section VII below.
258 See UNEP/OzL.Pro.7/INF.1, para. 28.
259 See UNEP/OzL.Pro.LG.1.3, para. 9. See also the proposal put forward by the Netherlands in UNEP/OzL.Pro.LG.1/CPR.1. See Thomas Gehring, *Dynamic International Regimes* (Peter Lang, 1994), pp. 314–317.
260 UNEP/OzL.Pro/WG.3/3/3, para. 44, (emphasis added).
261 See Lakshman D. Guruswamy, Geoffrey W. R. Palmer and Burns H. Weston (eds.), *International Environmental Law and World Order* (West Pub. Co. 1994), p. 1120.
262 See Section II(B) above.

the central aims of the NCP is, therefore, not to take controversial 'countermeasures' that would occasionally give rise to questions of State responsibility, but rather to seek 'amicable solutions' to expected non-compliance arising from *bona fides*.[263] In another case – not surprisingly – the NCP of the 1979 Convention on Long-Range Transboundary Air Pollution does not even provide for any sanctions.

Viewed in this light, we can see now that the Montreal NCP – which is (i) multilateral, (ii) flexible, (iii) simple and (iv) rapid[264] – is therefore designed carefully for applying the precautionary environmental 'principle' or approach to an urgent global environmental problem, that is, stratospheric ozone layer depletion (see Diagram below).[265] Furthermore, in the present case of the regulatory ozone régime, the evolving precautionary environmental 'principle' must receive global financial support for developing low-volume-ODS-consuming countries' (LVCs) capacities to fulfil their technical treaty obligations.[266]

It follows naturally that, in such situations, unless non-compliance or breaches results from malice or greed and are therefore considered strictly to be intentional or systematic non-compliance, the Ozone Meeting of the Parties will not resort to painful international sanctions against the party in question. As described above, any bad faith or intentional non-compliance would seriously endanger the value of the NCP.

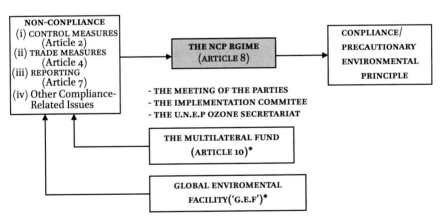

DIAGRAM 1 NCP in the 'self-contained' ozone régime

---

263   See Section IV(A.2) above.
264   See Introduction to this volume, and Sections IV and V(B) above.
265   See Atsuko Kanehara, 'Chikyu Kankyō Hogo ni okeru Songai Yobō no Hōri' ["Precautionary Remedies" in the Conventions on Global Environmental Protection], 93 *Kokusaiho Gaiko Zassi* [Journal of International Law and Diplomacy] (1994), pp. 448–490.
266   See Chapter 6 in this volume.

In addition, we should not overlook the fact that, even if the 'real guarantee' of treaty compliance is the system of collective sanctions, the measures termed 'sanctions' are not necessarily intended to be directly punitive or repressive, but rather 'coercive' in the sense that they would apply 'sufficiently strong pressure' on the defaulting Member States.[267]

Nevertheless, it does not necessarily follow that the principles and rules of customary international law and State responsibility have nothing to do with the avoidance or settlement of possible ozone disputes. Indeed, collective response measures required should be commensurate with the importance of the provision itself, as well as the nature and degree of compelling reasons behind non-compliance, frequency of non-compliance and length of non-compliance.[268] For example, international responsibilities arising from the violation of Article 4 obligations (TREMs) and continuing illegal trade in CFCs/ODSs will be handled differently and more strictly by the régime's agencies. It cannot be denied, perhaps, that the question of whether the NCP is a kind of conciliation, 'quasi-judicial' mechanism, or a mere institutionalised negotiation process would depend in part on the nature of the issues the specialised internal régime organs must handle.

While the NCP's flexibility has contributed to the effective implementation of the ozone treaties, it is still probable that the NCP will not often counterbalance the ultimate disadvantage of its considerable softness; we should therefore note the following statements by Professor Francesco Francioni:

> This question [whether soft enforcement procedures are exclusive of countermeasures] will arise whenever the soft implementation procedure has failed to satisfy a contracting party which, for instance, objects to an amicable compromise ... or when a state reiterate the breach or becomes a systematic defaulting state. In these instances it would have little sense to exclude the operation of ordinary countermeasures under customary international law or under the Vienna Convention on the Law

---

267 See J. Combacau, 'Sanctions', 9 *Encyclopedia of Public International Law* (North-Holland Pub. Co., 1982), pp. 337–340. See also Rosalyn Higgins, *Problems and Process: International Law and How We Use It* (Clarendon Press, 1994), pp. 13–16; Oscar Schachter, 'United Nations Law', 88 *AJIL* (1994), pp. 14–15. In practice, as Schermers and Blokker have pointed out, international institutions such as UN specialised organs, the WMO and the INF usually do not invoke the power to suspend a State's rights and privileges, and employ other means of securing compliance. See Henry G. Schermers and Niels M. Blokker, *International Institutional Law* (5th. rev. ed. Martinus Nijhoff, 2011), pp. 927–930.

268 See UNEP/OzL.Pro/WG/3/3/3, para. 44 (emphasis added) and a Discussion Paper from Canada (UNEP/OzL.Pro/WG.1/15/3).

of Treaties. *Soft law and soft remedies cannot be understood in such a way as to displace and curtail the operation of hard law.*[269]

VII   The Montreal NCP in Practice

A   *Ensuring Compliance with Reporting Requirements, Control Measures and Trade Restrictions*

(1)   The Reporting Requirements

As discussed earlier, international legal régimes are of no use if their legal rules are not put into operation in the sphere of domestic legal régimes.[270] Most international environmental agreements impose periodic reporting requirements regarding compliance with their treaty obligations.[271] Reports can be

---

269   Francioni, 'International "Soft Law": A Contemporary Assessment', in Vaughan Lowe and Malgosia Fitzmaurice (eds.), *Fifty Years of the International Court of Justice: Essays in Honour of Sir Robert Jennings* (Cambridge University Press, 1996), p. 178 (emphasis added).

270   See Soji Yamamoto, 'Chikyū Kankyō Kyōryoku no Hōteki Wakugumi [Characteristics of a Legal Framework for International Environmental Co-operation], *Juristo,* No. 1015 (1993), pp. 145–150 (in Japanese). For national implementation of international environmental law, see Catherine Redgwell, 'National Implementation', in Daniel Bodansky, Jutta Brunnée and Ellen Hey (eds.), *Oxford Handbook of International Environmental Law* (Oxford University Press, 2007), pp. 922–946.

271   See Michael Bothe, 'The Evaluation of Enforcement Mechanisms in International Environmental Law', in Rüdiger Wolfrum (ed.), *Enforcing Environmental Standards* (Springer, 1996), pp. 22–26; Alan E. Boyle, 'Saving the World? Implementation and Enforcement in International Environmental Law through International Institutions', 3 *JEL* (1991), pp. 236 et seq.; Patricia Birnie, Alan Boyle and Catherine Redgwell, *International Law and the Environment* (3rd ed. Oxford University Press, 2009), pp. 242–245; Alexandre Kiss, 'Compliance with International and European Environmental Obligations', *Hague YbkIL* (1996), pp. 51–52; Kal Raustiala, *Reporting and Review Institutions in 10 Multilateral Environmental Agreements* (Division of Early Warning and Assessment/UNEP, 2001). See, for example, the 1992 Biodiversity Convention (Article 26); the 1992 Climate Change Convention (Article 12(1)); the 1989 Basel Convention (Article 13); the 1991 Protocol to the Antarctic Treaty on Environmental Protection (Article 17); the 1988 NO_x Protocol (Article 8(1)); the 1985 SO_2 Protocol (Article 4); the 1976 Rhine Chloride Pollution Convention (Article 3(5)); the 1974 Paris Convention (Articles 11 and 17); the 1973 CITES Convention (Article 8(7)); the 1973 MARPOL Convention (Articles 6, 8 and 11); the 1972 World Heritage Convention (Article 11). Sands and Peel divide reporting requirements under environmental treaties into four types: (i) regular reporting requirements provided by international institutions to state parties, (ii) regular reporting by parties to international institutions or other parties, (iii) a party may be required to provide information to another party on certain occasions (for example, nuclear accidents) and (iv) a treaty may allow for a report to be submitted by a NGO to a party. See Philippe Sands and Jacqueline Peel, *Principles of International Environmental Law* (3rd ed. Cambridge University Press, 2012), pp. 629–630.

broadly divided into two categories, namely, (i) reports containing information on the overall implementation of a treaty and (ii) reports regarding the compliance with specific treaty obligations.[272] The national and regional reporting system of international environmental law has great importance for (i) assessing and judging the effectiveness of control measures and for (ii) adjusting the existing international standards set up by implementing treaty bodies. State administrations, including developed ones, usually devote much time to drafting this kind of data reports[273] and non-compliance with reporting requirements does not necessarily constitute a breach of a substantive international obligation.[274]

The Montreal Protocol requires Contracting Parties to provide the UNEP Ozone Secretariat with baseline and annual data on their production, imports and exports of each controlled substance that is conveniently divided into a group or the 'best possible estimates' of such data, provided actual data is not available.[275] Parties also have to report on the ozone activities in research, development, public awareness, and exchange of relevant information.[276] The names of the parties that have not fully complied with these reporting and other obligations are to be mentioned in the reports of the Implementation Committee and of the UNEP Secretariat.[277] Report by the Secretariat concerning Articles 7 and 9 of the Protocol is presented to the Meeting of the Parties, and used by both the Meeting of the Parties and the Multilateral Fund for various purposes not necessarily related to specific cases of non-compliance, including the assessment of progress being made in phasing out ODSs.[278]

Without timely and detailed reports, it will always be difficult for implementing agencies to spot particular State Parties that should be provided with

---

272 See Kamen Sachariew, 'Promoting Compliance With International Environmental Standards', 2 *YbkIEL*(1991), pp. 43 et seq.

273 See Alexandre Kiss 'Compliance with International and European Environmental Obligations', *Hague YbkIL* (1996), p. 52.

274 See Michael Bothe, 'International Obligations, Means to Secure Performance', 1 *Encyclopedia of Public International Law* (North-Holland Pub. Co., 1992), p. 103; Kamen Sachariew, 'Promoting Compliance with International Legal Standards', 2 *YbkIEL*(1991) p. 41.

275 See Article 7(1)-(2).

276 Article 9(3). See information by Boliva, Canada, Czech Republic, Germany, Islamic Republic of Iran, Kuwait, Norway, Romania and Slovenia, in UNEP/OzL.Pro.8/3 para. 29. At the Seventeenth Meeting of the Parties, the President of the Implementation Committee stated that reports submitted by the parties under Article 9 were decreasing over the last years. See UNEP/OzL.Conv.7/7-UNEP/OzL.Pro.17/11, para. 181.

277 See, for example, 'The Report of the Secretariat on Information Provided by the Parties in Accordance with Articles 7 and 9' (UNEP/OzL.Pro.8/3, 12 September 1996).

278 See UNEP/OzL.Pro/ImpCom/49/5/Rev.1, paras. 19–20.

THE MONTREAL NON-COMPLIANCE PROCEDURE   265

financial and technical assistance in implementing the ozone treaties. Hence, as Victor suggests, it is no exaggeration to say that the NCP's effectiveness depends on the supply of data reports about national performance and the ability to compare that information with international standards.[279] To date, on-the-spot investigations based on States' consent are not initiated by the Implementation Committee.[280]

Since its First Meeting in 1991, the Implementation Committee has dealt with a continuing problem of non-reporting or insufficient and late data reports from both parties and non-parties to the Protocol.[281] It is said that the quality of data reporting by parties 'can at best be called moderate',[282] and the major contributing factors of this problem are (i) low capacity to comply with such an obligation: (ii) an intention to maintain the confidentiality of reports regarding trade matters and/or (iii) other reasons (for example, change of government or administrative delays).[283] As for the data report for 1997/1998, although 139 parties reported required data for 1997 out of 166 parties, only 27 parties had done so for 1998.[284] In the Twentieth Meeting in July 1998, the Committee noted that the following 13 countries had never reported data: Bosnia-Herzegovina, Burundi, Chad, Comoros, Grenada, Honduras, Kiribati, Korea, Liberia, Marshall Islands, Micronesia, Mongolia and Vanuatu.[285] However, after nearly twenty years operation of the ozone régime since 1998, this situation seems to have been improved gradually. In 2016, 195 parties out

---

279   See UNEP/OzL.Pro.7/INF.1, para. 36. It is also important to note that environmental secretariat often lack the resources to accomplish their supervisory duties with regard to treaty compliance. The Ozone Secretariat has periodically received additional funds from the UNEP to compensate for incomplete contributions from parties. See United States General Accounting Office, *International Environment: International Agreements Are Not Well Monitored,* (January 1992) p. 20 and pp. 28 et seq.

280   K. Madhava Sarma, 'Compliance with the Multilateral Environmental Agreements to Protect the Ozone Layer', in Ulrich Beyerlin, Peter-Tobias Stoll and Rüdiger Wolfrum (eds.), *Ensuring Compliance with Multilateral Environmental Agreements* (Martinus Nijhoff, 2006), p. 33.

281   See also Feja Lesniewska, 'Filling the Holes: the Montreal Protocol's Non-Compliance Mechanism', in Malgosia Fitzmaurice, David M. Ong and Panos Merkouris (eds.), *Research Handbook on International Environmental Law* (Edward Elgar Publishing, 2010), pp. 480–481. Under Article 4 of Montreal the Protocol, trade restrictions will be imposed on 'non-treaty compliers'. See Chapter 4 in this volume.

282   See 20/18 *International Environment Reporter* (3 September 1997), p. 820; UNEP, 'Production and Consumption of Ozone-Depleting Substances 1986–1995: The Data Reporting System under the Montreal Protocol' (September 1997).

283   See UNEP/OzL.Pro/ImpCom/10/4, para. 14.

284   See UNEP/OzL.Pro/ImpCom/22/4, para. 13.

285   See UNEP/OzL.Pro/ImpCom/20/4, para. 17(a).

of 197 reported data for 2015 and 169 of those parties reported their data by 30 September 2016, as required under Article 7 of the Montreal Protocol.[286] However, two parties, Iceland and Yemen, had not reported their 2015 data[287] and the Twenty-Eighth Meeting of the Parties referred to their non-compliance with the Protocol in its Decision XXVIII/9.[288] The Twenty-Eighth Meeting of the Parties also required Yemen, which is Article 5 developing party, to work closely with the implementing agencies in reporting such data.[289]

Generally speaking, non-compliance with data reporting has been frequently observed in parties operating under Article 5 developing countries, rather than in Non-Article 5 parties.[290] The Implementation Committee, in its Third Meeting, explained that the principal reasons was 'the turnover of personnel in the Customs service, their lack of training and experience, and the lack of qualified specialists to train them'.[291] Indeed, 'training on data-monitoring and reporting could go a long way toward resolving reporting problems'.[292] Consequently, the Ozone Secretariat stressed the importance of the country studies and programmes being carried out by the implementing organs of the Multilateral Ozone Fund, namely, the UNDP, the UNEP and the World Bank.[293]

In 1993, the Implementation Committee invited nine parties that had persistently failed to provide reporting data to its Seventh Meeting.[294] At the Meeting, the representative of Costa Rica stated that incompleteness of data

---

286   See Decision XXVIII/9 in UNEP/OzL.Pro.28/12, para. 1.

287   See UNEP/OzL.Pro/ImpCom/58/4, para. 12.

288   See Decision XXVIII/9 in UNEP/OzL.Pro.28/12, para. 4.

289   See ibid., para. 5.

290   Reports of the Committee include a list of countries whose data reporting are missing or still insufficient. Perhaps, this would pressure those States into providing such data required. See UNEP, *Handbook for the Montreal Protocol on Substances That Deplete the Ozone Layer* (11th ed. 2017), pp. 377–488. See also Stephen O. Andersen and K. Madhava Sarma, *Protecting the Ozone Layer: The United Nations Story*, edited by Lani Sinclair (Earthsacn, 2002), pp. 276 et seq.

291   See UNEP/OzL.Pro/ImpCom/3/3, paras. 16 and 17. See also the Secretariat's Third Report of Data, in Jacob Werksman (eds.), *Improving Compliance with International Environmental Law* (1996) p. 119.

292   See UNEP/OzL.Pro/ImpCom/12/3, para. 46. See further, *UNEP's Efforts to Assist Data Reporting by Article 5 Countries*, in UNEP/OzL.Prp/ImpCom/12/3/Annex III.

293   See UNEP/OzL.Pro/ImpCom/3/3, para. 17. See Chapter 6 in this volume.

294   They include Belarus, Burkina Faso, Costa Rica, Islamic Republic of Iran, Italy, Maldives, Syrian Arab Republic, Togo, Trinidad and Tobago, and Ukraine. See UNEP/OzL.Pro/ImpCom/7/2. See also Winfried Lang, 'Ozone Layer', 5 *YbkIEL*(1994) pp. 161–162. The Reports of the Committee usually include the names of countries that do not participate in the meetings of the Committee, despite the fact that they were invited. Keutsch argues that this may serve as an 'inherent threat' to such parties to honour the invitation in order not to lose face. See A. Keutsch, 'Non-Compliance Procedures under the Montreal Protocol' in

was caused mainly by delays in receiving funds from the UNDP – that is to say, a lack of prompt financial assistance.[295] Belarus explained that difficulties in obtaining the data required stemmed from political and economic problems related to its recent independence.[296] The representative of Italy suggested that its failure was the result of purely bureaucratic matters and that forthcoming legislation would resolve the problems of non-reporting.[297] Regarding Yemen's non-compliance with Article 7 of the Protocol (HCFC data for 2009), at the Forty-Sixth Meeting of the Implementation Committee, representative of the UNEP explained that the country's environmental protection agency, including the national ozone unit, was unable to ensure a constant presence in its offices and to communicate effectively with local stakeholders.[298] In this respect, the Twenty-Third Meeting of the Parties urged Yemen to work closely with the implementing agencies to report the required data to the Secretariat as a matter of urgency.[299]

The Implementation Committee, considering the European Community's significant production and consumption impacts, once expressed 'particular concern' about non-reporting from some members of the European Community, including Belgium, Greece, Italy and Portugal, and at missing 1991 consumption data from the Commission of the European Community.[300] It is likely that some members of the European Union, or the European Union itself, tried to preserve the confidentiality of the business information concerned.[301]

In another case, the Implementation Committee decided to establish conditionality between the supply of technical data and MFL funding.[302] The Committee recommended that Mauritania be reclassified as a party not operating under Article 5 until it reported required data.[303] This implies that the government could not receive funds from the Montreal Multilateral Fund.[304] Furthermore, the Implementation Committee decided to take similar measures

---

     James Cameron, Jacob Werksman and Peter Roderick (eds.), *Improving Compliance with International Environmental Law* (Earthscan, 1996), p. 119.

295   See ibid., para. 7.

296   See ibid., para. 14.

297   See ibid., paras. 9 and 10.

298   See UNEP/OzL.Pro/ImpCom/46/5, para. 91.

299   See Decision XXIII/25.

300   See UNEP/OzL.Pro/ImpCom/5/3, para. 10. See also UNEP/OzL.Pro/ImpCom/3/3, para. 10.

301   See David G. Victor, *The Early Operation and Effectiveness of the Montreal Protocol's Non-Compliance Procedure* (International Institute for Applied Systems Analysis, 1996) p. 9.

302   On conditionality between the Multilateral Fund and compliance with the Protocol, see Chapter 6(III.D(4)) in this volume.

303   See UNEP/OzL.Pro/7/12, para 36.

304   See UNEP/OzL.Pro/ImpCom/12/3, note by the Secretariat at p. 3.

against three parties temporarily classified as Article 5 countries, namely, the Democratic People's Republic of Korea, Samoa and Liberia.[305] In case of Korea, it is reported that the country did not respond to the repeated communications by the Ozone Secretariat.[306] After the Twentieth Meeting held in July 1998, these countries finally transmitted the necessary data to the Secretariat, and they could maintain the status of Article 5 countries.[307]

(2)   The Control Measures of ODSS

Compliance with substantive control measures of ODSS, under Article 2, 2A to 2J and the corresponding measures in Article 5 and other relevant provisions, has formed the absolute basis of the international regulatory régime for the protection of the ozone layer. Since the operation of the NCP, as of 2016, the Meeting of the Parties, based on the recommendations by the Implementation Committee,[308] has identified over seventy parties' (potential) non-compliance with ODS-related control measures under the Montreal Protocol.[309] A majority of the non-complying parties are Article 5 countries, such as Bangladesh, Haiti and the Democratic People's Republic of Korea, and they are amount to more than fifty parties.[310] For example, the Democratic People's Republic of Korea exceeded its maximum allowable consumption of 78.0 ODP-tonnes for Hydrochlorofluorocarbons (HCFCS) for 2013 and, in November 2014, the Twenty-Sixth Meeting of the Parties decided that the party was in non-compliance with the consumption control measures under the Protocol for the ODSS.[311] However, at the Fifty-Second Meeting of the Implementation Committee, the Secretariat of the Multilateral Fund referred to the fact that, since July 1995, the Executive Committee had approved a total of $20.8 million in funding for institutional strengthening, investment and other projects, and the Fund's 2014–2016 business plan included funding for HCFC phase-out management plans for 2015;[312]

---

305   See ImpCom decisions regarding these countries in UNEP/OzL.Pro/ImpCom/20/4, (9 July 1998).

306   See UNEP/OzL.Pro/ImpCom/20/4, para. 10.

307   See UNEP/OzL.Pro/ImpCom/21/3 (7 December 1998), paras. 12–14.

308   See also Gilbert M. Bankobeza, *Ozone Protection* (Eleven International, 2005), p. 267.

309   See UNEP, *Handbook for the Montreal Protocol on Substances That Deplete the Ozone Layer* (11th ed. 2017), pp. 377–491.

310   See ibid. At the Eighteenth Meeting of the Parties, several parties stated that a number of 'patients' in developing countries depended on CFC-based products and converting production facilities to manufacture non-CFC alternatives was very costly for producers and took some years to achieve. See UNEP/OzL.Pro.18/10, para. 104.

311   See Decision XXVI/15 in UNEP, *Handbook for the Montreal Protocol on Substances That Deplete the Ozone Layer* (11th ed. 2017), p. 404.

312   See UNEP/OzL.Pro/ImpCom/52/4, para. 27.

THE MONTREAL NON-COMPLIANCE PROCEDURE   269

the Secretariat stated that 'activities in the Democratic People's Republic of Korea faced a number of challenges'.[313] In response, the Twenty-Sixth Meeting of the Parties cautioned the Democratic People's Republic of Korea, in accordance with item B of the Indicative List of Measures, and also suggested that the parties would consider measures consistent with item C of the List, including the possibility of actions available under Article 4, such as ensuring that the supply of HCHCs is ceased so that exporting parties are not contributing to a continuing situation of non-compliance.[314] At present, it is customary that, in such cases of non-compliance with the Protocol, the Meeting of the Parties refers to the possibility of taking measures under the items B and C of the Indicative List of Measures,[315] although, as K. Madhava Sarma mentioned, any further actions are not taken so far to suspend rights and privileges, as

---

313   See ibid.
314   See Decision XXVI/15, para. 7, in UNEP, *Handbook for the Montreal Protocol on Substances That Deplete the Ozone Layer* (11th ed. 2017), p. 404.
315   See, for example, Decision XIV/18 (Albania), Decision XIII/21 (Argentina), Decision XVIII/20 (Armenia), Decision X/20 (Azerbaijan), Decision XIV/19 (Bahamas), Decisions XIV/29, XVII/27 and XXI/17 (Bangladesh), Decision X/21 (Belarus), Decisions XIII/22 and XIV/33 (Belize), Decision XIV/20 (Bolivia), Decisions XIV/21, XV/30, XVII/28 and XXI/18 (Bosnia and Herzegovina), Decision XV/31 (Botswana), Decision XI/24 (Bulgaria), Decisions XIII/23, XIV/32 and XV/32 (Cameroon), Decisions XVI/22 and XVII/29 (Chile), Decision XVII/30 (China), Decisions XV/33 and XVIII/21 (Democratic Republic of the Congo), Decision XVIII/22 (Dominica), Decisions XVII/31, XVIII/23 and XX/16 (Ecuador), Decision XVIII/24 (Eritrea), Decision X/23 (Estonia), Decisions XIII/24 and XIV/34 (Ethiopia), Decision XVII/32 (Federated States of Micronesia), Decisions XVI/23 and XVII/33 (Fiji), Decision XXV/11 (France), Decision XIX/21 (Greece), Decisions XV/34, XVIII/26 and XXVI/16 (Guatemala), Decision XVI/24 (Guinea-Bissau), Decisions XV/35 and XVII/34 (Honduras), Decisions XVIII/27 and XIX/27 (Islamic Republic of Iran), Decisions XIII/19, XVII/35, XXV/12 and XXVI/13 (Kazakhstan), Decision XVIII/28 (Kenya), Decision XVII/36 (Kyrgyzstan), Decision X/24 (Latvia), Decision XVI/25 (Lesotho), Decisions XIV/25, XV/36, XVI/26, XVII/37, XXIII/23 and XXVII/11 (Libya), Decision X/25 (Lithuania), Decision XIV/26 (Maldives), Decisions XVIII/30 and XXI/20 (Mexico), Decision XV/23 (Morocco), Decisions XIV/22 and XV/38 (Namibia), Decision XIV/23 (Nepal), Decision XIV/30 (Nigeria), Decisions XVI/29 and XVIII/31 (Pakistan), Decision XV/40 (Papua New Guinea), Decisions XVIII/32 and XIX/22 (Paraguay), Decision XIII/25 (Peru), Decision XV/41 (Qatar), Decisions X/26, XIII/17, XIV/35 and XXIII/27 (Russian Federation), Decisions XIV/24, XV/42 and XVI/30 (Saint Vincent and the Grenadines), Decisions XIX/23, XXI/21 and XXII/15 (Saudi Arabia), Decision XVII/38 (Sierra Leone), Decision XX/18 (Solomon Islands), Decisions XVI/19, XX/19 and XXI/23 (Somalia), Decision XIII/20 (Tajikistan), Decisions XI/25 and XXI/25 (Turkmenistan), Decision XV/43 (Uganda), Decisions X/27 and XXIV/18 (Ukraine), Decisions XV/44 and XVII/39 (Uruguay), Decision X/28 (Uzbekistan), Decisions XXI/26 and XXII/18 (Vanuatu) and Decision XV/45 (Viet Nam).

provided by item C of the List.[316] Generally speaking, in accordance with recommendations adopted by the Meeting of the Parties and the Implementation Committee, most parties that had fallen into non-compliance with the Protocol, supported by the Ozone Secretariat, submit and implement plans of action, and return to compliance in reasonable period of time.[317]

In addition, some Non-Article 5 country parties are also found to be non-compliance with control measures under the Montreal Protocol.[318] For example, in October 2013, the Twenty-Fifth Meeting of the Parties decided France's non-compliance with production control measures of HCFCs under the Protocol.[319] In another case, in November 2006, the Eighteenth Meeting of the Parties identified Greece's non-compliance with Article 2 of the Protocol.[320] This was due to the fact that Greece did not have notified the Ozone Secretariat of prior to the date of a transfer of CFC production rights from the United Kingdom of 1,786 ODP-tonnes in 2004.[321] Further, non-compliance of the CEITs, including Russia, will be discussed below.

(3)   Trade with Non-Parties

The international ozone régime decided that, as we have observed, non-parties and non-complying States should be denied access to foreign markets for ODSs.[322] However, the Montreal Protocol does not currently impose any legally binding obligation to report on the implementation of Article 4 to the UNEP

---

316   See K. Madhava Sarma, 'Compliance with the Multilateral Environmental Agreements to Protect the Ozone Layer', in Ulrich Beyerlin, Peter-Tobias Stoll and Rüdiger Wolfrum (eds.), *Ensuring Compliance with Multilateral Environmental Agreements* (Martinus Nijhoff, 2006), p. 35. See also Hugh Adsett, Anne Daniel, Masud Husain and Ted L. McDorman, 'Compliance Committees and Recent Multilateral Environmental Agreements: The Canadian Experience with Their Negotiation and Operation', 42 *CYbkIL* (2005), pp. 120–121.

317   See, for example, UNEP/OzL.Conv.7/7-UNEP/OzL.Pro.17/11, paras. 176–177. However, there are always some exceptions. Some countries, such as Saint Vincent and Grenadines, had not submitted plans of action, despite requests from the Implementation Committee. See UNEP/OzL.Pro.15/9, para. 132.

318   See, for example, Decision X/20 (Azerbaijan), Decision X/21 (Belarus), Decision XI/24 (Bulgaria), Decision X/23 (Estonia), Decision XXIII/26 (European Union), Decision XXV/11 (France), Decision XIX/21 (Greece), Decisions XIII/19, XVII/35, XXV/12 and XXVI/13 (Kazakhstan), Decision X/24 (Latvia), Decision X/26 (Russian Federation), Decision XIII/20 (Tajikistan), Decisions X/27 and XXIV/18 (Ukraine) and Decision X/28 (Uzbekistan).

319   See Decision XXV/11.

320   See Decision XIX/21.

321   See ibid.

322   See Chapter 4(II) in this volume.

THE MONTREAL NON-COMPLIANCE PROCEDURE

Ozone Secretariat.[323] The parties are only encouraged to inform the Ozone Secretariat of the implementation of Article 4.[324] It is reported that both Article 5 and Non-Article 5 parties have introduced various national ozone laws and regulations to implement the TREMs provisions of the Protocol.[325]

In accordance with Decision IV/17C, regarding trade measures adopted by the Fourth Meeting of the Parties,[326] the Implementation Committee considered data reports from twenty-two non-parties.[327] The Implementation Committee observed that thirteen countries, including Belgium, Hong Kong and Vietnam, satisfied the requirements of the Decision IV/17C and that they thus should be exempt from the trade controls under Article 4.[328] In the Tenth Meeting of the Committee, one member stated that, rather than focusing on the formalities of data-reporting, the Committee should concern itself more with reports of dumping of obsolete technologies and the conclusion of joint venture agreements to construct CFC-production facilities in developing countries.[329] Nevertheless, this sensitive issue was not extensively discussed and we have only limited information on this matter.[330]

In November 2011, the Twenty-Third Meeting of the Parties decided the European Unions' non-compliance with Article 4 of the Protocol.[331] Although the European Union, as a party to all Amendments to the Montreal Protocol, was not permitted to export HCFCs to non-parties, according to its data report for 2009, the organisation exported 16.616 metric tonnes of HCFC-22 to Kazakhstan, a country that had not ratified either the Copenhagen or the Beijing

---

323   But see, for example, UNEP/OzL.Pro.4/6, Section III; UNEP/OzL.Pro.5/5 Add.1.

324   See, for example, Decision III/16 and Decision IV/17. See also Winfried Lang, 'Trade Restrictions as a Mean of Enforcing Compliance with International Environmental Law', in Rüdiger Wolfrum (ed.), *Enforcing Environmental Standards* (Springer, 1996), p. 270, noting the lack of data-reporting requirements 'may be traced back to a certain sense of political realism and to emerging doubts as to the full compatibility of Art. 4 with GATT-law'.

325   See UNEP/OzL.Pro.5/5 Add.1, 'Information on the Implementation of Article 4(3) of the Montreal Protocol' (13 September 1993).

326   See 'Application of Trade Measures under Article 4 to Non-Parties to the Protocol', in UNEP/OzL.Pro/4/15.

327   See UNEP/OzL.Pro/ImpCom/6/3, paras. 15–17. They included; Belgium, Comoros, Congo, Dominican Republic, Gabon, Guyana, Hong Kong, Jordan, Laos, Lithuania, Madagascar, Mali, Myanmar, Nicaragua, Poland, Sudan, Suriname, Turky, Uruguay, Vietnam, Yugoslavia.

328   See UNEP/OzL.Pro/ImpCom/6/3, paras 15–17.

329   See UNEP/OzL.Pro/ImpCom/10/4, para. 20.

330   See ibid., paras. 21–22.

331   See Decision XXIII/26. Kazakhstan ratified the Copenhagen on 28 June 2011, and the Beijing Amendment, on 19 September 2014.

Amendment to the Protocol.[332] At the Forty-Sixth Meeting of the Implementation Committee, the EU explained that, in 2009, HCFCs were exported by a Netherlands company through a harbour in Belgium, and this illegal export was detected because the company had included it in its annual report.[333] However, the Secretariat emphasised that the EU was responsible for this non-compliance case, since 'in the area of consumption, including reporting of consumption data and the issuing of import or export licences, responsibility lay with the European Union', and thus not with individual Member States.[334] Finally, the representative of the Netherlands stated that the risk profiles used by the Customs service had been updated and enhanced.[335] Also, the Twenty-Third Meeting of the Parties declared Russia's non-compliance with Article 4 of the Protocol, which had been engaged in trade with Kazakhstan.[336] However, according to the representative of the Ozone Secretariat, in 2010, there were no reports of ODSs, including HCFCs, to non-parties.[337]

As the TEAP/CEIT Report pointed out, it was widely known that, since January 1993, the Russian Federation had been in non-compliance with trade controls under Article 4 of the Ozone Protocol. This question is taken up in the next section below.

B   *Case Study: Non-Compliance by the Russian Federation and the Reactions of the NCP Organs*

Since early 1990s, issues concerning the non-compliance of the CEITs had formally been discussed in the Implementation Committee and in the Ozone Meeting of the Parties to the Protocol. Yet, it was not until 1995 that the Montreal NCP was invoked, for the first time, to handle the voluntary submission of anticipated non-compliance by several of the CEITs, which include the Russian Federation, Belarus, Bulgaria, Poland and the Ukraine. For the present, however, we shall concentrate on Russia's Non-Compliance case, rather than on the CEITs' treaty non-compliance as a whole.

(1)   The Russian Federation and the CEITs

There are twenty-seven States with their economies in a transitional state. They are divided into four groups: (i) successor States to the former Soviet Union (Armenia, Azerbaijan, Georgia, Kazakhstan, Kyrgyzstan, Moldova, the Russian

---

332   See UNEP/OzL.Pro/ImpCom/46/5, para. 59.
333   See UNEP/OzL.Pro/ImpCom/46/5, para. 62.
334   See UNEP/OzL.Pro/ImpCom/46/5, para. 71.
335   See UNEP/OzL.Pro/ImpCom/46/5, para. 72.
336   See Decision XXIII/27.
337   See UNEP/OzL.Pro/ImpCom/47/6, para. 15.

THE MONTREAL NON-COMPLIANCE PROCEDURE   273

Federation, Tajikistan, the Ukraine and Uzbekistan), (ii) Baltic States (Estonia, Latvia and Lithuania); (iii) Central/Eastern European States (Albania, Bulgaria, the Czech Republic, Hungary, Poland, Romania and Slovakia) and (iv) successor States to the former Yugoslavia (Bosnia-Herzegovina, Croatia, Macedonia, Slovenia and Yugoslavia – Serbia and Montenegro).[338] It is worth noting that the estimated 1994 consumption of ODSs in these States was approximately equal to a quarter of global consumption in that year.[339] In fact, at that time, the CEITs were contributing immensely to ozone depletion.

It is important to note that the Russian Federation exceeded sixty per cent of the consumption of controlled substances in the CEITs, and it is the only producer of these substances in the region.[340] Furthermore, the Russian Federation was the major exporter of controlled substances to twenty CEITs at least, and possibly some other countries outside the CEITs.[341] Hence, it is no exaggeration to say that, in the light of its considerable political and economic influence in the international community, the non-compliance behaviour of the Russian Federation undermines the global stability of the international ozone régime.

The former Soviet Union adopted the 1987 version of the Montreal Ozone Protocol on 10 November 1988. After the Russian Federation formally became an independent sovereign State on 24 August 1991,[342] it took over the obligations under the ozone treaties from the dissolved former Soviet Union.[343]

The Russian Government has employed legislative and other appropriate measures to comply with regulations of the Ozone Protocol. For example, the

---

338 When the 1987 version of the Montreal Protocol was signed, only eight of the twenty-seven States were sovereign States. See *The 1995 TEAP/CEIT Report*, p. 11.

339 See *The 1995 TEAP/CEIT Report*, p. 12.

340 See *The 1995 TEAP/CEIT Report*, p. 25.

341 See ibid.; UNEP/OzL.Pro.7/12, para. 43.

342 Russia's ODS production in 1994 was 10,000 ODP tonnes, and its ODS consumption in 1994 was 33.675 tonnes, respectively; it follows that Russia's ODS consumption per capita was 0.22 kg. See *The 1995 TEAP/CEIT Report*, p. 139.

343 According to a document entitled, *On the Ratification of the Agreement on the Creation of the Commonwealth of the Independent States*, 'For the purposes of the creating conditions necessary for the ratification of Article 11 of the said Agreement, to establish that the norms of the former USSR. shall apply on the territory of the RSFSR (that is, the Russian Federation) until the adoption of respective legislative acts of the RSFSR in that part which is not contrary to the Constitution of the RSFSR, legislation of the RSFSR, and the present Agreement'. See Decree of the RSFSR Supreme Soviet (12 December 1991), 17 *Rossiiskaya gazeta* (1991). The Russian Federation had already ratified the 1992 London Amendment in December 1991, but it had not ratified the 1992 Copenhagen Amendment. See also *Memorandum on Mutual Understanding on Issues of Succession to Treaties of the Former USSR having Mutual Interest* (6 July 1992).

274   CHAPTER 5

Russian Federation adopted the 1992 Environmental Act (Article 56 on ozone layer protection'); developed the national programme on the phaseout of ODSs and the introduction of alternative technologies; decided in 1993 to establish the commission on ozone layer protection under the Ministry for the Protection of the Environment: and in 1995, adopted a special act on the measures required to fulfil the obligations under the ozone treaties.[344] In the past, the Russian Federation declared that it was 'in principle complying with the basic provisions of the Montreal Protocol'.[345] Other domestic measures include, for example, the Ministerial Decree No. 1368 Reinforcing Controls over the Import and Export of Ozone-Depleting Substances (1999),[346] the Ministerial Decree No. 490 establishing regulatory measures for the manufacture and consumption of ozone-depleting substances in the Russian Federation (1999),[347] the Order No. 30 of the Ministry of Economic Development and Trade Reinforcing Measures on the Import and Export of Ozone-Depleting Substances (2000),[348] the Order No. 287 of the Ministry of Natural Resources and Ecology Validating Regulation on Issuance of Permits for Transboundary Movement of Ozone Depleting Substances and Produce Containing Them (2008)[349] and the Ministerial Decree No. 678 on the Arrangements for State Regulation of Export and Import of Ozone Depleting Substances (2009).[350]

---

344   See further *The 1995 TEAP/CEIT Report*, p. 29.
345   See UNEP/OzL.Pro/ImpCom/11/1/Annex II.
346   A summary of this order is available at: <https://www.ecolex.org/details/legislation/ ministerial-decree-no-1368-reinforcing-controls-over-the-import-and-export-of-ozone -depleting-substances-lex-faoc079002/?q=ozone+russia&type=legislation> (last visited on 31 January 2018).
347   A summary of this order is available at: <https://www.ecolex.org/details/legislation/ ministerial-decree-no-490-establishing-regulatory-measures-for-the-manufacture-and -consumption-of-ozone-depleting-substances-in-the-russian-federation-lex-faoc079001/ ?q=ozone+russia&type=legislation>(last visited on 31 January 2018).
348   A summary of this order is available at: <https://www.ecolex.org/details/legislation/ order-no-30-of-the-ministry-of-economic-development-and-trade-reinforcing -measures-on-the-import-and-export-of-ozone-depleting-substances-lex-faoc079003/?q =ozone+russia&type=legislation> (last visited on 31 January 2018).
349   A summary of this order is available at: <https://www.ecolex.org/details/legislation/ order-no-287-of-the-ministry-of-natural-resources-and-ecology-validating-regulation -on-issuance-of-permits-for-transboundary-movement-of-ozone-depleting-substances -and-produce-containing-them-lex-faoc091808/?q=ozone+russia&type=legislation> (last visited on 31 January 2018).
350   A summary of this order is available at: <https://www.ecolex.org/details/legislation/ ministerial-decree-no-678-on-the-arrangements-for-state-regulation-of-export-and -import-of-ozone-depleting-substances-lex-faoc094889/?q=ozone+russia&type=legislati on> (last visited on 31 January 2018).

THE MONTREAL NON-COMPLIANCE PROCEDURE   275

(2)   Russia's Non-Compliance Case

At the Eleventh Open-ended *Ad Hoc* Working Group held in May 1995, the Russian Federation submitted a joint statement, also speaking on behalf of Belarus, Bulgaria, Poland and the Ukraine, that it did not appear possible to completely phase out production and consumption by January 1996, due mainly to the difficult economic situations the CEITs were faced with.[351]

It is interesting to note that, to be fair, the Russian Federation did not initially intend to invoke the mechanics of the Montreal NCP. Instead, its original intention was to seek a special five-year grace period directly from the Meeting of the Parties.[352] That request was then first sent to the Implementation Committee.[353] The Government of the Russian Federation informed the Ozone Meeting of the Parties and the Implementation Committee of its anticipated treaty non-compliance.

Nevertheless, after 'considerable prodding' by the United States,[354] the Ozone Secretariat and the Implementation Committee agreed to accept this formal statement as a submission under paragraph 4 of the NPC under the Montreal Ozone Protocol. The Russian Federation did not attempt to deny this plausible interpretation by the Committee. As a result, the standing Implementation Committee was thus furnished with its first opportunity to address non-compliance matters concerning Article 2 control measures under the NCP.

At its Tenth Meeting, the Implementation Committee stated the simple fact that there were no treaty provisions that would allow any party a schedule for ODSs different from those of the Ozone Protocol, and it further suggested anticipated non-compliance by the Russian Federation should be addressed by a possible decision of the supreme decision-maker, the Ozone Meeting of the Parties, and not by adding an amendment to the Montreal Protocol.[355] The Committee then stated that: 'It should also be noted that the Russian Federation was the only one of the five Parties that had not reported data'.[356] The Committee also requested further information, including data on production

---

351   See UNEP/OzL.Prp/10/4, para. 31; 'United Nations Activities', 26/2–3 *EPL* (1996), p. 68. A subsequent statement made by the CEITs at the Twelfth Meeting of Open-ended Working Group read: '[T]he processed connected with political, geopolitical and social change, with the break from the previous economic system and the transition to a market economy, have demanded and continue to demand *great moral, material and financial outlays*' (emphasis added). See UNEP/OzL.Pro/ImpCom/11/1/Annex II.

352   See UNEP/OzL.Pro/ImpCom/11/1/Annex; *The 1995* TEAP/CEIT *Report*, p. 29.

353   See David G. Victor, *The Early Operation and Effectiveness of the Montreal Protocol's Non-Compliance Procedure,* (International Institute for Applied Systems Analysis, 1996), p. 28.

354   See Richard Benedick, *Ozone Diplomacy* (Harvard University Press, 1998), p. 281.

355   See *The 1995* TEAP/CEIT *Report*, p. 30.

356   See UNEP/OzL.Pro/ImpCom/10/4, para. 32.

and consumption of controlled substances and its compliance plan, for the elaboration of a committee recommendation.

Ultimately, since the Implementation Committee could not achieve an agreement with the Russian Federation, particularly regarding monitoring issues and trade controls as contained in draft decision VII/16,[357] those recommendations made by the standing Committee were then brought to the 1995 Ozone Meeting of the Parties, without a complete agreement by Russia.[358]

At the 1995 Vienna Ozone Meeting, the Russian Federation argued that 'it was not the Russian Federation but the former Soviet Union and that ratified the Montreal Protocol, Russia, as the successor Party, cannot be fully responsible for fulfilling its commitments', and that 'the collapse of the Soviet Union constituted an event "force majeure" or a "fundamental change in circumstances" that justifies flexibility in the application of the Protocol to Russia'.[359] As a result, at its Thirteenth Meeting, the Implementation Committee requested the Secretariat to seek clarification from the Legal Counsel of the United Nations on the status of the countries of the former Soviet Union regarding succession to the ozone treaties.[360]

After much discussion, and over the objections of the Russian Federation, the 1995 Vienna Ozone Meeting adopted by consensus, Decision VII/18 – broadly similar to Decision VII/16 – with regard to anticipated non-compliance by the

---

357 See UNEP/OzL.Pro/7/9/Rev.

358 See UNEP/OzL.Pro/7/12, para. 44; Jacob Werksman, 'Compliance and Transition: Russia's Non-Compliance Tests the Ozone Régime', 39 *ZaöRV* (1996), pp. 746–765.

359 Statement by the Minister of the Environment and Natural Resources of the Russian Federation (translated from Russian), cited in Jacob Werksman, 'Compliance and Transition: Russia's Non-Compliance Tests the Ozone Régime', 39 *ZaöRV* (1996), p. 760. Article 62 of the Vienna Convention on the Law of treaties is considered as customary international law. See *Fisheries Jurisdiction Case* (United Kingdom v. Iceland: Jurisdiction), *ICJ Reports* (1973), paras. 37–43; *Gabcikovo-Nagymaros Project Case* (Hungary/Slovakia), *ICJ Reports* (1997), para. 104. It is well-known that, in 1871, Russia similarly maintained the principle of *rebus sic stantibus* with regard to the Black Sea clause in the 1856 Peace Treaty.

360 See UNEP/OzL.Pro/ImpCom/13/3, para. 8(b). The Counsel's advice on this issue was as follows: 'as far as the former Republics are concerned, they are treated as newly independent States and legally distinct from the former Soviet Union. Under the practice of the Secretary-General as depositary of multilateral treaties, they could become Parties to the Convention and the Protocol only pursuant to an explicit expression of consent to do so by their respective Governments. Such consent can be expressed either by (i) depositing an instrument of accession or by (ii) explicitly succeeding to these instruments which were previously applied on their territory. The Secretary-General's practice does not include the concept of an "automatic succession". It is for a newly independent State to decide whether or not it should become a Party to any treaty deposited with the Secretary-General'. Information provided by G. M. Bankobeza of the UNEP Ozone Secretariat, 10 December 1997.

THE MONTREAL NON-COMPLIANCE PROCEDURE

Russian Federation.[361] Decision VII/18 required not only data reporting, that is, more detailed information on its firm commitments to the Ozone Protocol, but also the 'necessary action' to ensure that re-exports will be made from the CIS to any party to the Ozone Protocol.[362] In this sense, it can be said that the Ozone Meeting of the Parties consolidated, to some extent, the contents of the previous Decision VII/16 taken by the Implementation Committee.[363]

The representative of the Russian Federation, who considered such actions as 'discriminatory measures and sanctions against a Party', strongly disputed the paragraph addressing future trade restrictions – in vain however,[364] and thus regretted that 'it had not been able to accept the draft decision in its entirely.[365]

This example of the NCP in action nicely illustrates that, within the 'self-contained' ozone régime, a conflicting opinion defended by only one party – that is, the Russian Federation – may eventually have to reconcile with stated régime objectives.[366] This case thus explains the collective side of the Montreal NCP.

---

361 It should be noted that the Russian Federation called for a vote upon the Decision VII/18. See UNEP/OzL.Pro/7/12, para. 129.

362 See Decision VII/18 in UNEP/OzL.Pro/7/12. See also Decision VII/33, regarding illegal imports/exports of ODSS, in UNEP/OzL.Pro/7/12.

363 It may be argued that, in the light of the fact that the recommendations by the Commission were incorporated as a formal Decision of the Parties, the Commission developed quasi-judicial functions. The representative of the Russian Federation stated that such a stringent measure 'was not mentioned at all in the Implementation Committee's recommendations'. See UNEP/OzL.Pro/7/12, para. 128.

364 See 'Comments Made at the Time of Adoption of the Decisions', in UNEP/OzL.Pro/7/12, paras. 123–134. The Russian Federation insisted that the Meeting of the Parties should apply appropriate measures in accordance with the Indicative List of Measures (Annex V) in an ascending order of importance (that is, from assistance, cautions to sanctions). However, wording of the Montreal NCP does not necessarily prevent the Meeting of the Parties from choosing such 'appropriate measures' simultaneously, regardless the order of the List. However, in general, the Meeting of the Parties has taken the measures in question in ascending order. See Gilbert M. Bankobeza, *Ozone Protection* (Eleven International, 2005), p. 269.

365 See UNEP/OzL.Pro/7/12, para. 134.

366 The Secretariat noted: '[W]hen only one Party objected to a draft decision, that decision would be carried by consensus and the position of the dissenting Party would be clearly reflected in the report of the Meeting'; see UNEP/OzL.Pro/7/12, para. 130. However, as stated earlier, the procedures to adopt Decisions are rather complex and controversial, while Article 11(4) provides that the Meeting 'consider and undertake any additional action that may be required for the achievement of the purposes of this Protocol'. For instance, Article 40 of the Rules of Procedures for the Meeting of the Parties requires a two-third majority of the parties present and voting on all substantial matters. See UNEP/OzL.Pro.1/5/Annex I.

However, Decision VII/18, at the same time, allows the Russian Federation to export controlled substances to CIS parties operating under Article 2 of the Protocol, including Belarus and the Ukraine, and recommends, as an incentive, international assistance to help it comply with the ozone treaty obligations.[367] In reality, such funds would be indispensable for Russian lame-duck industries to virtually halt ODS production and then convert existing production capacity to less ozone-depleting HCFC or HCF production, although the Russian Federation, which preferred to use national production processes, was not willing to rely on transnational corporations' proprietary processes and licenses.[368]

It is important to note, however, that since the Russian Federation is, in the light of its high levels of consumption of ODSs, by no means a 'developing country' operating under Article 5 of the Protocol, this high-volume-ODS-consuming country is not entitled to receive funds from the Montreal Protocol's Multilateral Fund.[369] As a result, the only international mechanism which is ready to contribute the necessary funds for the possible non-compliance of Russia is the Global Environmental Facility (GEF), which has no official legal status within the international ozone régime.[370]

It was quite obvious that the Russian Federation wanted to ensure continuity of supplies of ODSS to developing countries to meet their 'basic domestic needs' – as permitted under the Protocol – and this fact supplies one of the rational reasons that it would not choose to withdraw from the legal régime for the protection of the ozone layer. Meanwhile, the Group of 77 and China, which were fearful of the consequences of Russian illegal trade of ODSs in their markets, tried in vain to add to Decision VII/18 clear wording that would ban export/re-export of controlled substances to Article 5 parties.[371] Therefore, the final text is not completely clear on this crucial point. At the Open-Ended Working Group held in September 1996, Kenya submitted an amendment proposal that reads as follows: 'to allow ... the Russian Federation to export substances controlled under the Montreal Protocol *only* to Parties operating under Article 2 of the Protocol ... *and not to any other Party, including those operating under Article 5 of the Protocol*'.[372] This proposal was killed by Russian

---

367   See ibid.

368   See *The 1995 TEAP/CEIT Report*, p. 40.

369   See Article 5 of the Ozone Protocol; Chapter 4 in this volume.

370   It is interesting to note that, similarly, under the 1992 Climate Change Convention the Russian Federation is not eligible for financial assistance from the Convention's Financial Mechanism (Article 4(3)).

371   See UNEP/OzL.Pro.8/CPR.1.

372   Emphasis original.

THE MONTREAL NON-COMPLIANCE PROCEDURE

opposition and by the hesitant Western countries, including the United States and the European Community.[373]

The Thirteenth Meeting of the Implementation Committee held in 1995 considered additional information offered by the Russian Federation in accordance with Decision VII/18.[374] As a result, the Committee emphasised unmet needs for further information and reiterated that the Russian Federation should monitor and report on the implementation of the trade restrictions.[375] The Committee further recommended that the GEF Council and other funding institutions should consider additional steps to expedite financial assistance for future projects. Although the information provided indicated discouraging signs of non-compliance for 1996, the Implementation Committee noted that the Russian Federation had taken 'important steps' to comply with Decision VII/18 and towards achieving full compliance with the control measures of the Protocol.[376] The Fourteenth Meeting of the Implementation Committee concluded that the Russian Federation satisfactorily answered all the questions raised by the Committee and that the information offered should be adequate for the purposes of the Fourteenth Meeting of the Committee.[377]

At the Seventeenth Meeting of the Implementation Committee, the representative of the Russian Federation reiterated his country's commitment to meeting its ozone treaty obligations, and also stated that a new federal phaseout programme would be implemented in cooperation with the international community and multilateral financing agencies. In this meeting, the Committee established that the Russian Federation had continued to produce ODSs during 1996 – contrary to the provisions of the Montreal Protocol and Decision VII/18 – and that Russia was still in non-compliance with the Protocol for 1996.[378] Moreover, the Implementation Committee resolutely decided that the Russian Federation had exported both new and reclaimed substances

---

373 See Richard Benedick, *Ozone Diplomacy* (Harvard University Press, 1998), p. 282 and Decision VIII/26(1). See also statement by Canada in the Open-Ended Working Group, in UNEP/OzL.Pro/WG.1/15/3, para. 4, suggesting that Decision VIII/26 could be implemented solely through a decision by the Parties to modify the NCP.

374 See UNEP/OzL.Pro/ImpCom/13/3, paras. 14–18. The Report of the Meeting says that, despite an invitation by the Committee, representatives of the Russian Federation was not present for most of the meeting.

375 See ibid.

376 See UNEP/OzL.Pro/ImpCom/13/3, para. 17.

377 See UNEP/OzL.Pro.8/2, para. 16. Victor says, however, that many observers are privately sceptical about the accuracy of the data provided by the Russian Federation. See David C. Victor, *The Early Operation and the Effectiveness of the Montreal Protocol's Non-Compliance Procedure* (International Institute for Applied Systems Analysis, 1996), p. 31.

378 See UNEP/OzL.Pro/ImpCom/17/3, para 25(b) and (c).

to – and also imported ODSs from – many developed and developing countries under the Montreal Protocol.[379] It was pointed out that 'there was a danger of a loss of credibility for the whole Montreal Protocol process if it was seen that Parties not operating under Article 5, which should have completed phase-out, were still importing and exporting controlled substances'.[380] After the Eighteenth Meeting of the Implementation Committee,[381] Russia's persistent non-compliance case was further discussed in the 1997 Montreal Ozone Meeting of the Parties, and the Ozone Meeting adopted Decision IX/31 based on the recommendations made by the Implementation Committee.[382]

In November 1998, the Tenth Meeting of the Parties adopted Decision X/26,[383] which is based on a draft decision (g)[384] made by the Implementation Committee. As with previous decisions regarding Russia's non-compliance, Decision X/26 provides that, as long as Russia is working toward and meeting the commitments in its country programme and the Special Initiative for ODS Production Closure and continue to report data indicating a decrease in imports and consumption, Russia should continue to receive international financial assistance. However, it is important that, under Decision X/26, the Parties cautioned Russia in accordance with item B of the Indicative List that 'in the event that the country fails to meet the commitments noted in prior decisions as well as in the above documents [the country programme and the Initiative] in the times specified, the Parties shall consider measures, consistent with item C of the indicative list of measures. These measures could include the possibility of actions that may be available under Article 4'.[385] Likewise, the serious possibility of taking 'countermeasures' was also mentioned in Decision X/20 (Azerbaijan), Decision X/21 (Belarus), Decision X/23 (Estonia), Decision X/24 (Latvia), Decision X/25 (Lithuania), Decision X/27 (Ukraine), and in Decision X/28 (Uzbekistan), although such punitive measures were not actually taken by the Meeting of the Parties against the Russian Federation and other non-complying Non-Article 5 country parties. If persistent non-compliance cases

---

379 See UNEP/OzL.Pro/ImpCom/17/3, para. 25(d).

380 UNEP.OzL.Pro/17/3, para. 23.

381 See UNEP/OzL.Pro/ImpCom/18/3.

382 See Decision IX/31 in UNEP/OzL.Pro.9/12. Decision IX/31 noted, for instance, that international financial assistance – the GEF in particular – should continue favourably with a view to furnishing funds for projects to implement the programme for the phaseout of the production/consumption of ODSs in the Russian Federation.

383 See UNEP/OzL.Pro.10/9, pp. 40–41.

384 See UNEP/OzL.Pro/ImpCom/21/3, pp. 17–18.

385 Decision X/26(3).

simply result from malice or wilful non-compliance, it may be clear that the Meeting of the Parties should seriously contemplate the growing possibility.

After the adoption of Decision X/26 by the Tenth Meeting of the Parties, at the Twelfth Meeting of the Parties in 2000, the President of the Implementation Committee expressed serious concern that 'the Russian Federation had not complied with its commitment to phase out CFCs under decision X/26, and had stockpiled large amounts of CFCs',[386] and in 2001, the Thirteenth Meeting of the Parties finally decided that the Russian Federation was in non-compliance with the phase-out benchmarks for 1999 and 2000 for the production and consumption of the ozone-depleting substances covered by Annex A to the Montreal Protocol.[387] Afterwards, however, at the Fourteenth Meeting of the Parties in 2002, the President of the Implementation Committee declared Russia's return to compliance: 'after successive recommendations of the Implementation Committee and decisions of Meetings of the Parties starting in 1995, ... the Russian Federation had now returned to compliance with its obligations. This was an illustration, he believed, of the success of the non-compliance system of the Montreal Protocol, a system widely regarded as a model for other multilateral environmental agreements.'[388] On 20 December 2000, the Russian Federation had closed the production of CFCs for end use, and their exports and imports had ceased on 1 March 2000.[389] In May 1999, the establishment of any new production facilities had also banned.[390] Thus, at the Twenty-Ninth Meeting of the Implementation Committee, the representative of the Russian Federation stated that these activities contributed to a reduction in production not only in the Russian Federation but throughout the former Soviet Union, and also to a reduction in illegal trade.[391]

VIII   Conclusions

Since the adoption of the 1987 version of the Ozone Protocol, the international legal régime for the protection of the ozone layer has been 'adjusting' itself to become more commensurate with the ecological impact of adverse effects

---

386   See UNEP/OzL.Pro.12/9, para. 66.
387   See Decision XIII/17. See also Decision XIV/35 (2002).
388   See UNEP/OzL.Pro.14/9, para. 133.
389   See UNEP/ OzL.Pro/ImpCom/29/3, para. 26.
390   See ibid.
391   See ibid. See also UNEP/ OzL.Pro/ImpCom/20/4, paras. 65–68; UNEP/ OzL.Pro/ImpCom/21/3, paras. 44–48; UNEP/ OzL.Pro/ImpCom/23/3, paras. 16–17; UNEP/ OzL.Pro/ImpCom/27/4, para. 15.

caused by severe ozone depletion. Now, the optional dispute settlement procedures of the 1985 Vienna Ozone Convention are effectively supplemented by a flexible dispute avoidance and settlement mechanism – the Montreal Non-Compliance Procedure.

As we have seen, it is fair to say that the Montreal NCP is essential to the operation of a regulatory rule-oriented ozone legal system in the comparatively weak realm of legal obligations of global environmental protection, and in reality, it has turned out to be a great step forward in strengthening the collective compliance or horizontal enforcement of international law principles of the environment, including the precautionary environmental 'principle' or approach and other widely accepted Stockholm/UNCED Principles. As the President of the Implementation Committee states, 'the ozone community had built a compliance system that was internationally regarded with respect and as a model to be emulated under other international agreements. The non-compliance procedure of the Montreal Protocol was a flexible and sophisticated system that continued to function successfully'.[392]

Therefore, we do not have to regret the absence of any reliable procedure of identifying, at an early stage, possible non-compliance with treaty obligations and of avoiding and settling multilateral ozone disputes. At the same time, however, the deterrent influence of the traditional dispute settlement procedures under the 1985 Vienna Ozone Convention should not be ignored. 'The possibility of resort to compulsory procedures may have a powerful impact on the dynamic and effectiveness of a treaty régime even if those procedures are in practice never used'.[393]

Yet, the standing Committee's régime-monitoring instruments within the NCP are largely limited to (i) extensive discussions on compliance matters, (ii) making recommendations to the Meeting of the Parties and (iii) making non-compliance transparent. In addition, the Committee can still deliberately duck certain issues, such as the legal status of monetary contributions to the financial mechanism, the Montreal Multilateral Fund, and the meaning of 'non-compliance' with the Protocol. Furthermore, the Implementation Committee – as an international conciliator – does not have formal decision-making power, while it is to report regularly to the Meeting of the Parties. Until now, the Committee is, as Széll observes, 'very careful not to exceed the scope of its mandate or the expectations of the Parties'.[394] Expanding the functions

---

392   See UNEP/OzL.Pro.27/12, para. 97.
393   See Alan E. Boyle, 'Settlement of Disputes Relating to the Law of the Sea and the Environment', 26 *Thesaurus Acroasium* (1996), p. 259.
394   See UNEP/OzL.Pro.7/INF.1, para. 29.

THE MONTREAL NON-COMPLIANCE PROCEDURE 283

of the NCP Committee, beyond the notion of an ozone dispute conciliator, would be hardly admissible.

While, in many cases, the Implementation Committee's recommendations are widely accepted by the régime Member States, unsettled questions regarding non-compliance must be ultimately referred to the supreme ozone agency, the Meeting of the Parties, which is entrusted with all the powers that are indispensable for the fulfilment of its objectives and purposes in protecting the ozone layer. It may be reasonable to suppose that the Committee's influence as a conciliator in the ozone régime depends in part on the extent to which the Meeting of the Parties follows the Committee's recommendations.

The weakness of the Montreal NCP, since the decisions as to what kind of recommendations should be made and which measures must be taken are left largely to the broad discretion of intergovernmental organs, that is, the Committee and/or the Meeting of the Parties, is that it remains questionable whether the political bodies consisting of government representatives can always act impartially and sincerely as trustees of the ozone layer.[395] Unlike international judicial institutions or human rights committees or commissions, the NCP operators or diplomats are not independent and they do not necessarily have 'professional' prestige. In addition, we should not overlook the confidential aspects of the Montreal NCP decision-making process that are often crucial to understanding the hidden meaning of decisions of the internal régime organs.[396]

It was in 1995 that the Montreal NCP started its active operation to handle the first formal (voluntary) submission of treaty non-compliance. As I have contended, the original intention of the NCP of the ozone régime was not to apply a sanction-related remedies, which are not very effective and often self-defeating. However, after looking at the above-mentioned fact that the Meeting of the Parties adopted Decision VII/18 by consensus, against the wishes of the Russian Federation (an action that might be regarded by some commentators as limited form of collective sanctions), we may argue that friendly confrontation may is beneficial to the effective operations of the existing Montreal

---

395 See Alan E. Boyle, 'Saving the World? Implementation and Enforcement of International Environmental Law Through International Institutions', 3 *JEL* (1991), pp. 229–245; Boyle, 'The Principle of Co-operation: Environment', in Vaughan Lowe and Colin Warbrick (eds.), *The United Nations and Principles of International Law: Essays in Memory of Michael Akehurst* (Routledge, 1994), pp. 129 et seq.

396 However, we need to remind ourselves of the fact that, in many case, internal international organs within treaty régimes are more suitable for interpretation of régime rules and settlement of disputes than other international tribunals external to them – often international legal régimes have, to a greater or lesser extent, their own 'jurisprudence'.

NCP. An ongoing lesson from Russia's non-compliance case is, simply, that, on suitable occasions, the internal environmental régime organs should exert appropriate multilateral pressure on Member States that persistently fail to comply with their treaty obligations, by applying not only bunches of carrots, but also the appropriate stick, carefully chosen to strike the right balance. If, in this first test on the Montreal NCP, the 1995 Meeting of the Parties had merely followed the Committee's rather soft recommendations, considerable doubts would have sprung up among the ozone régime members concerning the effectiveness of this new dispute avoidance and settlement procedure against non-compliance. Although it took more than five years, it is remarkable that, in 2002, the Implementation Committee confirmed the Russian Federation's return to compliance with the Montreal Protocol.

As a result, the Montreal NCP is now regarded as one of the most sophisticated dispute avoidance and settlement procedures for ensuring compliance with environmental obligations and fixed regulatory standards. As Rummel-Bulska observes: 'The main element that had led to the régime being considered as a model for other environmental treaties was mainly its preventive character and the readiness to assist rather than to sanction a Party considered not in compliance'.[397] Yet, it would be wrong to assume that the Meeting of the Parties will always ignore the possibility of taking 'countermeasures' in accordance with the Indicative List of the NCP. As explained above, at present, it is customary that, in cases of non-compliance with the Montreal Protocol, the Meeting of the Parties refers to the possibility of taking measures under the items B and C of the Indicative List of Measures.[398]

The experience of the Montreal NCP model will likely be helpful in designing other different non-compliance procedures under various international treaties of environmental protection. Yet it must be pointed out that, while the Montreal NCP has turned out to be the very prototype, each MEA should adopt a more suitable form of the NCP, depending on the nature and contents of its established legal obligations and types of potential environmental disputes.[399]

---

397 See UNEP/OzL.Pro.7/INF.1, para. 30.

398 However, as in other compliance mechanisms of MEAs, it is rare to resort to punitive measures. See also Jane Blumer, 'Compliance Regimes in Multilateral Environmental Agreements', in Jutta Brunnée, Meinhard Doelle and Lavanya Rajamani (eds.), *Promoting Compliance in an Evolving Climate Regime* (Cambridge University Press, 2012), p. 72.

399 For instance, the Montreal NCP model would not be suitable for the Basel Convention non-compliance régime. For a discussion, see Patrick Széll, 'Compliance Regimes for Multilateral Environmental Agreements: A Progress Report', 27/4 EPL (1997), p. 305.

Future global environmental treaties would do well to keep in mind the 'philosophy' of the Montreal NCP – collective soft enforcement.[400]

It is obvious that the NCP alone will not strengthen compliance with ozone treaty obligations, unless it is accompanied by the financial assistance and the transfer of technology required to improve State Parties' capacity to comply with them. Chapter 6 will examine whether the Montreal Protocol's compliance system has provided ozone régime members with sufficient inducements to comply with their international environment-related obligations.

---

400 See Section V above. Yet, it is important to note that, as Professor Boyle says, that 'the acceptance of more advanced models of institutional management and control remains limited, however, and does not justify the conclusion ... that the 'precautionary principle' has replaced national freedom to act in the absence of proof of harm'. See Alan E. Boyle, 'The Principle of Co-operation: Environment', in Vaughan Lowe and Colin Warbrick (eds.), *The United Nations and Principles of International Law: Essays in Memory of Michael Akehurst* (Routledge, 1994), p. 133.

CHAPTER 6

The Financial Mechanism of the Montreal Protocol and the International Transfer of Ozone-Friendly Technology: Capacity Building in the Ozone Régime

I   The Concept of Capacity Building in International Environmental Law

A   *The Definition of Capacity Building*

The provision of financial and technical aid to developing countries[1] – such as bilateral overseas development aid (ODA)[2] – has traditionally been considered as a moral, rather than a strictly legal, obligation of industrialised States. Philosophically speaking, it is meant to compensate for the wrongs perpetrated against the countries in the Third World during colonisation.[3] In this way, the ethical aspect of capacity building, under international development law in particular,[4] may be generally seen as a repeated, but often largely fruitless, demand for an improvement in North-South economic relations that benefits the

---

1   Developing countries include economically less-developed countries of Asia, Africa and Latin America. On the technical definition of 'developing countries' under the Montreal Protocol, see Chapter 3(III.E) in this volume. According to the Ozone Secretariat, as of January 2018, 147 of the 197 parties to the Montreal Protocol were classified as Article 5 developing countries. See at: <http://ozone.unep.org/en/article-5-parties-status> (last visited on 31 January 2018).

2   See, for example, Sam Johnston, 'Financial Aid, Biodiversity and International Law', in Michael Bowman and Catherine Redgwell (eds.), *International Law and the Conservation of Biological Diversity* (Kluwer Law International, 1996), pp. 271 et seq.; Laurence Boisson de Chazournes, 'Technical and Financial Assistance', in Daniel Bodansky, Juta Brunnée and Ellen Hey (eds.), *The Oxford Handbook of International Environmental Law* (Oxford University Press, 2007), pp. 950–952.

3   See Tang Chengyuan, 'Legal Aspects of the Global Partnership between North and South', in Najeeb Al-Nauimi and Richard Meese (eds.), *International Legal Issues Arising under the United Nations Decade of International Law* (Martinus Nijhoff, 1995), p. 210; Günther Handl, 'Environmental Protection and Development in Third World Countries: Common Destiny-Common Responsibility', 20 *NYUJILP* (1988), pp. 606–608.

4   On international law of development, see, for example, Ahmed Mahiou, 'Development, International Law of', in Rüdiger Wolfrum (ed.), *Max Planck Encyclopedia of Public International Law*, Vol. III (Oxford University Press, 2012), pp. 78–83; Guy Feuer and Hervé Cassan, *Droit international du développement* (2nd ed. Dalloz, 1991), pp. 1 et seq.

© KONINKLIJKE BRILL NV, LEIDEN, 2019 | DOI:10.1163/9789004290877_008

South. From a historical perspective, it is possible to argue that the concept of capacity building originated in the developing countries' movement for a New International Economic Order (NIEO), which won its first endorsement at the Sixth Special Session of the United Nations General Assembly in 1974.[5]

In the much narrower context of international environmental law and of its sectoral régimes, such as the ozone régime, the words 'capacity building' acquire more specific and/or different, technical meanings. In other words, capacity building is not exactly equal to traditional foreign financial aid that is designed to satisfy the basic human needs (BHNs) of those who are barely surviving on the margin of everyday life and/or promote an industrialising country's economic development (through ODA funds, for example).[6] One of the major objectives of capacity building is to enable aid-receiving countries to comply fully with the strict technical and legal obligations of specialised international environmental régimes

Capacity building in developing countries broadly falls into four categories:[7] (i) bilateral, regional or international environmental financial assistance in general; (ii) (associated) international technology transfer for environment protection purposes;[8] (iii) institutional strengthening for the implementation of environmental agreements (for example, the strengthening of administrative and legal capacities and improvements of data collection and analysis[9]) and (iv) the development of a recipient country's awareness of environmental

---

5 See Alan E. Boyle, 'Comment on the Paper by Diana Ponce-Nava', in Winfried Lang (ed.), *Sustainable Development and International Law* (Graham & Trotman/M. Nijhoff, 1995), p. 137. For an extensive discussion of the NIEO, see, for example, Kamal Hossain (ed.), *Legal Aspects of the New International Economic Order* (Frances Pinter, Nichols Publishing Company, 1980).

6 Yet, since 1990s, not only governments of industrialised countries but also the World Bank and other regional banks have made efforts to distinguish environmental aid from normal development assistance. See, for example, Wendy E. Franz, 'Appendix: The Scope of Global Environmental Financing – Cases in Context', in Robert O. Keohane and Marc A. Levy (eds.), *Institutions for Environmental Aid* (MIT Press, 1996), pp. 367–380.

7 See also John F.E. Ohiorhenuan and Stephen M. Wunker, *Capacity Building Requirements for Global Environmental Protection* (GEF Working Paper, No. 12, 1995), pp. 3–5; Lother Gündling, 'Compliance Assistance in International Environmental Law: Capacity Building through Financial and Technology Transfer', 39 *ZaöRV* (1996), pp. 800–802; Donald Kaniaru and Lal Kurukulasuriya, 'Capacity Building in Environmental Law', in Sun Lin et al. (eds.), *UNEP's New Way Forward: Environmental Law & Sustainable Development* (UNEP, 1995), pp. 172–179.

8 On the definition of 'technology transfer', see Section IV(A) below.

9 Non-compliance with data reporting has been frequently observed in Article 5 developing countries. See further Chapter 5(VII.A(1)) in this volume.

issues in general, including their political commitment to the legal obligations of environmental régimes.[10]

This characterisation of capacity-building is deeply associated with universal and effective participation of a growing number of developing States whose contributions as polluters to global environmental problems (for example, ozone depletion and global warming) are relatively minor. For the majority of poor developing countries, the protection of the global environment, such as the stratospheric ozone layer, may often be seen as merely an expensive problem, or an inescapable by-product of the industrialisation of the rich Northern States. In this context, the concept of capacity-building may be regarded as an effective, political bargaining tool for modern environmental negotiations that may eventually lead to the adoption of new international treaties on the protection of the environment. In other words, for most industrialising States that regard MEAs only as impediments to their economic growth, international financial resources for capacity building within environmental régimes have become the so-called 'carrots' that are required in advance of the establishment of environmental régimes.[11]

B   *Capacity Building and MEAs*

Treaty provisions concerning the ideas of capacity building – financial aid and technology transfer in particular – are already included in some international environmental agreements that precede the ozone régime.

With regard to environment protection funds, the 1972 UNESCO Convention for the Protection of the World Cultural and National Heritage introduced the World Heritage Fund (WHF) as a trust fund consisting of compulsory and voluntary contributions by contracting State Parties.[12] Likewise, in 1990, the

---

10   It has been pointed out that effectiveness of environmental law in developing States is impaired by corruption of government officials. See, for example, Michael G. Faure, *Enforcement Issues for Environmental Legislation in Developing Countries* (UNU/INTECH Working Paper No. 19, March 1995), pp. 18–19.

11   The 'principle' of 'common-but-differentiated responsibility' could be also understood in this similar context of capacity building.

12   See Articles 15 and 16. Each party pays one per cent of its contribution to the Regular Budget of the UNESCO to the World Heritage Fund. On this Fund, see, for example, Francesco Francioni (ed.), *The 1972 World Heritage Convention: A Commentary* (Oxford University Press, 2008), pp. 269–280; Peter H. Sand, 'The Potential Impact of the Global Environmental Facility of the World Bank, UNDP and UNEP', in Rüdiger Wolfrum (ed.), *Enforcing Environmental Standards: Economic Mechanisms as Viable Means?* (Springer, 1996), pp. 485–490. The World Heritage Fund has provided US$4 million annually to support its activities requested by States Parties. See UNESCO World Heritage Centre, 'Funding', at: <http://whc.unesco.org/en/funding/> (last visited on 31 January 2018).

Fourth Meeting of the Conference of the Parties of the 1971 Ramsar Convention established the Wetland Conservation Fund in order to assist developing country parties.[13] In addition to fund mechanisms within environmental treaties, the Environmental Convention Trust Funds were established in 1978 under the auspices of the UNEP for the greater implementation of legal obligations in particular environmental treaty régimes for sustainable development, though its relatively small budget for each treaty handicaps its current operations.[14]

With regard to technology transfer, the 1982 UNCLOS deals with marine technology transfer in two parts, that is, the provisions on the international sea-bed régime and Part XIV (Articles 266 to 274).[15] Under Articles 144 and 274, the International Sea Bed Authority[16] is required to train nationals of developing countries to make technical documentation on sea-bed mining available to developing States, and to assist these countries in the acquisition of sea-bed marine technology.[17] Under Article 266(1), State Parties are called on to cooperate in promoting the development and transfer of marine science and technology according to fair and reasonable terms and conditions.[18] The 1992 Climate Change Convention contains the 'classic environment technology

---

13   See Resolution C(4.3). In 1996, the Fund was renamed as the Ramsar Small Grants Fund (SGF) by Resolution VI.6. See Philippe Sands and Jacqueline Peel, *Principles of International Environmental Law* (3rd ed. Cambridge University Press, 2012), p. 494. Since its establishment, the Fund has provided over eight million Swiss Francs to over 240 projects from 110 countries. See Ramsar Convention Secretariat, 'Small Grants Fund', at: <https://www.ramsar.org/activity/small-grants-fund> (last visited on 31 January 2018).

14   See Peter H. Sand, 'The Potential Impact of the Global Environmental Facility of the World Bank, UNDP and UNEP', in Rüdiger Wolfrum (ed.), *Enforcing Environmental Standards: Economic Mechanisms as Viable Means?* (Springer, 1996), pp. 487 et seq.; Sand, 'Trust for the Earth: New Financial Mechanisms for Sustainable Development', in Winfried Lang (ed.), *Sustainable Development and International Law* (Graham & Trotman/Martinus Nijhoff, 1995), pp. 172–174; Rosalyn Higgins, Philippa Webb, Dapo Akande, Sandesh Sivakumaran and James Sloan, *Oppenheim's International Law: United Nations* (Oxford University Press, 2017), pp. 921–922.

15   See Alexander Proelss (ed.), *United Nations Convention on the Law of the Sea: A Commentary* (C.H. Beck, 2017), pp. 1764 et seq.

16   See generally Michael Wood, 'International Seabed Authority', in Rüdiger Wolfrum (ed.), *Max Planck Encyclopedia of Public International Law*, Vol. III (Oxford University Press, 2012), pp. 146–155.

17   See R.R. Churchill and A.V. Lowe, *The Law of the Sea* (Manchester University Press,1988), p. 302. The Agreement on the Implementation of Part XI of the UNCLOS revised the technology transfer régime on deep-sea bed mining.

18   See Alexander Proelss (ed.), *United Nations Convention on the Law of the Sea: A Commentary* (C.H. Beck, 2017), pp. 1770–1772. See also Articles 202–203 (Scientific and Technical Assistance to Developing States).

transfer clause'[19] (Article 4(5)) and, as with the Montreal Protocol, it has created conditionality between the compliance by industrialising countries and the effective transfer of technology and financial resources (Article 4(7)). Other modern MEAS also contain provisions on technology transfer. They include the 1992 Biodiversity Convention (Article 16),[20] the 1989 Basel Convention (Article 10) and the 1994 Sulphur Protocol to the 1979 Geneva LRTAP (Article 3).[21]

This chapter deals with the Montreal Protocol's Multilateral Fund (MLF) as a new capacity-building mechanism for its contracting parties.[22] After evaluating the 1987 version of the Montreal Protocol in the context of financial and technical assistance, Section II analyses the negotiation process of the Montreal Multilateral Fund, including the issues of international technology transfer regarding ODSS. Section III then investigates general aspects of the Financial Mechanism of the Protocol, including the Multilateral Fund, and also considers the role of international agencies within the framework of the Financial Mechanism. Section IV studies the current operation and effectiveness of the Multilateral Fund of the Protocol, focusing on the phaseout of ODSS and international transfer of ozone-friendly technology.

II   The Negotiation Process of the Montreal Multilateral Fund and Issues Related to Technology Transfer

A   *Capacity Building under the Vienna Ozone Convention and the Montreal Protocol*

The 1985 framework Ozone Convention adopted in Vienna neither centres much international attention on the need for special considerations to be given to developing countries, nor does it include a clause concerning additional multilateral financial assistance from industrially advanced Northern States. Article 4 of the Vienna Ozone Convention only provided that (i) the State

---

19   See Gaetan Verhoosel, 'International Transfer of Environmentally Sound Technology: The New Dimension of an Old Stumbling Block', 27/6 *EPL* (1997), p. 475.

20   See Mara Ntona, 'Technology Transfer', in Elisa Morgera and Jona Razzaque (eds.), *Biodiversity and Nature Protection Law* (Edward Elgar, 2017), pp. 358–368; Lyle Glowka, Françoise Burhenne-Guilmin and Hugh Synge, *A Guide to the Convention on Biological Diversity* (IUCN, 1994), noting that 'article 16 is probably the most controversial article' in the Convention.

21   See also the 1979 LRTAP (Article 8); the 1988 NO_x Protocol (Article 3); the 1991 VOC Protocol (Article 4).

22   On the role of the administrative trust funds for the Vienna Ozone Convention and the Montreal Protocol, see Gilbert M. Bankobeza, *Ozone Protection* (Eleven International, 2005), pp. 184–190.

Parties are to 'facilitate and encourage the exchange of scientific, technical, socio-economic, commercial and legal information relevant to this Convention'[23] and that (ii) they shall also 'co-operate, consistent with their national laws, regulations and practices and take into account in particular the needs of the developing countries, in promoting, directly or through competent international bodies, the development and transfer of technology and knowledge'.[24]

These treaty provisions indicate that, in most cases, global cooperation in transferring technology under the Vienna Ozone Convention is thus frequently subject to national laws regarding, for example, patents, trade secrets and the protection of confidential business or commercial information.[25] During the negotiation of the Vienna Convention, many experts considered that Article 4 contained an escape clause that could undermine the value of the Ozone Convention. In practice, it deterred industrialising developing States from participating in the international ozone régime.[26] Before the adoption of the 1987 Montreal Ozone Protocol, only a few developing countries[27] decided to become Contracting Parties to the framework Ozone Convention, that was regarded as merely an environmental régime of rich Northern States.

Since the negotiations of the 1987 Montreal Protocol were focused on technical and thorny issues of ODS emission reductions,[28] matters pertaining to the expected financial and technological assistance mechanism, including a multilateral fund and multilateral, regional and bilateral cooperation, were appropriately left to the Meeting of the Parties. Article 13(2) states that 'The Parties, at their first meeting, shall adopt by consensus financial rules for the operation of this Protocol'.[29] The 1989 First Meeting of the Parties was thus

---

23 See Article 4(1). For instance, socio-economic and commercial information include: (i) production and production capacity; (ii) use and use patterns; (iii) imports and exports: and (iv) the costs, risks and benefits of human activities which may indirectly modify the ozone layer and of the impacts of regulatory actions taken or being considered to control these activities. See Annex II(5).

24 Several developing States preferred 'consistent with' to 'subject to'. See UNEP/WG.94/8, p. 3.

25 See also Felix Bloch, *Technologietransfer zum internationalen Umweltschutz: Eine völkerrechtliche Untersuchung unter besonderer Berücksichtigung des Schutzes der Ozonschicht und des Weltklimas* (Peter Lang, 2007), pp. 132–133.

26 See, for example, UNEP/WG.94/8, p. 4.

27 These countries include Guatemala (11 September 1987, accession) and Mexico (14 September 1987).

28 See Chapter 3 in this volume for a full account of the Montreal NCP.

29 The Working Group on the Special Situation of Developing Countries noted that: '[W]hen the Financial Rules are drawn up it would be most important not to place undue financial burden on the developing countries whose contribution to depletion of the ozone layer is minimal'. See UNEP/WG.167/2, p. 32.

to begin deliberations on the means of fulfilling these treaty obligations, including the preparation of workplans.[30] Yet, as was described in Chapter 3 in this volume, it was agreed that a special provision in Article 5 of the Protocol should allow developing countries to delay their treaty compliance with ODS control measures for ten years.

According to Article 5(3) of the 1987 Ozone Protocol, State Parties are only required 'to facilitate bilaterally or multilaterally the provision of subsidies, aid, credits, guarantees or insurance programmes to Parties that are developing countries for the use of alternative technology and for substitute products'. Yet, it is important that Article 10(2) provides that any party or signatory to the Protocol can file a request to the UNEP Ozone Secretariat for technical assistance for the purposes of implementing or participating in the Ozone Protocol.

B   *The Negotiation of the Multilateral Fund and Technology Transfer*
The First Meeting of the Open-Ended Working Group of the Parties to the Montreal Protocol was held in August 1989 in order to develop modalities for finance-related mechanisms.[31] The Meeting was attended by representatives from twenty-two Contracting Parties and twelve non-Contracting Parties (for example, China, India and the Republic of Korea). The Executive Director of the UNEP officially opened the Meeting with an opening address which stated that, due mainly to the lack of financial resources, developing States were unable to comply with ozone treaty obligations without serious disruption of their development efforts. He also suggested that 'what they needed was concessional funding and outright grants *additional* to existing aid programmes'.[32] The Executive Director further indicated that the financial mechanisms of the Montreal Protocol would constitute an important precedent for those of a global climate change treaty.[33]

Delegates of industrialising States, led by Mexico, Venezuela, China and India, strongly advocated the establishment of a trust fund within the UNEP, or any other suitable institution, with 'legally enforceable obligations of contributions' for developed State Parties to the Ozone Protocol.[34] They also supported the view that the totality of funds should show an increase – that is, the concept of additionality – and that burden sharing must be implemented

---

30   See Articles 10(3) and 11(3)-(4).

31   See UNEP/OzL.Pro.WG.I(1)/3 (First Session of the First Meeting, held at UNEP headquarters in Nairobi from 21 to 25 August 1989).

32   See UNEP/OzL.Pro.WG.I(1)/3, para. 2 (emphasis in original).

33   See ibid.

34   See UNEP/OzL.Pro.WG.I(1)/3, paras. 9 and 34; Richard Benedick, *Ozone Diplomacy* (Harvard University Press, 1998), p. 153.

among the industrialised donor States.[35] However, industrialised donor States, including the United States, the United Kingdom and Japan, advocated the use of existing bilateral aid programmes and/or multilateral financial assistance from the World Bank. They considered that the concept of an 'International Environmental Facility', as a clearing house mechanism to identify and match bilateral and multilateral funding with individual projects, would be one of the acceptable alternatives to the creation of a new financial institution within the ozone régime, as long as it was external to existing international monetary organisations dominated by a handful of rich Northern States, including the United States.[36]

The Working Group also formulated a definition of transfer of technology in the context of financial aid, namely, 'facilitating access to environmentally safe alternative substances for Parties that are developing countries and assist them to make expeditious use of such alternatives' by meeting the incremental costs associated with transition from ODSs to alternatives and substitutes.[37] It was also agreed that incremental costs covered by the financial mechanism would include (i) production, (ii) use as an intermediate good and (iii) action at the consumer level.[38]

However, industrialising States insisted that free access to technical information and non-profit technology transfer of substitutes for ODSs should not be subject to trade concerns relating to matters of intellectual property rights, licences and patents.[39] We may notice here that the above definition of international technology transfer does not necessarily refer to the frequent situation in which certain Multinational Companies (MNCs) to sell patents for ODS emission control technology.[40] In the absence of promising economic benefits for these companies, the introduction of new technology would be difficult to achieve except by national regulations supported by socio-economic assistance from the government. In this context, the Director-General of the World Intellectual Property (WIPO) noted in a subsequent meeting that national governments have 'little space for manoeuvre with private industries beyond persuasion and incentives'.[41]

---

35 See UNEP/OzL.Pro.WG.I(1)/3, para. 26 (not officially agreed on the precise wording due to time constraints).

36 See UNEP/OzL.Pro.WG.I(1)/3, para. 9; Richard Benedick, *Ozone Diplomacy* (Harvard University Press, 1998), p. 153.

37 See Article 5(2) of the 1987 Montreal Protocol. See also UNEP/OzL.Pro.WG.II(2)/7.

38 For further details, see UNEP/OzL.Pro.WG.I(1)/3, para. 12.

39 See UNEP/OzL.Pro.WG.I(1)/3; Richard Benedick, *Ozone Diplomacy* (Harvard University Press, 1998), p. 153.

40 See Thomas Gehring, *Dynamic International Régimes* (Peter Lang, 1994), p. 289.

41 See UNEP/OzL.Pro.WG.II(2)/7, para. 7.

The meeting of the Bureau of the Montreal Protocol held in September 1989 recommended that the Second Working Group consider the creation of a binding financial mechanism based on compulsory contributions from industrialised countries and a situation in which private parties were not likely to release legal patents on ODS technologies.[42]

At the Open-Ended Working Group held in November 1989, a group of industrialising States, led by Mexico, put forward a new Article 10(bis) on transfer of technology and financial assistance. It provides that international technology transfer from industrialised to industrialising countries should be arranged on a 'preferential and non-commercial basis' and that an 'International Trust Fund' – proposed by an environmental NGO known as the World Resources Institute –[43] shall be established within the UNEP to meet fully the incremental costs.[44] The idea of the Trust Fund was comparatively modest compared to the 'Earth Fund' – the idea put forward by the Executive Director of the UNEP – that would institute a global levy on the use of the environment, in this case, the stratospheric ozone layer.[45]

The above-mentioned group of States also introduced an amendment to Article 5 of the Protocol which stated that the obligation of Article 5 parties or industrialising countries to comply with ODS control measures would be subject to the transfer of technologies and financial assistance as provided for in the new Article 10(bis).[46]

The Second Meeting of the Open-Ended Working Group was held in March 1990.[47] The Executive Director of the UNEP introduced the following six principles on which general agreement had been reached in previous formal and informal discussions:[48]

(i)   A new financial mechanism must be established and its funding must be additional to existing development assistance.

(ii) Contributions should be made on an assessed rather than a voluntary basis.

---

42   See UNEP/OzL.Pro.Bur.1/2, para. 8.

43   For further details, see UNEP/OzL.Pro.Mech.1/2, paras. 23–24. The other scheme put forward by the NGO was a pilot investment programme for Sustainable Resource Use, 'ECOVEST'. See ibid., para. 25.

44   See UNEP/OzL.Pro.WG.II(1)/5, p. 16.

45   See a note by Dr. M. Tolba, 'Transfer of Technology and the Financing of Global Environmental Problems: The Role of Users' Fees' (UNEP/OzL.Fin.1/2), para. 31.

46   See UNEP/OzL.Pro.WG.II(1)/5, Article 5(2), p. 14.

47   See UNEP/OzL.Pro.WG.II(2)/7, (26 February – 5 March 1990, second session, Geneva).

48   See a report of an informal consultations held in January 1990, UNEP/OzL.Pro.WG.II(2)/2; Thomas Gehring, *Dynamic International Régimes* (Peter Lang, 1994), pp. 290–291.

(iii) Existing bilateral and multilateral sources of funding should be maintained.

(iv) The UNEP, in its role as an Ozone Secretariat, should be assigned a major role in catalysing and coordinating the work of other organisations in a joint venture.

(v) Decisions on policies and criteria for the use of the resources should be assigned by the Contracting Parties. This will require an expansion of the role of the Ozone Secretariat.

(vi) While each country enjoys the prerogative to decide how to raise funds, the establishment of a user's fee for ozone-depleting activities has several advantages.[49]

However, the delegations from the industrialised donor State Parties pointed out the difficult and lengthy process that might be involved and they therefore defended their preference for existing financial and technical assistance through major international economic institutions – the World Bank in particular – over a new multilateral financial treaty institution. Some of them supported only the creation of a 'clearinghouse' to furnish objective information and to facilitate formal requests for possible assistance.[50] Indeed, the new financial mechanism was likely to form a historical precedent for the United States government, potentially the largest donor, to channel good money into a future CO_2 financial mechanism.[51] Recognising that they did not have much say in the present market-oriented political-economic systems, however, the developing States undoubtedly favoured it, strengthening the UNEP's moderating influence on the operation of the expected new environmental funding mechanism. Nevertheless, the issue remained unsettled.

The Second Meeting of the Parties was held in London, in June 1990, and, prior to that Meeting, the Forth Meeting of the Working Group managed to clear up several immediate problems, such as the voting procedures of the Executive Committee.[52] Developing States, such as India and China, considered that their ratification of the Protocol would depend not only on the expected

---

49 See UNEP/OzL.Pro.WG.II(2)/7, para. 6; Richard Benedick, *Ozone Diplomacy* (Harvard University Press, 1998), p. 155.

50 See ibid., pp. 155–156.

51 See Rene Bowser, 'History of the Montreal Protocol's Ozone Fund', 20 *International Environmental Reporter* (November 1991), p. 637; Richard Benedick, *Ozone Diplomacy* (Harvard University Press, 1998), p. 159.

52 See Thomas Gehring, *Dynamic International Régimes* (Peter Lang, 1994), pp. 296–298.

establishment of the ozone-related financial mechanism but also on sufficient guarantees for access to new technologies of ODSS.[53]

At the London Ozone Meeting, India argued that it was morally desirable that all CFC production should be stopped, but only after developing countries had received alternative technologies.[54] The delegation of Malaysia even stated that denying access to modern technology amounts to so-called 'environmental colonialism'.[55]

As Blake and Walters point out, underdeveloped countries, which depend on international technology transfer via major MNCs, generally consider that they have paid enough to the developed First World countries through the exploitation of their natural resources. They believe that technology is part of 'human heritage', not proprietary scientific knowledge (that is, the private property of the patentee) and they have a right of access to such technology to improve their standards of living.[56] On the other hand, industrialised countries generally regard patent protection as an incentive for the development of new technology. It is also true that the lack of a national legislative and regulatory régime with a limited enforcement mechanism has often reduced the attractiveness of making business investments in the Third World. In practice, it has also discouraged various bilateral or multilateral overseas investments.

It is important to note that, at this Meeting, the parties adopted the interim Montreal NCP. If developing countries have difficulties acquiring ozone-friendly technologies necessary to fully comply with the obligations of the ozone treaty, including control measures of ODSS, the internal treaty organs, such as the Implementation Committee and the Meeting of the Parties, are to decide future remedial measures for these matters, such as appropriate financial and/or technical assistance.[57]

After resolving major problems with the environmental fund, the parties to the Montreal Protocol decided to start operation of the Financial Mechanism on 1 January 1991 for an interim period of three years, prior to the Amendment entering into force and the establishment of the actual institutional mechanism. Accordingly, the Interim Multilateral Fund for the Implementation of the Montreal Protocol was established by the 1990 London Meeting based on a simple decision – Decision II/8 – of the Ozone Meeting of the Parties.

---

53   See M.W. Browne, '93 Nations move to ban Chemicals that harm Ozone', *New York Times* (30 June 1990).
54   See Karen T. Litfin, *Ozone Discourses* (Columbia University Press, 1994), p. 144.
55   See Richard Benedick, *Ozone Diplomacy* (Harvard University Press, 1998), p. 189.
56   See David H. Blake and Robert S. Walters, *The Politics of Global Economic Relations* (2nd ed. Prentice-Hall, 1983), p. 156.
57   For a full account of the Montreal NCP, see Chapter 5 in this volume,

It was thought that the Interim Fund would be transformed into the Montreal Protocol's Multilateral Fund on a permanent basis, as established by the Amendment.

However, at the 1992 Copenhagen Ozone Meeting, members of the European Community – France, Italy, the Netherlands and the United Kingdom, in particular – disputed the validity of such a transformation of the Fund and were unwilling to reaffirm their financial commitment to the Multilateral Fund beyond 1993. Nevertheless, not only Article 5 developing countries and small industrialised donor countries, but also the United States – which at the 1990 London Meeting had greatly preferred the GEF run by the World Bank – advocated the dominant and practical idea of establishing the Multilateral Fund.[58]

As a result, the Forth Meeting conclusively established the Financial Mechanism, including the Multilateral Fund. The Interim Fund only operated, therefore, until December 1992. In addition, the 1992 Copenhagen Meeting also decided that any resources remaining in the interim mechanism would be transferred to the new Multilateral Fund.

III   The Structure of the Financial Mechanism of the Montreal Protocol

A   *General Legal Aspects*

Initially, we will examine three fundamental aspects of the Multilateral Fund (MLF). First, the Multilateral Fund will meet agreed incremental costs for Article 5 countries' treaty compliance, on a grant or concessional basis and in accordance with criteria decided upon by the State Parties.[59] In this respect, the 1990 London Meeting adopted a detailed 'Indicative List of Categories of Incremental Cost' – which is utterly fundamental to project eligibility for the MLF, although it cannot be considered as definitive or exclusive, since it allows for costs not on the list to be met by the Fund (i) if they are identified and qualified and (ii) if they are found by the Executive Committee[60] to be consistent with any criteria decided by the parties.[61] Requests for financing the

---

58   See UNEP/OzL.Pro.4/15; Thomas Gehring and Sebastian Oberthür, 'The Copenhagen Meeting', 23/1 EPL (1993), p. 10. See also Richard Benedick, *Ozone Diplomacy* (Harvard University Press, 1998), pp. 209–212.

59   See Article 10(3-a).

60   See Section B(1) below.

61   Possible incremental costs include (i) cost of conversion of existing production facilities and equipments, (ii) costs arising from premature retirement or enforced idleness

incremental costs of an implementation project will be considered in accordance with several general principles, including cost effectiveness.[62] Defining the term 'incremental costs' is a difficult task and, in the meetings of the Executive Committee, some developing countries have tried to expand the list's coverage.[63]

Secondly, the MLF is to finance clearing-house functions concerning (i) assistance for industrialising countries by way of country-specific studies and technical cooperation to identify their need for cooperation, (ii) technical cooperation to meet these identified needs, (iii) the distribution of information and relevant materials as provided for in Article 9 and the conduct of workshops, training sessions and other related activities and (iv) the promotion and monitoring of other multilateral, bilateral and regional cooperation.[64]

Thirdly, the MLF finances the independent Fund Secretariat[65] and other related support costs.[66] It is important that the Fund does operate under the authority of the Meeting of the Parties and in accordance with this organ's overall policies.[67] Furthermore, the Financial Mechanism under Article 10 of the Montreal Protocol is 'without prejudice to any future arrangements that may be developed with respect to other environmental issues'.[68] As we shall see later, major internal treaty organs – the Meeting of the Parties, the Executive Committee and the Fund Secretariat – and pre-existing international organisations, such as the World Bank, the UNDP and the UNIDO, play important roles in the operation of the MLF.

The MLF will be financed by contributions from all State Parties not operating under Article 5(1) of the Ozone Protocol, including Russia and other CEITs, and funds are to be additional to other financial transfers to industrialising

---

and (iii) cost of establishing new facilities for substitutes of capacity equivalent to capacity lost when plants are converted or scrapped. See UNEP/OzL.Pro/2/3, Appendix I of Decision II/8; UNEP/OzL.Pro/4/15, Decision IV/18, Annex VIII. See also Consulting Engineers and Planners AS, *Study on the Financial Mechanism of the Montreal Protocol* (UNEP, March 1995), para. 214; Secretariat of the Multilateral Fund for the Implementation of the Montreal Protocol, *Executive Committee Primer – 2016 An introduction to the Executive Committee of the Multilateral Fund for the Implementation of the Montreal Protocol* (2016), Appendix 1: The Multilateral Fund, p. 2.

62 See further UNEP/OzL.Pro/2/3, Appendix 1 (Decision II/8) para. 1; UNEP/OzL.Pro/4/15, Decision IV/18, Section I(6).
63 See Richard Benedick, *Ozone Diplomacy* (Harvard University Press, 1998), pp. 257–258.
64 See Article 10(3-b).
65 See Section B(2) below.
66 See Article 10(3-c).
67 See Article 10(4).
68 See Article 10(10).

countries, such as existing bilateral or multilateral ODA flows. Contributions to the MLF – which is in convertible currency or in kind and/or in national currency – will be made based on the United Nations' scale of assessments[69] and on the scale of contributions decided by the annual Meeting of the Parties. There is no fixed date for making annual contributions to the Fund.[70]

Since 1991, the MLF has approved 6,791 projects and allocated grants collectively equivalent to $2.75 billion. Among them, over 5,500 projects have been completed so far, with 2,553 projects attempting to and/or contributing to the phaseout of ODS consumption and/or production.[71] In total, MLF projects have used less funding than initially planned by the Executive Committee, because some funds were returned to the MLF as a result of savings achieved during project preparation, and some projects were cancelled.[72] The distribution of the MLF is shown in the Figure below.

Bilateral and regional cooperation with low-volume-ODS-consuming States is regarded as a contribution to the Multilateral Fund up to a certain percentage,[73] provided that such cooperation (i) strictly relates to compliance with the provisions of the Ozone Protocol, (ii) provides additional resources and (iii) meets agreed incremental costs.[74] The amount representing the annual bilateral cooperation will be credited for the year designated by the non-Article 5 party as part of its contribution.[75] At its Seventh Meeting of 1995, the Executive Committee adopted guidelines for the cost assessment of bilateral and regional activities.[76] Furthermore, it should be noted that contributions

---

69 See Article 10(6). The United Nations scale of assessment is an index system based on country economic factors. See further Decision VII/37(4).

70 See UNEP/OzL.Pro/ExCom/10/40, para. 102. State Parties' pledges to contribute to the MLF is binding, provided that the approved budgets is consistent with Article 10 of the Montreal Protocol and the Terms of Reference of the MLF. See Gilbert M. Bankobeza, *Ozone Protection* (Eleven International, 2005), pp. 188–189 and 198–199.

71 See UNEP/OzL.Pro.24/INF/4, Annex: Final Report – Evaluation of the Financial Mechanism of the Montreal Protocol (28 September 2012), p. 14; UNEP/OzL.Pro.WG.1/32/4, p. 2.

72 See ibid.

73 See the Terms of Reference for the Multilateral Fund clarifies that such contributions would be counted up to a total of twenty per cent of the total contribution by that party as decided by the annual Ozone Meeting of the Parties (para. 9).

74 See Article 10(6).

75 See UNEP/OzL.Pro/ExCom/5/16: Annex IV, para. 12; Secretariat of the Multilateral Fund for the Implementation of the Montreal Protocol, *Executive Committee Primer – 2016 An introduction to the Executive Committee of the Multilateral Fund for the Implementation of the Montreal Protocol* (2016), p. 15.

76 See UNEP/OzL.Pro/ExCom/7/30, para. 82 and Annex IV.

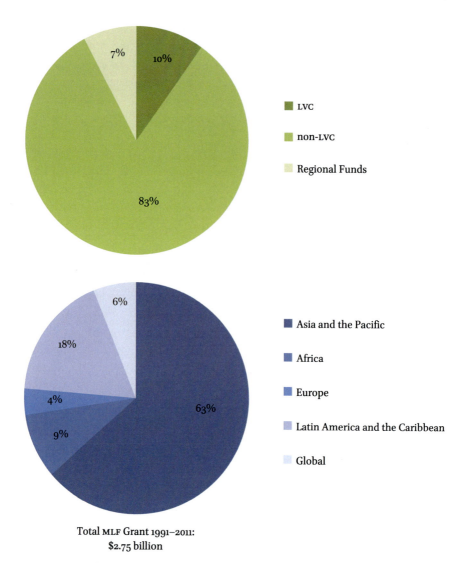

FIGURE 1   Distribution by Region and Country Consumption Level (UNEP/OzL.Pro.24/INF/4, Annex: Final Report – Evaluation of the Financial Mechanism of the Montreal Protocol (28 September 2012), p. 14; UNEP/OzL.Pro.WG.1/32/4, p. 40.).

may be received by those not party to the Montreal Protocol, as well as by other governmental, intergovernmental and non-governmental sources.[77]

---

77   See Annex IX(8).

It was also decided that the parties to the Protocol would decide on the programme budget of the Fund and on the percentage of contributions of individual Contracting Parties for each fiscal period. In addition, the resources of the Fund are to be disbursed with the concurrence of the beneficiary party.[78]

Finally, it is worth mentioning that, in order to clarify the nature and legal status of the Fund as a treaty body under international law, the 1994 Sixth Meeting of the Parties adopted Decision VI/16.[79] Decision VI/16 provides, for instance, that the Fund enjoys 'legal capacity as is necessary for the exercise of its functions and the protection of its interests ... to acquire and dispose of movable property and to institute legal proceedings in defence of its interests'. The MLF and the Fund Secretariat enjoy privileges and immunities in the host country, Canada.[80]

B *The Role of the International Agencies in the Financial Mechanism*

(1) The Executive Committee

As with the Implementation Committee of the NCP, the Executive Committee is a newly established permanent internal organ of the ozone régime.[81] The Executive Committee is assigned to 'develop and monitor the implementation of specific operational policies, guidelines and administrative arrangements for the purpose of achieving the objectives of the Multilateral Fund'.[82] In accordance with its Terms of Reference, the Executive Committee has carried out the following functions:[83]

(a) To develop and monitor the implementation of specific operational policies, guidelines and administrative arrangements, including the disbursement of resources;

---

78   See Article 10(7–8).

79   See UNEP/OzL.Pro.6/7, para. 103. Japan made a reservation on this Decision.

80   See Decision VI/16(b). See also Article 2 of the Agreement between the Government of Canada and the Multilateral Fund for the Implementation of the 1987 Montreal Protocol Regulating Matters Resulting from the Establishment in Canada of the Multilateral Fund and its Origin, reprinted in MFL Secretariat, 'Multilateral Fund for the Implementation of the Montreal Protocol: Policies, Procedures, Guidelines and Criteria' (as at July 1999), Annex I.2. See Winfried Lang, 'Ozone Layer', 5 *YbkIEL* (1994), p. 163, noting that several questions remain to be solved, for example, whether the Meeting of the Parties had a clear mandate to adopt such a decision, and whether it constitute in itself a 'valid source of international law'.

81   See Section III(B) in this volume.

82   See Article 10(5). See also Annex IX(5).

83   See the Terms of Reference of the Executive Committee as modified by Decisions IX/16, XVI/38 and XIX/11 of the Parties to the Montreal Protocol (para. 10), in *Executive Committee Primer – 2016 An introduction to the Executive Committee of the Multilateral Fund for the Implementation of the Montreal Protocol* (2016), Appendix 5, p. 2.

(b) To develop the plan and budget for the Multilateral Fund, including allocation of Multilateral Fund resources among the agencies identified in paragraph 5 of Article 10 of the Amended Protocol;

(c) To supervise and guide the administration of the Multilateral Fund;

(d) To develop the criteria for project eligibility and guidelines for the implementation of activities supported by the Multilateral Fund;

(e) To review regularly the performance reports on the implementation of activities supported by the Multilateral Fund;

(f) To monitor and evaluate expenditure incurred under the Multilateral Fund;

(g) To consider and, where appropriate, approve country programmes for compliance with the Protocol and, in the context of those country programmes, assess and where applicable approve all project proposals or groups of project proposals where the agreed incremental costs exceed $500,000;

(h) To review any disagreement by a Party operating under paragraph 1 of Article 5 with any decision taken with regard to a request for financing by that Party of a project or projects where the agreed incremental costs are less than $500,000;

(i) To assess annually whether the contributions through bilateral cooperation, including particular regional cases, comply with the criteria set out by the Parties for consideration as part of the contributions to the Multilateral Fund;

(j) To report annually to the meeting of the Parties on the activities exercised under the functions outlined above, and to make recommendations as appropriate;

(k) To nominate, for appointment by the Executive Director of UNEP, the Chief Officer of the Fund Secretariat, who shall work under the Executive Committee and report to it: and

(l) To perform such other functions as may be assigned to it by the Meeting of the Parties.

Unlike the Implementation Committee,[84] the Executive Committee has its own Rules of Procedure.[85] The Rules are to apply *mutatis mutandis* to the

---

84 See Chapter 5(IV.2(a)) in this volume.

85 See 'Rules of Procedure for Meetings of the Executive Committee for the Interim Multilateral Fund for the Implementation of the Montreal Protocol' in UNEP/OzL.Pro.3/11/Annex VI, in *Executive Committee Primer – 2016 An introduction to the Executive Committee of the Multilateral Fund for the Implementation of the Montreal Protocol* (2016), Appendix 5, pp. 1–4. The provisions of the Ozone Protocol prevail over the Rules of Procedure, however (Rule 20).

proceedings of any meeting of the Executive Committee. According to Rule 11, the Executive Committee will consist of seven parties from a group of industrialising countries operating under Article 5(1) and seven parties from a group of industrially advanced countries not operating under that article. Article 5 countries have organised themselves into three regions – Asia, Africa and Latin America and the Caribbean – and the donor countries have divided themselves into six groups – the European Union, the United States, Japan, Canada, Australia and New Zealand, the Nordic and EFTA countries and the Russian Federation.[86] Each group selects its own members of the Executive Committee and they must be formally endorsed by the Ozone Meeting of the Parties.[87]

Non-governmental organisations are allowed to participate in any meeting of the Executive Committee as observers.[88] NGOs are generally critical about MLF projects, particularly ones implemented by the IBRD, the World Bank. They had argued, for example, that the World Bank was too slow to implement its projects, that it largely controlled the decision-making of the Executive Committee;[89] that it frequently used chemicals that still destroy CFCs, or that are significant greenhouse gases:[90] and that it relied heavily on the recommendations of the Ozone Operations Resource Group (OORG), whose members had links with multilateral ODS-related MNCs.[91] At least, one MLF Fund project (World Bank-implemented HCFC-22 project in Mexico) was cancelled, as a result of NGOs' protests.[92] In the Fifteenth Meeting of the Executive Committee

---

86 See UNEP/OzL.Pro/ExCom/10/40, Annex I, para. 25.

87 The Twenty-Ninth Meeting of the Parties (2017) endorsed the selection of seven industrised State Parties – that is, Belgium, Canada (Vice-Chair), France, Japan, Norway, Slovakia and the United States, and seven Article 5 developing country parties – Argentina, Benin, the Dominican Republic, Grenada, India, Lebanon (Chair) and Nigeria, for one year beginning 1 January 2018 (Decision XXIX/22). See UNEP/OzL.Conv.11/7-UNEP/OzL. Pro.29/8, p. 48.

88 See Rules 6 and 7. See also Section V(D) below; Richard Benedick, *Ozone Diplomacy* (Harvard University Press, 1998), p. 223 (and endnote 3), noting that NGOs supported by the United States, Canada and the Netherlands appealed to the Third Meeting of the Parties to overrule a more restrictive proposal by the Executive Committee.

89 See Greenpeace, 'World Bank Gives More Excuses for Inaction on Ozone' (Press Release, 10 October 1994).

90 See ibid. But see also The World Bank, 'World Bank Assistance to 25 countries for Phasing out Harmful Ozone Depleting Substances Beginning to Produce Results', 7/4 *Environment Bulletin* (Winter 1995/96).

91 See Elizabeth R. DeSombre and Joanne Kauffman, 'The Montreal Protocol Fund: Partial Success Story', in Robert O. Keohane and Marc A. Levy (eds.), *Institutions for Environmental Aid* (MIT Press, 1996), p. 117.

92 See Richard Benedick, *Ozone Diplomacy* (Harvard University Press, 1998), pp. 260–261, reporting that the Friends of Earth was invited to an OORG meeting, and an OORG adviser

in 1994, the observers of two environmental NGOs, Greenpeace and Friends of Earth, and the representative of Denmark expressed concern at the Executive Committee approving many projects that would employ HCFCs or 'fifty per cent CFC reduced technology'.[93] The observer from Greenpeace argued, for instance, that the Executive Committee 'should ask for a full analysis of the scientific aspects and political considerations surrounding the use of CFCs'.[94]

With regard to the voting procedure, decisions of the Committee are to be made by consensus whenever possible. However, in a case where all efforts to achieve consensus have been exhausted and no agreement has been reached, a decisions will then be taken by a two-thirds majority of the parties representing both a majority of low-volume-ODS-consuming parties and a majority of industrialised State Parties not operating under Article 5(1).[95] This voting procedure, based on a harmonious North-South balance, is particularly significant since the voting strength of developing States in major international economic institutions, such as the World Bank and the IMF, is still less than one-third of the total, at most. At the 1992 Copenhagen Meeting, several government representatives stated that the MLF possessed a democratic character as reflected in its decision-making processes and a change in the structure of the Fund would be merely counterproductive.[96] To date, however, as with decision-making on control measures of ODSs, all fund decisions have been taken by consensus, and in practice, this two-third majority voting system has not been required yet.[97] However, the Executive Committee has encountered serious difficulties in achieving consensus particularly when a Member State of the Committee has had a direct interest in a given MLF project.[98] It is also suggested that some problems arising from the structure of the Executive Committee in itself – the turnover of Committee members and the inter-dependency of

---

and a USEPA representative corroborated an objection by the Friends of Earth to the Fund project.

93   See UNEP/OzL.Pro/ExCom/15/45, para. 113.

94   See ibid.

95   See the Rules of Procedure of the Executive Committee, Rule 17. On the utility of double majority, see Patrick Széll, 'Decision-Making under Multilateral Environmental Agreements', 26/5 EPL (1996), p. 213. Unlike this Multilateral Fund procedures, decisions by the GEF Council are made by consensus, and if these is a disagreement among members, then such decisions are to be taken based on a 'contribution-weighted voting procedure', but representing sixty per cent of the votes of all States.

96   See UNEP/OzL.Pro.4/15, para. 42.

97   See also Gilbert M. Bankobeza, *Ozone Protection* (Eleven International, 2005), p. 203.

98   See Consulting Engineers and Planners AS, *Study on the Financial Mechanism of the Montreal Protocol* (UNEP, March 1995), para. 228.

the Implementing Agencies in policy issue resolution – have often made some policy issues even much more complicated.[99]

In 1993, the Executive Committee established a Sub-Committee on Financial Matters at its Ninth Meeting to review and assess the existing financial arrangements and procedures and recommend modifications, where appropriate.[100] Subsequently, at the Twenty-first Meeting of the Committee, the Sub-Committee on Financial Matters was replaced by the 'Monitoring, Evaluation and Financial Sub-Committee' (MEF), which was (i) to review the cycle for business planning, the submission of work programmes and monitoring of approved projects and (ii) to make recommendations on these matters to the Committee.[101] The Executive Committee also established a sessional 'Project Review Sub-Committee' (PR).[102] For example, in 1996, three NGO representatives – one nominated by the environmental NGOs, one by industrial NGOs and one by NGOs from the academic community – were allowed to attend meetings of the Project Review Sub-Committee.[103] The membership of both Committees was balanced between non-Article 5 parties and Article 5 parties.[104] However, at its 40th meeting in 2003, the Executive Committee decided that certain planning activities affecting compliance should be addressed by the MLF's Executive Committee itself and therefore abolished both sub-committees for the year 2004 on a trial basis.[105]

---

99   See ibid., paras. 28 and 283.

100 See further UNEP/OzL.Pro/ExCom/9/20, paras. 31–32: Annex II.

101 See ExCom Decision 21/35, in UNEP/OzL.Pro/ExCom/21/36, para. 49. On its terms of reference, see MFL Secretariat, 'Multilateral Fund for the Implementation of the Montreal Protocol: Policies, Procedures, Guidelines and Criteria' (as at July 1999), Annex II.10.

102 See UNEP/OzL.Pro/ExCom/11/36, para. 156.8; UNEP/OzL.Pro/ExCom/15/45, para. 173. As for the Terms of Reference for the Sub-Committee, see UNEP/OzL.Pro/ExCom/15/45, para. 173.

103 See ExCom Decision 20/52, in UNEP/OzL.Pro/ExCom/20/72, para. 81 and its Annex II (amended terms of reference).

104 See ExCom Decision 23/6(a), in UNEP/OzL.Pro/23/68, para. 19.

105 See Decision 40/52. One representative stated that 'it might now be time to abolish both Sub-Committees, allowing more in-depth discussion of the issues within the Executive Committee as a whole, with some matters being initially addressed by small informal groups. It was stressed that if the Sub-Committees were retained, there would be a need to ensure balance in their workload and to avoid duplication of work', See UNEP/OzL.Pro/ExCom/40/50, para. 99. See also *Executive Committee Primer – 2016 An introduction to the Executive Committee of the Multilateral Fund for the Implementation of the Montreal Protocol* (2016), Appendix 1, p. 7; Multilateral Fund Secretariat, *Multilateral Fund for the Implementation of the Montreal Protocol: Policies, Procedures, Guidelines and Criteria* (As at November 2017), Chapter 2: Executive Committee, p. 15.

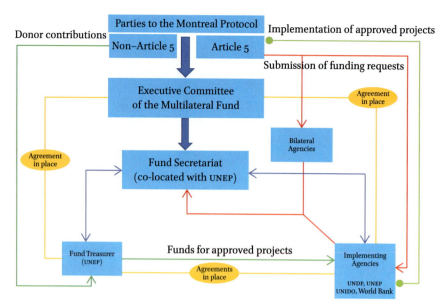

FIGURE 2   The Role of the Executive Committee in the MLF (*Executive Committee Primer – 2016 An Introduction to the Executive Committee of the Multilateral Fund for the Implementation of the Montreal Protocol* (2016), Appendix 1, p. 6)

(2)   The Multilateral Fund Secretariat

The Fund Secretariat of the Montreal Protocol, operating under the Chief Officer, is located in Montreal, Canada.[106] It is to consist of nine professional staff, which is broadly representative of the parties, with two staff members from Asia, two from Africa, one from North America, one from Latin America and two from Europe.[107]

---

106   See Decision IV/18 in UNEP/OzL.Pro/4/15. The officials of the Multilateral Fund Secretariat enjoy privileges and immunities necessary for the independent exercise of their functions of the Fund (Decision VI/16(b)). See Agreement Between The Government Of Canada And The Multilateral Fund For The Implementation Of The 1987 Montreal Protocol Regulating Matters Resulting From The Establishment In Canada Of The Multilateral Fund And Its Organs (Annex I.11), in Multilateral Fund Secretariat, *Multilateral Fund for the Implementation of the Montreal Protocol: Policies, Procedures, Guidelines and Criteria* (As at November 2017), Chapter 1: Financial Mechanism, p. 131. The Executive Committee thus accepted the offer of Canada to cover any additional costs relative to costs associated with UNEP Headquarters. See UNEP/OzL.Pro/ExCom/8/29 (Annex III, para. 3.3)).

107   See UNEP/OzL.Pro/ExCom/10/40, Annex I, para. 5; *Executive Committee Primer – 2016 An introduction to the Executive Committee of the Multilateral Fund for the Implementation of the Montreal Protocol* (2016), Appendix 1, p. 7. At present, the Fund Secretariat is

CAPACITY BUILDING IN THE OZONE RÉGIME

The tasks of the Fund Secretariat can be divided into seven categories:[108]

(i) Preparation and documentation for the meetings of the Executive Committee
(ii) Policy analysis and review
(iii) Analysis and review of programmes and fund activities
(iv) Monitoring the activities of the Implementing Agencies
(v) Communications and public relations
(vi) Administrative support, coordination and liaison for the Executive Committee
(vii) Financial management and monitoring of the Fund.

In addition, since 1997, the Fund Secretariat also have a monitoring and evaluation function.[109] The Fund Secretariat and the Implementing Agencies cooperate with parties to provide information on funding available for relevant projects to secure the necessary contacts and to coordinate projects financed from other sources with activities financed under the Montreal Protocol.[110] The Fund Secretariat also make the necessary arrangements for the meetings of the Committee and performs all other functions the Executive Committee requires.[111]

More specifically, the Fund Secretariat assesses and offers recommendations to the Executive Committee with regard to country programmes and work programmes developed by the Implementing Agencies.[112] It has been pointed out that 'although almost all projects brought before the ExCom [Executive Committee] are ultimately approved, many are withdrawn, postponed, or modified at the suggestion of the secretariat before they are brought forward'.[113] Thus,

---

comprised of sixteen professional and fourteen general service staff members. See at: <http://www.multilateralfund.org/aboutMLF/fundsecretariat/default.aspx>.

108 See UNEP/OzL.Pro/10/40, Annex I, para. 29; Terms of Reference for the Fund Secretariat, in Multilateral Fund Secretariat, *Multilateral Fund for the Implementation of the Montreal Protocol: Policies, Procedures, Guidelines and Criteria* (As at November 2017), Chapter 3: Fund Secretariat, Annex III.1, p. 17.

109 See *Executive Committee Primer – 2016 An introduction to the Executive Committee of the Multilateral Fund for the Implementation of the Montreal Protocol* (2016), Appendix 1, p. 8.

110 See the Terms of Reference for the Fund Secretariat, in UNEP/OzL.Pro.4/15, Annex IX, para. 22, p. 53.

111 See Rule 15 of the Rules of Procedure of the Executive Committee.

112 See Section IV(D.1–2) below.

113 See Elizabeth R. DeSombre and Joanne Kauffman, 'The Montreal Protocol Fund: Partial Success Story', in Robert O. Keohane and Marc A. Levy (eds.), *Institutions for Environmental Aid* (MIT Press, 1996), pp. 120–121.

308   CHAPTER 6

the Multilateral Fund Secretariat also assumes, to some extent, control over institutional oversight or supervisory mechanisms.

Finally, the Chief Officer submits bi-annual reports covering budget and financial issues to the Executive Committee and also report on activities, including those requiring actions by the Executive Committee.[114]

(3)   The Implementing Agencies

The Terms of Reference of the MLF provide that, under the supervision of the Executive Committee (i) Implementing Agencies are requested by the Committee – in the context of country programmes[115] – to cooperate with and assist the parties within their respective area of expertise and (ii) are invited by the Committee to develop an inter-agency agreement and specific agreements with the Executive Committee acting on behalf of the parties.[116]

The Executive Committee signed agreements with the UNEP (19 June 1991),[117] the UNDP (21 August 1991),[118] the UNIDO (22 October 1992)[119] and the World Bank (9 July 1991).[120] These agreements were adopted by the Forth Meeting of the Parties for use by the Multilateral Fund. These Implementing Agencies, which are not *ad hoc* treaty organisations but well established international

---

114   These tasks include, for example, the revision of current year's budget for the Secretariat and three-year plan and budget for the Fund. See further UNEP/OzL.Pro.ExCom/12Inf.6, p. 13; Multilateral Fund Secretariat, *Multilateral Fund for the Implementation of the Montreal Protocol: Policies, Procedures, Guidelines and Criteria* (As at November 2017), Chapter 3: Fund Secretariat, p. 3.

115   See Section IV(D.2) below.

116   See the Terms of Reference for the Fund Secretariat, in UNEP/OzL.Pro.4/15, Annex IX, para. 2, p. 51.

117   See UNEP/OzL.Pro/ExCom/5/Inf.4. See the Agreement between the Executive Committee of the Interim Multilateral Fund for the Implementation of the Montreal Protocol and the UNEP', in Multilateral Fund Secretariat, *Multilateral Fund for the Implementation of the Montreal Protocol: Policies, Procedures, Guidelines and Criteria (as at July 1999)*, Annex II.6.

118   See UNEP/OzL.Pro/ExCom/5/Inf.3. See the Agreement between the Executive Committee of the Interim Multilateral Fund for the Implementation of the Montreal Protocol and the UNDP', in Multilateral Fund Secretariat, ibid., Annex II.5.

119   See UNEP/OzL.Pro/ExCom/18/29, Annex IV. See the Agreement between the Executive Committee of the Interim Multilateral Fund for the Implementation of the Montreal Protocol and the UNIDO', in Multilateral Fund Secretariat, ibid., Annex II.7.

120   See UNEP/OzL.Pro/ExCom/5/Inf.2. See the Agreement between the Executive Committee of the Interim Multilateral Fund for the Implementation of the Montreal Protocol and the International Bank for Reconstruction and Development (World Bank)', in Multilateral Fund Secretariat, ibid., Annex II.8.

institutions, are to consult with the Executive Committee regarding the execution of their responsibilities for the MLF.[121]

It is stated that '[I]mplementing Agencies shall apply only those considerations relevant to effective and economically efficient programmes and projects which are consistent with any criteria adopted by the Parties'.[122] In identifying and selecting projects, the World Bank, the UNDP and the UNIDO have heavily relied on the frequent use of workshops and the contracts made by international experts.[123] In addition, it is pointed out that these Implementing Agencies are strongly influenced not only by firms in industrialising countries but also by the governments of Article 5 countries. As the Consulting Engineers and Planners (COWIconsult AS) of Denmark[124] observes, it is possible that this would come to contradict the root idea that Implementing Agencies are invited to participate in the Multilateral Fund by/on behalf of the Executive Committee as a higher decision-making institution.[125]

Finally, the Implementing agencies are entitled to receive support costs for their activities, having reached specific agreements with the Executive Committee.[126]

(a)   *The World Bank*[127]

The International Bank for Reconstruction and Development (IBRD) or the World Bank cooperates with and assist the Executive Committee in

---

121   See the Terms of Reference for the Fund Secretariat, in UNEP/OzL.Pro.4/15, Annex IX, para. 6, p. 51. Added to this, the heads of these agencies would meet at least once a year to report on their activities and consult on cooperative arrangements. See ibid.

122   See the Terms of Reference for the Fund Secretariat, in UNEP/OzL.Pro.4/15, Annex IX, para. 3, p. 51.

123   See Consulting Engineers and Planners AS, *Study on the Financial Mechanism of the Montreal Protocol* (UNEP, March 1995), para. 349.

124   In accordance with Decision IV/18(II.4) by the Forth Meeting of the Parties, the Team with support from Goss Gilroy Inc. of Canada was contracted by the UNEP to review and evaluate the effectiveness of the Financial Mechanism.

125   See Consulting Engineers and Planners AS, *Study on the Financial Mechanism of the Montreal Protocol* (UNEP, March 1995), paras. 307 et seq. As for the competition among the Implementing Agencies, see ibid., paras. 324–331.

126   See the Terms of Reference for the Fund Secretariat, in UNEP/OzL.Pro.4/15, Annex IX, para. 7, p. 51.

127   On the role of the World Bank in environmental protection, see Jacob Werksman, 'Greening Bretton Woods', in Philippe Sands (ed.), *Greening International Law* (Earthscan, 1993), pp. 65–84; Korinna Horta, 'The World Bank and the International Monetary Fund', in Jacob Werksman (ed.), *Greening International Institutions* (Earthscan, 1996), pp. 131–147; Kenneth Paddington, 'The Role of the World Bank', in Andrew Hurrell and

administering and managing the programme to finance the agreed incremental costs of Article 5 countries.[128] Regional development banks are also encouraged to participate in this process[129] and they are required to report as appropriate, based on the nature of their activities.[130] The World Bank (i) reports on activities relating to country programmes and on project proposals or groups of project proposals, including those which require the Executive Committee's approval and (ii) prepares a final report on operations financed by the Multilateral Fund.[131] The Bank administers and manages Montreal Protocol Operations through the Ozone Trust Fund (OTF),[132] and deals principally with Article 5 industrialising countries that are large consumers and producers of ODSs, such as India and China.[133]

It is interesting that each Implementing Agency, including the Bank, has taken a different approach to MLF project implementation.[134] In this respect, the World Bank has advanced a rather slow process that emphasises the importance of national execution through designated financial intermediaries and agents. The World Bank argues that 'there is no single more important aspect of project implementation than the establishment of local capacity to deal with the implementation of M.P. [Montreal Protocol] and ODS phaseout activities'.[135] Thus, under Bank projects, developing countries themselves are ultimately responsible for MLF project implementation. It had been suggested that a number of delays was caused by various disagreements between Article 5 countries and the World Bank regarding the flow of funds and taxation

---

Benedict Kingsbury (eds.), *International Politics of the Environment* (Clarendon Press, 1992), pp. 212–227; David Freestone. 'The World Bank and Sustainable Development', in Malgosia Fitzmaurice, David M. Ong and Panos Merkouris (eds.), *Research Handbook on International Environmental Law* (Edward Elgar, 2010), pp. 138–154.

128   See the Terms of Reference for the Fund Secretariat, in UNEP/OzL.Pro.4/15, Annex IX, paras. 4(c) and 16, pp. 51–52. The President of the World Bank is the Administer of this programme that operates under the authority of the Executive Committee. See ibid.

129   See the Terms of Reference for the Fund Secretariat, in UNEP/OzL.Pro.4/15, Annex IX, paras. 4(d) and 17, pp. 51–52.

130   See UNEP/OzL.Pro/ExCom/3/18/Rev.1, Annex III.

131   See UNEP/OzL.Pro/ExCom/3/18/Rev.1, Annex III. As for World Bank project preparation, see, for example, UNEP/OzL.Pro/ExCom/10/40, Annex I, paras. 72–81.

132   See *Executive Committee Primer – 2016 An introduction to the Executive Committee of the Multilateral Fund for the Implementation of the Montreal Protocol* (2016), Appendix 4, p. 16.

133   See Section V(C) below.

134   See *Executive Committee Primer – 2016 An introduction to the Executive Committee of the Multilateral Fund for the Implementation of the Montreal Protocol* (2016), Appendix 4, pp. 16–20.

135   See World Bank, 'Implementation Performance Review of Bank-Implemented Montreal Protocol Investment Operations' (December 1994), para. 8.

CAPACITY BUILDING IN THE OZONE RÉGIME

issues.[136] Nevertheless, it may be argued that the national execution of the MLF projects possesses the advantage of potentially promoting greater ownership of activities by the national government and of building national capacity for project development and implementation.[137]

Since 1991, the World Bank has supported the implementation of 700-plus investment and technical assistance phaseout activities in country recipients with more than $1 billion in grant approvals and it has contributed to a phaseout of more than 500,000 tons of ODS production and use.[138] At present, the Bank works with country partners in Argentina, China, Indonesia, Jordan, Vietnam and Thailand to implement $206 million in activities that deal with the first stage of HCFC consumption and production phaseout obligations.[139] Among them, since 1991, the partnership between the World Bank and China alone has phased out the consumption and production of more than 219,000 tons of ODSs from various sectors, such as refrigeration, air-conditioning, foam manufacturing, aerosol production and fire extinguishing.[140]

(b)   *The United Nations Development Programme (UNDP)*[141]

The UNDP cooperates with and assist the Executive Committee in feasibility and pre-investment studies and in other technical assistance measures.[142]

The UNDP is to:

(i)   Report on activities related to country programmes, including the activities of field offices;

(ii) Prepare periodic progress reports on projects;

(iii) Prepare an annual report on income and expenditures of previous years: and

(iv) Prepare a final report after completion and/or termination of each project.[143]

---

136   See Consulting Engineers and Planners AS, *Study on the Financial Mechanism of the Montreal Protocol* (UNEP, March 1995), para. 377.

137   See ibid., para. 488.

138   See World Bank, 'Brief: Montreal Protocol' (23 October 2013), at: <http://www.worldbank.org/en/topic/climatechange/brief/montreal-protocol> (last visited on 31 January 2018).

139   See ibid.

140   See ibid.

141   See, for example, Rosalyn Higgins, Philippa Webb, Dapo Akande, Sandesh Sivakumaran and James Sloan, *Oppenheim's International Law: United Nations* (Oxford University Press, 2017), pp. 661–662.

142   See the Terms of Reference for the Fund Secretariat, in UNEP/OzL.Pro.4/15, Annex IX, para. 4(b), p. 51.

143   See UNEP/OzL.Pro/ExCom/3/18/Rev.1, Annex III; Multilateral Fund Secretariat, *Multilateral Fund for the Implementation of the Montreal Protocol: Policies, Procedures, Guidelines and Criteria* (As at November 2017), Chapter 5: Implementing Agencies, p. 5. As for UNDP

The UNDP has established a Montreal Protocol Unit (MPU) that is located within its Sustainable Development Cluster, Bureau for Policy and Programme Support.[144] The MPU is responsible for programme development and technical project monitoring[145] and it also reports to the Executive Committee and the Multilateral Fund Secretariat.[146] Most of UNDP projects funded by MLF are implemented utilising the National Implementation Modality (NIM). It is said that the rationale for NIM comes from the fact that UNDP provides support through programmes and projects that are intended to strengthen national capacities and expand the options and opportunities available to partners and beneficiaries in programme countries.[147] Under UNDP projects, government organisations are responsible for the implementation of a development cooperation project in accordance with UNDP Regulations and Rules.[148]

According to the UNDP, although a significant part of its effort was dedicated to assisting private and public sector enterprises in their ODS elimination efforts during 1991–2000, since 2001, the UNDP has focused more on sector and national ODS phaseout programmes covering small and medium enterprises (SMEs).[149] Until September 2014, the UNDP had assisted partner countries access \$690.6 million in funding from the MLF and \$42.5 million from the GEF to eliminate ODSs. In addition, the UNDP has assisted 120 countries eliminate 67,870 tonnes of ODSs, which are amount to 5.08 billion tonnes reduction of CO_2-equivalent greenhouse gas emissions.[150]

---

     procedures for project development/implementation, see, for example, UNEP/OzL.Pro/ExCom/10/40, paras. 60–65 and its figure 2.

144   See Secretariat of the Multilateral Fund for the Implementation of the Montreal Protocol, *Executive Committee Primer – 2016 An introduction to the Executive Committee of the Multilateral Fund for the Implementation of the Montreal Protocol* (2016), Appendix 4, p. 1.

145   See UNEP/OzL.Pro/ExCom/10/40, para. 60.

146   See Secretariat of the Multilateral Fund for the Implementation of the Montreal Protocol, *Executive Committee Primer – 2016 An introduction to the Executive Committee of the Multilateral Fund for the Implementation of the Montreal Protocol* (2016), Appendix 4, p. 1.

147   See ibid.

148   See ibid. See also Ralph Luken and Tamas Grof, 'The Montreal Protocol's Multilateral Fund and Sustainable Development', in Donald Kaniaru (ed.), *The Montreal Protocol: Celebrating 20 Years of Environmental Progress – Ozone Layer and Climate Change* (Cameron May, 2007), pp. 71–73.

149   See *Protecting the Ozone Layer and Reducing Global Warming Results: Case Studies and Lessons Learned from UNDP's Montreal Protocol Programme* (November 2014), p. 5.

150   See ibid., p. 6.

(c)   *The United Nations Environment Programme (UNEP)*[151]

As previously noted, the UNEP (UN Environment) and its technical experts, the Nairobi-based Ozone Secretariat, have greatly contributed to the establishment and maintenance of the international legal ozone régime.[152]

The UNEP, as per its agreement between the Executive Committee of the interim MLF, has been set the following tasks:[153]

(i)   Political promotion of the objectives of the Montreal Protocol;

(ii)   Research and data-gathering, in accordance with the provisions of the Protocol: and

(iii) Clearing-house function, comprising the following activities.

   (a)   Assisting developing countries through country-specific studies and other technical cooperation to identify their needs for cooperation;

   (b)   Facilitating technical cooperation to meet these identified needs;

   (c)   Collecting and disseminating information and relevant materials, holding workshops and training sessions and other related activities for the benefit of developing country parties: and

   (d)   Facilitating and monitoring other multilateral regional and bilateral cooperation available to developing countries.

The UNEP, on the invitation of the Executive Committee, also acts as Treasure for the Fund.[154] The UNEP states that no additional charges are required for operating as Treasurer of the Fund and that all associated costs are covered by existing overheads assessed against the funds it receives in its role as one

---

151   See, for example, Rosalyn Higgins, Philippa Webb, Dapo Akande, Sandesh Sivakumaran and James Sloan, *Oppenheim's International Law: United Nations* (Oxford University Press, 2017), pp. 919–926.

152   See Chapters 2(II.B) and III(II) in this volume.

153   See the Terms of Reference for the Fund Secretariat, in UNEP/OzL.Pro.4/15, Annex IX, para. 4(a); UNEP/OzL.Pro/ExCom/10/40, Annex I, p. 23, para. 82; Multilateral Fund Secretariat, *Multilateral Fund for the Implementation of the Montreal Protocol: Policies, Procedures, Guidelines and Criteria* (As at November 2017), Chapter 5: Implementing Agencies, pp. 5–6. The Paris-based Industry and Environment Programme Activity Centre, in particular, takes on these clearinghouse and promotional activities. See also Rajendra M. Shende, 'Protecting the Ozone Layer: The Formulation of Country Programmes', *UNEP Industry and Environment* (October-December 1993), pp. 38–42.

154   See the Agreement between the UNEP as the Treasurer of the Interim Multilateral Fund for the Montreal Protocol and the Executive Committee of the Interim Multilateral Fund Established by the Parties to the Montreal Protocol', in Multilateral Fund Secretariat, 'Multilateral Fund for the Implementation of the Montreal Protocol: Policies, Procedures, Guidelines and Criteria' (as at July 1999), Annex II.4; Multilateral Fund Secretariat, *Multilateral Fund for the Implementation of the Montreal Protocol: Policies, Procedures, Guidelines and Criteria* (As at November 2017), Chapter 1: Financial Mechanism, p. 10; Gilbert M. Bankobeza, *Ozone Protection* (Eleven International, 2005), pp. 201–202.

of the implementing agencies.[155] As to implementation philosophy, the UNEP follows a bottom-up approach in identifying needs and in devising its programmes, and it utilises the TEAP and its TOCs (Technical Options Committees), as well as existing industry and government networks in both Article 5 and non-Article 5 countries.[156]

At its Thirty-Fifth Meeting in December 2001, the Executive Committee decided to approve the Compliance Assistance Programme (CAP) budget for the UNEP.[157] In order to identify countries that have difficulties in maintaining compliance or are at risk of being in non-compliance, with a focus on countries in post-conflict situations, the CAP activities are designed to cooperates with the Ozone Secretariat, the Multilateral Fund Secretariat and other Implementing Agency partners.[158] At present, the CAP provides country-specific compliance services and it operates 10 Regional Networks of Ozone Officers.[159] The CAP also provides a global information clearinghouse that serves national ozone units (NOUs) through information, communication, education, electronic knowledge management and capacity building activities.[160]

(d)   *The United Nations Industrial Development Organisation (UNIDO)*[161]
The Executive Committee invites the UNIDO to cooperate and assist in project development and implementation comprising pre-investment studies and other technical assistance matters.[162] The UNIDO, in its role as an Implementing Agency of the MLF, which deploys technology experts to provide concrete technology assistance to Article 5 developing States, believes that

---

155   See UNEP/OzL.Pro/ExCom/1/2, para. 13.
156   See Consulting Engineers and Planners AS, *Study on the Financial Mechanism of the Montreal Protocol* (UNEP, March 1995), paras. 322 and 374.
157   See Decision 35/36, in UNEP/OzL.Pro/ExCom/35/67, para. 69 and Annex VI; Multilateral Fund Secretariat, *Multilateral Fund for the Implementation of the Montreal Protocol: Policies, Procedures, Guidelines and Criteria* (As at November 2017), Chapter 5: Implementing Agencies, pp. 7–12.
158   See UN Environment/OzonAction, 'Projects and Services', at: <http://web.unep.org/ozonaction/news> (last visited on January 2018).
159   See Secretariat of the Multilateral Fund for the Implementation of the Montreal Protocol, *Executive Committee Primer – 2016 An introduction to the Executive Committee of the Multilateral Fund for the Implementation of the Montreal Protocol* (2016), Appendix 4, p. 6.
160   See UNEP/OzL.Pro.24/INF/4, Annex: Final Report – Evaluation of the Financial Mechanism of the Montreal Protocol (28 September 2012), pp. 23–25.
161   On the UNIDO, see generally Rosalyn Higgins, Philippa Webb, Dapo Akande, Sandesh Sivakumaran and James Sloan, *Oppenheim's International Law: United Nations* (Oxford University Press, 2017), pp. 664–665.
162   See UNEP/OzL.Pro/ExCom/8/29, Annex IV. On UNIDO's project cycle, see, for example, UNEP/OzL.Pro/ExCom/10/40, paras. 66–70 and its figure 3.

the institution is the best equipped to work on smaller projects.[163] The Environment Branch at the Programme Development and Technical Cooperation Division is responsible for MLF projects and, under the Branch, a Montreal Protocol Unit (MPU) and an Emerging Compliance Regimes (ECR) Unit work for implementing ODS phaseout programmes.[164]

UNIDO's MLF project cycle is, in general, as follows:[165]

(i)   Country's request through an official letter from the Government to the UNIDO for inclusion in the business plan.

(ii)   Submission and discussions concerning business plan. The Executive Committee notes the consolidated business plan for the Multilateral Fund.

(iii)   Draft business plan is presented to the UNIDO's Executive Board.

(iv)   Responsible staff is appointed by the Branch Director: request for funding for project preparation, discussion with the recipient country, discussion with the MLF Secretariat and the approval by the Executive Committee.

(v)   Submission of project proposals, discussion with the country, discussion with the MLF Secretariat and the approval by the Executive Committee.

(vi)   Project implementation takes place in cooperation with the national ozone units (NOU) and other national stakeholders.

(vii)   Projects are being implemented in accordance with the UNIDO's rules and regulations. Projects are requested to be registered in the UNIDO's Enterprise Resource Planning (ERP) system, including the portfolio and project management and the finance modules.

(viii) Most projects are implemented directly by the UNIDO without any financial intermediaries or executing agencies, including direct procurement of equipment and services.

(ix)   In some cases, implementation takes place with a more significant role of the Government through an agreement, which also respects the UNIDO's rules and regulations.

C   *The Global Environment Facility (GEF)*

The GEF, which is a World Bank's financial mechanism, was originally established in 1990 in order to help developing countries meet the 'agreed incremental costs' of activities related to the protection of the global environment in four major areas, namely, (i) global warming, (ii) pollution of

---

163   See UNEP/OzL.Pro/ExCom/10/40, Annex I, p. 40.

164   See Secretariat of the Multilateral Fund for the Implementation of the Montreal Protocol, *Executive Committee Primer – 2016 An introduction to the Executive Committee of the Multilateral Fund for the Implementation of the Montreal Protocol* (2016), Appendix 3, p. 12.

165   See ibid., p. 13.

international waters, (iii) destruction of biodiversity and (iv) the depletion of the stratospheric ozone layer.[166] In 1994, the GEF was restructured and replenished with over $ 2 billion (GEF II) and, as of at January 2018, 183 countries participate in the financial mechanism.[167] The GEF is jointly implemented by the UNDP, the UNEP and the World Bank, as Implementing Agencies under the GEF.[168] In addition, the functionally independent GEF Secretariat reports to and services the Council and Assembly of the GEF. Since its establishment, the GEF has received contributions from 39 donor countries and, at the last replenishment, 30 countries pledged a record $4.43 billion for the GEF-VI period (2014–2018).[169] As with the Multilateral Fund, participating developing countries are currently not required to contribute to the GEF funding.

The essential difference between the GEF and the Financial Mechanism of the Montreal Protocol is that the GEF utilises the Ozone Project Trust Fund (OTF) administered by the World Bank.[170] The relationship between the Multilateral Fund of the Ozone Protocol and the OTF consists of the following administrative procedure: once projects are approved by the Executive Committee, the UNEP then transfers funds from the Multilateral Fund to the

---

166 See texts in 30 *ILM* (1991), p. 1735 and 33 *ILM* (1994), p. 1273, in Patricia W. Birnie and Alan E. Boyle, *Basic Documents on International Law and the Environment* (Clarendon Press, 1995), p. 666. On the GEF, see, among others, Jacob Werksman, 'Consolidating Governance of the Global Commons: Insights from the Global Environmental Facility', 6 *YbkIEL* (1995), pp. 27–63; Helen Sjoberg, 'The Global Environmental Facility', in Jacob Werksman (ed.), *Greening International Institutions* (Earthscan, 1996), pp. 148–162; L. Boisson de Chazournes, 'Le Fonds por l'environnment mondial: recherche et conquéte de son identité', 13 *AFDI* (1995), pp. 612–632; Rosalyn Higgins, Philippa Webb, Dapo Akande, Sandesh Sivakumaran and James Sloan, *Oppenheim's International Law: United Nations* (Oxford University Press, 2017), pp. 917–918.

167 See Global Environment Facility, 'Countries (Participants)', at: <https://www.thegef.org/partners/countries-participants> (last visited on 31 January 2018).

168 See 'Principles of Cooperation among the Implementing Agencies', in Global Environment Facility, *Instrument for the Establishment of the Restructured Global Environment Facility* (March 2015), Annex D, p. 36.

169 See Global Environment Facility, 'Countries (Participants)', at: <https://www.thegef.org/partners/countries-participants> (last visited on 31 January 2018).

170 See World Bank, 'Establishment of the Global Environment Facility' (April 1991), Annex D and Supplement; International Bank for Reconstruction and Development Board of Governors, Resolution No. 487: Protection of the Global Environment', in Global Environment Facility, *Instrument for the Establishment of the Restructured Global Environment Facility* (March 2015), p. 59. The GEF bears several similarities with the Financial Mechanism of the Montreal Protocol. See Consulting Engineers and Planners AS, *Study on the Financial Mechanism of the Montreal Protocol* (UNEP, March 1995), Section 7.9.2.

OTF of the World Bank.[171] Furthermore, it is important to note that financial assistance under the GEF would be limited to those State Parties to the Montreal Protocol that had ratified the 1990 London Amendment.[172] Since the establishment of the Montreal Multilateral Fund, the subsidiary role of the GEF within the ozone treaty régime has been largely limited to middle-income countries and the CEITs, including the Russian Federation, which are ineligible for the Montreal Protocol Multilateral Fund.[173]

Since 1991, the GEF has assisted 18 countries in the CEITs to meet their ODS phaseout targets of the Protocol and it has supported 30 projects that have transferred new technologies, enhanced recycling operations, and provided training to reduce ODS use in these countries.[174] The GEF has invested $235 million in 29 projects that leveraged another $247 million from its partners.[175] To take a plain example, a GEF-funded project, which is the first GEF funding operation for ODSs phaseout in Russia, was structured as a framework project for a total of GEF grant amount of $60 million. It consisted of (i) an investment component to finance twenty-one sub-projects for ODSs phaseout in the aerosol and refrigeration sectors, (ii) a technical assistance component to strengthen project implementation and institutional capacity and (iii) a sub-grant processing component.[176] In addition, 'Initial Implementation of Accelerated hcfc Phaseout in the CEIT-Region – Uzbekistan' is one of the successful cases funded by the GEF and, at present, 99 per cent of ODSs have been eliminated in Uzbekistan.[177]

---

171 On the relationship between the GEF and the 1992 Climate Change Convention and the 1992 Biodiversity Convention, see, for example, L. Boisson de Chazournes, 'Le Fonds pour l'environnement mondial: recherche et conquéte de son identité', 13 *AFDI* (1995), pp. 15 et seq.

172 See UNEP/OzL.Pro.7/12, para. 51.

173 For a definition of the CEITs, see Chapter 5(VII.B) in this volume. For an analysis of ODS projects in the CEIT, see, for example, the World Bank's following reports, *Bulgaria: ODSs Phaseout Project* (October 1995); *Czech Republic: Technical Support and Investment Project for the Phaseout of ODSs* (August 1994); *Poland: ODSs Phaseout Project* (February 1997).

174 See Global Environment Facility, *Investing in the Phase-Out of Ozone-Depleting Substances: The GEF Experience* (November 2010), p. 9.

175 See Global Environment Facility, 'Ozone Layer Depletion', at: <https://www.thegef.org/partners/countries-participants> (last visited on 31 January 2018).

176 See further World Bank, *Russian Federation: Ozone Depleting Substance Consumption Phase-out Project* (May 1996); Global Environment Facility, *Investing in the Phase-Out of Ozone-Depleting Substances: The GEF Experience* (November 2010), p. 23.

177 See 'Uzbekistan: On the Road to adopt Ozone Friendly Technologies', *OzoNews*, Vol. XVI (15 November 2016), available at: <https://www.linkedin.com/pulse/ozonetwork-vol-xvi-vladan-galebović > (last visited on 31 January 2018).

In the middle of 1990s, the Study Team of the TEAP argued that the GEF had been more effective than the Montreal model of the Financial Mechanism in linking GEF resources not only to those of the regular programmes of the Implementing Agencies, but also to those of bilateral development agencies, NGOs, national governments and the private sector.[178]

D Strategies: Work Programmes, Country Programmes and Institutional Strengthening

For effective and efficient implementation of MLF projects for phasing out CFCs and other ODSs, régime members in the Montreal Protocol's Financial Mechanism – including Article 5 developing countries, developed State governments and four specialised international institutions – make use of the following three key concepts: (i) work programmes, (ii) country programmes, and (iii) institutional strengthening for project implementation.

(1) Work Programmes

The Executive Committee has invited the Implementing Agencies and other appropriate agencies, depending on their technical expertise, to develop work programmes in cooperation with potential recipient countries.[179]

It has been decided that the work programmes should specify, for example, types of activities and projects on which agreement has been reached between the Implementing Agency and the concerned party, and types of activities and projects which must be defined to allow the Executive Committee to review and monitor these Fund activities.[180] In developing these work programmes, there should be effective, result-oriented coordination among the operational units of all the Implementing Agencies.[181] Work programmes will be approved by the Executive Committee on an annual basis and will be reviewed bi-annually. Approval of work programmes should be based on project eligibility criteria.[182] Work programmes and amendments to them contain all the requests for activities other than investment projects submitted by each agency during the

---

178 See Consulting Engineers and Planners AS, *Study on the Financial Mechanism of the Montreal Protocol* (UNEP, March 1995), paras. 659–660.

179 See UNEP/OzL.Pro/ExCom/3/18/Rev.1, Annex III, Section II.2.1; Multilateral Fund Secretariat, *Multilateral Fund for the Implementation of the Montreal Protocol: Policies, Procedures, Guidelines and Criteria* (As at November 2017), Chapter 5: Implementing Agencies, pp. 23–24.

180 See further UNEP/OzL.Pro/ExCom/3/18/Rev.1, Annex III, Section II.2.2.

181 See UNEP/OzL.Pro/ExCom/3/18/Rev.1, para. 66.

182 See UNEP/OzL.Pro/ExCom/3/18/Rev.1, Annex III, Section II.2.3.

CAPACITY BUILDING IN THE OZONE RÉGIME

year. They include renewal of projects on institutional strengthening, project preparation, technical assistance, training and demonstration projects.[183]

Each Implementing Agency is responsible for the implementation and supervision of projects within its work programmes.[184] For instance, the UNEP's work programmes cover (i) information clearinghouse, (ii) training, and (iii) workshops, networking and country programmes for low-volume-ODSs consuming countries.[185] These activities are designed to contribute largely to capacity building in Article 5 industrialising countries.

(2)   Country Programmes

The Executive Committee has invited each Article 5 industrialising country that wish to receive support from the Multilateral Fund to develop a country programme and related projects, in accordance with paragraph 10(g) of the Terms of Reference of the Committee.[186]

Country programmes can be prepared by the countries themselves, or in cooperation with an Implementing Agency, or through bilateral cooperation.[187] In principle, the country programme is a prerequisite for investment support from the Multilateral Fund, though the Executive Committee often allows exceptions.[188] In addition, country programmes provide governments and Implementing Agencies with a strategic plan for phasing out ODSs, based on an assessment of the country's ODS consumption and production patterns, identification of priority investment projects and so forth.[189] The Study Team points out that the sense of government ownership of the country programme is an important contributing factor in the effectiveness of the country programme-related assistance.[190]

---

183   See Secretariat of the Multilateral Fund for the Implementation of the Montreal Protocol, *Executive Committee Primer – 2016 An introduction to the Executive Committee of the Multilateral Fund for the Implementation of the Montreal Protocol* (2016), p. 15.

184   See UNEP/OzL.Pro/ExCom/3/18/Rev.1, Annex III, Section II.2.5; Multilateral Fund Secretariat, *Multilateral Fund for the Implementation of the Montreal Protocol: Policies, Procedures, Guidelines and Criteria* (As at November 2017), Part VIII: Country Programme, p. 5.

185   See UNEP/OzL.Pro/ExCom/10/40, para. 83.

186   See UNEP/OzL.Pro/ExCom/3/18/Rev.1, Annex III, Section II.1.1; Multilateral Fund Secretariat, *Multilateral Fund for the Implementation of the Montreal Protocol: Policies, Procedures, Guidelines and Criteria* (As at November 2017), Chapter 5: Implementing Agencies, pp. 23–24.

187   See UNEP/OzL.Pro/ExCom/10/40, Annex I: Executive Summary, para. 12.

188   See Consulting Engineers and Planners AS, *Study on the Financial Mechanism of the Montreal Protocol* (UNEP, March 1995), para. 484.

189   See ibid. See also Richard Benedick, *Ozone Diplomacy* (Harvard University Press, 1998), p. 256.

190   See ibid., paras. 488–491 and 59 et seq.

The Executive Committee has decided that country programmes should be viewed as flexible instruments which set out the framework for that country's actions to meet the requirements of the Montreal Ozone Protocol.[191] The Executive Committee also requested governments to present to the Executive Committee information on progress being made in the implementation of country programmes on an annual basis, in accordance with the decision of the Executive Committee on the implementation of country programmes.[192]

(3)   Institutional Strengthening for Project Implementation

Support for institutional strengthening within a developing country, which formulates one of the basic components of capacity building,[193] is often an essential element in achieving the objectives of the Montreal Protocol and the MLF. This is particularly true at the stage when an Article 5 country has just become a party to the Protocol. In this initial phase, the stakeholders and the general public have to be aware of a number of fundamental ozone-related issues.[194] In this context, so-called 'national ozone units' – 'local counterparts' to the Protocol's institutions – have been established in more than seventy developing countries.[195] At present, many stakeholders regard activities regarding institutional strengthening as 'the most effective non-investment project types and a fundamental component contributing to the overall success of the Montreal Protocol model'.[196]

It might seem surprising, however, that the issue of institutional capacity building was not originally included in the Indicative List of Incremental Cost Categories.[197] It was at its 1992 Seventh Meeting that the Executive Committee decided to allocate limited funding for activities and assistance related to institutional strengthening on case-by-case basis.[198] It is pointed out that a number of non-Article 5 countries regard this kind of expenditure as an overhead

---

191   See UNEP/OzL.Pro/ExCom/5/16, para. 28a; Multilateral Fund Secretariat, *Multilateral Fund for the Implementation of the Montreal Protocol: Policies, Procedures, Guidelines and Criteria* (As at November 2017), Part VIII: Country Programme, p. 5.

192   See UNEP/OzL.Pro/ExCom/17/60, Decision 17/34, para. 57.

193   See Section I above.

194   See UNEP/OzL.Pro/ExCom/5/16, para. 28d; UNEP/OzL.Pro/ExCom/19/52, para. 36.

195   See Richard Benedick, *Ozone Diplomacy* (Harvard University Press, 1998), p. 255.

196   See UNEP/OzL.Pro.24/INF/4, Annex: Final Report – Evaluation of the Financial Mechanism of the Montreal Protocol (28 September 2012), p. 26.

197   See also Multilateral Fund Secretariat, *Multilateral Fund for the Implementation of the Montreal Protocol: Policies, Procedures, Guidelines and Criteria* (As at November 2017), Chapter 10: Institutional Strengthening, p. 5.

198   See Consulting Engineers and Planners AS, *Study on the Financial Mechanism of the Montreal Protocol* (UNEP, March 1995), para. 62.

CAPACITY BUILDING IN THE OZONE RÉGIME   321

element which will increase the administrative cost of the operation of the Fund.[199]

The main objective of institutional strengthening is to provide necessary resources to an eligible country to enable it to strengthen an institutional mechanism that facilitates the expeditious implementation of projects to phaseout of CFCs and ODSS, as well as to ensure effective liaison between the country, on the one hand, and the Committee, the Fund Secretariat and Implementing Agencies on the other.[200] The main elements of institutional strengthening include (i) office equipment, (ii) personnel cost and (iii) operational cost (for example, costs of post and telecommunication, stationery, maintenance of equipment and creation of awareness).[201] Provided that a recipient country for institutional strengthening projects assigns a full-time ozone officer to manage its ozone unit and that it institutes a national licensing system to control ODS imports, 'a threshold level of annual funding' will be allocated to the country.[202] Until December 1995 a total of only about $10 million had been approved for sixty-one countries for institutional capacity building, including country programmes and workshops to enhance data reporting capabilities of developing countries,[203] and, since its Seventh Meeting in 1992, the Executive Committee has approved $123,895,821, plus agency support costs of $7,210,170 for institutional strengthening projects, which represents less than 4 per cent of the total funds approved under the MLF.[204] In this respect, the UNEP's Study Team pointed out that shifting more emphasis on institutional strengthening not only lead to a faster project implementation but also to overall ODS phase-out.[205] Subsequently, in 2009, the Twenty-First Meeting of the Parties stated that 'the heavy workload and future challenges that Article 5 Parties still have to face looking towards the consolidation of CFC, halon and carbon

---

199   See Consulting Engineers and Planners AS, *Study on the Financial Mechanism of the Montreal Protocol* (UNEP, March 1995), para. 74.

200   See UNEP/OzL.Pro/ExCom/7/30, para. 74.2; Multilateral Fund Secretariat, *Multilateral Fund for the Implementation of the Montreal Protocol: Policies, Procedures, Guidelines and Criteria* (As at November 2017), Chapter 10: Institutional Strengthening, p. 5.

201   See UNEP/OzL.Pro/ExCom/19/52, para. 6.

202   See Secretariat of the Multilateral Fund for the Implementation of the Montreal Protocol, *Executive Committee Primer – 2016 An introduction to the Executive Committee of the Multilateral Fund for the Implementation of the Montreal Protocol* (2016), Appendix 2, pp. 8–9.

203   See UNEP/OzL.Pro/ExCom/19/52, para. 9. For details of activities of the Implementing Agencies in assisting data reporting, see, for example, UNEP/OzL.Pro/ImCom/8/3, Section III; UNEP/OzL.Pro/ImCom/14/4, Section V; Chapter 5(VII.A(1)) in this volume.

204   See UNEP/OzL.Pro/ExCom/78/7, para. 16.

205   See Consulting Engineers and Planners AS, *Study on the Financial Mechanism of the Montreal Protocol* (UNEP, March 1995), para. 58.

tetrachloride phase-out, the phase-out of methyl bromide and the accelerated HCFC phase-out' and it asked the Executive Committee to extend financial support for institutional strengthening funding for Article 5 Parties beyond 2010.[206] It is expected that additional funding for institutional strengthening will be required for the implementation of the Kigali Amendment.[207]

(4)   The Conditionality between MLF Funding and Compliance
        with the Protocol

It appears that the relationship between the MLF funding and compliance with the Protocol's requirements has been gradually strengthened. As with Article 4 trade restrictions considered in Chapter 4 in this volume, loss of the MLF funding can also be regarded as a certain 'stick' within the ozone régime. Yet, as far as is known, the Executive Committee has never formally raise non-compliance problems regarding Fund operations at the meetings of the Implementation Committee of the NCP. In addition, Fund-related decisions by the Executive Committee (and the Meeting of the Parties) have been monitored almost entirely by the Executive Committee and the Multilateral Fund Secretariat. As Victor noted, 'the link between the MLF and the Non-Compliance Procedure remains surprisingly weak'.[208]

As described in Chapter 5 in this volume, in the case of Mauritania, the Implementation Committee of the NCP decided to create conditionality between the MLF funding and the supply of baseline data.[209] The Meeting of the Parties adopted Decision VI/5, stating that an Article 5 developing country will lose its status 'if it does not report base-year data as required by the Protocol within one year of the approval of its country programme and its institutional strengthening by the Executive Committee'. In addition, the GEF has made funding of ozone-related projects in the CEITs conditional on compliance with the Montreal Protocol and its 1990 London Amendment. The World Bank requires recipient countries to be members of and in compliance with all relevant environmental agreements.[210]

---

206   See Decision XXI/29 (Institutional Strengthening).
207   See UNEP/OzL.Pro/ExCom/78/11, paras. 104 and 107; UNEP/OzL.Pro/ExCom/78/7, paras. 17–18.
208   See David C. Victor, *The Early Operation and Effectiveness of the Montreal Protocol's Non-Compliance Procedure* (International Institute for Applied Systems Analysis, 1996), pp. 17 and 24.
209   On the international base level, see Chapter 3(III.B(2)) in this volume.
210   See David C. Victor, *Early Operation of the Montreal Protocol's Non-Compliance Procedure* (International Institute for Applied Systems Analysis, 1996), p. 25.

As noted in Chapter 3 in this volume, by using the international financial aid, some Article 5 countries enjoying a grace period[211] had built industrial plants capable of producing or using CFCs or other destructive chemicals (for example, India). Indian firms were selling CFCs to the Middle East.[212] In this context, the Executive Committee decided in 1995 that it would prohibit any grants for India's conversion of factories that had installed ODS capacity after July 1995.[213] In addition, it is also important that the Implementation Committee has persistently stated that parties in non-compliance with control measures under Article 2 and/or 4 of the Montreal Protocol had already been given a certain amount of financial assistance from the MLF (or the GEF) for their domestic implementation of the environmental treaty.[214] This may be seen as a kind of political pressure for those non-complying countries.

IV   Special Considerations for the International Transfer of Ozone-Friendly Technology

A   *International Technology Transfer*

To begin with, the term technology transfer[215] is defined in UNCTAD's Draft International Code of Conduct on the Transfer of Technology as the transfer of systematic knowledge for 'the manufacture of a product, for the application of a process or for the rendering of a service and does not extend to the transactions involving merely the sale or mere lease of goods'.[216] Although technology

---

211   See Chapter 3(III.E) in this volume.

212   See 'Holed Up: Chemicals Production/Controlling CFCs', 337 *The Economist* (9 December 1995), p. 690.

213   See Franck Biermann, *Financing Environmental Policies* (1997), pp. 44–45, cited in Richard Benedick, *Ozone Diplomacy* (Harvard University Press, 1998), p. 258. On MLF projects in India, see World Bank, *Ozone Projects Trust Fund Grant: Technical Support and Investment Project* (*ODS Phaseout 1*) (July 1994) and *Ozone Projects Trust Grant: Phaseout of Ozone Depleting Substances* (*ODS Phaseout II*) (February 1995).

214   See, for example, Decision XIII/21 (Argentina), Decisions XIV/23 and XVI/27 (Nepal), Decisions XVI/29 and XVIII/31 (Pakistan), Decision XV/40 (Papua New Guinea), Decisions XVIII/32 and XIX/22 (Paraguay), Decision XIII/25 (Peru), Decision XV/41 (Qatar), Decisions XIV/24 and XVI/30 (Saint Vincent and the Grenadines), Decisions XXI/21 and XXII/15 (Saudi Arabia), Decision XVII/38 (Sierra Leone), Decision XX/18 (Solomon Islands), Decision XXI/25 (Turkmenistan), Decision XV/43 (Uganda), Decisions XV/44 and XVII/39 (Uruguay), Decisions XXI/26 and XXII/18 (Vanuatu) and Decision XV/45 (Viet Nam).

215   On technology transfer in international environmental law, see also Section I(B) above.

216   See TD/CODE TOT/47. However, this code was not universally accepted. See Michael Waibel and William Alford, 'Technology Transfer', in Rüdiger Wolfrum (ed.), *Max Planck*

covered by patent has territorial protection, it is possible that environmentally-friendly technology can be transferred to third parties – or developing countries in the present case – through the transfer of the property rights on the technology, or by the granting of a user's licence.

More recently, according to Chapter 34 of Agenda 21, environmentally sound technology is defined as being 'less polluting, using all resources in a more sustainable manner, recycling more of their wastes and products, and handling residual wastes in a more acceptable manner than the technologies for which they were substitutes'.[217] In regard to this point, it is also important that Agenda 21 emphasises that environmentally sound technologies are 'total systems which include know-how, procedures, goods and services, and equipment as well as organisational and managerial procedures'.[218] Furthermore, Principle 9 of the Rio Declaration states that:

> States should cooperate to strengthen endogenous capacity-building for sustainable development by improving scientific understanding through exchanges of scientific and technological knowledge, and by enhancing the development, adaptation, diffusion and transfer of technologies, including new and innovative technologies.[219]

B *International Technology Transfer of ODS Reduction*

It may be said that the cost of ozone-friendly technology is particularly costly as it requires new, or additional, foreign investment, additional supervision, re-training of personnel and so forth.[220] Article 5 industrialising countries that need technology transfer for ODS reduction can be generally divided into three categories, that is, (i) importers of ODSs-related products and components (most of newly industrialising States belong to this category), (ii) users of ODSS in the manufacturing process (for example, Egypt, Tunisia, Turkey and Taiwan) and (iii) 'self-sufficient' producers/users of ODSS (for example,

---

Encyclopedia of Public International Law, Vol. IX (Oxford University Press, 2012), pp. 808–809. In addition, The United Nations General Assembly Resolution 36/192 adopted in 1981 states that: 'The General Assembly [recognises] that environmental deficiencies generated by the conditions of under-development pose grave problems and can best be remedied by accelerated development through the transfer of substantial quantities of financial and technical assistance'.

217 See paras. 34.1 and 34.2. See also Felix Bloch, *Technologietransfer zum internationalen Umweltschutz: Eine völkerrechtliche Untersuchung unter besonderer Berücksichtigung des Schutzes der Ozonschicht und des Weltklimas* (Peter Lang, 2007), pp. 92 et seq.

218 See para. 34.3.

219 See also Chapter 34 of Agenda 21, para. 34.18.

220 See, for example, UNEP/WG.78/6.

Argentina, Brazil, China, India, Indonesia, Korea, Mexico and Venezuela).[221] It is clear that the last category of developing countries is not necessarily affected by Article 4 trade restrictions under the Protocol, and therefore, they persistently demanded the establishment of new financial mechanisms and funding additional to existing bilateral or multilateral aid programmes.[222]

The international transfer of technology, which is necessary to enable developing countries in their compliance with the Montreal Protocol, involves, *inter alia*: (i) identification of needs, (ii) acquisition of patents, (iii) acquisition of designs, (iii) adaptation of technology for local assimilation, (iv) identification and procurement of appropriate equipment and materials, (v) training of personnel and (vi) technical assistance.[223] In light of these lists, it must be emphasised that, as Chapter 34 of Agenda 21 states, 'Environmentally sound technologies are not just individual technologies, but total systems which include know-how, procedures, goods and services, and equipments as well as organisational and material procedures'.

New Article 10A of the Montreal Protocol as amended in 1990 requires State Parties to take every practicable step, consistent with the programmes supported by the financial mechanism to ensure the transfer of the best available, environmentally safe substitutes and related technologies under fair and most favourable conditions. Not only developed country parties but also the CEITS currently assume the obligation of providing technology transfer to Article 5 developing countries. Yet, it is obvious that, in the light of the Protocol text itself and its *travaux préparatoires*, parties to the Protocol are not required to compel their industries to transfer relevant technology under any circumstances. For instance, industrialised State Parties are not obliged to export environmentally sound technology of ODSS to developing countries that do not provide adequate intellectual property protection.[224] This is in line with the TRIPs Agreement that requires Member States to respect the principles of the MFN and national treatment, and to provide other intellectual-property-related protections. However, it is still true that some other information may be obtained from academic and government exchanges, scientific publications and international institutions, including various technical organisations.[225]

---

221 See Kempe Ronald Hope, 'International Trade and International Technology to Eliminate ODSS', 8 *International Environmental Affairs* (1996), p. 36.

222 See Section II(B) above.

223 See UNEP/OzL.Pro/ExCom/18/63, para. 9.

224 See Robert Housman et al. (eds.), *The Use of Trade Measures in Select Multilateral Environmental Agreements* (UNEP, 1995), p. 86.

225 See, for example, E/CN.17/1993/10, Section II; Section IV(2) below.

V The Operation of the Financial Mechanism of the Montreal Protocol

A The Effectiveness of the Montreal Multilateral Fund

Since 1991, as at November 2017, the Executive Committee has held eighty meetings and it approved the expenditure of approximately $3.6 billion for the implementation of projects, including industrial conversion, technical assistance, training and capacity building.[226] In total, the Committee has approved 144 country programmes, 144 HCFC phaseout management plans and has also funded for the establishment and the operating costs of ozone offices in 145 Article 5 country parties.[227] In addition, the Executive Committee has so far approved a total of $12.5 million for projects for the implementation of the HFC phase-down.[228]

A quick but objective judgement of the effectiveness of the Financial Mechanism of the Montreal Protocol and its Multilateral Fund will depend on the global phaseout of ODSs, that is, the amounts of controlled ODSs phased out and the international transfer of environmentally sound technologies of ODS emission reductions. However, it should not be forgotten that the MFL is only one of the important factors that will affect ODS phaseout processes in Article 5 developing countries. Among others are, for example, existing international market forces,[229] issues of illegal foreign trade in ODSs,[230] the grace period given to Article 5 developing countries in the Third World,[231] the effectiveness of the Montreal NCP, political, economic and social factors at national level[232] and so forth.

---

226 See UNEP/OzL.Pro/ExCom/79/51, Annex I (Trust Fund for the Multilateral Fund For The Implementation of the Montreal Protocol, as at 30 June 2017, Figure 1: Status of the Fund from 1991–2017; information provided by the Secretariat of the Multilateral Fund for the Implementation of the Montreal Protocol, at: http://www.multilateralfund.org/default .aspx> (last visited on 31 January 2018).

227 See ibid.

228 See ibid.

229 See Richard Benedick, *Ozone Diplomacy* (Harvard University Press, 1998), pp. 266–267, noting that some members of industries in developing countries consider that the MLF as a new bureaucratic mechanism may be of doubtful utility.

230 See Chapter 3(IV.F) and Chapter 5(VII.A) in this volume.

231 See Chapter 3(III.E) in this volume. For example, ten Article 5 countries, namely, China, India, Mexico, Thailand, Yugoslavia, Brazil, Indonesia, Saudi Arabia, Malaysia and Argentina, accounted for an unconstrained consumption of approximately 150,000 ODP tonnes, which was over seventy per cent of total estimated ODS consumption in Article 5 countries. See Consulting Engineers and Planners AS, *Study on the Financial Mechanism of the Montreal Protocol* (UNEP, March 1995), para. 796.

232 Obviously, India lacked the will to realise the Montreal Protocol's stated purposes. See Richard Benedick, *Ozone Diplomacy* (Harvard University Press, 1998), pp. 248–251.

(1)   The Phaseout of Controlled ODSS

In accordance with Decision XXII/2, the Twenty-Second Meeting of the Parties to the Protocol approved in 2010 the terms of reference[233] and funding for an evaluation and recommendations of the Financial Mechanism of the Montreal Protocol.[234] This evaluation was done by an independent evaluator, ICF International in Washington, DC,[235] and supervised by a steering panel, which was selected from eight members, that is, Austria, Canada, Colombia, India, Japan, Nigeria, the former Yugoslav Republic of Macedonia and the United States.[236] According to the evaluation report, during 1993 to 2011, MLF projects have contributed to the phaseout of 256,153 ODP tonnes of consumption and 192,628 ODP tonnes of production in Article 5 country parties.[237] Over 180,000 ODP tonnes of CFC consumption and 85,000 ODP tonnes of CFC production were phased out by MLF-funded activities.[238] Furthermore, MLF projects have led to the phaseout of 80,000 ODP tonnes of consumption and over 100,000 ODP tonnes of production of Carbontetrachloride, Halons, Methylbromide and 1,1,1-trichloroethane, equivalent to 72,000 MT consumption and 73,000 MT of production.[239] In total, about 90 per cent of phaseout of ODS consumption and production in Article 5 countries is attributed to MLF-funded projects (see Figure 3).

Furthermore, it is pointed out that, during the period 1993 to 2011, the total reduction in consumption and production of ODSS having global warming potentials is estimated at 1,387 million metric tonnes of carbon dioxide equivalent ($MMTCO_2eq$) and 943 $MMTCO_2eq$, respectively, and the MLF has also contributed to the prevention of global warming.[240]

(2)   The Transfer of Technology of ODSS

In the middle of 1990s, the UNEP's Study Team reported that it had found no evidence of serious flaws in international technology transfer supported by the Fund, or of systematic bias and inappropriate advice on technology choice, though some enterprises in Article 5 countries suggested that licence fees for

---

233   Annex to Decision XXII/2.

234   See UNEP/OzL.Pro.22/9, pp. 26–29.

235   See UNEP/OzL.Pro.24/INF/4, Annex: Final Report – Evaluation of the Financial Mechanism of the Montreal Protocol (28 September 2012), p. 1.

236   See Decision XXII/2, para. 3, UNEP/OzL.Pro.22/9, p. 26.

237   See UNEP/OzL.Pro.24/INF/4, Annex: Final Report – Evaluation of the Financial Mechanism of the Montreal Protocol (28 September 2012), p. 14.

238   See ibid.

239   See ibid., pp. 14–15.

240   See UNEP/OzL.Pro.24/INF/4, Annex: Final Report – Evaluation of the Financial Mechanism of the Montreal Protocol (28 September 2012), pp. 16–19.

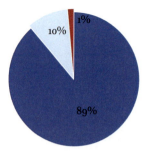
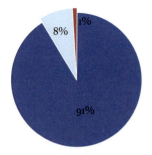

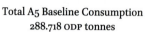

FIGURE 3   ODS phase-out attributed to MLF projects (1993–2010) UNEP/OzL.Pro.24/INF/4, Annex: *Final Report – Evaluation of the Financial Mechanism of the Montreal Protocol* (28 September 2012), p. 11

technology transfer were high and that production licences for alternative substances are in reality difficult to obtain.[241] The Study Team stated that the major current barrier to the international technology transfer was the slow pace of MLF project implementation.[242] It is interesting to note here that, at the Meeting of the WTO Trade and Environment Committee,[243] India argued that although developing countries adhered to the international consensus to phase out certain environmentally injurious substances under MEAs, 'substitute technologies were not transferred by multilateral enterprises on "fair and most favourable terms", as required in Article 16 of the Biodiversity Convention and Article 10A of the Montreal Protocol'.[244] India further suggested that certain projects were not being cleared under the Financial Mechanism of the

---

241   See Consulting Engineers and Planners AS, *Study on the Financial Mechanism of the Montreal Protocol* (UNEP, March 1995), paras. 54, 106 and 551. See also UNEP/OzL.Pro/ExCom/18/63, para. 13. But see, for example, UNEP/OzL.Pro.7/12, para. 79.
242   See Consulting Engineers and Planners AS, *Study on the Financial Mechanism of the Montreal Protocol* (UNEP, March 1995), para. 107; Stephen O. Andersen, K. Madhava Sarma and Kristen N. Taddonio, *Technology Transfer for the Ozone Layer* (Earthscan, 2007), p. 249.
243   On the WTO's CTE, see Chapter 4(I.B) in this volume.
244   See PRESS/TE009 (1 May 1996). See also Stephen O. Andersen, K. Madhava Sarma and Kristen N. Taddonio, *Technology Transfer for the Ozone Layer* (Earthscan, 2007), pp. 162–163.

Montreal Protocol due to their very high costs.[245] The Meeting of the Parties often requests the Executive Committee to 'expeditiously' identify steps that can practically be taken to eliminate impediments to the transfer of ozone-friendly technologies to Article 5 countries[246] and the Beijing Declaration (1999) and the Ouagadougou Declaration (2000) also refers to the importance of technology transfer under the ozone régime.[247]

With regard to the effectiveness of technology transfer under the MLF, the above-mentioned evaluation report by ICF International suggests that, at present, technology selection is not systematically referred to in projects documentation, nor recorded in any data management system of the MLF.[248] Thus, the report recommends that the Executive Committee should consider instituting a mechanism to systematically record technology selection under the MLF.

VI   Conclusions

It may concluded from the above that the establishment of the Montreal Protocol's Multilateral Fund, as an expression of international solidarity concerning the ozone régime, was indispensable (i) for universal and effective participation of hesitant sovereign States – particularly developing countries in the Third World – and (ii) for future build-up of Article 5 industrialising States' capability to fully comply with the stringent environmental treaty obligations and rules, including control measures of CFCs/ODSs and reporting requirements under Article 7 of the Montreal Protocol. It may be easily assumed that, without the Multilateral Fund, the precautionary environmental 'principle' or approach for the protection of the ozone would never be universally observed in the international community. Due to the participation by a number of Third World countries, including India and China, the Vienna Ozone Convention and the dynamic Protocol were transformed from a mere 'North-oriented régime' into an international legal régime in the field of global environmental protection.

With regard to the two points just mentioned above, it is especially important that the MLF has been managed not only by an existing international financial

---

245   See ibid. But see Richard Benedick, *Ozone Diplomacy* (Harvard University Press, 1998), pp. 247–248, noting that such a view is 'more negotiating rhetoric than reality'.

246   See, for example, Decision IX/14.

247   See also Gilbert M. Bankobeza, *Ozone Protection* (Eleven International, 2005), pp. 206–207.

248   See UNEP/OzL.Pro.24/INF/4, Annex: Final Report – Evaluation of the Financial Mechanism of the Montreal Protocol (28 September 2012), pp. 40–41 and 50.

organisation, the World Bank – which is often dominated by developed OECD countries – and three United Nations agencies (UNDP, UNIDO, UNEP), but also by new internal treaty organs within the ozone régime, namely, the Executive Committee, equally representing both developed and developing State Parties, and the independent Multilateral Fund Secretariat, which is carefully selected on the basis of the principle of equitable geographic distribution. In addition, it must not be forgotten that the 'democratic' supreme body of the environmental régime, the Meeting of the Parties regularly exercises 'parental' control over the operation of the Financial Mechanism of the Montreal Protocol, although the Meeting, unlike the Executive Committee, does not necessarily formulate specific MLF policies. This structure encourages the legitimate expectation that the Northern régime members will not necessarily dominate the South.

Furthermore, it is also important to note that there exists a linkage between the 'effective implementation of the financial co-operation and transfer of technology' and gradual development of capacity building in Third World countries.[249] As described, not only major IGOs but also various NGOs that are interested in ozone-related activities directly participate in the process of capacity building for Article 5 developing countries.

In spite of delays in implementation of MLF projects, the Fund has contributed, to an appreciable extent, to the phaseout of controlled ODSs and the international transfer of ozone-friendly technology. In addition, the institutional régime actors of the Mechanism – the Executive Committee, the Implementing Agencies and the Multilateral Fund Secretariat – continue their organised steady efforts towards improving the operations and effectiveness of the Financial Mechanism of the Montreal Protocol.

Finally, there are just two particularly recommendations. In the first place, the Executive Committee should put more emphasis on an institutional strengthening aspect of capacity building for Article 5 developing countries. It is certain that this will help resolve the thorny issues of treaty non-compliance with Article 7 data reporting requirements, which is frequently observed in a number of developing State Parties to the Protocol. In the second place, since fragmentary official reports on projects alone do not necessarily

---

249   See Article 5(4) as amended in 1990. In this respect, Article 4(7) of the 1992 Climate Change Convention similarly states that 'The extent to which developing country Parties will effectively implement their commitments under the Convention will depend on the effective implementation by developed country Parties of their commitments under the Convention related to financial resources and transfer of technology ...'.

constitute effective and efficient international supervision of MLF-supported projects, the Executive Committee should therefore continue to develop not only a systematic approach to policy development, but also a monitoring and evaluation system for the Multilateral Fund for achieving the Montreal Protocol's objectives.

PART 5

Conclusions

CHAPTER 7

The International Legal Régime for the Protection of the Ozone Layer

Part I of this volume (Chapter 1) analysed international legal régimes for the environment, focusing on law-making, international environmental cooperation, soft enforcement of treaties by international bodies and non-governmental organisations. The international regulatory régime for ozone was conceptually characterised as a self-contained environmental regime for obligations *erga omnes* in the sphere of general international law.

Part II (Chapters 2 and 3) was devoted to a detailed analysis of the international treaties for the protection of the ozone layer. Chapter 3 examined the Vienna Ozone Convention in the context of modern international law of environmental protection. Chapter 3 dealt with the gradual internationalisation of ODS regulatory measures under the Montreal Protocol as amended and adjusted, as well as national implementation and enforcement of the ozone treaties.

Part III (Chapter 4) discussed extensively the relationship between Article 4 TREMS of the Montreal Protocol and the WTO/GATT law régime. It was established that, when viewed in its entirety, Article 4 trade restrictions appear to be compatible with the stringent trade rules of the WTO/GATT law.

Part IV (Chapters 5 and 6) examined the compliance system of the ozone régime. In Chapter 5, the dispute avoidance and settlement system of the Montreal Protocol, that is, the Non-Compliance Procedure (NCP), and the functions of the internal treaty organs were closely examined. Chapter 6 then investigated the Financial Mechanism of the Montreal Protocol, including the Multilateral Fund.

It is not my intention to provide a detailed summary of the arguments contained in this study in Part V (Chapter 7). Instead, this Chapter is primarily intended as a provisional evaluation of a dynamic international régime for the protection of the ozone layer in the field of public international law.

The basic role of international legal régimes has been to organise 'partly unorganised society'[1] that still lacks a centralised supreme authority. Another, directly corresponding role of international legal régimes is to regulate previously unregulated areas of international relations. International legal régimes

---

1   On this concept, see Georg Schwarzenberger, *A Manual of International Law* (5th ed. Stevens & Sons Limited/Frederick A. Praeger, 1967), pp. 8–15.

© KONINKLIJKE BRILL NV, LEIDEN, 2019 | DOI:10.1163/9789004290877_009

are not strictly meant to be supranational law-making institutions or supranational enforcement mechanisms, although they may contribute to the establishment of such organisations in the future.[2]

Until the early 1980s, global protection of upper atmospheric ozone in the stratosphere had been an unregulated area of international environmental relations. Nation States were quite free to deplete the ozone shield that preserve the environment. Apart from the customary principles and rules of international environment protection law considered in Chapter 2 above (for example, Stockholm Principle 21 and Rio Principle 2), States were under no particular obligations under international law to protect the ozone layer.

However, the creation of the international ozone régime (that is, the 1985 Vienna Ozone Convention and the 1987 Montreal Protocol) dramatically changed this situation.

Faced with conflicting scientific evidence, ozone negotiators finally decided to take the framework convention-implementing protocol approach: the Convention laid down the legal basis for future international environmental cooperation, particularly in scientific research and information exchange; the subsequent implementing Protocol then introduced detailed ODS regulations and standards within its international instruments, which has been adjusted by the Meeting of the Parties. At present the stratospheric ozone layer enjoys the international legal status of the common concern of mankind, having *erga omnes* character. The rapid entry into force of the ozone treaties indicated that multilateral treaty régimes could provide an efficient legal means of global law-making.[3] The ozone régime has been widely regarded as a global precautionary régime for the protection of the environment.

What future benefits will the ozone régime produce? According to a report by Applied Research Consultants for Environment Canada,[4] the global benefits of the ODS phaseout over the years from 1987 to 2060 include the avoidance of (i) 19.1 million cases of non-melanoma skin cancer, (ii) 1.5 million cases of melanoma skin cancer (about sixty per cent would have been in women), (iii) 333,500 death as a result of skin cancer, (iv) 129 million cases of cataracts,

---

2 See Hans J. Morgenthau, *Politics among Nations: The Struggle for Power and Peace* (4th ed. Knopf, 1962), Chapters 29-30, arguing that United Nations organs, such as the UNESCO, would not help establish the world government and that 'a world community must antedate a world state'.

3 See Patricia Birnie, Alan Boyle and Catherine Redgwell, *International Law and the Environment* (3rd ed. Oxford University Press, 2009), p. 16.

4 See 'Costs and Benefits of the Montreal Protocol', 25 *OzonAction Newsletter* (January 1998), p. 6. See, in detail, ARC Research Consultants, *Global Benefits and Costs of the Montreal Protocol on Substances That Deplete the Ozone Layer* (Environment Canada, 1997).

(v) U.S. $238,000 million worth of damage to the world sheries avoided, (v) $191,000 million worth of damage to agricultural production and (vi) 30,000 million worth of damage to PVC plastic products in the building industry.

The Montreal Protocol's concept of international environmental cooperation has been well translated into partnership at the national level: parties – both Non-Article 5 and Article 5 countries – have made considerable efforts to meet the legal requirements of the Montreal Protocol. Many are ahead of the Protocol's reduction schedules, and only a small number of Article 5 countries are not fully complying with Article 2 control provisions of the Protocol. The problem of illegal trade in ODSs, for which Russia and two Article 5 countries, China and India, had been the main supply sources, has been tackled in earnest by the parties. Rising CFC prices – which rocketed in the summer of 1996 as a result of high demand and low availability – suggested that black market trade has gradually declined.[5] In order to counter the illegal trade in CFCs or ODSs, the Meeting of the Parties has taken additional measures to further strengthen the existing Montreal NCP régime and to institute an import and export licensing system for trade in ODSs.

The strict trade restrictions on ODSs provided for in Article 4 of the Protocol will continue to be valuable for the maintenance of the ozone régime. During the negotiations leading to the 1987 Montreal Protocol, the United States strongly argued that 'without restrictions on imports of ozone-depleting chemicals from non-parties, there would be a strong incentive for the development of "pollution havens"'.[6] This concern, voiced by the United States' government was, well founded: when trade controls for non-parties fully entered into force (that is, during the period from 1990 to 1993), the number of Article 5 developing countries roughly doubled.[7] The Montreal Protocol's TREMs therefore allowed universal participation by all State Parties, including LVCs, thus avoiding a situation in which potential CFC-producing countries remained outside the ozone régime to pick up the abandoned market shares of other countries.

The question to what extent WTO dispute settlement bodies take into account multilateral environmental agreements and general international environmental law in the interpretation of WTO/GATT rules on trade-related environmental measures is a very interesting one.[8] The trade controls of Article 4

---

5 See Richard Benedick, *Ozone Diplomacy* (Harvard University Press, 1998), p. 276.
6 See discussion paper submitted by the United States, 'GATT Considerations and the Ozone Protocol' (4 September 1987), p. 1.
7 See Richard Benedick, *Ozone Diplomacy* (Harvard University Press, 1998), p. 243.
8 See Ernst-Ulrich Petersmann, *The GATT/WTO Dispute Settlement System* (Kluwer Law International, 1997), p. 120. As Professor Petersmann indicated in his articles, this will include, for example, Stockholm Principle 21 and Rio Principle 2.

of the Montreal Protocol are an integral part of the international ozone régime that is based on general international law of the environment. In this respect, the customary principles and rules of interpretation of international law, as codified in the Vienna Convention on the Law of Treaties, are to be welcomed.

The Montreal Protocol's compliance system should be also highly acclaimed. The Montreal NCP – as an internally instituted dispute settlement system consistent with the consensus building of communication within an international régime[9] – can be regarded as an unprecedented procedural régime that is designed to operate obligations *erga omnes,* that is, towards the global protection of the ozone layer.[10] The Montreal NCP is therefore meant to overcome the recognised deficiencies of general international law regarding global environmental protection. The standing Implementation Committee within the NCP, which is not an *ad hoc* organ, (i) has taken up many non-compliance issues concerning the ODS control measures, reporting requirements and trade restrictions in good time and effectively controlled and/ or resolved them, (ii) tactfully classified Non-Article 5 and Article 5 countries based on the available ODS data and (iii) created a tentative conditionality between treaty compliance by developing countries and MLF funding.

The Implementation Committee of the NCP, the Meeting of the Parties to the Protocol and the Implementing Agency of the World Bank, which deals with the GEF funding, are making collaborative and organised efforts at solving various non-compliance cases. Yet, the Montreal NCP is not meant to supplant traditional settlement procedures. Professor Handl points out that 'where basic constituent principles and "hard" legal parameters are concerned, disputes should be amended both technically and politically to formal third-party decision making "in accordance with international law" narrowly defined'.[11] For instance, it is possible that breaches of treaty obligations under Article 4 of the Montreal Protocol may be dealt with by appropriate traditional dispute settlement procedures.

---

9 See Thomas Gehring, 'International Environmental Regimes', 1 *YbkIEL* (1990), p. 37; Chapter v in this volume.

10 See also Tomohito Usuki, 'Chikyu Kankyō Hogo Jōyaku ni okeru Funsō Kaiketsu Tetsuduki no Hatten [Development of Dispute Settlement Procedures in Global Environmental Conventions], in Takane Sugihara (ed.), *Funsō Kaiketsu no Kokusaihō* [International Law for Dispute Settlement: Essays in Celebration of Judge Shigeru Oda's Seventieth Birthday] (Sanseido, 1997), pp. 182-183 (in Japanese). Of course, as Ragazzi says, an risk of proliferation of candidates of obligations *erga omnes* should be avoided carefully, since the use and abuse of this concept is essentially a question of political nature. See Maurizio Ragazzi, *The Concept of International Obligations Erga Omnes* (Clarendon Press, 1997), p. 217.

11 Günther Handl, 'Controlling Implementation of and Compliance with International Environmental Commitments: The Rocky Road from Rio', 5 *Colorado JEP* (1994), p. 330.

Although often criticised as a slow implementation mechanism, the Financial Mechanism of the Montreal Protocol – the Multilateral Fund and MLF projects in particular – has contributed to the strengthening of Article 5 developing countries' capacity to comply with the ozone treaties. As Ambassador Benedick suggested, it is important to note that the Multilateral Fund is designed to fill a gap.[12] The MLF funding is indispensable not only for key Article 5 countries, such as China and India, but also for the remaining many LVC parties and their industries, whose access to initial investment capital and ozone-friendly technologies would be severely restricted. The international transfer of technologies cannot be fully acieved in the absence of an equitable global financial agency, such as the Montreal Protocol's MLF.

As with the Implementation Committee of the NCP, the Executive Committee of the MLF signals the potential conditionality between the implementation of the ozone treaties and MLF funding. For instance, the Executive Committee decided in 1995 that it would prohibit any grants for India's conversion of factories that had installed ODS capacity after July 1995.[13]

The Montreal Protocol's decision-making procedures may deserve special attention of international lawyers and international relations scholars. Under Article 2(9), adjustments of ODS control measures are binding on all the parties. Although this two-thirds majority voting procedure – 'a great novelty in international environmental law'[14] – has never been used so far, its political impact on 'the parameters of the expectations'[15] shared by ozone régime members cannot be ignored. It is uncertain, however, whether other environmental régimes should follow the precedent that was adopted in circumstances in which the total elimination of CFCs was widely anticipated among all prospective parties to the Protocol.[16] Perhaps such a revolutionary approach would be unacceptable in the majority of MEAs. However, it is important to note at the same time that this new voting system is designed to reflect the opinions of developing country parties by requiring double majorities of both Non-Article 5

---

12 See Richard Benedick, *Ozone Diplomacy* (Harvard University Press, 1998), p. 267.

13 By using the MLF funding, India had built new industrial plants capable of producing or using CFCs and other destructive chemicals. See Chapter 6(III.D(4)) in this volume.

14 Johan G. Lammers (Rapporteur), 'Second Report of the International Committee on Legal Aspects of Long-Distance Air Pollution', *Report of the Sixty-Third Conference, held at Warsaw, August 21st to August 27th, 1988*, International Law Association (1988), p. 231, cited in Patrick Széll, 'Decision Making under Multilateral Environmental Agreements', 26/5 EPL (1996), p. 213.

15 See Jacob Werksman, 'The Conference of Parties to Environmental Treaties', in Werksman (ed.), *Greening International Institutions* (Earthscan, 1996), p. 61.

16 See Patrick Széll, 'Decision Making under Multilateral Environmental Agreements', 26/5 EPL (1996), p. 213. See also Chapter 3(III.C) in this volume.

and Article 5 countries. This new approach based on a North-South balance has also been adopted in the Executive Committee's decision-making structure.

Attention should be also directed towards the role of non-governmental organisations in the ozone régime's establishment and maintenance. Environmental NGOs actively participate in the periodic meetings of the Meeting of the Parties, the Executive Committee of the MLF and the Open-Ended Working Group of the Parties to the Protocol. The functions of environmental NGOs in the context of compliance monitoring at international and national levels are particularly worthly of mention. Information regarding potential non-compliance derived from environmental NGOs might – without any governmental support – reach the Montreal NCP through the UNEP Ozone Secretariat. In addition, NGOs may organise community pressure to enforce non-binding recommendations and decisions of the Implementation Committee of the NCP and of the Meeting of the Parties. In the meetings of the Executive Committee, NGOs often criticise MLF projects that might be regarded as not necessarily visionary from an environmental perspective. As Professor Alexandre Kiss puts, it is true that 'the most powerful .... tool for ensuring compliance with international environmental obligations is public awareness and the will to impose upon governments the protection of the environment values which are essential for the survival of humanity'.[17]

It must be emphasised that the international ozone treaties, which forms a highly technical treaty régime, demonstrate that Stockholm/Rio Principles, including the customary international law of the environment, can be observed in an international environmental community of over 190 States. The Vienna Ozone Convention claimed to implement Principle 21 of the 1972 Stockholm Declaration and, for the first time, referred to the term 'precautionary measures' in international environment protection law. Now the Montreal Protocol, as amended and adjusted, contains stringently binding controls on CFCS and ODSS, which will help to avoid, or at least mitigate, the adverse consequences of global ozone depletion. In addition, the ozone régime should be regarded as the first MEA that specifically addressed the principle of common-but-differentiated responsibilities: the régime (i) operates a ten-years grace period, (ii) created the Financial Mechanism of the Montreal Protocol, including the MLF, and (iii) includes provisions for basic domestic needs in Article 5.

The ozone régime also shows equal considerations for the interests of developing countries. As noted, under the present ozone régime, (i) decisions on ODS adjustments are made by a two thirds majority of the parties, representing

---

17   Alexandre-Charles Kiss, 'Compliance with International and European Environmental Obligations', *Hague YbkIL* (1996), p. 54.

a majority of both Non-Article 5 developed and Article 5 developing countries and (ii) the Executive Committee of the MLF consists of seven parties from a group of Article 5 industrialising countries operating and seven parties from a group of Non-Article 5 industrially advanced countries. The ozone régime will be arguably the first international cooperation régime for the environment that successfully achieves the delicate balance of economic and political interests of both Northern and Southern nations. This kind of international legal régimes – with an equitable institutional mechanisms – can contribute to the achievement and maintenance of the globally recognised customary principle of sustainable development and its two constituent elements, development and environmental protection.

Finally, it must be noted that the adoption of the Kigali Amedments is likely to change the basic nature of the ozone treaty régime we have observed in this work. A treaty régime, which regulates both ODSs and substances that have high global warming potentials (GWP), but with zero ozone-depletion potentials, will no longer be regarded as a sectoral or fragmented international law system. This event may be the real beginning of the evlotion of the 'Convention on the Law of Global Air', suggested at the 1989 Ottawa Meeting of Legal and Policy Experts on the Protection of the Atmosphere.[18] It will be very interesting to see how the synergies between the ozone régime and the climate change régime will develop each other, in the coming decades.

The international ozone régime may be seen as a 'comparatively autonomous legal system' or 'self-contained' régime in international law. As Professor Thomas Gehring has pointed out, a sectoral régime controlled by a supreme political organ often seems separate from long-established traditional principles and rules of public international law. Nevertheless, the legal régime for the protection of the ozone layer has been based on the ever-changing system of principles and rules of international law considered in this study. The interaction between the ozone régime and general international law should be correctly understood, and the impact of the ozone régime on the development of international law and international environmental law should not be underestimated.

---

18   See Peter H. Sand, 'UNCED and the Development of International Environmental Law', 3 *YbkIEL* (1992), p. 7; Chapter 1(III) in this volume.

APPENDIX I

The 1985 Vienna Convention for the Protection of the Ozone Layer

Preamble
The Parties to this Convention,

Aware of the potentially harmful impact on human health and the environment through modification of the ozone layer,

Recalling the pertinent provisions of the Declaration of the United Nations Conference on the Human Environment, and in particular principle 21, which provides that "States have, in accordance with the Charter of the United Nations and the principles of international law, the sovereign right to exploit their own resources pursuant to their own environmental policies, and the responsibility to ensure that activities within their jurisdiction or control do not cause damage to the environment of other States or of areas beyond the limits of national jurisdiction",

Taking into account the circumstances and particular requirements of developing countries,

Mindful of the work and studies proceeding within both international and national organizations and, in particular, of the World Plan of Action on the Ozone Layer of the United Nations Environment Programme,

Mindful also of the precautionary measures for the protection of the ozone layer which have already been taken at the national and international levels,

Aware that measures to protect the ozone layer from modifications due to human activities require international co-operation and action, and should be based on relevant scientific and technical considerations,

Aware also of the need for further research and systematic observations to further develop scientific knowledge of the ozone layer and possible adverse effects resulting from its modification,

Determined to protect human health and the environment against adverse effects resulting from modifications of the ozone layer,

HAVE AGREED AS FOLLOWS:

Article 1: Definitions

For the purposes of this Convention:

1. "The ozone layer" means the layer of atmospheric ozone above the planetary boundary layer.
2. "Adverse effects" means changes in the physical environment or biota, including changes in climate, which have significant deleterious effects on human health or on the composition, resilience and productivity of natural and managed ecosystems, or on materials useful to mankind.
3. "Alternative technologies or equipment" means technologies or equipment the use of which makes it possible to reduce or effectively eliminate emissions of substances which have or are likely to have adverse effects on the ozone layer.
4. "Alternative substances" means substances which reduce, eliminate or avoid adverse effects on the ozone layer.
5. "Parties" means, unless the text otherwise indicates, Parties to this Convention.
6. "Regional economic integration organization" means an organization constituted by sovereign States of a given region which has competence in respect of matters governed by this Convention or its protocols and has been duly authorized, in accordance with its internal procedures, to sign, ratify, accept, approve or accede to the instruments concerned.
7. "Protocols" means protocols to this Convention.

Article 2: General obligations

1. The Parties shall take appropriate measures in accordance with the provisions of this Convention and of those protocols in force to which they are party to protect human health and the environment against adverse effects resulting or likely to result from human activities which modify or are likely to modify the ozone layer.
2. To this end the Parties shall, in accordance with the means at their disposal and their capabilities:
   (a) Co-operate by means of systematic observations, research and information exchange in order to better understand and assess the effects of human activities on the ozone layer and the effects on human health and the environment from modification of the ozone layer;
   (b) Adopt appropriate legislative or administrative measures and co-operate in harmonizing appropriate policies to control, limit, reduce or prevent human activities under their jurisdiction or control should it be found that these activities have or are likely to have adverse effects resulting from modification or likely modification of the ozone layer;

1985 VIENNA CONVENTION FOR THE PROTECTION OF THE OZONE LAYER   345

  (c) Co-operate in the formulation of agreed measures, procedures and standards for the implementation of this Convention, with a view to the adoption of protocols and annexes;

  (d) Co-operate with competent international bodies to implement effectively this Convention and protocols to which they are party.

3. The provisions of this Convention shall in no way affect the right of Parties to adopt, in accordance with international law, domestic measures additional to those referred to in paragraphs 1 and 2 above, nor shall they affect additional domestic measures already taken by a Party, provided that these measures are not incompatible with their obligations under this Convention.

4. The application of this article shall be based on relevant scientific and technical considerations.

Article 3: Research and Systematic Observations

1. The Parties undertake, as appropriate, to initiate and co-operate in, directly or through competent international bodies, the conduct of research and scientific assessments on:

  (a) The physical and chemical processes that may affect the ozone layer;

  (b) The human health and other biological effects deriving from any modifications of the ozone layer, particularly those resulting from changes in ultra-violet solar radiation having biological effects (UV-B);

  (c) Climatic effects deriving from any modifications of the ozone layer;

  (d) Effects deriving from any modifications of the ozone layer and any consequent change in UV-B radiation on natural and synthetic materials useful to mankind;

  (e) Substances, practices, processes and activities that may affect the ozone layer, and their cumulative effects;

  (f) Alternative substances and technologies;

  (g) Related socio-economic matters; and as further elaborated in annexes I and II.

2. The Parties undertake to promote or establish, as appropriate, directly or through competent international bodies and taking fully into account national legislation and relevant ongoing activities at both the national and international levels, joint or complementary programmes for systematic observation of the state of the ozone layer and other relevant parameters, as elaborated in annex I.

3. The Parties undertake to co-operate, directly or through competent international bodies, in ensuring the collection, validation and transmission of research and observational data through appropriate world data centres in a regular and timely fashion.

Article 4: Co-operation in the Legal, Scientific and Technical Fields

1. The Parties shall facilitate and encourage the exchange of scientific, technical, socio-economic, commercial and legal information relevant to this Convention as further elaborated in annex II. Such information shall be supplied to bodies agreed upon by the Parties. Any such body receiving information regarded as confidential by the supplying Party shall ensure that such information is not disclosed and shall aggregate it to protect its confidentiality before it is made available to all Parties.

2. The Parties shall co-operate, consistent with their national laws, regulations and practices and taking into account in particular the needs of the developing countries, in promoting, directly or through competent international bodies, the development and transfer of technology and knowledge. Such co-operation shall be carried out particularly through:

   (a) Facilitation of the acquisition of alternative technologies by other Parties;

   (b) Provision of information on alternative technologies and equipment, and supply of special manuals or guides to them;

   (c) The supply of necessary equipment and facilities for research and systematic observations;

   (d) Appropriate training of scientific and technical personnel.

Article 5: Transmission of Information

The Parties shall transmit, through the secretariat, to the Conference of the Parties established under article 6 information on the measures adopted by them in implementation of this Convention and of protocols to which they are party in such form and at such intervals as the meetings of the parties to the relevant instruments may determine.

Article 6: Conference of the Parties

1. A Conference of the Parties is hereby established. The first meeting of the Conference of the Parties shall be convened by the secretariat designated on an interim basis under article 7 not later than one year after entry into force of this Convention. Thereafter, ordinary meetings of the Conference of the Parties shall be held at regular intervals to be determined by the Conference at its first meeting.

2. Extraordinary meetings of the Conference of the Parties shall be held at such other times as may be deemed necessary by the Conference, or at the written request of any Party, provided that, within six months of the request being communicated to them by the secretariat, it is supported by at least one third of the Parties.

3. The Conference of the Parties shall by consensus agree upon and adopt rules of procedure and financial rules for itself and for any subsidiary bodies it may establish, as well as financial provisions governing the functioning of the secretariat.

4. The Conference of the Parties shall keep under continuous review the implementation of this Convention, and, in addition, shall:

(a) Establish the form and the intervals for transmitting the information to be submitted in accordance with article 5 and consider such information as well as reports submitted by any subsidiary body;

(b) Review the scientific information on the ozone layer, on its possible modification and on possible effects of any such modification;

(c) Promote, in accordance with article 2, the harmonization of appropriate policies, strategies and measures for minimizing the release of substances causing or likely to cause modification of the ozone layer, and make recommendations on any other measures relating to this Convention;

(d) Adopt, in accordance with articles 3 and 4, programmes for research, systematic observations, scientific and technological co-operation, the exchange of information and the transfer of technology and knowledge;

(e) Consider and adopt, as required, in accordance with articles 9 and 10, amendments to this Convention and its annexes;

(f) Consider amendments to any protocol, as well as to any annexes thereto, and, if so decided, recommend their adoption to the parties to the protocol concerned;

(g) Consider and adopt, as required, in accordance with article 10, additional annexes to this Convention;

(h) Consider and adopt, as required, protocols in accordance with article 8;

(i) Establish such subsidiary bodies as are deemed necessary for the implementation of this Convention;

(j) Seek, where appropriate, the services of competent international bodies and scientific committees, in particular the World Meteorological Organization and the World Health Organization as well as the Co-ordinating Committee on the Ozone Layer, in scientific research, systematic observations and other activities pertinent to the objectives of this Convention, and make use as appropriate of information from these bodies and committees;

(k) Consider and undertake any additional action that may be required for the achievement of the purposes of this Convention.

5. The United Nations, its specialized agencies and the International Atomic Energy Agency, as well as any State not party to this Convention, may be represented at meetings of the Conference of the Parties by observers. Any body or agency, whether national or international, governmental or non-governmental, qualified in fields relating to the protection of the ozone layer which has informed the secretariat of its wish to be represented at a meeting of the Conference of the Parties as an observer may be admitted unless at least one-third of the Parties present object. The admission and participation of observers shall be subject to the rules of procedure adopted by the Conference of the Parties.

Article 7: Secretariat

1. The functions of the secretariat shall be:

   (a) To arrange for and service meetings provided for in articles 6, 8, 9 and 10;

   (b) To prepare and transmit reports based upon information received in accordance with articles 4 and 5, as well as upon information derived from meetings of subsidiary bodies established under article 6;

   (c) To perform the functions assigned to it by any protocol;

   (d) To prepare reports on its activities carried out in implementation of its functions under this Convention and present them to the Conference of the Parties;

   (e) To ensure the necessary co-ordination with other relevant international bodies, and in particular to enter into such administrative and contractual arrangements as may be required for the effective discharge of its functions;

   (f) To perform such other functions as may be determined by the Conference of the Parties.

2. The secretariat functions will be carried out on an interim basis by the United Nations Environment Programme until the completion of the first ordinary meeting of the Conference of the Parties held pursuant to article 6. At its first ordinary meeting, the Conference of the Parties shall designate the secretariat from amongst those existing competent international organizations which have signified their willingness to carry out the secretariat functions under this Convention.

Article 8: Adoption of Protocols

1. The Conference of the Parties may at a meeting adopt protocols pursuant to Article 2.

2. The text of any proposed protocol shall be communicated to the Parties by the secretariat at least six months before such a meeting.

Article 9: Amendment of the Convention or Protocols

1. Any Party may propose amendments to this Convention or to any protocol. Such amendments shall take due account, *inter alia*, of relevant scientific and technical considerations.

2. Amendments to this Convention shall be adopted at a meeting of the Conference of the Parties. Amendments to any protocol shall be adopted at a meeting of the Parties to the protocol in question. The text of any proposed amendment to this Convention or to any protocol, except as may otherwise be provided in such protocol, shall be communicated to the Parties by the secretariat at least six months before the meeting at which it is proposed for adoption. The secretariat

shall also communicate proposed amendments to the signatories to this Convention for information.

3. The Parties shall make every effort to reach agreement on any proposed amendment to this Convention by consensus. If all efforts at consensus have been exhausted, and no agreement reached, the amendment shall as a last resort be adopted by a three-fourths majority vote of the Parties present and voting at the meeting, and shall be submitted by the Depositary to all Parties for ratification, approval or acceptance.

4. The procedure mentioned in paragraph 3 above shall apply to amendments to any protocol, except that a two-thirds majority of the parties to that protocol present and voting at the meeting shall suffice for their adoption.

5. Ratification, approval or acceptance of amendments shall be notified to the Depositary in writing. Amendments adopted in accordance with paragraphs 3 or 4 above shall enter into force between parties having accepted them on the ninetieth day after the receipt by the Depositary of notification of their ratification, approval or acceptance by at least three-fourths of the Parties to this Convention or by at least two-thirds of the parties to the protocol concerned, except as may otherwise be provided in such protocol. Thereafter the amendments shall enter into force for any other Party on the nineteenth day after that Party deposits its instrument of ratification, approval or acceptance of the amendments.

6. For the purposes of this article, "Parties present and voting" means Parties present and casting an affirmative or negative vote.

Article 10: Adoption and Amendment of Annexes

1. The annexes to this Convention or to any protocol shall form an integral part of this Convention or of such protocol, as the case may be, and, unless expressly provided otherwise, a reference to this Convention or its protocols constitutes at the same time a reference to any annexes thereto. Such annexes shall be restricted to scientific, technical and administrative matters.

2. Except as may be otherwise provided in any protocol with respect to its annexes, the following procedure shall apply to the proposal, adoption and entry into force of additional annexes to this Convention or of annexes to a protocol:

    (a) Annexes to this Convention shall be proposed and adopted according to the procedure laid down in article 9, paragraphs 2 and 3, while annexes to any protocol shall be proposed and adopted according to the procedure laid down in article 9, paragraphs 2 and 4;

    (b) Any party that is unable to approve an additional annex to this Convention or annex to any protocol to which it is party shall so notify the Depositary, in writing, within six months from the date of the communication of the adoption by the Depositary. The Depositary shall without delay notify all

Parties of any such notification received. A Party may at any time substitute an acceptance for a previous declaration of objection and the annexes shall thereupon enter into force for that Party;

(c) On the expiry of six months from the date of the circulation of the communication by the Depositary, the annex shall become effective for all Parties to this Convention or to any protocol concerned which have not submitted a notification in accordance with the provision of subparagraph (b) above.

3. The proposal, adoption and entry into force of amendments to annexes to this Convention or to any protocol shall be subject to the same procedure as for the proposal, adoption and entry into force of annexes to the Convention or annexes to a protocol. Annexes and amendments thereto shall take due account, *inter alia*, of relevant scientific and technical considerations.

4. If an additional annex or an amendment to an annex involves an amendment to this Convention or to any protocol, the additional annex or amended annex shall not enter into force until such time as the amendment to this Convention or to the protocol concerned enters into force.

Article 11: Settlement of Disputes

1. In the event of a dispute between Parties concerning the interpretation or application of this Convention, the parties concerned shall seek solution by negotiation.

2. If the parties concerned cannot reach agreement by negotiation, they may jointly seek the good offices of, or request mediation by, a third party.

3. When ratifying, accepting, approving or acceding to this Convention, or at any time thereafter, a State or regional economic integration organization may declare in writing to the Depositary that for a dispute not resolved in accordance with paragraph 1 or paragraph 2 above, it accepts one or both of the following means of dispute settlement as compulsory:

(a) Arbitration in accordance with procedures to be adopted by the Conference of the Parties at its first ordinary meeting;

(b) Submission of the dispute to the International Court of Justice.

4. If the parties have not, in accordance with paragraph 3 above, accepted the same or any procedure, the dispute shall be submitted to conciliation in accordance with paragraph 5 below unless the parties otherwise agree.

5. A conciliation commission shall be created upon the request of one of the parties to the dispute. The commission shall be composed of an equal number of members appointed by each party concerned and a chairman chosen jointly by the members appointed by each party. The commission shall render a final and recommendatory award, which the parties shall consider in good faith.

1985 VIENNA CONVENTION FOR THE PROTECTION OF THE OZONE LAYER 351

6. The provisions of this Article shall apply with respect to any protocol except as provided in the protocol concerned.

Article 12: Signature

This Convention shall be open for signature by States and by regional economic integration organizations at the Federal Ministry for Foreign Affairs of the Republic of Austria in Vienna from 22 March 1985 to 21 September 1985, and at United Nations Headquarters in New York from 22 September 1985 to 21 March 1986.

Article 13: Ratification, Acceptance or Approval

1. This Convention and any protocol shall be subject to ratification, acceptance or approval by States and by regional economic integration organizations. Instruments of ratification, acceptance or approval shall be deposited with the Depositary.

2. Any organization referred to in paragraph 1 above which becomes a Party to this Convention or any protocol without any of its member States being a Party shall be bound by all the obligations under the Convention or the protocol, as the case may be. In the case of such organizations, one or more of whose member States is a Party to the Convention or relevant protocol, the organization and its member States shall decide on their respective responsibilities for the performance of their obligation under the Convention or protocol, as the case may be. In such cases, the organization and the member States shall not be entitled to exercise rights under the Convention or relevant protocol concurrently.

3. In their instruments of ratification, acceptance or approval, the organizations referred to in paragraph 1 above shall declare the extent of their competence with respect to the matters governed by the Convention or the relevant protocol. These organizations shall also inform the Depositary of any substantial modification in the extent of their competence.

Article 14: Accession

1. This Convention and any protocol shall be open for accession by States and by regional economic integration organizations from the date on which the Convention or the protocol concerned is closed for signature. The instruments of accession shall be deposited with the Depositary.

2. In their instruments of accession, the organizations referred to in paragraph 1 above shall declare the extent of their competence with respect to the matters governed by the Convention or the relevant protocol. These organizations shall also inform the Depositary of any substantial modification in the extent of their competence.

3. The provisions of article 13, paragraph 2, shall apply to regional economic integration organizations which accede to this Convention or any protocol.

Article 15: Right to vote

1. Each Party to this Convention or to any protocol shall have one vote.
2. Except as provided for in paragraph 1 above, regional economic integration organizations, in matters within their competence, shall exercise their right to vote with a number of votes equal to the number of their member States which are Parties to the Convention or the relevant protocol. Such organizations shall not exercise their right to vote if their member States exercise theirs, and vice versa.

Article 16: Relationship between the Convention and its Protocols

1. A State or a regional economic integration organization may not become a party to a protocol unless it is, or becomes at the same time, a Party to the Convention.
2. Decisions concerning any protocol shall be taken only by the parties to the protocol concerned.

Article 17: Entry into Force

1. This Convention shall enter into force on the ninetieth day after the date of deposit of the twentieth instrument of ratification, acceptance, approval or accession.
2. Any protocol, except as otherwise provided in such protocol, shall enter into force on the ninetieth day after the date of deposit of the eleventh instrument of ratification, acceptance or approval of such protocol or accession thereto.
3. For each Party which ratifies, accepts or approves this Convention or accedes thereto after the deposit of the twentieth instrument of ratification, acceptance, approval or accession, it shall enter into force on the ninetieth day after the date of deposit by such Party of its instrument of ratification, acceptance, approval or accession.
4. Any protocol, except as otherwise provided in such protocol, shall enter into force for a party that ratifies, accepts or approves that protocol or accedes thereto after its entry into force pursuant to paragraph 2 above, on the ninetieth day after the date on which that party deposits its instrument of ratification, acceptance, approval or accession, or on the date which the Convention enters into force for that Party, whichever shall be the later.
5. For the purposes of paragraphs 1 and 2 above, any instrument deposited by a regional economic integration organization shall not be counted as additional to those deposited by member States of such organization.

Article 18: Reservations

No reservations may be made to this Convention.

Article 19: Withdrawal

1. At any time after four years from the date on which this Convention has entered into force for a Party, that Party may withdraw from the Convention by giving written notification to the Depositary.

2. Except as may be provided in any protocol, at any time after four years from the date on which such protocol has entered into force for a party, that party may withdraw from the protocol by giving written notification to the Depositary.

3. Any such withdrawal shall take effect upon expiry of one year after the date of its receipt by the Depositary, or on such later date as may be specified in the notification of the withdrawal.

4. Any Party which withdraws from this Convention shall be considered as also having withdrawn from any protocol to which it is party.

Article 20: Depositary

1. The Secretary-General of the United Nations shall assume the functions of depositary of this Convention and any protocols.

2. The Depositary shall inform the Parties, in particular, of:

    (a) The signature of this Convention and of any protocol, and the deposit of instruments of ratification, acceptance, approval or accession in accordance with articles 13 and 14;

    (b) The date on which the Convention and any protocol will come into force in accordance with article 17;

    (c) Notifications of withdrawal made in accordance with article 19;

    (d) Amendments adopted with respect to the Convention and any protocol, their acceptance by the parties and their date of entry into force in accordance with article 9;

    (e) All communications relating to the adoption and approval of annexes and to the amendment of annexes in accordance with article 10;

    (f) Notifications by regional economic integration organizations of the extent of their competence with respect to matters governed by this Convention and any protocols, and of any modifications thereof.

    (g) Declarations made in accordance with article 11, paragraph 3.

Article 21: Authentic Texts

The original of this Convention, of which the Arabic, Chinese, English, French, Russian and Spanish texts are equally authentic, shall be deposited with the Secretary-General of the United Nations.

IN WITNESS WHEREOF the undersigned, being duly authorized to that effect, have signed this Convention.

DONE AT VIENNA ON THE 22ND DAY OF MARCH 1985

Annex I: Research and Systematic Observations

1. The Parties to the Convention recognize that the major scientific issues are:

   (a) Modification of the ozone layer which would result in a change in the amount of solar ultra-violet radiation having biological effects (UV-B) that reaches the Earth's surface and the potential consequences for human health, for organisms, ecosystems and materials useful to mankind;

   (b) Modification of the vertical distribution of ozone, which could change the temperature structure of the atmosphere and the potential consequences for weather and climate.

2. The Parties to the Convention, in accordance with article 3, shall co-operate in conducting research and systematic observations and in formulating recommendations for future research and observation in such areas as:

   (a) *Research into the physics and chemistry of the atmosphere*

      (i) Comprehensive theoretical models: further development of models which consider the interaction between radiative, dynamic and chemical processes; studies of the simultaneous effects of various man-made and naturally occurring species upon atmospheric ozone; interpretation of satellite and non-satellite measurement data sets; evaluation of trends in atmospheric and geophysical parameters, and the development of methods for attributing changes in these parameters to specific causes;

      (ii) Laboratory studies of: rate coefficients, absorption cross-sections and mechanisms of tropospheric and stratospheric chemical and photochemical processes; spectroscopic data to support field measurements in all relevant spectral regions;

      (iii) Field measurements: the concentration and fluxes of key source gases of both natural and anthropogenic origin; atmospheric dynamics studies; simultaneous measurements of photochemically-related species down to the planetary boundary layer, using *in situ* and remote sensing instruments; intercomparison of different sensors, including co-ordinated correlative measures for satellite instrumentation; three-dimensional fields of key atmospheric trace constituents, solar spectral flux and meteorological parameters;

      (iv) Instrument development, including satellite and non-satellite sensors for atmospheric trace constituents, solar flux and meteorological parameters;

   (b) *Research into health, biological and photodegradation effects*

      (i) The relationship between human exposure to visible and ultra-violet solar radiation and (a) the development of both non-melanoma and melanoma skin cancer and (b) the effects on the immunological system;

(ii) Effects of UV-B radiation, including the wavelength dependence, upon (a) agricultural crops, forests and other terrestrial ecosystems and (b) the aquatic food web and fisheries, as well as possible inhibition of oxygen production by marine phytoplankton;

(iii) The mechanisms by which UV-B radiation acts on biological materials, species and ecosystems, including: the relationship between dose, dose rate, and response; photorepair, adaptation, and protection;

(iv) Studies of biological action spectra and the spectral response using polychromatic radiation in order to include possible interactions of the various wavelength regions;

(v) The influence of UV-B radiation on: the sensitivities and activities of biological species important to the biospheric balance; primary processes such as photosynthesis and biosynthesis;

(vi) The influence of UV-B radiation on the photodegradation of pollutants, agricultural chemicals and other materials;

(c) *Research on effects on climate*

(i) Theoretical and observational studies of the radiative effects of ozone and other trace species and the impact on climate parameters, such as land and ocean surface temperatures, precipitation patterns, the exchange between the troposphere and stratosphere;

(ii) The investigation of the effects of such climate impacts on various aspects of human activity;

(d) *Systematic observation on:*

(i) The status of the ozone layer (i.e. the spatial and temporal variability of the total column content and vertical distribution) by making the Global Ozone Observing System, based on the integration of satellite and ground-based systems, fully operational;

(ii) The tropospheric and stratospheric concentrations of source gases for the HO_x, NO_x, ClO_x and carbon families;

(iii) The temperature from the ground to the mesosphere, utilizing both ground-based and satellite systems;

(iv) Wavelength-resolved solar flux reaching, and thermal radiation leaving, the Earth's atmosphere, utilizing satellite measurements;

(v) Wavelength-resolved solar flux reaching the Earth's surface in the ultra-violet range having biological effects (UV-B);

(vi) Aerosol properties and distribution from the ground to the mesosphere, utilizing ground-based, airborne and satellite systems;

(vii) Climatically important variables by the maintenance of programmes of high-quality meteorological surface measurements;

(viii) Trace species, temperatures, solar flux and aerosols utilizing improved methods for analyzing global data.

356 APPENDIX I

3. The Parties to the Convention shall co-operate, taking into account the particular needs of the developing countries, in promoting the appropriate scientific and technical training required to participate in the research and systematic observations outlined in this annex. Particular emphasis should be given to the intercalibration of observational instrumentation and methods with a view to generating comparable or standardized scientific data sets.

4. The following chemical substances of natural and anthropogenic origin, not listed in order of priority, are thought to have the potential to modify the chemical and physical properties of the ozone layer.

(a) **Carbon substances**

(i) *Carbon monoxide (CO)*

Carbon monoxide has significant natural and anthropogenic sources, and is thought to play a major direct role in tropospheric photochemistry, and an indirect role in stratospheric photochemistry.

(ii) *Carbon dioxide (CO_2)*

Carbon dioxide has significant natural and anthropogenic sources, and affects stratospheric ozone by influencing the thermal structure of the atmosphere.

(iii) *Methane (CH_4)*

Methane has both natural and anthropogenic sources, and affects both tropospheric and stratospheric ozone.

(iv) *Non-methane hydrocarbon species*

Non-methane hydrocarbon species, which consist of a large number of chemical substances, have both natural and anthropogenic sources, and play a direct role in tropospheric photochemistry and an indirect role in stratospheric photochemistry.

(b) **Nitrogen substances**

(i) *Nitrous oxide (N_2O)*

The dominant sources of N_2O are natural, but anthropogenic contributions are becoming increasingly important. Nitrous oxide is the primary source of stratospheric NOx, which play a vital role in controlling the abundance of stratospheric ozone.

(ii) *Nitrogen oxides (NO_x)*

Ground-level sources of NO_x play a major direct role only in tropospheric photochemical processes and an indirect role in stratosphere photochemistry, whereas injection of NO_x close to the tropopause may lead directly to a change in upper tropospheric and stratospheric ozone.

(c) Chlorine substances

    (i)   *Fully halogenated alkanes, e.g. CCl_4, $CFCl_3$ (CFC–11), CF_2Cl_2 (CFC–12), $C_2F_3Cl_3$ (CFC– 113), $C_2F_4Cl_2$ (CFC–114)*

        Fully halogenated alkanes are anthropogenic and act as a source of ClO_x which plays a vital role in ozone photochemistry, especially in the 30–50 km altitude region.

    (ii)   *Partially halogenated alkanes, e.g. CH_3Cl, CHF_2Cl (CFC–22), CH_3CCl_3, $CHFCl_2$ (CFC–21)*

        The sources of CH_3Cl are natural, whereas the other partially halogenated alkanes mentioned above are anthropogenic in origin. These gases also act as a source of stratospheric ClO_x.

(d) Bromine substances

Fully halogenated alkanes, e.g. CF_3Br

These gases are anthropogenic and act as a source of BrO_x, which behaves in a manner similar to ClO_x.

(e) Hydrogen substances

    (i)   *Hydrogen (H_2)*

        Hydrogen, the source of which is natural and anthropogenic, plays a minor role in stratospheric photochemistry.

    (ii)   *Water (H_2O)*

        Water, the source of which is natural, plays a vital role in both tropospheric and stratospheric photochemistry. Local sources of water vapor in the stratosphere include the oxidation of methane and, to a lesser extent, of hydrogen.

Annex II: Information Exchange

1.   The Parties to the Convention recognize that the collection and sharing of information is an important means of implementing the objectives of this Convention and of assuring that any actions that may be taken are appropriate and equitable. Therefore, Parties shall exchange scientific, technical, socioeconomic, business, commercial and legal information.

2.   The Parties to the Convention, in deciding what information is to be collected and exchanged, should take into account the usefulness of the information and the costs of obtaining it. The Parties further recognize that co-operation under this annex has to be consistent with national laws, regulations and practices regarding patents, trade secrets, and protection of confidential and proprietary information.

3. *Scientific information*

This includes information on:

(a) Planned and ongoing research, both governmental and private, to facilitate the co-ordination of research programmes so as to make the most effective use of available national and international resources;

(b) The emission data needed for research;

(c) Scientific results published in peer-reviewed literature on the understanding of the physics and chemistry of the Earth's atmosphere and of its susceptibility to change, in particular on the state of the ozone layer and effects on human health, environment and climate which would result from changes on all time-scales in either the total column content or the vertical distribution of ozone;

(d) The assessment of research results and the recommendation for future research.

4. Technical information

This includes information on:

(a) The availability and cost of chemical substitutes and of alternative technologies to reduce the emissions of ozone-modifying substances and related planned and ongoing research;

(b) The limitations and any risks involved in using chemical or other substitutes and alternative technologies.

5. *Socio-economic and commercial information on the substances referred to in annex I*

This includes information on:

(a) Production and production capacity;

(b) Use and use patterns;

(c) Imports/exports;

(d) The costs, risks and benefits of human activities which may indirectly modify the ozone layer and of the impacts of regulatory actions taken or being considered to control these activities.

6. *Legal information*

This includes information on:

(a) National laws, administrative measures and legal research relevant to the protection of the ozone layer;

(b) International agreements, including bilateral agreements, relevant to the protection of the ozone layer;

(c) Methods and terms of licensing and availability of patents relevant to the protection of the ozone layer.

APPENDIX II

The Montreal Protocol on Substances That Deplete the Ozone Layer*

As adjusted and amended by the Second Meeting of the Parties (London, 27–29 June 1990) and by the Fourth Meeting of the Parties (Copenhagen, 23–25 November 1992) and further adjusted by the Seventh Meeting of the Parties (Vienna, 5–7 December 1995) and further adjusted and amended by the Ninth Meeting of the Parties (Montreal, 15–17 September 1997) and by the Eleventh Meeting of the Parties (Beijing, 29 November – 3 December 1999) and further adjusted by the Nineteenth Meeting of the Parties (Montreal, 17–21 September 2007) and further amended by the Twenty-Eighth Meeting of the Parties (Kigali, 10-15 October 2016).

Preamble

The Parties to this Protocol,

Being Parties to the Vienna Convention for the Protection of the Ozone Layer,

Mindful of their obligation under that Convention to take appropriate measures to protect human health and the environment against adverse effects resulting or likely to result from human activities which modify or are likely to modify the ozone layer,

Recognizing that world-wide emissions of certain substances can significantly deplete and otherwise modify the ozone layer in a manner that is likely to result in adverse effects on human health and the environment,

Conscious of the potential climatic effects of emissions of these substances,

Aware that measures taken to protect the ozone layer from depletion should be based on relevant scientific knowledge, taking into account technical and economic considerations,

Determined to protect the ozone layer by taking precautionary measures to control equitably total global emissions of substances that deplete it, with the ultimate objective of their elimination on the basis of developments in scientific knowledge, taking into account technical and economic considerations and bearing in mind the developmental needs of developing countries,

---

* Reprinted from *Handbook for the Montreal Protocol on Substances That Deplete the Ozone Layer* Twelfth ed., 2018, pp. 2–34.

Acknowledging that special provision is required to meet the needs of developing countries, including the provision of additional financial resources and access to relevant technologies, bearing in mind that the magnitude of funds necessary is predictable, and the funds can be expected to make a substantial difference in the world's ability to address the scientifically established problem of ozone depletion and its harmful effects,

Noting the precautionary measures for controlling emissions of certain chlorofluorocarbons that have already been taken at national and regional levels,

Considering the importance of promoting international co-operation in the research, development and transfer of alternative technologies relating to the control and reduction of emissions of substances that deplete the ozone layer, bearing in mind in particular the needs of developing countries,

HAVE AGREED AS FOLLOWS:

Article 1: Definitions

For the purposes of this Protocol:

1. "Convention" means the Vienna Convention for the Protection of the Ozone Layer, adopted on 22 March 1985.
2. "Parties" means, unless the text otherwise indicates, Parties to this Protocol.
3. "Secretariat" means the Secretariat of the Convention.
4. "Controlled substance" means a substance in Annex A, Annex B, Annex C, Annex E or Annex F to this Protocol, whether existing alone or in a mixture. It includes the isomers of any such substance, except as specified in the relevant Annex, but excludes any controlled substance or mixture which is in a manufactured product other than a container used for the transportation or storage of that substance.
5. "Production" means the amount of controlled substances produced, minus the amount destroyed by technologies to be approved by the Parties and minus the amount entirely used as feedstock in the manufacture of other chemicals. The amount recycled and reused is not to be considered as "production".
6. "Consumption" means production plus imports minus exports of controlled substances.
7. "Calculated levels" of production, imports, exports and consumption means levels determined in accordance with Article 3.
8. "Industrial rationalization" means the transfer of all or a portion of the calculated level of production of one Party to another, for the purpose of achieving economic efficiencies or responding to anticipated shortfalls in supply as a result of plant closures.

Article 2: Control Measures

1. *Incorporated in Article 2A.*

2. *Replaced by Article 2B.*

3. *Replaced by Article 2A.*

4. *Replaced by Article 2A.*

5. Any Party may, for one or more control periods, transfer to another Party any portion of its calculated level of production set out in Articles 2A to 2F, Articles 2H and 2J, provided that the total combined calculated levels of production of the Parties concerned for any group of controlled substances do not exceed the production limits set out in those Articles for that group. Such transfer of production shall be notified to the Secretariat by each of the Parties concerned, stating the terms of such transfer and the period for which it is to apply.

5 *bis*. Any Party not operating under paragraph 1 of Article 5 may, for one or more control periods, transfer to another such Party any portion of its calculated level of consumption set out in Article 2F, provided that the calculated level of consumption of controlled substances in Group I of Annex A of the Party transferring the portion of its calculated level of consumption did not exceed 0.25 kilograms per capita in 1989 and that the total combined calculated levels of consumption of the Parties concerned do not exceed the consumption limits set out in Article 2F. Such transfer of consumption shall be notified to the Secretariat by each of the Parties concerned, stating the terms of such transfer and the period for which it is to apply.

6. Any Party not operating under Article 5, that has facilities for the production of Annex A or Annex B controlled substances under construction, or contracted for, prior to 16 September 1987, and provided for in national legislation prior to 1 January 1987, may add the production from such facilities to its 1986 production of such substances for the purposes of determining its calculated level of production for 1986, provided that such facilities are completed by 31 December 1990 and that such production does not raise that Party's annual calculated level of consumption of the controlled substances above 0.5 kilograms per capita.

7. Any transfer of production pursuant to paragraph 5 or any addition of production pursuant to paragraph 6 shall be notified to the Secretariat, no later than the time of the transfer or addition.

8. (a) Any Parties which are Member States of a regional economic integration organization as defined in Article 1 (6) of the Convention may agree that they shall jointly fulfil their obligations respecting consumption under this Article and Articles 2A to 2J provided that their total combined calculated level of consumption does not exceed the levels required by this Article and Articles 2A to 2J. Any such agreement may be extended to include obligations respecting consumption or production under Article 2J provided that the total combined calculated level of consumption or

production of the Parties concerned does not exceed the levels required by Article 2J.

(b) The Parties to any such agreement shall inform the Secretariat of the terms of the agreement before the date of the reduction in consumption with which the agreement is concerned.

(c) Such agreement will become operative only if all Member States of the regional economic integration organization and the organization concerned are Parties to the Protocol and have notified the Secretariat of their manner of implementation.

9. (a) Based on the assessments made pursuant to Article 6, the Parties may decide whether:

   (i) Adjustments to the ozone depleting potentials specified in Annex A, Annex B, Annex C and/or Annex E should be made and, if so, what the adjustments should be;

   (ii) Adjustments to the global warming potentials specified in Group 1 of Annex A, Annex C and Annex F should be made and, if so, what the adjustments should be; and

   (iii) Further adjustments and reductions of production or consumption of the controlled substances should be undertaken and, if so, what the scope, amount and timing of any such adjustments and reductions should be;

(b) Proposals for such adjustments shall be communicated to the Parties by the Secretariat at least six months before the meeting of the Parties at which they are proposed for adoption;

(c) In taking such decisions, the Parties shall make every effort to reach agreement by consensus. If all efforts at consensus have been exhausted, and no agreement reached, such decisions shall, as a last resort, be adopted by a two-thirds majority vote of the Parties present and voting representing a majority of the Parties operating under Paragraph 1 of Article 5 present and voting and a majority of the Parties not so operating present and voting;

(d) The decisions, which shall be binding on all Parties, shall forthwith be communicated to the Parties by the Depositary. Unless otherwise provided in the decisions, they shall enter into force on the expiry of six months from the date of the circulation of the communication by the Depositary.

10. Based on the assessments made pursuant to Article 6 of this Protocol and in accordance with the procedure set out in Article 9 of the Convention, the Parties may decide:

(a) whether any substances, and if so which, should be added to or removed from any annex to this Protocol, and

MONTREAL PROTOCOL ON SUBSTANCES THAT DEPLETE THE OZONE LAYER 363

(b) the mechanism, scope and timing of the control measures that should apply to those substances;

11. Notwithstanding the provisions contained in this Article and Articles 2A to 2J Parties may take more stringent measures than those required by this Article and Articles 2A to 2J

Article 2A: CFCS

1. Each Party shall ensure that for the twelve-month period commencing on the first day of the seventh month following the date of entry into force of this Protocol, and in each twelve-month period thereafter, its calculated level of consumption of the controlled substances in Group I of Annex A does not exceed its calculated level of consumption in 1986. By the end of the same period, each Party producing one or more of these substances shall ensure that its calculated level of production of the substances does not exceed its calculated level of production in 1986, except that such level may have increased by no more than ten per cent based on the 1986 level. Such increase shall be permitted only so as to satisfy the basic domestic needs of the Parties operating under Article 5 and for the purposes of industrial rationalization between Parties.

2. Each Party shall ensure that for the period from 1 July 1991 to 31 December 1992 its calculated levels of consumption and production of the controlled substances in Group I of Annex A do not exceed 150 per cent of its calculated levels of production and consumption of those substances in 1986; with effect from 1 January 1993, the twelve-month control period for these controlled substances shall run from 1 January to 31 December each year.

3. Each Party shall ensure that for the twelve-month period commencing on 1 January 1994, and in each twelve-month period thereafter, its calculated level of consumption of the controlled substances in Group I of Annex A does not exceed, annually, twenty-five per cent of its calculated level of consumption in 1986. Each Party producing one or more of these substances shall, for the same periods, ensure that its calculated level of production of the substances does not exceed, annually, twenty-five per cent of its calculated level of production in 1986. However, in order to satisfy the basic domestic needs of the Parties operating under paragraph 1 of Article 5, its calculated level of production may exceed that limit by up to ten per cent of its calculated level of production in 1986.

4. Each Party shall ensure that for the twelve-month period commencing on 1 January 1996, and in each twelve-month period thereafter, its calculated level of consumption of the controlled substances in Group I of Annex A does not exceed zero. Each Party producing one or more of these substances shall, for the same periods, ensure that its calculated level of production of the substances does not exceed zero. However, in order to satisfy the basic domestic needs of the Parties

operating under paragraph 1 of Article 5, its calculated level of production may exceed that limit by a quantity equal to the annual average of its production of the controlled substances in Group I of Annex A for basic domestic needs for the period 1995 to 1997 inclusive. This paragraph will apply save to the extent that the Parties decide to permit the level of production or consumption that is necessary to satisfy uses agreed by them to be essential.

5. Each Party shall ensure that for the twelve-month period commencing on 1 January 2003 and in each twelve-month period thereafter, its calculated level of production of the controlled substances in Group I of Annex A for the basic domestic needs of the Parties operating under paragraph 1 of Article 5 does not exceed eighty per cent of the annual average of its production of those substances for basic domestic needs for the period 1995 to 1997 inclusive.

6. Each Party shall ensure that for the twelve-month period commencing on 1 January 2005 and in each twelve-month period thereafter, its calculated level of production of the controlled substances in Group I of Annex A for the basic domestic needs of the Parties operating under paragraph 1 of Article 5 does not exceed fifty per cent of the annual average of its production of those substances for basic domestic needs for the period 1995 to 1997 inclusive.

7. Each Party shall ensure that for the twelve-month period commencing on 1 January 2007 and in each twelve-month period thereafter, its calculated level of production of the controlled substances in Group I of Annex A for the basic domestic needs of the Parties operating under paragraph 1 of Article 5 does not exceed fifteen per cent of the annual average of its production of those substances for basic domestic needs for the period 1995 to 1997 inclusive.

8. Each Party shall ensure that for the twelve-month period commencing on 1 January 2010 and in each twelve-month period thereafter, its calculated level of production of the controlled substances in Group I of Annex A for the basic domestic needs of the Parties operating under paragraph 1 of Article 5 does not exceed zero.

9. For the purposes of calculating basic domestic needs under paragraphs 4 to 8 of this Article, the calculation of the annual average of production by a Party includes any production entitlements that it has transferred in accordance with paragraph 5 of Article 2, and excludes any production entitlements that it has acquired in accordance with paragraph 5 of Article 2.

Article 2B: Halons

1. Each Party shall ensure that for the twelve-month period commencing on 1 January 1992, and in each twelve-month period thereafter, its calculated level of consumption of the controlled substances in Group II of Annex A does not exceed, annually, its calculated level of consumption in 1986. Each Party producing one

MONTREAL PROTOCOL ON SUBSTANCES THAT DEPLETE THE OZONE LAYER 365

or more of these substances shall, for the same periods, ensure that its calculated level of production of the substances does not exceed, annually, its calculated level of production in 1986. However, in order to satisfy the basic domestic needs of the Parties operating under paragraph 1 of Article 5, its calculated level of production may exceed that limit by up to ten per cent of its calculated level of production in 1986.

2.   Each Party shall ensure that for the twelve-month period commencing on 1 January 1994, and in each twelve-month period thereafter, its calculated level of consumption of the controlled substances in Group II of Annex A does not exceed zero. Each Party producing one or more of these substances shall, for the same periods, ensure that its calculated level of production of the substances does not exceed zero. However, in order to satisfy the basic domestic needs of the Parties operating under paragraph 1 of Article 5, its calculated level of production may, until 1 January 2002 exceed that limit by up to fifteen per cent of its calculated level of production in 1986; thereafter, it may exceed that limit by a quantity equal to the annual average of its production of the controlled substances in Group II of Annex A for basic domestic needs for the period 1995 to 1997 inclusive. This paragraph will apply save to the extent that the Parties decide to permit the level of production or consumption that is necessary to satisfy uses agreed by them to be essential.

3.   Each Party shall ensure that for the twelve-month period commencing on 1 January 2005 and in each twelve-month period thereafter, its calculated level of production of the controlled substances in Group II of Annex A for the basic domestic needs of the Parties operating under paragraph 1 of Article 5 does not exceed fifty per cent of the annual average of its production of those substances for basic domestic needs for the period 1995 to 1997 inclusive.

4.   Each Party shall ensure that for the twelve-month period commencing on 1 January 2010 and in each twelve-month period thereafter, its calculated level of production of the controlled substances in Group II of Annex A for the basic domestic needs of the Parties operating under paragraph 1 of Article 5 does not exceed zero.

Article 2C: Other fully halogenated CFCS

1.   Each Party shall ensure that for the twelve-month period commencing on 1 January 1993, its calculated level of consumption of the controlled substances in Group I of Annex B does not exceed, annually, eighty per cent of its calculated level of consumption in 1989. Each Party producing one or more of these substances shall, for the same period, ensure that its calculated level of production of the substances does not exceed, annually, eighty per cent of its calculated level of production in 1989. However, in order to satisfy the basic domestic needs

of the Parties operating under paragraph 1 of Article 5, its calculated level of production may exceed that limit by up to ten per cent of its calculated level of production in 1989.

2. Each Party shall ensure that for the twelve-month period commencing on 1 January 1994, and in each twelve-month period thereafter, its calculated level of consumption of the controlled substances in Group I of Annex B does not exceed, annually, twenty-five per cent of its calculated level of consumption in 1989. Each Party producing one or more of these substances shall, for the same periods, ensure that its calculated level of production of the substances does not exceed, annually, twenty-five per cent of its calculated level of production in 1989. However, in order to satisfy the basic domestic needs of the Parties operating under paragraph 1 of Article 5, its calculated level of production may exceed that limit by up to ten per cent of its calculated level of production in 1989.

3. Each Party shall ensure that for the twelve-month period commencing on 1 January 1996, and in each twelve-month period thereafter, its calculated level of consumption of the controlled substances in Group I of Annex B does not exceed zero. Each Party producing one or more of these substances shall, for the same periods, ensure that its calculated level of production of the substances does not exceed zero. However, in order to satisfy the basic domestic needs of the Parties operating under paragraph 1 of Article 5, its calculated level of production may, until 1 January 2003 exceed that limit by up to fifteen per cent of its calculated level of production in 1989; thereafter, it may exceed that limit by a quantity equal to eighty per cent of the annual average of its production of the controlled substances in Group I of Annex B for basic domestic needs for the period 1998 to 2000 inclusive. This paragraph will apply save to the extent that the Parties decide to permit the level of production or consumption that is necessary to satisfy uses agreed by them to be essential.

4. Each Party shall ensure that for the twelve-month period commencing on 1 January 2007 and in each twelve-month period thereafter, its calculated level of production of the controlled substances in Group I of Annex B for the basic domestic needs of the Parties operating under paragraph 1 of Article 5 does not exceed fifteen per cent of the annual average of its production of those substances for basic domestic needs for the period 1998 to 2000 inclusive.

5. Each Party shall ensure that for the twelve-month period commencing on 1 January 2010 and in each twelve-month period thereafter, its calculated level of production of the controlled substances in Group I of Annex B for the basic domestic needs of the Parties operating under paragraph 1 of Article 5 does not exceed zero.

Article 2D: Carbon Tetrachloride

1. Each Party shall ensure that for the twelve-month period commencing on 1 January 1995, its calculated level of consumption of the controlled substance in Group II of Annex B does not exceed, annually, fifteen per cent of its calculated level of consumption in 1989. Each Party producing the substance shall, for the same period, ensure that its calculated level of production of the substance does not exceed, annually, fifteen per cent of its calculated level of production in 1989. However, in order to satisfy the basic domestic needs of the Parties operating under paragraph 1 of Article 5, its calculated level of production may exceed that limit by up to ten per cent of its calculated level of production in 1989.

2. Each Party shall ensure that for the twelve-month period commencing on 1 January 1996, and in each twelve-month period thereafter, its calculated level of consumption of the controlled substance in Group II of Annex B does not exceed zero. Each Party producing the substance shall, for the same periods, ensure that its calculated level of production of the substance does not exceed zero. However, in order to satisfy the basic domestic needs of the Parties operating under paragraph 1 of Article 5, its calculated level of production may exceed that limit by up to fifteen per cent of its calculated level of production in 1989. This paragraph will apply save to the extent that the Parties decide to permit the level of production or consumption that is necessary to satisfy uses agreed by them to be essential.

Article 2E: 1,1,1-Trichloroethane (Methyl Chloroform)

1. Each Party shall ensure that for the twelve-month period commencing on 1 January 1993, its calculated level of consumption of the controlled substance in Group III of Annex B does not exceed, annually, its calculated level of consumption in 1989. Each Party producing the substance shall, for the same period, ensure that its calculated level of production of the substance does not exceed, annually, its calculated level of production in 1989. However, in order to satisfy the basic domestic needs of the Parties operating under paragraph 1 of Article 5, its calculated level of production may exceed that limit by up to ten per cent of its calculated level of production in 1989.

2. Each Party shall ensure that for the twelve-month period commencing on 1 January 1994, and in each twelve-month period thereafter, its calculated level of consumption of the controlled substance in Group III of Annex B does not exceed, annually, fifty per cent of its calculated level of consumption in 1989. Each Party producing the substance shall, for the same periods, ensure that its calculated level of production of the substance does not exceed, annually, fifty per cent of its calculated level of production in 1989. However, in order to satisfy the basic

domestic needs of the Parties operating under paragraph 1 of Article 5, its calculated level of production may exceed that limit by up to ten per cent of its calculated level of production in 1989.

3. Each Party shall ensure that for the twelve-month period commencing on 1 January 1996, and in each twelve-month period thereafter, its calculated level of consumption of the controlled substance in Group III of Annex B does not exceed zero. Each Party producing the substance shall, for the same periods, ensure that its calculated level of production of the substance does not exceed zero. However, in order to satisfy the basic domestic needs of the Parties operating under paragraph 1 of Article 5, its calculated level of production may exceed that limit by up to fifteen per cent of its calculated level of production for 1989. This paragraph will apply save to the extent that the Parties decide to permit the level of production or consumption that is necessary to satisfy uses agreed by them to be essential.

Article 2F: Hydrochlorofluorocarbons

1. Each Party shall ensure that for the twelve-month period commencing on 1 January 1996, and in each twelve-month period thereafter, its calculated level of consumption of the controlled substances in Group I of Annex C does not exceed, annually, the sum of:

    (a) Two point eight per cent of its calculated level of consumption in 1989 of the controlled substances in Group I of Annex A; and

    (b) Its calculated level of consumption in 1989 of the controlled substances in Group I of Annex C.

2. Each Party producing one or more of these substances shall ensure that for the twelve-month period commencing on 1 January 2004, and in each twelve-month period thereafter, its calculated level of production of the controlled substances in Group I of Annex C does not exceed, annually, the average of:

    (a) The sum of its calculated level of consumption in 1989 of the controlled substances in Group I of Annex C and two point eight per cent of its calculated level of consumption in 1989 of the controlled substances in Group I of Annex A; and

    (b) The sum of its calculated level of production in 1989 of the controlled substances in Group I of Annex C and two point eight per cent of its calculated level of production in 1989 of the controlled substances in Group I of Annex A.

    However, in order to satisfy the basic domestic needs of the Parties operating under paragraph 1 of Article 5, its calculated level of production may exceed that limit by up to fifteen per cent of its calculated level of production of the controlled substances in Group I of Annex C as defined above.

MONTREAL PROTOCOL ON SUBSTANCES THAT DEPLETE THE OZONE LAYER   369

3.   Each Party shall ensure that for the twelve month period commencing on 1 January 2004, and in each twelve-month period thereafter, its calculated level of consumption of the controlled substances in Group I of Annex C does not exceed, annually, sixty-five per cent of the sum referred to in paragraph 1 of this Article.

4.   Each Party shall ensure that for the twelve-month period commencing on 1 January 2010, and in each twelve-month period thereafter, its calculated level of consumption of the controlled substances in Group I of Annex C does not exceed, annually, twenty-five per cent of the sum referred to in paragraph 1 of this Article. Each Party producing one or more of these substances shall, for the same periods, ensure that its calculated level of production of the controlled substances in Group I of Annex C does not exceed, annually, twenty-five per cent of the calculated level referred to in paragraph 2 of this Article. However, in order to satisfy the basic domestic needs of the Parties operating under paragraph 1 of Article 5, its calculated level of production may exceed that limit by up to ten per cent of its calculated level of production of the controlled substances in Group I of Annex C as referred to in paragraph 2.

5.   Each Party shall ensure that for the twelve-month period commencing on 1 January 2015, and in each twelve-month period thereafter, its calculated level of consumption of the controlled substances in Group I of Annex C does not exceed, annually, ten per cent of the sum referred to in paragraph 1 of this Article. Each Party producing one or more of these substances shall, for the same periods, ensure that its calculated level of production of the controlled substances in Group I of Annex C does not exceed, annually, ten per cent of the calculated level referred to in paragraph 2 of this Article. However, in order to satisfy the basic domestic needs of the Parties operating under paragraph 1 of Article 5, its calculated level of production may exceed that limit by up to ten per cent of its calculated level of production of the controlled substances in Group I of Annex C as referred to in paragraph 2.

6.   Each Party shall ensure that for the twelve-month period commencing on 1 January 2020, and in each twelve-month period thereafter, its calculated level of consumption of the controlled substances in Group I of Annex C does not exceed zero. Each Party producing one or more of these substances shall, for the same periods, ensure that its calculated level of production of the controlled substances in Group I of Annex C does not exceed zero. However:

(a)   Each Party may exceed that limit on consumption by up to zero point five per cent of the sum referred to in paragraph 1 of this Article in any such twelve-month period ending before 1 January 2030, provided that such consumption shall be restricted to the servicing of refrigeration and air-conditioning equipment existing on 1 January 2020;

(b) Each Party may exceed that limit on production by up to zero point five per cent of the average referred to in paragraph 2 of this Article in any such twelve-month period ending before 1 January 2030, provided that such production shall be restricted to the servicing of refrigeration and air-conditioning equipment existing on 1 January 2020.

7. As of 1 January 1996, each Party shall endeavour to ensure that:

(a) The use of controlled substances in Group I of Annex C is limited to those applications where other more environmentally suitable alternative substances or technologies are not available;

(b) The use of controlled substances in Group I of Annex C is not outside the areas of application currently met by controlled substances in Annexes A, B and C, except in rare cases for the protection of human life or human health; and

(c) Controlled substances in Group I of Annex C are selected for use in a manner that minimizes ozone depletion, in addition to meeting other environmental, safety and economic considerations.

Article 2G: Hydrobromofluorocarbons

Each Party shall ensure that for the twelve-month period commencing on 1 January 1996, and in each twelvemonth period thereafter, its calculated level of consumption of the controlled substances in Group II of Annex C does not exceed zero. Each Party producing the substances shall, for the same periods, ensure that its calculated level of production of the substances does not exceed zero. This paragraph will apply save to the extent that the Parties decide to permit the level of production or consumption that is necessary to satisfy uses agreed by them to be essential.

Article 2H: Methyl bromide

1. Each Party shall ensure that for the twelve-month period commencing on 1 January 1995, and in each twelve-month period thereafter, its calculated level of consumption of the controlled substance in Annex E does not exceed, annually, its calculated level of consumption in 1991. Each Party producing the substance shall, for the same period, ensure that its calculated level of production of the substance does not exceed, annually, its calculated level of production in 1991. However, in order to satisfy the basic domestic needs of the Parties operating under paragraph 1 of Article 5, its calculated level of production may exceed that limit by up to ten per cent of its calculated level of production in 1991.

2. Each Party shall ensure that for the twelve-month period commencing on 1 January 1999, and in the twelve-month period thereafter, its calculated level of consumption of the controlled substance in Annex E does not exceed, annually,

seventy-five per cent of its calculated level of consumption in 1991. Each Party producing the substance shall, for the same periods, ensure that its calculated level of production of the substance does not exceed, annually, seventy-five per cent of its calculated level of production in 1991. However, in order to satisfy the basic domestic needs of the Parties operating under paragraph 1 of Article 5, its calculated level of production may exceed that limit by up to ten per cent of its calculated level of production in 1991.

3.   Each Party shall ensure that for the twelve-month period commencing on 1 January 2001, and in the twelve-month period thereafter, its calculated level of consumption of the controlled substance in Annex E does not exceed, annually, fifty per cent of its calculated level of consumption in 1991. Each Party producing the substance shall, for the same periods, ensure that its calculated level of production of the substance does not exceed, annually, fifty per cent of its calculated level of production in 1991. However, in order to satisfy the basic domestic needs of the Parties operating under paragraph 1 of Article 5, its calculated level of production may exceed that limit by up to ten per cent of its calculated level of production in 1991.

4.   Each Party shall ensure that for the twelve-month period commencing on 1 January 2003, and in the twelve-month period thereafter, its calculated level of consumption of the controlled substance in Annex E does not exceed, annually, thirty per cent of its calculated level of consumption in 1991. Each Party producing the substance shall, for the same periods, ensure that its calculated level of production of the substance does not exceed, annually, thirty per cent of its calculated level of production in 1991. However, in order to satisfy the basic domestic needs of the Parties operating under paragraph 1 of Article 5, its calculated level of production may exceed that limit by up to ten per cent of its calculated level of production in 1991.

5.   Each Party shall ensure that for the twelve-month period commencing on 1 January 2005, and in each twelve-month period thereafter, its calculated level of consumption of the controlled substance in Annex E does not exceed zero. Each Party producing the substance shall, for the same periods, ensure that its calculated level of production of the substance does not exceed zero. However, in order to satisfy the basic domestic needs of the Parties operating under paragraph 1 of Article 5, its calculated level of production may, until 1 January 2002 exceed that limit by up to fifteen per cent of its calculated level of production in 1991; thereafter, it may exceed that limit by a quantity equal to the annual average of its production of the controlled substance in Annex E for basic domestic needs for the period 1995 to 1998 inclusive. This paragraph will apply save to the extent that the Parties decide to permit the level of production or consumption that is necessary to satisfy uses agreed by them to be critical uses.

5 *bis*. Each Party shall ensure that for the twelve-month period commencing on 1 January 2005 and in each twelve-month period thereafter, its calculated level of production of the controlled substance in Annex E for the basic domestic needs of the Parties operating under paragraph 1 of Article 5 does not exceed eighty per cent of the annual average of its production of the substance for basic domestic needs for the period 1995 to 1998 inclusive.

5 *ter*. Each Party shall ensure that for the twelve-month period commencing on 1 January 2015 and in each twelve-month period thereafter, its calculated level of production of the controlled substance in Annex E for the basic domestic needs of the Parties operating under paragraph 1 of Article 5 does not exceed zero.

6. The calculated levels of consumption and production under this Article shall not include the amounts used by the Party for quarantine and pre-shipment applications.

Article 2I: Bromochloromethane

Each Party shall ensure that for the twelve-month period commencing on 1 January 2002, and in each twelvemonth period thereafter, its calculated level of consumption and production of the controlled substance in Group III of Annex C does not exceed zero. This paragraph will apply save to the extent that the Parties decide to permit the level of production or consumption that is necessary to satisfy uses agreed by them to be essential.

Article 2J: Hydrofluorocarbons

1. Each Party shall ensure that for the twelve-month period commencing on 1 January 2019, and in each twelve-month period thereafter, its calculated level of consumption of the controlled substances in Annex F, expressed in CO_2 equivalents, does not exceed the percentage, set out for the respective range of years specified in subparagraphs (a) to (e) below, of the annual average of its calculated levels of consumption of Annex F controlled substances for the years 2011, 2012 and 2013, plus fifteen per cent of its calculated level of consumption of Annex C, Group I, controlled substances as set out in paragraph 1 of Article 2F, expressed in CO_2 equivalents:
    (a) 2019 to 2023: 90 per cent
    (b) 2024 to 2028: 60 per cent
    (c) 2029 to 2033: 30 per cent
    (d) 2034 to 2035: 20 per cent
    (e) 2036 and thereafter: 15 per cent

2. Notwithstanding paragraph 1 of this Article, the Parties may decide that a Party shall ensure that, for the twelve-month period commencing on 1 January 2020, and in each twelve-month period thereafter, its calculated level of consumption of the controlled substances in Annex F, expressed in CO_2 equivalents, does not

exceed the percentage, set out for the respective range of years specified in sub-paragraphs (a) to (e) below, of the annual average of its calculated levels of consumption of Annex F controlled substances for the years 2011, 2012 and 2013, plus twenty-five per cent of its calculated level of consumption of Annex C, Group I, controlled substances as set out in paragraph 1 of Article 2F, expressed in CO_2 equivalents:

(a)   2020 to 2024: 95 per cent

(b)   2025 to 2028: 65 per cent

(c)   2029 to 2033: 30 per cent

(d)   2034 to 2035: 20 per cent

(e)   2036 and thereafter: 15 per cent

3.   Each Party producing the controlled substances in Annex F shall ensure that for the twelve-month period commencing on 1 January 2019, and in each twelve-month period thereafter, its calculated level of production of the controlled substances in Annex F, expressed in CO_2 equivalents, does not exceed the percentage, set out for the respective range of years specified in subparagraphs (a) to (e) below, of the annual average of its calculated levels of production of Annex F controlled substances for the years 2011, 2012 and 2013, plus fifteen per cent of its calculated level of production of Annex C, Group I, controlled substances as set out in paragraph 2 of Article 2F, expressed in CO_2 equivalents:

(a)   2019 to 2023: 90 per cent

(b)   2024 to 2028: 60 per cent

(c)   2029 to 2033: 30 per cent

(d)   2034 to 2035: 20 per cent

(e)   2036 and thereafter: 15 per cent

4.   Notwithstanding paragraph 3 of this Article, the Parties may decide that a Party producing the controlled substances in Annex F shall ensure that for the twelve-month period commencing on 1 January 2020, and in each twelve-month period thereafter, its calculated level of production of the controlled substances in Annex F, expressed in CO_2 equivalents, does not exceed the percentage, set out for the respective range of years specified in subparagraphs (a) to (e) below, of the annual average of its calculated levels of production of Annex F controlled substances for the years 2011, 2012 and 2013, plus twenty-five per cent of its calculated level of production of Annex C, Group I, controlled substances as set out in paragraph 2 of Article 2F, expressed in CO_2 equivalents:

(a)   2020 to 2024: 95 per cent

(b)   2025 to 2028: 65 per cent

(c)   2029 to 2033: 30 per cent

(d)   2034 to 2035: 20 per cent

(e)   2036 and thereafter: 15 per cent

5. Paragraphs 1 to 4 of this Article will apply save to the extent that the Parties decide to permit the level of production or consumption that is necessary to satisfy uses agreed by the Parties to be exempted uses.

6. Each Party manufacturing Annex C, Group I, or Annex F substances shall ensure that for the twelve-month period commencing on 1 January 2020, and in each twelve-month period thereafter, its emissions of Annex F, Group II, substances generated in each production facility that manufactures Annex C, Group I, or Annex F substances are destroyed to the extent practicable using technology approved by the Parties in the same twelve-month period.

7. Each Party shall ensure that any destruction of Annex F, Group II, substances generated by facilities that produce Annex C, Group I, or Annex F substances shall occur only by technologies approved by the Parties.

Article 3: Calculation of Control Levels

1. For the purposes of Articles 2, 2A to 2J and 5, each Party shall, for each group of substances in Annex A, Annex B, Annex C, Annex E or Annex F, determine its calculated levels of:

   (a) Production by:

      (i) multiplying its annual production of each controlled substance by the ozone depleting potential specified in respect of it in Annex A, Annex B, Annex C or Annex E, except as otherwise specified in paragraph 2;

      (ii) adding together, for each such Group, the resulting figures;

   (b) Imports and exports, respectively, by following, *mutatis mutandis*, the procedure set out in subparagraph (a); and

   (c) Consumption by adding together its calculated levels of production and imports and subtracting its calculated level of exports as determined in accordance with subparagraphs (a) and (b). However, beginning on 1 January 1993, any export of controlled substances to non-Parties shall not be subtracted in calculating the consumption level of the exporting Party; and

   (d) Emissions of Annex F, Group II, substances generated in each facility that generates Annex C, Group I, or Annex F substances by including, among other things, amounts emitted from equipment leaks, process vents and destruction devices, but excluding amounts captured for use, destruction or storage.

2. When calculating levels, expressed in CO_2 equivalents, of production, consumption, imports, exports and emissions of Annex F and Annex C, Group I, substances for the purposes of Article 2J, paragraph 5 *bis* of Article 2 and paragraph 1 (d) of Article 3, each Party shall use the global warming potentials of those substances specified in Group I of Annex A, Annex C and Annex F.

MONTREAL PROTOCOL ON SUBSTANCES THAT DEPLETE THE OZONE LAYER   375

Article 4: Control of Trade with non-Parties

1.   As of 1 January 1990, each party shall ban the import of the controlled substances in Annex A from any State not party to this Protocol.

1 *bis.* Within one year of the date of the entry into force of this paragraph, each Party shall ban the import of the controlled substances in Annex B from any State not party to this Protocol.

1 *ter.* Within one year of the date of entry into force of this paragraph, each Party shall ban the import of any controlled substances in Group II of Annex C from any State not party to this Protocol.

1 *qua.* Within one year of the date of entry into force of this paragraph, each Party shall ban the import of the controlled substance in Annex E from any State not party to this Protocol.

1 *quin.* As of 1 January 2004, each Party shall ban the import of the controlled substances in Group I of Annex C from any State not party to this Protocol.

1 *sex.* Within one year of the date of entry into force of this paragraph, each Party shall ban the import of the controlled substance in Group III of Annex C from any State not party to this Protocol.

1 *sept.* Upon entry into force of this paragraph, each Party shall ban the import of the controlled substances in Annex F from any State not Party to this Protocol.

2.   As of 1 January 1993, each Party shall ban the export of any controlled substances in Annex A to any State not party to this Protocol.

2 *bis.* Commencing one year after the date of entry into force of this paragraph, each Party shall ban the export of any controlled substances in Annex B to any State not party to this Protocol.

2 *ter.* Commencing one year after the date of entry into force of this paragraph, each Party shall ban the export of any controlled substances in Group II of Annex C to any State not party to this Protocol.

2 *qua.* Commencing one year of the date of entry into force of this paragraph, each Party shall ban the export of the controlled substance in Annex E to any State not party to this Protocol.

2 *quin.* As of 1 January 2004, each Party shall ban the export of the controlled substances in Group I of Annex C to any State not party to this Protocol.

2 *sex.* Within one year of the date of entry into force of this paragraph, each Party shall ban the export of the controlled substance in Group III of Annex C to any State not party to this Protocol.

2 *sept.* Upon entry into force of this paragraph, each Party shall ban the export of the controlled substances in Annex F to any State not Party to this Protocol.

3.   By 1 January 1992, the Parties shall, following the procedures in Article 10 of the Convention, elaborate in an annex a list of products containing controlled substances in Annex A. Parties that have not objected to the annex in accordance

with those procedures shall ban, within one year of the annex having become effective, the import of those products from any State not party to this Protocol.

3 *bis.* Within three years of the date of the entry into force of this paragraph, the Parties shall, following the procedures in Article 10 of the Convention, elaborate in an annex a list of products containing controlled substances in Annex B. Parties that have not objected to the annex in accordance with those procedures shall ban, within one year of the annex having become effective, the import of those products from any State not party to this Protocol.

3 *ter.* Within three years of the date of entry into force of this paragraph, the Parties shall, following the procedures in Article 10 of the Convention, elaborate in an annex a list of products containing controlled substances in Group II of Annex C. Parties that have not objected to the annex in accordance with those procedures shall ban, within one year of the annex having become effective, the import of those products from any State not party to this Protocol.

4. By 1 January 1994, the Parties shall determine the feasibility of banning or restricting, from States not party to this Protocol, the import of products produced with, but not containing, controlled substances in Annex A. If determined feasible, the Parties shall, following the procedures in Article 10 of the Convention, elaborate in an annex a list of such products. Parties that have not objected to the annex in accordance with those procedures shall ban or restrict, within one year of the annex having become effective, the import of those products from any State not party to this Protocol.

4 *bis.* Within five years of the date of the entry into force of this paragraph, the Parties shall determine the feasibility of banning or restricting, from States not party to this Protocol, the import of products produced with, but not containing, controlled substances in Annex B. If determined feasible, the Parties shall, following the procedures in Article 10 of the Convention, elaborate in an annex a list of such products. Parties that have not objected to the annex in accordance with those procedures shall ban or restrict, within one year of the annex having become effective, the import of those products from any State not party to this Protocol.

4 *ter.* Within five years of the date of entry into force of this paragraph, the Parties shall determine the feasibility of banning or restricting, from States not party to this Protocol, the import of products produced with, but not containing, controlled substances in Group II of Annex C. If determined feasible, the Parties shall, following the procedures in Article 10 of the Convention, elaborate in an annex a list of such products. Parties that have not objected to the annex in accordance with those procedures shall ban or restrict, within one year of the annex having become effective, the import of those products from any State not party to this Protocol.

MONTREAL PROTOCOL ON SUBSTANCES THAT DEPLETE THE OZONE LAYER   377

5.   Each Party undertakes to the fullest practicable extent to discourage the export to any State not party to this Protocol of technology for producing and for utilizing controlled substances in Annexes A, B, C, E and F.

6.   Each Party shall refrain from providing new subsidies, aid, credits, guarantees or insurance programmes for the export to States not party to this Protocol of products, equipment, plants or technology that would facilitate the production of controlled substances in Annexes A, B, C, E and F.

7.   Paragraphs 5 and 6 shall not apply to products, equipment, plants or technology that improve the containment, recovery, recycling or destruction of controlled substances, promote the development of alternative substances, or otherwise contribute to the reduction of emissions of controlled substances in Annexes A, B, C, E and F.

8.   Notwithstanding the provisions of this Article, imports and exports referred to in paragraphs 1 to 4 ter of this Article may be permitted from, or to, any State not party to this Protocol, if that State is determined, by a meeting of the Parties, to be in full compliance with Article 2, Articles 2A to 2J and this Article, and have submitted data to that effect as specified in Article 7.

9.   For the purposes of this Article, the term "State not party to this Protocol" shall include, with respect to a particular controlled substance, a State or regional economic integration organization that has not agreed to be bound by the control measures in effect for that substance.

10. By 1 January 1996, the Parties shall consider whether to amend this Protocol in order to extend the measures in this Article to trade in controlled substances in Group I of Annex C and in Annex E with States not party to the Protocol.

Article 4A: Control of Trade with Parties

1.   Where, after the phase-out date applicable to it for a controlled substance, a Party is unable, despite having taken all practicable steps to comply with its obligation under the Protocol, to cease production of that substance for domestic consumption, other than for uses agreed by the Parties to be essential, it shall ban the export of used, recycled and reclaimed quantities of that substance, other than for the purpose of destruction.

2.   Paragraph 1 of this Article shall apply without prejudice to the operation of Article 11 of the Convention and the non-compliance procedure developed under Article 8 of the Protocol.

Article 4B: Licensing

1.   Each Party shall, by 1 January 2000 or within three months of the date of entry into force of this Article for it, whichever is the later, establish and implement a system for licensing the import and export of new, used, recycled and reclaimed controlled substances in Annexes A, B, C and E.

2. Notwithstanding paragraph 1 of this Article, any Party operating under paragraph 1 of Article 5 which decides it is not in a position to establish and implement a system for licensing the import and export of controlled substances in Annexes C and E, may delay taking those actions until 1 January 2005 and 1 January 2002, respectively.

2 *bis*. Each Party shall, by 1 January 2019 or within three months of the date of entry into force of this paragraph for it, whichever is later, establish and implement a system for licensing the import and export of new, used, recycled and reclaimed controlled substances in Annex F. Any Party operating under paragraph 1 of Article 5 that decides it is not in a position to establish and implement such a system by 1 January 2019 may delay taking those actions until 1 January 2021.

3. Each Party shall, within three months of the date of introducing its licensing system, report to the Secretariat on the establishment and operation of that system.

4. The Secretariat shall periodically prepare and circulate to all Parties a list of the Parties that have reported to it on their licensing systems and shall forward this information to the Implementation Committee for consideration and appropriate recommendations to the Parties.

Article 5: Special Situation of Developing Countries

1. Any Party that is a developing country and whose annual calculated level of consumption of the controlled substances in Annex A is less than 0.3 kilograms per capita on the date of the entry into force of the Protocol for it, or any time thereafter until 1 January 1999, shall, in order to meet its basic domestic needs, be entitled to delay for ten years its compliance with the control measures set out in Articles 2A to 2E, provided that any further amendments to the adjustments or Amendment adopted at the Second Meeting of the Parties in London, 29 June 1990, shall apply to the Parties operating under this paragraph after the review provided for in paragraph 8 of this Article has taken place and shall be based on the conclusions of that review.

1 *bis*. The Parties shall, taking into account the review referred to in paragraph 8 of this Article, the assessments made pursuant to Article 6 and any other relevant information, decide by 1 January 1996, through the procedure set forth in paragraph 9 of Article 2:

    (a) With respect to paragraphs 1 to 6 of Article 2F, what base year, initial levels, control schedules and phase-out date for consumption of the controlled substances in Group I of Annex C will apply to Parties operating under paragraph 1 of this Article;

    (b) With respect to Article 2G, what phase-out date for production and consumption of the controlled substances in Group II of Annex C will apply to Parties operating under paragraph 1 of this Article; and

MONTREAL PROTOCOL ON SUBSTANCES THAT DEPLETE THE OZONE LAYER   379

(c)   With respect to Article 2H, what base year, initial levels and control schedules for consumption and production of the controlled substance in
Annex E will apply to Parties operating under paragraph 1 of this Article.

2.   However, any Party operating under paragraph 1 of this Article shall exceed neither an annual calculated level of consumption of the controlled substances in
Annex A of 0.3 kilograms per capita nor an annual calculated level of consumption of controlled substances of Annex B of 0.2 kilograms per capita.

3.   When implementing the control measures set out in Articles 2A to 2E, any Party
operating under paragraph 1 of this Article shall be entitled to use:

(a)   For controlled substances under Annex A, either the average of its annual
calculated level of consumption for the period 1995 to 1997 inclusive or
a calculated level of consumption of 0.3 kilograms per capita, whichever
is the lower, as the basis for determining its compliance with the control
measures relating to consumption.

(b)   For controlled substances under Annex B, the average of its annual calculated level of consumption for the period 1998 to 2000 inclusive or a calculated level of consumption of 0.2 kilograms per capita, whichever is the
lower, as the basis for determining its compliance with the control measures relating to consumption.

(c)   For controlled substances under Annex A, either the average of its annual
calculated level of production for the period 1995 to 1997 inclusive or a
calculated level of production of 0.3 kilograms per capita, whichever is the
lower, as the basis for determining its compliance with the control measures relating to production.

(d)   For controlled substances under Annex B, either the average of its annual
calculated level of production for the period 1998 to 2000 inclusive or a
calculated level of production of 0.2 kilograms per capita, whichever is the
lower, as the basis for determining its compliance with the control measures relating to production.

4.   If a Party operating under paragraph 1 of this Article, at any time before the control measures obligations in Articles 2A to 2J become applicable to it, finds itself
unable to obtain an adequate supply of controlled substances, it may notify this
to the Secretariat. The Secretariat shall forthwith transmit a copy of such notification to the Parties, which shall consider the matter at their next Meeting, and
decide upon appropriate action to be taken.

5.   Developing the capacity to fulfil the obligations of the Parties operating under
paragraph 1 of this Article to comply with the control measures set out in Articles 2A to 2E and Articles 2I and 2J, and with any control measures in Articles 2F
to 2H that are decided pursuant to paragraph 1 *bis* of this Article, and their implementation by those same Parties will depend upon the effective implementation

of the financial co-operation as provided by Article 10 and the transfer of technology as provided by Article 10A.

6. Any Party operating under paragraph 1 of this Article may, at any time, notify the Secretariat in writing that, having taken all practicable steps it is unable to implement any or all of the obligations laid down in Articles 2A to 2E and Articles 2I and 2J, or any or all obligations in Articles 2F to 2H that are decided pursuant to paragraph 1 *bis* of this Article, due to the inadequate implementation of Articles 10 and 10A. The Secretariat shall forthwith transmit a copy of the notification to the Parties, which shall consider the matter at their next Meeting, giving due recognition to paragraph 5 of this Article and shall decide upon appropriate action to be taken.

7. During the period between notification and the Meeting of the Parties at which the appropriate action referred to in paragraph 6 above is to be decided, or for a further period if the Meeting of the Parties so decides, the non-compliance procedures referred to in Article 8 shall not be invoked against the notifying Party.

8. A Meeting of the Parties shall review, not later than 1995, the situation of the Parties operating under paragraph 1 of this Article, including the effective implementation of financial co-operation and transfer of technology to them, and adopt such revisions that may be deemed necessary regarding the schedule of control measures applicable to those Parties.

8 *bis.* Based on the conclusions of the review referred to in paragraph 8 above:

    (a)   With respect to the controlled substances in Annex A, a Party operating under paragraph 1 of this Article shall, in order to meet its basic domestic needs, be entitled to delay for ten years its compliance with the control measures adopted by the Second Meeting of the Parties in London, 29 June 1990, and reference by the Protocol to Articles 2A and 2B shall be read accordingly;

    (b)   With respect to the controlled substances in Annex B, a Party operating under paragraph 1 of this Article shall, in order to meet its basic domestic needs, be entitled to delay for ten years its compliance with the control measures adopted by the Second Meeting of the Parties in London, 29 June 1990, and reference by the Protocol to Articles 2C to 2E shall be read accordingly.

8 *ter.* Pursuant to paragraph 1 *bis* above:

    (a)   Each Party operating under paragraph 1 of this Article shall ensure that for the twelve-month period commencing on 1 January 2013, and in each twelve-month period thereafter, its calculated level of consumption of the controlled substances in Group I of Annex C does not exceed, annually, the average of its calculated levels of consumption in 2009 and 2010. Each Party operating under paragraph 1 of this Article shall ensure that for the twelve-month period commencing on 1 January 2013 and in each twelve-month period thereafter, its calculated level of production of the controlled substances in Group I of Annex C does not exceed, annually, the average of its calculated levels of production in 2009 and 2010;

(b) Each Party operating under paragraph 1 of this Article shall ensure that for the twelve-month period commencing on 1 January 2015, and in each twelve-month period thereafter, its calculated level of consumption of the controlled substances in Group I of Annex C does not exceed, annually, ninety per cent of the average of its calculated levels of consumption in 2009 and 2010. Each such Party producing one or more of these substances shall, for the same periods, ensure that its calculated level of production of the controlled substances in Group I of Annex C does not exceed, annually, ninety per cent of the average of its calculated levels of production in 2009 and 2010;

(c) Each Party operating under paragraph 1 of this Article shall ensure that for the twelve-month period commencing on 1 January 2020, and in each twelve-month period thereafter, its calculated level of consumption of the controlled substances in Group I of Annex C does not exceed, annually, sixtyfive per cent of the average of its calculated levels of consumption in 2009 and 2010. Each such Party producing one or more of these substances shall, for the same periods, ensure that its calculated level of production of the controlled substances in Group I of Annex C does not exceed, annually, sixty-five per cent of the average of its calculated levels of production in 2009 and 2010;

(d) Each Party operating under paragraph 1 of this Article shall ensure that for the twelve-month period commencing on 1 January 2025, and in each twelve-month period thereafter, its calculated level of consumption of the controlled substances in Group I of Annex C does not exceed, annually, thirtytwo point five per cent of the average of its calculated levels of consumption in 2009 and 2010. Each such Party producing one or more of these substances shall, for the same periods, ensure that its calculated level of production of the controlled substances in Group I of Annex C does not exceed, annually, thirty-two point five per cent of the average of its calculated levels of production in 2009 and 2010;

(e) Each Party operating under paragraph 1 of this Article shall ensure that for the twelve-month period commencing on 1 January 2030, and in each twelve-month period thereafter, its calculated level of consumption of the controlled substances in Group I of Annex C does not exceed zero. Each such Party producing one or more of these substances shall, for the same periods, ensure that its calculated level of production of the controlled substances in Group I of Annex C does not exceed zero. However:

(i) Each such Party may exceed that limit on consumption in any such twelve-month period so long as the sum of its calculated levels of consumption over the ten-year period from 1 January 2030 to 1 January 2040, divided by ten, does not exceed two point five per cent of the average of its calculated levels of consumption in 2009 and 2010, and provided that such consumption shall be restricted to the servicing of refrigeration and air-conditioning equipment existing on 1 January 2030;

(ii) Each such Party may exceed that limit on production in any such twelve-month period so long as the sum of its calculated levels of production over the ten-year period from 1 January 2030 to 1 January 2040, divided by ten, does not exceed two point five per cent of the average of its calculated levels of production in 2009 and 2010, and provided that such production shall be restricted to the servicing of refrigeration and air-conditioning equipment existing on 1 January 2030.

(f) Each Party operating under paragraph 1 of this Article shall comply with Article 2G;

(g) With regard to the controlled substance contained in Annex E:

(i) As of 1 January 2002 each Party operating under paragraph 1 of this Article shall comply with the control measures set out in paragraph 1 of Article 2H and, as the basis for its compliance with these control measures, it shall use the average of its annual calculated level of consumption and production, respectively, for the period of 1995 to 1998 inclusive;

(ii) Each Party operating under paragraph 1 of this Article shall ensure that for the twelve-month period commencing on 1 January 2005, and in each twelve-month period thereafter, its calculated levels of consumption and production of the controlled substance in Annex E do not exceed, annually, eighty per cent of the average of its annual calculated levels of consumption and production, respectively, for the period of 1995 to 1998 inclusive;

(iii) Each Party operating under paragraph 1 of this Article shall ensure that for the twelve-month period commencing on 1 January 2015 and in each twelve-month period thereafter, its calculated levels of consumption and production of the controlled substance in Annex E do not exceed zero. This paragraph will apply save to the extent that the Parties decide to permit the level of production or consumption that is necessary to satisfy uses agreed by them to be critical uses;

(iv) The calculated levels of consumption and production under this subparagraph shall not include the amounts used by the Party for quarantine and pre-shipment applications.

8 qua

(a) Each Party operating under paragraph 1 of this Article, subject to any adjustments made to the control measures in Article 2J in accordance with paragraph 9 of Article 2, shall be entitled to delay its compliance with the control measures set out in subparagraphs (a) to (e) of paragraph 1 of Article 2J and subparagraphs (a) to (e) of paragraph 3 of Article 2J and modify those measures as follows:

(i)   2024 to 2028: 100 per cent

(ii) 2029 to 2034: 90 per cent

(iii) 2035 to 2039: 70 per cent

(iv) 2040 to 2044: 50 per cent

(v)   2045 and thereafter: 20 per cent

(b) Notwithstanding subparagraph (a) above, the Parties may decide that a Party operating under paragraph 1 of this Article, subject to any adjustments made to the control measures in Article 2J in accordance with paragraph 9 of Article 2, shall be entitled to delay its compliance with the control measures set out in subparagraphs (a) to (e) of paragraph 1 of Article 2J and subparagraphs (a) to (e) of paragraph 3 of Article 2J and modify those measures as follows:

(i)   2028 to 2031: 100 per cent

(ii) 2032 to 2036: 90 per cent

(iii) 2037 to 2041: 80 per cent

(iv) 2042 to 2046: 70 per cent

(v)   2047 and thereafter: 15 per cent

(c) Each Party operating under paragraph 1 of this Article, for the purposes of calculating its consumption baseline under Article 2J, shall be entitled to use the average of its calculated levels of consumption of Annex F controlled substances for the years 2020, 2021 and 2022, plus sixty-five per cent of its baseline consumption of Annex C, Group I, controlled substances as set out in paragraph 8 *ter* of this Article.

(d) Notwithstanding subparagraph (c) above, the Parties may decide that a Party operating under paragraph 1 of this Article, for the purposes of calculating its consumption baseline under Article 2J, shall be entitled to use the average of its calculated levels of consumption of Annex F controlled substances for the years 2024, 2025 and 2026, plus sixty-five per cent of its baseline consumption of Annex C, Group I, controlled substances as set out in paragraph 8 *ter* of this Article.

(e) Each Party operating under paragraph 1 of this Article and producing the controlled substances in Annex F, for the purposes of calculating its production baseline under Article 2J, shall be entitled to use the average of its calculated levels of production of Annex F controlled substances for the years 2020, 2021 and 2022, plus sixty-five per cent of its baseline production of Annex C, Group I, controlled substances as set out in paragraph 8 *ter* of this Article.

(f) Notwithstanding subparagraph (e) above, the Parties may decide that a Party operating under paragraph 1 of this Article and producing the controlled substances in Annex F, for the purposes of calculating its production baseline under Article 2J, shall be entitled to use the average of its calculated levels of production of Annex F controlled substances for the years 2024, 2025 and 2026, plus sixty-five per cent of its baseline production of Annex C, Group I, controlled substances as set out in paragraph 8 *ter* of this Article.

(g) Subparagraphs (a) to (f) of this paragraph will apply to calculated levels of production and consumption save to the extent that a high-ambient-temperature exemption applies based on criteria decided by the Parties.

9. Decisions of the Parties referred to in paragraph 4, 6 and 7 of this Article shall be taken according to the same procedure applied to decision-making under Article 10.

Article 6: Assessment and Review of Control Measures

Beginning in 1990, and at least every four years thereafter, the Parties shall assess the control measures provided for in Article 2 and Articles 2A to 2J on the basis of available scientific, environmental, technical and economic information. At least one year before each assessment, the Parties shall convene appropriate panels of experts qualified in the fields mentioned and determine the composition and terms of reference of any such panels. Within one year of being convened, the panels will report their conclusions, through the Secretariat, to the Parties.

Article 7: Reporting of Data

1. Each Party shall provide to the Secretariat, within three months of becoming a Party, statistical data on its production, imports and exports of each of the controlled substances in Annex A for the year 1986, or the best possible estimates of such data where actual data are not available.

2. Each Party shall provide to the Secretariat statistical data on its production, imports and exports of each of the controlled substances
   - in Annex B and Groups I and II of Annex C for the year 1989;
   - in Annex E, for the year 1991,
   - in Annex F, for the years 2011 to 2013, except that Parties operating under paragraph 1 of Article 5 shall provide such data for the years 2020 to 2022, but those Parties operating under paragraph 1 of Article 5 to which

subparagraphs (d) and (f) of paragraph 8 *qua* of Article 5 applies shall provide such data for the years 2024 to 2026;

or the best possible estimates of such data where actual data are not available, not later than three months after the date when the provisions set out in the Protocol with regard to the substances in Annexes B, C, E and F respectively enter into force for that Party.

3. Each Party shall provide to the Secretariat statistical data on its annual production (as defined in paragraph 5 of Article 1) of each of the controlled substances listed in Annexes A, B, C, E and F and, separately, for each substance,

 – Amounts used for feedstocks,
 – Amounts destroyed by technologies approved by the Parties, and
 – Imports from and exports to Parties and non-Parties respectively,

for the year during which provisions concerning the substances in Annexes A, B, C, E and F respectively entered into force for that Party and for each year thereafter. Each Party shall provide to the Secretariat statistical data on the annual amount of the controlled substance listed in Annex E used for quarantine and pre-shipment applications. Data shall be forwarded not later than nine months after the end of the year to which the data relate.

3 *bis*. Each Party shall provide to the Secretariat separate statistical data of its annual imports and exports of each of the controlled substances listed in Group II of Annex A and Group I of Annex C that have been recycled.

3 *ter*. Each Party shall provide to the Secretariat statistical data on its annual emissions of Annex F, Group II, controlled substances per facility in accordance with paragraph 1 (d) of Article 3 of the Protocol.

4. For Parties operating under the provisions of paragraph 8 (a) of Article 2, the requirements in paragraphs 1, 2, 3 and 3 bis of this Article in respect of statistical data on production, imports and exports shall be satisfied if the regional economic integration organization concerned provides data on production, imports and exports between the organization and States that are not members of that organization.

Article 8: Non-compliance

The Parties, at their first meeting, shall consider and approve procedures and institutional mechanisms for determining non-compliance with the provisions of this Protocol and for treatment of Parties found to be in noncompliance.

Article 9: Research, Development, Public Awareness and Exchange of Information

1. The Parties shall co-operate, consistent with their national laws, regulations and practices and taking into account in particular the needs of developing

countries, in promoting, directly or through competent international bodies, research, development and exchange of information on:

(a) best technologies for improving the containment, recovery, recycling, or destruction of controlled substances or otherwise reducing their emissions;

(b) possible alternatives to controlled substances, to products containing such substances, and to products manufactured with them; and

(c) costs and benefits of relevant control strategies.

2. The Parties, individually, jointly or through competent international bodies, shall co-operate in promoting public awareness of the environmental effects of the emissions of controlled substances and other substances that deplete the ozone layer.

3. Within two years of the entry into force of this Protocol and every two years thereafter, each Party shall submit to the Secretariat a summary of the activities it has conducted pursuant to this Article.

Article 10: Financial Mechanism

1. The Parties shall establish a mechanism for the purposes of providing financial and technical cooperation, including the transfer of technologies, to Parties operating under paragraph 1 of Article 5 of this Protocol to enable their compliance with the control measures set out in Articles 2A to 2E, Article 2I and Article 2J, and any control measures in Articles 2F to 2H that are decided pursuant to paragraph 1 *bis* of Article 5 of the Protocol. The mechanism, contributions to which shall be additional to other financial transfers to Parties operating under that paragraph, shall meet all agreed incremental costs of such Parties in order to enable their compliance with the control measures of the Protocol. An indicative list of the categories of incremental costs shall be decided by the meeting of the Parties. Where a Party operating under paragraph 1 of Article 5 chooses to avail itself of funding from any other financial mechanism that could result in meeting any part of its agreed incremental costs, that part shall not be met by the financial mechanism under Article 10 of this Protocol.

2. The mechanism established under paragraph 1 shall include a Multilateral Fund. It may also include other means of multilateral, regional and bilateral co-operation.

3. The Multilateral Fund shall:

(a) Meet, on a grant or concessional basis as appropriate, and according to criteria to be decided upon by the Parties, the agreed incremental costs;

(b) Finance clearing-house functions to:

(i) Assist Parties operating under paragraph 1 of Article 5, through country specific studies and other technical co-operation, to identify their needs for co-operation;

MONTREAL PROTOCOL ON SUBSTANCES THAT DEPLETE THE OZONE LAYER   387

(ii)   Facilitate technical co-operation to meet these identified needs;

(iii) Distribute, as provided for in Article 9, information and relevant materials, and hold workshops, training sessions, and other related activities, for the benefit of Parties that are developing countries; and

(iv)   Facilitate and monitor other multilateral, regional and bilateral co-operation available to Parties that are developing countries;

(c)   Finance the secretarial services of the Multilateral Fund and related support costs.

4.   The Multilateral Fund shall operate under the authority of the Parties who shall decide on its overall policies.

5.   The Parties shall establish an Executive Committee to develop and monitor the implementation of specific operational policies, guidelines and administrative arrangements, including the disbursement of resources, for the purpose of achieving the objectives of the Multilateral Fund. The Executive Committee shall discharge its tasks and responsibilities, specified in its terms of reference as agreed by the Parties, with the co-operation and assistance of the International Bank for Reconstruction and Development (World Bank), the United Nations Environment Programme, the United Nations Development Programme or other appropriate agencies depending on their respective areas of expertise. The members of the Executive Committee, which shall be selected on the basis of a balanced representation of the Parties operating under paragraph 1 of Article 5 and of the Parties not so operating, shall be endorsed by the Parties.

6.   The Multilateral Fund shall be financed by contributions from Parties not operating under paragraph 1 of Article 5 in convertible currency or, in certain circumstances, in kind and/or in national currency, on the basis of the United Nations scale of assessments. Contributions by other Parties shall be encouraged. Bilateral and, in particular cases agreed by a decision of the Parties, regional co-operation may, up to a percentage and consistent with any criteria to be specified by decision of the Parties, be considered as a contribution to the Multilateral Fund, provided that such co-operation, as a minimum:

(a)   Strictly relates to compliance with the provisions of this Protocol;

(b)   Provides additional resources; and

(c)   Meets agreed incremental costs.

7.   The Parties shall decide upon the programme budget of the Multilateral Fund for each fiscal period and upon the percentage of contributions of the individual Parties thereto.

8.   Resources under the Multilateral Fund shall be disbursed with the concurrence of the beneficiary Party.

9.   Decisions by the Parties under this Article shall be taken by consensus whenever possible. If all efforts at consensus have been exhausted and no agreement

reached, decisions shall be adopted by a two-thirds majority vote of the Parties present and voting, representing a majority of the Parties operating under paragraph 1 of Article 5 present and voting and a majority of the Parties not so operating present and voting.

10. The financial mechanism set out in this Article is without prejudice to any future arrangements that may be developed with respect to other environmental issues.

Article 10A: Transfer of Technology

Each Party shall take every practicable step, consistent with the programmes supported by the financial mechanism, to ensure:

(a) that the best available, environmentally safe substitutes and related technologies are expeditiously transferred to Parties operating under paragraph 1 of Article 5; and

(b) that the transfers referred to in subparagraph (a) occur under fair and most favourable conditions.

Article 11: Meetings of the Parties

1. The Parties shall hold meetings at regular intervals. The Secretariat shall convene the first meeting of the Parties not later than one year after the date of the entry into force of this Protocol and in conjunction with a meeting of the Conference of the Parties to the Convention, if a meeting of the latter is scheduled within that period.

2. Subsequent ordinary meetings of the parties shall be held, unless the Parties otherwise decide, in conjunction with meetings of the Conference of the Parties to the Convention. Extraordinary meetings of the Parties shall be held at such other times as may be deemed necessary by a meeting of the Parties, or at the written request of any Party, provided that within six months of such a request being communicated to them by the Secretariat, it is supported by at least one third of the Parties.

3. The Parties, at their first meeting, shall:

(a) adopt by consensus rules of procedure for their meetings;

(b) adopt by consensus the financial rules referred to in paragraph 2 of Article 13

(c) establish the panels and determine the terms of reference referred to in Article 6;

(d) consider and approve the procedures and institutional mechanisms specified in Article 8; and

(e) begin preparation of workplans pursuant to paragraph 3 of Article 10.

The Article 10 in question is that of the original Protocol adopted in 1987.]

4.   The functions of the meetings of the Parties shall be to:

   (a)   review the implementation of this Protocol;

   (b)   decide on any adjustments or reductions referred to in paragraph 9 of Article 2;

   (c)   decide on any addition to, insertion in or removal from any annex of substances and on related control measures in accordance with paragraph 10 of Article 2;

   (d)   establish, where necessary, guidelines or procedures for reporting of information as provided for in Article 7 and paragraph 3 of Article 9;

   (e)   review requests for technical assistance submitted pursuant to paragraph 2 of Article 10;

   (f)   review reports prepared by the secretariat pursuant to subparagraph (c) of Article 12;

   (g)   assess, in accordance with Article 6, the control measures;

   (h)   consider and adopt, as required, proposals for amendment of this Protocol or any annex and for any new annex;

   (i)   consider and adopt the budget for implementing this Protocol; and

   (j)   consider and undertake any additional action that may be required for the achievement of the purposes of this Protocol.

5.   The United Nations, its specialized agencies and the International Atomic Energy Agency, as well as any State not party to this Protocol, may be represented at meetings of the Parties as observers. Any body or agency, whether national or international, governmental or non-governmental, qualified in fields relating to the protection of the ozone layer which has informed the secretariat of its wish to be represented at a meeting of the Parties as an observer may be admitted unless at least one third of the Parties present object. The admission and participation of observers shall be subject to the rules of procedure adopted by the Parties.

Article 12: Secretariat

For the purposes of this Protocol, the Secretariat shall:

   (a)   arrange for and service meetings of the Parties as provided for in Article 11;

   (b)   receive and make available, upon request by a Party, data provided pursuant to Article 7;

   (c)   prepare and distribute regularly to the Parties reports based on information received pursuant to Articles 7 and 9;

   (d)   notify the Parties of any request for technical assistance received pursuant to Article 10 so as to facilitate the provision of such assistance;

(e) encourage non-Parties to attend the meetings of the Parties as observers and to act in accordance with the provisions of this Protocol;

(f) provide, as appropriate, the information and requests referred to in sub-paragraphs (c) and (d) to such non-party observers; and

(g) perform such other functions for the achievement of the purposes of this Protocol as may be assigned to it by the Parties.

Article 13: Financial Provisions

1. The funds required for the operation of this Protocol, including those for the functioning of the Secretariat related to this Protocol, shall be charged exclusively against contributions from the Parties.

2. The Parties, at their first meeting, shall adopt by consensus financial rules for the operation of this Protocol.

Article 14: Relationship of this Protocol to the Convention

Except as otherwise provided in this Protocol, the provisions of the Convention relating to its protocols shall apply to this Protocol.

Article 15: Signature

This Protocol shall be open for signature by States and by regional economic integration organizations in Montreal on 16 September 1987, in Ottawa from 17 September 1987 to 16 January 1988, and at United Nations Headquarters in New York from 17 January 1988 to 15 September 1988.

Article 16: Entry into Force

1. This Protocol shall enter into force on 1 January 1989, provided that at least eleven instruments of ratification, acceptance, approval of the Protocol or accession thereto have been deposited by States or regional economic integration organizations representing at least two-thirds of 1986 estimated global consumption of the controlled substances, and the provisions of paragraph 1 of Article 17 of the Convention have been fulfilled. In the event that these conditions have not been fulfilled by that date, the Protocol shall enter into force on the ninetieth day following the date on which the conditions have been fulfilled.

2. For the purposes of paragraph 1, any such instrument deposited by a regional economic integration organization shall not be counted as additional to those deposited by member States of such organization.

3. After the entry into force of this Protocol, any State or regional economic integration organization shall become a Party to it on the ninetieth day following the date of deposit of its instrument of ratification, acceptance, approval or accession.

Article 17: Parties Joining after Entry into Force

Subject to Article 5, any State or regional economic integration organization which becomes a Party to this Protocol after the date of its entry into force, shall fulfil forthwith the sum of the obligations under Article 2, as well as under Articles 2A to 2J and Article 4, that apply at that date to the States and regional economic integration organizations that became Parties on the date the Protocol entered into force.

Article 18: Reservations

No reservations may be made to this Protocol.

Article 19: Withdrawal

Any Party may withdraw from this Protocol by giving written notification to the Depositary at any time after four years of assuming the obligations specified in paragraph 1 of Article 2A. Any such withdrawal shall take effect upon expiry of one year after the date of its receipt by the Depositary, or on such later date as may be specified in the notification of the withdrawal.

Article 20: Authentic Texts

The original of this Protocol, of which the Arabic, Chinese, English, French, Russian and Spanish texts are equally authentic, shall be deposited with the Secretary-General of the United Nations.

IN WITNESS WHEREOF THE UNDERSIGNED, BEING DULY AUTHORIZED TO THAT EFFECT, HAVE SIGNED THIS PROTOCOL.

DONE AT MONTREAL THIS SIXTEENTH DAY OF SEPTEMBER, ONE THOUSAND NINE HUNDRED AND EIGHTY SEVEN.

APPENDIX II

ANNEX A: Controlled substances

Group	Substance	Ozone-Depleting Potential*	100-Year Global Warming Potential
Group I			
CFCl₃	(CFC-11)	1.0	4,750
CF₂Cl₂	(CFC-12)	1.0	10,900
C₂F₃Cl₃	(CFC-113)	0.8	6,130
C₂F₄Cl₂	(CFC-114)	1.0	10,000
C₂F₅Cl	(CFC-115)	0.6	7,370
Group II			
CF₂BrCl	(halon-1211)	3.0	
CF₃Br	(halon-1301)	10.0	
C₂F₄Br₂	(halon-2402)	6.0	

* These ozone depleting potentials are estimates based on existing knowledge and will be reviewed and revised periodically.

ANNEX B: Controlled substances

Group	Substance	Ozone-Depleting Potential
Group I		
CF₃Cl	(CFC-13)	1.0
C₂FCl₅	(CFC-111)	1.0
C₂F₂Cl₄	(CFC-112)	1.0
C₃FCl₇	(CFC-211)	1.0
C₃F₂Cl₆	(CFC-212)	1.0
C₃F₃Cl₅	(CFC-213)	1.0
C₃F₄Cl₄	(CFC-214)	1.0
C₃F₅Cl₃	(CFC-215)	1.0
C₃F₆Cl₂	(CFC-216)	1.0
C₃F₇Cl	(CFC-217)	1.0
Group II		
CCl₄	carbon tetrachloride	1.1
Group III		
C₂H₃Cl₃*	1,1,1-trichloroethane* (methyl chloroform)	0.1

MONTREAL PROTOCOL ON SUBSTANCES THAT DEPLETE THE OZONE LAYER   393

ANNEX C: Controlled substances

Group	Substance	Number of isomers	Ozone- Depleting Potential*	100-Year Global Warming Potential***
Group I				
$CHFCl_2$	(HCFC-21)**	1	0.04	151
CHF_2Cl	(HCFC-22)**	1	0.055	1810
CH_2FCl	(HCFC-31)	1	0.02	
C_2HFCl_4	(HCFC-121)	2	0.01–0.04	
$C_2HF_2Cl_3$	(HCFC-122)	3	0.02–0.08	
$C_2HF_3Cl_2$	(HCFC-123)	3	0.02–0.06	77
$CHCl_2CF_3$	(HCFC-123)**	–	0.02	
C_2HF_4Cl	(HCFC-124)	2	0.02–0.04	609
$CHFClCF_3$	(HCFC-124)**	–	0.022	
$C_2H_2FCl_3$	(HCFC-131)	3	0.007–0.05	
$C_2H_2F_2Cl_2$	(HCFC-132)	4	0.008–0.05	
$C_2H_2F_3Cl$	(HCFC-133)	3	0.02–0.06	
$C_2H_3FCl_2$	(HCFC-141)	3	0.005–0.07	
CH_3CFCl_2	(HCFC-141b)**	–	0.11	725
$C_2H_3F_2Cl$	(HCFC-142)	3	0.008–0.07	
CH_3CF_2Cl	(HCFC-142b)**	–	0.065	2310
C_2H_4FCl	(HCFC-151)	2	0.003–0.005	
C_3HFCl_6	(HCFC-221)	5	0.015–0.07	
$C_3HF_2Cl_5$	(HCFC-222)	9	0.01–0.09	
$C_3HF_3Cl_4$	(HCFC-223)	12	0.01–0.08	
$C_3HF_4Cl_3$	(HCFC-224)	12	0.01–0.09	
$C_3HF_5Cl_2$	(HCFC-225)	9	0.02–0.07	
$CF_3CF_2CHCl_2$	(HCFC-225ca)**	–	0.025	122
CF_2ClCF_2CHClF	(HCFC-225cb)**	–	0.033	595
C_3HF_6Cl	(HCFC-226)	5	0.02–0.10	
$C_3H_2FCl_5$	(HCFC-231)	9	0.05–0.09	
$C_3H_2F_2Cl_4$	(HCFC-232)	16	0.008–0.10	
$C_3H_2F_3Cl_3$	(HCFC-233)	18	0.007–0.23	
$C_3H_2F_4Cl_2$	(HCFC-234)	16	0.01–0.28	
$C_3H_2F_5Cl$	(HCFC-235)	9	0.03–0.52	
$C_3H_3FCl_4$	(HCFC-241)	12	0.004–0.09	
$C_3H_3F_2Cl_3$	(HCFC-242)	18	0.005–0.13	
$C_3H_3F_3Cl_2$	(HCFC-243)	18	0.007–0.12	
$C_3H_3F_4Cl$	(HCFC-244)	12	0.009–0.14	
$C_3H_4FCl_3$	(HCFC-251)	12	0.001–0.01	
$C_3H_4F_2Cl_2$	(HCFC-252)	16	0.005–0.04	
$C_3H_4F_3Cl$	(HCFC-253)	12	0.003–0.03	
$C_3H_5FCl_2$	(HCFC-261)	9	0.002–0.02	
$C_3H_5F_2Cl$	(HCFC-262)	9	0.002–0.02	
C_3H_6FCl	(HCFC-271)	5	0.001–0.03	

Group	Substance	Number of isomers	Ozone-Depleting Potential*
Group II			
$CHFBr_2$		1	1.00
CHF_2Br	(HBFC-22B1)	1	0.74
CH_2FBr		1	0.73
C_2HFBr_4		2	0.3–0.8
$C_2HF_2Br_3$		3	0.5–1.8
$C_2HF_3Br_2$		3	0.4–1.6
C_2HF_4Br		2	0.7–1.2
$C_2H_2FBr_3$		3	0.1–1.1
$C_2H_2F_2Br_2$		4	0.2–1.5
$C_2H_2F_3Br$		3	0.7–1.6
$C_2H_3FBr_2$		3	0.1–1.7
$C_2H_3F_2Br$		3	0.2–1.1
C_2H_4FBr		2	0.07–0.1
C_3HFBr_6		5	0.3–1.5
$C_3HF_2Br_5$		9	0.2–1.9
$C_3HF_3Br_4$		12	0.3–1.8
$C_3HF_4Br_3$		12	0.5–2.2
$C_3HF_5Br_2$		9	0.9–2.0
C_3HF_6Br		5	0.7–3.3
$C_3H_2FBr_5$		9	0.1–1.9
$C_3H_2F_2Br_4$		16	0.2–2.1
$C_3H_2F_3Br_3$		18	0.2–5.6
$C_3H_2F_4Br_2$		16	0.3–7.5
$C_3H_2F_5Br$		8	0.9–1.4
$C_3H_3FBr_4$		12	0.08–1.9
$C_3H_3F_2Br_3$		18	0.1–3.1
$C_3H_3F_3Br_2$		18	0.1–2.5
$C_3H_3F_4Br$		12	0.3–4.4
$C_3H_4FBr_3$		12	0.03–0.3
$C_3H_4F_2Br_2$		16	0.1–1.0
$C_3H_4F_3Br$		12	0.07–0.8
$C_3H_5FBr_2$		9	0.04–0.4
$C_3H_5F_2Br$		9	0.07–0.8
C_3H_6FBr		5	0.02–0.7
Group III			
CH_2BrCl	bromochloromethane	1	0.12

* Where a range of ODPs is indicated, the highest value in that range shall be used for the purposes of the Protocol. The ODPs listed as a single value have been determined from calculations based on laboratory measurements. Those listed as a range are based on estimates and are less certain. The range pertains to an isomeric group. The upper value is the estimate of the ODP of the isomer with the highest ODP, and the lower value is the estimate of the ODP of the isomer with the lowest ODP.

** Identifies the most commercially viable substances with ODP values listed against them to be used for the purposes of the Protocol.

*** For substances for which no GWP is indicated, the default value 0 applies until a GWP value is included by means of the procedure foreseen in paragraph 9 (a) (ii) of Article 2.

MONTREAL PROTOCOL ON SUBSTANCES THAT DEPLETE THE OZONE LAYER

ANNEX D*: A list of products** containing controlled substances specified in Annex A

Products	Customs code number
1. Automobile and truck air conditioning units (whether incorporated in vehicles or not)	....
2. Domestic and commercial refrigeration and air conditioning/heat pump equipment***	....
e.g. Refrigerators	....
Freezers	....
Dehumidifiers	....
Water coolers	....
Ice machines	....
Air conditioning and heat pump units	....
3. Aerosol products, except medical aerosols	....
4. Portable fire extinguisher	....
5. Insulation boards, panels and pipe covers	....
6. Pre-polymers	....

* This Annex was adopted by the Third Meeting of the Parties in Nairobi, 21 June 1991 as required by paragraph 3 of Article 4 of the Protocol.

** Though not when transported in consignments of personal or household effects or in similar non-commercial situations normally exempted from customs attention.

*** When containing controlled substances in Annex A as a refrigerant and/or in insulating material of the product.

ANNEX E: Controlled substances

Group	Substance	Ozone-Depleting Potential
Group I		
CH_3Br	methyl bromide	0.6

ANNEX F: Controlled substances

Group	Substance	100-Year Global Warming Potential
Group I		
CHF_2CHF_2	HFC-134	1,100
CH_2FCF_3	HFC-134a	1,430
CH_2FCHF_2	HFC-143	353
$CHF_2CH_2CF_3$	HFC-245fa	1,030
$CF_3CH_2CF_2CH_3$	HFC-365mfc	794
CF_3CHFCF_3	HFC-227ea	3,220
$CH_2FCF_2CF_3$	HFC-236cb	1,340
CHF_2CHFCF_3	HFC-236ea	1,370
$CF_3CH_2CF_3$	HFC-236fa	9,810
$CH_2FCF_2CHF_2$	HFC-245ca	693
$CF_3CHFCHFCF_2CF_3$	HFC-43-10mee	1,640
CH_2F_2	HFC-32	675
CHF_2CF_3	HFC-125	3,500
CH_3CF_3	HFC-143a	4,470
CH_3F	HFC-41	92
CH_2FCH_2F	HFC-152	53
CH_3CHF_2	HFC-152a	124
Group II		
CHF_3	HFC-23	14,800

APPENDIX III

Non-Compliance Procedure (1998)

The following procedure has been formulated pursuant to Article 8 of the Montreal Protocol. It shall apply without prejudice to the operation of the settlement of disputes procedure laid down in Article 11 of the Vienna Convention.

1. If one or more Parties have reservations regarding another Party's implementation of its obligations under the Protocol, those concerns may be addressed in writing to the Secretariat. Such a submission shall be supported by corroborating information.

2. The Secretariat shall, within two weeks of its receiving a submission, send a copy of that submission to the Party whose implementation of a particular provision of the Protocol is at issue. Any reply and information in support thereof are to be submitted to the Secretariat and to the Parties involved within three months of the date of the dispatch or such longer period as the circumstances of any particular case may require. If the Secretariat has not received a reply from the Party three months after sending it the original submission, the Secretariat shall send a reminder to the Party that it has yet to provide its reply. The Secretariat shall, as soon as the reply and information from the Party are available, but not later than six months after receiving the submission, transmit the submission, the reply and the information, if any, provided by the Parties to the Implementation Committee referred to in paragraph 5, which shall consider the matter as soon as practicable.

3. Where the Secretariat, during the course of preparing its report, becomes aware of possible noncompliance by any Party with its obligations under the Protocol, it may request the Party concerned to furnish necessary information about the matter. If there is no response from the Party concerned within three months or such longer period as the circumstances of the matter may require or the matter is not resolved through administrative action or through diplomatic contacts, the Secretariat shall include the matter in its report to the Meeting of the Parties pursuant to Article 12 (c) of the Protocol and inform the Implementation Committee, which shall consider the matter as soon as practicable.

4. Where a Party concludes that, despite having made its best, bona fide efforts, it is unable to comply fully with its obligations under the Protocol, it may address to the Secretariat a submission in writing, explaining, in particular, the specific circumstances that it considers to be the cause of its noncompliance. The

Secretariat shall transmit such submission to the Implementation Committee which shall consider it as soon as practicable.

5. An Implementation Committee is hereby established. It shall consist of 10 Parties elected by the Meeting of the Parties for two years, based on equitable geographical distribution. Each Party so elected to the Committee shall be requested to notify the Secretariat, within two months of its election, of who is to represent it and shall endeavour to ensure that such representation remains throughout the entire term of office. Outgoing Parties may be re-elected for one immediate consecutive term. A Party that has completed a second consecutive two-year term as a Committee member shall be eligible for election again only after an absence of one year from the Committee. The Committee shall elect its own President and Vice-President. Each shall serve for one year at a time. The Vice-President shall, in addition, serve as the rapporteur of the Committee.

6. The Implementation Committee shall, unless it decides otherwise, meet twice a year. The Secretariat shall arrange for and service its meetings.

7. The functions of the Implementation Committee shall be:

    (a) To receive, consider and report on any submission in accordance with paragraphs 1, 2 and 4;

    (b) To receive, consider and report on any information or observations forwarded by the Secretariat in connection with the preparation of the reports referred to in Article 12 (c) of the Protocol and on any other information received and forwarded by the Secretariat concerning compliance with the provisions of the Protocol;

    (c) To request, where it considers necessary, through the Secretariat, further information on matters under its consideration;

    (d) To identify the facts and possible causes relating to individual cases of non-compliance referred to the Committee, as best it can, and make appropriate recommendations to the Meeting of the Parties;

    (e) To undertake, upon the invitation of the Party concerned, information-gathering in the territory of that Party for fulfilling the functions of the Committee;

    (f) To maintain, in particular for the purposes of drawing up its recommendations, an exchange of information with the Executive Committee of the Multilateral Fund related to the provision of financial and technical cooperation, including the transfer of technologies to Parties operating under Article 5, paragraph 1, of the Protocol.

8. The Implementation Committee shall consider the submissions, information and observations referred to in paragraph 7 with a view to securing an amicable solution of the matter on the basis of respect for the provisions of the Protocol.

NON-COMPLIANCE PROCEDURE (1998)   399

9.   The Implementation Committee shall report to the Meeting of the Parties, including any recommendations it considers appropriate. The report shall be made available to the Parties not later than six weeks before their meeting. After receiving a report by the Committee the Parties may, taking into consideration the circumstances of the matter, decide upon and call for steps to bring about full compliance with the Protocol, including measures to assist the Parties' compliance with the Protocol, and to further the Protocol's objectives.

10. Where a Party that is not a member of the Implementation Committee is identified in a submission under paragraph 1, or itself makes such a submission, it shall be entitled to participate in the consideration by the Committee of that submission.

11. No Party, whether or not a member of the Implementation Committee, involved in a matter under consideration by the Implementation Committee, shall take part in the elaboration and adoption of recommendations on that matter to be included in the report of the Committee.

12. The Parties involved in a matter referred to in paragraphs 1, 3 or 4 shall inform, through the Secretariat, the Meeting of the Parties of the results of proceedings taken under Article 11 of the Convention regarding possible non-compliance, about implementation of those results and about implementation of any decision of the Parties pursuant to paragraph 9.

13. The Meeting of the Parties may, pending completion of proceedings initiated under Article 11 of the Convention, issue an interim call and/or recommendations.

14. The Meeting of the Parties may request the Implementation Committee to make recommendations to assist the Meeting's consideration of matters of possible non-compliance.

15. The members of the Implementation Committee and any Party involved in its deliberations shall protect the confidentiality of information they receive in confidence.

16. The report, which shall not contain any information received in confidence, shall be made available to any person upon request. All information exchanged by or with the Committee that is related to any recommendation by the Committee to the Meeting of the Parties shall be made available by the Secretariat to any Party upon its request; that Party shall ensure the confidentiality of the information it has received in confidence.

Indicative list of measures that might be taken by a meeting of the Parties in respect of non-compliance with the Protocol

A.   Appropriate assistance, including assistance for the collection and reporting of data, technical assistance, technology transfer and financial assistance, information transfer and training.

B. Issuing cautions.

C. Suspension, in accordance with the applicable rules of international law concerning the suspension of the operation of a treaty, of specific rights and privileges under the Protocol, whether or not subject to time limits, including those concerned with industrial rationalization, production, consumption, trade, transfer of technology, financial mechanism and institutional arrangements.

Select Bibliography

Abe, Y., 'Implementation System of the WTO Dispute Settlement Body: A Comparative Approach', 6 *Journal of East Asia and International Law* (2013), 7.

Adsett, H., A. Daniel, M. Husain and T.L. McDorman, 'Compliance Committees and Recent Multilateral Environmental Agreements: The Canadian Experience with Their Negotiation and Operation', 42 *CYbkIL* (2005), 91.

Alam, S., S. Atapattu, C.G. Gonzalez and J. Razzaque (eds.), *International Environmental Law and the Global South* (Oxford University Press, 2015).

Aman, A.C., 'The Earth as Eggshell Victim: A Global Perspective on Domestic Regulation', 102 *Yale Law Journal* (1993), 2107.

Amerasinghe, C.F., *Local Remedies in International Law* (2nd ed. Cambridge University Press, 2004).

Andersen, S.O. and K.M. Sarma, *Protecting the Ozone Layer: The United Nations Story*, edited by Lani Sinclair (Earthsacn, 2002).

Andersen, S.O. and K.N. Taddonio, *Technology Transfer for the Ozone Layer* (Earthscan 2007).

Baker, B., 'Protection, Not Protectionism: Multilateral Environmental Agreement and the GATT', 26 *Vanderbilt Journal of Transnational Law* (1993a), 437.

Baker, B. 'Eliciting Non-Party Compliance with Multilateral Environmental Treaties: U.S. Legislation and the Jurisdictional Bases for Compliance Incentives in the Montreal Protocol', 35 *GYbkIL* (1993b), 333.

Bales, J.S., 'Transnational Responsibility and Recourse for Ozone Depletion', 19 *Boston College International and Comparative Law Review* (1996), 259.

Bankobeza, G.M., *Ozone Protection* (Eleven International, 2005).

Barnhoorn, L.A.N.M., 'Diplomatic Law and Unilateral Remedies', 25 *NYbkIL* (1994), 39.

Barratt-Brown, E., 'Building a Monitoring and Compliance Regime under the Montreal Protocol', 16 *Yale Journal of International Law* (1991), 519.

Baxter, R., 'Multilateral Treaties as Evidence of Customary International Law', 41 *BYbkIL* (1965–1966), 275.

Beacham, G., 'International Trade and the Environment: Implications of the General Agreement on Tariffs and Trade for the Future of Environmental Protection Efforts', 3 *Colorado Journal of International Environmental Law and Policy* (1992), 655.

Benedek, W., K. De Feyter, M.C. Kettemann and C. Voigt, *The Common Interest in International Law* (Intersentia, 2014).

Benedick, R.E., *Ozone Diplomacy. New Directions in Safeguarding the Planet* (Enlarged ed. Harvard University Press, 1998).

Benedick, R.E., 'Science Inspiring Diplomacy: The Improbable Montreal Protocol', in C. Zerefos, G. Contopoulos and G. Skalkeas, *Twenty Years of Ozone Decline:*

Proceedings of the Symposium for the 20th Anniversary of the Montreal Protocol (Springer, 2009).

Bernauer, T., 'The Effect of International Environmental Institutions: How We Might Learn More', 49 *International Organisations* (1995), 351.

Beyerlin, U., P.-T. Stoll, and R. Wolfrum (eds.), *Ensuring Compliance with Multilateral Environmental Agreements* (Martinus Nijhoff, 2006).

Biermann, F., *Saving the Atmosphere: International Law, Developing Countries and Air Pollution* (Peter Lang, 1995).

Bilder, R.B., 'The Settlement of Dispute in the Field of the International Law of the Environment', 144 *Recueil des cours* (1975), 139.

Birnie, P., 'The Role of International Law in Solving Certain Environmental Conflicts', in J.E. Carroll (ed.), *International Environmental Diplomacy* (Cambridge University Press, 1988).

Birnie, P., 'Legal Techniques of Settling Disputes: The "Soft Settlement" Approach', in W.E. Butler (ed.), *Perestroika and International Law* (Kluwer Academic Publishers, 1990).

Birnie, P., 'Environmental Protection and Development', 20 *Melbourne University Law Review* (1995), 67.

Birnie, P., and A.E. Boyle, *International Law of the Environment* (Clarendon Press, 1992).

Birnie, P., and A.E. Boyle *Basic Documents on International Law and the Environment* (Clarendon Press, 1995).

Birnie, P., and A. Boyle, C. Redgwell, *International Law and the Environment* (3rd ed. Oxford University Press, 2009).

Biswas, A.K. (ed.), *The Ozone Layer: Proceeding of the Meeting of Experts Designated by Governments, International and Nongovrnment Organisations on the Ozone Layer Organised by the United Nations Environmental Programme in Washington D.C., 1–9 March 1977* (Pergamon Press, 1979).

Bleckmann, A., *Völkerrecht* (Nomos, 2001).

Bloch, F., *Technologietransfer zum internationalen Umweltschutz: Eine völkerrechtliche Untersuchung unter besonderer Berücksichtigung des Schutzes der Ozonschicht und des Weltklimas* (Peter Lang, 2007).

Bodansky, D., J. Brunnée and L. Rajamani, *International Climate Change Law* (Oxford University Press, 2017).

Boisson de Chazournes, L., 'La mise en œuvre du droit international dans le domaine de la protection de l'environnement: enjeux et défis', 99 *RGDIP* (1995a), 37.

Boisson de Chazournes, L., 'Le Fonds sur l'environnement mondial, recherche et conquête de son identité', 41 *AFDI* (1995b), 612.

Borràs, S., 'Comparative Analysis of Selected Compliance Procedures under Multilateral Environmental Agreements', in S. Maljean-Dubois and L. Rajamani (eds.), *Implementation of International Environmental Law* (Martinus Nijhoff, 2011).

SELECT BIBLIOGRAPHY

Bos, M., *A Methodology of International Law* (North-Holland, 1984).

Bothe, M., 'Compliance Control beyond Diplomacy: The Role of Non-Governmental Actors', 27/4 *EPL* (1997), 293.

Bothe, M., (ed.), *Trends in Environmental Policy and Law* (E. Schmidt, 1980).

Bowett, D.W., *The Law of International Institutions* (4th ed. Sweet & Maxwell, 1982).

Bowett, D.W., 'Contemporary Developments in Legal Techniques in the Settlement of Disputes', 180 *Recueil des cours* (1983), 169.

Bowser, R., 'History of the Montreal Protocol's Ozone Fund', 20 *International Environmental Reporter* (1991), 636.

Bowman, M.J., and C. Redgwell, *International Law and the Conservation of Biological Diversity* (Kluwer Law International, 1995).

Boyle, A.E., 'Marine Pollution under the Law of the Sea Convention', 79 *AJIL* (1985), 347.

Boyle, A.E., 'State Responsibility and International Liability for Injurious Consequences of Acts not Prohibited by International Law: Necessary Distinction?' 39 *ICLQ* (1990a), 1.

Boyle, A.E., 'Chernobyl and the Development of International Environmental Law', in W.E. Butler (ed.), *Perestroika and International Law* (Kluwer Academic Publishers, 1990b).

Boyle, A.E., 'Saving the World? Implementation and International Environmental Law through International Institution,' 3 *JEL* (1991a), 229.

Boyle, A.E., 'State Responsibility for Breach of Obligations to Protect the Global Environment', in W.E. Butler (ed.), *Control Over Compliance with International Law* (Kluwer Academic Publishers, 1991b).

Butler, W.E. 'International Law and the Protection of the Global Atmosphere: Concepts, Categories and Principles', in D. Freestone and R. Churchill (eds.), *International Law and Global Climate Change* (Graham & Trotman/Martinus Nijhoff, 1991).

Butler, W.E. 'The Principle of Co-operation: Environment', in V. Lowe and C. Warbrick (eds.), *The United Nations and the Principles of International Law* (Routledge, 1994).

Butler, W.E. and M.R. Anderson (eds.), *Human Rights Approaches to Environmental Protection* (Oxford University Press, 1996).

Butler, W.E. and M.R. Anderson, 'Settlement of Disputes Relating to the Law of the Sea and the Environment', 26 *Thesaurus Acroasium* (Sakkoulas Publications, 1997a), 295.

Butler, W.E. and M.R. Anderson, 'Remedying Harm to International Common Spaces and Resources: Compensation and Other Approaches', in P. Wetterstein (ed.), *Harm to the Environment* (Clarendon Press, 1997b).

Butler, W.E. and M.R. Anderson, 'Soft Law in International Law-Making', in M.D. Evans (ed.), *International Law* (4th ed. Oxford University Press, 2014).

Butler, W.E. and M.R. Anderson, 'Relationship between International Environmental Law and Other Branches of International Law', in D. Bodansky, J. Brunnée and L. Rajamani, *International Climate Change Law* (Oxford University Press, 2017).

Butler, W.E. and M.R. Anderson (ed.), *Environmental Regulation and Economic Growth* (Claredon Press, 1994).

Butler, W.E. and M.R. Anderson and D. Freestone, *International Law and Sustainable Development: Past Achievements and Future Challenges* (Oxford University Press, 1999).

Butler, W.E. and M.R. Anderson and C. Chinkin, *The Making of International Law* (Oxford University Press, 2007).

Brack, D., *International Trade and the Montreal Protocol* (The Royal Institute of International Affairs, 1996).

Bree, A., *Harmonization of the Dispute Settlement Mechanisms of the Multilateral Environmental Agreements and the World Trade Agreements* (Erich Schmidt, 2003).

Brownlie, I., 'A Survey of International Customary Rules of Environmental Protection', 13 *NRJ* (1973), 179.

Brownlie, I., *Principles of Public International Law* (7th ed. Oxford University Press, 2008).

Brunnée, J., *Acid Rain and Ozone Layer Depletion: International Law and Regulation* (Transnational Publishers, 1988).

Brunnée, J., '"Common Interest" - Echoes from an Empty Shell?', 49 *ZaöRV* (1989), 791.

Brunnée, J., and S. Toope, 'Environmental Security and Freshwater Resources: A Case for International Ecosystem Law', 6 *YbkIEL* (1994), 1.

Brunnée, J., and M. Doelle and L. Rajamani (eds.), *Promoting Compliance in an Evolving Climate Regime* (Cambridge University Press, 2012).

Buckley, R., 'International Trade, Investment and Environmental Regulation: An Environmental Management Perspective', 27 *JWT* (1993),101.

Caldwell, L., *International Environmental Policy* (2nd ed. Duke University Press, 1990).

Camble, J.K., 'Reservations to Multilateral Treaties: A Macroscopic View of State Practice', 74 *AJIL* (1980), 372.

Cameron, J. and J. Robinson, 'The Use of Trade Provisions in International Environmental Agreements and Their Compatibility with the GATT', 5 *YbkIEL* (1994), 3.

Campiglio, L. (eds.). *The Environment after Rio: International Law and Economics* (Graham & Trotman/Martinus Nijhoff, 1994).

Canan, P. and N. Reichman, *Ozone Connections* (Greenleaf, 2002).

Carlarne, C.P., K.R. Gray and R.G. Tarasofsky (eds.), *The Oxford Handbook of International Climate Change Law* (Oxford University Press, 2016).

Caron, D., 'La protection de la couche d'ozone stratosphérique et la structure de l'activité normative internationale en matière d'environnement', 36 *AFDI* (1990), 704.

Caron, D., 'Protection of Stratospheric Ozone Layer and the Structure of International Environmental Law-Making', 14 *Hastings International and Comparative Law Review* (1991), 755.

SELECT BIBLIOGRAPHY

Carlson, S.N., 'The Montreal Protocol's Environmental Subsidies and GATT: A Needed Reconciliation', 29 *Texas ILJ* (1994), 211.

Charney, J.I., 'Universal International Law', 87 *AJIL* (1993), 529.

Charnovitz, S., 'Exploring the Environmental Exceptions in GATT Article XX', 25 *JWT* (1991), 37.

Chayes, A. and A.H. Chayes, *The New Sovereignty* (Harvard University Press, 1995).

Cheyne, I., 'Environmental Unilateralism and the WTO/GATT System', 24 *Georgia Journal of International and Comparative Law* (1995), 433.

Chinkin, C.M., 'The Challenge of Soft Law: Development and Change in International Law', 38 *ICLQ* (1989), 850.

Chittick, D.R., 'The Transfer of Chlorofluorocarbon Technologies: A Case-Study in Industry Cooperation', 7 *ATAS Bulletin* (1992), 194.

Churchill, R.R. and D. Freestone, *International Law and Global Climate Change* (Graham & Trotman, 1991).

Churchill, R.R. and G. Kütting and L.M. Warren, 'The 1994 UN ECE Sulphur Protocol', 7 *JEL* (1995), 169.

Conrad, C.R., *Processes and Production Methods (PPMs) in WTO Law* (Cambridge University Press, 2011).

Cook, E. (ed.), *Ozone Protection in the United States* (World Resources Institute, 1996).

Cooper, C.A., 'The Management of International Environmental Disputes in the Context of Canada-United States Relations: A Survey and Evaluation of Techniques and Mechanisms', 14 *CYbkIL* (1986), 247.

Cot, J.P., *International Conciliation* (Europa Publications, 1972).

Cottier, T. and K.N. Schefer, 'Non-Violation Complaints in WTO/GATT Dispute Settlement: Past, Present and Future', in E.-U. Petersmann (ed.), *International Trade Law and the GATT/WTO Dispute Settlement System* (Kluwer Law International, 1997).

Crawford, J., *The International Law Commission's Articles on State Responsibility* (Cambridge University Press, 2002).

Crawford, J. and A. Pellet, S. Olleson (eds.), *The Law of International Responsibility* (Oxford University Press, 2010).

D'Amato, A, 'Trashing Customary International Law', 81 *AJIL* (1987), 101.

Davidson, C.B., 'The Montreal Protocol: The First Step toward Protecting the Global Ozone Layer', 20 *NYJILP* (1988), 793.

Davey, W.J., *Non-Discrimination in the World Trade Organization* (Martinus Nijhoff, 2012).

Degan, V.D., *Sources of International Law* (Martinus Nijhoff, 1997).

Dörr, O. and K. Schmalenbach (eds.), *Vienna Convention on the Law of Treaties: A Commentary* (Springer, 2012).

Dott, L. and H. Schiff, *The Ozone War* (Doubleday & Company, 1978).

Dunoff, J.L., 'Institutional Misfits: The GATT, the ICJ and Trade-Environment Disputes', 15 *Michigan JIL* (1994), 1043.

Dupuy, P.M., 'Soft Law and the International Law of the Environment' 12 *Michigan JIL* (1990a), 420.

Dupuy, P.M., 'The International Law of State Responsibility: Revolution or Evolution?', 11 *Michigan JIL* (1990b), 105.

Dupuy, P.M., 'Humanity and the Environment', 2 *Colorado Journal of International Environmental Law and Policy* (1991), 201.

Dupuy, P.M., and J.E. Viñuales, *International Environmental Law* (Cambridge University Press, 2015).

Ebbesson, J., *Compatibility of International and National Environmental Law* (Kluwer Law International, 1996).

El-Kholy, O.A. and M.K. Tolba (eds.), *The World Environment 1972-1992* (Chapman and Hall, 1992).

Enders, A. and A. Porges, 'Successful Conventions and Conventional Success: Saving the Ozone Layer', in K. Anderson and K Blackhurst, (eds.), *The Greening of World Trade Issues* (Harvester Wheatsheaf, 1992).

Engfeldt, L., 'The United Nations and the Human Environment: Some Experience', 27 *International Organisations* (1973), 393.

Fabian, P. and M. Dameris, *Ozone in the Atmosphere: Basic Principles, Natural and Human Impacts* (Springer, 2014).

Fahey, D.W., 'The Montreal Protocol Protection of Ozone and Climate', 14 *Theoretical Inquiries in Law* (2013), 21.

Flinterman, C., B. Kwiatkowska, and J.G. Lammers, *Transboundary Air Pollution: International Legal Aspects of the Co-operation of States* (Martinus Nijhoff, 1986).

Fitzmaurice, M.A., 'International Environmental Law as a Special Field', 25 *NYbkIL* (1994), 181.

Francioni, F. 'International "Soft Law": A Contemporary Assessment', in V. Lowe and M. Fitzmaurice (eds.), *Fifty Years of the International Court of Justice* (Cambridge University Press, 1996).

Francioni, F. and T. Scovazzi (eds.), *International Responsibility for Environmental Harm* (Graham & Trotman/Kluwer Academic Publishers Group, 1991).

Frank, T., 'Some Instances of Fairness in Establishing Environmental Normative Systems', 240 *Recueil des cours* (1993), 1.

Frank, T., *Fairness in International Law and Institutions* (Clarendon Press, 1995).

Freestone, D., 'The Road from Rio: International Environmental Law after the Earth Summit', 6 *JIL* (1994), 193.

Freestone, D., and E. Hey, *The Precautionary Principle and International Law* (Kluwer Law International, 1996).

French, D., '1997 Kyoto Protocol to the 1992 UN Framework Convention on Climate Change', 10 *JEL* (1998), 227.

SELECT BIBLIOGRAPHY

Gehring, T., 'International Environmental Regimes: Dynamic Sectoral Legal Systems', 1 *YbkIEL* (1990), 35.

Gehring, T., *Dynamic International Regimes: Institutions for International Environmental Governance* (Peter Lang, 1992).

Goldie, L.F.E., 'Special Régimes and Pre-Emptive Activities in International Law', 11 *ICLQ* (1962), 670.

Gong, X., 'Undertaking the Common but Differentiated Responsibilities: China's Decision to Accept the Two Amendments to the Montreal Protocol on Substances that Deplete the Ozone Layer', 4 *Journal of East Asia and International Law* (2011), 515.

Goyal, A., 'Do Environmental Subsidies under Montreal Protocol Offend SCM Agreement of WTO? An Analysis', 44 *Indian JIL* (2004), 521.

Gündling, L., 'Status in International Law of the Principle of Precautionary Action', 5 *IJECL* (1990), 23.

Gündling, L., 'Compliance Assistance in International Environmental Law: Capacity Building through Financial and Technology Transfer', 39 *ZaöRV* (1996), 796.

Handl, G., 'Territorial Sovereignty and the Problem of Transnational Pollution', 69 *AJIL* (1975), 50.

Handl, G., 'Environmental Protection and Development in Third World Countries: Common Destiny – Common Responsibility', 20 *NYUJILP* (1988), 603.

Handl, G., 'Environmental Security and Global Change: The Challenge to International Law', 1 *YbkIEL* (1990), 3.

Handl, G., 'Controlling Implementation of and Compliance with International Environmental Commitments: The Rocky Road from Rio', 5 *Colorado Journal of International Environmental Law and Policy* (1994), 305.

Hass, P., 'Banning Chlorofluorocarbons: Epistemic Community Efforts to Protect Stratospheric Ozone', 46 *International Organisations* (1992), 215.

Heimsoeth, H., 'The Protection of the Ozone Layer', 10 *EPL* (1983), 34.

Hey, E., 'The Precautionary Concept in Environmental Policy and Law: Institutionalising Caution', 4 *Georgetown International Environmental Law Review* (1992), 303.

Hohmann, H., *Precautionary Legal Duties and Principles of Modern International Environmental Law* (Martinus Nijhoff, 1994).

Hunt, K.J., 'International Environmental Agreements in Conflict with GATT: Greening GATT after the Uruguay Round Agreement', 30 *International Lawyer* (1996), 163.

Hurdec, R.E., *The GATT Legal System and World Trade Diplomacy* (2nd ed. Butterworth Legal Publishers, 1990).

Hurlbut, D., 'Beyond the Montreal Protocol: Impact on Nonparty States and Lessons for Future Environment Protection Regimes', 4 *Colorado Journal of International Environmental Law and Policy* (1993), 344.

Hurlock, M.H., 'The GATT, U.S. Law and the Environment: A Proposal to Amend the GATT in Light of the Tuna/Dolphin Decision', 92 *Columbia LR* (1992), 2098.

Iluyomade, B.O., 'The Scope and Content of a Complaint of Abuse of Right in International Law', 16 *AJIL* (1975), 47.

Iwasawa, Y., *WTO no Funsō Shori* [WTO Dispute Settlement] (Sanseido, 1995) (in Japanese).

Iwasawa, Y., 'Kokusai Gimu no Tayōsei' [Diversity of International Obligations: Focusing on Obligations *Erga Omnes*], in J. Nakagawa and K Teraya. (eds.), *Kokusaihōgaku no Chihei* [Horizon of International Law: Essays in Honour of Yasuaki Onuma] (Toshindo, 2008), 123 (in Japanese).

Iwasawa, Y., 'Domestic Application of International Law', 378 *Recueil des cours* (2015), 21.

Jachtenfuchs, M., 'The European Community and the Protection of Ozone Layer', 18 *Journal of Common Market Studies* (1990), 261.

Jackson, J.H., *The World Trading System* (2nd ed. MIT Press, 1997).

Jackson, J.H. and W.J. Davey, and A.O. Sykes, *Legal Problems of International Economic Relations* (6th ed. West, 2013).

Johnston, D.M. and P. Finkle, 'Acid Precipitation in North America: The Case for Transboundary Co-operation', 14 *Vanderbilt JTL* (1981), 787.

Kanehara, A., 'The Significance of the Japanese Proposal of "Predge and Review" Process in Growing International Environmental Law', 35 *Japanese Annual of International Law* (1992), 1.

Kanehara, A., 'Chikyu Kankyō Hogo ni okeru Songai Yobō no Hōri' ["Precautionary Remedies" in the Conventions on Global Environmental Protection], 93 *Kokusaiho Gaiko Zassi* [Journal of International Law and Diplomacy] (1994), 448 (in Japanese).

Kanehara, A., 'Wakugumi Jōyaku' [Framework Convention], in S. Yamamoto (ed.), *Kokusaikankyōhō no Jūyō Kōmoku* [Basic Points of International Environmental Law] (Japan Energy Law Institute, 1995) (in Japanese).

Kaniaru, D. (ed.), *The Montreal Protocol: Celebrating 20 Years of Environmental Progress* (Cameron May, 2007).

Kennedy, D., *International Legal Structures* (Nomos, 1987).

Kim, D.-W., *Non-Violation Complaints in WTO Law* (Peter Lang, 2006).

Kindt, J. and S. Menefee, 'The Vexing Problem of Ozone Depletion in International Law and Policy', 24 *Texas ILJ* (1989), 261.

Kingsbury, B., 'The Tuna-Dolphin Controversy, the World Trade Organization, and the Liberal Project to Reconceptualize International Law', 6 *YbkIEL* (1994a), 1.

Kingsbury, B., 'Environment and Trade: The GATT/WTO Regime in the International Legal System', in A.E. Boyle (ed.), *Environmental Regulation and Economic Growth* (Clarendon Press, 1994b).

Kingsbury, B. and A. Hurrell (eds.), *The International Politics of the Environment* (Clarendon Press, 1992).

SELECT BIBLIOGRAPHY

Kirgis, F.L. Jr., 'Standing to Challenge Human Endeavours that could Change the Climate', 84 *AJIL* (1990), 525.

Kirgis, F.L. Jr., *International Organizations in Their Legal Setting* (2nd ed. West Publishing, 1993).

Kiss, A., 'Mechanisms of Supervision of International Environmental Rules', in F. Kalshoven, P.J. Kuyper and J.G. Lammers (eds.), *Essays on the Development of the International Legal Order* (Sijthoff & Noordhoff, 1980).

Kiss, A., 'La notion de patrimoine commun de l'humanité', 175 *Recueil des cours* (1982), 98.

Kiss, A., *Droit international de l'environment* (Pedone, 1989).

Kiss, A. and D. Shelton, *International Environmental Law* (3rd ed. Transnational Publishers, 2004).

Klein, D., M.P. Carazo, M. Doelle, J. Bulmer and A. Higham (eds.), *The Paris Agreement on Climate Change: Analysis and Commentary* (Oxford University Press, 2017).

Klein, E., *Statusverträge im Völkerrecht* (Springer, 1980).

Klein, E., 'Self-Contained Regime', in R. Wolfrum (ed.), *Max Planck Encyclopedia of Public International Law*, Vol. IX (Oxford University Press, 2012), 98.

Koskenniemi, M., 'Breach of Treaty or Non-Compliance? Reflections on the Enforcement of the Montreal Protocol', 3 *YbkIEL* (1992), 123.

Kotera, A., 'GATT no Kokusaihō teki Chii' [International Legal Status of the GATT], 38 *Bōeki to Kanzei* [Trade Journal] (1990), 39 (in Japanese).

Kotera, A., 'Kokusai Regīmu no Ichi' [Position of International Régimes], in M. Iwamura et al. (eds.), *Kokusai Shakai to Hō* [International Community and Law] (Iwanami-Koza Series, volume 2), (Iwanami Shoten, 1997) (in Japanese).

Kotera, A., *WTO Taisei no Hō Kōzō* [Legal Structure of the WTO Regime] (University of Tokyo Press, 2000) (in Japanese).

Kotera, A., *Paradigm Kokusaihō* [Basic Structure of International Law] (Yuhikaku, 2004) (in Japanese).

Kummer, K., *International Management of Hazardous* (Clarendon Press, 1995).

Kuyper, P.J., 'The Law of GATT as a Special Field of International Law', 25 *NYbkIL* (1994), 227.

Lammers, J., 'Efforts to Develop a Protocol on Chlorofluorocarbons to the Vienna Convention for the Protection of the Ozone Layer', 1 *Hague Yearbook of International Law* (1988), 255.

Lammers, J. and C. Flinterman, B. Kwiatkowska (eds.), *Transboundary Air Pollution* (Martinus Nijhoff, 1986).

Lammers, J., 'The Mechanism of Decision-making under the Vienna Convention and the Montreal Protocol for the Protection of the Ozone Layer', in G. Kreijen et al. (eds.), *Sovereignty, and International Governance* (Oxford University Press, 2002).

Lang, J., 'The Ozone Layer Convention: a New Solution to the Question of Community Participation in "Mixed" International Agreements', 23 *CMLR* (1986), 157.

Lang, W., 'Diplomacy and International Environmental Law-Making: Some Observations', 3 *YbkIEL* (1992), 108.

Lang, W., 'International Environmental Agreements and the GATT: The Case of Montreal Protocol', 3-4 *Internationaler Handel und Umwelt* (1993), 364.

Lang, W., 'Is the Protection of the Environment a Challenge to the International Trading System?', 7 *Georgetown International Environmental Law Review* (1995a), 463.

Lang, W., 'Regimes and Organizations in the Labyrinth of International Institutions', in Lang, *Völkerrecht in Zeitverantwortung – Ausgewählte Schriften zu Diplomatie, Umweltschutz, internationale Organisationen und Integration* (Heribert Franz Köck (ed.), NWV Verlag, 2006).

Lang, W., (ed.), *Sustainable Development and International Law* (Graham & Trotman/ Martinus Nijhoff, 1995b).

Lang, W., (ed.), *The Ozone Treaties and Their Influence on the Building of Environmental Régimes* (Austrian Ministry of Foreign Affairs, 1996).

Lang, W. and H. Neuhold, K. Zemanek (eds.), *Environmental Protection and International Law* (Graham & Trotman/Martinus Nijhoff, 1992).

Lawrence, P.M., 'International Legal Regulation for Protection of the Ozone Layer: Some Problems of Implementation', 2 *JEL* (1990), 17.

Lesniewska, F., 'Filling the Holes: The Montreal Protocol's Non-Compliance Mechanism', in M. Fitzmaurice, D.M. Ong, and P. Merkouris (eds.), *Research Handbook on International Environmental Law* (Edward Elgar Publishing, 2010).

Litfin, K., *Ozone Discourses* (Columbia University Press, 1994).

Liu, N., V. Somboon and C. Middleton, 'Illegal Trade in Ozone Depleting Substances', in E. Lorraine and W.H. Schaedla (eds.), *Handbook of Transnational Environmental Crime* (Edward Elgar, 2016).

Lukashuk, I.I., 'The Principle *Pacta Sunt Servanda* and the Nature of Obligation under International Law', 83 *AJIL* (1989), 513.

Maljean-Dubois, S. and L. Rajamani (eds.), *Implementation of International Environmental Law* (Martinus Nijhoff, 2011).

McNair, A.D., 'Treaties Producing Effects «Erga Omnes»', in *Scritti di diritto internazionale in Onore di Tomaso Perassi*, Vol. 2 (Dott. A. Giuffrè, 1957), 25.

Merrills, J.G., *International Dispute Settlement* (6th ed. Cambridge University Press, 2017).

Morita, A., 'Kokusai Kontorōru (contrôl international) Riron no Rekishiteki Tenkai' [The Historical Development of the Theory of International Supervision: Focusing on the Legal Concept Based on its Functions', 95 *Kokusaiho Gaiko Zasshi* [*Journal of International Law and Diplomacy*] (1996), 313 (in Japanese).

SELECT BIBLIOGRAPHY

Morita, A., *Kokusai Kontorōru no Riron to Jikkō* [International Control: Theory and Practice] (University of Tokyo Press, 2000) (in Japanese).

Morikawa, T., 'Kokusai Seido no Taiseiteki Kōka' [International Régimes Producing Effects *Erga Omnes*], 2 *Yokohama Kokusai Keizai Hogaku* [Yokohama Journal of International Economic Law] (1993), 1 (in Japanese).

Morrisette, P.M., 'The Evolution of Policy Responses to Stratospheric Ozone Layer', 29 *NRJ* (1989), 793.

Mosler, H., *The International Society as a Legal Community* (Sijthoff & Noordhoff, 1980).

Murase, S., 'Perspectives from International Economic Law on Transnational Environmental Issues', 253 *Recueil des cours* (1995), 287.

Murray, T. and I. Walter, 'Quantitative Restrictions, Developing Countries, and GATT', 11 *JWT* (1977), 391.

Nadelmann, E.A., 'Global Prohibition Regimes: The Evolution of Norms in International Society', 44 *International Organisations* (1990), 479.

Nanda, V.P., 'Global Warming and International Environmental Law – A Preliminary Inquiry', 30 *Harvard ILJ* (1989), 375.

Nolte, G. (ed.), *Treaties and Subsequent Practice* (Oxford University Press, 2013).

Ntambirweki, J., 'The Developing Countries in the Evolution of an International Environmental Law', 14 *Hasting International and Comparative Law Review* (1991), 905.

O'Connell, M.E., 'Enforcing the New International Law of the Environment', 35 *GYbkIL* (1992), 292.

O'Connor, J.F., *Good Faith in International Law* (Dartmouth Publishing Company, 1991).

Okowa, P.N., 'Procedural Obligations in International Environmental Agreements', 67 *BYbkIL* (1996), 275.

Onuma, Y., *International Law in a Transcivilizational World* (Cambridge University Press, 2017).

Ott, H., 'The New Montreal Protocol: A Small Step for the Protection of the Ozone Layer, a Big Step for International Law and Relations', 2 *Law and Politics in Africa and Asia* (1991), 188.

Ott, H., *Umweltregime im Völkerrecht* (Nomos, 1998).

Palmer, G., 'New Ways to Make International Environmental Law', 86 *AJIL* (1992), 259.

Papasavva, S. and W.R. Moomaw, 'Adverse Implications of the Montreal Protocol Grace Period for Developing Countries', 9 *International Environmental Affairs* (1997), 219.

Parson, E.A., *Protecting the Ozone Layer: Science and Strategy* (Oxford University Press, 2003).

Patlis, J.M., 'The Multilateral Fund of the Montreal Protocol: A Prototype for Financial Mechanisms in Protecting Global Environment', 25 *Cornell ILJ* (1992), 181.

Patterson, E., 'GATT and the Environment: Rules Changes to Minimize Adverse Trade and Environmental Effects', 26 *JWT* (1992), 99.

Paul, V., 'The Abuse of Rights and Bona Fides in International Law' 28 *Österreichische Zeitschrift für öffentliches Recht und Völkerrecht* (1977), 121.

Peel, J., Science and Risk Regulation in International Law (Cambridge University Press, 2010).

Petersmann, E.-U., 'Violation-Complaints and Non-Violation Complaints in Public International Trade Law', 34 *GYbkIL* (1991), 175.

Petersmann, E.-U., 'International Competition Rules for the GATT-MTO World Trade and Legal System', 27 *JWT* (1993a), 35.

Petersmann, E.-U., 'International Trade Law and International Environmental Law': Prevention and Settlement of International Environmental Disputes in GATT', 27 *JWT* (1993b), 43.

Petersmann, E.-U., *International and European Trade Law and Environmental Law after Uruguay Round* (Kluwer Law International, 1996).

Petersmann, E.-U., *The GATT/WTO Dispute Settlement System* (Kluwer Law International, 1997).

Petsonk, C.A., 'Recent Developments in International Organisations: The Role of the United Nations Environment Programme (UNEP) in the Development of International Environmental Law', 5 *AUJILP* (1990), 351.

Pisillo-Mazzeschi, R., 'The Due Diligence Rule and the Nature of the International Responsibility of States', 35 *GYbkIL* (1992), 9.

Posencranz, A., 'The ECE Convention of 1979 on Long-Range Transboundary Air Pollution', 75 *AJIL* (1981), 975.

Ragazzi, M., *The Concept of International Obligations Erga Omnes* (Oxford University Press, 1997).

Rege, V., 'GATT Law and Environment-Related Issues Affecting the Trade of Developing Countries', 28 *JWT* (1994), 95.

Rama-Montaldo, M., 'International Legal Personality and Implied Powers of International Organisations', 14 *BYbkIL* (1970), 111.

Read, J.F., 'The Trail Smelter Dispute', 1 *CYbkIL* (1963), 213.

Redgwell, C., 'Transboundary Pollution: Principles, Policy and Practice', in T. Koh, R. Beckman, H.D. Phan and S. Jayakumar (eds.), *Transboundary Pollution: Evolving Issues of International Law and Policy* (Edward Elgar, 2015).

Reistein, R.A., 'Trade and the Environment: The Case for and against Unilateral Actions', in W. Lang (ed.), *Sustainable Development and International Law* (Martinus Nijhoff/ Graham & Trotman, 1995).

Sachariew, K., 'The Definition of Thresholds of Tolerance for Transboundary Environment Injury under International Law: Development and Present Status', 37 *NILR* (1990), 193.

Sachariew, K., 'Promoting Compliance with International Environmental Legal Standards: Reflections on Monitoring and Reporting Mechanisms', 2 *YbkIEL* (1991), 31.

SELECT BIBLIOGRAPHY

Sand, P.H., *Marine Environment Law in the United Nations Environment Programme: An Emergent Eco-Regime* (Cassell Tycooly, 1988).

Sand, P.H., *Lessons Learned in Global Environmental Governance* (World Resources Institute, 1990).

Sand, P.H., 'New Approaches to Transnational Environmental Disputes', 3 *International Environmental Affairs* (1991), 193.

Sand, P.H., 'UNCED and the Development of International Environmental Law', 3 *YbkIEL* (1992a), 3.

Sand, P.H., 'International Economic Instruments for Sustainable Development: Sticks, Carrots and Games', 26 *Indian YbkIL* (1996), 1.

Sand, P.H., 'Whither CITES? The Evolution of a Treaty Regime in the Borderland of Trade and Environment', 8 *EJIL* (1997), 29.

Sand, P.H., (ed.), *The Effectiveness of International Environmental Agreements* (Grotius Publications, 1992b).

Sands, P., 'International Law in the Field of Sustainable Development', 66 *BYbkIL* (1995), 303.

Sands, P. (ed.), *Greening International Law* (Earthcan, 1993).

Sands, P. and J. Peel, *Principles of International Environmental Law* (3rd ed. Cambridge University Press, 2012).

Sarma, K.M., 'Compliance with the Multilateral Environmental Agreements to Protect the Ozone Layer', in U. Beyerlin, P.-T. Stoll and R. Wolfrum (eds.), *Ensuring Compliance with Multilateral Environmental Agreements* (Martinus Nijhoff, 2006).

Sato, T., *Evolving Constitutions of International Organisations* (Kluwer Law International, 1996).

Schachter, O., 'Recent Trends in International Law Making', 12 *Australian YbkIL* (1989), 1.

Schachter, O., *International Law in Theory and Practice* (Martinus Nijhoff, 1991).

Schermers, H.G. and N.M. Blokker, *International Institutional Law: Unity and Diversity* (5th. rev. ed. Martinus Nijhoff, 2011).

Schneider, J., *World Public Order of the Environment* (University of Toronto Press, 1979).

Schoenbaum, T.J., 'Free International Trade and Protection of the Environment: Irreconcilable Conflicts', in 'Agora: Trade and Environment', 86 *AJIL* (1992), 700.

Schoenbaum, T.J., 'International Trade and Protection of the Environment: The Continuing Search for Reconciliation', 91 *AJIL* (1997), 268.

Schrijver, N., *Sovereignty over Natural Resources: Balancing Rights and Duties* (Cambridge University Press, 1997).

Schrijver, N., *The Evolution of Sustainable Development in International Law* (Martinus Nijhoff, 2008).

Schrijver, N. and O. Kuik, P. Peters (eds.), *Joint Implementation to Curb Climate Change* (Kluwer Academic, 1994).

Schrijver, N. and F. Weiss (eds.), *International Law and Sustainable Development: Principles and Practice* (Martinus Nijhoff, 2004).

Schultz, J., 'Environmental Reform of the GATT/WTO International Trading System', 18 *World Competition* (1994), 77.

Schultz, J., 'The GATT/WTO Committee on Trade and the Environment: Toward Environmental Reform', 89 *AJIL* (1995), 423.

Seidl-Hohenveldern, I., 'International Economic "Soft Law"', 163 *Recueil des cours* (1979), 165.

Shh, W.C., 'Multilateralism and the Case of Taiwan in the Trade Environment Nexus: The Potential Conflict between CITES and GATT/WTO', 30 *JWT* (1996), 109.

Shibata, A., 'Ensuring Compliance with the Basel Convention – Its Unique Features', in U. Beyerlin, P.-T. Stoll, and R. Wolfrum (eds.), *Ensuring Compliance with Multilateral Environmental Agreements* (Martinus Nijhoff, 2006).

Simma, B., 'Self-Contained Regimes', 16 *NYbkIL* (1985), 111.

Simma, B., 'The Antarctic Treaty as a Treaty Providing an "Objective Regime"', 19 *Cornell ILJ* (1986), 189.

Simma, B. and D. Pulkowski, 'Leges Speciales and Self-Contained Régimes', in J. Crawford, A. Pellet, and S. Olleson (eds.), *The Law of International Responsibility* (Oxford University Press, 2010).

Skilton, T.E., 'GATT and the Environment in Conflict: The Tuna-Dolphin Dispute and the Quest for an International Conservation Strategy', 26 *Cornell ILJ* (1993), 455.

Skubiszewski, K. 'Enactment of Law by International Organisation', 41 *BYbkIL* (1965–1966), 198.

Springer, A.L., *The International Law of Pollution* (Quoroum Books, 1983).

Subedi, S.P., *Land and Maritime Zones of Peace in International Law* (Clarendon Press, 1996).

Széll, P., 'Decision-Making under Multilateral Environmental Agreements', 26/5 *EPL* (1996), 210.

Széll, P., 'Compliance Regimes for Multilateral Environmental Agreements: A Progress Report', 27/4 *EPL* (1997), 304.

Talbot, L.B., 'Recent Development in the Montreal Protocol on Substances that Deplete the Ozone Layer: The June 1990 Meeting and Beyond', 26 *International Lawyer* (1992), 145.

Tam, C.J., *Enforcing Obligations Erga Omnes in International Law* (Cambridge University Press, 2005).

Tarasofsky, 'Ensuring Compatibility between MEAs and GATT/WTO', 7 *YbkIEL* (1996), 52.

Teraya, K., 'Kokusaihō ni okeru "Chikara (Power)"' ['Power' in the Science of International Law], in Y. Onuma (ed.), *Kokusaishakai ni okeru Hō to Chikara* [Law and Power in International Society] (Nihonhyoronsha, 2008), 103 (in Japanese).

SELECT BIBLIOGRAPHY

Thirlway, H., *The Sources of International Law* (Oxford University Press, 2014).

Tolba, M.K. and O.A. El-Kholy (eds.), *The World Environment 1972–1992* (Chapman & Hall, 1992).

Treves, T. et al. (eds.), *Non-Compliance Procedures and Mechanisms and the Effectiveness of International Environmental Agreements* (T.M.C. Asser Press, 2009).

Trip, J., 'The UNEP Montreal Protocol: Industrial and Developing Countries Sharing the Responsibility for Protecting the Stratospheric Ozone Layer', 20 *NYUJILP* (1988), 733.

Twum-Barima, R. and L.B. Campbell, *Protecting the Ozone Layer Through Trade Measures: Reconciling the Trade Provisions of the Montreal Protocol and the Rules of the GATT* (UNEP, 1994).

Ulfstein, G. (ed.), *Making Treaties Work* (Cambridge University Press, 2007).

Usuki, T., 'Chikyu Kankyō Hogo Jōyaku ni okeru Funsō Kaiketsu Tetsuduki no Hatten' [Development of Dispute Settlement Procedures in Global Environmental Conventions], in T. Sugihara (ed.), *Funsō Kaiketsu no Kokusaihō* [International Law for Dispute Settlement: Essays in Celebration of Judge Shigeru Oda's Seventieth Birthday] (Sanseido, 1997) (in Japanese).

Usuki, T., 'Kankyō Hogo ni kansuru Nankyoku Jōyaku Sisutemu no Henyō' [Protection of the Antarctic Environment: From Resourcism to Earth-patriotism], 49 *Hokudai Hogaku Ronshu* [Hokkaido Law Review] (1998), 769 (in Japanese).

Utton, A.E., 'International Environmental Law and Consultation Mechanisms', 12 *Columbia JTL* (1973), 56.

Verdross, A. and B. Simma, *Universelles Völkerrecht* (3rd ed. Duncker & Humblot, 1984).

Victor, D.G., *The Early Operation and Effectiveness of the Montreal Protocol's Non-Compliance Procedure* (International Institute for Applied Systems Analysis, 1996a).

Victor, D.G., *The ILO System of Supervision and Compliance Control: A Review and Lessons for Multilateral Environmental Agreements* (International Institute for Applied Systems Analysis, 1996b).

Villapando, S., 'Some Archeological Explorations on the Birth of Obligations *Erga Omnes*', in *Liber Amicorum Raymond Ranjeva: l'Afrique et le droit international: variations sur l'organisation internationale* (A. Pedone, 2013).

Villiger, M.E., *Commentary on the 1969 Vienna Convention on the Law of Treaties* (Martinus Nijhoff, 2009).

Viñuales, J.E. (ed.), *The Rio Declaration on Environment and Development: A Commentary* (Oxford University Press, 2015).

Virally, M., 'Good Faith in Public International Law', 77 *AJIL* (1983), 130.

von Bogdandy, 'The Non-Violation Procedure of Article XXIII:2, GATT: Its Operation and Rationale', 26 *JWT* (1992), 95.

Ward, H., 'Trade and Environment in the Round-And After', 6 *JEL* (1994), 263.

Weiss, E.D., *In Fairness to Future Generations* (United Nations University, 1989).

Weksman, J., 'Trade Sanctions under the Montreal Protocol', 1 *RECIEL* (1992), 69.

Weksman, J., 'Consolidating Governance of the Global Commons: Insights from the Global Environmental Facility', 6 *YbkIEL* (1995), 27.

Weksman, J., 'Compliance and Transition: Russia's Non-Compliance Test the Ozone Régime', *ZaöRV* (1996a), 750.

Weksman, J. (ed.), *Greening International Institutions* (Earthscan, 1996b).

Weksman, J. and J. Cameron, P. Roderick (ed.), *Improving Compliance with International Environmental Law* (Earthscan, 1996).

Wettestad, J., 'Acid Lessons? LRTAP Implementation and Effectiveness', 7 *Global Environmental Change* (1997), 235.

Williams, S., 'The Protection of the Ozone Layer in Contemporary International Law', 10 *International Relations* (1990), 167.

Wolfrum, R., 'Purposes and Principles of International Environmental Law', 33 *GYbkIL* (1990), 308.

Wolfrum, R., (ed.), *Enforcing Environmental Standards: Economic Mechanisms as Viable Means?* (Springer, 1996).

Wood, A., 'The Multilateral Fund for the Implementation of the Montreal Protocol', 5 *International Environmental Affairs* (1993), 335.

Yamin, F. and J. Depledge, *The International Climate Change Regime* (Cambridge University Press, 2004).

Yokota, Y., 'The Role of the Committee of Experts in the ILO's Supervisory Mechanism: Reflections on Ten Years' Experience as a Member', in R. Wolfrum, M. Seršić and T.M. Šošić (eds.), *Contemporary Developments in International Law: Essays in Honour of Budislav Vukas* (Brill/Martinus Nijhoff, 2016).

Yoshida, O., '"Soft Enforcement" of Treaties: The Montreal Non-Compliance Procedure and the Functions of the Internal International Institutions', 10 *Colorado Journal of International Environmental Law and Policy* (1999), 95.

Yoshida, O., 'Kokusaihō ni okeru "Kokusai Regīmu" no Shintenkai' [Developments of "International Régimes" in International Law], 99 *Kokusaiho Gaiko Zasshi* [Journal of International Law and Diplomacy] (2000), 259 (in Japanese).

Yoshida, O., *The International Legal Régime for the Protection of the Stratospheric Ozone Layer* (Kluwer Law International, 2001).

Yoshida, O., 'Organising International Society? Legal Problems of International Régimes between Normative Claims and Political Realities,' 9 *ARIEL* (2006), 63.

Yoshida, O., 'Hans Keruzen no Konpon Kihan Ronkou' [Reflections on Hans Kelsen's Basic Norm in International Law], 44 *Tsukuba Hosei* [Tsukuba University Journal of Law and Politics] (2008), 103 (in Japanese).

Yoshida, O., 'Procedural Aspects of the International Legal Regime for Climate Change: Early Operation of the Kyoto Protocol Compliance System', 4 *Journal of East Asia and International Law* (2011), 41.

SELECT BIBLIOGRAPHY

Yoshida, O. and A. Sakota, 'Kokusai Ozonsō Hogo Jōyaku Rejīmu ni okeru NGO no Yakuwari' [The Role of NGOs in the International Legal Régime for the Protection of the Ozone Layer], in *Kankyo Sisaku ni okeru Jūmin Sanka, NGO Katsudō ni kansuru Hōgaku oyobi Gyōseigaku teki Kenkyū* [Legal and Administrative Studies on Public Participation and NGO Activities in Environmental Measures] (Japan Environment Protection Agency, October 1998) (in Japanese).

Zaelke, D., S.O. Andersen and N. Borgford-Parnell, 'Strengthening Ambition for Climate Mitigation: The Role of the Montreal Protocol in Reducing Short-lived Climate Pollutants', 21 *RECIEL* (2012), p. 231.

Zamora, S., 'Is There Customary International Economic Law?', 32 *GYbkIL* (1989), 9.

Zerefos, C., G. Contopoulos and G. Skalkeas (eds.), *Twenty Years of Ozone Decline – Proceedings of the Symposium for the 20th Anniversary of the Montreal Protocol* (Springer, 2009).

Zoller, E., *La bonne foi en droit international public* (A. Pedone, 1977).

Index

acid rain   42n, 66, 79n, 82n

adverse effects   42, 66–68, 72, 95, 146–147, 211, 281
   and the Vienna Ozone Convention   67–68

Agenda   21, 324–325

air pollution, transboundary   66–67, 76, 212
   and ozone depletion   66–67

air space   69

Antarctica   69–70, 76, 126
   See also ozone hole

Arctic   126–127, 146
   See also ozone hole

Argentina   104, 126, 220, 311, 325

Australia   53, 100, 104, 126, 218, 220, 303

Austria   218, 327

basic norm (of international law)   16

Basel Convention   3, 19, 23, 30, 38, 42, 84, 86, 119, 165, 168, 179, 196–197, 206, 214, 235, 263n, 290

basic domestic needs   113, 124–125, 129, 135, 137, 140n, 141

Belgium   267, 271, 271, 278

Benedick, Richard E.   97, 157, 339

Biodiversity Convention   26n, 38, 71–72, 74, 86, 119, 206, 214, 224n, 263n, 290, 328

Birnie, Patricia   17, 82, 240

Bonn Convention   29n, 37

Boyle, Alan   33, 72, 82, 240

Brazil   104, 325

Bromochloromethane (CH2BrCl)   140, 145

Canada   53, 56, 63, 100–105, 108–109, 122, 144, 146, 220, 232, 279n, 301, 303, 305, 327
   CFC regulation   56

capacity building   31–32, 49, 85, 286–292, 314, 324, 326, 330
   See also Multilateral Fund
   and the Vienna Ozone Convention   290–291
   meaning   31, 286–288

Carbontetrachloride (CC14)   2, 98, 105, 112, 127, 129–130, 133, 145, 327

CEITS   225, 229, 231, 232n, 260, 270, 272–273, 275, 298, 317, 322

CFCS   2–3, 18, 53–58, 60–65, 68, 79, 94, 83, 94, 98, 100–101, 103–109, 111–113, 115–116, 120–122, 125–139, 141–142, 144–145, 168–171, 172n, 173–174, 180, 183, 195, 201, 213, 222, 230n, 259, 268n, 270–271, 281, 296, 303–304, 321, 323, 327, 329, 339–340

Chlorofluorocarbons
   See CFCS

China   110, 124n, 130, 137–138, 142, 147, 220, 240, 278, 292, 295, 310–311, 325, 329, 339

CITES Convention   23n, 30, 31n, 34, 37, 62, 165, 168, 178–179, 196, 197n, 198, 200, 203, 205–206, 263n

climate change   4, 141–143, 215, 242, 292, 341

Climate Change Convention (UNFCCC)   22–23, 26, 32, 71–72, 74, 84, 86, 99, 119, 141, 144, 224n, 263n, 289, 330n
   See also Kyoto Protocol

common-but-differentiated responsibilities   32, 123–124, 288n, 340

common concern of mankind (CCM)   44, 46, 71–73, 76, 95, 336

common heritage of mankind (CHM)   70–72

common (community) interests   14, 18

compliance   13, 28, 34, 37–38, 88, 91, 102, 124, 158, 195, 211–212, 215–216, 221, 226, 228, 255, 260, 299, 305, 322
   See also non-compliance
   definitions   221

conciliation, international   35, 92, 245–248, 250, 262
   and Non-Compliance Procedure (NCP)   245–247

Conference of the Parties   17, 19, 26, 61
   and the Vienna Ozone Convention   88–90

conservation   70, 78n, 80n, 192, 204–205

control measures
   See Montreal Protocol

Copenhagen Amendment/Adjustment
   See Meeting of the Parties

countermeasures   40–41, 198, 225, 258–259, 261, 280, 283

country programmes
   See Multilateral Fund

INDEX

customary (international) law 17–18, 24, 26, 42, 68–69, 75, 77, 81, 94, 178, 213, 222, 240–242, 258, 262, 340
and environmental protection 17–18

damage, environmental 33, 47, 78, 123, 205, 222
See also State responsibility
Denmark 53
developing countries, Article 5
See Montreal Protocol
developed countries, non-Article 5
See Montreal Protocol
disputes, environmental 33, 93, 211–213, 260
dispute settlement 61, 89, 92–94, 212–213, 216, 230, 244–246, 249, 251, 253, 256–257, 282, 335, 337–338
and environmental treaties 92–93
and the Ozone Convention
See Vienna Ozone Convention
due diligence 25–26, 77–79, 81, 85
DuPont 2

Egypt 104, 137, 324
environmental impact assessment (EIA) 20, 28, 80–81
equity, international 32
See also common-but-differentiated responsibilities
essential use 132–134
European Community/European Union 41, 43, 53–57, 60–65, 100–106, 108–109, 114, 116, 118–120, 134, 136–140, 167, 191, 193n, 217n, 218–220, 267, 272, 279, 297, 303
CFC regulation 56–57
Executive Committee (Montreal Protocol) 32, 158, 233, 236n, 237, 295, 297–299, 301–316, 318–323, 326, 329–331, 339–341
and NGOs 38
functions 301–305
membership 303
Rules of Procedure 302
Terms of Reference 301–302, 319
voting procedure 304

Finland 53, 59, 61–62, 76, 88, 100
France 120, 297
funds, environmental 31, 288–289
See also Multilateral Fund

GATT 12, 171, 173, 176–186, 190–207, 249–252
Article XX, Preamble conditions 191–193
Article XX(b) 193–194, 196, 198–200, 201, 205–206
Article XX(g) 202–205
subsidies 179, 244n
GEMS 91
Germany 56, 119, 140
global commons 13, 165
Global Environment Facility (GEF) 31, 216–217, 278–279, 297, 280n, 304n, 315–318, 322–323, 338
global warming 32, 66, 127, 143, 144n, 288, 315
good faith 14–16, 49, 193, 227
good neighbourliness 75
grace periods
See Montreal Protocol
Greece 267, 270
greenhouse gases 146

Halons 2, 98, 101, 105, 107–109, 111, 113–114, 121, 127, 129–130, 134–135, 141, 145, 171, 172n, 195, 327
HBFCS 3, 112, 145
HCFCS 2, 112, 127–129, 131–132, 134–137, 139, 140n, 141–145, 148–149, 268, 270–272, 278, 303–304, 311, 326
human rights 13, 31, 41, 68, 176n, 213, 216n, 227, 235, 254
Hydrobromofluorocarbons
See HBFCS
HFCS 121, 127–128, 142–148, 150, 154n, 156–157, 172, 278, 326
Hydrochlorofluorocarbons
See HCFCS
Hydrofluoroolefins (HFOS) 148

ICAO 88n, 111
illegal trade in CFCS/ODSS 125, 133, 136–137, 143, 175, 262, 278, 281, 326
ILO 254–257
IMF 244, 304
IMO 28, 79
Implementation Committee 39, 48, 115, 131, 149, 158, 213, 219–221, 224, 227–238, 245–249, 257, 259–261, 264–268, 270–272, 275–277, 279–284, 296, 301, 322, 338–340

420 INDEX

Implementation Committee (*cont.*)
  See also Non-Compliance Procedure
    and confidentiality of information
    219, 230n, 234–235, 247, 265, 267
    functions   233–237
    members   233
    Rules of Procedure   236
India   110, 124n, 130, 137–138, 190, 292,
    295–296, 310, 325, 326n, 329, 339
industrial rationalization   113n
institutional strengthening   31
International Court of Justice (ICJ)   35n, 39,
    44, 93–94, 186, 212n, 257
international development law   286
international environmental law   1, 17,
    32, 42, 65, 167, 199–200, 213, 228, 231,
    268–287, 336–337, 341
International Law Commission (ILC)   73,
    178, 222
International Law Association (ILA)   24n,
    36, 66, 69n
international régimes   4, 9–50
    definitions   9–16
    regulatory régimes   9, 16–21, 24, 26, 42,
      335
    self-contained régimes   9, 39–48
    territorial régimes   13
international society   13
Italy   267, 297

Japan   56, 62, 100–101, 142, 172n, 188, 231n,
    293, 303
    CFC regulation   57, 152–156
joint implementation   114, 118–120

Kelsen   16
Kenya   104, 232, 278
Kiss, Alexandre-Charles   232, 340
Korea   175, 268–269, 292, 325
Kyoto Protocol   23, 32, 99, 128n, 141–144,
    214–215

Lang, Winfried   19, 171n, 186
Law of Treaties (1969)   15, 24, 26n, 45n, 62,
    170n, 176, 181, 183–185, 189, 191n, 193, 243,
    245, 276n, 338
like products   173–174
LRTAP Convention   4, 22, 25, 62, 65–66,
    70–71, 74, 82, 86, 87n, 88n, 95, 112, 114,
    213, 230, 233n, 236n, 261, 290

EMEP Protocol   22
  NOx Emissions Protocol   22
  Sulphur Emissions Protocols   22–23, 112,
    114, 116n, 119, 122n, 124, 290
  VOCs Emissions Protocol   22–23
  POPs Protocol   23
  Heavy Metals Protocol   23
  Gothenburg Protocol   23

Malaysia   98n, 144n, 296, 326n
Mauritania   149n, 267, 322
MEAS   3, 30n, 38, 163–168, 184–190, 206–208,
    213, 244, 284n, 288, 290, 328, 339
  categories   165
  meaning   164–165
Meeting of the Parties (Montreal
    Protocol)   48, 90, 149, 198, 218–219,
    224–228, 230–232, 234n, 238–240, 247,
    260–261, 264, 269–270, 272, 275, 277,
    280–282, 291, 296, 298–299, 302–303,
    322, 329–330, 336–338, 340
  First Meeting (1989)   128–130, 132, 135,
    236, 291
    Helsinki Declaration   23n, 129, 218
  Second Meeting (1990)   110, 219, 231,
    238n, 296–297
    London Amendment/Adjustment
    116n, 117–118, 132, 135n, 171, 259n,
    322
  Third Meeting (1991)   48, 172, 226, 243
  Fourth Meeting (1992)   110–111, 131–133,
    220, 222, 226, 243, 271, 297, 304,
    308
    Copenhagen Amendment and
    Adjustment   117–118, 131–133, 135, 171,
    259n, 271–272
  Fifth Meeting (1993)   134, 172
  Sixth Meeting (1994)   134, 301, 322
  Seventh Meeting (1995)   134–137, 242,
    276, 299
    Vienna Adjustment   117, 134–135, 171,
    259n
  Eighth Meeting (1996)   137
  Ninth Meeting (1997)   112, 220, 280
    Montreal Amendment/
    Adjustment   117–118, 138n, 171, 175,
    259n
  Tenth Meeting (1998)   113, 220–221,
    280–281
  Eleventh Meeting (1999)   139–141

INDEX   421

Beijing Amendment/
Adjustment   117–118, 139–141, 171,
259n, 271–272
Beijing Declaration   329
Twelfth Meeting (2000)   138, 281
Ouagadougou Declaration   329
Thirteenth Meeting (2001)   147, 281
Fourteenth Meeting (2002)   221, 281
Eighteenth Meeting (2006)   141–142,
268n, 270
Nineteenth Meeting (2007)   141–143
Montreal Adjustment   117, 171, 259n
Twentieth Meeting (2008)   143–144
Twenty-First Meeting (2009)   144, 321
Twenty-Second Meeting (2010)   146, 327
Twenty-Third Meeting (2011)   144n, 146,
271–272
Twenty-Fourth Meeting (2012)   146
Twenty-Fifth Meeting (2013)   146, 270
Twenty-Sixth Meeting (2014)   146, 268
Twenty-Seventh Meeting (2015)   146
Twenty-Eighth Meeting (2016)   147–149,
232, 266
Kigali Amendment   117–118, 128n,
143–150, 152, 156, 171–172, 322, 341
and NGOs   38
decisions   239–243
legal nature   239–244
implied powers   241
Rules of Procedure   239, 241
Methylbromide (CH_3Br)   3, 112, 133–136,
140–141, 145, 327
Methylchloroform ($C_2H_3Cl_3$)   1–2, 98, 105,
112, 127, 129–130, 133, 135, 145
Mexico   292, 294, 325
Montevideo Meeting (1981)   59–61
Montreal Protocol   38, 41, 45–48, 71, 87,
89n, 91, 94, 97–159, 165, 169–172,
174–175, 179–180, 183–185, 187, 190,
195–201, 206, 208, 212, 215–217, 220–223,
225–226, 228, 231, 238–239, 240–241,
243–244, 251, 259–260, 264, 266, 268,
270–271, 273–274, 276, 278, 282, 284,
290–292, 296–302, 307, 310, 312–313,
315–317, 320, 322–323, 325–331,
335–341
amendments/adjustments
mechanisms   32, 116–118, 339
control measures   47, 111–150, 171–175,
336–337, 340–341

developing countries, Article 5   98, 113,
121–122, 125, 128, 135–137, 140n, 141–142,
145, 148, 150, 157, 170n, 221–222, 225,
228, 233–234, 246, 258–260, 266, 271,
278, 297, 303–305, 309–310, 313–314,
319–324, 326–327, 329–330, 337–338,
340–341
developed countries, non-Article 5   98,
113, 125, 133–134, 136–137, 139, 142, 145,
148–151, 157, 227, 233, 259, 266, 270–271,
280, 299, 304–305, 314, 320, 337–341
grace periods   32, 121–125, 340
Implementation Committee
See Implementation Committee
Meeting of the Parties
See Meeting of the Parties
Multilateral Fund
See Multilateral Fund
negotiation (text of 1987)   100–109
Secretariat (UNEP)   34, 48, 91–92,
110n, 188, 215, 219–220, 228–232,
234, 238, 243, 246, 264, 265n,
266–268, 270–272, 275–276,
277n, 314, 340
trade with non-parties   30, 35, 45–46,
270–272, 292, 295
licensing system   136, 175, 337
Montreal Rules (ILA)   66–67
Multilateral Fund   31–32, 38, 87, 110, 122,
124–125, 131, 133, 136, 158, 179, 216,
223–224, 233–234, 237, 242, 244, 264,
266–268, 278, 282, 296–331, 335,
338–341
See also Global Environment Facility
country programmes   279, 302, 307–308,
319–321
effectiveness and assessment   326–329
Executive Committee
See Executive Committee
Implementing Agencies   237n, 266–267,
305, 307–310, 314, 316, 318–319, 321, 330,
338
UNDP   266, 308–309, 311–312, 330
UNEP   266, 313–314, 330
UNIDO   308–309, 314–315, 330
World Bank   266, 298, 303, 308–311,
317, 338
incremental costs   294, 297–299, 302, 320
institutional strengthening   268, 320–322
legal capacity   301

Multilateral Fund (*cont.*)
    Secretariat in Montreal   268, 298, 301–302, 306–308, 312, 314–315, 321–322, 330
    subsidies   244
    technology transfer
      See technology transfer
    Terms of Reference   308
    work programmes   307, 318–319

NAFTA   165, 235
natural law   14
Netherlands   56, 218, 260n, 272, 297
New Zealand   53, 100, 303
NGOS   14, 28, 36–38, 43, 55n, 58, 60, 89, 100, 109, 133n, 134, 142, 157, 188n, 189, 227, 229, 230–231, 234–235, 237, 294, 303–305, 318, 335, 340
    and Conference of the Parties   89
    and Executive Committee   303
    and Implementation Committee   39, 234–235
    and Meeting of the Parties
      See Meeting of the Parties
    and Non-Compliance Procedure (NCP)
      See Non-Compliance Procedure (NCP)
NIEO   287
non-compliance   16, 34–35, 46, 115–116, 121–122, 212, 218–219, 221–227, 229–230, 232, 234–240, 246, 248, 254, 261–262, 264, 266–272, 275, 278–284, 314, 323, 330, 338, 340
    Albania   269n
    Argentina   269n
    Armenia   269n
    Azerbaijan   269n, 270n
    Bahamas   269n
    Bangladesh   122, 229n, 230n, 236n, 269n
    Belarus   266n, 269n, 270n
    Belize   269n
    Bolivia   269n
    Bosnia-Herzegovina   269n
    Botswana   269n
    Bulgaria   269n, 270n
    Burkina Faso   266n
    Burundi   265n
    Cameroon   269n
    CEITS
      See CEITS

Chad   122, 265
Chile   269n
China   269n
Comoros   122, 265
Congo   269n
Costa Rica   266n
Dominica   122, 269n
EU   270n, 271–272
Ecuador   269n
Eritrea   269n
Estonia   269n, 270n
Ethiopia   269n
Fiji   269n
France   270n
Greece   269n, 270n
Guatemala   269n
(Guinea-Bissau)   269n
Grenada   265
Honduras   122, 269n
Iran   266n, 269n
Israel   236n
Italy   266n
Kazakhstan   236n, 269n, 270n
Kenya   122, 269n
Korea   265, 268–269
Kyrgyzstan   269n
Latvia   269n, 270n
Lesotho   269n
Liberia   265
Libya   269n
Lithuania   269n
Maldives   266n, 269n
Marshall Islands   265
Mexico   269n
Micronesia   265, 269n
Mongolia   122, 265
Morocco   122, 269n
Namibia   269n
Nepal   269n
Nigeria   122, 269n
Pakistan   269n
Papua New Guinea   122, 269n
Paraguay   122, 269n
Peru   269n
Qatar   269n
Saint Vincent and the Grenadines   269n
Samoa   122
Saudi Arabia   269n
Sierra Leone   269n

INDEX

Solomon Islands 122, 269n
Somalia 269n
Syria 266n
Russia
   See Russian Federation
Tajikistan 269n, 270n
Togo 266n
Trinidad and Tobago 266n
Turkmenistan 269n
Uganda 269n
Ukraine 266n, 269n, 270n
Uruguay 269n
Uzbekistan 269n, 270n
Vanuatu 269n
Viet Nam 269n
Non-Compliance Procedure (NCP) 35,
   39, 41, 47, 110, 115–116, 131, 136, 158,
   175, 186–187, 190, 198, 211–285, 296,
   301, 322, 326, 335, 337–338,
   340
   and Kyoto Protocol 215
   and settlement procedures under
   the Vienna Ozone Convention 224–226
   and NGOs 39, 230–231
   Implementation Committee
      See Implementation Committee
   Indicative List of Measures 222, 237, 240,
      242, 248, 260, 269–270, 280, 284
   reporting 263–268
non-governmental organisations
   See NGOS
Norway 53, 56, 61–62, 76, 100, 187n, 231n
   CFC regulation 56
NO_x 18

objective régimes 12–13
obligations *erga omnes* 18n, 43–47, 72–73,
   117, 182, 216, 335–336, 338
OECD 43, 57, 137, 330
ODPS 111, 114–115, 270, 326n, 327
ODSS 18, 46, 53, 83, 90, 94, 98, 101–105,
   108, 110, 112–118, 120–121, 125–126, 128,
   130–140, 143, 145–146, 151–154, 159,
   168–172, 175, 180, 183, 195–198, 213, 215,
   217, 220, 222–223, 239, 259, 262, 264,
   268, 272–274, 278–280, 291–294, 296,
   299, 303–304, 310–312, 317, 319, 321, 324,
   326–330, 335–341
OORG 303

Open-ended Working Group 38–39,
   122n, 130, 146, 275, 279n, 292, 294,
   340
outer space 70, 76
ozone 1
ozone depleting potentials
   See ODPS
ozone depleting substances
   See ODSS
ozone depletion 1, 24, 33, 42, 53, 59, 66–69,
   82–83, 87, 94–95, 144, 158–159, 168, 217,
   242, 273, 281, 288, 340–341
ozone hole 2, 126
   Antarctic ozone hole 2, 126
   and the Arctic 126–127
ozone layer 44, 46–50, 54, 68–76, 82, 94–95,
   112, 125, 127, 140, 142, 146, 152, 158, 170,
   195, 199–200, 204–206, 215, 247, 261,
   278, 281, 283, 288, 294, 316, 335–336,
   338, 341
   legal status 68–73

Paris Agreement (2015) 99, 215
prior informed consent 20, 84, 143
prior notification and consultation 19, 80
polluter pays principles 43
pollution 43, 71, 121n, 199, 211
PPMS 172–173, 202
precautionary principle/approach 32–33,
   42, 49, 53, 74, 79–85, 98, 125, 196, 258,
   261, 282, 329
preventive action 32–33, 74–75, 79–80, 94

Ramsar Convention 37, 289
regional economic integration
   organization 65, 118–120
reporting, in general 34, 263–264
   categories 264
Rio Declaration 75, 83, 123
   Principle 2 32, 75, 85, 200
   Principle 9 324
   Principle 12 202
   Principle 19 20n
Russian Federation 142, 148, 150, 220, 232n,
   234n, 236n, 242–243, 248, 260, 270,
   272–281, 283–284, 298, 303
   non-compliance 236n, 239n, 270n,
      275–281
   ozone regulations 273–274

INDEX

sanctions 30–31, 34, 49, 170, 243, 283
Sands, Philippe 207, 263n
scientific knowledge 18, 26, 81, 106, 296
Secretariat of MEAs, in general 25, 33n, 90–91
self-contained régimes 39–48, 242, 258, 277, 335, 341
shared natural resources 69–70
soft law 23–25, 27–28, 70, 128–129, 242
State responsibility 40, 42–43, 47, 67, 211, 222, 225, 261–262
   and ozone depletion 41–42
   environmental damage
   See damage, environmental
   due diligence
      See due diligence
Stockholm Declaration 23n, 62, 74, 79–80, 121n
Stockholm Principle 21 32, 74–77, 81, 85, 89n, 95, 200, 340
stratosphere 1–2
sustainable development 29, 49, 123, 166n, 199, 206, 289, 324, 341
   meaning 29n
Sweden 53, 56, 59, 61–63, 76, 100
   CFC regulation 56
Switzerland 53, 59, 88, 100, 188, 220

Taiwan 324
TEAP 111, 130, 131n, 157, 159, 232, 272, 314
technology transfer 31, 61, 86, 124, 285, 237–238, 287, 289–291, 293–294, 296, 323–325, 327–330
   See also capacity building
   and environmental treaties 289–290
   and MLF
      See Multilateral Fund
   definitions 323–333
Thailand 175
Tolba, Mostafa 54, 107–108
Toronto Group 53–54, 56, 60–61, 63, 100, 106, 116
troposphere 1, 71

UNCED 282
UNCLOS 62, 65n, 70, 74, 75n, 85n, 92, 289

UNDP 31, 266–267, 298, 316
UNEP 28, 31, 34, 46, 53–54, 56–59, 61–62, 65, 67n, 68n, 76, 90–92, 97, 98n, 100–101, 107, 111, 128, 137, 144, 147, 157–158, 188n, 232, 265n, 266–267, 289, 292, 294–295, 302, 308, 313–314, 319, 327, 330, 316, 321
UNEP Regional Sea Conventions 23
UNEP/CCOL 56–59, 71, 90
United States 31, 53, 55, 63, 94, 100–106, 108–109, 120, 134, 137n, 138, 141, 144, 146, 167, 169, 171, 196, 202, 205, 217n, 218, 221, 224, 275, 279, 293, 295, 297, 303, 327
   ODS regulation 55–56
United Kingdom 56, 63, 88, 102, 120, 220, 232, 270, 293, 297
USSR (Soviet Union) 48, 62, 100–101, 105n, 115–116, 229, 272–273, 276, 281

Venezuela 104
Vienna Ozone Convention 25, 31n, 45, 48n, 53–68, 71, 74, 76, 79, 82, 85–98, 110–111, 118, 123, 129, 134, 146, 151, 170, 190, 201, 211–212, 218–220, 222, 224–226, 228, 233, 239–240, 282, 291, 329, 335–336, 340
   assessment 94–95
   Conference of the Parties 88–90, 95
      Rules of Procedure 90
   dispute settlement 93–94
   Funding 87–88
   negotiation 54–64
   Secretariat 90–92

WMO 56, 90, 111, 127n, 147, 159, 262n
work programmes
   See Multilateral Fund
World Bank 31, 287n, 293, 295, 297, 315–316, 322, 338
World Charter for Nature 20n, 23n, 80
World Heritage Convention 37, 263n
World Resources Institute 294
WTO (trade law) 12, 166–167, 176, 179–180, 182, 184–190, 203, 207, 250, 252, 337
   CTE 92, 166, 184n, 187–189, 199n, 202, 207–208, 328

INDEX

dispute settlement 180–182, 186–190, 249–254

DSU 180, 189, 250–251, 253

GATT

See GATT

TRIPS 180, 251, 325

WTO/GATT 41, 46, 48, 163, 166, 168, 175–176, 180–186, 188–190, 204, 206, 208, 244, 249, 252–254, 335, 337

Printed in the United States
By Bookmasters